SAMUEL RICHARDSON

a reference guide

A
Reference
Guide
to
Literature

Arthur Weitzman
Editor

SAMUEL RICHARDSON
a reference guide

SARAH W.R. SMITH

G.K.HALL&CO.
70 LINCOLN STREET, BOSTON, MASS.

Library of Congress Cataloging in Publication Data

Smith, Sarah W. R.
   Samuel Richardson : a reference guide.

   Bibliography: p.
   Includes index.
   1.   Richardson, Samuel, 1689-1761—Bibliography
I. Title.
Z8744.19.S6 1984 [PR3666]   016.823'6   83-18557
ISBN 0-8161-8170-5

This publication is printed on permanent/durable acid-free paper
MANUFACTURED IN THE UNITED STATES OF AMERICA

To

Sarah May Buck

and

Robert Lee Wolff

gentle readers

Contents

The Author

Sarah Smith received her bachelor's degree from Radcliffe College, studied at the University of London on a Fulbright fellowship, and returned to Harvard to write her Ph.D. thesis on Samuel Richardson. She has taught at Northeastern University and Tufts University, and is now in the Department of English at Boston University. She is field editor for the late eighteenth and early nineteenth century sections of the Twayne's English Authors Series, and is currently at work on a study of Richardson and Fielding.

Preface

The following bibliography offers an annotated list of publications by Richardson and criticism of his work, arranged by date from 1723 to 1978. These items should be noted:

1. Only the most significant editions of Richardson's works have been included: editions during his lifetime, modern editions, important foreign editions, and editions offering a version of his text significantly different from his own. Space has precluded listing the numerous other editions of his work.

2. Early or rare books have been marked with a library location. United States libraries are listed by their abbreviations in the National Union Catalogue. Numerous foreign libraries were kind enough to contribute to this study; they are listed by readily recognizable abbreviations (Bib. Naz. Centrale) or by their full names (Statni knihovna ČSR, Saltykov-Shchedrin).

3. Although novels based on Richardson's works are not strictly speaking Richardsonian criticism, their prevalence says something about the Richardsonian vogue in the eighteenth century. Richardsonian fiction that contains criticism of him has been listed in the body of the bibliography. For the curious, I have listed some other novels, plays, and poetry in the Appendices.

4. Work too recent to be listed in the body of the bibliography, but which has come to my attention during its compiling, is listed in the Appendix on Recent Work.

Acknowledgments

Because Richardson's influence extended throughout Europe, and because traces of it have often survived only in rare or unique editions, I owe a great debt to the research of others. Over one hundred librarians and their staffs were kind enough to search their library holdings for material on Richardson and for editions of his works. Private persons too numerous to mention--academic colleagues, booksellers and collectors--have very generously shared with me their special knowledge and have allowed me to examine editions and Richardson association items.

The staffs of the following libraries have given continuing aid and support: the British Library at the British Museum; the Bibliothèque nationale; the Bibliothèque de l'Arsénal; the Forster Collection of the Victoria and Albert Museum; Yale University Library; Cambridge University Library; Columbia University Library; the New York Public Library; and Widener and Houghton Libraries at Harvard University. I owe special thanks to Joseph Komidar, Jean Butt, Myra Siegenthaler, and Margaret Gooch of Wessell Library, Tufts University.

Like all students of Richardson, I owe a great debt to Professors T.C. Duncan Eaves and Ben D. Kimpel, whose Samuel Richardson: A Biography has transformed our sense of Richardson's life, and to the editorial and bibliographic work of Professor John Carroll. To name the many others whose work has revitalized Richardson studies in the past twenty years would be a pleasant task, but one too large to carry out here; I am grateful to them, and particularly to those with whom I have had the pleasure of reading and discussing Richardson.

Some initial research on this study was done while I was writing my dissertation at Harvard under Reuben J. Brower. The debt I owe to him, as mentor, model, and friend, extends far beyond the bounds of this book.

Funding for this study has been provided by the Frank Knox Fellowship at Harvard University and by a Faculty Research Grant from Tufts University, which has also given generous support for the preparation of the manuscript through its Work-Study program.

This manuscript was typed, formatted and indexed at the Computer Center of Tufts University by a group of students under my direction; George Stalker, Director of Academic Computing, wrote the formatting and indexing programs. To George, Carolyn Neipris, Mary Ellin Barrett, Stephen Pietrantoni, Rebecca Saunders, and Diane Wysocki, many thanks for your work. Thanks also to the secretaries of the English Department at Tufts, Ann Parker, Elizabeth Matchett, and Linda Scola, and to my friends and colleagues there.

To David Maxwell Tufts, who was kind enough to translate the Russian catalogue entries, <u>spasibo</u>!

Great thanks are due to Arthur Weitzman, field editor at G.K. Hall, and to the staff of the Hall Bibliographical Series, in particular Janice Meagher, for their patience and care.

Special thanks for moral support are due to Christine and Sacha and to Elaine.

And last and best—thank you, dear Fred.

Introduction

To open <u>Pamela</u> is to stand at the beginning of an era in fiction. Richardson's first book, and its successors <u>Clarissa</u> and <u>Sir</u> <u>Charles</u> <u>Grandison</u>, did not take out a patent on the novel, or epistolary fiction, or psychological studies, or moral realism, or well-structured fiction. Rather, apart from their importance in themselves, they provided a pattern combining all these elements. The importance of that pattern, its prevalence in the cultural life of Europe in the past two centuries, we are only beginning to recognize.

Richardson made a comfortable living printing other men's books and came late, though not wholly surprisingly, to his own. Born in Mackworth, Derbyshire, in July or August 1689, he lived in extreme poverty during his childhood and seems to have been largely self-educated. Some talent for fiction declared itself in him early; at eleven he was expressing himself through fictional correspondents and he later wrote to Johannes Stinstra that he had told his "Schoolfellows" stories "from my Head . . . I recollect, that I was early noted for having Invention." His first choice of profession, the Anglican priesthood under which so many authors sheltered, was closed to him by his parents' poverty and "I chose [the profession] of a Printer, . . . as what I thought would gratify my Thirst after Reading."

All Richardson's life was lived in the printing and bookselling world. It not only supported him (far better than his novels ever did) but educated him. He told Stinstra, "I read but as a Printer," and like many of his fellow middle-class artists, he posed as a simple, hardly educated man, but we should understand by this not that he was a literary <u>naif</u> but that he probably knew no language but his own. As Erich Poetzsche suggests, his acquaintance with literature may well have been comparatively large. He did not know the classics in the original, but like many other middle-class artists, had some acquaintance with them in translation and did not find them proper material for imitation. He read little fiction; he seems to have preferred drama (particularly Steele and, apparently, Charles Johnson), and his favorite leisure reading was history and theology.

The twentieth-century reader is likely to underestimate the importance of such reading; not only were the clergy "our most famous Masters and most correct Writers of English," but questions of epistemology, vital to the emergent novel, were discussed almost exclusively in theological terms. The most integrated treatment of the relationships between experience and mental change, a central question in Richardson's new fiction, is found in the religious poetry of the period, especially among those early Sentimentalists who transmitted "Modern" impulses in literature in the early eighteenth century. Among the output of Richardson's printing house, thus among books he certainly knew, is a remarkable preponderance of works by these Moderns: Joseph Mitchell, Thomas Edwards, Elizabeth Singer Rowe, Dennis, Hill, Dyer, Savage, Mallet, Young, and Thomson. Hill, Young, and Edwards were Richardson's close friends and correspondents. Richardson's reading as described by Poetzsche shows the same bias toward what might be considered the Modern classics: Milton, Butler, Dryden, Watts, Prior, and Cowley. He shared the school's admiration for Shakespeare and unlike any but his "pre-Romantic" contemporaries (Thomson, Edwards, the Wartons, and Young) he admired Spenser.

In short, Richardson's profession seems to have given him a fairly good education in contemporary literature with certain strengths in history and theology and a bias toward Modernist writing. Moreover, printing gave him early training in writing. In any business concerned with the making of books there are always small writing jobs to do; Richardson seems to have taken his full share. What precisely he produced before Pamela will always be a matter for speculation. We hear of a sheet on "The Duties of Wives to Husbands," no copy of which has yet been found, a set of rules for his printing office (1734), a letter originally written for his nephew and published as The Apprentice's Vade Mecum (1733), a pamphlet against playhouses (1734) that put him on the opposite side of the controversy from Henry Fielding, and possibly a leader for a political newspaper, The True Briton, early in his career (1723). It is tempting to speculate that Richardson may have written for some periodical, perhaps the Weekly Miscellany or even the Gentleman's Magazine in its early years. In 1736 he wrote a set of verses that were published in the Gentleman's Magazine. To them Edward Cave, the editor, prefaced the note that " . . . the Publick is often agreeably entertain'd by his Elegant Disquisitions in Prose." This seems to promise rather more than what we know Richardson to have written before 1736, and something of a higher order than the literary pursuits Richardson described to Stinstra: "Indexes, Prefaces, and sometimes . . . honest Dedications . . . " Even these dull honest creatures, however, have seldom been identified.

We know, however, that among his printer's duties was editing. From the mid-1730s he took on the official functions of an editor (a job he had done silently for years before), possibly for the 1737

edition of The Complete English Tradesman, more certainly for James
Mauclerc's Christian's Magazine in the same year, and quite possibly
for the 1738 edition of Defoe's Whole Tour thro' the Island of Great
Britain. For the Society for the Encouragement of Learning he took
on the tremendous Negotiations of Sir Thomas Roe . . ., the first
volume of which, the only one to appear, runs over 900 pages. In
1739 he produced an edition of Aesop's Fables, bringing together
Samuel Croxall's and Sir Roger l'Estrange's texts to create his own
"modernized" and apolitical version. (In effect, of course, it was
Richardsonized as well, the first of Richardson's works to show his
distinct literary personality; but this would hardly have been
apparent to early readers, Richardson included.) Finally, of course,
before writing Pamela Richardson had half-finished a commissioned
book of sample letters for tradesmen, his closest approach yet to
fiction. The Familiar Letters are excellent reading, clever short
stories in letters, and Pamela came from a pen of even greater
skill; again one may wonder what caused such flowering so quickly.
Was it more than the simple explosive coming together of a writer
with his form? Had the booksellers who commissioned the Familiar
Letters read some of those "elegant disquisitions"? We shall
probably never know. But it seems evident that, through these
productions of the 1730s, Richardson had served an apprenticeship in
writing that helped to create the novels.

The novels stand by themselves. There were only three: Pamela,
first appearing in 1740; Clarissa, the greatest of them, which came
out in three installments in 1747-48; and the now underrated Sir
Charles Grandison (1753-54). A second part of Pamela, Pamela in her
Exalted Condition (often shortened to Pamela II), first appeared in
1741; it has usually been considered a separate, minor work.
Richardson himself printed every edition of the enormous books
appearing in his lifetime and revised them, sometimes radically,
from edition to edition; the resulting textual problems have not
yet been fully addressed. Pamela was also radically revised during
the 1750s for an edition that did not appear until 1801.

In amplification or defense of his novels he wrote a number of
short articles and pamphlets and compiled several book-length
supplements. Among the first are his contribution to the
Gentleman's Magazine in 1749, answering Haller's objections to
Clarissa, and his Two Letters Concerning Sir Charles Grandison
(1754). The second group includes Clarissa's purported Meditations
Collected from the Sacred Books . . . (1750), as well as Letters
and Passages Restored from the Original Manuscripts of the History
of Clarissa (1751) and A Collection of the moral and instructive
Sentiments, Maxims, Cautions, and Reflections, Contained in the
Histories of Pamela, Clarissa, and Sir Charles Grandison . . .
(1755). Pamela II, above, should to some extent be considered
another book of the same kind. In 1753 he was a victim of
commercial espionage; the Irish pirate publisher George Faulkner
suborned one of Richardson's employees to get the sheets of the

first volumes of <u>Grandison</u>, and Richardson published several versions of his side of the story. He also wrote several short independent works of moral instruction, including his contribution to Johnson's <u>Rambler</u>, No. 97 (1751); six letters against duelling, not published until 1765; and perhaps, though it is highly questionable, a moral fable called "The Contented Porter," which appeared in 1799.

Richardson wrote little criticism and published none under his own name. He silently collaborated with Edward Young in the Modernist manifesto, <u>Conjectures</u> <u>on</u> <u>Original</u> <u>Composition</u> (1759); as McKillop (1925) points out, Richardson's contribution went beyond simple editorial help to a modification of Young's argument. But his best criticism seems to have been expressed privately and was not systematic. Much of it is to be found in Richardson's major unpublished literary work, his own letters. A quite reliable selection from them was published by John Carroll in 1964, partially replacing Anna Laetitia Barbauld's six-volume edition of the <u>Correspondence</u> (1804), which is not textually reliable. However, no edition is as inclusive or reliable as the manuscript letters themselves, a virtually complete guide to which has been published in T.C. Duncan Eaves and Ben D. Kimpel's <u>Samuel</u> <u>Richardson:</u> <u>A</u> <u>Biography</u>; it covers letters both from and to Richardson. The largest single collection of the letters, in the Forster Collection of the Victoria and Albert Museum London, is now available on microfilm from the English firm Micro Methods Ltd.

Writing, printing and correspondence occupied Richardson after his success as before it. The major event of his public life was his election in 1754 to the mastership of the Stationers' Company. Typically, he seems to have been elected to heal a split in the organization, as the one man upon whom all could agree. He remained active in business and the Company until close to his death, on July the fourth, 1761;he was buried in St. Bride's, Fleet Street, to whose restored vaults he has recently been returned.

To say, as Eaves and Kimpel do, that Richardson was "as close to being original as a writer can be" is in a sense to make it difficult to understand his appeal. Like the Moderns he was in search of a rhetorical form that could combine grandeur with simplicity and escape the biases of classically based, aristocratically oriented rhetoric. Like theirs his early work (at least) depended heavily on the rhetoric of the Bible and signaled an attempt to work out a Biblical authenticity of perception. Dramatists before him had explored some of his concerns ; the moral dilemmas of contemporary bourgeois life found frequent expression on stage. Richardson drew heavily on the romance, using it to establish a tradition (but not an identity) for his characters. Epistolary fiction was by no means new. However, no one befoe him had combined a consciously tragic story like <u>Clarissa</u> or a morally serious one like <u>Pamela/</u> <u>or</u> <u>Grandison</u> with the informal familiar letter. Rhetorically this was quite new; Richardson seems to have been among the first writers to recognize that the plain-style "new way of writing" was particularly applicable to fiction, that the novel could attain grandeur from its subject alone rather than through formal rhetorical heightening. He was certainly not the first to see the advantages of a hero or heroine not already defined by class, or to connect lack of class definition with the need to explore the self and define one's singular moral nature. His power over the writing of his time did not come, as has been too often suggested, from his knowing nothing of it. Rather, Richardson's power was precisely that he was not new.

But he was different; and from almost the moment that <u>Pamela</u> appeared Richardson's fiction fascinated his contemporaries. The fascination was by no means confined to England; similar questions of ethics, social morality, style and feeling were being posed by the very different bourgeoisies emerging in France and Germany, as well as by those that would appear more slowly elsewhere in Europe. Marivaux had already prepared the way in France for a fiction very like Richardson's; Prévost and Gellert would quickly adapt him. Perhaps because Prévost and Gellert perceived themselves as his supporters, Richardson became the central point of this emerging literary school. In this sense we can speak of a book as owing an allegiance to Richardson's sort of writing, of showing a Richardsonian influence or being part of a Richardsonian school. Moreover, some novelists-- not few, and not always the worst--borrowed from Richardson's novels elements of their style, characterization, and sentiment, and this is "Richardsonian" too. It is hard to separate the general development of the literary sensibility from the specific imitation of Richardson, since they so often overlapped. Richardsonian fiction formed a significant and perhaps the major element of Sentimental fiction: idealizing, dialectical, emotional, concerned with establishing a new, "harmonious" society. It also served as the ancestor of record for fiction of a very different sort, for instance the <u>sensiblerie</u> of Mackenzie and Baculard d'Arnaud or the work of Sade.

Richardson's presence in eighteenth-century European fiction can thus hardly be overestimated. Among the novelists who showed or expressed a debt to him are Diderot, Rousseau, Goethe, Mme de Staël, Restif de la Bretonne, Sade, Henry Fielding, Sarah Fielding (whose <u>Governess,</u> <u>or</u> <u>Little</u> <u>Female</u> <u>Academy</u>, the first novel for children, was written under his influence), Elizabeth Inchbald, Robert Bage, Godwin, Holcroft, Clara Reeve, Fanny Burney, Frances Moore Brooke, Henry Brooke, Henry Mackenzie, Edward Kimber, J.C.A. Musaeus, Dusch, Mme Riccoboni, Maria Geertruida de Cambon, Hermes, Baculard d'Arnaud, Sophie de la Roche, Nicolai, Achim von Arnim, J.H. Miller, Elisabeth Wolff and Agathe Deken, Pietro Chiari, Mme de Genlis, Rhijnvis Feith, Charles Brockden Brown, Frances Sheridan, Tieck, Choderlos de Laclos, Ugo Foscolo, Karamzin, Gellert, and Jane

Austen.   One piles up names not to exhaust them or the reader, nor
to sound merely impressive, but to suggest that no major novelist of
the   eighteenth   century remained untouched by him, that the list of
unimportant writers who took material from him is close to   endless,
and that therefore the "Richardsonian" school had a permanent effect
on the development of the classical novel.

This school comprises every level of writing from   the   creative
transformations   of   Laclos   and   Austen   to   the   most   shameless
imitations, for which   the   Germans   have   coined   the   useful   word
Richardsonaden.   Some   attempts   have   already been made to put the
major works of this school into context;   much remains to be   done.
No   bibliography   properly   yet   covers   the   English fiction of the
period or that of any of the European countries except the French,
and   until   that   research   is   done   our   sense of Richardson's real
influence (or anyone else's) remains largely based on guesswork.   It
is   beyond   the   aspirations   of   this   bibliography   to correct the
situation.   In the meantime, though, a few things can be said   about
the   nature   of   the school and the potential difficulties in dealing
with it.

First, a familiar problem with Richardson studies: we   cannot
assume   that the persons who wrote in a Richardsonian style, even in
English, read what we can agree is a standard text of   Richardson's
novels.   There is no standard text.   Even among the editions printed
by Richardson himself there are   such   large   differences   as   those
between   the   subtly wrong Lovelace of the first edition of Clarissa
and the much more obvious villain   of   the   third.   When   we   say,
blithely,   that   such-and-such an author "imitated Clarissa," we are
speaking at a certain level not of a single book but of   a   nexus   of
related   texts.   The   differences among them are hardly significant
when we speak of Richardson's influence over,   say,   Frances   Moore
Brooke;   over Laclos, Diderot, or Austen, though, they may well be
important.

And   these   are   only   the   English,   authorized   versions   of
Richardson's   texts.   Most   of   the foreign writers and not a few of
the English read versions that   Richardson   had   never   dreamed   of.
What,   for   instance,   did   Diderot   read,   an   English   or a French
Clarissa? It matters; Prévost's Lettres angloises, ostensibly a
translation   of   Clarissa,   was   actually   a drastic revision of the
book, abridged by half and much prettified.   For some   time--perhaps
into the nineteenth century-- the standard French Clarissa consisted
of this book "completed" by sections of what Prévost had   left   out,
translated   by   J.-B.   Suard   in   1762.   Prévost's Grandison, the
Nouvelles lettres angloises, was beyond   even   completion;   it   was
only   one-quarter   as   long   as   Richardson's   original,   and   the
Correspondance litteraire in 1758 characterized   it   as   "absolutely
mutilated." These   translations   circulated outside France as well:
Archenholz complained of them in 1782, and they served as the   basis
for   further   translations,   for   instance into Spanish and Russian.
Princess Aline in Eugen Onegin read Grandison in French or   in   the

Russian translation from French, and most even of educated Europe did no better.

Nor was Prévost's the only shortened version available. The reading world was showered with abridgments, adaptations, and transformations of the three books: for children, for illiterates, for the Youth of Both Sexes, for the Moral Reader, for Young German Maidens, for Loyal French Citizens, and even for rakes. (The curious reader may find these in Appendix A.) They were openly less authorized versions, for a less educated public, but their cumulative effect was enormous. Possibly the best of these is The Paths of Virtue Delineated (1756), a spirited and pleasant rendition of the three novels as non-epistolary novelettes. Almost alone among this class of adaptation, The Paths of Virtue Delineated lets the stories speak for themselves, with no obtrusive moralizing. Often enough, though, the adaptations were covert criticism, showing uneasiness at the "difficult" epistolary mode or at the possibility of misunderstanding Richardson's morality. The fortunes of Clarissa in the nineteenth century would be heavily influenced by such adaptations in both Europe and England.

But of course we are assuming that the followers of the Richardsonian school read any Richardson, even Prévost's. So many "Richardsonian" writers practiced their craft in the second part of the eighteenth century that the essentials of his sort of writing could well be gathered at a second or third remove. (This is one reason why it is difficult to speak of the influence of Richardson himself after 1800, although there clearly continues to be a Richardsonian sensibility in fiction; the school he headed had simply become too large.) The school comprised not only mere imitation, though there was plenty of that, but creative use of a form; it extended from Richardson himself to an explosively multiplying group of writers who were not tabulae rasae and who did not in all cases wholly approve of Richardson's techniques. Austen read Richardson; but she also read Fanny Burney, who read Richardson; and Fanny Burney read Frances Moore Brooke and Frances Sheridan, who read Richardson; and Frances Sheridan, who knew Richardson, must also have read Sarah Fielding, who knew Richardson too—and also read Richardson. And Richardson, who knew (and read) Sarah Fielding and Frances Sheridan, may also have read Eliza Haywood, who read Richardson. Richardson's novels themselves, particularly Sir Charles Grandison, developed out of a nexus that includes David Simple, Felicia to Charlotte, Jemmy and Jenny Jessamy, and Amelia, as well as, of course, Tom Jones.

No single formula will cover every manifestation of Richardsonian intent; what writers found valuable in the school changed from decade to decade. Its first concerns included increased social and psychological realism and a serious interest in investigating moral problems in contemporary life. The choice of a female protagonist allowed, to some degree, the separation of this psychological and moral realism from some of the other aspects of social life--for instance from the need to work. At its best, such fiction allowed some of the allegorical grandeur of the old romance to rub off on the new realism: moral didacticism combined pleasantly with realism of character to give characters like Pamela an elusive moral grandeur. This view of character as individual, yet morally representative, led directly to the emergent Bildungsromane, the fiction of Sarah Fielding, Gellert's Schwedische Graefin, and such minor successes as Eliza Haywood's late works.

A major theme of this school was the double nature of the person: both individual and moral representative. After Clarissa the quality of being morally representative was often felt to have tragic implications. In Sir Charles Grandison the very quality of exemplarity seemed to become tragic; it was because they were exemplary, and not merely through external pressures, that Sir Charles, Harriet and Clementina suffered so greatly. The nobility of finding one's own moral code and sticking to it, "living to one's self," implied a necessary difference from one's surroundings--not a rejection of the world so much as a transcendence of it. It is to Richardson's credit that he recognized how quixotic such actions could be; he is able to take a remarkably shifting, questioning attitude to his hero, a man who can very nearly play both Prince Hamlet and the Fool. Only in the light of such an ennobled conception of individuality can one understand the appeal of Werther or such a Sentimental avorton as Harley, the Man of Feeling. But few of the noble individuals of the Richardsonaden pretend to such ambiguity.

The theme of the private vs. the public self was mirrored in the epistolary novel. Richardson's chief innovation in the formal technique of fiction was of course the multiple-narrator epistolary form, the "symphonic novel" or Briefwechselroman. As practiced by the Richardsonians, the form required an editor who "found" and "arranged" a bundle of letters to tell a story. Within the story, two or more principal narrators wrote to confidant(e)s; the story was filled out by a number of minor correspondents. The reading of letters silently or aloud, their sharing, their forging, stealing, loss, regaining, their fragmentation, served as objective correlatives of the private self operating uneasily in a public world.

We tend now to think of the "best" examples of the form as those in which differentiation of character and significant overlap in the narrative allow disagreement about the meaning of events. But this may not have been true for its eighteenth-century practitioners. As Peter Sabor has pointed out, one of Fielding's objections to the form was that it tended toward solipsism. Many of the authors of the Richardsonaden, unhappy with any but clear moral points, seem to have found solipsism a major problem. Although the "editor" could serve as moral mediator by suppressing, arranging, and sometimes desperately commenting on the letters (as Richardson himself had done in the third edition of Clarissa) his role was necessarily limited. Most of the morality had to be expressed through the characters, and the more individualized they became, the more difficult it was to make them mere examples of virtue rewarded and vice punished.

For this reason, authors who felt at home with clear moralities often used Richardson's characters as stereotypes to indicate their own characters' moral nature. Clarissa became a shorthand for a suffering maiden, who was always to be considered a martyr to the wiles of a cruel masculine world. Harriet Byron and Clementina became exemplary virgins, Dull English and Colorful Foreign, with a great tendency to fall in love with men mysteriously unable to marry them. Such imitation often extended to specific character traits, scenes imitated from Richardson's originals, and even names: some Charlottish and Annaish characters were actually given the names of their originals. This imitative system was capable of nice distinctions. If one wished to imply that one's rake, though wild enough, was capable of reform, one compared him in some way with Mr. B., often by involving him in a scene stolen recognizably from Pamela. Sten Liljegren (1937.3) notes the extraordinary number of summerhouse scenes in German fiction at this period; many, though not all, were used in this way. A rake who was not slated for reform but who could be pitied would be given something of Lovelace, while a rake without any redeeming qualities would become Sir Hargrave Pollexfen. (This may help to explain the near-ubiquity of the kidnapping scene from Grandison, Sir Hargrave's only memorable moment.)

The most interesting of the "Richardsonian" characters were Lovelace and Grandison. From about 1770 onward, even the least skilled of the Richardsonians began to find a special interest in Lovelace. More than Clarissa, he was capable of tragic treatment; his sin was the Romantic virtue of the overreacher, and he began to represent the Sentimental questioning of received morality. The most interesting aspect of this fascination appears in the tendency, among some Sentimental writers of the last part of the century, to conflate him with Grandison, the other man who "lived to his own heart." In Holcroft's Anna St. Ives the tendency is mature: Frank, Anna, and Coke Clifton share and are admired for their exigence, in fact to a degree they admire each other for it, and it eventually reconciles them and allows Clifton's villainy to be turned to good. The conflation of cleaving to a standard of moral grandeur with cleaving to any standard at all signaled the increasing tendency of the Sentimental novel to fall into the very solipsism Fielding had feared.

Using Richardson's characters as moral indices limited the kind of characterization available to practitioners of the Richardsonaden: there are no major women characters who reform in Richardson's novels and so the women of the Richardsonaden tended to be typecast as suffering saints. Some aspects of Richardson's fiction depended on the flexibility of characterization of his originals; his imitators could not dramatize flexible characters and so some important parts of Richardson's novel structure, for instance the scenes of persuasion, were muffed or avoided. Thus, rather than mimicking Richardson's own balance of aspiring rationality and emotional turmoil, the writers of imitative Richardsonian fiction concentrated on scenes of emotion, especially emotion between "bad" active males and "good" passive females. All this did not happen in a vacuum: many factors, including sheer lazy writing, pushed the fiction in the directions it took. But we can see in such patterns the characteristic opposition of nineteenth-century fiction: on the one hand, deep exploration of character; on the other, the melodrama and stereotyping characteristic of many Victorian novels.

As early as 1780 the Richardsonian school presented a divided front. "Richardsonian fiction" might be anything from minute description of psychological change (the Richardson that we associate with Flaubert and James) to sexual melodrama. It is only to be expected that some of the readers brought up on Richardsonaden would find the slow, careful Richardson himself rather a disappointment, as Crabbe's Belinda Waters did (1834), while for others Richardson would be tarred with melodrama. Moreover, his social morality was becoming old-fashioned; the radical novels of the French Revolution drew on his work, but there is implicit criticism of him in the reaction to François de Neufchateau's dramatization of Pamela (1793), the ending of which was attacked as counter-revolutionary, and in such adaptations as Robert le Suire's Paméla française (1803), in which B. became encitoyenné, not Pamela ennobled. As realism became a less experimental style, Richardson's innovations in writing were overlooked or misunderstood; realism was bourgeois, old-fashioned, or associated with lack of artistic intention, and Richardson's deviations from realism were attacked as primitive or were simply ignored. There were few writers who, like Châteaubriand (1836), could separate the individual style from its context. The success of such adaptations as De kleine Grandison (1782) and the abridged American pamphlets gave Richardson a reputation as a writer for adolescents and children-- morally reliable, old-fashioned, and suitably dull. On the other hand, the parent who investigated the actual novels was bound to be shocked, and the adult and often scabrous explorations of morality in later eighteenth-century fiction, for instance the work of Restif de la Bretonne and Sade, who ascribed their darkness back to Richardson's example, gave further reason to consider him morally dubious, repellent, and--because less graphic--equally dull. Apparently Richardson could fit into none of the categories his works had created.

From about 1825, then, the three novels became biblia abiblia, important works that nobody read. "Nobody" did not include everybody; Balzac, Ruskin, George Eliot, Meredith, and the popular novelist Charlotte Yonge read even Grandison, and Meredith's and

Yonge's references to the book imply that they expected other
educated people had read it too. (A parody of <u>Grandison</u> published
in 1878 seems to imply the same.) However, it was difficult for
those without access to a large library even to find the book; it
had no complete edition between 1824 and 1883, and it was not
separately published unabridged from the 1820s until 1973--close to
a hundred and fifty years. <u>Pamela</u> continued to be published
frequently--indeed, it is possible that in some form <u>Pamela</u> has
<u>never</u> been out of print--but many of these editions were abridged or
bowdlerized. We hear of "sixpenny <u>Pamelas</u>" for sale at the corner
shop in 1892, when the cook of a friend of Augustine Birrell rushed
out to buy one; I have found no copy of any of these sixpenny
editions, but since the cook finished hers before dinner it was
almost certainly abridged. It "was constantly reprinted for sale
among the poor," Birrell says, and it had gained a reputation as a
servant-girl's delight. However, it was felt to be rather naughty
because of the attempted rape scenes; many "unabridged" Victorian
editions, like Archer's of 1873, are slightly bowdlerized.

    <u>Clarissa</u> underwent the most interesting transformations. It was
fairly familiar to readers in both England and France in the
nineteenth century--that is, a book with the title <u>Clarissa</u> was;
however, in anything like complete form it was published exactly
once, by the indefatigable Bernhard Tauchnitz, between the Scott
edition of 1824 and the Stephen edition of 1883. Robert Louis
Stevenson complained in 1877 that it was "one of the rarest [as it
is] certainly one of the best of books"; he himself had been able
to find it only in the even earlier Mangin edition of 1811. There
may have been unabridged or comparatively unabridged versions in
French and German. But the other editions of <u>Clarissa</u> during these
years, editions that were far more popular than any in the collected
works, in fact, <u>all</u> the <u>Clarissas</u> that exerted any influence on the
nineteenth-century popular conception of Richardson were
abridgments, and abridgments with ferocious purpose.

    Chief among these in influence and sensation value was Jules
Janin's French <u>Clarissa</u> of 1846. Written under the influence of
Villemain's <u>Lectures</u> as well as, one suspects, Ducray-Duminil and
Eugène Sue, Janin's <u>Clarissa</u> at least made no pretensions to be
Richardson's. His introduction reflected frankly that he felt
Richardson was no longer of much interest to the nineteenth century;
he promised to "demolish" the book in order to "select from these
gross materials the most beautiful parts of the monument . . .".
The result is really extraordinary--one of the gamier novels of the
period, with almost no important similarities to Richardson's
original--and it proved very popular, going into several editions in
German as well as the original French and reaching the stage in
theatrical adaptations. It was published in America (in French) and
may have had some slight effect on Richardson's American reputation
as a destroyer of morals.

What attracted the French to Janin´s <u>Clarissa</u>, the daring story and the character of Lovelace, repulsed the English. L.B. Lang believed as late as 1889 that <u>Clarissa</u> could not be read by unmarried women; in 1869 even the unshakeable Margaret Oliphant was ashamed to like Lovelace and could admit her feelings only privately. Richardson´s morality proved a sticking-point for many of his nineteenth-century critics, who felt that he shared--perhaps exaggerated--the crudity of his century. Four English abridgments, appearing almost simultaneously between 1868 and 1874, tried to purge <u>Clarissa</u> of its unfortunate frankness and moral ambiguity.

All four of these impose on <u>Clarissa</u> the utilitarian moral precepts and much of the style of a Victorian novel. In all four the editors show uneasiness at the epistolary form, pruning it in the interests of moral clarity, realism, and "story." Replacing the original almost-unmediated letters with a combination of epistolary fragments and linking narrative, all four ride roughshod over Richardson´s psychological complexities to preserve the "essential" of his characterization: Clarissa´s virginal innocence and Lovelace´s vice. In this the Milner and Sowerby edition of 1870 is perhaps the worst offender; of its 364 pages only 158 are given to the period before the rape, and Clarissa emerges a martyr. Somewhat more acceptable is the E.S. Dallas three-volume abridgment published in 1868, which describes itself as an attempt to prune Richardson of excessive moralizing. However, what Dallas removes from the dialogue he dramatizes in the action, turning Clarissa into a sentimental mid-Victorian victim. H. Buxton Forman, reviewing the book in 1869, apologized for its "ultra-moralizing," apparently not aware of Dallas´s extensive changes. A third abridgment, Mrs. Harriet Ward´s, appeared in the same year as Dallas´s and proved far more popular, but it is hardly better than the Milner and Sowerby edition. Such abridgments make sense if <u>Clarissa</u> is to be thought of as a victim-heroine, whose interest lies wholly in her "ruin" and fading away; but in fact they point out only how far the Victorian deathbed is from what Richardson had in mind.

C.H. Jones´s edition of <u>Clarissa</u> (1874) is a little less moralistic than these three, but psychologically no more accurate. It held the stage even longer than Mrs. Ward´s, preserving a Victorian version of <u>Clarissa</u> well into our time. The last edition of the Jones <u>Clarissa</u> I have traced was published in 1939, but so frequently was it reprinted in the sixty-five years of its glory that it is still readily available today.

Much of the nineteenth-century criticism of Richardson, and his popular reputation in the period, thus rested on a near-universal ignorance of Richardson´s texts. The first task of modern criticism was to remove those textual corruptions and get back to an idea of the novels based on the novels themselves. So far it has failed badly. Textually Richardson studies are still in a chaos; over two hundred years after Richardson wrote his books, the only really reliable editions of them are those he printed. The most frequently reprinted twentieth-century edition of a Richardson book, the <u>Pamela</u> kept in print by Everyman's Library since 1914, is unfortunately based on an extremely corrupt nineteenth-century text. The decision to take the third edition as the copy-text for the Everyman <u>Clarissa</u>, though more defensible, seems increasingly debatable. Scholars such as Shirley van Marter, John Carroll, Philip Gaskell, and Peter Sabor have done excellent recent work on the textual evolution of <u>Clarissa</u> and <u>Pamela</u>. Although the task is as enormous as <u>Clarissa</u> itself, their discoveries, the increasing interest of eighteenth-century scholars in Richardson, and the availability of computerized editing methods ought to open the way for scholarly editions of <u>Clarissa</u> and <u>Pamela</u> comparable to the recent edition of <u>Sir Charles Grandison</u> by Jocelyn Harris (now itself out of print).

But complete editions have caused problems too. After the excessive gentility of the Victorian <u>Clarissas</u>, the republication of complete if not accurate texts in 1901 and 1902 seemed to unveil a Richardson of appalling frankness. Such remarks as Sir Charles Grandison's prediction about Mrs. O-Hara (Emily's "mother will tell the world, that we live together") had disappeared from Victorian abridgments. But the shock of Richardson was not merely a matter of a felt vulgarity; in the first enthusiasm of Freudian criticism, readers of Richardson made the discovery that this paragon of virtue had taken as one of his subjects the portrayal of sexual aberration. Critics were appalled that a man who had such extensive understanding of the psychopathology of sex should be so naive, or so presumptuous, to speak of a moral order as well. It is an oddly nineteenth-century understanding of moralities, this idea that sex (even aberrant sex) should be either free of the moral order or incompatible with it. But it speaks in such divergent early twentieth-century criticism as Joseph Wood Krutch's righteous shock at the vulgarity of <u>Clarissa</u>, Priestley's Coleridgean unease at the "curiously unhealthy hothouse atmosphere" of the books, and Lawrence's triumphant insistence that the "slightly indecent . . . titillations" of <u>Pamela</u> were as pornographic as any work of his own. More recent writers have suggested more sophisticated psychological approaches, for instance, explaining that the novels continue to appeal because they provide psychological allegories of universal unconscious trends or case-studies of the bourgeoisie in eighteenth-century England.

The rediscovery of Richardson, together with much of value in the eighteenth-century novel, has been due to the efforts of many scholars to understand the intellectual coherence of the period. The first attempts to place Richardson in an eighteenth-century intellectual context came during the 1870s, led by Erich Schmidt in 1875, and good scholarly studies of his relationship to his period began to be published around 1890, with the work of men like Max Gassmeyer, J.G. Robertson, and Joseph Texte. Historical understanding of Richardson advanced on a number of fronts. First and of great value was the attempt to establish a decent biography.

A number of biographical-critical works, such as those of Dobson and Thomson at the turn of the century, drew together the known facts but made little advance over their sources. Not even his birthplace was known; a long, plaintive correspondence about it extended through decades of <u>Notes</u> <u>and</u> <u>Queries</u>. This and many other biographical questions have been resolved only with the publication of T.C. Duncan Eaves and Ben D. Kimpel's brilliant <u>Samuel</u> <u>Richardson:</u> <u>A</u> <u>Biography</u> (1971), the result of a quarter- century of effort.

After the discovery of the man himself came some attempt to connect his works with the mainstream of English and European fiction—a task made harder because, as we have said, the fiction itself is still largely uncharted. its extent is still undefined. Critics from Schmidt on discovered an interlocking network of influence, which they first expressed as speculation about the influence of one individual on another: Robert Chasles on Prevost, Rousseau on Goethe, Marivaux on Richardson. For instance, the question of whether <u>Marianne</u> had influenced <u>Pamela</u> was a favorite critical theme for a few years after World War I. But more recent studies have concentrated instead on the attractiveness of certain themes, forms, and subjects to the generality of writers in the period, and this has led to many valuable studies of lesser contemporary novels. The work of Tompkins (1930), Black (1933), Singer (1933), and Mayo (1948), among others, has been augmented in recent years by the work of critics such as Robert Adams Day, John J. Richetti, François Jost, Natascha Wurzbach, and Jerry C. Beasley. Recent feminist criticism by Nancy Kipnis Miller, Margaret Doody, Mary Poovey and others has recuperated women's novels of the period, casting valuable light on (for example) the popularity of female protagonists and the question of "heroism". From 1919 onward the work of Lawrence Marsden Price added to our knowledge of Richardson in Germany, while Richardson's connection with the French eighteenth century has been studied by critics such as Servais Etienne (1922) and Christian Pons (1969), as well as by Bernard Facteau, Daniel Mornet, Paul Van Tieghem, and many others. The recent bibliographical study by Angus Martin, Vivienne Mylne, and Richard Frautschi, the <u>Bibliographie</u> <u>du</u> <u>genre</u> <u>romanesque</u> <u>français</u> <u>1750-1800</u> (1977), is the first sustained attempt to chart the French fiction of the later eighteenth century and gives invaluable information on the prevalence of the <u>roman</u> <u>anglais</u>. Laurent Versini and June Sigler Siegel have studied Richardson's relationship to Laclos and Diderot and some indicative work has been done on the Prévost translations—through which, of course, and not through his original texts, Richardson was most familiar to Continental writers. Prof. Dimiter Daphinoff of the University of Bern is currently working on a new general study of Richardson in Europe.

To study the "Richardsonian" novel, as these critics have told us, is to study a complex of European relationships between the consumers and audience of fiction, the emergent bourgeoisies, and the themes and forms of what they read. This complex is hardly yet explored. Even in England itself, and in the relationship between Richardson's fiction and the moral, social, and religious milieu from which he came, the complexity of the relationship has only recently been recognized. Until about 1950 Richardson was considered a "Puritan" writer, a term used sloppily and judgmentally. The connection between this "Puritanism" and aspects of Richardson's fiction was explored disapprovingly, largely by Freudians intent on exploring submerged themes. More recently, a far more sophisticated and largely sympathetic view has been expressed by such writers as John Dussinger, Carey McIntosh, Allan Wendt, and Michael Bell. With a better definition of "Puritanism," aided in large part by Ian Watt's classic The Rise of the Novel (1957), there has grown up an appreciation of the connection between belief and literary form. In this light such concepts as "realism," "sentimentalism" and the epistolary form take on new qualities. Sheldon Sacks' classic study, Fiction and the Shape of Belief, and several of Martin Battestin's books on Fielding have drawn persuasive connections between moral intention, realism, and form, providing excellent background material for Richardson studies; criticism of Richardson himself has recently connected the formal requirements of religiously oriented realism to social purposiveness and the epistolary form. In such a morally motivated realism may lie the solution to the old problem of whether Richardson espouses "realism" or "idealism" in psychology. Dussinger has noted that the epistolary and journal forms naturally show conflict of mind--a conflict that may be exemplary because leading to reform and salvation--and Edward W. Copeland has written interestingly on the possible relationships between such morally motivated forms and the demi-allegories of Richardson's fiction. The same attention that has been given to "Puritanism" has not yet been given to Sentimentalism, its later and more secular descendant; a notable exception, however, is R.F. Brissenden's excellent Virtue in Distress (1974).

Such studies have led to what is possibly the most fertile current strand of Richardsonian criticism, discussion of his language itself. As Châteaubriand foretold in 1836, the re-separation of Richardson's style from bourgeois style has once again allowed readers to see Richardson's own distinctive linguistic structures. Eric Erämetsä has shown how much his style has in common with that of the later Sentimentalists--a community that may influence such writers as Goethe. The work of authors such as Wolfgang Folkierski shows Richardson's style to be, under its realistic surface, highly structured and distinctively suited to painting mental conflict. Comparisons of Richardson's writing with classical rhetoric, the rhetoric of tragedy, and Biblical and

theological language show him using language allusively with great
skill. Structural criticism, with its interest in linguistics, is
providing more means of exploring Richardson's style and connecting
style with the other structures of his fiction, such as repetitive
characterization and recurring situations.

The neglect of _Grandison_ is among the most striking failures of
current Richardsonian criticism.   Until a very few years ago,
discussion of Richardson's novels usually included only the first
two, and most of the general studies of eighteenth-century fiction,
even the most intelligent, have passed _Grandison_ by. (Margaret
Doody's brilliant synthesis of modern Richardson studies, _A Natural
Passion_, is a welcome exception; Gary Kelly's otherwise outstanding
Jacobin Novelists, on the other hand, seems flawed by his failure to
recognize patterns taken from _Grandison_.) The least that can be said
for _Grandison_ is that it is far too important to current Richardson
criticism to be neglected as it has.   It is the culmination of
Richardson's work as an author, the most skilful example of his
epistolary style, the end-point of his ideas on characterization and
social morality. Having said this, we can, if we wish, go on
actually to like it; some of the most sensitive Richardson critics
of recent years have done so.

Two current works deserve special mention. W.B. Warner's
Reading Clarissa, a study of the novel through reader-response
criticism, appeared in 1979; though Warner's approach and
conclusions have been widely quarreled with, the book provides a new
way of formulating questions of meaning and structure in
Richardson's greatest novel. And a new piece of Richardsoniana, a
partial dramatization of _Sir Charles Grandison_, possibly by Jane
Austen, it brings up once again the question of Richardson's
influence over her; it has been recently edited by Brian Southam.

Abbreviations

I have adopted the abbreviated periodical names used in the MLA International Bibliography and the library abbreviations used in the National Union Catalogue. Foreign libraries are referred to by readily recognizable abbreviations (Bib. Naz. Marciana) or by full names (Saltykov-Shchedrin, Országos Széchényi Konytvar). The following abbreviations are also used:

ADB	Allgemeine Deutsche Bibliothek
Block	Andrew Block. The English Novel 1740–1850 . . . London: Dawsons of Pall Mall, 1968.
BM	British Library at the British Museum, London
BZK	Bayerische Zentralkatalog
E&K	T.C. Duncan Eaves and Ben D. Kimpel. Samuel Richardson: A Biography. Oxford: Clarendon, 1971.
JVFD	Journal von und fur Deutschland
MMF	Angus Martin, Vivienne Mylne, and Richard Frautschi. Bibliographie du genre romanesque français 1751–1800. London: Mansell; Paris: France-Expansion, 1977.
RNB	"Richardson in Nederland: Een Bibliografie." Documentatieblad van de Werkgroep 18e Eeuw, Instituut voor Nederlandistiek van de Universiteit van Amsterdam, September 1979, pp. 19–70.
Sale	W.M. Sale. Samuel Richardson: A Catalogue of his Literary Career with Historical Notes. New Haven: Yale University Press, 1936.
Wilpert-Gühring	G. von Wilpert and A. Gühring. Erstausgaben deutscher Dichtung. Munich: Suhrkamp, 1967.

List of Major Works

Pamela, or Virtue Rewarded, 1740. (Continuation, Pamela in her Exalted Condition, 1741.)

Clarissa, or the History of a Young Lady (1747-48).

The History of Sir Charles Grandison (1753-54).

A full list of Richardson's works will be found in the Preface.

Writings By and About Richardson, 1723-1978

1723

1   [RICHARDSON, SAMUEL.] The True Briton, 1, no. 6 (June 21).
     This number of The True Briton is supposed by John
     Nichols to have been written by Richardson, but the
     evidence is inconclusive. For a summary of Richardson's
     involvement with the affair, see E&K, p. 21 ff.

1733

1   [RICHARDSON, SAMUEL.] The Apprentice's Vade Mecum, or, Young
     Man's Pocket-Companion. London: Printed for J. Roberts .
     . . and sold by J. Leake, at Bath, 1734 [1733], 108 pp.
     Detailed discussion of duties of apprenticeship--legal,
     extralegal, and moral; a general manual of middle-class
     young manhood. Third part is against Deism and
     freethinking.
     Reviewed in Weekly Miscellany, December 1, 1733, and its
     objections to theatre-going reprinted there, December 8,
     1733 and (abridged) March 8, 1735; see 1954.2, p. 72, and
     E&K, p. 60.

1734

1   [RICHARDSON, SAMUEL.] Rules and Orders to be Observed by the
     Members of this Chapel. [Dated August 30.] BM MSS. Add.
     27,799, f. 88 (Place Papers). Printed in 1947.1, pp.
     30-32.
     Regulations for the printers and compositors of
     Richardson's printing-house.

1735

1   [RICHARDSON, SAMUEL.] A Seasonable Examination of the Pleas
     and Pretensions of the Proprietors of, and Subscribers to,
     Play-houses, Erected in Defiance of the Royal License, with
     Some Brief Observations on the Printed Case of the Players
     belonging to Drury-Lane and Covent-Garden Theatres.
     London: Printed for T. Cooper, 29 pp.

Richardson attacks the "growing Evil" of the theaters and expresses himself in agreement with the censorship of the stage; opposes the spread of the theaters for moral and legal reasons and calculates how much the new theater would gain or lose by being closed, finding it an acceptable loss. See 1954.2 for discussion and evidence of authorship.

1736

1   [RICHARDSON, SAMUEL.] Verses. Gentleman's Magazine 6, no. 1: 51.
        Invited to dinner by the editors, Richardson replies in rhyme to say that he is pre-engaged.

1737

1   [DEFOE, DANIEL, and others.] The Complete English Tradesman, Directing him in the Several Parts and Progress of Trade. From his First Entering upon Business, to his Leaving Off. 4th ed. 2v. London: C. Rivington, 1738 [1737].
        1943.5 speculates that Richardson may have been involved in editing this edition; see also E&K, pp. 71-72.

2   MAUCLERC, JAMES. The Christian's Magazine, or Treasure. London: Printed for the Author by S. Richardson, n.d., 416 pp. BM.
        Richardson made some suggestions for, or helped to edit, this Latitudinarian, anti-Deist religious compendium, which can be dated by its entry in the SR (November 8, 1737) and its appearance in the December 1737 GM register of books (7:770). See Sale, p. xi; E&K, p. 70. Another edition (q.v.) appeared in 1748.

1738

*1 [DEFOE, DANIEL, and others.] A Tour thro' the Whole Island of Great Britain. 2d ed.
        See 1975.19 and E&K, pp. 72-76, for argument that this

version of the <u>Tour</u> was revised by Richardson with the help of others. Sale, item 28, argues differently.

Reviewed in <u>History of the Works of the Learned</u> 5 (March 1739): 194-97.

<u>1739</u>

1   RICHARDSON, SAMUEL. <u>Aesop´s Fables, with instructive Morals and Reflections, Abstracted from all Party Considerations, Adapted To All Capacities; and design´d to promote Religion, Morality, and Universal Benevolence . . . The Life of Aesop prefixed</u>, by <u>Mr. Richardson</u>. London: Printed for J. Osborn Jr., 1740 [1739], 228 pp. CtY.

A revision of Croxall´s and (principally) L´Estrange´s editions, with the political reflections largely omitted and the rest rearranged, rewritten, or reinterpreted to give it a distinctly Richardsonian moral cast. See E&K, pp. 76-79, for a summary of Richardson´s changes for this edition.

<u>1740</u>

1   RICHARDSON, SAMUEL. <u>The Negotiations of Sir Thomas Roe, in his Embassy to the Ottoman Porte</u>. . . . London: Printed by Samuel Richardson for the Society for the Encouragement of Learning; sold by G. Strahan, C. Rivington, P. Vailland . . . J. Osborn, Jr., 910 pp. BM.

Richardson provided the detailed table of contents for these letters of a seventeenth-century British statesman and, with some help from John Ward, Professor of Rhetoric at Gresham College, London, wrote the dedication and preface (see Sale, p. 7), which are now, in MS, in the British Museum (BM Add. MSS 6211, f. 53). Well-thought-of, according to the <u>History of the Works of the Learned</u> in its review (1740[1]: 346-60), the book was a financial failure; see E&K, pp. 80-83. MS 708/1-2 at Trinity College, Dublin, consists of materials for Richardson´s edition of the <u>Negotiations</u>, including a "Catalogue of such pieces among Sir Thomas Roe´s papers as were omitted" from the book, probably in Richardson´s hand.

2   [RICHARDSON, SAMUEL.] <u>Pamela: or, Virtue Rewarded</u>. <u>In</u> <u>a</u>
     <u>Series</u> <u>of</u> <u>Familiar</u> <u>Letters</u> <u>from</u> <u>a</u> <u>Beautiful</u> <u>Young</u> <u>Damsel,</u>
     <u>to</u> <u>her</u> <u>Parents</u>. <u>Now</u> <u>first</u> <u>published</u> <u>in</u> <u>order</u> <u>to</u> <u>cultivate</u>
     <u>the</u> <u>Principles</u> <u>of</u> <u>Virtue</u> <u>and</u> <u>Religion</u> <u>in</u> <u>the</u> <u>Minds</u> <u>of</u> <u>the</u>
     <u>Youth</u> <u>of</u> <u>Both</u> <u>Sexes</u>. . . . 2v. London: C.   Rivington
     & J. Osborn. 1741 [1740]. PPRF, NIC.
          The first edition, published November 6,   1740;   Sale,
     item 5.   A letter inserted in this edition had previously
     been published in the <u>Weekly</u> <u>Miscellany</u> (October 11),
     according to E&K, p.   60n16, which lists two further
     references to <u>Pamela</u> in the same magazine;   the editor's
     preface was reprinted there on December 13, and a letter
     and a poem by Aaron Hill appeared on February 28, 1741. It
     was reviewed in the <u>History</u> <u>of</u> <u>the</u> <u>Works</u> <u>of</u> <u>the</u> <u>Learned</u>
     1740 (2): 433-39;   the <u>GM</u>, (1741):250-51;   the <u>London</u>
     <u>Magazine</u> 10 (1741): 250-51, 303 (material on <u>Shamela</u>),
     358; the <u>Bibliothèque</u> <u>britannique</u> 17 (1741):   27-60
     (largely   summary);   the   <u>Göttingische</u>   <u>Zeitungen</u> <u>von</u>
     <u>gelehrten</u> <u>Sachen</u>, February 23, 1741 (first review to
     suggest a connection between <u>Pamela</u> and Marivaux); the
     <u>Bibliothèque</u> <u>raisonnée</u> 28, 2 (1741):   417-27 (hostile);
     the <u>Journal</u> <u>de</u> <u>Verdun</u> 5 (1742):   108 ff. (praises
     naturalness); by the abbé Goujet in the <u>Bibliothèque</u>
     <u>françoise</u> <u>ou</u> <u>Histoire</u> <u>littéraire</u> <u>de</u> <u>la</u> <u>France</u> 35, 2 (1742):
     319 ff.; in the <u>Mercure</u> <u>de</u> <u>France</u>, December 1742; in the
     <u>Laerde</u> <u>Tidender</u> in 1742 and 1743, according to R.M.
     Stolpe, <u>Dagspressen</u> <u>i</u> <u>Danmark</u> (Hannaford, item 133);   and,
     perhaps by Haller, in the <u>Zurcher</u> <u>freymuthige</u> <u>Nachrichten</u> 1
     (1744): 19-20, 106-7, and 6 (1749) 107. (Cf.   Hannaford,
     item 312.) Early reactions to it came frequently in the
     form of letters to the "editor," Richardson, many of which
     are preserved in the Forster MSS.

                              <u>1741</u>

1   ANON. <u>The</u> <u>Life</u> <u>of</u> <u>Pamela</u>. <u>Being</u> <u>a</u> <u>full</u> <u>and</u> <u>particular</u>
     <u>relation</u> <u>of</u> <u>the</u> <u>birth</u> <u>and</u> <u>advancement</u> <u>of</u> <u>that</u> <u>fortunate</u> <u>and</u>
     <u>beautiful</u> <u>young</u> <u>damsel</u>. . . . London: Printed for C.
     Whitefield, 495 pp. MH, CtY.
          A retelling of <u>Pamela</u> in straight narrative, with some
     changes and elaborations, a few new subplots, and
     considerable sheer plagiarism;   numerous copper plates,
     some interesting. Sale, item 78.

2   ---. <u>Memoirs</u> <u>of</u> <u>the</u> <u>Life</u> <u>of</u> <u>Lady</u> <u>H----,</u> <u>the</u> <u>Celebrated</u>
       <u>Pamela</u>. London: [T. Cooper], 59 pp. BM.
            Purports to be the life of Lady Hannah Heselrige,
       supposedly the original of Pamela; leaves out much of
       Richardson's explicit sexuality, changes the story greatly.
       Indirect criticism of <u>Pamela</u> for keeping the reader "in
       Suspense by the artful Clue of Romantic Amusements," p. 1.
       The only known copy lacks a title page, but the book is
       advertised in the <u>London</u> <u>Magazine</u>, December, 1741, as being
       printed by Cooper. Sale, item 77.

*3   ---. <u>Pamela</u> <u>Bespiegeld,</u> <u>Of,</u> <u>Het</u> <u>beruchte</u> <u>Boek</u> <u>het</u> <u>welk</u> <u>onder</u>
       <u>der</u> <u>Titel:</u> Pamela, of de beloonde Deugd, <u>Nu</u> <u>al</u> <u>binnen</u> <u>'t</u>
       Jaar viermaal <u>in</u> <u>het</u> Engelsch <u>gedrukt,</u> <u>in</u> <u>het</u> Fransch <u>reeds</u>
       <u>getranslateert</u> <u>is,</u> <u>en</u> <u>in</u> <u>het</u> Nederduits <u>ook</u> <u>overgezet</u> <u>en</u>
       <u>uitgegeven</u> <u>worden</u> <u>zal,</u> Zedelyk beschouwd en onderzocht, in
       een Brief aan den Uitgever, <u>uit</u> <u>het</u> Engels <u>vertaald.</u> <u>Waar</u>
       <u>by</u> <u>vooraf</u> <u>geplaatst</u> <u>is</u> <u>een</u> <u>kort</u> <u>UYTTREKZEL</u> <u>Van</u> <u>het</u> <u>gemelde</u>
       <u>Boek,</u> <u>Benevens</u> <u>een</u> <u>VOOR-REDEN</u> <u>Van</u> <u>den</u> <u>Overzetter.</u> . . .
       [Pamela Contemplated; Or, The notorious Book, which under
       the title, <u>Pamela or Virtue Rewarded</u>, has within this year
       been printed <u>four</u> <u>times</u> in English, is already translated
       into French, and is to be translated and printed in Dutch,
       <u>Morally</u> <u>regarded</u> <u>and</u> <u>investigated</u>, in a Letter to the
       Editor, translated from the English. Preceded by a short
       abstract of the abovementioned book, with a preface by the
       translator.] Amsterdam: Dirk Swart, 107 pp. Kongelige
       Bib.
            Source: <u>RNB</u>, item 15. 1969.17, pp. xxiii ff.,
       discusses this as if it were several books bound together;
       however, it is a single publication drawing together
       elements of <u>Pamela</u> and <u>Pamela</u> <u>Censured</u>, as well as what
       appears to be original criticism.

4   ---. <u>Pamela</u> <u>censured:</u> <u>in</u> <u>a</u> <u>letter</u> <u>to</u> <u>the</u> <u>editor:</u> <u>showing</u>
       <u>that</u> <u>under</u> <u>the</u> <u>specious</u> <u>pretence</u> <u>of</u> <u>cultivating</u> <u>the</u>
       <u>principles</u> <u>of</u> <u>virtue</u> <u>in</u> <u>the</u> <u>minds</u> <u>of</u> <u>the</u> <u>youth</u> <u>of</u> <u>both</u>
       <u>sexes,</u> <u>the</u> <u>most</u> <u>artful</u> <u>and</u> <u>alluring</u> <u>amorous</u> <u>ideas</u> <u>are</u>
       <u>convey'd</u>. . . . London: J. Roberts, 59 pp. TxU, MH,
       ICU, CtY.
            Attacks <u>Pamela</u> on moral grounds.

5   ---. <u>Pamela</u> <u>in</u> <u>High</u> <u>Life:</u> <u>or,</u> <u>Virtue</u> <u>Rewarded.</u> <u>In</u> <u>a</u> <u>Series</u>
       <u>of</u> <u>Familiar</u> <u>Letters</u> <u>from</u> <u>Pamela</u> <u>to</u> <u>her</u> <u>Parents.</u> <u>Carefully</u>
       <u>extracted</u> <u>from</u> <u>Original</u> <u>Manuscripts,</u> <u>communicated</u> <u>to</u> <u>the</u>

Editor by her Son. . . . London: Printed for Mary
Kingman. MH.
  Spurious continuation of Pamela, highly moralistic,
carries story through her death. Sale, item 69.

5A   ---. London Magazine 10: 250-51, 304, 358.
          Three short poems for and against Pamela.

*5B   BENNET, GEORGE. Pamela, or Virtue Rewarded: A Heroick Poem.
          Quoted in Scots Magazine, October 1741.
          Source: Wiles, Serial Publication in England, p. 255.

6   [DANCE, JAMES?] [JAMES LOVE, pseud.] Pamela, or, Virtue
          Triumphant. A Comedy. As it was intended to be Acted at
          the Theatre Royal in Drury-Lane. London: Samuel Lyne, 96
          pp. CtY.
          See 1935.9. Dottin identifies this play as by Lyne, but
          unjustifiably.

Fielding, Henry. See Keyber, Conny.

7:      [GIFFARD, HENRY.] Pamela. A Comedy. As it is perform'd
          Gratis, at the Late Theater in Goodman's-Fields. London:
          H. Hubbard, 66 pp. BM.
          Dramatic version of Pamela, in which Garrick played the
          original Jack Smatter (Richardson's Jackey). Dottin calls
          it an "indigne travestissement" (1930.5, p. 516); it is
          remarkable chiefly for the number and comparative
          coarseness of its comic characters. The epilogue
          indirectly criticizes Pamela for "low" themes. Sale, item
          74; a pirated edition.

*8   ---. Pamela, a Comedy. . . . London: Jo. Miller, 54 pp.
          Another edition of 1741.7: Pirated. Source: Sale,
          item 73.

9   ---. Pamela, a Comedy. . . . London: J. Robinson, 1742
          [1741], 74 pp. BM.
          The authorized edition of 1741.7. Sale, item 71.

10   [HAYWOOD, ELIZA?] Anti-Pamela: or, Feign'd Innocence
          Detected, in a Series of Syrena's Adventures. A narrative
          which has really its foundation in truth and nature; and
          at the same time that it entertains, by a vast variety of
          surprizing incidents, arms against a partial credulity, by

shewing <u>the</u> <u>mischiefs</u> <u>that</u> <u>frequently</u> <u>arise</u> <u>from</u> <u>a</u> <u>too</u>
<u>sudden</u> <u>admiration.</u> <u>Publish'd</u> <u>as</u> <u>a</u> <u>necessary</u> <u>caution</u> <u>to</u> <u>all</u>
<u>young</u> <u>gentlemen</u>. London: J. Huggonson, 286 pp. BM.
　　Eliza Haywood is usually identified as the author of
this attempt to capitalize on <u>Pamela</u>; the book is
concerned with <u>Pamela</u>, however, for only its first episode,
after which it becomes a straight Haywooden <u>roman</u>
<u>scandaleux</u>. It is partly epistolary and letters play a
large role in its plot.

11　[KELLY, JOHN.] <u>Pamela's</u> <u>Conduct</u> <u>in</u> <u>High</u> <u>Life.</u> <u>Published</u> <u>from</u>
　　<u>her</u> <u>Original</u> <u>Papers.</u> <u>To</u> <u>which</u> <u>are</u> <u>prefix'd,</u> <u>Several</u>
　　<u>Curious</u> <u>Letters</u> <u>written</u> <u>to</u> <u>the</u> <u>Editor</u> <u>on</u> <u>the</u> <u>Subject</u>. 2v.
　　London: Ward & Chandler, John Wood, Charles Woodward,
　　Thomas Waller. BM (Vol. 1 only); Trinity College, Dublin
　　(Vol. 1 only).
　　　　Epistolary, with a framing epistolary narrative (the
　　"several curious letters"). Criticism of <u>Shamela</u> and
　　<u>Pamela</u> <u>Censured</u>; defense of <u>Pamela</u> from immodesty and
　　attempt to follow Richardson stylistically but to improve
　　on him in epistolary realism. No plot, many
　　interpolations. See 1930.6, 1936.1.

12　---. <u>Pamela's</u> <u>Conduct</u> <u>in</u> <u>High</u> <u>Life.</u> . . . Dublin:
　　Printed for George Faulkner and Oliver Nelson. Trinity
　　College, Dublin (Vol. 1 only).
　　　　Pirated edition. Kelly advertised his "continuation" of
　　<u>Pamela</u> in the <u>Country</u> <u>Journal,</u> <u>London</u> <u>Daily</u> <u>Post</u>, and
　　<u>General</u> <u>Advertiser</u>, among other papers, and drew
　　Richardson's wrath; their advertisements and
　　counter-advertisements are discussed at length in E&K, pp.
　　136-39.

13　[KEYBER, CONNY, pseud.] [HENRY FIELDING?] <u>An</u> <u>Apology</u> <u>for</u> <u>the</u>
　　<u>Life</u> <u>of</u> <u>Mrs.</u> <u>Shamela</u> <u>Andrews.</u> <u>In</u> <u>which,</u> <u>the</u> <u>many</u>
　　<u>notorious</u> <u>falshoods</u> <u>and</u> <u>misreprsentations</u> [sic] <u>of</u> <u>a</u> <u>book</u>
　　<u>called</u> <u>Pamela</u> <u>are</u> <u>exposed</u> <u>and</u> <u>refuted;</u> <u>and</u> <u>all</u> <u>the</u>
　　<u>matchless</u> <u>Arts</u> <u>of</u> <u>that</u> <u>young</u> <u>Politician</u> <u>set</u> <u>in</u> <u>a</u> <u>true</u> <u>and</u>
　　<u>just</u> <u>Light.</u> <u>Together</u> <u>with</u> <u>A</u> <u>Full</u> <u>Account</u> <u>of</u> <u>all</u> <u>that</u>
　　<u>passed</u> <u>between</u> <u>her</u> <u>and</u> <u>Parson</u> <u>Arthur</u> <u>Williams;</u> <u>whose</u>
　　<u>Character</u> <u>is</u> <u>represented</u> <u>in</u> <u>a</u> <u>manner</u> <u>something</u> <u>different</u>
　　<u>from</u> <u>that</u> <u>which</u> <u>he</u> <u>bears</u> <u>in</u> <u>Pamela.</u> <u>The</u> <u>whole</u> <u>being</u> <u>exact</u>
　　<u>Copies</u> <u>of</u> <u>authentick</u> <u>Papers</u> <u>delivered</u> <u>to</u> <u>the</u> <u>Editor.</u>
　　<u>Necessary</u> <u>to</u> <u>be</u> <u>had</u> <u>in</u> <u>all</u> <u>Families.</u> . . . London:
　　Printed for A. Dodd, 71 pp.

The most famous parody of Pamela, published April 4,
1741, is almost certainly assignable to Fielding. 1928.2,
p. 68, summarizes the reasons for thinking so:
Richardson, a man with many publishing contacts, said it
was Fielding's; Fielding did not like Cibber or Middleton,
who are pilloried in the text; Fielding preferred the
obsolescent "hath" and doth," as does the author of
Shamela; Fielding used "Booby" in Joseph Andrews as it is
used here [and compare his epilogue to Charles Johnson's
Caelia, 1732, in which "not one marrying Booby will come
nigh" the heroine - SWRS]; Fielding used the locution
"just and true Light" in advertising Jonathan Wild in the
Miscellanies, 1742; Fielding admired Parson Oliver, whose
name is given to a character in Shamela. In short, "it
seems unlikely that two men with such similar outlook and
powers of description should have been living at the same
time, and even more so that one of them should never (as it
would seem) have ventured beyond an anonymous brochure." J.
Paul de Castro (N&Q, 12th ser. 1 (1916): 22-24) adds the
fact of Fielding's acquaintance with Dodd and sets out
further linguistic parallels. See also 1936.10; C.R.
Greene, MLN 59 (1944): 571; 1936.5; J.C. Maxwell, N&Q
193 (1948): 364-65; C.B. Woods, PQ 25 (1946): 248-72.
Fielding sneers at Pamela under his own name in the
Miscellanies(1743) 1:91.

14   ---. An Apology for the Life of Mrs. Shamela Andrews. .   .
      . London: A. Dodd, 69 pp.
         The second edition, with the typo in the title page
      corrected, published November, 1741. Reproduced as ARS,
      no. 57:(1956).

15   ---. An Apology for the Life of Mrs. Shamela Andrews. .   .
      . Dublin: Oliver Nelson, 71 pp.
         Pirated edition, with the typo in the title page
      corrected.

16   PARRY, JAMES. The True Anti-Pamela; or, Memoirs of Mr.
      James Parry, late Organist of Ross in Herefordshire. In
      which are inserted, His Amours with the celebrated Miss
      T--- of Monmouthshire. Written by Himself, In Two Parts
      Compleat. Part I: Memoirs of his Life and Amours. Part
      II: Genuine Letters of Love and Gallantry. London:
      Printed for the Author; and sold by the Booksellers in
      Town and Country, 378 pp.

The title is the closest resemblance to <u>Pamela</u>.

*17   ---. <u>The True Anti-Pamela</u>. . . .
A second edition. Source: Sale. Another edition
appeared in 1770.

18   ---. <u>The True Anti-Pamela</u>. . . . Dublin: Thomas
Armitage, 324 pp. BM.
Probably a pirated edition.

19   POVEY, CHARLES. <u>The Virgin in Eden, or the State of
Innocency. Deliver'd by way of image and description.
Presenting a nobleman, a student, and heiress, on their
progress from Sodom to Canaan. With the parable of the
shepherd, Zachariah, and Mary who dwelt in thatched
tenements, secluded from noise and snares. Their holy
living and dying. To which are added, Pamela's letters
proved to be immodest romances painted in images of virtue;
masquerades in disguise, that receiv'd birth now vice
reigns in triumph, and swells in streams even to a deluge.
. . .The decree of God appoints these records to be kept
in every house, in every kingdom and state, from one
generation to another, till the great fall of nature.
Wrote by the author of the sheets entitled, Torments after
death</u>. . . . London: J. Roberts, pp. 68-71. BM.
Accuses Richardson of inflaming his readers by showing
Pamela undressed and through the character of Mrs. Jewkes.
Sale, item 75.

*20   ---. <u>The Virgin in Eden</u>. . . .
A second issue of 1741; source: Sale, item 76. Divine
intervention, as noted by Povey above, was doubtless the
cause for two purported later issues of this book, of which
no copies have been traced, before its last appearance in
1767.

21   [RICHARDSON, SAMUEL.] <u>Letters written to and for particular
friends, on the most important occasions. Directing not
only the requisite style and forms to be observed in
writing familiar letters; but how to think and act justly
and prudently, in the common concerns of human life.
Containing one hundred and seventy-three letters. None of
which were ever before published</u>. London: Printed for C.
Rivington, J. Osborn, and J. Leake at Bath, 280 pp. MH,
DLC, CtY.

Downs's edition of the <u>Familiar</u> <u>Letters</u> (1928) notes the
connection of this compendium with the later novels.
1934.6 notes that selections from it were appearing in
letter-writing manuals as late as 1924.

22   ---. <u>Letters</u> <u>written</u> <u>to</u> <u>and</u> <u>for</u> <u>particular</u> <u>friends</u>. . . .
        Dublin: Printed for George Faulkner, 268 pp. CtY.
        Pirated edition.

23   ---. <u>Pamela, or Virtue Rewarded</u>. . . . 2d ed. 2v.
        London: Printed for C. Rivington and J. Osborn. MH.
        Sale, item 6; appeared mid-February, 1741.

24   ---. <u>Pamela, or Virtue rewarded</u>. . . . 3d ed. 2v.
        London: Printed for C. Rivington and J. Osborn. MH.
        Sale, item 7; appeared in March, 1741.

25   ---. <u>Pamela, or Virtue Rewarded</u>. . . . 4th ed. 2v.
        London: Printed for C. Rivington and J. Osborn. MH.
        Sale, item 8; appeared in May, 1741.

26   ---. <u>Pamela, or Virtue Rewarded</u>. . . . 5th ed. 2v.
        London: Printed for C. Rivington and J. Osborn. MH.
        Sale item 9; appeared September 22, 1741. Each of
        these editions contains changes from the previous
        one--substantial changes in the cases of the second and
        fifth editions; see E&K, pp. 124-25.

27   ---. <u>Pamela, or Virtue Rewarded. In a Series of familliar</u>
        [!] <u>Letters from a beautiful young damsel, to her parents.</u>
        <u>. . To which are perfix'd</u> [!], <u>extracts from several</u>
        <u>curious letters</u>. . . . London: Mary Kingman. MH.
        Pirated edition in 20 numbers.

28   ---. <u>Pamela, or Virtue Rewarded. In a series of familiar</u>
        <u>letters</u>. . . . 2v.? Dublin: Printed by R. Reilly,
        for G. Ewing and G. Faulkner.
        First pirated Irish edition. Vol. 1 only? See
        1742.18. Sale, item 5.

29   ---. <u>Pamela, or Virtue Rewarded. In a Series of Familiar</u>
        <u>Letters from a Beautiful Young Damsel to her Parents: And</u>
        <u>Afterwards, In her Exalted Condition, Between Her, and</u>
        <u>Persons of Figure and Quality, Upon the Most Important and</u>
        <u>Entertaining Subjects, in Genteel Life. The Third and</u>

Fourth <u>Volumes</u>. <u>Published in order to Cultivate the</u>
<u>Principles of Virtue and Religion in the Minds of the Youth</u>
<u>of Both Sexes</u>. Vols. 3 and 4. London: Printed for
Samuel Richardson: and Sold by C. Rivington and J.
Osborn, 1742 [1741].
   The first edition of <u>Pamela in her Exalted Condition</u>,
published December 7, 1741. Sale, item 15.

*30   ---. <u>Pamela of de Beloonde Deugd</u>. <u>In een reeks van</u>
      <u>gemeenzaame brieven</u>. <u>Naar den Vierden druk uit het Engels</u>
      <u>vertaald</u>. Translated by Johannes Stinstra? 4v.
      Amsterdam: Gerrit Tielenburg, 1741-42.
         Source. <u>RNB</u>, item 1. A second edition appeared in 1742
      (<u>RNB</u>, item 2, which corrects 1969.17, pp. xxiii ff. See
      also Jan te Winkel, <u>De Ontwikkelingsgang der Nederlandsche</u>
      <u>Letterkunde</u>, Haarlem, 1908-21, 4, part 1: 133; 1938.3, p.
      357n1). A third edition appeared in 1744 (<u>RNB</u>, item 3) and
      one from another publisher in 1747 (<u>RNB</u>, item 4).

31   ---. <u>Pamela; ou, La Vertu recompensée</u>. <u>Traduit de l'anglois</u>
      . . . Translator unknown. 2v. London: T. Woodward &
      J. Osborn. Cty, IU, NjP, CSt, MWiW-C.
         The translator's identity is an intriguing question.
      Roddier asserts that it was not Prévost (see 1956.7); the
      frequent eighteenth-century attributions of it to him are
      apparently based on no evidence, and the style of
      translation is not his. It was almost certainly not
      translated by Aubert de la Chesnaye des Bois; see 1743.1.
      In his (or her?) preface the translator states that he
      prepared the translation "avec la participation de
      l'Auteur"; material that later reached the English <u>Pamela</u>
      was actually published here first.
         The French <u>Pamela</u> was reprinted with great frequency,
      two or three editions often appearing in a single year;
      for reasons of space these have been omitted.

32   SHENSTONE, WILLIAM. Letter of July 22, 1741, to the Rev.
      Richard Jago, "in the Manner of <u>Pamela</u>." Published in
      1939.4.
         That is, with the pen "go[ing] scrattle, scrattle"
      through masses of meaningless detail. Shenstone read all
      three novels and criticized them for prolixity and,
      occasionally, for style; however, he praised Richardson
      for "nice observation" and morality. See 1939.4.

<u>1742</u>

*1   ANON. <u>Lettre</u> <u>à</u> <u>Madame</u> <u>de</u> *** <u>sur</u> <u>l´Anti-Pamela</u>.
         Source: Hannaford, item 335.

*2   ---. <u>Lettre</u> <u>à</u> <u>Monsieur</u> <u>l´Abbé</u> <u>Des</u> <u>Fontaines</u> <u>sur</u> <u>"Pamela."</u>
         Amiens, August 7, 1742.
              Source: Hannaford, item 131. Suggests that Richardson
         learned from the French novelists; attacks Desfontaines
         for liking a novel that "attacks France." Reply to 1742.7.

*3   ---. Poem. <u>Le</u> <u>Magasin</u> <u>des</u> <u>événemens</u> <u>de</u> <u>tous</u> <u>genres</u> 4:
         76-80.
              Source: Hannaford, item 340. Doggerel verse retelling
         of <u>Pamela</u>, criticizing character of heroine.

*4   ---. "Pamela the Second." <u>Universal</u> <u>Spectator,</u> <u>and</u> <u>Weekly</u>
         <u>Journal</u>, April 24, May 8.
              A "dramatic poem" based on a case "similar to"
         Pamela´s--though not as similar as the author asserts.
         Praises morality of <u>Pamela</u>. Sources: 1969.3 and E&K, pp.
         133-34.

*5   [DANCE, JAMES?] [JAMES LOVE, pseud.] <u>Pamela:</u> <u>a</u> <u>comedy</u>.
         Dublin: Printed by and for Oliver Nelson. Trinity
         College, Dublin.
              Source: Catalog of the library of Trinity College,
         Dublin.

6   [DEFOE, DANIEL, and others.] OTHERS.] <u>A</u> <u>Tour</u> <u>thro´</u> <u>the</u> <u>Whole</u>
         <u>Island</u> <u>of</u> <u>Great</u> <u>Britain</u> <u>. . . by a Gentleman.</u> <u>The</u> <u>Third</u>
         <u>Edition.</u> <u>With</u> <u>very</u> <u>great</u> <u>Additions,</u> <u>Improvements</u> <u>and</u>
         <u>Corrections;</u> <u>which</u> <u>bring</u> <u>it</u> <u>down</u> <u>to</u> <u>the</u> <u>Year</u> <u>1742</u>. 4v.
         London: J. Osborn, S. Birt, D. Browne, J. Hodges, A.
         Millar, J. Whiston, & J. Robinson.

7   DESFONTAINES, PIERRE F.G., abbé. Letter 429. <u>Observations</u>
         <u>sur</u> <u>les</u> <u>Ecrits</u> <u>modernes</u> 29: 193-214.
              Letter 429 of July 28, 1742, is devoted to <u>Pamela</u>.
         Desfontaines finds it one of the most natural books he has
         ever read, not depending on unusual events or melodrama,
         and to some appearing boring; the style may seem "négligé
         et plat, parce qu´il est simple et naturel," p. 205.
         Illusion is necessary to fiction, and <u>Pamela</u>, almost alone
         of modern fiction, creates a successful illusion; it is

also an excellent treatise of morality in action. The epistolary style is essential to the book, the letters helping the denouement and giving added verisimilitude because they motivate the narrator's detailed recollection of events; the style is exactly what it should be to touch our hearts. A few daring episodes, necessary to the action, leave no bad impression. For its unity of action and character, Desfontaines finds in it "en quelque sorte les qualites d'un Poeme exact et regulier" p. 206, and if all novels were like it Pere Poree would have had nothing to say against fiction. However, the material after the marriage should be cut. Notes the <u>Lettre</u> <u>sur</u> <u>Pamela</u>.

7   EDGE, Mr. <u>Pamela:</u> <u>or,</u> <u>Virtue</u> <u>Rewarded.</u> <u>An</u> <u>Opera</u> <u>Alter'd</u> <u>from</u> <u>the</u> <u>Comedy,</u> <u>call'd</u>, Pamela, <u>by</u> <u>Mr.</u> <u>Edge</u>. . . . Newcastle: Printed by J. White and Sold by the Booksellers, 47 pp. CtY, MH.
     Adapted from Giffard's <u>Pamela</u>, in a hurry, "for . . . several different Persons were writing on that Subject at the same Time. . . . " p. vii. Uninspired. Reprinted in 1975 with Dance's, Giffard's, and Goldoni's adaptations (see under 1974.23).

8   FIELDING, HENRY. <u>History</u> <u>of</u> <u>the</u> <u>Adventures</u> <u>of</u> <u>Joseph</u> <u>Andrews</u> <u>and</u> <u>of</u> <u>his</u> <u>friend</u> <u>Mr.</u> <u>Abraham</u> <u>Adams.</u> <u>Written</u> <u>in</u> <u>imitation</u> <u>of</u> <u>the</u> <u>manner</u> <u>of</u> <u>Cervantes</u> . . . 2v. London: Andrew Millar.
     Published on February 22, 1742, and frequently republished, including two more editions in London in the same year and one in Dublin, pirated. As the publishing history of <u>Joseph</u> <u>Andrews</u> is more properly a subject for a Fielding bibliography, we will note no more editions of this, the most sublime and enduring of the "Antipamelas." For a recent study of its relationship to <u>Pamela</u>, see 1978.11.

9   [GIFFARD, HENRY.] <u>Pamela:</u> <u>a</u> <u>Comedy</u>. . . . London: Printed for J. Robinson, 76 pp.
     Sale, item 72.

10   [HAYWOOD, ELIZA.] <u>Anti-Pamela</u>. . . . London: F. Cogan, 286 pp. CtY.
     Sale, item 65. Second issue of first edition.

11   ---. The Virtuous Villager, or Virgin's Victory: Being the
        Memoirs of a very Great Lady at the Court of France.
        Written by Herself. . . . Translated from the Original,
        by the Author of La Belle Assemblee. 2v. London: Francis
        Cogan. BM.
             Actually by the translator of La Belle Assemblée; the
        considerably altered original of The Virtuous Villager is
        the Paysanne parvenue of Charles de Fieux, chevalier de
        Mouhy. Pamela and anti-Pamela stories dot the book;
        Charlotta's is one of the latter, and the duke who
        debauches her lists a series of men who have married
        beneath themselves and regretted it (1:15-16), but the
        Virtuous Villager, late plain Jeannetta, has been raised to
        the glory of being Marchioness de L-- V--- because of her
        virtue; "it is to that alone I am indebted for the good
        Fortune I enjoy" (1:34). Haywood is apparently to some
        degree capitalizing on Pamela both ways.

11A   HURD, RICHARD. Letter to Cox Macro, November 7. BM Add. MSS
        32,557, f.47. Printed in 1956.5, p. 63.
             Criticizes Pamela.

12   JOLYOT DE CRÉBILLON, PIERRE PROSPER. Letter to L.
        Chesterfield, July 26. Printed by Maty, 1:ix-x.
             "Without Pamela," Crébillon fils writes, "we should not
        know here what to read or to say." Chesterfield does not
        mention the book in reply, August 26.

13   [MARQUET, l'abbé?] Lettre sur Pamela. Londres: n.p., 42 pp.
        BM.
             Reviewing a "bad translation" of Pamela, "le meuble à la
        mode," p. 3, the author finds that "malgré la négligeance
        du style, . . . [ce livre] m'a touché et même attendri,"
        p. 4, and that the subject and moral (the whole world
        bends before beauty and virtue) are well-chosen for women.
        However, many details are undignified and, if not immoral,
        perhaps a bit off-color. The book should end with the
        marriage.

*14   PARRY, JAMES. True anti-Pamela. . . . London.
             Source: NCBEL.

*15   [RICHARDSON, SAMUEL.] Letters written to and for particular
        Friends. . . .
             Second edition. Source: Sale, item 22 (supplied by

advertisements; no copy has been located).

*15   ---. <u>Pamela, or Virtue Rewarded. In a Series of Familiar</u>
<u>Letters from a Beautiful Young Damsel to her Parents: And</u>
<u>Afterwards, In her Exalted Condition,Between Her and</u>
<u>Persons of Figure and Quality, Upon the Most Important and</u>
<u>Entertaining Subjects in Genteel Life.</u> . . . <u>The Second</u>
<u>Edition.</u> London: Printed for S. Richardson and sold by
J. Osborn and J. Rivington.
         Second edition of Vols. 3 and 4 of <u>Pamela</u>. Sale, item
16.

17   ---. <u>Pamela, or Virtue Rewarded, In a Series of Familiar</u>
<u>Letters From a Beautiful Young Damsel to her Parents: and</u>
<u>Afterwards, In her Exalted Condition, between Her and</u>
<u>Persons of Figure and Quality, upon the Most Important and</u>
<u>Entertaining Subjects, in Genteel Life. In Four Volumes.</u>
<u>Publish'd in order to cultivate the Principles of Virtue</u>
<u>and Religion in the Minds of the Youth of Both Sexes. The</u>
<u>Sixth Edition, Corr'd. and Embellish'd with Copper Plates,</u>
<u>Design'd and Engrav'd by Mr. Hayman, and Mr. Gravelot.</u>
London: Printed for S. Richardson, and Sold by J. Osborn
and John Rivington. MH, BM, BN, CtY, NjP, OO, CSmH.
         Vol. 1 carries the additional title-page material:
"Vol. I, to which is prefixed an ample table of contents
. . ," and Vols. 3 and 4 label themselves, correctly, as
the third edition of <u>Pamela in her Exalted Condition</u>; this
is the first edition of either in the larger octavo format.
Sale, items 10, 17.

18   ---. <u>Pamela, or Virtue Rewarded</u>. . . .   2nd ed.   2v.
Dublin: Printed by S. Powell, for G. Ewing and W.
Smith, and G. Faulkner. NIC, InU; Trinity College,
Dublin. (All have Vol. 2 only.)
         In all copies found of the "first and second Irish
editions" (see 1741.27), Vol. 1 is of the first edition
and Vol. 2 of the second. It is possible that Reilly
printed the first volume for Ewing and Faulkner in 1741 and
that Powell printed the second for the larger conger under
date 1742. See Sale, items 5,6.

19   ---. <u>Pamela, or Virtue Rewarded</u>. . . .   4v.   "6th ed."
Dublin: Printed for George Ewing and William Smith and
George Faulkner. PBm; Trinity College, Dublin.
         Reported by PBm in <u>NUC</u>; TCD has a made-up edition in

which Vol. 1 is "the sixth edition," Vol. 2 is from
1742.18, and Vols. 3 and 4 are "the first edition." They
are in fact the first Irish edition of <u>Pamela</u> <u>in</u> <u>her</u>
<u>Exalted</u> <u>Condition</u>.

20   ---.   <u>Pamela,</u> <u>or</u> <u>Virtue</u> <u>Rewarded</u>. . . . 5th ed.   2v.   in
1.   London , Printed, Philadelphia: Reprinted and Sold by
B. Franklin, 1742-43.   MWA.
The only known copy of the first novel published in
America.

21   ---.   <u>Pamela,</u> <u>or</u> <u>La</u> <u>Vertu</u> <u>récompensée.</u>   <u>Trad.</u>   <u>de</u>   <u>l´anglois.</u>
. . . 4v.   London: Chez Jean Osborne.   CtY, NjP, BN.

22   ---.   <u>Pamela,</u> <u>ou</u> <u>La</u> <u>Vertu</u> <u>récompensée.</u>   . . .   Vols.   3-4.
London: Thomas Woodward.
Source: Uffizio di Informazioni Bibliografiche, Bib.
Naz. Centrale Vittorio Emanuele II, Roma.

23   ---.   <u>Pamela;</u>   <u>ou,</u>   <u>La</u>   <u>Vertu</u>   <u>récompensée.</u>   <u>Traduit</u>   <u>de</u>
<u>l´Anglois.</u>   4v.   Amsterdam: Aux depens de la Compagnie.
NIC, OU; Nat. Lib. Greece (Vols. 1-2 only); BZK; Bib.
Naz. Marciana; Saltykov-Shchedrin.
Illustrated.

24   ---.   <u>Pamela</u> <u>oder</u> <u>die</u> <u>belohnte</u> <u>Tugend.</u>   <u>Aus</u> <u>dem</u> <u>Engländischen</u>
<u>Richardsons</u>   <u>übersetzt</u>   <u>von</u>   <u>M.</u>   Translated by Johann
Mattheson.   2v. in 1.   Franckfurt und Leipzig: n.p.   NjP.
See also 1938.3, p.   357n2, and Goedeke, <u>Grundriss</u>, 3d
ed., 4, pt.   1:576.

25   ---.   <u>Pamela,</u> <u>oder</u>   <u>die</u>   <u>Belohnte</u>   <u>Tugend</u> <u>eines</u>   <u>armen,</u> <u>doch</u>
<u>wunderschönen</u> <u>Dienstmädchens.</u> <u>. . .</u> <u>Aus</u> <u>dem</u> <u>Englischen</u>
<u>übersetzt</u> <u>von</u> <u>Mattheson.</u>   Translated by   Johann   Mattheson.
2v.   Hamburg: n.p.   Saltykov-Shchedrin.
Source: Saltykov-Shchedrin Catalogue.

26   [VILLARET, CLAUDE?] <u>Antipamela</u> <u>or</u> <u>Mémoires</u> <u>de</u> <u>M.</u> <u>D***.</u>
<u>Traduit</u> <u>de</u> <u>l´anglois</u>. "Londres": n.p., 152 pp.   BN.
Querard and Barbier suggest that Villaret wrote this;
it was actually published in Paris. As satire or criticism
it is peripheral. Republished in 1743 (source:
Saltykov-Shchedrin Catalogue).

<u>1743</u>

1   [AUBERT DE LA CHESNAYE DES BOIS, F. A.?] <u>Lettres</u> <u>Amusantes et</u>
     <u>critiques,</u> <u>Sur</u> <u>les</u> <u>Romans</u> <u>en</u> <u>general</u> <u>Anglois</u> <u>et</u> <u>Francois,</u>
     <u>tant</u> <u>anciens</u> <u>que</u> <u>modernes.</u> <u>Addressées</u> <u>a</u> <u>Mylady</u> <u>W**</u>.
     Paris: Gissey; Bordelet: David Fils, pp. 43-78, 122-24.
     BN, NNC.
          Almost certainly by Aubert de la Chesnaye des Bois,
     although a MS notation in the BN copy, in an
     eighteenth-century hand, gives the author's name as M.
     Neuville Montadou. If Aubert wrote this, he could hardly
     have translated <u>Pamela</u>. The author of the <u>Lettres</u> pans
     both the original and the French translation, finding them
     low, <u>grossier</u>, and incredible, and preferring to them
     "<u>Pamela</u> <u>ou</u> <u>Mémoires</u> <u>de</u> <u>Myledy</u> <u>B.</u>" and <u>Anti-Pamela</u> <u>ou</u>
     <u>Memoires</u> <u>de</u> <u>M*** D***</u>. Cut by two-thirds, however, <u>Pamela</u>
     might make an excellent novel. Replies to Desfontaines's
     eulogy of <u>Pamela</u> disparagingly.
          I have seen no copy of Mme Riccoboni's novel with the
     title as the author of the <u>Lettres</u> gives it.

2   [BOISSY, LOUIS DE.] <u>Pamela</u> <u>en</u> <u>France</u> <u>ou</u> <u>La</u> <u>Vertu</u> <u>mieux</u>
     <u>éprouvée</u>. First performed by the Comédiens italiens
     ordinaires du Roi, March 4, 1743. Published as 1745.2.
          In verse; satiric; suggests Pamela should not resist
     B. Reviewed by the Marquis d'Argenson (<u>Notices</u> <u>sur</u> <u>les</u>
     <u>Oeuvres</u> <u>de</u> <u>théâtre</u>. Edited by H. Lagrave. <u>SVEC</u>, 43
     [1966]: 700) and in 1755.1. See 1967.13, p. 21; 1931.3,
     p. 118. Claude Godard d'Aucourt wrote a play about the
     failure of this and P.-C. Nivelle de la Chaussée's
     versions of <u>Pamela</u>, <u>La</u> <u>Déroute</u> <u>des</u> <u>Pamela</u> (1928.6, p. 171;
     1935.6, p. 167).

3   DESFONTAINES, PIERRE F.G., ABBÉ. <u>Observations</u> <u>sur</u> <u>les</u> <u>Ecrits</u>
     <u>modernes</u> 32: 95-96.
          Review of an abridgment of <u>Pamela</u>, <u>Mémoires</u> <u>de</u> <u>Pamela</u>;
     according to Desfontaines it was popular. (I have traced
     no copy of this book; it is not in the BN or the Arsénal,
     unless Desfontaines has not well remembered the title.)

4   ---. <u>Observations</u> <u>sur</u> <u>les</u> <u>Ecrits</u> <u>modernes</u> 33:189-91, 313 ff.
     Reviewing <u>Joseph</u> <u>Andrews</u>, which Desfontaines apparently

believes is a continuation in good faith of <u>Pamela</u>, he
again praises <u>Pamela</u> but finds it impossible to reread.

5   [HAYWOOD, ELIZA?] <u>Anti-Pamela</u> . . . <u>Traduit</u> <u>de</u> <u>l´anglois</u>
     <u>par</u> <u>D.</u> <u>M*****</u> [E. de Mauvillon]. Amsterdam and Leipzig:
     Arkstee & Merkus. CtY.

6   ---. <u>De</u> <u>Anti-Pamela,</u> <u>of</u> <u>de</u> <u>valsche</u> <u>Eenvoudigheit,</u> <u>Outdekt</u> <u>in</u>
     <u>de</u> <u>gevallen</u> <u>van</u> <u>Syrena</u> <u>Tricksy</u> . . . <u>Uit</u> <u>het</u> <u>Engelsch</u>
     <u>vertaalt.</u> [Anti-Pamela, or False Innocence Detected, in
     the Adventures of Syrena Tricksy . . . Translated from
     the English.] Amsterdam: Arent van Huyssteen, 311 pp.
     Koninklikje Bib.; Univbib. Amsterdam.
          <u>RNB</u>, item 16.

7   LA CHAUSSÉE, PIERRE-CLAUDE NIVELLE DE. <u>Pamela.</u>
          Produced 1743; published as 1762.14. According to
     d´Origny´s <u>Annales</u> <u>du</u> <u>Théâtre</u> <u>italien</u>, 1788, it was so
     monumentally unsuccessful that it spawned a <u>mot.</u> "Comment
     va Paméla?--Elle pâme, hélas!" See 1928.6, p. 171;
     1930.4, p. 118, calls it "languissant et efféminé";
     1938.3, pp. 360-61, describes it.

*8   RICHARDSON, SAMUEL. <u>Mémoires</u> <u>de</u> <u>Pamela.</u> Abridger unknown.
          Source: 1743.3.

9   ---. <u>Pamela</u> <u>eller</u> <u>Den</u> <u>belonnede</u> <u>Dyd,</u> <u>forst</u> <u>skrevet</u> <u>i</u> <u>Engelsk,</u>
     <u>og</u> <u>nu</u> <u>i</u> <u>Dansk</u> <u>oversat</u> <u>af</u> <u>L.</u> [Barthold Joh. Lodde].
     Preface by J.G. Anchersen. 4 parts. Copenhagen:
     1743-46.
          Source: <u>Bibliotheca</u> <u>Danica</u>, 4:484. Anchersen´s preface
     praises <u>Pamela</u>, takes issue with critics of it.

10   W---, J---. <u>Pamela:</u> <u>or</u> <u>the</u> <u>Fair</u> <u>Imposter.</u> Dublin: Thomas
     Chrichlow, 42 pp. BM.
          A poem in heroic couplets, in imitation of <u>The</u> <u>Rape</u> <u>of</u>
     <u>the</u> <u>Lock.</u> An anti-<u>Pamela</u> in which "the fairest, but
     vainest in the Town" plays the "subtile Game" of catching
     Sir Blunder, while amorous of Williams. Sir Blunder
     eventually comes to discover her perfidy but fails to get a
     divorce. She is not to blame, however; it was "her
     stars." J--- W--- may be Irish, as, contrary to the usual
     practice, the poem was published first in Dublin, in London
     the next year.

1744

1   COLLYER, MARY. <u>Felicia</u> <u>to</u> <u>Charlotte</u>: <u>being</u> <u>Letters</u> <u>from</u> <u>a</u>
     <u>Young</u> <u>Lady</u> <u>in</u> <u>the</u> <u>Country</u> <u>to</u> <u>Her</u> <u>Friend</u> <u>in</u> <u>Town.</u>
     <u>Containing</u> <u>a</u> <u>Series</u> <u>of</u> <u>the</u> <u>most</u> <u>interesting</u> <u>Events,</u>
     <u>interspersed</u> <u>with</u> <u>Moral</u> <u>Reflections;</u> <u>chiefly</u> <u>tending</u> <u>to</u>
     <u>prove,</u> <u>that</u> <u>the</u> <u>Seeds</u> <u>of</u> <u>Virtue</u> <u>are</u> <u>implanted</u> <u>in</u> <u>the</u> <u>Mind</u>
     <u>of</u> <u>Every</u> <u>Reasonable</u> <u>Being</u>. 2v. London: R. Griffiths &
     G. Woodfall. BM.
         The novels of the Latitudinarian Mary Collyer, a friend
     of Richardson's, are among the first to show striking
     similarities to his, as Albrecht von Haller notes in his
     translation of <u>Felicia</u> <u>to</u> <u>Charlotte</u> in 1753. (See also
     Helen Sard Hughes. "An Early Romantic Novel." <u>JEGP</u> 15
     (1916): 564-98, which argues for Richardson's influence.)
     This collection of letters shows similarities of plot,
     outlook, style, characters, and language to <u>Pamela</u>. It was
     reprinted in 1749 (<u>ex</u> <u>post</u> <u>Clarissa</u>?).

2   [FIELDING, SARAH.] <u>The</u> <u>Adventures</u> <u>of</u> <u>David</u> <u>Simple</u>: <u>Containing</u>
     <u>an</u> <u>Account</u> <u>of</u> <u>his</u> <u>Travels</u> <u>through</u> <u>the</u> <u>Cities</u> <u>of</u> <u>London</u> <u>and</u>
     <u>Westminster,</u> <u>In</u> <u>the</u> <u>Search</u> <u>of</u> <u>a</u> <u>Real</u> <u>Friend.</u> <u>By</u> <u>a</u> <u>Lady.</u>
     2v. London: A. Millar.
         "[Richardson's] general influence on <u>David</u> <u>Simple</u> is
     evident, in the effusion of sentiment, in the analysis of
     women's misfortunes, and in the copybook, sometimes
     infantile, character of the moralising" (1928.3). See also
     F.H. Dudden, <u>Henry</u> <u>Fielding</u> (Oxford: Clarendon, 1952),
     1:506. The Oxford English Novels edition of 1973 contains
     an introduction by Malcolm Kelsall drawing attention to
     Sarah Fielding's dissimilarities from Richardson.

*3   HOLBERG, LUDVIG. <u>Moralske</u> <u>tanker</u>. Copenhagen: n.p.
         Source: Hannaford, item 139. Summarizes criticism of
     <u>Pamela</u>; believes Pamela is not hypocritical but rather
     sincerely religious; the book shows an example of "just
     Sentiments . . . Virtue and Honour." Dr. Peter Shaw
     plagiarized these comments in <u>The</u> <u>Reflector</u> in 1750,
     according to Hannaford.

4   W---, J---. <u>Pamela,</u> <u>or,</u> <u>the</u> <u>Fair</u> <u>Imposter.</u> <u>A</u> <u>Poem,</u> <u>in</u> <u>Five</u>
     <u>Cantos</u>. London: Printed for E. Bevins . . . and sold
     by J. Roberts, 46 pp. MH.
         See 1743.16.

<u>1745</u>

*1   ANON. Article. <u>Daily Advertiser</u>, April 23, 1745.
          <u>Pamela</u> is pictured in a waxwork of over 100 figures. (A
      second   waxwork,   picturing   Pamela   in   her   "exalted
      condition," is advertised in the August 8   issue.) Source:
      Hannaford.

*2   W.,A. [PSEUD.] <u>Enormous Abomination of the Hoop-Petticoat</u>.
      London. P. 4.
          Prose fiction including <u>Pamela</u> criticized as distraction
      from better reading. Source: Hannaford, item 141.

3   BOISSY, LOUIS DE.   <u>Pamela en France: ou La Vertu mieux</u>
      <u>éprouvée</u>. Paris: J. Clousier, 80 pp. BN.
          See 1743.2.

3   GELLERT, CHRISTIAN FURCHTEGOTT.   <u>Die Betschwester, ein</u>
      <u>Lustspiel in drey Aufzugen</u>. In <u>Neue Beytrage zum Vergnügen</u>
      <u>des Verstandes und Witzes</u>. Bremen & Leipzig: n.p.   2,
      part 2: [83]-168. MH.
          Contains   a   discussion   of   <u>Pamela</u>;   a   foolish   Frau
      Richardinn   complains that her daughter has been given "ein
      Buch ze lesen, ich weis nicht, ob es Pemala oder Pamela
      hiess.   Gewiss, es war ein Liebesbuch, und auf dem Kupfer
      stund der Teufel hinter einer Frau, und wollte   sie
      verführen." Although it has been recommended from the
      pulpit by a priest, "wenn es zehn Priester gethan haben, so
      soll meine Tochter keinen Roman lesen." However, a good
      character praises it. (Act 2, scene 1.)

4   HIGHMORE, JOSEPH, TRUCHY, L., AND BENOIST, A.   Twelve plates
      illustrating <u>Pamela</u>. London: 12 double pl. folio. NN.
          Described in 1951.2, in which an account of its origins
      is given.

*5   LE BLANC, JEAN-BERNARD, abbé. Letter 30. <u>Lettres d´un</u>
      <u>François</u>. 2v. Amsterdam: n.p., 1:279-80.
          Sources: 1967.13, p. 16; Hannaford, item 333.
      According to Hannaford, Le Blanc believes <u>Pamela</u> to be
      propaganda for a Society for the Reformation of Manners.
      *6 MILLER, JAMES. <u>The Picture</u>. London.
          <u>Pamela</u> criticized for ruining young people.   Source:
      Hannaford, item 140.

*6   MILLER, JAMES. <u>The Picture</u>. London.
          <u>Pamela</u> criticized for ruining young people.   Source:
      Hannaford, item 140.

<u>1746</u>

1　　BODMER, J.J., BREITINGER, J.J. <u>Der Mahler der Sitten. Von</u>
　　　<u>neuem ubersehen und starck vermehret</u>. . . 2v. Zurich:
　　　Conr. Orell u. Comp. BM.
　　　　　Considerably revised and augmented reprint of the
　　　<u>Discourse der Mahlern</u>, in which <u>Pamela</u> is newly included in
　　　the list of recommended reading, possibly at the suggestion
　　　of Gottsched (see 1926.5, p. 12n20); see also 1937.3, p.
　　　57.

2　　GELLERT, C.F. <u>Leben der schwedischen Gräfin von G</u>. 2 parts.
　　　Leipzig: Hahn, 1746-48. BM.
　　　　　The "first modern German novel" has often been
　　　considered to be influenced by Richardson, whom Gellert
　　　certainly admired, although Prevost may well also be an
　　　influence. In some ways, e.g., the exoticism of the
　　　love-situations, it anticipates <u>Clarissa</u> and <u>Grandison</u>. On
　　　the question of influence see 1937.3, pp. 67-69, 125-27;
　　　1911.2; 1949.1; and Hugo Friedrich, <u>L´Abbé Prévost in</u>
　　　<u>Deutschland</u>, 1929. Price (1932.7, p. 196f.) calls it "the
　　　first sign of Richardson´s influence in Germany," although
　　　by 1953 (pp. 173-74) he feels it "shares with <u>Pamela</u> its
　　　moral intent, and almost nothing more." 1902.2 discusses
　　　the relationship of the <u>Schwedische Gräfin</u> to French,
　　　English, and German novels. See also Hannaford, item 155.

3　　[RICHARDSON, SAMUEL.] <u>Letters Written to and for Particular</u>
　　　<u>Friends, on the Most Important Occasions. Directing not</u>
　　　<u>only the requisite style and forms to be observed in</u>
　　　<u>writing familiar letters; but how to think and act justly</u>
　　　<u>and prudently in the common concerns of human life</u>. The
　　　Third Edition. London: J. Osborn & J. and J.
　　　Rivington; Bath: J. Leake, 272 pp.
　　　　　Sale, item 23.

4　　---. <u>Pamela: or, Virtue Rewarded. . . .In four volumes.</u>
　　　<u>The Sixth Edition</u>. . . . London: J. Osborn & J. and
　　　J. Rivington.
　　　　　The fourth edition of <u>Pamela in her Exalted Condition</u>.
　　　Sale, items 12, 18.

5　　---. <u>Pamela, ovvero La virtu premiata</u>. Translated by D.V.S.
　　　4v. Venice: G. Bettinelli.
　　　　　1938.3 suggests a date of 1744-45, p. 357n3. CtY, MH,

and Nat. Lib. Greece have an edition dated 1749; its
place of publication, given as Venice, is probably Naples,
according to MH.

<u>1747</u>

1   EDWARDS, THOMAS. Letter Book of Thomas Edwards. MSS. Bodl.
     1007.12. (Vol. 4) Letters 1747÷1752.
         Letters 76, 103, 162, 210, 223, 231, 247, 268, 280, 296,
     306, 316, 335, and 338 are to Richardson; they contain
     material on <u>Clarissa</u>, <u>Grandison</u>, Richardson's health, a
     lost print of Richardson, and Edwards's scholarly projects
     (in which Richardson took great interest).

2   [FIELDING, HENRY.] Preface. <u>Familiar</u> <u>Letters</u> <u>between</u> <u>the</u>
     <u>Principal</u> <u>Characters</u> <u>in</u> <u>David</u> <u>Simple</u> [by Sarah Fielding].
     2v. London: Printed for the Author, and sold by A.
     Millar, 1:3-22.
         Fielding attacks the epistolary novel as a genre--an
     extraordinary performance, if meant to commend his sister's
     book.

*3   [RICHARDSON, SAMUEL.] <u>Aesop's</u> <u>Fables</u>. . . . 2d ed.
     London: J. Osborn?
         Sale, item 2; deduced from advertisements.

4   ---. <u>Clarissa.</u> <u>Or,</u> <u>The</u> <u>History</u> <u>of</u> <u>a</u> <u>Young</u> <u>Lady:</u>
     <u>Comprehending</u> <u>the</u> <u>Most</u> <u>Important</u> <u>Concerns</u> <u>of</u> <u>Private</u> <u>Life.</u>
     <u>And</u> <u>particularly</u> <u>shewing</u> <u>the</u> <u>Distresses</u> <u>that</u> <u>may</u> <u>attend</u> <u>the</u>
     <u>Misconduct</u> <u>both</u> <u>of</u> <u>Parents</u> <u>and</u> <u>Children</u> <u>in</u> <u>Relation</u> <u>to</u>
     <u>Marriage.</u> <u>Published</u> <u>by</u> <u>the</u> <u>Editor</u> <u>of</u> <u>Pamela.</u> . . 7v.
     London: Printed for S. Richardson: and Sold by A.
     Millar, J. and J. Rivington, John Osborn, and J. Leake,
     at Bath, 1747-48.
         Volumes 1 and 2 were published on December 1, 1747; 3
     and 4, on April 28, 1748; and 5-7, on December 6, 1748.
     3-7 have imprint, "Printed for S. Richardson: and sold by
     John Osborn, Andrew Millar, J. and J. Rivington, and J.
     Leake at Bath. 1748." Described completely in <u>A</u> <u>Catalogue</u>
     <u>of</u> <u>the</u> <u>Books</u> <u>of</u> <u>Harry</u> <u>Elkins</u> <u>Widener</u> (Philadelphia:
     privately printed, 1918), 2:88-89. Sale, item 32.

5   --- AND CARTER, ELIZABETH. Correspondence 1747-1753.
       See 1812.5.

                              1748

1   ANON. "A Short Character of Clarissa." GM 18:548-50.
            An alleged letter from Cibber's character, Sir Charles
       Easy, designed to arouse interest in the book, precedes
       Lovelace's letter on annual marriages.   Since Cibber had
       read Clarissa in manuscript, the letter may be his.

*1A   BIRCH, THOMAS. Letters of January 19 and December 20.
       Printed in The Orrery Papers. Edited by Emily Charlotte
       Boyle, Countess of Cork and Orrery.   London: 1903.
       2:14,49.
            Clarissa is too long and not as well-liked as Pamela,
       but the last volumes are more varied and interesting.
       Source: Hannaford, item 271.

2   BROCKES, B.H.   Irdisches Vergnugen in Gott.   Hamburg:
       1721-48. Vol. 9 (1748); 556.
            Praise of Pamela as popular philosophy; see 1938.3, p.
       354, and 1926.5, pp. 13-15.

3   [DEFOE, DANIEL, and others.] others.] A Tour thro' the Whole
       Island of Great Britain . . . The Fourth Edition, with
       very great Additions, Improvements, and Corrections; which
       bring it down to the Year 1748. 4v. London: S. Birt, T.
       Osborne, D. Browne, J. Hodges, J.   Osborn, A.   Millar,
       and J. Robinson.
            Extensive revisions. Sale, item 29.

4   [FIELDING, HENRY.] The Jacobite's Journal, no.   5 (Jan.   2,
       1747/8).
            An appreciation of Clarissa, based on the first two
       volumes.   "Such Simplicity, such Manners, such deep
       Penetration into Nature; such Power to raise and alarm the
       Passions, few Writers, either ancient or modern, have been
       possessed of." The Works of Henry Fielding. The Jacobite's

Journal (n.p.: Wesleyan University Press; Oxford: Oxford
University Press, 1975), pp. 119-20; cf. pp. lx, 188.

5   MAUCLERC, JAMES. The Christian's Magazine. . . . London:
    Printed for the author and sold by A. Hodges, 416 pp.
    NjP, TxU have on film.
        The second publication; see E&K, p. 70.

6   MONTAGU, ELIZABETH.   Letter to the Duchess of Portland,
    September, 1748. Printed in E. Huchon, Mrs. Montagu
    1720-1800, London: John Murray, 1907, p. 23.
        She has read Clarissa before publication, in MS or
    sheets; praises it highly, though in a presumably later
    letter she feels it is too long and not sufficiently
    elegant, while Lovelace is "an unnatural compound of too
    many inconsistencies" (1907.3, p. 83).

7   OXFORD SCHOLAR, AN. [pseud.] The Parallel; or, Pilkington
    and Phillips Compared. Being Remarks upon the Memoirs of
    those two celebrated Writers.   London: Printed for M.
    Cooper, p. 6.
        Criticizes Pamela for inadequate morality and excessive
    realism; compares it unfavorably with Joseph Andrews.   See
    1968.3.

8   [RICHARDSON, SAMUEL.] Clarissa. . . . 7v. Dublin: George
    Faulkner, 1748-49. Trinity College, Dublin.
        Vol. 1-4, 1748; 5-7, 1749.

9   RICHARDSON, SAMUEL. Clarissa, Die Geschichte eines vornehmen
    Frauenzimmers, von demjenigen herausgegeben, welcher die
    Geschichte der Pamela geliefert hat: und nunmehr aus dem
    Englischen in das Deutsche übersetzt.   Translated by
    Michaelis. 8 parts? Frankfort & Leipzig: n.p., 1748-49?
    Öst. Nationalbib; Saltykov-Shchedrin.

10 ---. Clarissa, Die Geschichte eines vornehmen Frauenzimmers.
    . . .   8 parts. in 6 vol. Göttingen: Verlegts Abram
    Vandenhoeck, 1748-53. Öst. Natlbib.; Sächs. Landesbib.
    (destroyed); Bib. Naz. Braidense (filed as Historia
    Clarissae ex angelico germanice).

1749·

1   ANON. <u>The History of Tom Jones, the Foundling, in his Married</u>
     <u>State</u>. Dublin: S. Powell, 232 pp. BM.
          A quick attempt to capitalize on Fielding's novel, this
     book draws on elements of <u>Pamela in her Exalted Condition</u>,
     e.g., the jealousy subplot and the domestic-conduct advice.

2   --- [SARAH FIELDING?]. <u>Remarks on Clarissa, Addressed to the</u>
     <u>Author, Occasioned by some Critical Conversations on the</u>
     <u>Characters and Conduct of that Work</u>. . . London: J.
     Robinson, 54 p. BM, CtY.
          Three dialogues and an exchange of letters in which the
     principal objections to <u>Clarissa</u> are discussed and
     dismissed. Notable remarks on the epistolary form, the
     roles of "pride" and "hypocrisy," and the division of the
     narrative among Clarissa, Lovelace, and Belford. 1931.3,
     p. 279, suggests it was a publicity piece; the general
     level of the writing is high, and Richardson attributes it
     to Sarah Fielding in the FMSS copy. Sale, item 84.
     Reprinted 1974.

3   CLELAND, JOHN. <u>Memoirs of a Woman of Pleasure</u>. 2v. London:
     "G. Fenton" [Ralph Griffiths?], [1749?].
          See 1963.3. Bibliographical information from "Pisanus
     Fraxi."

4   FIELDING, HENRY. <u>The History of Tom Jones a Foundling</u>. 6v.
     London: A. Millar.
          "<u>Tom Jones</u> . . . est plein d'allusions malignes à
     Richardson," Aurélien Digeon asserts (1920.2, p. 219):
     e.g., Book 14, chap. 1. Its relationship to Richardson's
     work is frequently discussed; see index under "Fielding,
     Henry".

5   FIELDING, SARAH. <u>The Governess: or, Little Female Academy</u>.
     . . . London: Printed for the Author, and Sold by A.
     Millar.
          Jill E. Grey, introducing the modern edition of <u>The</u>
     <u>Governess</u> (Oxford University Press, 1968), notes
     Richardson's influence over this, "the first novel written
     for children." Richardson suggested textual changes in <u>The</u>
     <u>Governess</u> (see 1804.5, 2:61-64), a service he also
     performed for Jane Collier's and Sarah Fielding's joint
     production, <u>The Cry</u>; he printed this and a number of later

25

novels for Sarah Fielding. (Jane Collier mentions him in
her Art of Ingeniously Tormenting [London: A. Millar,
1753, p. 88--a mention of Clarissa; Sarah Fielding
praises Grandison as a romantic hero in the preface to her
Lives of Cleopatra and Octavia [London: A. Millar, 1757,
p. iii].) Richardson's influence over Sarah Fielding is
evident, says Grey, in the endeavor "to cultivate an early
inclination to Benevolence, and a Love of Virtue, in the
Minds of Young Women" (from the dedication to The
Governess), to mingle moral influence with entertainment,
and to create model characters. The book went through
numerous later editions in English and foreign languages.

6 HAGEDORN, FRIEDRICH VON. Letter to J.J. Bodmer, September
   28. Reprinted in Poetische Werke, ed. Joh. Joachim
   Eschenburg. Hamburg: Carl Ernst Bohn, 1800. 5:110-11.
       "Jetzo lese und bethräne ich die Klarissa. . . .
   Dieses Buch muss ganz, oder gar nicht, gelesen werden. Es
   enthält Alles, was die Tugend verehren, und das Laster
   verabscheuen und beklagen lehrt." Such virtue and vice are
   believable on larger stages, but remain ideal in the
   private sphere. The common reader will not easiy give
   Richardson the attention he needs.

7 HALLER, ALBRECHT VON. Bibliothèque raisonnée des Ouvrages des
   Savans de l'Europe 42: no. 1 (January-March), 324-36.
       Largely favorable criticism of Clarissa. "The chief
   herald of Richardson in Germany [at this time] was Haller
   in Gottingen," says 1926.5, which refers the reader to
   numerous other examples of Haller's commendation of
   Richardson, including a series of reviews of books in the
   Göttingische gelehrte Anzeigen, 1750-1765 (1926.5, p.
   17n34). Haller also wrote briefly on Clarissa in the
   Göttingische Zeitungen von gelehrten Sachen (1748):274-75.

8 ---. GM 19:245-46, 345-47;
       Anonymous translation of 1749.7. Richardson replied in
   1749.10.

9 RICHARDSON, SAMUEL. Answer to the Letter of a Very Reverend
   and Worthy Gentleman Objecting to the Warmth of a
   Particular Scene in the History of Clarissa. [London:
   Samuel Richardson], 11 pp. Forster Collection.
       Defends the fire scene in Clarissa. See 1961.3 and E&K,
   pp. 291-92.

10   ---. "Answer to the Remarks on the History of Clarissa." <u>GM</u>
      19:347-49.
          Reply to Haller, defending <u>Clarissa</u>.

11   ---. <u>Clarissa</u>. <u>Or, The History of a Young Lady</u> . . . 2d
      ed. . . . <u>To Which is prefixed, a table of contents for
      the whole</u>. London: Printed for S. Richardson, and sold
      by J. Osborn, A. Millar, J. and J. Rivington, and J.
      Leake, at Bath.
          Only volumes 1-4 were reprinted for the second edition.
      Sale, item 33.

12   VOLTAIRE (pseud. of FRANÇOIS-MARIE AROUET). <u>Nanine, ou Le
      Préjugé vaincu</u>. First presented at the Comédie française,
      June 16, 1749. Paris: Le Mercier & Lambert, 108 pp.
          An elegant French version of the <u>Pamela</u> plot, with the
      "correction"--to be followed next year by Goldoni´s <u>Pamela
      nubile</u>--that Pamela is a noblewoman in disguise. 1928.6
      discusses this play, <u>Charlot ou La Comtesse de Givry</u>
      (1767), and <u>Le Droit du Seigneur</u> (1762) as examples of
      Voltaire´s adaptations of Richardson´s themes. D´Argenson
      comments on <u>Nanine</u> and the social order in <u>Notices sur les
      Oeuvres de théâtre</u>, ed. H. Lagrave, <u>SVEC</u> 43 (1966):300;
      Gerstenberg compares it and <u>Pamela</u> in the <u>Neuer Buchersaal
      der schönen Wissenschaft und freyen Kunste</u> 10 (1750):72;
      1938.3 discusses it, pp. 361-62. Source for bibliographic
      information: G. Bengescu, "Notice bibliographique," in
      <u>Oeuvres complètes de Voltaire</u>. Paris: Garnier, 50
      (1882):492.

                            <u>1750</u>

*1   ANON. <u>The History of Charlotte Summers, the Fortunate Parish
      Girl</u>. 2v. London: Printed for the Author; sold by
      Corbett . . . n.d.
          Published in late 1749 or early 1750; 1965.21, vol. 3,
      p. 4n1, suggests 1749. In the third edition (Dublin,
      1753), 130-31, there is praise for <u>Tom Jones</u> and <u>Clarissa</u>;
      although the book is a self- confessed imitation of
      Fielding, some plot details are taken from <u>Clarissa</u>.

*2   POLYCLETUS UND CRITO [pseuds.] Correspondence on Vols. 5 and
       6 of Clarissa. Zurcher freymuthige Nachrichten. Reprinted
       in Die critischen Nachrichten aus dem Reiche der
       Gelehrsamkeit, Pts. 44-46.
           Source: 1925.7; pp. 171-73. Debate on the moral
       rightness of the tragic ending of Clarissa; Richardson is
       justified and compared to Homer. Gerstenberg praised the
       "diderotische Enthusiasmus" of this correspondence in the
       Hamburgische Neue Zeitung, September 5, 1768 (1938.3, p.
       353n3).

3   CHAPONE, HESTER MULSO. Three letters on filial obedience.
       Published in The Posthumous Works of Mrs. Chapone.
       Containing her Correspondence with Mr. Richardson . . .
       Vol. 1. London: John Murray, 1807; pp. 19-156.
           The letters, dated from late 1750 to early 1751, concern
       the question of Clarissa's obedience to her parents;
       Richardson's opinions are discussed at length.

*3A   CHAPONE, SARAH KIRKHAM. Remarks on Mrs. Muilman's Letter to
       the Right Honourable the Earl of Chesterfield . . .
       London. P. 19.
           Compliments Richardson, "the most masterly intellectual
       Painter" of the time, for his portraits of "Men of Honour"
       in Clarissa. Source: Hannaford, item 278.

4   CHESTERFIELD, PHILIP DORMER STANHOPE, earl of. Letter to Mme
       du Boccage, October 13 (o.s.), 1750. In Letters of Lord
       Chesterfield. Vol. 4. Edited by Bonamy Dobree (London
       and New York: Eyre & Spottiswoode, 1932), p. 1,589.
           "Si Prevot traduit notre Clarice, il doit l'abreger
       d'une bonne moitie; il y a un furieux superflu et en meme
       temps un interet touchant, et des situations interessantes.
       Celui qui l'a ecrite . . . est un libraire [sic] qui
       manque de savoir et de style, mais qui connait le coeur."
       Perhaps Chesterfield was kinder to Richardson himself; see
       E&K, p. 405.

5   DELANY, MARY GRANVILLE. Letters concerning Clarissa. In The
       Autobiography and Correspondence of Mary Granville, Mrs.
       Delany. Edited by Lady Llanover. 3v. London: R.
       Bentley, 1861. Vol. 2, pp. 523, 561, 603, 614.
           Largely laudatory. Mrs. Delany was a friend of the
       Richardsons.

6   GOLDONI, CARLO.   Pamela.   First   performed   Mantua   1750;
     published as 1756.4.
         Goldoni's remarkably   successful   adaptation   was   first
     called Pamela;   after the composition of Pamela maritata
     (1759) it was likely to be confounded with its sequel,   and
     the   name   was   changed   first   to Pamela fanciulla (in the
     Pasquali edition of the Opere, 1761), and later, in the
     Venice edition of 1788, to Pamela nubile.   See 1756.4 for
     discussion.

7   JOHNSON, SAMUEL. The Rambler No. 4. March 31.
         Discusses the ethical effect of fiction,   especially   on
     the young, and the bad effect of mixed characters. 1948.7,
     p.   99 argues that this is an implicit defense   of
     Richardson and an attack on Tom Jones.

8   KLOPSTOCK, FRIEDRICH GOTTLOB.   "An die todte   Clarissa."
     [Poem.] Reprinted in Werke. Ed. Karl August Schleiden.
     Munich: Carl Hanser Verlag, 1954, pp. 34-35.
         Written as a Liebesode for Meta Moller in 1750 or 1751
     and first published in 1771; the two mourn the death of
     Clarissa but celebrate the hour in which she left her
     picture behind.

9   MATY, ---.   Laudatory   epigram   on   Clarissa.   Journal
     Britannique 3:438.
         "The Work is Nature's . . . " Hannaford, item 314,
     ascribes to a Mr. Graham.

*10 RAMLER, J. Critische Nachrichten.
         Asserts that Richardson is the equal of Homer, in a
     piece plagiarized from the Zurcher freymuthige Nachrichten.
     Source: 1925.7, pp. 171-73.

11   [RICHARDSON, SAMUEL.] Letters written to and for particular
     friends, on the most important occasions. . . . The
     fourth edition. London: J.   Osborn & J.   and J.
     Rivington, and J.   Leake at Bath, 272 pp. MH.
         Sale, item 24.

12   ---.   Meditations Collected from the Sacred Books;   and
     Adapted to the Different Stages of a Deep Distress;
     Gloriously Surmounted by Patience, Piety, and Resignation.
     Being those mentioned in the History of Clarissa as drawn
     up by her for her own use. To each of which is prefixed a

Short Historical Account, Connecting it with the Story.
London: J. Osborn: A. Millar, J. and J. Rivington, and
James Leake at Bath, 84 pp. MH.
    Thirty-six meditations, four of which also appear in the
novel. Sale, item 38, suggests that this very rare book
was never actually offered for sale.

13   WORTLEY MONTAGU, MARY, lady. Letter to Lady Bute, October 20,
      1755. Published in 1965.21, Vol. 2, p. 470.
          Letter on *Pamela*'s "very extrodinary (and I think
undeserv'd) success." Lady Mary frequently discussed
Richardson with Lady Bute; see 1965.21.

1751

1   ANON. <u>An Essay on the New Species of Writing Founded by Mr.
      Fielding</u>. London: William Owen.
          1936.5 and 1974.26 feel that Richardson is censured here
for "not altogether unexceptionable" language, but the
straw man of record is the author of <u>Charlotte Summers</u>.

*2   ---. <u>Den belønnede dyd, eller Pamela sødskende barn</u>.
      Copenhagen.
          Supposedly an abridgment; I have seen no copy. Source:
<u>NCBEL</u>. Perhaps same as 1743.9?

*3   TUGENDLICHEN, CLARISSA PAMELA. [pseud.] Letter. <u>Der Redliche</u>
      2 (for 1751): 320ff.
          1925.7, p. 180-81, notes as first recorded appearances
of Richardson in Nurnberg, but see below.

*4   W. [pseud.] "Gedanken von der Gelehrsamkeit der Frauenzimmer
      nebst dem Entwurf einer galanten Bibliothek." <u>Der Redliche</u>
      1 (for 1751): 202ff.
          Recommends <u>Clarissa</u>. Source: 1925.7; p. 180.

5   [GRIMM, FRIEDRICH MELCHIOR, baron?] <u>Correspondance littéraire</u>.
      January 25. Reprinted in 1877.2, 2:24-25.
          Reviews the first part of Prevost's translation of
<u>Clarissa</u>, which has made "beaucoup plus de bruit à Paris
que . . . de succes" but merits serious examination.
The characters are the most interesting part of the work:
Clarissa wise above her age, but attractive; Lovelace a

paradoxical and fascinating mixture of artifice and
passion; Anna Howe a pleasing original. "Je la crois . .
. toujours dans la nature, mais dans une nature où
personne n´est." The moral reflections are fine, but the
book is overlong. "J´ai éprouvé dans la lecture de ce
livre une chose qui n´est pas ordinaire, le plaisir le plus
vif et l´ennui le plus assommant." (For convenience we have
filed all material from the Correspondance under Grimm´s
name, as editor and principal writer.)

6   LA PORTE, JOSEPH DE, abbé. Observations sur la Littérature
     moderne. 4 (Oct.-Dec. 1751): 109-24.
         Praises Clarissa for physical naturalism. See 1967.13,
     p. 19n17. Other mentions: 5(1752):290; 7(1752):116-38.

7   RICHARDSON, SAMUEL. Clarissa. Or, the History of a Young
     Lady . . . 3rd ed. 8v. London: Printed for S.
     Richardson: and sold by J. Osborn, A. Millar, J. and J.
     Rivington, and by J. Leake, at Bath. NIC, CtY, CaBVaU.
         Sale, item 34. The text was greatly altered, the most
     important alterations being made to "blacken Lovelace´s
     character." The third edition has become the standard text,
     but its primacy is currently being questioned by Shirley
     Van Marter and others.

8   RICHARDSON, SAMUEL. Clarissa. Or, The History of a Young
     Lady. . . . 4th ed. 7v. London: Printed for S.
     Richardson: and sold by J. Osborn, A. Millar, J. and J.
     Rivington, and J. Leake, at Bath.
         Octavo edition. Sale, item 35.

9   ---. Lettres Angloises, ou Histoire de Miss Clarisse Harlove.
     Translated, introduced, and considerably altered by A.F.
     Prévost d´Exiles. 6v. Dresden: George Conrad Walther,
     1751-52. Öst. Natlbib., Sächs. Landesib., BZK.

10   ---. Lettres Angloises, ou Histoire de Miss Clarisse Harlove.
     Translated, altered, and introduced by Prévost. 12 parts
     in 6v. London: J. Nourse, 1751-52? BN, Sorbonne,
     Besançon.
         UCLA reports an edition in 7v.
         See 1927.10 for an examination of the changes Prévost
     introduced into Clarissa. Prévost´s introduction details
     some of them, made in order to adapt Richardson to French
     tastes. Richardson had the introduction translated (FMSS

XV,2, fols. 62-72) and was considerably annoyed.

*11   ---. Clarissa. 2v. Dublin.
       An abridgment. Reprinted 1756.7?
       Source: Book Auction Records 25: 492.

12   ---. Letters and Passages Restored from the Original
       Manuscripts of the History of Clarissa. To which is
       subjoined, A Collection of Such of the Moral and
       Instructive Sentiments, Cautions, Aphorisms, Reflections
       and Observations Contained in the History, as are Presumed
       to Be of General Use and Service. Digested under Proper
       Heads. Published for the sake of doing Justice to the
       Purchasers of the Two First Editions of That Work. London:
       Printed for S. Richardson: and sold by John Osborn,
       Andrew Millar, J. and J. Rivington, and by J. Leake, at
       Bath, 311 pp. MH, CtY.
          Sale, item 37. Only one edition of this extremely rare
       book was published; it is likely that the material was not
       "restored" to but simply written for the third edition, in
       order to make Lovelace less attractive.

*13   ---. [German edition of Letters and Passages Restored to
       Clarissa, published in Dresden.]
       Source: 1925.7, p. 11n12 from GGA, 1751, p. 605.

14   ---. Rambler, no. 97, February 19, 1751.
          Richardson's contribution to Johnson's periodical was
       the most popular number of the run; it compares women of
       his youth to those now. The introduction by Johnson
       contains perhaps the most famous phrase written about
       Richardson: he "taught the passions to move at the command
       of virtue . . . ." Frequently reprinted, e.g. in The
       Yale Edition of the Works of Samuel Johnson, Vol. 4.   Ed.
       W.J. Bate, J.M. Bullitt, and L. Powell (New Haven and
       London: Yale University Press, 1969); 153-59.

15   UZ, JOHANN PETER. Letter to J.W.L. Gleim, October 29, 1751.
       Briefwechsel zwischen Gleim und Uz. Edited by Carl
       Schüddekopf.Bibliothek des Litteratur-Vereins in Stuttgart
       218 (1899): 233.
          They agree that the ending of Clarissa is far too
       tragic. (Compare his "Lines to Grotzner" in 1753
       [Hannaford, item 375].)

1752

*1   ANON. Criticism of Richardson. Maendelyke Uittreksels, of de
      Boekzaal der geleerde Werrelt. Part 75 (December): 730.
           Source: 1965.17, p. 22.

*2   ---. Review of Clarissa. Nouvelles critiques du royaume des
      savants.
           Discusses ending of Clarissa. Source: 1931.3, p. 256.

3   KENRICK, WILLIAM. Fun: A Parodi-tragi-comical Satire.
      London: T. Stamper.
           Among the ingredients in the Three Witches´ spell for
      Dulness is "the Virtue of Pamela . . . [and] Clarissa,"
      p. 4.

4   LENNOX, CHARLOTTE. The Female Quixote. 2v. London: Andrew
      Millar.
           Margaret Dalziel, in an appendix to her edition of The
      Female Quixote (London, Oxford, New York: Oxford
      University Press, 1973, pp. 418-27), details Richardson´s
      contributions to the book. He and Johnson criticized it
      and influenced it heavily. His works are discussed p. 253
      of the 1973 ed., in which he is compared with Johnson and
      Young, and p. 377, in which his books are preferred to
      romances. On p. 314 Lennox echoes his idea of Protestant
      nunneries.

5   RICHARDSON, SAMUEL. Clarissa: of, De historie van eene jonge
      juffer, waarin de gewigtigste belangen des gemeenen leevens
      vervat zijn . . . Translated by Johannes Stinstra.   8v.
      Haarlingen: F. van der Plaats, 1752-55.
           Stinstra contributed prefaces as well as the
      translation, the first into Dutch of Clarissa. See
      1969.17; RNB item 6.

*6   ---. Letters written to and for particular friends, on the
      most important occasions. . . . The fifth edition.
      London: Printed for T. Longman and C. Hitch, J. and J.
      Rivington, and J. Leake, at Bath.
           Sale, item 25.

*7   ---. Letters written to and for particular friends . . .
      The fifth edition. London: Printed for T. Longman and C.
      Hitch and L. Hawes, J. Hodges, J. and J. Rivington, and

J. Leake at Bath.
Sale, item 26. Second issue of this edition; the title page is a cancel.

1753

*1   ANON. Article. Dublin Spy, November 5.
A violent invective against Richardson for wanting to sell his own sheets of Sir Charles Grandison in Ireland, rather than allowing the book to be pirated. Source: 1919.6, p. 17.

2   ---. Article. GM 23 (July-December): 465-66.
Partial reprint of The Case of Samuel Richardson of London, Printer. Summarizes what George Faulkner, the Dublin pirate, has done; reprints Arthur Murphy's letter from "Jonathan Swift" in The Gray's Inn Journal of October 13 and summarizes the rest of Murphy's article; with Richardson, urges the passage of a copyright law.

3   ---. Letter. GM 23 (July-December); 511-13.
A commendatory letter, in a style not at all dissimilar to Richardson's, praising Grandison for its qualites touchantes, its exact descriptions of interior and external character, its clever conversation, and its energy of expression, and justifying it comparative lack of incident. The book "may in a great measure supply the place of the tutor and boarding school" through giving its readers a knowledge of the polite world. "But besides heart-moving incidents [sic] and instructive conversations, there are in this work curious particulars in geography . . . " and the author reprints the Mont Cenis passage, possibly the only one in the book not written by Richardson. E&K, p. 406, suggest that Hester Mulso may have had a hand in this letter.

4   ---. Exchange of letters. De Nederlandsche Spectator 5; 139-41. Letter from "Lugthart" and answer by "Editor" defending Richardson's morality. Source: 1965.17, pp. 27-28; 1969.17, p. xxi.

5   ---. Review of <u>Grandison</u>. <u>Nouvelles Littéraires</u> 117
      (December 30). Reprinted in <u>Les Cinq Années Littéraires,
      ou Nouvelles Littéraires</u> . . . 4v. La Haye: Ant.   de
      Groot et Fils for Pierre Gosse, Jr., 1754, 4:271.
           Finds <u>Sir Charles Grandison</u> amusing and boring by turns,
      and thinks the epistolary form old-fashioned.

6   CHESTERFIELD, PHILIP DORMER STANHOPE, earl of.   Letter to
      David   Mallet, November 5.   Reprinted in 1936.5, pp.
      219-20.
           Even though it is overlong, with too much mere talk, <u>Sir
      Charles</u> Grandison amuses Chesterfield; Richardson mistakes
      high life "but never . . . nature, and he has surely
      great   knowledge   and   skill   both   in   painting   and   in
      interesting the heart. He has even coined some words for
      those little secret movements that are admirable."

7   [DEFOE, DANIEL, and others.] <u>A Tour thro' the Whole Island of
      Great   Britain</u>.   . . <u>The Fifth Edition. With very Great
      Additions, Improvements, and Corrections; which bring it
      down to the year 1753</u>. 4v. London: for S. Birt, T.
      Osborne, D. Browne, T. and T. Longman, C. Hitch and L.
      Hawes, J. Hodges, A. Millar, J. Robinson and J. and J.
      Rivington.
           Richardson served as co-editor for this edition.   Sale,
      item 30.

*8   [FAULKNER, GEORGE?] <u>The Case of Samuel Richardson against the
      Dublin Pirates</u>. Dublin: n.p, 8 pp.
           The Dublin pirates strike back.   Characteristically,
      this   pamphlet   might   be   mistaken   by   the   unwary   for
      Richardson's well-publicized original, for which see below.
      Source: Sale, p. 66.

*9   [FAULKNER, GEORGE.] <u>Dublin Journal</u> (November 3).
           Defends his conduct in the piracy episode; Source:
      Sale, p. 66.

10   [GRIMM, FRIEDRICH MELCHIOR, baron.] <u>Correspondance littéraire</u>.
      June 15. Reprinted in 1877.2, 2: 248.
           Through its variety of styles <u>Clarissa</u> is perhaps the
      most surprising work ever written, a "prodige continuel aux
      yeux du connaisseur." It is hardly surprising that it has
      had only mediocre success, "[car] le vrai sublime n'est
      fait que pour être senti de quelques âmes privilégiées."

*11   HALLER, ALBRECHT von.   Preface to <u>Felicia</u> <u>oder</u> <u>Natur</u> <u>und</u>
       <u>Sitten</u> <u>in</u> <u>der</u> <u>Geschichte</u> <u>eines</u> <u>adeligen</u> <u>Frauenzimmers</u> <u>auf</u>
       <u>dem</u> <u>Lande</u>. <u>Aus</u> <u>dem</u> <u>Englischen</u> [of Mary Collyer's <u>Felicia</u>
       <u>to Charlotte</u>] <u>von</u> <u>Haller</u>. Hamburg und Leipzig.
            Preface compares the heroine of this book to
       Richardson's heroines and Amelia, and discusses the
       contemporary novel in a manner influenced by Richardson's
       work. Haller's alterations to the novel show the influence
       of Richardson's novels. Source: 1932.7, p. 192n7.

12   HILL, AARON. <u>The</u> <u>Works</u> <u>of</u> <u>the</u> <u>Late</u> <u>Aaron</u> <u>Hill</u>, <u>Esq</u>;   <u>.</u>   <u>.</u>   <u>.</u>
       <u>Consisting</u> <u>of</u> <u>Letters</u> <u>on</u> <u>Various</u> <u>Subjects</u>, <u>and</u> <u>of</u> <u>Original</u>
       <u>Poems</u>, <u>Moral</u> <u>and</u> <u>Facetious</u>. <u>With</u> <u>an</u> <u>Essay</u> <u>on</u> <u>the</u> <u>Art</u> <u>of</u>
       <u>Acting</u>. 4v.   London: Printed for the Benefit of the
       Family. BM.
            Richardson subscribed generously to, and may have been
       concerned in the production of, this attempt to aid Hill's
       family. Letters and poems to him appear in 1, 267-269;
       vol. 2, <u>passim</u>; and 4, pp. 64-66. (See 1913.1.)

13   LESSING, G.E. Review of <u>Felicia</u>. <u>Berlinische</u> <u>privilegierte</u>
       <u>Zeitung</u>, May 17.   Repr. in <u>Sämt</u>. <u>Schriften</u>, ed. K.
       Lachmann and F. Muncker, 3rd ed. (Stuttgart: 1886-1924),
       5:165.
            Testifies to the striking popularity of <u>Pamela</u>.   See
       1938.3, p. 354.

14   MURPHY, ARTHUR. <u>Gray's</u> <u>Inn</u> <u>Journal</u>, No. 3 (October 13).
            A letter from "Jonathan Swift" deplores the Dublin
       piracy of <u>Sir</u> <u>Charles</u> <u>Grandison</u>.

15   [RICHARDSON, SAMUEL.] <u>Aesop's</u> <u>Fables</u> . . .   [New edition.]
       London: Printed by S. Richardson for T. and T. Longman,
       C. Hitch and L. Hawes, T. Hodges, I. and I. Rivinton
       [sic], G. Keith and R. Dodsley, n.d., 220 pp. and 25
       engraved 1.
            Sale, item 3.

16   RICHARDSON, SAMUEL. <u>Aesop's</u> <u>Fables</u> <u>.</u> <u>.</u> <u>.</u> <u>by</u> <u>Mr.</u>
       <u>Richardson</u>.   York: T. Wilson and R. Spence, n.d., 192
       pp. and 25 engraved 1. Private collection.
            Another edition from the London one of the same year;
       the title-page cut has been re-engraved in reverse, the
       comma is missing after "Religion" in the same place, and
       there are no brackets around the signature marks for B and

C. Unlike the London edition, it is not anonymous. Not
listed in Sale. Dating courtesy of Mr. A.R. Heath.

17:    ---. Address to the Public. London: [S. Richardson], 7p.
CtY, Forster Collection.
Richardson's grievances against the Dublin pirates. A
somewhat different version of The Case of Samuel Richardson
of London.

18   ---. The Case of Samuel Richardson, of London, printer; with
regard to the Invasion of his Property in The History of
Sir Charles Grandison, By Publication, by certain
Booksellers in Dublin. [London: Samuel Richardson], one
folio sheet. CtY.
Like the preceding, dated Sept. 13, 1753. Both
describe the action of his workman and the Dublin printers
in pirating Grandison. Sale, item 44.

19   ---. The History of Sir Charles Grandison. In a Series of
Letters. Publish'd from the Originals, by the Editor of
Pamela and Clarissa. 7v. London: Printed for S.
Richardson; and sold by C. Hitch and L. Hawes, J. and
J. Rivington, Andrew Millar, R. and J. Dodsley, and J.
Leake in Bath, 1753-54. [All vols. are dated 1754.]
The duodecimo first edition, published simultaneously
with the second edition in octavo. Sale, item 39.

20   ---. The History of Sir Charles Grandison. . . . 6v.
London: Printed for S. Richardson; and sold by C. Hitch
and L. Hawes, J. and J. Rivington, Andrew Millar, R.
and J. Dodsley, and J. Leake in Bath, 1753-54. [All
vols. are dated 1754.]
The octavo edition; Sale, item 40.

21   ---. The History of Sir Charles Grandison . . . 7v.
London, Printed by S. Richardson, and Dublin, Reprinted
and sold by the booksellers, 1753- 54. CtY PPRF.
The pirated edition. See Sale, pp. 65-70, and 1933.10.

22   WHITEHEAD, WILLIAM. Article. The World. May 10.
Excepts Richardson and Fielding from a general
condemnation of novels. Reprinted in 1970.31.

<u>1754</u>

1   ---. Review of <u>Grandison</u>. <u>Monthly Review</u> 10: 70-71.
         Does <u>Grandison</u> cause more pleasure or pain? Pleasure,
     if one considers its good sense, its excellent sentiments,
     its judicious observations and moral reflections; disgust,
     through the absurdity of the epistolary method, its extreme
     verbosity, its frequently affected language and the
     inconsistency of its characterization.

*2   ---. Review of <u>Grandison</u>. <u>Neue Zeitungen von Gelehrten
     Sachen</u> (Leipzig), p. 736.
         Source: 1969.11, p. 563.

[Campbell, Alexander?] See "Lover of Virtue".

3   COWPER, WILLIAM. "An Ode on Reading Mr. Richardson´s History
     of Sir Charles Grandison." Written 1754(?). A MS is in
     FMSS. Published in <u>Cowper: Poetical Works</u>. Ed. H.S.
     Milford. London: Oxford University Press, 1967, pp.
     283-84, and (a variant) in 1966.7.
         Goodness cannot work unaided by the Divine, Cowper
     concludes.

*3A EVANS, CADWALLADER. Letter of February 12. Printed in
     <u>Monthly Magazine</u> 40 (1815): 512.
         <u>Grandison</u> is accused of prolixity but has many
     advocates; few of his friends have read it. Source:
     Hannaford, item 300.

4   [GRIMM, FRIEDRICH MELCHIOR, baron.] <u>Correspondance littéraire</u>,
     August 15. Reprinted in 1877.1, 2:391.
         Again draws attention to <u>Clarissa</u>; it requires <u>génie</u>,
     not merely <u>esprit</u>, to create a Lovelace. 1975.20, p. 147,
     remarks on Grimm´s early appreciation of Richardson.

5   LOVER OF VIRTUE, A. [pseud.] <u>Critical Remarks on Sir Charles
     Grandison, Clarissa and Pamela. Enquiring, Whether they
     have a Tendency to corrupt or improve the public Taste and
     Morals. In a Letter to the Author. By a Lover of Virtue</u>.
     L: J. Dowse, 61 pp.
         Praises the purpose of <u>Grandison</u>, but Richardson´s
     actual practice has fallen short both stylistically and
     morally, e.g., in his treatment of the passions. The men
     are too good (Grandison) or not sufficiently inventive in

their wickedness; the women, Clarissa excepted, are not the paragons of virtue that Richardson believes. <u>Clarissa</u> will live; the other two books, no. The author, apparently a Deist, attacks Richardson and Hill for their anti-Deism; thus Mrs. Chapone's theory that Fielding wrote this will not stand, as he also attacked Deism. Sale, item 86. The author may be Alexander Campbell.

6   [PLUMMER, FRANCIS?] <u>A Candid Examination of the History of Sir Charles Grandison. In a letter to a lady of distinction, published by permission.</u> London: Dodsley, 46 pp. NN.
        Attacks the length of <u>Grandison</u>, Sir Charles's vanity and chastity, the courtship, the too-frequent faintings, praise, and crying; but finds much good conversation and excellent characters and scenes, including Charlotte G—— and everything in Italy. Concludes, somewhat regretfully, that "<u>it is low.</u>"

7   RICHARDSON,SAMUEL. <u>An Address to the Public, on the Treatment which the Editor of the History of Sir Charles Grandison has met with, from certain Booksellers and Printers in Dublin.</u> . . . [London: Samuel Richardson.] BM, CtY.
        Sale, item 45. Dated February 1, 1754.

8   ———. <u>The History of Sir Charles Grandison. In a Series of Letters Publish'd from the Originals, by the Editor of Pamela and Clarissa.</u> 7v. . . . <u>The Third Edition.</u> London: Printed for S. Richardson, and sold by C. Hitch and L. Hawes, J. and J. Rivington, Andrew Millar, R. and J. Dodsley, James Leake, in Bath, and by R. Mann, in Dublin.
        Sale, item 41.

9   ———. <u>Geschichte Herrn Carl Grandison. In Briefen entworfen von dem Verfasser der Pamela und der Clarissa. Aus dem Englischen übersetzt</u> . . . Translated by C.F. Gellert (and others?). 7v. Leipzig: M.G. Weidmann, 1754-55.
        Schmid (1792.15) says Schwabe translated <u>Grandison</u> into German, and Price believes him; but the anonymous editor of 1953.5 cites (note 7a) Reich's letter to Richardson of May 10, 1754 (1804.2, 5:297) and other sources to support Gellert. E&K, p. 415, suggest that the translation may

have been completed by some other hand. Gellert seems at
least to have kept an eye on it throughout; see his letter
to Count Moritz von Brühl, Jan. 14, 1756. Grandison is
also discussed in Gellert's letters to von Brühl of Dec.
12, 1754, and August 3, 1755, and von Brühl's to Gellert of
Oct. 18, 1755.

10   RICHARDSON, SAMUEL. Pamela; or, Virtue Rewarded.   .   .   .
      7th ed. [5th ed. of Pamela in her Exalted Condition.] 4v.
      London: Printed for J. Hodges; and J. and J.
      Rivington.
           Sale, items 13, 19.

11   ---. Two Letters Concerning Sir Charles Grandison [Copy of a
      Letter to a Lady, who was Solicitous for an Additional
      Volume to the History of Sir Charles Grandison; Answer to
      a Letter from a Friend, who had objected to Sir Charles
      Grandison's Offer to allow his Daughters by Lady Clementina
      . . . to be educated Roman Catholics]. [London: Samuel
      Richardson], 4 pp. each. Bodleian, Forster Collection.
           Richardson details in the first the reasons, artistic
      and personal, why Grandison will not be further continued;
      in the second, his reasoning in allowing his hero to
      compromise on the religious question where daughters were
      concerned. (The objections to the compromise are
      feminist.) Described by Sale, item 46. The letter from Cox
      Macro that occasioned the second letter is in the British
      Museum (B.M. Add. MS. 32,557, II, fo. 175) and in FMSS.
      XV, fo. 57; a draft of Richardson's answer is in FMSS.XV,
      4, fo. 23, and his letter is in the B.M. (Add. MS.
      32,557, II, fos. 176-77).

12   WILLIAMS, ANNA, revised by Samuel Johnson. "Verses to Mr.
      Richardson on his History of Sir Charles Grandison." GM 24:
      40.
           Compares Richardson to the epic poets; his name will
      long outshine Fielding's. Grandison is finer than
      Clarissa, and Clementina is the finest part of Grandison.
      Boswell is the authority for Johnson's being concerned in
      the revision. The poem was republished in her Miscellanies
      in Prose and Verse (London: T. Davies, 1766), pp. 31-34.

1755

1   ANON. [possibly A.F. Prévost d´Exiles.] Review of Goldoni´s
     Pamela nubile and other imitations of Pamela. Journal
     étranger (February): 176-200.
         Approves of Goldoni´s works as the first Italian plays
     combining decency, truth to nature, nobility of character
     and vivid expression; however, criticizes the near-rape
     and Pamela´s willingness to think about B even before he
     has encouraged her. Also notices Nanine and Paméla en
     France.

2   FIELDING, HENRY. The Journal of a Voyage to Lisbon . . .
     London: A. Millar, 276 pp.
         Austin Dobson believes that Fielding´s mention of
     "authors, who often fill a whole sheet with their own
     praises, to which they sometimes set their own names,
     and sometimes a fictitious one" is yet another dig at the
     prefatory material of Pamela; but Fielding´s attitude
     toward Richardson had changed since Shamela, and there were
     many other, more current books that sinned in the same way.

3   [FRÉRON, ELIE CATHERINE.] L´Année littéraire . . .   8 (for
     1755): 136-42.
         Defends Prévost´s translation of Grandison, which he has
     "hewn" from the English original as a sculptor hews a
     statue from a block of wood; largely a summary of the
     action through Grandison´s first visit to Bologna.

4   JAQUIN OR JACQUIN, l´abbé. Entretiens sur les Romans. Paris:
     Duchesne, preface and pp. 100-01. BN.
         Attacks the epistolary novel; feels that Pamela,
     Clarissa, and Tom Jones are "forgotten."

5   KIDGELL, JOHN. The Card. 2v. London: John Newberry. BM.
         Amiably parodies the Clementina situation of mixed
     religions and introduces characters from Richardson as part
     of a parody-pastiche of contemporary novelists, who also
     include Smollett and Fielding. See particularly in vol.
     1, pp. xii-xiii, 174; vol.2, pp. 68, 83, 94n, 294-96.
     Reviewed by the Monthly Review 12 (1755): 117÷21, which
     notes the parody of Grandison.

*6   [PLUMMER, FRANCIS?] A Candid Examination of the History of Sir
     Charles Grandison. . . .
         Sale lists a possible second and a third edition in
     1755; see items 87, 88.

7   RICHARDSON, SAMUEL. A Collection of the moral and instructive
     Sentiments, Maxims, Cautions, and Reflections, Contained in
     the Histories of Pamela, Clarissa, and Sir Charles
     Grandison . . . To which are subjoined, two letters from
     the editor of those works. Introduction by Benjamin
     Kennicott. London: Printed for Samuel Richardson, 420 pp.
     NN.
          Sale, item 47. The two letters are reprinted from
     1754.11. The Collection is described in 1804.2, 5:48 as
     "the pith and marrow of nineteen volumes," a sentiment that
     may have been held more widely than by Richardson's
     friends; Sale describes a card-game engraved with mottoes
     from this book, and the game is known to have gone into
     nine editions. Kennicott's introduction praises
     Richardson, comparing him to Plutarch. See 1968.5.

8   ---. Nouvelles lettres angloises, ou Histoire du chevalier
     Grandison, par l'auteur de Paméla et de Clarisse.
     Translated and extensively altered with an introduction by
     A.F. Prévost d'Exiles. 8v. in 4. Amsterdam, 1755-56
     [1755-58].
          See 1927.10 for the numerous changes introduced into
     this version--one can hardly say translation--of
     Richardson's novel. Prévost's introduction praises
     Richardson's genius.

9   ---. [Letters written to and for particular persons, on the
     most important occasions. . . . The sixth edition.
     London: T. Longman, C. Hitch and L. Hawes, J. Hodges,
     J. and J. Rivington, and J. Leake at Bath], 272 pp.
     CtY.
          Sale, item 27. The Yale copy, the title page of which
     is missing, was used as the text for 1928.7 and contains MS
     annotations. The title is supplied from an advertisement
     in the Public Advertiser, July 1, 1755.

10   WORTLEY MONTAGU, LADY MARY. Letter to Lady Bute, October 20,
     Reprinted in 1965.21, 3:91-97.
          Richardson's knowledge of high life and his morality, as
     expressed in Grandison, do not please Lady Mary; his ideas
     of medicine are false, his morality low and foolish, his
     knowledge of society nil. She approves of Protestant
     nunneries.

1756

1   ANON. Review. <u>Critical Review</u> 1: 261.
        In a review of <u>The Supposed Daughter, or Innocent Impostor</u>, Richardson is criticized for prolixity. See Smollett to Richardson, August 10, 1756, in which Smollett discusses this article. See also 1928.7, which ascribes the review to Fulke Greville.

2   ---. <u>Mercure de France</u> (January), pp. 50-78.
        Long letter on <u>Grandison</u>. Is it "a sermon," unrealistic, or highly moral? 1754.1 is cited. A rejoinder is in the <u>Journal encyclopédique</u> 2 (February): 32-38.

3   GIBBON, EDWARD. Letter to Catherine Porten, ca. November 15, Reprinted in <u>Letters of Edward Gibbon</u>, ed. J.E. Norton (London: Cassell and Co., 1956), 1:37.
        He urges her to read <u>Sir Charles Grandison</u>, which is "much superior to <u>Clarissa</u>."

4   GOLDONI, CARLO. <u>Pamela: Commedia di Carlo Goldoni . . . Pamela: A Comedy by Charles Goldoni. Translated into English with the Italian Original</u>. London: J. Nourse, 192 pp. BM.
        A dual-language version of Goldoni's play (1750.6) with its first English translation, a spirited, perhaps too spirited, rendition of the original. ("Maledetto amore" becomes "Rot your love!") Goldoni's introduction contains interesting material on his idea of sentimental comedy and his principal change to the plot of Richardson's original, making Pamela noble, an alteration also made by Voltaire. Much more is made of Lady Davers' resentment at Pamela's supposed low birth; Pamela's virtue is called to witness that she is noble. ("Ah, che la virtu di Pamela dovea farmi avvertito, che abietto il di lei sangue non fosse!" Act 3, scene 11.)
        Goldoni explained in his <u>Memoirs</u> that he had changed the ending of the play in order to remain realistic in Italian terms; a nobleman in Venice who married a commoner would deprive his children of any claim to nobility (see 1938.3, p. 355). However, this was often lost on critics of the play. See e.g. the <u>Monthly Review</u> 17 (July 1757): 47-50. The play was reviewed by Gottsched in 1760; see Hannaford, item 192.

5   ---. Pamela, oder: Die belohnte Tugend. Ein Lustspiel in
       drey Handlungen, aus dem italienischen . . . Translated
       by ? Danzig: n.p.   126 pp.   BM.   See 1938.3, pp.
       371-372.

*6   [GRIMM, FRIEDRICH MELCHIOR, and DENIS DIDEROT?] Correspondance
       littéraire, January 1756. Printed in 1877.2.
            Review Prévost's Nouvelles lettres anglaises and find it
       an inferior work.

7   RICHARDSON, SAMUEL.   An Abridgment of Clarissa: or, The
       History of a Young Lady. Comprehending the Most Important
       Concerns of Private Life, and Particularly Shewing the
       Distresses that may Attend the Misconduct both of Parents
       and Children, in Relation to Marriage. Abridged by ?   2v.
       Dublin: W. Sleater. ICU, National Library of Ireland.

8   ---. Pamela, ovvero La Virtu Premiata. Traduzione
       dall'Inglese.   4v.   Venice: Presso Di Domenico, e
       Manfredi. Ed a spese di Giacomo-Antonio Venaccia. MH;
       Vatican (2v. only).
            Part I only.

9   ---. Histoire de Sir Charles Grandison, contenue dans une
       Suite de Lettres, publiées sur les Originaux, par l'Editeur
       de Paméla et de Clarisse. Translated by G.J. Monod. 7v.
       Gottingen and Leiden: Elie Luzac Fils. Bib. Jagiellońska
       (vols. 2-7); BN; Württ. Landesbib. (vols. 4-7);
       Statni knihovna ČSR.
            Unlike Prevost's, a full translation. See E&K, pp.
       415-16, for information on it.

10   ---. Histoire de Sir Charles Grandison . . . Translated by
       G.J.   Monod. 7v.   Leipzig: Chez les Héritiers de G.M.
       Weidmann. Württ. Landesbib. (vols. 1-3); BN (lacks 1
       vol.); NIC (complete): Courtesy of Mr. Williston R.
       Benedict (Trebizond Rare Books) and Mr.   Charles B.
       McNamara, Cornell.

11   ---. Historie van den Ridder-Baronet Karel Grandison. In
       een' reeks van gemeenzaame brieven, uit de Oorsprongkelyken
       in 't licht gebragt, door den Uitgeever van Pamela en
       Clarissa. En nu naar den derden Druk, uit het Engelsch
       overgezet. Translated by a group supervised by Johannes
       Stinstra. 7v. Harlingen: Folkert van der Plaats;

Amsterdam: Kornelis van Tongerlo, 1756-57. Koninklikje
Bibliotheek, WU.
    Grandison in Dutch. RNB, item 7. For the circumstances
of translation, see 1969.17, letter 21, Sept. 19, 1755.

12   ---. The Paths of Virtue Delineated; or, the History in
      Miniature of the Celebrated Pamela, Clarissa Harlowe, and
      Sir Charles Grandison, Familiarized and Adapted to the
      Capacities of Youth. Abridged and adapted [by Oliver
      Goldsmith?] London: R. Baldwin, 239 pp. ICU, MH.
          The preface , by the anonymous adapter, discusses the
      potential of the novel to serve as an example or "living
      picture" to educate youth; apologizes for omitting some
      fine touches of the original. But the adaptations
      themselves are extraordinarily well done, brisk
      storytelling without moralizing, unusual for abridgments of
      Richardson. We know that Richardson and Goldsmith became
      acquainted about 1756 (E&K, pp. 461- 462), and that
      Goldsmith was engaged in work for children at this time,
      but nothing more solid supports the tempting traditional
      identification. The second edition (1764) was the source
      of many American abridgments, according to Sale, p. 134.
      Reviewed (favorably) by the Critical Review 1:315-16,
      perhaps as an apology from Smollett for 1756.1;
      (unfavorably) by the Monthly Review 14:581-82.

*13   WIELAND, CHRISTOPH MARTIN. Sympathien. As Soul approuches
      [sic] Soul. S.o.O. 1756.
          Source: Wilpert & Gühring, pp. 138-139. Sympathien
      was translated into English in 1795 as The Sympathy of
      Souls (London: Printed for the Editor and sold by E.
      Beetham, Bladon, Byfield, and Hawksworth, Chapple, n.d.);
      I have seen only this edition. In it there are frequent
      references to Grandison; Chapter VIII is an ecstatic paean
      to Clementina.

                              1757

1   KLOPSTOCK, META. Letter to her sisters, May 13, 1757.
      Reprinted in H. Tiemann, ed., Meta Klopstock, geborene
      Moller, Briefwechsel mit Klopstock, ihrer Verwandten und
      Freunden. 3v. N.p.: Maximilian-Gesellschaft, 1956,
      2:617-18.

Frederick of Prussia is the Lovelace of the Seven Years´ War, Maria Theresa the Clarissa. Compare Klopstock´s remarks to his future wife, quoted 3:737; he compliments her epistolary style by calling her "Clärchen" or "Clary." (Courtesy of Prof. Kevin Hilliard)

2 RICHARDSON, SAMUEL. Sittenlehre für die Jugend in der auserlesensten Aesopischen Fabeln mit dienlichen Betrachtungen zur Beförderung der Religion und der allgemeinen Menschenliebe vorgestellet. Aus dem Englischen übertragen und mit einem Vorrede von Gotthold Ephraim Lessing. Mit Kupfern. Translated with a preface by G.E. Lessing. Leipzig: Weidmann, 368 pp. InU, MH.
   The preface is reprinted in Sämt. Schriften, ed. Lachmann and Muncker, 3d ed., 1886-1924, 7: 75ff.; Lessing praises Pamela and discourses on the value of an edition of Aesop for youth.

3 ZACHARIAE, FRIEDRICH WILHELM. Die Vier Stufen des weiblichen Älters. Rostock: Johann Christian Koppe, p. 14.
   For novels, the young woman may read only Richardson´s; only his works are pure.

1758

1 FRÉRON, ELIE CATHERINE. Review of Nouvelles Lettres anglaises. L´Année littéraire 4 (for 1758): 3-20.
   Reports on the publication of the last part of Prevost´s translation of Grandison. Mrs. "Bémont´s" discovery of Clementina´s passion for Grandison and Clementina´s attempt to convert him are reprinted in detail. Treats the book as one of Prévost´s works.

2 GRIMM, FRIEDRICH MELCHIOR, baron. Review of Nouvelles lettres anglaises. Correspondance littéraire, August 1, 1758. Repr. 1877.2, 4: 24-25.
   Prévost has "absolument estropié" Grandison, even cutting the masterstrokes of the book in the episodes involving Clementina. Monod´s translation, though awkward, is preferable. Grimm concludes that few modern works show as much genius as Richardson´s. See also 1877.2, 3:161.

3   MARMONTEL, JEAN-FRANÇOIS, abbé. Review of <u>Nouvelles</u> <u>Lettres</u>
      <u>anglaises</u>. <u>Mercure</u> <u>de</u> <u>France</u> (August), pp. 79-95.
           This first version of the "Essai sur les Romans
      considérés du cote moral" (see 1819.2) reviews the last
      half of Prevost's <u>Grandison</u>, incidentally summarizing some
      of Prevost's more startling innovations. Praises
      Richardson for his delicacy and animation, the truth of his
      writing, and "la magie de l'ordonnance" with which he
      groups his strikingly realized characters. However,
      Richardson's too-great detail slows the pace of the
      narrative.

4   ROUSSEAU, JEAN-JACQUES. <u>Lettre</u> <u>à</u> <u>M.</u> <u>d'Alembert</u> <u>sur</u> <u>les</u>
      <u>Spectacles</u>. First published 1750. Repr. ed. L, Brunel.
      Paris: Hachette, 1896, p. 124n.
           Rousseau expresses his admiration of <u>Clarissa</u>: "no
      other book ever approached it."

5   WEBSTER, WILLIAM. <u>A</u> <u>Plain</u> <u>Narrative</u> <u>of</u> <u>Facts,</u> <u>or</u> <u>the</u> <u>Author's</u>
      <u>Case . . .</u>. London: J. Noon, p. ii.
           Expresses his gratitude to Richardson, who forgave him a
      debt of £90 and offered further help during a crisis.

<u>1759</u>

1   BEATTIE, JAMES. Letter to Dr. John Ogilvie, August 20.
      Printed in <u>An</u> <u>Account</u> <u>of</u> <u>the</u> <u>Life</u> <u>and</u> <u>Writings</u> <u>of</u> <u>James</u>
      <u>Beattie,</u> <u>Lit.D.</u> <u>. .</u> <u>.Including</u> <u>Many</u> <u>of</u> <u>his</u> <u>Original</u>
      <u>Letters</u>. Ed. Sir William Forbes. 3v. Edinburgh: Arch,
      Constable & Co; London: Longman, Hurst, Rees, and Orme,
      T. Cadell and W. Davies, and John Murray, 1807, 1:
      46-57.
           A long letter discussing Richardson, who shows great
      knowledge of human nature; he does not write to amuse and
      will not suit those who read only for amusement. Beattie
      has felt tedium in reading <u>Clarissa</u>, but now feels no part
      is superfluous. Defends Richardson's "perfect characters";
      we should have perfect models before us. However, Clarissa
      is humanly imperfect as well, in her heart though not in
      her behavior. Finds Richardson's pathos superior to that
      of all other novel-writers, hardly excelled even in the
      best tragedy, and generally commends his style. "To have
      raised it above the familiar had been faulty." Compare

1783.2.
   Mrs. Piozzi's copy of this book, now in the British
Museum (10856.ee.9), contains extensive marginal comments
on this letter. P. 47, Beattie writes, "He delineates
some characters with masterly and distinguishing strokes";
Mrs. Piozzi underlines "some" and writes "all." P. 48,
Beattie discusses "the progress of the story"; Mrs.
Piozzi comments, "There is no Story--A Man gets a Girl from
her Parents--violates her Free Will, and She dies of a
broken heart. That is all the Story--But the Book's merit
is in so filling up this Inelegant Outline as to make it
the ´wisest, virtuousest, discreetest, best´ of all
possible Novels.--a Picture replete with Character, and
luminous with well-contrasted Clear-obscure;--Grace in each
Page, Expression in each Line." P. 49, Beattie suggests
that Richardson should have "disposed of all the parts of
his work in such a manner, as that the reader . . .
should never be tempted to pass over any part." Mrs.
Piozzi comments, "All that is better done by 20 Writers
than by Richardson." P. 54, Beattie and Piozzi agree that
Clarissa's inability to remember when she has last seen
Mrs. Sinclair (it was during the drugged rape) is tragic
and "delightfully intolerable." P. 55, Mrs. Piozzi is not
sure that she agrees with Beattie in his commendation of
the long-uncertain ending of Clarissa. But on the whole,
she concludes, p. 57, "His Criticisms on Clarissa are the
very best extant."

2   BLAIR, HUGH. Lectures on Rhetoric and Belles Lettres.
    Delivered 1759. Printed in 2v. London: W. Strahan, T.
    Cadell; Edinburgh: W. Creech, 1783. 2:309-10.
       Richardson is the most moral of English novelists, but
    he spins out stories to an "immeasurable length."

3   DU DEFFAND, MARIE ANNE, marquise. Letter of October 28, 1759,
    to Voltaire. Printed in Correspondance complète de Mme.
    la Marquise du Deffand, ed. M. de Lescure. 2v. Paris:
    Plon, 1865, 1: 250.
       Recommends to him Richardson's novels, "des traités de
    morale en action, qui sont très-intéressants et peuvent
    être fort utiles; l'auteur . . . me paraît avoir bien
    de l'esprit," though she is sure Voltaire will find them
    too long.

4   MENDELSSOHN, MOSES.   Briefe,   die   neueste   Litteratur
     betreffend.   No. 66 (November 8).   Printed in Briefe . .
     . 3d. ed. 24 parts.   Berlin and Stettin: Friedrich
     Nicolai, 1767, part 21, pp. 1-23.
          Wholly virtuous characters are easier to create than
     ideals;   Grandison   was   easier to conceive of than
     Clementina, and perhaps Clarissa easier than Lovelace.

5   RICHARDSON, SAMUEL.   Clarissa; or, The History of a Young
     Lady . . .   4th ed.   8v.   London: Printed for S.
     Richardson.
          Compare the fourth edition of 1751. Sale, item 36.

6   ---.   Geschichte Herrn Carl Grandison. In Briefen entworfen.
     . . .   Zweyte verbesserte und mit Kupfern versehene
     Auflage. Aus dem Englischen übersetzt. Translated by C.F.
     Gellert   (and   others?).   7v.   Leipzig: In   der
     Weidmannischen Handlung. BM, MdBJ, MH, IU, CtY, Sachs.
     Landesbib.

Smith, Adam. Theory of Moral Sentiments.
          See 1790.10.

7   YOUNG, EDWARD.   [with   suggestions   and   corrections   by
     Richardson] Conjectures on Original Composition, in a
     Letter to the Author of Sir Charles Grandison. London: A.
     Millar and R. and J. Dodsley, 114 pp.
          "How shall I rejoice to read . . .   such noble
     instances of the doctrines you advance in favour of the
     moderns!" wrote Richardson to Young on May 10, 1757.   He
     was disingenuous;   though Young wrote the first draft of
     this important document on the Moderns, its final version
     was greatly influenced by Richardson's comments on the
     issues it had raised. (Sale reports, p. 98, that Johnson
     may have given some advice as well.) Richardson's role is
     discussed in 1925.4 and in E&K, pp. 432-436; see also the
     Monthly Magazine correspondence on the subject (42 [1816],
     331-335; 44 [1817], 327-330; 46 [1818], 43-45).   Sale,
     item 49.   A second edition and a pirated edition were
     published the same year (Sale, item 49 and page 97).

<u>1760</u>

*1   ANON. <u>Louisa, or Virtue in Distress</u>.
        "Lady G--- is one of the most imitated of Richardson´s
        characters; most of our modern novels abound with a Lady
        G---." P. x. Quoted by 1950.7, p. iv.

1A   ---. "On the Present State of Literature in England."
        <u>Imperial Magazine</u> 1: 686-87.
        Finds Richardson´s writings too long and not
        sufficiently varied, but this is a minority view.

2   ---. <u>The Polite Lady: or, A Course of Female Education, in a
        Series of Letters, from a Mother to her Daughter</u>. London:
        J. Newbery, p. 143. Private collection.
        Recommends the reading of novels including Richardson´s,
        which are put in the company of <u>Telemaque</u>, <u>Le Grand Cyrus</u>,
        and <u>Rasselas</u> as respectable reading for a young girl.

3   COLMAN, GEORGE. <u>Polly Honeycombe. A Dramatic Novel in One
        Act . . .</u> London: T. Becket and T. Davies, 60 pp.
        Much of Polly´s romantic delusions stem from the
        (mis)reading of <u>Clarissa</u>. She compares her favored
        Scribble to "Bob Lovelace," refers to <u>Clarissa</u> while she
        tries to get herself locked up, and thinks of her family
        and suitor-<u>en-titre</u> as Harlowes and Solmes. Scribble,
        having apparently read in the same source, hides in a
        closet.

4   GOLDONI, CARLO. <u>Pamela maritata</u>. First performed 1760 at the
        Teatro Capricana, Rome. Printed in Bologna: Stamperia di
        S. Tommaso d´Aquino, 1765. CtY.
        A little bit of Richardson, a little bit of <u>Othello</u> . .
        . See 1928.6; 1938.3, pp. 366-367; the play was
        reviewed by Baretti in <u>La Frusta</u>, no. 22 (August 15,
        1764).

5   LUSSAN, MARGUERITE DE. <u>The Life and Heroic Actions of Balbe
        Berton, Chevalier de Grillon. Translated from the French
        by a Lady, and revised by Mr. Richardson, Author of
        Clarissa, Grandison, etc.</u> Translated anonymously. 2v.
        London: H. Woodgate and S. Brooks. NNC.
        The "revisions by Mr. Richardson" consisted in
        suggesting additional notes to the Paris massacre and the
        assassination of Henry IV (Richardson to Lady Bradshaigh,
        June 20, 1760). Sale, item 50. A second edition the next
        year; Sale, item 51.

7   MENDELSSOHN, MOSES. <u>Briefe, die neueste Litteratur</u>
     <u>betreffend</u>. Letters 122-24 (August 21, 28; September 4).
     Printed in edition with 1759.8, 7: 113-50.
          A long discussion of <u>Clementina von Porretta</u>, which
     Mendelssohn finds far inferior to Richardson´s original.
     Again makes distinction between ideal poetic beauty and
     virtuous characters; the latter are interesting only when
     suffering. "Bey solche Gesinnungen konnte ich unmöglich
     einen Charakter wie Carl Grandisons für theatralisch gut
     halten," p. 126, especially when he is given nothing to
     do. Jeronymo draws the viewer interest away from
     Clementina, whom we so seldom see that we know nothing of
     her.

8   [MONTAGU, ELIZABETH.] Dialogue 28. In Lyttelton, George,
     baron. <u>Dialogues of the Dead</u>. London: W. Sandby, pp.
     317-19.
          Praises Richardson for presenting patterns of virtue in
     Grandison and Clarissa; also praises Fielding for his
     moral tendency. (Since the dialogue was printed under
     Lyttelton´s name, it has often been wrongly attributed to
     him.)

9   MUSÄUS, JOHANN KARL AUGUST VON. <u>Grandison der Zweyte, oder</u>
     <u>Geschichte des Herrn von N</u>. 3v. Eisenach: M.G.
     Griesbach. ICU, BM.
          Herr von N., having read <u>Sir Charles Grandison</u> once too
     often, becomes Grandison <u>à la</u> Quixote, converting his
     sleepy Kargfeld ("Barren-field") into Karlsfeld, giving his
     servants English names, and endowing his former tutor,
     Lampert Willibald, with the heavy mantle of Dr. Bartlett.
     His nephew and niece, Baron von F. and Amalia, plot to
     hoax him; Amalia´s brother, in England, writes von N. of
     meetings at Grandison Hall with the characters of the novel
     and Richardson himself. The result is "a frenzy of plots
     and counterplots" (1958.6, p. 337). The book is
     epistolary and depends for its full effect, of course, on a
     good knowledge of <u>Grandison</u>.

10   "THEOPHILA" [PSEUD.]. <u>The History of Sir Charles Grandison</u>
     <u>Spiritualized in Part</u>. . . London.
          "Theophila" considers <u>Sir Charles Grandison</u> as an
     allegory of the soul´s journey to Heaven. Described by
     1911.6.

11   WIELAND, CHRISTOPH MARTIN. <u>Clementina</u> <u>von</u> <u>Porretta</u>. <u>Ein</u>
      <u>Trauerspiel</u>. <u>Von</u> <u>dem</u> <u>Verfasser</u> <u>der</u> <u>Lady</u> <u>Johanna</u> <u>Grāy</u>.
      Zurich: bey Orell & Co., 230 pp. BM.
           1760.7 gives a perceptive review of Wieland's play, a
      long-drawn-out dramatization of the Italian episodes of
      <u>Grandison</u>, focused on Clementina as tragic heroine. There
      is no Harriet Byron in the play; Grandison chooses simply
      Clementina or religion, while Clementina, separated from
      him for life and fated to enter a nunnery, looks forward to
      a life with him beyond the grave.

12   YOUNG, EDWARD. [with additions by Richardson]. <u>Edward</u> <u>Youngs</u>
      <u>Bedanken</u> <u>über</u> <u>die</u> <u>Originalwerke</u> <u>in</u> <u>einem</u> <u>Schreiben</u> <u>an</u>
      <u>Samuel</u> <u>Richardson</u>. Translated by H.E. von Teubern.
      Leipzig: Heinsii Erben.
           <u>Conjectures</u> <u>on</u> <u>Original</u> <u>Composition</u> in German. Teubern
      was also a writer of minor novels in the Sentimental style,
      influenced at several removes by Richardson. Republished
      in 1761.

                              <u>1761</u>

1   ANON. Letter 13 (April 5). <u>L'Année</u> <u>littéraire</u> 2 (for 1761):
      289-330.
           Reviews <u>La</u> <u>Nouvelle</u> <u>Héloïse</u> and compares Richardson and
      Rousseau. The latter has obviously used <u>Clarissa</u> for his
      model; the form of the book, the epistolary novel, has
      been brought to France by Richardson's fiction. Claire is
      Anna Howe, M. d'Orbe is Hickman, and "par la fureur de
      raisonner et de vouloir analyser tout," p. 306, Julie is
      drawn from Clarissa. The author blames Rousseau for
      failing to introduce vicious characters into his book
      comparable to Gélin in <u>Cléveland</u> and Lovelace. See also
      1895.3, p. 283.

2   "S." [PSEUD.] Review of <u>La</u> <u>Nouvelle</u> <u>Héloïse</u>. <u>Briefe,</u> <u>der</u>
      <u>neueste</u> <u>Litteratur</u> <u>betreffend</u>. Published in same edition
      as 1759.8; 10: 255 ff.
           Finds that speech of real fire and passion, speech that
      individualizes character, is to be found in Richardson but
      not Rousseau.

*3   ANON. Review of English <u>Nouvelle Héloïse</u>. <u>Critical</u> <u>Review</u>
       12: 242-45.
            Reviews <u>Eloisa</u>, comparing Richardson and Rousseau.
       Reprinted in part in 1970.31. Other contemporary reprints
       (see Hannaford, item 196).

4   ---. <u>GM</u> 53: 334, 924; 54: 448.
            Eulogies and tributes on the death of Richardson.

5   ---. "Parallèle entre la Clarice de Richardson et la nouvelle
       Eloise de M. Rousseau." <u>Journal</u> <u>étranger</u> (December), pp.
       184-95.
            A translation of an article from the <u>Critical</u> <u>Review</u>
       compares Richardson and Rousseau. Richardson's greatest
       eulogy is to have been taken as a model by Rousseau;   the
       first remains inimitable in the art of copying Nature,
       while the second has greatly surpassed his master in
       profundity of reflection and concision of style.
       Richardson's heroine is ideal and a little cold, while
       Rousseau's Julie and St.-Preux are fallible, human, and
       thus interesting to us. Rousseau is more   profound,
       animated, ingenious, and elegant; Richardson more natural,
       interesting, varied, and dramatic. Rousseau excites our
       admiration, Richardson our tears. Richardson's book is
       more unified, while Rousseau's digressions are works of
       genius.   Richardson is a realist and Rousseau a
       philosopher.

6   ---. <u>London</u> <u>Magazine</u> 30: 448.
            Obituary of Richardson.

*7   GOODWORTH, FRAU. [pseud.] "Ob in Grandisons Geschichte
       Clementine oder Henriette Byron den Vorzug verdiene."
       <u>Nordische</u> <u>Aufseher</u>.
            Harriet Byron gets the palm. Possibly written by the
       editor of <u>Der</u> <u>Nordische</u> <u>Aufseher</u>, Cramer. Source: 1925.7,
       pp. 175-76.

8   GRIMM, FRIEDRICH MELCHIOR, baron. <u>Correspondance</u> <u>littéraire</u>,
       February. Reprinted 1877.2.
            Review of <u>La</u> <u>Nouvelle</u> <u>Héloïse</u>, comparing Richardson and
       Rousseau.

*9   MUSENHOLD, DER PLAUDERER, and SINCERINUS. [pseuds.] <u>Der
      Sammler</u>, pp. 9ff., 43ff., 76ff.
          Three letters attacking and defending the translation of
      Goldoni, <u>Pamela oder die bekrönte Unschuld</u>, currently
      playing in Strasburg. Source: 1925.7, pp. 173-75.

10   ---. <u>Scots Magazine</u> 23: 391.
      Obituary of Richardson.

11   CARTER, ELIZABETH. Epitaph on Richardson. Written 1761;
      published in <u>Universal Magazine</u>, February 1786, p. 77, and
      in <u>Annual Register, or a View of the History, Politics, and
      Literature, for the Year 1761</u>. Sixth Edition. London: J.
      Dodsley, 1796, pp. 259-60. BM.
          Benevolence, wisdom, fancy draw readers to Richardson's
      works; friendship, love, charity, and innocence mourn for
      him.

12   [DEFOE, DANIEL, and others.] <u>A Tour thro' the Whole Island of
      Great Britain . . . The Sixth Edition. With very great
      Additions, Improvements, and Corrections; which bring it
      down to the Year 1761</u>. 4v. London: For D. Browne, T.
      Osborne, C. Hitch and L. Hawes, A. Millar, J. Buckland,
      J. Rivington, S. Crowder and Co., W. Johnston, T.
      Longman, T. Lowndes, B. Law and Co., T. Caslon, and G.
      Kearsl[e]y, 1761-62. [Volumes 2 and 4 are dated 1761; in
      those volumes Crowder, Johnston, and Law are missing from
      the imprint.]
          The last edition supervised by Richardson.

13   DIDEROT, DENIS. <u>Discours sur la Poésie dramatique</u>. (Ca.
      1761.) Published in <u>Oeuvres complètes</u>, ed. Assézat &
      Tourneux. Paris: Garnier, 1875, 7:380.
          "C'est la peinture des mouvements qui charme, surtout
      dans les romans domestiques. Voyez avec quelle
      complaisance l'auteur de <u>Pamela</u>, de <u>Grandison</u>, et de
      <u>Clarisse</u> s'y arrête. Voyez quelle force, quel sens, et
      quel pathétique elle donne à son discours! Je vois le
      personnage, soit qu'il parle, soit qu'il se taise, je le
      vois, et son action m'affecte plus que sa parole . . . "
      Interestingly, p. 370, he does not count Richardson among
      "les Anglais."

*14   HERVEY, JAMES. A Treatise on the Religious Education of
        Daughters. London: J. Rivington.
            Praises Clarissa as "admirably calculated to instruct
        and entertain." Source: Hannaford, item 202.

15   ROUSSEAU, JEAN-JACQUES. Lettres de Deux Amants, Habitans
        d´une petite Ville au pied des Alpes. 6v. Amsterdam
        [Paris]: n.p.
            Better known by its half-title, Julie ou la Nouvelle
        Héloïse was frequently compared to Richardson´s Clarissa
        (see above). Rousseau himself made comments on his
        predecessor´s work in the preface and, according to Janin
        (1846.5, p. xvinl), in Letter 82. According to Bernardin
        de St.-Pierre, "il [Rousseau] ne parloit de Richardson,
        auteur de Clarisse, qu´avec enthousiasme. Voulant comparer
        son Héloïse a Clarisse[, il disait]: ´Je n´ai fait qu´un
        tableau; il a fait une galerie . . . ." (La Vie et les
        Ouvrages de Jean-Jacques Rousseau. Edition critique . .
        . par Maurice Souriau. Paris: Société nouvelle de
        Librairie et d´Edition, 1907, p. 140.) But in the
        Confessions Rousseau was less generous, feeling that
        Richardson had made his characters distinctive and filled
        his book with incidents, but that Clarissa was inferior to
        Rousseau´s own book in the simplicity of its subject and
        the sustained interest kept up through only three
        characters and a very simple story. Characters and
        incidents could easily be made; Richardson´s book was
        comparatively barren of ideas. (The passage is early in
        Book XI; in the Pleiade edition, pp. 537-38.) Of the many
        discussions of the two books, the most sustained, still
        useful, is 1895.3. 1782.9, p. 158, says that Richardson
        read and annotated a copy of the English translation; its
        location is not known, and apparently he did not like it.
        (E&K, p. 605n55.)

*16   SMOLLETT, TOBIAS GEORGE. A Continuation of the Complete
        History of England. London: J. Rivington, 4:128.
            Richardson is praised for aligning virtue and the
        passions and for "a sublime system of ethics, an amazing
        knowledge and command of the human nature." Source:
        Hannaford, item 201. Possibly still another apology for
        1756.1; see 1928.7.

1762

*1   ANON. Journal étranger, March.
      Morden's narrative of the funeral. Source: CBFL.

*2   ---. "L'Histoire de Clarisse." Observations sur la
      littérature moderne 4 (1762): 109-24.
      Source: CBFL.

*3   ---. A New and General Biographical Dictionary. London.
      10:142-43.
         Richardson's motives for writing are virtuous, but "the
      novels do not always have the effect intended; he puts too
      much reliance on Shaftesbury's system of human nature"
      (Hannaford, item 203).

4   [DIDEROT, DENIS.] "Eloge de Richardson." Journal étranger 8
      (January): 5-38.
         Probably the single best-known criticism of Richardson,
      reputedly written in a single night after Diderot heard of
      the novelist's death, the "Eloge" is an ecstatic paean to
      the power of Richardson's characters, his moral force, and
      the tragic grandeur of his works. Diderot puts him on a
      level with Homer.   The "Eloge" appeared as a pamphlet
      shortly afterward (Paris: Quillau, 1762, 33 pp.); it was
      customarily reprinted in later editions of Prevost's
      translations and found wide circulation elsewhere, in
      French and in translation.   1967.13, p.   22, notes
      contradictions in Diderot's idea of Richardson's
      universality;   1957.20, pp. 148 ff., summarizes Diderot's
      references to Richardson in his published works and
      correspondence.

5   GELLERT, C.F. Letter to an anonymous lady, March   22.
      Reprinted in Vie et Lettres de Gellert.   . . 3v.
      (Utrecht: J. van Schonhoven & Co., 1775), 2: 227.
         The lady's step-parents say that weeping over Clarissa
      and Clementina is not morally good for her; Gellert
      replies that though the books are admirable they may be
      dangerous for an over-sensible heart. She must not forget
      that there are men capable of being loved, though
      Grandisons do not exist.

6   [GRIMM, FRIEDRICH MELCHIOR, baron.] Correspondance littéraire,
      January 15. Reprinted in 1877.2, 5: 23.
         Recommends Diderot's Eloge.

7   ---. <u>Correspondance littéraire</u>, June 1. Reprinted in 1877.2,
         5: 99.
                 Reviews <u>Mémoires pour servir à l'Histoire de la Vertu</u>,
         the French translation of Sheridan's <u>Miss Sidney
         Bid[d]ulph</u>. "C'est le sort des grands ouvrages de produire
         quantité de mauvaises copies. Richardson en a bien fait
         faire. <u>Miss Bidulph</u> et la <u>Nouvelle Héloïse</u> ne seront pas
         les dernières."

8   HAMANN, J.G. <u>Leser und Kunstrichter</u>. Reprinted in <u>Sämt</u>.
         <u>Schriften</u>, ed. Friedrich Roth (Berlin: G. Reimer, 1821),
         2: 409.
                 Young men now care for no women but the ideal Miss Byron
         and the Swedish Countess.

9   HIGHMORE, JOSEPH, L. TRUCHY, and A. BENOIST. Twelve plates
         illustrating <u>Pamela</u>.
                 Another edition of 1745.3. Noted by <u>TLS</u> (1920.1).

*10   LA CHAUSSÉE, PIERRE-CLAUDE NIVELLE DE. <u>Paméla</u>. Paris.
         Source: <u>NCBEL</u>. See 1743.8.

11   RICHARDSON, SAMUEL. <u>Lettres angloises ou Histoire de miss
         Clarisse Harlove, tome VII</u>. Trans. Jean-Baptiste-Antoine
         Suard. Lyon: Frères Périsse, 158 pp. BN.
                 A translation of some material from <u>Clarissa</u> omitted by
         Prévost. According to the BN catalogue, Suard's volume was
         published with Prévost's translation in the editions of
         1766, 1777, 1783, and 1784. It consists of Diderot's
         <u>Eloge</u>, Morden's account of the funeral (previously
         published in 1762.3), Clarissa's posthumous letters, and
         Clarissa's will. Described by 1975.20, pp. 152-53.

12   WARTON, JOSEPH. <u>Essay on the Genius and Writings of Pope</u>.
         <u>The Second Edition, Corrected</u>. London: R. and J.
         Dodsley, p. 274.
                 "But of all representations of madness, that of
         Clementina, in the History of Sir Charles Grandison, is the
         most deeply interesting. I know not whether even the
         madness of Lear is [so] wrought up, and expressed by so
         many little strokes of nature, and genuine passion. Shall
         I say it is pedantry to prefer and compare, the madness of
         Orestes in Euripedes, to this of Clementina?" I have not
         had access to the first edition (1756) and do not know
         whether this passage also appears there.

<u>1763</u>

*1   ANON. "Observations sur Clarice." <u>Journal encyclopédique</u>,
      March.
           Source: 1967.13, p. 23n31.

*1A   "PHILOTIMOS" [PSEUD.] <u>London Chronicle</u> 13:143.
           A statue should memorialize Richardson. Source:
      Hannaford, item 350.

*2   DIDEROT, DENIS. "Eloge de Richardson." Translated into Dutch
      in <u>De Vaderlandsche Letteroefeningen</u> 3: 135-43, 165-74.
           Source: 1965.17; p. 28.

3   GOLDONI, CARLO. <u>Die verehelichte Pamela.</u> <u>Ein Lustspiel</u> <u>.</u> <u>.</u>
      <u>.</u> Translated by J.G. von Laudes. Vienna: In der
      Krausischen Buchladen. 94 pp. Wiener Natbib.
           <u>Pamela maritata</u> in German; republished, altered, in
      1768. Both versions are discussed in 1938.3, p. 369n3,
      374-76.

4   [GRIMM, FRIEDRICH MELCHIOR, baron.] <u>Correspondance littéraire</u>,
      February. Reprinted in 1877.2.
           In a dialogue on novels, Grimm distinguishes between
      emotion as such and tragic emotion. Though <u>Pamela</u> is
      excellent, <u>Clarissa</u> alone has the latter, the true
      sublimity of terror. <u>La nouvelle Héloïse</u> is inferior to
      both <u>Amelia</u> and <u>Grandison</u>; in both of the latter the style
      is more varied, the characters more real. "L´essentiel
      dans ce genre d´ouvrage, c´est que l´auteur n´y paraisse
      jamais." Sir Charles he does not care for. "Ce n´est parce
      que je ne trouve un tel caractère dans la nature; mais je
      l´aurais voulu d´une teinte plus sombre; il ne me paraît
      pas outré. Grandison ne me paraît pas trop parfait, comme
      on a dit; mais il parle un peu trop, parfois même il
      disserte; et moi, je l´aurois voulu homme de peu de
      paroles, taciturne, toujours agissant, ne parlant jamais.
      De cette manière, il aurait eu un caractère plus
      intéressant et plus vrai, et tout cette emphase qui vous
      choque aurait disparu." Nor does he like it that every
      enterprise of Grandison´s succeeds; "cela est contre
      l´expérience de la vie."

<u>1764</u>

*1   ANON. <u>Anecdotes</u> <u>of</u> <u>Polite</u> <u>Literature</u>. London. 2:ii,78-79.
          Rousseau preferred to Richardson, who is "tedious,"
      "trifling," "verbose" and "uninteresting." Source:
      Hannaford, item 206.

*1A   ---. <u>Der</u> <u>Zufriedene</u> 3: 14 ff.
          Recommends Richardson, but notes problems with the
      idealism of his works. Source: 1925.7; pp. 181-82.

2   BARETTI, GIUSEPPE. <u>La</u> <u>Frusta</u>, Nos. 17 (June 1), 22 (August
      15). Reprinted in <u>Scrittori</u> <u>d'Italia</u>, ed. Luigi Picconi
      (Bari: Giuseppe Laterza e Figli, 1937), Vol. 74, part 2,
      34-41, 171-90.
          No. 17 censures <u>Pamela</u> <u>nubile</u>; while praising the
      artistic goal of preaching virtue, feels that Goldoni has
      not accomplished this and has not understood the English
      character. No. 22 directs similar criticism toward <u>Pamela</u>
      <u>maritata</u>. Goldoni's heroine is rewarded for her virtue by
      having been a contessa from the day of her birth and having
      found a <u>sciocco</u> and bestial husband.

3   CHIARI, PIETRO, abate. <u>Pamela</u> <u>als</u> <u>Mutter.</u> <u>Ein</u> <u>ruhrendes</u>
      <u>Lustspiel</u> <u>in</u> <u>drey</u> <u>Aufzugen.</u> . . . <u>Von</u> <u>einem</u>
      <u>Oesterreichischen</u> <u>Ritter.</u> . . . Trans. Joseph Anton
      von Riegger. Wien: Kraussischen Buchladen. 131 pp. MH
      (catalogued under Riegger)
          1938.3, p. 370n3, notes later editions of 1765 and
      1771. A translation of 1759.4, adapting freely (see
      1938.3, pp. 376-77) to the sentimentally inclined Viennese
      taste. Josef von Sonnenfels reviewed it very unfavorably
      in the <u>Briefe</u> <u>über</u> <u>die</u> <u>wienerische</u> <u>Schaubühne</u>, October 7,
      1768.

4   ROUSSEAU, JEAN-JACQUES. Letter to M. Panckouck, May 27,
      1764. Quoted in 1846.11, p. xv.
          Discusses abridging Richardson.

5   WALPOLE, HORACE. Letter to Sir Horace Mann, December 20,
      1764. Reprinted in <u>Correspondence</u> <u>of</u> <u>Horace</u> <u>Walpole</u> (New
      Haven: Yale University Press; London: Oxford University
      Press, 1960), Vol. 22, p. 271.
          Notes that the <u>Lettres</u> <u>du</u> <u>marquis</u> <u>de</u> <u>Roselle</u> are
      imitated from "a most woeful" standard, "the works of

Richardson, who wrote those deplorably tedious lamentations, <u>Clarissa</u> and <u>Sir Charles Grandison</u>, which are pictures of high life as conceived by a bookseller, and romances as they would be spiritualized by a Methodist minister . . . ".

<u>1765</u>

1   ABBT, THOMAS [B.]. <u>Briefe, die neueste Litteratur betreffend</u>. No. 314. Berlin: Bey Friedrick Nicolai. Pt. 21, pp. 145-72,
    Largely a summary of <u>Grandison der Zweyte</u>, which Abbt reviews favorably. He notes that the book laughs at persons who take sentimentalism seriously in real life, not at <u>Grandison</u>, but (pp. 145-49) points out some failures in Richardson's book. These include Harriet Byron, Dr. Bartlett, Sir Charles's modesty, the plot, and the first two volumes. The interest of the book leans too much toward Clementina and away from Sir Charles, and the long letters are unlifelike.

2   BICKERSTAFFE, ISAAC. <u>The Maid of the Mill. A Comic Opera. As it is performed at the Theatre Royal in Covent Garden. The music compiled, and the words written by the author of Love in a Village</u>. London: J. Newbery, 83 pp.
    This operetta was first acted in 1765 and is based loosely on <u>Pamela</u>; Richardson's heroine becomes Patty, B. is ennobled as Lord Aimworth, and Ralph, as Mrs. Inchbald pointed out in 1808, may owe his being to a hint of Richardson's about a ne'er-do-well brother of Pamela. The music was by Samuel Arnold. The play was extremely popular from its first performances; Newbery published at least six editions of it in 1765 alone, and it held the stage and was frequently reprinted into the nineteenth century.

3   GOETHE, J.W. VON. Letter to his sister Cornelia, December 6. Reprinted in 1937.3, p. 78.
    Goethe advises her not to read novels, though making an ambiguous exception for Richardson's. "Du bist eine Narrin mit deinem Grandison . . . du sollst keine Romane mehr lesen, als die ich erlaube . . . Grand[ison], Cla[rissa]

und Pa[mela] sollen vielleicht ausgenommen werden." In the
same place Liljegren collects several later references of
Goethe to Richardson's novels, including a poem of November
6, 1768 to Friederike Oeser: "Denn will sich einer nicht
bequemen/Des Grandisons ergebner Knecht/Zu sein, und alles
blindlings anzunehmen./Was der Dictator spricht,/Den lacht
man aus, den hört man nicht."

*4   RICHARDSON, SAMUEL, translated by Friedrich Wilhelm Streit.
      Die Wege der Tugend, oder die Geschichte der berühmten
      Pamela, der Clarissa Harlowe, und des Ritters Carl
      Grandisons, ins Kleine gebracht. Aus dem Englischen
      übersetzt. Altenburg.
           German translation of The Paths of Virtue Delineated.
      Sources: Goedeke, Grundriss, 3d ed., 4,1: 576; 1938.3,
      p357n5.

5   RICHARDSON, SAMUEL. "Six Original Letters upon Duelling.
      Written by Mr. Samuel Richardson, Author of the History of
      Sir Charles Grandison, &c." Candid Review and Literary
      Repository 1 (March 1765): 227÷31. CtY.
           To and from Thomas Gillies and two bellicose gentlemen,
      Andrew Crisp and John Orme (apparently not the lachrymose
      Orme of Grandison). Sale, item 57. Yale's is the only
      copy known.

6   STEFFENS, J.H. Clarissa: ein bürgerliches Trauerspiel.
      Zelle: George Conrad Gsellius, 96 pp. BM.
           Steffens, the rector of the school at Zelle, specialized
      in adaptations from novels; the BM also has his Cleveland
      and Tom Jones. His Clarissa is one long death-scene.
      Clarissa is already am Sterbebett as "Bellford" retails to
      a convenient listener how "Löwelace" betrayed her--as in
      many other scenes in the play, he finds it most dramatic to
      do so by standing about on the stage reading her letters
      aloud. Lovelace and Frau Smith condole over Clarissa's
      letter, "I am going to my Father's house." In Act 2
      Belford, Lovelace, and Hickman talk about Clarissa's
      virtue. In Act 3 she has ordered her coffin; her
      "Sterbelied" is sung, and as she dies and Anna Howe
      arrives, Lovelace and Morden fight at the door of her room,
      allowing her betrayer to die in a chair by her bedside.
      "It is the handwriting on the wall!" intone the survivors.

1766

*1   ANON. "A Critical Examination of the Respective Merits of
      Voltaire, Rousseau, Richardson, Smollett, and Fielding."
      Universal Museum NS 2:391-93. Reprinted in the London
      Chronicle 20:247; Royal Magazine 15:146-49.
           Richardson is compared with Rousseau; the former is
      more pathetic, the latter more "florid." Source:
      Hannaford, item 208.

 2   FORDYCE, REV. JAMES. Sermons to Young Women. The Sixth
      Edition, Corrected. 2v. London: A. Millar and T.
      Cadell, J. Dodsley, J. Payne, 1: 71-72. BM.
           I have not seen the first edition, published in 1765.
      Fordyce remarks in Sermon IV that among the few books young
      women may read are those of Richardson, who is "well
      entitled to the first rank" among novelists for his
      morality and his attention to the best interests of the
      female sex. Although Clarissa's early conduct is
      exceptionable, she later exhibits "a sanctity of sweetness
      and manner" [sic] that Fordyce has never seen in a book of
      similar character, but that it is perfectly possible for an
      ordinary woman to emulate.

 2A   GOLDONI, CARLO. Nova Comedia intitulada, A Mais Heroica
      Virtude, ou a Virtuosa Pamella, composta no idioma italiano
      e traduzida ao gosto portuguez. Translated anonymously.
      Lisbon: n.p., 47 pp. BM.
           Three acts in verse; translated and altered from
      Goldoni.

*3   RICHARDSON, SAMUEL. Het pad der deugd, als lieflyk en
      vreedzaam, schetsgewyze, vertoond in de geschiedenissen van
      Pamela, Clarissa, en Grandison. Dordrecht: Abraham
      Blusse. 450 pp.
           Sources: 1969.17, xxv-xxvi; Univbib. Amsterdam; RNB
      item 9.
           Reviewed in De Vaderlandsche Letteroefeningen 6: 464-65
      (1965.17, p. 25).

1767

*1   ANON. De Philosooph, No. 57 (February 2, 1767), p. 35.
           Clarissa is somewhat exceptionable on moral grounds,
      though less so than Fielding's work. Women take more

interest in Richardsonian novels than in chivalric tales.
Source: 1965.17, pp. 25-26.

2   GOLDONI, CARLO, altered by G. G. Bottarelli. La Buona
     Figliuola Maritata, a new comic opera . . . [in Italian
     and English]. London: W. Griffin, 71 pp. BM.
     Pamela maritata as a comic opera.

3   HERDER, JOHANN GOTTFRIED. Königsbergschen Gelehrten und
     Politischen Zeitungen auf das Jahr 1767. No. 66, August
     17. Reprinted in Bernhard Suphan and Carl Redlich, edd.
     Sämtliche Werke . . . (Hildesheim: Georg Olms
     Verlagsbuchhandlung, 1968), 4:225-226.
          A review of Diderot's Ehrengedächtnis, presumably
     published in German in this year, though I have seen no
     edition. It is "voll Feuer, voll Seele, voll Sentiments,
     voll Leben."

*4   SONNENFELS, JOSEF VON. In his journal Theresie und Eleonore
     (1767).
          "Which Richardson novels should a young girl read?--None
     of them! They're all immoral." Source: 1953.5, 170-171;
     1925.7; 176-178.

                              1768

*1   ANON. "Clary." Der Menschenfreund, eine moralisch-satyrische
     Wochenschrift (Frankfurt), 275-288, 292-304.
          Discussed in 1925.7; pp. 178-180.

*2   ---. "Parallèle entre la Clarice de Richardson et la Nouvelle
     Héloïse de M. Rousseau." in Baculard d'Arnaud and Suard,
     edd. Variétés littéraires 3: 392-403.
          Source: CBFL.

*3   SONNENFELS, JOSEF VON. Briefe über die wienerische Schaubühne
     2, pt.8, May 20. Reprinted in Wiener Neudrucke (Vienna:
     1884)7:146.
          Protests Goldoni's solution to the Pamela problem: " .
     . . ist die Tugend ausschlüssend ein Erb des Adels?"
     Source: 1938.3, p. 355.

1769

*1   ANON. Review of Dutch translation of <u>La Nouvelle Clarice</u>. <u>De</u>
<u>Nieuwe Vaderlandsche Oefeningen</u> 2: 474-75; 3: 144.
Source: 1969.17, p. xxvii.

2   BARTHE, NICOLAS T. <u>La Jolie Femme:</u>   <u>ou La Femme du Jour</u>.
Lyons: 1769. Excerpted in <u>GM</u> 40 (October 1770): 454-56.
Eulogy of Richardson and Fielding. Richardson's work is
realistic; the morality is excellent. Barthe's favorite
of the novels is <u>Grandison</u>, which he prefers to Plutarch
and to Plato as "the book which most inspires virtue."
Fielding seems a genius of a similar character in his
realism, knowledge of the heart, and simple morality. He
is less sublime than Richardson and makes us weep less,
though he is more cheerful, original, and engaging.
"Richardson is more grand, more formed on models which will
live throughout all ages; the other is more simple, more
instructive . . . "

3   DU DEFFAND, MARIE ANNE, marquise. Letter to Horace Walpole,
July 4, 1769. Quoted in 1969.19, p. 154.
"J'aime tous les détails domestiques. . . .c'est ce
qui me fait préférer les romans de Richardson à ceux de La
Calprenède, et à tous nos romanciers."

4   GELLERT, C.F. <u>Sämtliche Schriften</u> . . . First published
Leipzig: 1769. Repub. 10v. Leipzig: M.G. Weidmanns
Erben und Reich, und Caspar Fritsch, 1784.
"With men like Gellert, Richardson was the object of an
inconceivable worship," 1937.3 notes, p. 124. Gellert
prizes Richardson above all for his qualities as a teacher
of ethics. In his lecture, "Von dem Ursachen des Vorzugs
der Alten von den Neuern in den schonen Wissenschaften . .
. " (1767), he asserts that men are becoming better
because artists are discovering new and more sublime
character types. "Wo waren die Clarissen und Grandisone,
ehe Richardson schrieb?" (5: 278) In his
<u>Inaugural-dissertation</u>, "Von dem Einflusse der schönen
Wissenschaften auf das Herz und die Sitten" (originally
delivered in Latin), he echoed the idea: "I should not be
surprised if a single good book, such as <u>Grandison</u>, for
instance, or <u>Clarissa</u>, doesn't inspire in an attentive

reader more noble and virtuous sentiments than a whole
library of moral works do in a savant who reads them only
to have read them, to discuss them and show his erudition."
(5:89) In the last lecture of the second part of his
Moralische Vorlesungen, he supports their ethical qualities
and defends them against any charge of immorality,
expressing his gratitude emotionally: "Ich habe ehedem
über den siebenten Theil der Clarissa und den fünften des
Grandisons mit einer Art von süsser Wehmuth einige der
merkwürdigsten Stunden für mein Herz verweinet; dafür
danke ich dir noch itzt, Richardson!" (6:258) But he also
praises Richardson's realism, noting in his Praktische
Abhandlung von dem guten Geschmacke in Briefen Richardson's
ability to differentiate his characters' letters, making
them write as if they were living people. (4:92) 1937.3
discusses Gellert's debt to Richardson, p. 53 and
elsewhere.

5   [HERMES, JOHANN TIMOTHEUS.] Sophiens Reise von Memel nach
    Sachsen. 5v. Leipzig: Johann Friedrich Junius,
    1769-1773.
        "Richardson has furnished much of the detail of thought
    and action" of Sophiens Reise, 1937.3 notes (p. 70), and
    especially in the earlier part of the book Hermes arranges
    frequent occasions to refer to Grandison (1:44 ff., 56,
    331). Later in the novel (5: 385 f.) he criticizes
    Richardson for Clementina's madness--"Weil sein Unding
    Clementine, diese Erkennutnislose, Glaubenslose Romerin,
    wahnwitzig ist, so mus[s]ten seither soviel Romanheldinnen
    wahnwitzig werden? Was ist der Philosoph, wenn er das
    weibliche Herz nicht kennt?" But, as Liljegren notes (229),
    even this criticism is half-hearted. The novel contains a
    Grandison-figure and a heroine persecuted à la
    Pamela/Clarissa/Harriet by a seducer; the resemblance is
    strengthened in the second edition (6v. Leipzig: Junius,
    1774-76).

6   ---. The History of Pamela: or, Virtue Rewarded. Abridged
    from the works of Samuel Richardson, esquire . . .
    London: F. Newberry, 166 pp. NjP.

1770

*1   ANON. Clary ein Schauspiel. Frankfurt.
       1926.5, p. 12, speculates that this play may have been
       based on Clarissa; neither he nor I has seen a copy.

*2   ---. Das Wochenblatt ohne Titel, 1770, 1771.
       Recommends reading Richardson to attain culture;
       source: 1925.7, p. 182n24.

3   BARETTI, GIUSEPPE. Letter to Francesco Cercano, December 29,.
       Quoted in Lettere Istruttive, Descrittive e Familiari di
       Giuseppe Baretti Torinese (Messina: Giuseppe Pappalardo,
       1825), p. 186.
          Baretti remembers Richardson as one of his best friends
       in England and weeps still over his death; mentions the
       three novels. Of Clarissa, "la storia . . . e favolosa
       da un capo all'altro, e basta leggerla per vedere che e
       tale. . . [Richardson] era uomo che conosceva poco il
       mondo, ma il cuore umano lo intendeva meglia d'ogni altro."

*4   MUSAEUS, J.K.A. VON. De Nieuwe Grandison. 2v. 1770-71.
       Source: Kalff, 6 (1910): 11. 1969.17, p.
       xxvii-xxviii identifies it as a translation of 1760.9.

*5   RICHARDSON, SAMUEL or ANON.? Histoire de Paméla en liberté.
       Frankfurt?
       Source: NCBEL, from Heinsius 4:159 and/or 1926.5, p.
       11n12? Same as 1771.4 and 1771.5?

1771

1   [MEADES, ANNA.] The History of Sir William Harrington.
       Written Some Years Since, And revised and corrected by the
       late Mr. Richardson, Author of Sir Charles Grandison,
       Clarissa, &c. Now First Publish'd, in Four Volumes .
       London: John Bell; York: C. Etherington. BM.
          Long ascribed to Thomas Hull, Sir William Harrington is
       now known to be Meades'; see 1935.10 and 1968.21, both of
       whom draw on the Richardson-Meades correspondence preserved
       in the BM (Add. MS. 28,097). The running title is A
       Description of Modern Life; it is a symphonic epistolary
       novel including marriages, rakes, reform, moralizing, and
       an alarming tendency, on the part of nearly all the
       characters, to quote from Richardson's works at climactic

moments.

2   ---, trans. by "E." <u>Geschichte</u> <u>Sir</u> <u>Wilhelm</u> <u>Harrington</u> <u>vor</u>
      <u>einigen</u> <u>Jahren</u> <u>entworfen</u> <u>und</u> <u>von</u> <u>dem</u> <u>Verfasser</u> <u>des</u> <u>Sir</u> <u>Carl</u>
      <u>Grandison</u> <u>nachgesehen</u> <u>und</u> <u>verbessert.</u> <u>Aus</u> <u>dem</u> <u>Englischen</u>
      <u>übersetzt.</u> 4 pts. Leipzig: Joh. Fried. Junius. BM,
      Wiener Stadt- und Landesbib.

*3   PERREAU, JEAN-ANDRÉ. <u>Clarisse,</u> <u>drame</u> <u>en</u> <u>cinq</u> <u>actes</u> <u>et</u> <u>en</u>
      <u>prose.</u> Paris.
           Sources: 1935.2, p. 60n24; MMF under "Perreau,
      <u>Lettres</u> <u>illinoises,</u>" 1772. His <u>Lettres</u> <u>illinoises</u>, a
      sentimental epistolary novel, which I have not seen, sounds
      quite promising as a <u>Richardsonade.</u>

*4   RICHARDSON, SAMUEL. <u>Histoire</u> <u>de</u> <u>Paméla.</u> Frankfurt.
           Source: Kayser, vol.5 (1836), p. 112, quoted in
      1938.3, p. 357n2. Same as 1771.5 and 1770.5?

5   ---,translated and abridged by ? <u>L'Histoire</u> <u>de</u> <u>la</u> <u>vertueuse</u>
      <u>Paméla,</u> <u>dans</u> <u>le</u> <u>temps</u> <u>de</u> <u>sa</u> <u>liberté,</u> <u>jusqu'à</u> <u>son</u> <u>mariage.</u>
      <u>Traduit</u> <u>de</u> <u>l'anglois</u> <u>de</u> <u>Mr.</u> <u>Grandisson</u> [<u>sic</u>]. <u>Vol.</u> <u>I:</u>
      <u>Histoire</u> <u>de</u> <u>la</u> <u>vertueuse</u> <u>villageoise</u> <u>Paméla,</u> <u>dans</u> <u>le</u> <u>tems</u>
      <u>de</u> <u>sa</u> <u>liberté,</u> <u>et</u> <u>de</u> <u>ses</u> <u>chastes</u> <u>amours,</u> <u>jusqu'à</u> <u>son</u>
      <u>Mariage</u> <u>avec</u> <u>son</u> <u>Maître</u> <u>le</u> <u>Comte</u> <u>de</u> <u>B***.</u> <u>Traduit</u> <u>de</u>
      <u>l'Anglois,</u> <u>sur</u> <u>le</u> <u>Journal</u> <u>qu'elle</u> <u>en</u> <u>a</u> <u>dressé</u> <u>elle-même.</u>
      3v. in 2. Francfort, Leipzig, et La Haye: aux dépens de
      la Compagnie. BM; Nat. Lib. Greece has Vol.2,pt.2 only.
           Volume II has separate title and consists of two
      volumes, separately paginated: "<u>Volume</u> <u>II:</u> <u>Mémoirs</u>
      <u>journaliers,</u> <u>ou</u> <u>Tableau</u> <u>de</u> <u>l'amour</u> <u>conjugal</u> <u>et</u> <u>des</u> <u>jours</u> <u>de</u>
      <u>bonheur</u> <u>de</u> <u>Paméla,</u> <u>peints</u> <u>par</u> <u>elle-même</u> <u>à</u> <u>ses</u> <u>parents</u>"and
      "<u>Volume</u> <u>II.</u> <u>Pt.</u> <u>II:</u> <u>Journal</u> <u>des</u> <u>jours</u> <u>de</u> <u>bonheur</u> <u>de</u>
      <u>Paméla,</u> <u>depuis</u> <u>sa</u> <u>rencontre</u> <u>avec</u> <u>Milady</u> <u>Davers,</u> <u>soeur</u> <u>au</u>
      <u>Comte</u> <u>de</u> <u>B.</u>" The three volumes (184, 152, and 162 pp.
      respectively) cover only <u>Pamela</u> <u>I</u>, and not all of that,
      beginning with the kidnapping to Lincolnshire and
      summarizing the previous story. The first volume is in a
      combination of letters and narrative; the second and third
      volumes are all letters. The paragraphs, curiously, are
      numbered, and the illustrations are mostly allegorical or
      of moral scenes in the work. Another edition of this work
      may have been published in 1776.

6   SCHMID, C.H.   Das   Parterr.   Erfurt: Verlegs   E.A.G.
     Griessbach, p.   274.   BM.
          In a review of Beaumarchais's Eugénie, performed Oct.
     17, 1770, in Leipzig, Schmid says, "Es wird von Lesern und
     Zuschauerns verlassen, worüber ich mich auch von Herzen
     freue.   Gleiches Schicksal werden immer die Romanstücke in
     der Folge erfahren, so sehr sie auch anfangs, durch einige
     glänzende Sentimens [sic] und Situationen, aus Richardson
     gestohlen.   Denn in der That ist Richardson die Quelle der
     meisten   französischen Dramas, so wie der Eugenie." 1950.6,
     p.   20, calls this "exaggeration."

                              1772

*1   ANON.   "Von   der   Erziehung   des   Töchter." Wochenblatt für
     rechtschaffene Eltern 2.
          Richardson is a powerful influence for   good;   however,
     he encourages the young to strive for impossible virtues,
     in doing which they neglect the conventional ones. Source:
     1925.7, pp. 182-183.

*2   DIDEROT, DENIS. [Eloge de Richardson.] In De Algemeene
     Oefenschool   van Konsten en Wetenschappen, 6 (1772?),
     303-324.
          Dutch translation of the Eloge; see 1965.17, pp.
     28-29.

3   [MEADES, ANNA.] Les Moeurs du jour ou histoire de Sir William
     Harrington, écrite du vivant de M. Richardson, éditeur de
     Pamela, Clarisse, et Grandison, revue et retouchée par lui
     sur le manuscrit de l'auteur, traduction de l'anglois. 4v.
     Amsterdam: D.J. Changuion. Arsenal
          Other editions in 1772, 1773,   1778 (Uff.   Inf.
     Centrale, Bib. Naz. Centrale Vitt. Emanuele, Roma), 1785
     (BN), and 1786.

                              1773

1   GRAVES, RICHARD, Rev. The Spiritual Quixote, or The Summer's
     Ramble of Mr. Geoffrey Wildgoose. A Comic Romance . . .
     3v. London: J. Dodsley. BM.

In the preface, Graves remarks, " . . . I am convinced that Don Quixote or Gil Blas, Clarissa or Sir Charles Grandison will furnish more hints for correcting the follies and regulating the morals of young persons, and impress them more forcibly on their minds, than volumes of severe precepts . . . "

2 MERCIER, LOUIS-SEBASTIEN. Du Théâtre, ou Nouvel Essai sur l'Art dramatique. Amsterdam: E. van Harrevelt, p. 326n.
Richardson's works are "poèmes auxquels nous n'avons rien de comparable dans toute l'antiquité." He is the master of one style, Voltaire of the other, and his works have attracted readers of both sexes and of every age and class, some of whom have been so fascinated by them as to forget to eat, drink or sleep for several days. Richardson must be a favorite among men of taste. Hannaford, item 217, cites other praise of Richardson by Mercier.

1774

1 BACULARD D'ARNAUD, FRANÇOIS - THOMAS. "Preface." Nouvelles historiques. Paris: Delalain, pp. 14-15. BN.
In reply to a "man of genius" who complained of Clarissa, "Je suis fâché que Richardson ait mis sous nos yeux cette triste leçon de l'expérience; pour l'honneur du roman et de l'humanité, il falloit que Clarisse fut récompensée de tant d'épreuves cruelles qu'elle a essuyées," the author defends Richardson's tragic ending; there is no one who would not rather be Clarissa in misery than Lovelace happy. Baculard d'Arnaud believes that reading Grandison is more profitable than reading history. The Nouvelles historiques show a distinctly Richardsonian tint.

2 BLANKENBURG, C.F. VON. Versuch über den Roman. Leipzig und Liegnitz: David Siegerts Witwe, 546 pp. BM.
In the "Vorbericht," Blankenburg apologizes for praising Fielding above Richardson—"ich schätze Richardson; aber die Wahrheit höher, als ihn." And Fielding is the more realistic writer, an observation he expands on pp. 399-400; Fielding is the poet of observation, while Richardson's gift is Nachbildung. On pp. 67÷68 he discusses the sort of realism he means; he would like to

have seen Sir Charles Grandison developing into the man he
is, so as to show us the answer to the important question:
"Kann der Mensch auch das werden, was der Mann ist?" We
need a man in the process of becoming Grandison, "ein
werdenden Grandison"; he thinks of attempting such a novel
himself, but meanwhile believes that Tom Jones is the model
novel because it shows characters in process of
development.
　　On p. 137 a footnote makes a minor criticism of
Grandison; we are so caught up in the story and the
interesting character (sehr anziehend) of Clementina that
we forget his principal character, Harriet--perhaps more
than forget her.
　　1875.3, p. 12, discusses Blankenburg, as does 1932.7,
pp. 200-01, 224-25; p. 225n27 cites a review of the book
in ADB, 43, pt.2 (1775): 348 [I have not found this review
there]. The Versuch über den Roman was republished as nos.
29-30 of the Deutsche Litteraturdenkmale series (Heilbronn:
Gebr. Henniger, 1888-89, 527 pp.), with a good index.

*3   LENZ, JACOB M.R.. Der Hofmeister od. Vortheile der
      Privaterziehung. Eine Komödie. Leipzig: in der
      Weygandschen Buchhandlung.
　　　"Was ist Grandison, der abstrahierte, geträumte, gegen
      einen Rebhuhn, der dasteht!" Die Soldaten (1775.2) shows a
      similar antipathy to Pamela, but in Der Engländer (1777)
      Lenz seems bemused by Lovelace and the Italian subplot of
      Grandison. Source: 1932.7; p. 227.

4   OGILVIE, Dr. JOHN. Philosophical and Critical Observations
      on the Nature and Characters of Various Species of
      Composition. 2v. London: G. Robinson, 1:339, 342-343
      fn. BM.
　　　Richardson shows "the wanderings of the human heart" and
      the delineation of "first impressions made upon the
      susceptible mind by interesting objects," 339; in this
      sort of writing, Marivaux, Crébillon and Sterne are the
      masters. Fielding's genius is to show familiar characters
      in original combinations. However, a comparison of
      Clarissa and Parson Adams shows Fielding creating a true
      original. Compare his and Beattie's letters with 1926.2,
      pp. 218-19, which misrepresents them.

<u>1775</u>

*1   ANON. <u>De</u> <u>Opmerker</u> 3: 100.
          Defends Sir Charles Grandison´s perfection.   Source:
       1965.17; p. 26.

2   AIKIN, JOHN AND ANNA LAETITIA AIKIN (later BARBAULD).   "An
       Enquiry into those Kinds of Distress which Excite Agreeable
       Sensations." In their <u>Miscellaneous</u> <u>Pieces,</u> <u>in</u> <u>Prose</u>.
       Second ed. London: J. Johnson, pp. 205-7.
          Distress is pitied only when its effects are unseen;
       Richardson admirably excites pathos by keeping Clarissa
       unstained by her misfortunes. But Clarissa is too perfect
       to be wholly sympathetic.

3   LENZ, JACOB M.R..   <u>Die</u> <u>Soldaten.</u> <u>Eine</u> <u>Komödie</u>.   Leipzig:
       Weidmanns Erben und Reich, 119 pp.
          Countess La Roche refers to <u>Pamela</u> as the cause of the
       seduction of the heroine, Marie, since the book has made
       lower-class women look above their station for husbands and
       lovers.   "Ihr einziger Fehler war,...dass Sie die Pamela
       gelesen haben, das gefährlichste Buch, das eine Person aus
       ihrem Stande lesen kann." Act 3, scene 10. Marie is often
       shown writing letters and attracts Desportes by remarking
       coquettishly, "Ich schreib´ gar zu gern." There is a
       summerhouse scene <u>à</u> <u>la</u> <u>Pamela</u>. Discussed in 1937.3, pp.
       87-89.

<u>1776</u>

*1   ANON. <u>De</u> <u>Vaderlander</u> 2: 219.
          Richardson´s novels are above Aristotelian rules;
       <u>Clarissa</u> and <u>Grandison</u> are such masterpieces that they give
       rise to new rules. Source: 1965.17, p. 26.

*2   ---. <u>Das</u> <u>Deutsche</u> <u>Museum</u>, pp. 1048-50 (1875.3) or p.   280
       (as corrected in the copy of Schmidt in the BM).
          "Das Ideal der Dichtkunst ist der leidenschaftliche
       Mensch.   Ihr Gegenstand ist Handlung und die Summe der
       Kraft, die eine Handlung hervorbringen, ist hier das Mass
       ihre Vollkommenheit.   Der Würger des keuschesten Weibes,
       das je in den Armen eines Mannes lag, ist Othello,
       dichtrisch vollkommer, als der ganze göttliche Grandison."

Quoted in 1875.3, p. 17.

3   DUSCH, J.J.. <u>Geschichte</u> <u>Carl</u> <u>Ferdiners,</u> <u>von</u> <u>dem</u> <u>Verfasser</u> <u>der</u>
     <u>Moralischen</u> <u>Briefe</u> <u>zur</u> <u>Bildung</u> <u>des</u> <u>Herzens</u>. 6 pts. in 3v.
     Breslau und Leipzig: Verlegts J.E. Meyer, 1777
     [1776?]-80. MH, NjP.
         "The indebtedness to Richardson and his <u>Clarissa</u> . . .
     is out of doubt.   But we find much which we can explain
     only by means of <u>Grandison</u>," says Liljegren of this book
     (p.   178).   Among the points of resemblance are the
     Lovelacish Ferdiner and the Hickmanesque Dankwart, an
     abduction scene in which Julie is rescued by Ferdiner, a
     summerhouse incident between Julie and Ferdiner, duels,
     madness through disappointment in love, and an extended,
     Clarissalike death scene (spreading itself over   1500
     pages!).   In Volume 1, part 2, pp. 16-18, two characters
     discuss <u>Clarissa</u> and decide that, although Hickman is the
     better man, Lovelace is far more attractive. See 1937.3,
     pp. 176-78, 195, 199-201, 218-19, 231-32, 241.   The book
     was reviewed by Merck in the <u>Teutscher</u> <u>Mercur</u> 3 (1776):
     261, according to 1932.7, p. 225.

                              <u>1777</u>

*1   ANON. <u>Nouvelle</u> <u>bibliothèque</u> <u>d´un</u> <u>homme</u> <u>de</u> <u>goût</u>.   Paris.
     4:81-82.
         Richardson combines sharply accentuated character-types
     and vivid detail. Source: Hannaford, item 226.

2   [KNOX, VICESIMUS.] <u>Essays,</u> <u>Moral</u> <u>and</u> <u>Literary</u>.   2v.   London:
     Edward and Charles Dilly, "1778-79" [1777-78], 1:171;
     2:185-92.
         Does not like novels in general and finds Richardson´s
     "inflaming."

3   PRIESTLEY, JOSEPH.   <u>A</u> <u>Course</u> <u>of</u> <u>Lectures</u> <u>on</u> <u>Oratory</u> <u>and</u>
     <u>Criticism</u>. London: J. Johnson, p. 81. BM.
         <u>Clarissa</u> shows fiction-writing having the advantage over
     history in arousing passion.   (The <u>Lectures</u> were first
     delivered at the Academy at Warrington in 1762.)

*4   RICHARDSON, SAMUEL, trans. Christian Felix Weisse. <u>Sammlung</u>
      <u>der</u> <u>gemeinnützigen</u> <u>Lehren,</u> <u>Warnungen,</u> <u>und</u> <u>moralischen</u>
      <u>Anmerkungen</u> <u>aus</u> <u>der</u> <u>Werken</u> <u>des</u> <u>Herrn</u> <u>Sam.</u> <u>Richardson,</u>
      <u>Verfasser</u> <u>der</u> <u>Pamela,</u> <u>Clarissa,</u> <u>und</u> <u>Grandison</u>. Leipzig.
          Source: <u>JVFD</u> 9 (1792): 17; quoted in 1926.5, p.
      10n11. (See 1792.7.) German translation of <u>A</u> <u>Collection</u> <u>of</u>
      <u>the</u> <u>Moral</u> <u>and</u> <u>Instructive</u> <u>Sentiments</u> . . . (1755.7).

                          <u>1778</u>

1   GRANT, ANNE, of Loggan. Letter to Miss Ewing of Glasgow, Oct.
     3, 1778. Printed in <u>Letters</u> <u>from</u> <u>the</u> <u>Mountains:</u> <u>being</u> <u>the</u>
     <u>Real</u> <u>Correspondence</u> <u>of</u> <u>a</u> <u>Lady,</u> <u>between</u> <u>the</u> <u>Years</u> <u>1773</u> <u>and</u>
     <u>1807</u>. 2d ed. 3v. London: Luke Hansard for Longmans,
     Hurst, Rees and Orme; J. Hatchard, and Mrs. Cook, 1807,
     2:45-48. BM.
         Complains that young people now think <u>Clarissa</u> languid,
     tedious and unlifelike, but "I know nothing . . . equal
     to [her] death-bed" (47) and though "we must be so just to
     the other sex as to think Lovelace almost an impossibility
     . . . if such a being could exist he would think and act
     like Lovelace."

2   HERDER, JOHANN GOTTFRIED VON. <u>Über</u> <u>die</u> <u>Wirkung</u> <u>der</u> <u>Dichtkunst</u>
     <u>auf</u> <u>die</u> <u>Sitten</u> <u>der</u> <u>Völker</u> <u>in</u> <u>alten</u> <u>und</u> <u>neuen</u> <u>Zeiten</u>. First
     published 1778. In <u>Werke</u>, ed. Bernhard Suphan. Berlin:
     Weidmannsche Buchhandlung, 1883, 8: 422.
         Comparison between Fielding and Richardson; Fielding is
     the representative of realistic fiction, while Richardson
     represents the too-strained ideal class of fiction.
     However, is the realistic sort best? Should novels open
     one's eyes only to the worst of one's century, or try to
     better the times?

3   LA HARPE, JEAN FRANÇOIS DE. "Des Romans." In <u>Oeuvres</u>. Paris:
     Pissot, 3:337÷88.
         Richardson is treated on pp. 365-73. <u>Pamela</u> and <u>Sir</u>
     <u>Charles</u> <u>Grandison</u> are cold novels, and Lovelace is
     completely unnatural--could a man of pride act in such a
     way with the woman he intends to marry? But Clarissa
     herself leaves a profound and "celestial" impression.
     Richardson lacks one essential talent for writing, to know
     when to stop. La Harpe prefers Fielding--"le premier roman

du monde, c´est <u>Tom Jones</u>."

4   PIOZZI, HESTER LYNCH (THRALE). Letter to Samuel Johnson, November 11, 1778. Published in <u>Letters</u> <u>To</u> <u>and</u> <u>From</u> <u>the</u> <u>Late</u> <u>Samuel</u> <u>Johnson</u> . . . <u>Published</u> <u>by</u> <u>Hester</u> <u>Lynch</u> <u>Piozzi</u>. 2v. London: A. Strahan and T. Cadell, 1788, 2: 30-31. BM.
      "´Tis nature, ´tis truth, and what I delight in still more, ´tis general nature, not particular manners, that Richardson represents." He is translatable, as Fielding is not; while Fielding´s works are genre pictures, Richardson is of the greater Italian school of universal nature.

1779

*1   CAVENDISH, GEORGINA, duchess of DEVONSHIRE. <u>The</u> <u>Sylph</u>. London. 2:22-23.
      <u>Pamela</u> encourages young women to try to marry above their station. Source: Hannaford, item 231.

2   RICHARDSON, SAMUEL. <u>Den</u> <u>Engelske</u> <u>Baroneten</u> <u>Sir</u> <u>Charles</u> <u>Grandisons</u> <u>Historia;</u> <u>I</u> <u>En</u> <u>Samling</u> <u>af</u> <u>Bref,</u> <u>Efter</u> <u>Originalerne</u> <u>til</u> <u>trycket</u> <u>befordrade</u> <u>Af</u> <u>Herr</u> <u>Sam.</u> <u>Richardsson</u> [<u>sic</u>], <u>Auctor</u> <u>til</u> <u>Pamela</u> <u>och</u> <u>Clarissa</u>. <u>Ofwersatt</u> <u>ifran</u> <u>Engelskan</u>. 2v. Stockholm: Trykt i Kongl. Tryckeriet, 1779-1800 [<u>sic</u>]. Univbib. Uppsala.
      <u>Grandison</u> in Swedish abridgment.

1780

*1   ANON. <u>Lovelace</u> <u>og</u> <u>Clarissa</u> <u>elder</u> <u>den</u> <u>dramatiske</u> <u>bortforelse</u>. Copenhagen.
      Source: <u>NCBEL</u>, from <u>CBEL</u>; not in <u>Bib.</u> <u>Danica</u> or otherwise findable.

2   LESSING, K.G.. <u>Die</u> <u>Mätresse</u>. First published 1780. Reprinted in <u>DLD</u> 28, ed. Eugen Wolff. Heilbronn: Gebr. Henniger, 1887.
      Wolff contributes a helpful essay to the 1887 edition of <u>Die</u> <u>Mätresse</u> , citing Richardson´s novels as the most important of the sources for Lessing´s play (see 1887.1).

The drama concerns male-female differences in rank and
includes a kidnapping. Wolff notes the wider popularity of
these themes in German drama of the period including works
by Lenz, Wagner, Gemmingen (<u>Der</u> <u>Deutsche</u> <u>Hausvater</u>),
Schröder (<u>Der</u> <u>Vetter</u> <u>in</u> <u>Lissabon</u>), Klinger (<u>Der</u> <u>Derwisch</u>),
Grossman (<u>Nicht</u> <u>mehr</u> <u>als</u> <u>sechs</u> <u>Schlüssel</u>), and Schiller´s
<u>Kabale</u> <u>und</u> <u>Liebe</u>. Of these Wolff prefers <u>Die</u> <u>Mätresse</u> for
the rigor with which the consequences are worked out.

3   MORE, HANNAH. Letter to her sister, 1780. Quoted (from the
    <u>Memoirs</u> <u>of</u> <u>Hannah</u> <u>More</u>, New York, 1835, 1:101) in Wilbur
    Cross. <u>The</u> <u>History</u> <u>of</u> <u>Henry</u> <u>Fielding</u> (New Haven: Yale
    University Press, 1918), 3:159.
        Johnson has been "really angry" with her only once, when
    she alluded to <u>Tom</u> <u>Jones</u>.   ". . . He went so far as to
    refuse to Fielding the great talents which are ascribed to
    him, and broke out into a noble panegyric upon his
    competitor Richardson; who, he said, was as superior to
    him in talents as in virtue, and whom he pronounced to be
    the greatest genius that had shed its lustre on this path
    of literature."

4   RICHARDSON, SAMUEL. <u>Sir</u> <u>Carl</u> <u>Grandisons</u> <u>Historie</u> <u>i</u> <u>en</u> <u>Samling</u>
    <u>af</u> <u>Breve</u>. <u>Oversat</u> <u>af</u> <u>Engelsk</u> [by Hans Christian Amberg].
    7v. Copenhagen: Trykt hos P.H. Hoecke, 1780-82. BN;
    Kongelige Bibliotek, Copenhagen.

                           <u>1781</u>

1   ANON. <u>L´Année</u> <u>littéraire</u> 4 (for 1781):   184.
        As part of a review of the Richardsonian <u>Histoire</u> <u>de</u>
    <u>Miss</u> <u>Elise</u> <u>Warwick,</u> <u>trad.</u> <u>angl.</u> 2 pts. (Amsterdam: D.
    Changuion; Paris: Mérigot le jeune, 1781), the author
    praises Richardson at the expense of his imitators for
    "l´invention, le plan, les caractères, la force & la vérite
    du dialogue," as well as for moral instruction: "Peut-on
    lire <u>Clarice</u> & <u>Grandisson</u> sans être pénétré de respect pour
    la vertu & d´horreur pour le vice?" But there are few
    novels like his.
        I have encountered no copy of <u>Miss</u> <u>Elise</u> <u>Warwick</u>.

2   JOHNSON, SAMUEL. "Life of Rowe." In <u>Prefaces, Biographical</u>
        <u>and Critical, to the Works of the English Poets</u> . . .
        London: Printed by J. Nichols, for C. Bathurst, J.
        Buckland, W. Strahan [etc.], Vol. 6.
            Remarks that the character of Lovelace was taken from
        that of Rowe´s Young Lothario.

3   MUSAEUS, J.K.A. VON. <u>Der deutsche Grandison</u>. 2v. Eisenach:
        J.G.E. Wittekindt.
            Much changed version of 1760.9; see 1910.2, 1937.3, pp.
        62-66, 73, 179-80, 215-18, and also A. Ohlmer, <u>Musaeus als</u>
        <u>saatirischen Romanschriftsteller</u> (Hildesheim: 1912), and
        E. Kost, <u>Die Technik des deutschen Romans von Musaeus bis</u>
        <u>Goethe</u> (Tubingen: 1891). Price, from whom come the last
        two citations, asserts that "the two editions of
        [Musaeus´s] work stand as convenient landmarks in the
        history of the German novel"--1953.5, p. 189. The
        introduction to this edition summarizes the change in the
        German literary scene from Musaeus´s own point of view. In
        1759 or ´60 "es gab eben so viele vaterlandische Pamelen,
        Clarissen, Lovelacen, Grandisons, als es jetzt Lotten,
        Werther, Siegwarte, Southeime, Adolphe giebt." But now the
        situation is changed and readers can hardly remember the
        old sentimental fiction. The satire of <u>Der deutsche</u>
        <u>Grandison</u>, appropriately, is no longer directed
        specifically against <u>Grandison</u>.

4   SHERLOCK, MARTIN. <u>Letters on Several Subjects</u>. 2v. London:
        J. Nichols, T. Cadell, P. Elmsley, H. Payne, and N.
        Conant, 1: letters II, III, XVII-XIX. BM.
            P. 22--"Archimedes, Newton, Shakespeare and Richardson"
        are among the greatest geniuses, those distinguished by "a
        sound judgment and a superior imagination. . . The
        greatest effort of genius that perhaps was ever made, was
        forming the plan of Clarissa Harlowe. The second was
        executing that plan." Pp. 27÷31, reading <u>Clarissa</u> and
        weeping are indexes to sensibility. 134-40, "Richardson is
        admirable for every species of delicacy," delicacy of wit
        among them. Letter 18 discusses Richardson´s one
        misfortune, not to know the ancients; if he had he would
        not have satiated the reader as he has done. However,
        Sherlock defends the perfection of Richardson´s characters.
        [John Duncombe, in his edition of Sherlock´s <u>Works</u>, 1802,
        lays more stress on Richardson´s prolixity--see his
        footnote at 2:64.] Letter 19 shows Sherlock´s admiration of

Richardson´s pathos, especially in <u>Clarissa</u>; but one must read the whole book, not isolated letters, to feel its effect. (152-55) When translated into German in 1782, says 1926.5, pp. 28-29, this book reawakened interest in Richardson. Sherlock´s <u>Lettres d´un voyageur anglais</u>("Londres"[Geneva]: 1779) also contains praise of Richardson; see Hannaford, item 232.

1782

1   ANON. [J.H. MEISTER?] <u>Correspondance littéraire</u>, April. Reprinted in <u>Correspondance littéraire</u> Paris; Buisson, 1813, vol.1, part 3, pp. 374 ff.
      Review of <u>Les Liaisons dangereuses</u> with references to <u>Clarissa</u>. Madame de Merteuil is "un vrai Lovelace en femme," Valmont loves the Présidente no more than Lovelace did Clarissa, and Valmont´s letters to his huntsman and their replies are worthy of comparison with Lovelace´s and Joseph Leman´s.

2   ARCHENHOLZ, J.W. VON. <u>England und Italien</u>. First published 1782. Republished: 5 pts. Carlsruhe: C.G. Schmieder, 1791, 3:63-66. BM.
      The excellence of <u>Tom Jones</u> makes it worthy of being in everyone´s hands, but <u>Clarissa</u> is written for the ages. The best minds of its day never tired of praising it. Grandison, an English ideal, should not be transported to Germany. But <u>Grandison</u> should not be compared with Richardson´s masterwork, <u>Clarissa</u>, which one knows only through miserable French and German translations; "hier ist alles Natur." Clarissa and Lovelace are painted with genius. But one must read <u>Clarissa</u> straight through, all at once; Archenholz knows German intellectuals who have been frightened by its length.

3   CAMBON, MARIA GEERTRUIDA de. <u>De Kleine Grandisson, of de Gehoorzaame Zoon. In eene Reeks van Brieven en Saamenspraaken. Door Mevrouwe de Weduwe de Cambon, Gebooren Van der Werken</u>. 2v. ´s Gravenhaage: H.H. Van Drecht. Univbib. Amsterdam (2 copies)
      <u>RNB</u> item 21. This is the original appearance of the enormously long-lived children´s book sometimes attributed to Arnaud Berquin; see MMF 87.35, 1787.2, 1790.1,2,3, and

1791.2. In its original Dutch and in English its success
was flourishing enough, but in French, in Berquin's
adaptation, it endured for nearly a century--the last of
the seventeen editions listed in the BN Catalogue, surely
only a selection of those published, dates from 1885. I
have read only the Berquin version, for which see 1787.2.

4   CHAPONE, HESTER MULSO. Letter to Elizabeth Carter, about
     1782. In The Works of Mrs. Chapone (London: John Murray,
     1807), 1:175-76; see also 27÷33.
         She has been reading Pamela, in a scream, to her deaf
     aunt and it "appeared somewhat different from what I
     thought of it thirty years ago; yet I still see, in each
     of Richardson's works, amazing genius, unpolished indeed,
     either by learning or knowledge of polite life, but making
     its way to the heart by strokes of nature that perhaps
     would have been lost, or at least weakened, by the
     re[s]traints of critical elegance. It is only from the
     ignorant that we can now have any thing original . . ."
     Earlier she refers to Richardson's correspondence with her
     on filial obedience in marriage, to Grandison, and to his
     prolixity, which she "honors"; a long good book is better
     than a short good book.

5   CHODERLOS DE LACLOS, PIERRE-AMBROISE-FRANÇOIS. Les Liaisons
     dangereuses, ou Lettres recueillies dans une société, et
     publiées pour l'instruction de quelques autres, par M. C .
     . . de L . . . . 4v. Amsterdam et Paris: Durand.
         1968.44 has argued that Laclos's debt to Richardson was
     comparatively minor; however, it is sometimes difficult to
     separate the influence of Richardson himself from the sense
     that many authors had of belonging to a "school" of which
     Richardson was the patron saint. In this Laclos certainly
     concurred (see 1785.2 and 1787.4). Like much Richardsonian
     fiction, his is as far as possible from the moral climate
     of Richardson's own works; most notably, rather than
     balancing the moral impact of the work between a virtuous
     and a vicious figure, he follows current French taste in
     concentrating his attention on the vicious Valmont and
     Merteuil. The conflict of motives in Valmont is, if not
     more complex, certainly more fully realized than that in
     Lovelace. Laclos's novel is the brilliant transformation
     of many tendencies in French imitation of Richardson, but
     unlike most it does not slavishly follow the Richardsonian
     pattern of character relationships or events.

Stylistically, as epistolary fiction, it is the only work
on a level with Richardson´s own.

6   GENLIS, STEPHANIE-FELICITÉ DUCREST de ST.-AUBIN, comtesse de.
     Adèle et Théodore, ou Lettres sur l´éducation . . . 3v.
     Paris: n.p., 3:257-58, 417. BM.
         Richardson´s novels are praised for offering a picture
     of the human heart as it really is, reasonable and unhurt
     by passion; Clarissa is recommended for reading at 16, the
     other two novels at 17. Mme. de Genlis´s Rousseauist
     fiction is modern in recommending a number of novels as
     respectable parts of a young person´s education. See
     1786,4.

7   MORE, HANNAH. "Sensibility." In her Sacred Dramas . . .
     London: T. Cadell, p. 283.
         Sensibility is not defined by weeping at Richardson´s
     heroines, but More "first caught that flame" of sensibility
     from him. 8 NICHOLS, JOHN. Biographical and Literary
     Anecdotes of William Bowyer, Printer, F.S.A. . . .
     London: Printed By and For the Author, pp. 156-60, 306,
     310, 645; 89-90, verses to Richardson.
         Anecdotes about Richardson, frequently reprinted
     elsewhere. See 1812.1.

                          1783

1   BACULARD D´ARNAUD, FRANÇOIS THOMAS. "The New Clementina, from
     the French of the celebrated M. [Baculard] d´Arnaud."
     Universal Magazine 75:295-96.
         Obviously not the first appearance, which I have not
     found. Defense of the madness of Clementina, prefixed to a
     story about a bride who went mad at the death of her
     bridegroom.

2   BEATTIE, JAMES. Dissertations Moral and Critical. London:
     W. Strahan, pp. 567-70.
         In his "On Fables and Romances," he includes Grandison
     and Clarissa under the rubric or the "New Romance," as
     examples of works that are "serious, and Poetically
     arranged," that is, that begin in the middle of the story
     to shorten the time of the action. Since the characters
     are their own "relaters," the action is partly epic and

partly dramatic. Richardson's epistolary form has the charm of variety of style and of preserving suspense, but "this mode of narration can hardly fail . . . to be encumbered with repetitions", and Richardson becomes tedious. He is, moreover, too pathetic, and his favorite characters play too much the prude; Allworthy is better than Clementina or Grandison. Richardson has great knowledge of human nature. But how could he write a character like Lovelace, who in life would succeed far better than Richardson's character does, and who dies not as a result of his crimes but because of his slight "inferiority to his antagonist in the use of the small sword"? (569) Compare 1759.1.

*3   BIEVRE, Monsieur. Le Séducteur. Paris.
       A verse drama in three acts, based on Clarissa. Source: 1935.2, p. 60n24.

4   DIDEROT, DENIS. Elogio di Richardson autore dei romanzi morali Clarissa, Grandisson, Pamela ec. [!] Traduzion dal francese. Premessa ancora al volgarizzamento della prima delle sudette Opere, che si sta pubblicando per Associazione. [Venice:] Dalla stamperia Valvasense a S. Gio. Novo. Bib. Comunale dell'Archiginnasio.

5   FEITH, RHIJNVIS. Julia. First published 1783. Amsterdam: Elwe en Langeveld, 1786, 116 pp. BM.
       An ecstatic novel, non-epistolary, popularly supposed to be influenced by Richardson but showing more the influence of Sterne's Sentimental Journey. However, in the "Apologie van Julia," Feith praises Richardson as an "onsterfelijken schrijver" whose novels are "Liefdesgeschiedenissen, welke edeler menschen aan de maatschappij en nieuwe bewoners aan den hemel gegeven hebben." In 1779, though, he had said of Richardson (Brieven Messchert, vol.1, quoted in 1910.3, p. 182), "Ongelukkige Maatschappij, waar Richardson der Leermeester der jeugd is! Hij is de gevaarlijkste aller vergiftmengeren." He preferred Clarissa, found Grandison "minder schoon," and Pamela "behaagt [hem] in het geheel niet." 1910.3, p. 11. His Ferdinand en Constantia (1785) has Richardsonian elements.

6   [JONES, Rev. JOHN.] "Mr. Samuel Richardson, Printer (A Great Genius)." GM 53: 924-25.
       Information on Richardson's eleven-year-old letter "in

character" and his relationship to Edward Young. Martha
Bridgen replies in GM 54 (1784):488 that her father did not
attend Christ's Hospital.

6   MORITZ, CARL PHILLIPP. Reisen eines Deutschen in England.
     See 1903.5.

7   RICHARDSON, SAMUEL. Miss Clarissa Harlowes Historie i en
     Samling af Breve. Oversat af Engelsk [by Hans Christian
     Amberg]. 8v. Copenhagen: Tryckt hos P.H. Hoecke,
     1783-88. BN; Det kongelige Bibliotek, Copenhagen.
          From Vol. 5 onward "J.W. Thiele" is added to the
     imprint.

8   ---. Pamela eller den Belonta Dygden. I Korthet forfattad.
     Ofwersattning. Wasteras. Nat. Lib. Scotland; Univbib.
     Uppsala.

                         1784

1   MÜLLER, JOHANN GOTTWERTH. Die Herren von Waldheim eine
     komische Geschichte vom Verfasser des Siegfried von
     Lindenburg. 4 pts. in 2. Gottingen: Dieterich. NIC.
          "Unsers Bedünkens haben die Grandisone, die Siegwarte,
     die Leiden Werthers u.s.w. eine Menge alberne Köpfe
     vollends zu Narren gemacht," 1937.3, p. 250n7, quotes
     Müller, from the preface to Die Herren von Waldheim. But
     the book shows Müller softening the anti-Richardsonian
     stance of his Siegfried von Lindenburg, Liljegren believes.

2   SCHILLER, FRIEDRICH. Kabale und Liebe ein bürgerliches
     Trauerspiel in fünf Aufzugen. . . Mannheim: In der
     Schwanischen Hofbuchhandlung, 176 pp. BM.
          Liljegren calls this "his contribution to the domestic
     drama in imitation of Richardson"--1937.3, p. 108, and
     Wolff (1887.1) also notes Schiller's use of Richardson as a
     source. Schiller would think less of Richardson in later
     years; see his Briefe (ed. Jonas. 6v. Stuttgart,
     Leipzig, etc.: Deutsche Verlags-Anstalt, 1894-96). At
     2:286 of the Briefe he feels that because of the engagement
     of the affections, Tom Jones pleases the reader far more
     than Grandison (letter to Körner, Feb. 23, 1793), and in a
     letter to Wolfgang von Goethe, July 2, 1796, he prefers the

treatment of emotions in Wilhelm's Therese to Richardson's
(5:3). His Geisterseher is partly epistolary but draws
only vaguely on Richardson (in the interpolated story of
the Incomprehensible).

1785

1   ADAMS, ABIGAIL. Letter to Lucy Cranch, August 27, 1785. In
     Letters of Mrs. Adams . . . with an Introductory Memoir
     by . . . Charles Francis Adams. 4th ed. Boston:
     Wilkins, Carter & Co., 1848, pp. 261-62.
         Justifies ideal characters, but finds Richardson's
     neither too idealized nor too odious.

2   CHODERLOS DE LACLOS, PIERRE-AMBROISE-FRANÇOIS. "De
     l'Education des femmes." Written 1785. Reprinted in
     Oeuvres complètes. Paris: Gallimard, 1951, p. 479.
         Clarissa is an educational treatise, showing how much
     difficulty a virtuous young woman can get into from an
     outwardly venial fault. "There can be few more useful
     pieces of reading."

3   FONTANES, LOUIS JEAN PIERRE, MARQUIS DE. Letter to J.
     Joubert, November 29. In Les Correspondants de J.
     Joubert. Ed. Paul de Raynal. Paris: Calmann Lévy, 1883,
     p. 30.
         Richardson is now unread at Paris; Pamela is scorned,
     Grandison read only for Clementina, and even Clarissa
     placed far below Fielding's novels. Parisians would find
     the English opinion of him unbelievable.

4   HAYLEY, WILLIAM. Marcella; a Tragedy, of Three Acts . . .
     In Poems and Plays . . . London: T. Cadell, 6:1-76.
     BM.
         A Richardson association item; Hayley was given the
     subject of this tragedy by Young, who had it from
     Richardson. But Hayley has "made considerable alterations"
     in the plot. In Barcelona, Marcella reluctantly engages
     herself to Lupercio, but immediately afterward meets
     Mendoza; they fall in love. She has said that if Lupercio
     loses the ring she has given him her promise is void, and
     now she asks a servant, Hernandez, to arrange that the ring
     is lost. Hernandez rather mistakes her meaning and kills

Lupercio. But Hernandez wants Marcella; she virtuously refuses, he rapes her, she goes mad, and there is a rash of suicides (Marcella leaves a rather long letter). Richardson seems overpowered by John Ford.

5   MACKENZIE, HENRY. "On Novel Writing." The Lounger, No. 20 (June 18).
     The Richardsonian Mackenzie apparently attacks Richardsonian fiction. "The principal danger of novels, as forming a mistaken and pernicious system of morality, seems to me to arise from that contrast between one virtue or excellence and another, that war of duties which is to be found in many of them, particularly in that species called the sentimental." In these the extraordinary virtues are likely to be preferred over the everyday. Sentimentalists favor imaginary virtues and relieve imaginary distresses rather than real ones. However, although the novel has been reproached for "faultless monsters" of virtue, mixed characters are a greater evil.

6   MORITZ, KARL PHILIPP. Anton Reiser. Ein psychologischer Roman. Berlin: F. Maurer, 1785-94, 2:164-65.
     Speaks of the confusion in his mind caused by seeing a Pamela play in 1776, Clarissa oder das unbekannte Dienstmädchen; after this he no longer understood his fellow men clearly.

7   PRATT, SAMUEL JACKSON ["Courtney Melmoth"]. Miscellanies by Mr. Pratt. In Four Volumes. London: T. Becket, 3:122-23. BM.
     Criticizes Richardson for poetical license in the distribution of rewards and punishments according to merit--"this cannot be allowed, for it is not altogether true"--and for drawing his protagonists without faults. Sir Charles and Clarissa are bad; Pamela is worse than either. "We must take care, while Human Nature is our Subject, not to paint . . . larger than the life." He much prefers Fielding and Smollett, and would like Rousseau except for his voluptuousness. Originally printed in the Westminster Magazine 4 (1776):521, according to Hannaford, item 225, who notes references to and pastiches of Richardson in Pratt's novels The Pupil of Pleasure (1776) and Excessive Sensibility (1787).

8   REEVE, CLARA. The Progress of Romance. 2v. Colchester:
       Printed for the Author by W. Keymer, and Sold by Him;
       London: G.G.J. and J. Robinson, 1:133-41.
           The characters of Reeve's symposium compare Richardson
       and Fielding; Richardson's prolixity is defended, he is
       praised for his morality and characterization, and the
       three novels are compared. Pamela is preferable for the
       "sweetness" of the heroine and the originality of the book;
       Clarissa, with the highest graces, has the most faults.
       Reeve had praised Richardson earlier in the preface to The
       Champion of Virtue (1777); see also the exchange of
       letters between her and Anna Seward in the GM, 1786.
           Another edition of The Progress of Romance appeared in
       Dublin in 1785; it was republished by the Facsimile Text
       Society in New York, 1930.

9   RICHARDSON, SAMUEL, trans. PIERRE LE TOURNEUR. Clarisse
       Harlowe. Traduction nouvelle et seule complète par Le
       Tourneur. Faite sur l'ed. orig. rev. par Richardson,
       ornée de figures du célèbre [Daniel] Chodowiecki. 10v.
       Genève: Barde; Paris: Moutarde, Merigot, 1785-86.
       Genève.
           Edition in octavo.

10   ---, trans. PIERRE LE TOURNEUR. Clarisse Harlowe . . .
       14v. Genève: Barde, Manget et Comp., 1785-86. Genève;
       Bib. de l'Archiginnasio.
           Edition in 16mo.
           The Journal des Savants reviewed Le Tourneur's
       translation in September 1785 (pp. 629-30), preferring it
       to Prévost's: "Clarisse, le chef d'oeuvre des romans
       anglais, est devenu le premier des nôtres." However,it did
       not have the success of Prévost's --perhaps because it came
       at a period when the great rage for Richardson's works was
       beginning to pass, perhaps because the French preferred a
       version tailored to their taste.

*11   ---. Klarissa, oder Geschichte eines jungen Frauenzimmers aus
       dem Englischen des Richardson neu übersetzt. Bibliothek
       der Romane. Mannheim: Reichard, 1785-1791.
           Source: 1950.6, p. 89. A sample of the proposed
       translation appeared in the Bibliothek der Romane 12
       (1785): 257 ff.

<u>1786</u>

*1   ---. Life of Richardson. <u>Traduction</u> <u>du</u> <u>Plutarque</u> <u>anglois,</u>
      <u>contenant</u> <u>la</u> <u>vie</u> <u>des</u> <u>Hommes</u> <u>les</u> <u>plus</u> <u>illustres</u> <u>de</u>
      <u>l'Angleterre</u> <u>et</u> <u>de</u> <u>l'Irlande</u> . . . Paris: Couturier
      [etc.], 11:188 ff. Bib. nat. de Québec.

2   BRIDGEN, EDWARD [L.] Memoir of Richardson. <u>Universal</u> <u>Magazine</u>
      78: 17-21, 73-77.
           A biographical character and eulogy quoting liberally
      from Rousseau, Baculard d'Arnaud, Johnson, Young, Diderot,
      Hill, Sherlock, Elizabeth Carter, and Hester Mulso Chapone.

3   CUMBERLAND, RICHARD. The Observer, No. 46. Reprinted in <u>The</u>
      <u>Observer</u> . . . 5v. London: Charles Dilly, 1786,
      2:152-58.
           Comparison of Richardson and Fielding.   The epistolary
      style, though less natural, is better suited to pathos,
      while Fielding's suits comedy better.   <u>Clarissa</u>, though
      generally allowed by prudent parents to children, will lead
      young girls to artificiality, not forming either "natural
      manners or natural style." "As to the characters of
      Lovelace, the heroine herself, and the heroine's parents, I
      take them all to be beings of another world." The
      connection between the elopement and Clarissa's miseries is
      unclear.
           Originally published as No. 27 of the periodical in
      1785; see 1970.31, pp. 332-35.

4   GENLIS, STÉPHANIE-FÉLICITÉ DUCREST de ST.-AUBIN, comtesse de.
      <u>Mémoires</u> <u>inédits</u> <u>de</u> <u>Mme</u> <u>la</u> <u>Comtesse</u> <u>de</u> <u>Genlis</u> <u>sur</u> <u>le</u> XVIIIe
      <u>siècle</u> . . . 10v. Paris: Ladvocat, 1825, 3:303-5. BN.
           Records a meeting between herself and Edward Bridgen,
      Richardson's son-in-law, in 1786, and Mme de Tessé's
      tearful reaction to viewing "Richardson's grave."

*5   NÉE DE LA ROCHELLE, JEAN-FRANÇOIS. <u>Clarisse</u> <u>Harlove,</u> <u>drame</u> <u>en</u>
      <u>3</u> <u>actes</u> <u>et</u> <u>en</u> <u>prose</u>. Paris: Née de la Rochelle, 95 pp.
      BN.
           See 1935.2, pp. 61-62.

6   REEVE, CLARA, AND SEWARD, ANNA. Exchange of letters. <u>GM</u> 56:
      15-17, 117.
           Anna Seward indignantly attacks Reeve for daring to

prefer <u>Pamela</u>, "that dim dawn of an illustrious genius," to Richardson´s other work. Reeve defends herself and mentions her friendship with Anne Richardson. "A Constant Reader" disagrees with Reeve, <u>GM</u> 56:288–89; Anna Seward writes on Richardson again in <u>GM</u> 58 (1788):818,1005–6,1168–71.

                              1787

*1   ANON. <u>Olla Podrida</u>. No. 15.
           Attacking novels as such, praises <u>Grandison</u> and <u>Clarissa</u>. Source: 1948.7, pp. 155–56.

2   CAMBON, MARIA GEERTRUIDA de, and ARNAUD BERQUIN. <u>Le Petit Grandisson, traduction libre du hollandois</u>. 4 pts. Paris: Au bureau de l´<u>Ami des Enfants</u>.
           According to MMF, the first French edition of 1782.3 (see their item 87.35). Told in letters written to his mother by a Guillaume D., who has had the dubious good fortune to settle in England and make the acquaintance of Charles Grandison jr. The book crawls with moral sentiments, including a persuasion-out-of-a-duel scene that confronts Charles, <u>aet</u>. 14, with a potential duellist of 18. Cameo appearances by Sir Charles himself, Lady Grandison, and "Mr. Bartlet." Although the book is epistolary, it makes no attempt at emulating Richardson´s stylistic or psychological complexity; but, like other of the Richardsonian adaptations for children, it is important in the history of children´s literature. It was long popular in both English and French and was frequently published in French in London, perhaps as a text for English pupils learning French.

3   [CANNING, GEORGE.] <u>The</u> [Eton] <u>Microcosm</u>. No. 26 (May 14, 1787). Reprinted in <u>The Microcosm: A Periodical Work, by Gregory Griffin</u>. Windsor: C. Knight, and sold by G.G.J. and J. Robinson and Mr. Debrett, London, pp. 303–06. BM.
           <u>Tom Jones</u> is too early put into the hands of children; although the schoolboy Canning admires Fielding´s book, <u>Sir Charles Grandison</u> far better suits children as an object of imitation.

4   CHODERLOS de LACLOS, P.-A.-F., and RICCOBONI, M.-J.
      Correspondence. Les Liaisons dangereuses . . . Nouvelle
      édition augmentée d´une correspondance avec Mde Riccoboni .
      . . 4v. N.p.: n.p. BM.
            In the separately paged correspondence at the end of
      this edition, Laclos defends himself from "ornamenting
      vice" by saying, "Il faut faire la même reproche au peintre
      de Lovelace." Mme Riccoboni argues against this.

*5   GOLDONI, CARLO. La bella Inglesa Pamela en el estado de
      soltera, primera parte; id. en el estado de casada, 2da
      parte; comedias escritas en prosa en italiano por el
      abogado Carlos Goldoni, y traducidas en verso castellano.
      Madrid: Libreria de Quiroga.
            Source: 1930.5, p. 56, from advertisements.

5A   HAWKINS, Sir JOHN. The Life of Samuel Johnson. London:
      Printed for J. Buckland, J. Rivington and Sons, T. Payne
      and Sons . . . , pp. 216-17, 382-85.
            Richardson´s vivid imagination, ability to attract young
      women, generosity, unconversability, and lack of humor.

6   MARMONTEL, JEAN-FRANÇOIS. Essai sur les Romans, considérés du
      côté moral. First published 1787.
            Revision of 1758.5; see 1819.3.

7   RICHARDSON, SAMUEL. Pamela, ili Nagrazhdennaja dobrodetel´,
      angliiskoe tvorenie g. Richardsona. V 4 ch. Per. s.
      fr. g. P.P. Chertkova. Spb. [Pamela, or Virtue
      Rewarded, from the English of Mr. Richardson, in 4 parts.
      Translated from the French by P.P. Chertkov. St.
      Petersburg: n.p.] All-Union State Library, Moscow; Bib.
      Akad. Nauk SSSR; Saltykov-Shchedrin.

8   SEWARD, ANNA. Letter of May 10. Letters of Anna Seward:
      Written between the Years 1784 and 1807. Edinburgh:
      George Ramsay & Co. and Archibald Constable & Co., and
      sold by Longman, Hurst, Rees, Orme and Brown, and William
      Miller, and John Murray, London, 1:293.
            Though she likes Fielding, whose "romances" are
      "excellent," she cannot understand the taste that would

prefer him to Richardson, whose "immortal volumes [are] .
. . the highest efforts of genius in our language, next
to Shakespeare´s plays." She writes in the same year in
Variety that in the character of Sophia in Tom Jones a girl
may find sanctions for attaching herself to a libertine,
but in Clarissa, never.

1788

*1   ANON. "Gedachten over ´t Leezen van Vercierde Geschiedenissen
      en Romans." De Nieuwe Vaderlandsche Letteroefeningen 3:
      97-98.
          Praises Clarissa and Stinstra´s prefaces.   Source:
      1969.17, p. xxii.

2   PORRETT, ROBERT. Clarissa; or, the Fatal Seduction. A
      Tragedy, in Prose. Founded on Richardson´s celebrated
      Novel of Clarissa Harlowe. London: Printed for the Author
      [by subscription], 136 pp. BM.
          One of the wilder of the Richardsonian adaptations,
      featuring two ripe Victorian stage villains in Young
      Harlowe and Arabella, a chorus of chairmen, and a corps of
      banditti (who gang-rape Clarissa). Unexpected incursions
      into the play from the original novel, as well as from the
      mad   scenes   in   Shakespeare   and   Dr.   Faustus.
      Incomprehensible without the novel. Described in 1964.27.

3   SCHULZ, J.C.F., trans. and adapt. Albertine: Richardsons
      Clarissen nachgebildet und zu einen lehrreichen Lesebuch
      fur deutsche Mädchen bestimmt. 5v. Berlin: A.   Wever,
      1788-89. BN.
          A condensation of Clarissa for the German taste, set in
      Berlin. See the preface to Volume I for Schulz´s ideas on
      what was and was not suitable for German adolescent taste.
      Winterfeld is Schulz´s Lovelace, Albertine his Clarissa;
      the latter´s death-scene is a literal rendering from
      Richardson. The book was reviewed in ADB 88, 2 (1798);
      162-67, which had respect for both it and its English
      original but suggested it could have been shortened even
      more; Schiller, writing to Körner on April 25, 1788, found
      it "sehr lesbar."

<u>1789</u>

1   ANON.   "Lothario: or, The Accomplished Villain." <u>Mass.</u>   <u>Mag.</u>
     1:   443-45.
          1932.3 points to this and other   short   stories   in   the
     <u>Massachusetts</u>   <u>Magazine</u>   (e.g.   "Innocent   Simplicity
     Betrayed," 1:   470-73, 539-41;   "The Libertine and Duellist
     Reclaimed," 1:   205-8)   as   indicating   the   influence   of
     Richardson over early fiction in the Colonies.   While   this
     is   true   (see   the indicative, if overdone, 1960.5), it is
     not so true in   specific   cases   as   Brown   would   have   us
     believe.   "The   plot   of   <u>Clarissa</u>,"   for   instance,   is   not
     "closely   followed"   in   "Innocent   Simplicity   Betrayed"
     (1932.3, p.   7?)

2   BENNETT, JOHN.   <u>Letters</u> <u>to</u> <u>a</u> <u>Young</u> <u>Lady</u>.   First   published
     1789.   2v.   Hartford: Hudson and Goodwin, 1791, 2:58-64.
          Letters XX and XXI concern Richardson.   He is the master
     of   the   human   heart,   though   prolix and clumsy;   Bennett
     enthuses over his characters as moral types,   feeling   that
     Clarissa's   story   encourages   greatness   in a young woman,
     Harriet Byron's encourages   loveliness.   Bennett   strongly
     prefers   <u>Grandison</u>;   <u>Clarissa</u>   leaves   "too   melancholy
     impressions.   Her distresses are too deep and too   <u>unvaried</u>
     for   sensibility   to   bear."   Though Grandison is a perfect
     model, Bennett does not mind;   so is Christ [!].

*3   CLAUDIUS, GEORG   KARL   [FRANZ   EHRENBURG].   <u>Leonore</u>   <u>Schmidt</u>.
     <u>Nach</u> <u>Richardsons</u> <u>Pamela</u>.   2v.   Leipzig, 1789-91.
          Source: Goedeke, third   ed.,   4, 1:   625,   quoted   by
     1926.5, p.   10n8.   (Query: Could this <u>Leonore</u> <u>Schmidt</u> be
     the same as Schulz's <u>Leonore</u> and the author be Schulz,   not
     Claudius?   If this were so, however, <u>Leonore</u> <u>Schmidt</u> would
     probably have been published in Berlin.)

4   TWINING, THOMAS.   <u>Aristotle's</u> <u>Treatise</u> <u>on</u> <u>Poetry,</u> <u>Translated</u>
     <u>by</u> <u>Thomas</u> <u>Twining</u> . . .   London: Payne and Sons;   White
     and Son;   Robson and Clarke . . . , 119-20n.
          "Is not the Lovelace of Richardson . . .   more out   of
     nature . . .   than   the   Caliban of Shakespeare?   The
     latter is, at least,   consistent,   I can   <u>imagine</u>   such   a
     monster   as   Caliban: I never could imagine such a man as
     Lovelace."

<u>1790</u>

1   CAMBON, MARIA GEERTRUIDA de. <u>Young</u> <u>Grandison.</u> <u>A</u> <u>Series</u> <u>of</u>
     <u>Letters</u> <u>from</u> <u>Young</u> <u>Persons</u> <u>to</u> <u>their</u> <u>Friends.</u> <u>Translated</u>
     <u>from</u> <u>the</u> <u>Dutch</u> <u>of</u> <u>Mme</u> <u>de</u> <u>Cambon,</u> <u>with</u> <u>Alterations</u> <u>and</u>
     <u>Improvements.</u> 2v. London: Johnson. BM, ICN, PPL, NcD,
     PPULC.
         First (?) English translation of 1782.3, probably from
     Berquin's intermediate French version. Flexner and others
     give it to Mary Wollstonecraft, though it has sometimes
     been ascribed to John Hall.

*2   ---. <u>De</u> <u>kleine</u> <u>Klarissa</u> <u>door</u> <u>M.G.</u> <u>de</u> <u>Cambon</u> <u>Gebn</u> <u>van</u> <u>der</u>
     <u>Werken.</u> . . . 4 pts. in 2v.? 's Hage: I.F. Jacobs
     de Age. Private collection of Mr. C.F. Van Veen.
         <u>RNB</u>, item 23. The engraved title page of this book,
     designed by J.J. de Cambon, has led to the suggestion that
     he wrote this and even <u>De</u> <u>Kleine</u> <u>Grandisson</u>. This J.J. de
     Cambon may be the same person who wrote the Richardsonian
     <u>Clementina</u> <u>Bedford</u>, which has its own bibliographical
     mysteries. <u>RNB</u> lists <u>De</u> <u>kleine</u> <u>Klarissa</u> as having been
     published in 1791, the year after its first apparent
     translation, below. It is an improving book for girls, with
     little resemblance to <u>Clarissa</u>, more to <u>Grandison</u>.

3   ---. <u>Letters</u> <u>and</u> <u>Conversations</u> <u>between</u> <u>Several</u> <u>Young</u> <u>Ladies</u>
     <u>on</u> <u>Interesting</u> <u>and</u> <u>Improving</u> <u>Subjects.</u> <u>Translated</u> <u>from</u> <u>the</u>
     <u>Dutch</u> <u>of</u> <u>Madame</u> <u>de</u> <u>Cambon.</u> <u>Abridged</u> . . . London:
     Printed for J. Mawman [etc.?], 177 pp. NN.
         The first of a number of English editions of <u>De</u> <u>kleine</u>
     <u>Klarissa</u>.

4   GOETHE, J.W. VON. <u>Faust.</u> <u>Ein</u> <u>Fragment</u>. Leipzig: Goschen,
     168 pp.
         Only in a bibliography of Richardson would one even
     consider listing <u>Faust</u> as a <u>Richardsonade</u>. However, 1937.3
     notes many connections between <u>Faust</u> and Richardson's
     works, including the character of Gretchen, the drugged
     rape (though in <u>Faust</u> it is not the victim who is drugged),
     the treatment of the seduction-scene, the definition of
     virtue as chastity, the summerhouse location, the duel,
     Gretchen's insanity, and her death.

5   HAWKESWORTH, DR. JOHN. Lines on Richardson. <u>GM</u> 60: 692.
         Expresses grief over his death; presumably written
     about 1761.

6   HITCHCOCK, DR. ENOS. <u>Memoirs of the Bloomsgrove Family.</u> <u>In</u>
      <u>a Series of Letters</u> . . . <u>Containing Sentiments on Modes</u>
      <u>of Domestic Education</u> . . . Boston: Thomas and Andrews,
      pp. 86-87. MB, MH.
           Believes that Richardson is not totally safe on moral
      grounds, laying "open scenes, which it would have been
      safer to have kept concealed," p. 87, but "among all
      writings which unite sentiment with character, and present
      images of life, Richardson's, perhaps, may be placed at the
      head of the list," p. 86. The <u>Mass.</u> <u>Mag.</u> review of the
      book (2 [1790]: 758) condemned Richardson simply for being
      a novelist--"that pernicious reading, which too frequently
      engages female attention."

7   [KNOX, VICESIMUS, ed.] <u>Elegant</u> <u>Epistles;</u> <u>or.</u> <u>A</u> <u>Copious</u>
      <u>Collection of Familiar and Amusing Letters</u> . . . London:
      Charles Dilly, 815 pp. <u>MH.</u>
           Brief extracts from Richardson's correspondence are
      included in this, according to A.J.H., 1933.4. Other
      editions of the book were published in 1790 (Dublin), 1791,
      1795, 1807, 1821, and 1822.

8   MACAULAY, CATHERINE. <u>Letters</u> <u>on</u> <u>Education.</u> London: C.
      Dilly, pp. 145-47.
           Richardson's novels corrupt the minds of young people.

9   RICHARDSON, SAMUEL. <u>Clarissa, die Geschichte eines vornehmen</u>
      <u>Frauenzimmers</u> . . . <u>Neuverdeutscht von Ludwig Theobul</u>
      <u>Kosegarten.</u> Translated by L.T. Kosegarten. 8v. Leipzig:
      Graff, 1790-93. Nat. Lib. Scotland; Sachs. Landesbib.
      OC (destroyed in World War II); BZK; Deutsche Staatsbib.
      1926.5, pp. 8-9, and 1792.15, p. 21, have information
      on this edition.

*10   ---. <u>Klarissa,</u> <u>oder,</u> <u>die</u> <u>Geschichte</u> <u>eines</u> <u>jungen</u>
      <u>Frauenzimmers,</u> <u>aus</u> <u>dem</u> <u>Englischen</u> <u>des</u> <u>Herrn</u> <u>Richardson,</u>
      <u>Verfassers der Pamela, und des Sir Karl Grandison, neu</u>
      <u>übersetzt.</u> Translated anonymously. 16v. Mannheim:
      1790-91.
           Sources: 1926.5, p. 8n4; 1792.15, pp. 21-22. Not
      the same as the Kosegarten translation.

11   SMITH, ADAM. <u>The Theory of Moral Sentiments</u> . . . <u>The</u>
      <u>Sixth Edition, with Considerable Additions and Corrections.</u>
      2v. London: A. Strahan and T. Cadell, and W. Creech,

and J. Bell & Co. at Edinburgh, 1:350. BM.
Warning against both false affections and none, Smith
praises "poets and romance writers," Richardson among them,
for "painting the refinements and delicacies of love and
friendship, and ... all other private and domestic
affections . . . [They] are in such cases much better
instructors than Zeno, Chrysippus, or Epictetus." Smith
revised the Theory of Moral Sentiments at the beginning of
the winter 1789-90. 1926.2 incorrectly dates this opinion
1759.

1791

*1   BURNS, ROBERT. Letter to Dr. John Moore. Printed in Letters
      of Robert Burns. Edited by J. De Lancy Ferguson. 2v.
      Oxford: Clarendon, 1931, 1:58-59.
         Richardson can paint the human heart, but his characters
      are not of this world. Source: Hannaford, item 275.

2   CAMBON, MARIA GEERTRUIDA de. The History of Little Grandison.
      London: John Stockdale. 174 pp. BM.
         An abridged edition, not the same as 1790.1. Another
      edition of this version of De kleine Grandison was
      published by Stockdale in 1797; it is also in the BM.

3   CHÉNIER, ANDRÉ. "Elégie XIV." Written summer 1791. Published
      in Oeuvres posthumes. Paris: Guillaume, 1826, pp.
      173-74; in Oeuvres complètes, ed. Gérard Walter. Paris:
      Pléiade, 1950, pp. 57÷58, as "Elégie II".
         Among the "fantômes si beaux à nos pleurs tant aimés"
      are Clarissa and Clementina.

4   FRANKLIN, BENJAMIN. Mémoires de la vie privée . . . First
      published Paris: 1791. As The Autobiography of Benjamin
      Franklin, edited by Leonard W. Labarree et al. New Haven:
      Yale University Press, 1964, p. 72.
         With Bunyan and Defoe, Richardson agreeably mingles
      dialogue and narration.

5   LA ROCHE, SOPHIE VON. Briefe über Mannheim. Zurich: Orell,
      Gessner, Fussli & Co., p. 356. BM.
         Records her disillusionment with idealistic novels, such
      as the ones she wrote.

6   RICHARDSON, SAMUEL. <u>Dostopamyatnaja zhizn´ devitsy Klarissy</u>
      <u>Garlov, istinnaja povest´; angliiskoe tvorenie g.</u>
      <u>Richardsona. S prisovokupleniem k tomu ostavshikhsja po</u>
      <u>smerti Klarissy pisem i dukhovnago eja zaveshchanija.</u>
      <u>Pereveli s frants. jaz. N.P. Osipov i Petr</u>
      <u>Kil´djushevskii.</u> Ch. 1-6. Vo grade sv. Petra, tip.
      Sytina, 1791-1792. [The Memorable Life of the Maiden
      Clarissa Harlowe, a True Story, in Six Parts. The English
      work of Mr. Richardson, with the addition of the
      posthumous letters and her last will and testament.
      Translated from the French by N. Osipov and Petr
      Kil´djushevskii. (Unfinished.) 6 pts. St. Petersburg:
      Sytin, 1791-92.] All-Union State Library, Moscow; Bib.
      Akad. Nauk SSSR.

7   ---. <u>The Paths of Virtue Delineated; or, The History in</u>
      <u>Miniature of the Celebrated Clarissa Harlowe</u> . . .
      Philadelphia: W. Woodhouse, 135 pp.

                          <u>1792</u>

*1   ---. <u>Clarisse ou La Vertu malheureuse. Comédie-tragédie en</u>
      <u>cinq actes et en vers.</u> Paris.
          Source: 1935.2, p. 60n24.

2   ---. Portrait of Richardson. <u>GM</u> 62: 784.

3   BADEN, CHARLOTTE. <u>Den fortsatte Grandison, tilligemed et Brev</u>
      <u>til Forfatterinden, hendes Svar, og en Fortaelling.</u> [The
      Continued Grandison, Together with a Letter to its
      Authoress, Her Answer, and an Introduction.] Copenhagen:
      Printed by Mattings for Sebastian Popp, 129 pp. (of which
      1-93 only are the continuation). BM.
          A Danish continuation of <u>Grandison</u>, in letters,
      concentrating on the Italian episodes; very favorable to
      Richardson.

4   CAMBON, MARIA GEERTRUIDA de. <u>De kleine Grandisson verkort, en</u>
      <u>in Themata´s of kleine Leeslesjens geschikt; waar achter</u>
      <u>gevoegd zijn. Algemeene Grondregelen der Fransche Taal,</u>
      <u>tot gebruik der Fransche Schoolen, door P. Sazerac.</u>
      Amsterdam: J.R. Poster.
          <u>RNB</u>, item 25. A second edition was published without

date of issue, attributed to "A.R." (<u>RNB</u>, item 30); a third edition appeared in 1831 (<u>RNB</u>, item 29).

*5   KARAMZIN, NIKOLAI MIHAELOVICH. "Bednaya Liza" [Poor Liza]. In <u>Moskovskii Zhurnal</u>.
     Popularly supposed to indicate Richardson's influence in Russia, although largely a mere Sentimental fiction: Liza, seduced and abandoned, drowns herself. [Courtesy of Prof. Daniel LaFerrière and Harvard University Library. I have seen only an English translation.] Karamzin proclaimed Richardson as "the most artistic painter of man's moral nature."

*6   LEMERCIER, [LOUIS-JEAN-] NEPOMUCÈNE. <u>Lovelace</u>. First staged 1792. MS in Bib. du Théâtre français (according to 1935.2, p. 60n24). Not printed.
     "In 1792 appeared 'Lovelace', which was, on its revival in 1795, named 'Clarisse Harlowe' as well; in fact, critics use either title. 'Le goût des institutions anglaises, qui dominait à cette époque, lui inspirait [i.e. à Lemercier] le drame . . . ', but 'le roman de Clarisse . . . devait perdre sur la scène tous ses avantages; aussi le "Lovelace" de M. Lemercier, quoique fort bien écrit et dialogué, n'a pas eu de succès.'" 1924.2, p. 55, quoting from the <u>Journal des Comédiens</u>, June 11, 1840, and the <u>Mémoires . . . de F. Chéron</u>. Edited by F. Hervé-Bazin, 1882.

7   [SCHMID, C.H.] "Über die verschiedenen Verdeutschungen von Richardson's Klarisse." <u>JVFD</u> 9, part 1: 16-35. BM.
     Discusses <u>Albertine</u>, the translation of 1748-53, and the Kosegarten and Mannheim translations of 1790-91. Discussed in 1950.6 and 1926.5 and Price's <u>C.H. Schmid</u> (1950).

8   SMITH, CHARLOTTE. <u>Desmond</u>. 3v. London: G.G.J. & J. Robinson. BM.
     A <u>Briefwechselroman</u> influenced by <u>Sir Charles Grandison</u> with occasional references to Richardson's works themselves, e.g. at 2:172-73: "The great name of Richardson (and great it certainly deserves to be) makes . . . those scenes, those descriptions pass uncensured in Pamela and Clarissa, which are infinitely more improper for the perusal of young women than any that can be found in the novels of the present day . . . "

1793

*1   ANON.   O Richardsone.   Per.   s frants.   Fedor   Puchkov.
      "Sankt-Peterburgskii Merkurii," 1793, ch.   IV, s.   156-72.
      ["On Richardson." Trans.   from French by Feodor Puchkov.
      St.   Petersburg Mercury 4 (for 1793):   156-72.] All-Union
      State Lib., Moscow.

2   AIKIN, JOHN.   Letters from   a   Father to his Son . . .
      London: J. Johnson, pp.   82-83.
          Distinguishes between an unreal character like Amadis de
      Gaul and an uncommon one like Grandison.

3   FRANÇOIS   DE   NEUFCHÂTEAU,   NICOLAS-LOUIS.   François   de
      Neufchâteau, auteur de Paméla, à la Convention nationale .
      . . 21 septembre 1793. Paris: C.F.   Patris, 53 pp.   BN.
          Defends his use of Richardson's ending against the
      charge that to reward virtue with a title was
      counterrevolutionary.

4   ---.   Pamela, ou la vertu récompensée . . . First performed
      August 1, 1793, by the Comédiens français. Published as
      1795.2.

5   RICHARDSON, SAMUEL.   The Pleasing History of Pamela; or,
      Virtue Rewarded . . . Boston: S.   Hall, 96 pp.   CtY.
          Illustrated.

6   ---.   Angliskija pis'ma, ili Istorija kavalera Grandisona,
      tvorenie g.   Richardsona sochinitelja Pamely i Klarisy.
      Perevedeno s frantsuzskago A. Kondratovichem.   Izhdiveniem
      I.   Sitina.   Ch.   1-8.   Vo grade sv. Petra, tip. Sytina,
      1793-94. [English Letters, or the History of the Chevalier
      Grandison, the work of Mr.   Richardson, the creator of
      Pamela and Clarissa.   Translated from the French by
      A[leksandr] Kondratovich, (printed at) the expense of I.
      Sytin.   8 pts.   St.   Petersburg: Sytin, 1793-94.]
      All-Union State Library, Moscow; Bib. Akad.   Nauk SSSR.

7   ---.   Angliskija pis'ma . . . Moskva, tip.   Selivanovskogo
      i tovarishcha.   [English Letters, or the History of the
      Chevalier Grandison . . . Moscow: Selivanovsky & Co.]
      Bib.   Akad.   Nauk SSSR has parts 4-5, 7, 8 only.

8   ---. De Geschiedenis van Sir Charles Grandison Verkort.   Ten
      nutte der Nederlandsche jeugd uit het Engelsch vertaald.
      Leyden, 219 pp. Koninklikje Bib.

9   THOMAS, ALEXANDER. Essay on Novels: A Poetical Epistle.
      Edinburgh: P.   Hill and J. Watson & Co., pp. vi, 2-4,
      7-9. BM.
          Praises   Richardson's   originality   and   power   of
      influencing the passions; though cannot deny Richardson is
      sometimes tedious, Clarissa is true poetry;   prefers him
      (and Fielding, Rousseau, and Goethe) to Virgil, Milton, and
      Homer.

1794

1   RICHARDSON, SAMUEL. Clara Harlowe; novela. Tr. del inglés
      al francés por Le Tourneur, siguiendo en todo la ed. orig.
      rev. por su autor Richardson, y del francés al castellano,
      por Joseph Marcos Gutierrez. 11v. Madrid: Benito Cano,
      1794-96. Bib. Nac. de Mexico, Nat. Lib. of Chile.
          Imprint varies. Coe cites a 5 1/2 page review of this
      translation   in   the   Memorial   Literario   of December
      1794--1935.2, p. 59.

2   ---. Pamela Andrews, ó La Virtud Recompensada: Escrita en
      Inglés Por Thomas [sic] Richardson. Traducida al
      Castellano, Corregida y acomodada á nuestras costumbres,
      por el traductor. 6v. Madrid: Don Antonio Espinosa. MH.
          Pamela I only. Translator's preface, I, i-ix, is a
      general introduction showing the value of the work. From
      internal evidence, translated from the French rather than
      Richardson's English; e.g., part of the translator's
      introduction is lifted from the "Avis des nouveaux
      Editeurs" of the Prévost edition.

1795

1   D'ISRAELI, ISAAC. The Literary Character, Illustrated by the
      History of Men of Genius.
          See 1818.1.

2   FRANÇOIS DE NEUFCHÂTEAU, NICOLAS-LOUIS. <u>Paméla, ou La Vertu</u>
     <u>récompensée, comédie en cinq actes, et en vers,</u>
     <u>représentée, pour la première fois, par les Comédiens</u>
     <u>français, le 1er auguste</u> [<u>sic</u>] <u>1793, et remise au théâtre</u>
     <u>de la rue Feydeau, le 6 thermidor l'an troisième</u> [1795].
     <u>Par le citoyen François de Neufchâteau</u>. Paris: Barba, an
     III, 104 pp. BN.
         The prologue, "Aux Femmes," refers to his imprisonment
     for having written <u>Paméla</u>; this is a sad time for France,
     and humanity is a beastly race, but Heaven has created
     women to sweeten it. The play itself is an adaptation of
     Goldoni in Alexandrines, with touches designed to make it
     attractive to the Revolutionary audience. Bonfil and
     Pamela love each other; he wishes that he or she were in
     another <u>état</u>, but he cannot wed her because of his rank.
     Artur and Bonfil have a spirited debate about class
     intermarriage, the rights of man, and natural law. Sir
     Ernold arrives, a pre-Revolutionary beau and <u>un grand fat</u>.
     Mme Jeffre (=Jervis) is a revolutionary, preaching the
     natural equality of man, and tries to get Pamela married
     off, but Mr. Andrews, coming to get her, reveals that his
     name is Auspingh and gives a gallant defense of
     Latitudinarianism. All truly virtuous people are alike,
     they agree, and the ending is happy. See 1793.3,4.

3   GOETHE, J.W. VON. <u>Wilhelm Meisters Lehrjahre.</u> <u>Ein Roman</u>.
     4v. Berlin: Unger, 1795-96, part 5, ch. 7.
         The hero of a novel ought to be passive, a
     "retardierende Person," allowed pathos rather than tragedy;
     Richardson's Grandison, Clarissa, Clementina and Pamela are
     cited as examples. 1932.7, pp. 230-31, contends that
     <u>Wilhelm Meister</u> in its various versions shows Goethe in
     transition from a Richardsonian to a Fieldingesque (i.e.,
     idealistic to realistic) idea of fiction. The fragment,
     "Die Bekenntnisse einer schönen Seele," is discussed as
     Richardsonian fiction by 1937.3, p. 140, 247-48.

4   ---. <u>Clarissa; or The History of a Young Lady . . .</u>
     <u>Abridged from the Works of Samuel Richardson, esq. . . .</u>
     <u>The first Boston edition, adorned with cuts</u>. Boston:
     Samuel Hall, 142 pp. CtY, NjP, MB, RPJCB, MH.

1796

1   ANON. Algemeene Konst en Letter-bode, part 6 (December 1796),
        141-42.
            New Dutch editions of Clarissa and Sir Charles Grandison
        are announced. "Two moral novels, both of which must be
        viewed as the first and only ones of their kind, are
        continually held in all of Europe to be the greatest of
        masterworks by people of judgment and taste." Source:
        1969.17, p. xxiv.

2   BECKFORD, WILLIAM. [Lady Harriet Marlow.] Modern   Novel
        Writing: or, The Elegant Enthusiast;   and Interesting
        Emotions of Arabella Bloomville. A Rhapsodical Romance .
        . . 2v. London: G.G. and J. Robinson. BM.
            William Beckford's parody of his half-sister Lady
        Hervey's fiction expands to include many of the favorite
        cliches of the period, including Richardson. At 1:120-28,
        the elegant Arabella undergoes the second rape attempt from
        Pamela nearly verbatim; Miss Macnamara, 1: 181-82, seems
        a takeoff on Charlotte Grandison, while the grandson of Sir
        Charles himself makes an appearance on 1:185, disapproving
        of his grandfather. The Elegant Enthusiast implies
        Richardson is old-fashioned, but assumes Beckford's readers
        have read him.

3   RICHARDSON, SAMUEL. Pamela, ili nagrazhdennaja dobrodetel' .
        . . Novyi per. s fr. 4 ch. Smolensk: Sytin. [Pamela,
        or Virtue Rewarded. .   .   .   A new translation from
        French. 4 pts. Smolensk: Sytin.] All-Union State
        Library, Moscow; Bib. Akad. Nauk SSSR.

1797

*1 ---. The Adviser, No. 5 (March 11), No. 11 (May 13).
        Edinburgh.
            Praise for Richardson's ideal characters. Source:
        1948.7.

*2 ---. Encyclopedia Britannica. 1797 edition.
            1926.2 and 1935.8 note the great disparity of space
        given to Richardson (98 lines) and Fielding (37). By the
        ninth edition (1879), however, Fielding had three pages to

Richardson's one.

3   ---. Monthly Review 2d. ser. 22: 283.
      Reviewing The Italian, compares Richardson's,
      Fielding's, and Burney's works to the new Gothic fiction
      and finds the former better.

3A   DARWIN, ERASMUS. Plan for the Conduct of Female Education .
      . . Derby: J. Drewry . . . for J. Johnson, London,
      p. 36.
      Richardson's novels are too voluminous and full of
      objectionable passages to be useful for schools.

3B   GODWIN, WILLIAM. "Of Choice in Reading." The Enquirer.
      London: G.G. and J. Robinson, pp. 134-35.
      "It would not perhaps be adventurous to affirm that more
      readers have wished to resemble Lovelace, than . . .
      Grandison."

4   HERDER, JOHANN GOTTFRIED VON. Briefe zu Beförderung der
      Humanität. In Werke. Edited by Bernhard Suphan. Berlin:
      Weidmannische Buchhandlung, 1883 ff., 18; 208.
      English writers are hardly received so well in England
      itself as in Germany; "Richardsons drei Romane haben in
      Deutschland ihre goldne Zeit erlebt . . ." Earlier, in
      1796 (18:109), Herder says that Richardson and Fielding
      made "epochs" in their time in Germany, and in a letter of
      1795 (17:400) he feels that a taste for Richardson's
      "herrschende Werke" is a sign of piety and trueness of
      heart--now becoming old-fashioned, as is Richardson.

5   MOORE, JOHN. "The Commencement and Progress of Romance."
      Preface to The Works of . . . Smollett. London: B.
      Law [etc.], 1:lxxxvii-lxxxix. BM.
      Both Fielding and Richardson are followers of Cervantes,
      advocates of human realism rather than of the idealism of
      earlier romances. Richardson "introduced a new species of
      romance, in which the persons concerned are supposed to be
      the relators of what passes; and the sentiments are
      expressed as they arise on the first impression, and while
      the relator is still ignorant of the events that are to
      follow." The advantage of this is variety of style, in
      which Richardson surpasses Rousseau; its disadvantages,
      repetition and length. Grandison is too formal,
      Richardson's heroines sometimes too prudish, "but he
      describes the operations of the passions with a truth and
      minuteness that evinces a great knowledge of human nature."

Clementina´s   madness   and   Clarissa´s   distress   are
masterfully done. "He was conscious [however] that his
strength lay in the pathetic, and by this perhaps he was
led to prolong scenes of sorrow till the spirits of the
reader   are   fatigued,   and   the   luxury   of   sympathy   is
over-powered." Lovelace is striking and animated, genuinely
witty,   inventive,   accomplished,   and if young men waited to
acquire his accomplishments before   imitating   his   rakery,
"the   exhibition of his portrait would do little harm," but
the character has excited fascination   among   women   and   a
spirit of emulation among men.

6   WILBERFORCE, WILLIAM. A Practical View of the Prevailing
     Religious System of Professed Christians, in the Higher and
     Middle Classes in This Country, Contrasted with Real
     Christianity. London: T.   Cadell and W. Davies, pp.
     282, 385n., 429-30, 436-41.
        Attacks sensibility in Sterne and Rousseau--"the persons
     in whom" the qualities of generous emotion and exquisite
     sensibility "most abound, are often far from conducting to
     the peace and comfort of their nearest relations," 282, and
     Wilberforce feels in general that sensibility´s "goodness
     of heart" is a sham;   but Richardson´s characters are
     really influenced by their religion.

                              1798

1   "M."[PSEUD.] Lady´s Monthly Museum . . . 1: 434-37. BM.
        Notes the number of novels that were indebted to the
     "censurable passages which occur in Clarissa, Pamela,
     etc."; in former times, when novels were bought cheaply by
     the manuscript, this practice of copying the bad bits
     "rendered their performances totally improper for the eye
     of   an   innocent   female." But better pay for novelists has
     meant better and more original novels.

2   BENNET, JOHN. Letters to a Young Lady on a Variety of Useful
     and   Interesting   Subjects. 2v.   Boston.   (Originally
     published: Warrington: For the Author, 1789.)
        Richardson is excepted from Bennett´s general dislike of
     novels and romances; to be good, a girl should continually
     study Clarissa, and to be lovely, Harriet Byron.

3   FOSTER, HANNAH WEBSTER. <u>The</u> <u>Boarding</u> <u>School;</u> <u>or,</u> <u>Lessons</u>
      <u>from</u>   <u>a</u>   <u>Preceptress</u>   <u>to</u>   <u>her</u>   <u>Pupils;</u>   <u>Consisting</u>   <u>of</u>
      <u>Information,</u> <u>Instruction,</u> <u>and</u> <u>Advice</u> . . . <u>To</u> <u>which</u> <u>is</u>
      <u>Added,</u> <u>A</u> <u>Collection</u> <u>of</u> <u>Letters,</u> <u>Written</u> <u>by</u> <u>the</u> <u>Pupils,</u> <u>to</u>
      <u>their</u> <u>Instructor,</u> <u>their</u> <u>Friends,</u> <u>and</u> <u>Each</u> <u>Other.</u>   Boston:
      Printed by T. Thomas and E.T. Andrews. Sold by them, by
      C. Bingham, and the other booksellers in Boston . . .
      252 pp. MH.
           1932.3 quotes a reference to Richardson, p. 161; he is
      admired for his "beauties" but distrusted for the effect
      Lovelace might have on the minds of the young. The whole
      book shows the odd connection, in this period, between
      epistolary "fiction" (or, at least, the reading of
      fictional letters) and moral tone, a connection deriving
      largely from Richardson.

4   RICHARDSON, SAMUEL. <u>The</u> <u>History</u> <u>of</u> <u>Miss</u> <u>Clarissa</u> <u>Harlowe,</u>
      <u>Comprehending</u> <u>the</u> <u>Most</u> <u>Important</u> <u>Concerns</u> <u>of</u> <u>Private</u> <u>Life,</u>
      <u>and</u> <u>Shewing</u> <u>Wherein</u> <u>the</u> <u>Arts</u> <u>of</u> <u>a</u> <u>Designing</u> <u>Villain,</u> <u>and</u>
      <u>the</u> <u>Rigour</u> <u>of</u> <u>Parental</u> <u>Authority,</u> <u>Conspired</u> <u>to</u> <u>Complete</u> <u>the</u>
      <u>Ruin</u> <u>of</u> <u>a</u> <u>Virtuous</u> <u>Daughter.</u> <u>Abridged</u> <u>from</u> <u>the</u> <u>Works</u> <u>of</u>
      <u>Samuel</u> <u>Richardson,</u> <u>Esq.</u> . . . Philadelphia: Printed
      for the Booksellers, 117 pp. MB, NN, CtY, MiU-C.

5   --- trans. "E.T.D.T." <u>Historia</u> <u>del</u> <u>Caballero</u> <u>Carlos</u>
      <u>Grandison,</u> <u>escrita</u> <u>en</u> <u>ingles</u> <u>por</u> <u>Samuel</u> <u>Richardson</u> <u>autor</u> <u>de</u>
      <u>la</u> <u>Clara</u> <u>Harlowe</u> <u>y</u> <u>de</u> <u>la</u> <u>Pamela</u> <u>Andrews,</u> <u>y</u> <u>puesta</u> <u>en</u>
      <u>Castellano</u> <u>por</u> <u>E.T.D.T.</u> 6v. Madrid: Josef Lopez. MH,
      CLSU, Bib. nac. de Mexico.
           A translation from Prévost's <u>Nouvelles</u> <u>lettres</u>
      <u>angloises</u>, not directly from English.

                              <u>1799</u>

1   [AUSTEN, JANE?] [Sir Charles Grandison: a drama.] [1799?]
      Published   as   <u>Jane</u>   <u>Austen's</u>   ´<u>Sir</u>   <u>Charles</u>   <u>Grandison</u>.´
      Transcribed and edited by Brian Southam; foreword by L.
      David Cecil. Oxford: Clarendon, 1980 [1981], 150 pp.
           This fragmentary manuscript of a drama based on
      <u>Grandison</u> serves (at least) as one more evidence of
      Austen's long literary involvement with Richardson. She
      appears to have been deeply influenced by Richardson in her
      youth, but her appreciation of his qualities as a writer

                                101

was   early modified by a sense of the unreality of
Richardsonian cliches. We may see both tendencies at work
in early fiction such as Love and Freindship; Lady Susan
shows her skilled in the epistolary model, but rather
impatient with it. Northanger Abbey allows her to parody
the form: Catherine's sister Sarah "neither insisted on
Catherine's writing by every post, nor exacted her promise
of transmitting the character of every new acquaintance,
nor a detail of every interesting conversation that Bath
might produce." As late as Sanditon Sir Edward Denham has
been badly influenced by "all the impassioned, and the most
exceptionable parts of Richardson's [novels];   and such
Authors as have since appeared to tread in Richardson's
steps, so far as Man's determined pursuit of Woman in
defiance of every opposition of feeling and convenience is
concerned .   .   . " (see 1817.3).   Henry   Austen's
Biographical Notice of Austen, J.E. Austen-Leigh's Memoir,
and Austen's own letters (edited by R.W. Chapman. Oxford:
Clarendon, 1932) contain further references to Richardson,
particularly to Grandison.
    Austen's Grandison itself has recently appeared as a
literary artifact to be quarreled over in James Ivory's
film Jane Austen in Manhattan.

*2   BISSET, ROBERT. "History of Literature and Science for the
      Year   1799."   The   Historical, Biographical, Literary,
      Scientific Magazine 1: 55-56.
          Richardson, "instead of portraits and historical
      paintings," drew "fancy pictures," and although "few or
      none" equal him "in that kind of writing, yet it was a much
      easier   imitation" than Fielding's realism.   Source:
      1926.2, p. 265.

*3   BROWN, CHARLES BROCKDEN.   Correspondence with Henrietta G.
      [an abandoned Sentimental novel].
          "I am a disciple of that religion and philosophy of
      which the effects are to be seen in Clarissa. O best of
      men! most eloquent of writers! It is from thy immortal
      production that I have imbibed the love of virtue; of
      moral harmony and beauty. From thee also have I gathered
      critical instruction, and learned to speak and write,"
      Brown rhapsodizes to the spirit of Richardson;   quoted by
      1960.5, p. 44.

4   ---. <u>Ormond; or, The Secret Witness</u>. First published 1799.
     Edited with an introduction, chronology and bibliography by
     Ernest Marchand. American Fiction Series. New York:
     American Book Co., 1937, 333 pp.
         Ormond is a Lovelace, Constantia Dudley his Clarissa,
     though with almost Grandisonian touches. Female
     friendship; penknife scene; attempted rape scene.
     Marchand's introduction to the 1937 edition refers to the
     influence of Richardson over Brown as expressed in the
     epistolary form and the seduction theme; like 1960.5, pp.
     76-78, he finds Richardson's influence "almost omnipresent
     in the early American novel." Brown's <u>Clara Howard</u> and <u>Jane
     Talbot</u> also show the general influence of Richardson.

5   [RICHARDSON, SAMUEL?] "The Contented Porter." <u>Satirical,
     Humorous, and Familiar Pieces</u>. Ed. George Nicholson?
     Ludlow: George Nicholson, pp. 27-28. BM.
         Anecdote about value of work; everything the (highly
     unimaginative) porter wants to do, he can do and also work.
     Attributed to Richardson by the BM Catalogue; although the
     piece is skillful and lively enough, the attribution is
     very questionable.

18XX

1   RICHARDSON, SAMUEL. <u>A letter from Samuel Richardson, esq.,
     formerly a member of the Company of Stationers and given by
     them to the youths bound at their hall</u>. London:
     Stationers' Hall. CtY.
         Reprinted frequently throughout the century as a present
     to all apprentices bound to the Company of Stationers. The
     custom lasted until after 1945. Text is slightly modified
     version of 1733.1, parts 1 and 2.

180X

1   GENERALI, PIETRO. [Pamela nubile.] [Venice? 180-?], 379 pp.
     with music. MB.
         MS of unpublished opera.

1800

*1   ANON. Clarice. Venice.
      Prose drama in three acts. Source: 1935.2, p. 60n24.

*2   ---. Pamela, dramma comico.
      Source: 1928.6.

*2A   ---. "Eulogy on Richardson. An Original Letter" and
      "Objections to Richardson's Clarissa." Monthly Magazine
      3:163-67, 321-23.
          "R.P." gives high praise to Richardson's perfect
      characters;   another   correspondent   argues   that the
      characters are not perfect-- virtue is equated with rank
      and wealth, filial duty is sometimes ignored, and the
      characters suffer from a too-delicate nature. Source:
      Hannaford, items 461 and 462.

3   [HAMILTON, ELIZABETH.] Memoirs of Modern Philosophers. 3v.
      Bath: R.   Crutwell for G.G. and J. Robinson, London.
      BM.
          Written against William Godwin; has a sneering
      reference to Clarissa, a subplot parodying Clarissa, and a
      Clarissa-like death scene.   See 1936.10, p. 122, for
      discussion.

4   HERDER, JOHANN GOTTFRIED. Kalligone. First published 1800.
      Reprinted in Bernard Suphan and Carl Redlich, edd.
      Sämtliche Werke .   .   .   Hildesheim: Georg   Olms
      Verlagsbuchhandlung, 1968, 22:150.
          Refers to emotional effects of Richardson's works;
      "Welche geheimste Kammer des Herzens blieb Richardsons,
      Fieldings,   Sternes,   Friedrich   Richters   Romanen
      verschlossen?"

5   SADE, DONATIEN A.F. DE, comte dit marquis de SADE. "Idée sur
      les romans." Les Crimes de l'Amour, nouvelles héroïques et
      tragiques, précédée d'une Idée sur les romans. 4v. Paris:
      Massé. Volume 1, prefatory material.
          Praises Richardson and Fielding for having opened to us
      the secrets of the human heart, "véritable dédale de la
      nature."

6   SMITH, CHARLOTTE. <u>Letters</u> <u>of</u> <u>a</u> <u>Solitary</u> <u>Wanderer</u>.   3v.
      London: Sampson Low, 1800-01, 1:25-26.
           Richardson's realism is more difficult to write than the
      currently   fashionable   fantastic   tales;   though   his
      minuteness is tedious, his knowledge of the human heart
      endures.

7   STAËL-HOLSTEIN, GERMAINE DE. <u>De</u> <u>la</u> <u>Littérature,</u> <u>considérée</u>
      <u>dans</u> <u>ses</u> <u>rapports</u> <u>avec</u> <u>les</u> <u>institutions</u> <u>sociales.</u> . . .
      2v. Paris: Maradan, 1:284-85.
           Ardent praise of <u>Clarissa</u> and <u>Tom</u> <u>Jones</u>; representative
      of Staël's attitude toward Richardson, for whom
      "l'enlèvement de Clarisse a été le grand événement de [sa]
      jeunesse." (See Lady Blennerhassett, <u>Mme</u> <u>de</u> <u>Staël</u> et son
      <u>temps</u> [Paris: Louis Westhausser, 1890], 1:185.)

8   WORDSWORTH, WILLIAM. <u>Lyrical</u> <u>Ballads</u> <u>with</u> <u>Other</u> <u>Poems</u> . . .
      2d ed. 2v. London: T.N. Longman and O. Rees, 1:xxxi.
           Wordsworth only reluctantly rereads the "distressful
      parts" of <u>Clarissa</u>; it is too painfully passionate.

                              <u>1801</u>

*1   ANON. <u>Memorial</u> <u>Literario</u> part 1 (1801), p. 40.
           Praise of Richardson. "Cervantes puede muy bien ser
      comparado   a Fielding,   y   aun   le   aventaja;   pero   que
      novelista sera comparable con Richardson, el Homero,
      digamoslo asi, de las novelas?" Source: 1935.2, pp.
      59-60n21.

2   BALLANCHE, P.S., <u>fils</u>. <u>Du</u> <u>Sentiment</u> <u>considérée</u> <u>dans</u> <u>ses</u>
      <u>Rapports</u> <u>avec</u> <u>la</u> <u>Littérature</u> <u>et</u> <u>les</u> <u>Arts</u>. Lyon: Ballanche
      et Barette; Paris: Calixte Volland, p. 221.
           Unmixed praise for Richardson's sublimity and purity.

3   RICHARDSON, SAMUEL. <u>Pamela,</u> <u>or</u> <u>Virtue</u> <u>rewarded.</u> <u>In</u> <u>a</u> <u>series</u>
      <u>of</u> <u>letters</u> <u>from</u> <u>a</u> <u>beautiful</u> <u>young</u> <u>damsel</u> <u>to</u> <u>her</u> <u>parents;</u>
      <u>and</u> <u>afterwards</u> <u>in</u> <u>her</u> <u>exalted</u> <u>condition,</u> <u>between</u> <u>her,</u> <u>and</u>
      <u>persons</u> <u>of</u> <u>figure</u> <u>and</u> <u>quality</u> . . . <u>A</u> <u>new</u> <u>edition,</u> <u>the</u>
      <u>14th,</u> <u>with</u> <u>numrous</u> <u>corrections</u> <u>and</u> <u>alterations</u>.   4v.
      London: Printed for J. Johnson [etc.].
           The "genteel" edition, incorporating Richardson's last
      corrections.   See 1967.8, 1977.15, and 1978.4 for further

information on this edition, reprinted most recently by
Penguin (edited by Peter Sabor, with an introduction by
Margaret Doody), 1981.

1802

1   ANON. New England Quarterly, no. 3. Boston: H.   Sprague,
     p. 157.
          Richardson's novels are recommended to a father who is
     perplexed   about   what   to let his daughter read; but "one
     novel in six months is sufficient." Mentioned in 1932.3, p.
     68.

2   FOSCOLO, UGO. Ultime lettere di Iacopo Ortis. Italia: n.p.,
     246 pp.
          Clarissa is mentioned in Letter 45, and certain scenes
     have   similarities   with Richardsonian ones, although the
     similarities   are   not   close.   Marchesi,   Romanzi   et
     romanzieri italiani nel Settecento (Bergamo: 1903), p.
     304,   draws   attention   to   stylistic and   thematic
     similarities.   1911.4, p.   282, comments, "Le Ultime
     lettere   .   .   .   risalgono a [Richardson], sia pure
     attraverso il Werther."

3   STAËL-HOLSTEIN, GERMAINE DE. Delphine.   4v.   Geneva: J.J.
     Paschoud. MH, CtY, ICU, MdBJ.
          Praise for the "English novels": "Les romans qu'on ne
     cessera jamais d'admirer, Clarisse, Clémentine, Tom Jones,
     la Nouvelle Héloïse, Werther, etc., ont pour but de révéler
     ou de retracer une foule de sentiments dont se compose, au
     fond de l'âme, le bonheur ou le malheur de l'existence . .
     . "

1803

1   ANON. Zhizn' Samuela Richardsona, avtora zhizn' Klarissy,
     Grandisona i Pamely, s privosokupleniem pokhval'nogo emu
     slova, sochinennogo g. Diderotom. Per.s fr. Smolensk:
     pri Guberniskom pravleni. [The Life of Samuel Richardson,
     author of the Lives of Clarissa, Grandison, and Pamela,
     with the addition of the eulogy composed by Mr. Diderot.

Translated from French. Smolensk: at the Provincial
Administration.] All-Union State Library, Moscow; Bib.
Akad. Nauk SSSR.

2   BACULARD D´ARNAUD, FRANÇOIS THOMAS. Les Epreuves du
sentiment. In Oeuvres . . . Paris: Laporte, Maradan,
vols. 1-5.
The preface to the Epreuves defines his idea of
sentiment, discusses briefly his debt to Richardson. The
collection itself contains a number of histoires anglaises
dramatizing that debt. Fanni, ou Paméla, histoire anglaise
(1:1-82) reprints his Nancy, ou la nouvelle Paméla (1762;
see Appendix A) under yet another title. Clary, ou La
retour à la vertu récompensée, histoire anglaise (1:139-99)
opens with its heroine reading "la divine Clarisse, ce chef
d´oeuvre de l´immortel Richardson," a trouble she need
hardly take, as she has personally experienced most of it
and much of Pamela. Julie, anecdote historique (1:201-88)
is largely a selection of good and bad deathbeds, as is
Amélie, anecdote anglaise (1:291-391). Comparison of
Amélie with the newspaper article it is based on (in
Courrier de l´Europe 6, No. 11 [July 6, 1779], p. 14)
shows that Arnaud added to the story important plot
elements, including its pervasive necrophilia, apparently
derived from his reading of Clarissa.
See also Arnaud´s Délassements de l´homme sensible, 12v.
Paris: Buisson, 1783-87, for more evidence of his debt to
Richardson.

3   PORTER, JANE. "Preface." Thaddeus of Warsaw. 4v. London:
Printed by A. Strahan for T.N. Longman and O. Rees.
The novels of Richardson are "unequalled"; he writes
"epic poems in prose." Jane Porter´s heroes are idealized
types who perhaps owe something to her liking for
Grandison.

1804

1   JEFFREY, FRANCIS, lord JEFFREY. Review of Richardson´s Life
and Correspondence. Edinburgh Review 5: 23-44. Reprinted
Folcroft, Pa.: Folcroft Press, 1969.
Mrs. Barbauld´s Life is worth more than all the rest of
the publication; he finds the correspondence itself

boring, with compliments, health, and the novels its only
staples.   The review is largely of the novels themselves.
Jeffrey notes Richardson's excellence   at giving us the
whole of his characters' lives, so as to make us intimate
with them.   The "probability" of a mode of writing is not
the issue, since no reader will think of probability in the
midst of an interesting story.   The epistolary style is
adapted   to   favor   characters, sentiments, and feelings at
the expense of story.   Richardson's good people are "too
wise   and   too   formal   ever to appear in the light of
desirable comnpanions," while "his vicious ones   have
charm." His characters' gaiety is girlish and silly and
"the diction throughout heavy, vulgar, and embarrassed,"
but the novels [i.e. Clarissa] are too powerfully tragic
to make us notice their defects; they will be read with
admiration when the Correspondence is forgotten.

2   RICHARDSON, SAMUEL.   The Correspondence of Samuel Richardson .
       . . selected from the original manuscripts, bequeathed by
       him to his family, to which are prefixed a biographical
       account of the author and observations on his writings.
       Edited with an introduction by Anna Laetitia Barbauld. 6v.
       London: R.   Phillips.   Reprinted: 6v. New York: AMS
       Press, 1966.
          A selection from the complete Richardson correspondence,
       including only letters from persons not living in 1804,
       with the exception of those from Susanna Highmore.   Some
       letters, since disappeared, are available only here (see
       E&K's list of letters).   However, the texts are not
       reliable;   as noted by E&K, Poetzsche, Pettit, Carroll and
       others,   Mrs.   Barbauld   rewrote   the   Richardson
       correspondence frequently,   massively,   and   silently.
       Barbauld's "Life of Richardson" prefixed to Volume 1 is one
       of the most comprehensive early appreciations of
       Richardson, and still valuable.   She notes the influence of
       Defoe;   distinguishes three types of fiction (xxi-xxviii);
       compares Fielding with Richardson;   and writes intelligent
       appreciations of the three novels.
          Reviewed by The Anti-Jacobin Review and Magazine 19
       (1804):   167-77;   The Imperial Review 2: 414-30; The
       British Critic 24 (November 1804): 507;   Algemeene Konst
       en Letter-bode Pt. 2, No. 35 (August 17, 1804): 97; and
       Maendelyke Uitreksels Pt. 183 (July 1806):420.   (Source
       for Dutch reviews: 1965.17, p. 30.) The Literary Magazine
       2 (October 1804): 523-33, gives a highly favorable review;

the reviewer has been tentatively identified as Charles
Brockden Brown. (See Ernest Marchand, "The Literary
Opinions of Charles Brockden Brown," SP 31 [1934]: 554.)
Richard Lovell Edgeworth writes to Barbauld, Sept. 4,
1804, that he and eight other readers are devouring
Richardson's Correspondence; they "love the man as much as
we admire the author" but are pleased with the censure of
Richardson's "indecent passages". (A.L. Le Breton,
Memoirs of Mrs. Barbauld, London: George Bell and Sons,
1874, pp. 94-96.) It is apparently after reading the
Correspondence that Blake writes to William Hayley, July
16, 1804, that "Richardson has won my heart" and he intends
to read "Clarissa, etc." over again. But Robert Southey
reacts differently; writing on November 27, 1804, he fumes
that "Richardson's correspondence I should think worse than
anything of any celebrity that ever was published, if the
life prefixed did not happen to be quite as bad."
(Selections from the Letters of Robert Southey, ed. J.W.
Warter, London: Longman, Brown, Green, and Longmans, 1856,
1: 289.) Jeffrey's review appears above.

3   RICHARDSON, SAMUEL. Letter to Thomas Verren Richardson.
     Imperial Review 2: 609-16.
         First publication of letter to Richardson's nephew,
     written probably during the summer of 1732, which was the
     basis of the Apprentice's Vade Mecum. Thomas Verren
     Richardson was apprenticed to Samuel Richardson on August
     1, 1732, and died November 8 of the same year.

*4   ---. Historia da virtuosa feliz Clara Harlowe. Lisbon: tip.
     Rollandiana, 1804-18. Bib. Nac. de Lisboa.
         Multivolume; translated into Portuguese from the French
     translation of Le Tourneur. Source: Catalog of the Bib.
     Nac. de Lisboa.

                              1805

*1   ANON. Memorial Literario, Part 2 (1805): p. 166.
         Praise of Richardson. Source: 1935.2, p. 60.

2   COLERIDGE, SAMUEL TAYLOR. Notebook entry of 1805. Published
     in Anima Poetae from the unpublished note-books of Samuel
     Taylor Coleridge. Ed. Ernest Hartley Coleridge. London:

William Heinemann, 1895, pp. 166-67.
    It costs him some exertion not to be "vexed that I must
admire, aye, greatly admire Richardson. His mind is so
very vile a mind, so oozy, hypocritical, praise-mad . . .
." Richardson did not know the difference between
observation and meditation.

*3   [DRUZHININ, A.V.] Klarissa: Roman. Izlozhenie Druzhinina. V
      kn.: Druzhinin Sobranie Sochinen ii, t.v, SPb., 1805.
      [Clarissa: A Novel. An Account by (A.V.) Druzhinin.   In
      Collected Works of Druzhinin, Vol. 5. St. Petersburg.]
          Source: Catalog of the All-Union State Library, Moscow.

4   RICHARDSON, SAMUEL. Pamela, Clarissa en Grandison.   Verkort.
      Verbeterde uitgave.   Amsterdam: J.   Ten Brink, 473 pp.
      Koninklikje Bib.
          "Improved" Dutch translation of The Paths of Virtue
      Delineated. RNB, item 13.

*5   SANDERSON, THOMAS. "On Novels." In Life and Literary Remains
      of Thomas Sanderson. Ed. Rev. J. Lowthian. Carlisle:
      1829.
          Sanderson believes that "none except Shakespeare has
      displayed such a profound knowledge of human nature" and
      praises Richardson´s minute delineation of human motive.
      Source: 1926.2, p.   271, which suggests the footnote added
      by Lowthian twenty-four years later is an index of
      Richardson´s fall from favor: "Some persons will smile at
      the praise bestowed upon Richardson."

1806

1   CUISIN, PIERRE. Le Bâtard de Lovelace et la Fille naturelle
      de la Marquise de Merteuil, ou les Moeurs vengées. 4v.
      Paris: Martinet. BN.
          The villain-hero declaims, "LOVELACE! . . . mon
      illustre père moral" and "veu[t] venger sa [Lovelace´s]
      mort sur tout le sexe" of Clarissas (2: 57; 1: 43).
      Symphonic epistolary form; Richardsonian plot elements
      taken to a sort of surreal extremity (five simultaneous
      drugged rapes;   bizarre variants on claustration).
      Interest in Richardsonian stylistic elements; Cuisin´s
      Lovelace discourses on "writing to the moment," the letter

as an expression of the passions, and the importance of an
individual style. Cuisin's later <u>Clémentine, orpheline et
androgyne</u> (1820) has nothing to do with Richardson.

1807

1   PENNINGTON, REV. MONTAGU. <u>Memoirs</u> <u>of</u> <u>the</u> <u>Life</u> <u>of</u> <u>Mrs.</u>
    <u>Elizabeth</u> <u>Carter</u>. London: F.C. and J. Rivington, pp.
    69-70.
        Richardson's letter to Elizabeth Carter of Dec.   18,
    1747, apologizing for inserting the "Ode to Wisdom" into
    <u>Clarissa</u>, reprinted with commentary.

2   PIOZZI, HESTER THRALE.   Marginalia;   comments on Beattie's
    criticism of Richardson.
        See 1759.2.

*3 RICHARDSON, SAMUEL. <u>Pamela</u> <u>Andrews, ou a virtude recompensada</u>
    <u>escrita</u> <u>em inglês</u> . . . Lisboa: Of. de João Rodrigues
    Neves. Bib. Nac. de Lisboa.
        Source: Catalog of the Bib. Nac. de Lisboa.

1808

1   BARBAULD, A.L. <u>La</u> <u>Vie</u> <u>de</u> <u>Samuel</u> <u>Richardson</u> <u>avec</u> <u>l'examen</u>
    <u>critique</u> <u>de</u> <u>ses</u> <u>ouvrages.</u> <u>Translated</u> <u>by</u> <u>J.J.</u> <u>Leuliette</u>.
    . . . Paris: Dentu, 230 pp. BZK; Saltykov-Shchedrin.
        French translation of Mrs.   Barbauld's prefatory
    material to the <u>Correspondence</u>.

2   CARTER, ELIZABETH, and CATHERINE TALBOT. <u>A</u> <u>Series</u> <u>of</u> <u>Letters</u>
    <u>between</u> <u>Mrs.</u> <u>Elizabeth</u> <u>Carter</u> <u>and</u> <u>Miss</u> <u>Catherine</u> <u>Talbot</u> .
    . . Ed. by the Rev. Montagu Pennington. 2v. London:
    F.C. and J. Rivington.
        Extensive personal and literary commentary on Richardson
    dated from 1742-1761.

3   COLERIDGE, SAMUEL TAYLOR. <u>Lectures</u> <u>on</u> <u>Shakespeare, 1808</u>. In
    <u>Complete</u> <u>Works</u>. Ed. W.G. Shedd. New York: Harper &
    Brothers, 1853, 4:226.
        "Richardson evinces an exquisite perception of minute

feeling, but there is a want of harmony, a vulgarity in his sentiment; he is _only_ interesting." His novels are immoral; "the lower passions of our nature are kept through seven or eight volumes in a hot-bed of interest." Fielding is less pernicious; in him laughter drives away sensuality.

4   LAMB, CHARLES. "Characters of Dramatic Writers, Contemporary with Shakespeare." In _The Works of Charles and Mary Lamb_. Ed. E.V. Lucas. 7v. London: Methuen and Co., 1903-05, 1:43.
      " . . . The precise, strait-laced Richardson has strengthened Vice, from the mouth of Lovelace, with entangling sophistries and abstruse pleas against her adversary Virtue, which Smedley, Villiers, and Rochester, wanted depth of libertinism enough to have invented."

5   MANGIN, EDWARD. _Essay on Light Reading_. London: James Carpenter, pp. 112-17.
      Although most novels "will eventually be found only in the cabinets of the most curious and reprobate," Richardson's novels are fine, ethical, clearly written, and inspirational, if a little old-fashioned.

6   MORE, HANNAH. _Coelebs in Search of a Wife. Comprehending Observations on Domestic Habits and Manners, Religion and Morals_. 2v. London: 1808, 2: 210-11.
      Praise of Richardson for his just view of human nature, his realism, and his psychological perspicacity. He has given us "exemplifications of elegantly cultivated minds combined with the sober virtues of domestic economy" in his heroines; he shows the triumph of religion and reason over the passions. (Quoted from 3d ed. 2v. London: T. Cadell and W. Davies, 1809, 2: 165-66.)

*7   RICHARDSON, SAMUEL. _Pamela, Clarissa en Grandison. Verkort. Met platen_. Amsterdam: J. Ten Brink, 473 pp. Koninklijke Bib.
      Source: _RNB_, item 14; Catalog of the Koninklijke Bibliothek.

8   ---. "A series of original letters of the late Mr. Richardson to Miss Wescomb." In _European Magazine_ 53: 370-72, 429; 54: 10-13, 94-98, 190-92.
      Letters 1746/7-1755; almost exclusively personal.

1809

1   SMITH, JAMES. Review of A New System of Domestic Cookery.
     The London Review 1: 31.
         The coauthor of Rejected Addresses puts Fielding
     decidedly above Richardson.

2   [SMITH, SYDNEY.] Review of Coelebs in Search of a Wife.
     Edinburgh Review 14: 146.
         "Sir Charles Grandison is less agreeable than Tom Jones;
     but it is more agreeable than Sherlock and Tillotson; and
     teaches religion and morality to those who would not seek
     it in [them]."

3   STOCKDALE, PERCIVAL. Memoirs of the Life and Writings of
     Percival Stockdale. 2v. London: Longman, Hurst, Rees,
     and Orme, 1:93-98.
         In Stockdale's boyhood Richardson was read as he
     deserved, but now his works are "buried" and "despised".

1810

1   BARBAULD, ANNA LAETITIA. "Richardson." In The British
     Novelists. 50v. London: F.C. and J. Rivington,
     1:i-xlvi.
         Material reworked from her introduction to the
     Correspondence.

*2   GREEN, THOMAS. Extracts from the Diary of a Lover of
     Literature. Ipswich. P. 77.
         Prefers Grandison, which portrays the "lesser manners"
     that form civilized life, to Clarissa, which deals with
     "the higher morals, engrafted on the fiercer passions."
     Source: Hannaford, item 435.

*3   GRIFFIN, RICHARD. Specimens of the Novelists and Romancers.
     First printed London 1810. Republished New York: 1831,
     2:43-44.
         Indicates how Pamela affected humble people in the late
     eighteenth century. Source: Hannaford, item 436.

4   SCHEDONI, PIETRO. <u>Delle</u> <u>Influenze</u> <u>morale</u>:   <u>opera</u> <u>di</u> <u>Pietro</u>
      <u>Schedoni</u>. Modena: Societa Tipografica 1: 305n.
           Richardson´s works would be perfect if it were not for
      the too-free and vicious language of Lovelace, which cannot
      be restrained by the language of virtue. However, he feels
      that Richardson is, with Fénelon, the only guide capable of
      getting him through the moral dangers of <u>romanzi</u>. Cf. his
      remarks   on Goldoni´s <u>Pamela</u> and <u>Pamela</u> <u>maritata</u>, 1:
      221-24.

5   [SCOTT, SIR WALTER.] Review of <u>Fatal</u> <u>Revenge,</u> <u>or</u> <u>The</u> <u>Family</u> <u>of</u>
      <u>Montorio</u>. <u>Quarterly</u> <u>Review</u> 3: 340.
           "The elegant and fascinating productions . . .[of]
      Richardson, Mackenzie, and Burney . . . of which it was
      the object to exalt virtue and degrade vice; to which no
      fault could be objected unless that they unfitted here and
      there a romantic mind for the common intercourse of life,
      while they refined perhaps a thousand whose faculties could
      better bear the fair ideal which they presented--these have
      entirely vanished from the shelves of the circulating
      library."

                              <u>1811</u>

1   BRUNTON, MARY.   <u>Self-Control</u>. <u>A</u> <u>Novel</u>.   2d   ed.   3v.
      Edinburgh: George   Ramsay   for   Manners   and   Miller,
      Edinburgh; Longman, Hurst, Rees, Orme and Brown, London.
           Non-epistolary but has Richardsonian plot elements: an
      upper-class seducer and a lower-class woman, who faints
      when propositioned;   the obligatory kidnap, by another
      seducer;   a Grandison character with a Charlotte-like
      sister. <u>Grandison</u> criticized for "formality," 1:   135.
      Her <u>Discipline</u> contains less obvious Richardsonian
      elements, and she refers to Richardson favorably in her
      letters (excerpts from which are collected with her
      <u>Emmeline</u>, 1819).

2   GOETHE, J.W. von. <u>Aus</u> <u>meinem</u> <u>Leben</u>: <u>Dichtung</u> <u>und</u> <u>Wahrheit</u>.
      6v. Stuttgart, Tübingen: Cotta, 1811-22.
           Notes Richardson´s influence on the refinement and
      codifying of middle-class morals and in the criticism of
      the morals of the upper classes (3:   295 ff.).   "Only
      Richardson´s endless details" would give an idea of his

sister Cornelia´s character (2: 31). 1937.3 comments extensively, pp. 81-83.

3   RICHARDSON, SAMUEL. The Works of Samuel Richardson. With a sketch of his life and writings, by the Rev. Edward Mangin . . . 19 v. London: J. Carpenter and W. Miller. Vols. 1-4, Pamela; 5-12, Clarissa; 13-19, Grandison.

*4 WEST, JANE. Letters to a Young Lady. London. 2:453-54.
    "Praises Clarissa and Grandison for moral excellence, pathetic and descriptive power, and devout and pious sentiment." Source: Hannaford, item 518.

1812

1   NICHOLS, JOHN. Literary Anecdotes of the Eighteenth Century .
    . . 7 v. London: Printed for the Author . . ., 1812-13.
    7: 351 indexes considerable material on Richardson, most of which is familiar from other sources; it is divided between biographical material and judgments by his contemporaries. In Nichols´ supplementary Vol 8 (London: Printed for the Author, 1814, pp. 506-7), there is material on Anne Richardson´s death-date and epitaph. There is no indexed material on Richardson in Vol. 9.

2   RICHARDSON, SAMUEL, and CARTER, ELIZABETH. "Original Letters of Miss Elizabeth Carter and Mr. Richardson." Monthly Magazine 35: 533-543.
    Letters 1747-1753, largely personal gossip, material relating to the printing of the "Ode to Wisdom," and some reaction to Clarissa; Elizabeth Carter praises the ending (Dec. 16, 1748) and Richardson replies the next day that he has had difficulty getting readers to accept it.

1813

*1 ANON. "Clarisse Harlowe, aan hare Moeder, bij hare Doodkist zittenden." Almanak voor het Verstand en Hart voor ´t jaar 1814. Amsterdam: 1814 [1813], pp. 97-103.
    Source: RNB, item 27.

2   AIKIN, JOHN. <u>General Biography</u>. London: John Stockdale; Longman, Hurst, Rees, Orme, and Brown . . ., 8: 539-41.

      Critical and biographical article on Richardson. In his work "the sense of tediousness is lost in sympathic emotion" (540). Although <u>Clarissa</u> is now considered the greater work, Aikin considers <u>Grandison</u> a book of "more compass, invention, and entertainment; and the part of Clementina has, perhaps, no equal in delicate delineation." His style is low, however.

3   COLERIDGE, SAMUEL TAYLOR. "Lecture 1." <u>Lectures on Shakespeare, 1813-14</u>. in <u>Coleridge's Shakespeare Criticism</u>. London: Bohn's Library, 1904, pp. 465-66.

      Fielding's genius was limited to observation; Richardson was better at "depicting that species of character which no observation could touch."

4   RICHARDSON, SAMUEL, and YOUNG, EDWARD. "One Hundred and Forty-Eight Original Letters between Dr. Edward Young and Mr. Richardson." <u>Monthly Magazine</u> 36 (July-Dec. 1813): 418-23; 37 (Jan.-June 1814): 138-42, 326-30; 38 (July-Dec. 1814): 429-34; 39 (Jan.-June 1816): 230-33; 40 (July-Dec. 1815):134-37; 41 (Jan.-June 1816): 230-33; 42 (July-Dec. 1816): 39-41, 331-35; 43 (Jan.-June 1817): 327-329; 44 (July-Dec. 1817): 327-30; 45 (Jan.-June 1818): 43-45; 46 (July-Dec. 1818): 238-39; 47 (Jan.-June 1819): 134-37.

      Extensive and valuable commentary on <u>Clarissa</u>, <u>Grandison</u>, the <u>Conjectures</u> (for Richardson's role, see letters CVIII, CXI), and Richardson's moral and literary goals.

<u>1814</u>

1   DUNLOP, JOHN COLIN. <u>The History of Fiction: being an account of the most celebrated prose works of fiction</u>. London: Longman, Brown, Green and Longmans, 3: 372-76.

      Richardson must be placed at the head of the class of writers of serious English novels. His object is "to show the superiority of virtue"; his chief merit "consists in the delineation of character." But Lovelace "seems

incompatible with human nature" and Grandison is a
faultless monster. <u>Clarissa</u>, and its heroine, are his
masterpieces; <u>Pamela</u> is an apprentice-work in comparison
with the other two novels. In the third edition of 1845
(London: Longman, etc., p. 411) the criticism of
<u>Grandison</u> is amplified by the inclusion of Warton's
comments on Clementina.

1815

*1   ANON. Review. <u>Edinburgh</u> <u>Review</u> 25:485.
      Notices decline of Richardson's reputation in England.
Translations of his work have removed blemishes in diction
but also his distinctive style and portrayal of English
manners. Source: Hannaford, item 421.

1   GERSTENBERG, HEINRICH WILHELM von. "Clarissa." <u>Vermischte</u>
      <u>Schriften, von ihm selbst gesammelt</u> . . . Altona: J.F.
      Hammerich, 1815-16. 2 (1815): 255-58.
      Ecstatic ode on Clarissa's death and journey to Heaven.
See 1916.1.

2   HAZLITT, WILLIAM. Review of Fanny Burney's <u>The</u> <u>Wanderer</u>.
      <u>Edinburgh</u> <u>Review</u> 24: 326 ff.
      Much on Richardson; revised for his lecture on the
English Comic Writers (1819.2).

3   RÉMUSAT, CLAIRE E.J.G de VERGENNES, comtesse de. Letter of
      June 10, 1815, to Mme de Nansouty. <u>Correspondance</u> <u>de</u> <u>M.</u>
      <u>de</u> <u>Rémusat</u>, edited by Paul de Rémusat. Paris:
      Calmann-Lévy, 1883 ff., 1: 70-71.
      She makes time for the daily reading of <u>Clarissa</u>.

4   WRAXALL, SIR NATHANIEL. <u>Memoirs</u> . . . First published
      1815. Edited by Henry B. Wheatley. London: Bickers and
      Son, 1884, 1: 37-38.
      Fielding, though greatly eminent in novel-writing, will
never be known outside his own country; Clarissa and
Clementina will go everywhere, because Richardson gave us
the kernel of life, Fielding only the husk of manners. [In
part he is quoting Johnson; see 1897.1, 1: 282.]

<u>1816</u>

1   HIGHMORE, JOSEPH. <u>GM</u> 86:577-78.
         Two letters of Joseph Highmore, dated July 1 and July
     18, 1761, describe Richardson's apoplectic attack and a
     visit with the widowed Mrs. Richardson.

<u>1817</u>

1   EDGEWORTH, MARIA. <u>Ormond.</u> First published *1817. In <u>Works</u>.
     London: Baldwin and Cradock, 1832-33, 18: 89-91.
         Henry Ormond, who has been encouraged to vice by reading
     <u>Tom Jones</u>, is reformed by reading <u>Sir Charles Grandison</u>.
     Though he at first finds the characters stiff, he soon is
     impressed by their superiority to those in <u>Tom Jones</u> and
     finds Sir Charles more worthy of emulation.

<u>1818</u>

1   D'ISRAELI, ISAAC. <u>Literary Character, Illustrated by the</u>
     <u>History of Men of Genius</u>. 2nd ed. London: John Murray,
     p. 169.
         "A Homer and a Richardson, like Nature, open a volume
     large as life itself--embracing a circuit of human
     existence!" Draws attention to the circumstantiality of
     Richardson's realism.

*2   RICHARDSON, SAMUEL. <u>Hanes Pamela; neu, Ddiweisdeb wedi ei</u>
     <u>wobrywo</u> . . . Caerfyrddin. ICN.
         <u>Pamela</u> in Welsh.

<u>1819</u>

*1   BOWLES, WILLIAM LISLE. "An Answer to some Observations of
     Thomas Campbell . . . " In <u>The Invariable Principles of</u>
     <u>Poetry</u>. Bath: Richard Cruttwell.
         <u>Clarissa</u> is praised for truth to nature and for pathos;
     Richardson's art is based upon the passions. Source:
     Hannaford, item 397.

1A   HAZLITT, WILLIAM. <u>Lectures on the English Comic Writers</u>.
     London: Taylor and Hessey, pp. 233-39.

Praises Richardson´s intense intellectual consciousness
of his characters, their implications and
effects--"laboured, and yet completely effectual" (238-39).
Though Fielding had a better idea of the practical results
of human nature in action, Richardson was better able to
"speculat[e] upon [its] possible results, and combin[e it]
in certain ideal forms of passion and imagination, which
was [his] real value." Hazlitt likes Richardson´s exactness
of detail, his "high finishing from imagination . . .
There is an artificial reality about his works, which is no
where else to be met with." (233) Hazlitt does not find his
works overlong; "we listen with the same attention as we
should to the particulars of a confidential communication."
(243) Praise of Richardson´s originality and his pathos,
pp. 222-23.

2   MARMONTEL, JEAN-FRANCOIS, abbé. "Essai sur les Romans
considérés du côté moral." <u>Oeuvres complètes</u> . Paris:
Verdière, 1819, 10:287÷361.
Richardson is treated specifically on pp. 327; 337÷46.
Marmontel finds his <u>Clarissa</u> and <u>Grandison</u>, with <u>Télémaque</u>,
almost the only exceptions to the general viciousness of
novels and also compares his work to Prévost´s, finding the
greatest possible similarity between the two, though
wondering at the vagaries of Prévost´s translations.
Defends <u>Clarissa</u> against the charge of slowness; "cette
lenteur est celle d´un orage qui grossit insensiblement et
qui gronde avant d´éclater . . ." (339). Does not find
Grandison too good, except for the envious and vain; the
character is not in the least romanesque. Quotes liberally
from his <u>Mercure de France</u> article of August 1758 (q.v.),
praising Richardson´s capacity for dramatization ("on ne
lit pas, on voit ce qu´il raconte") and suggesting that
Richardson´s suspense depends upon our impatience with the
form: "on jette la lettre, mais on la reprend, et il
attache, quoiqu´il impatiente; ou plutôt il n´impatiente
que par la raison qu´il attache: car rien n´est plus
inquiétant qu´une action intéressante qui ne court point au
dénouement." (343) Defines the <u>roman anglais</u> with reference
to <u>Grandison</u>.

3   RICHARDSON, SAMUEL, and SMOLLETT, TOBIAS G. "Letters between
Smollett and Richardson." <u>Monthly Magazine</u> 48 (July-Dec.):
326-28;
Mostly concerns the <u>History of England</u> and the <u>Universal

<u>History</u>; letters date from 1756-60.

1820

*1   ANON. "Het Landmeisje." <u>Almanak</u> <u>aan</u> <u>Bevalligheid</u> <u>en</u> <u>Deugd</u>
      <u>gewijd</u>. Amsterdam. Pp. 79 ff.

2   COLERIDGE, SAMUEL TAYLOR. Letter of April 8, 1820. <u>Collected</u>
      <u>Letters</u> <u>of</u> <u>Samuel</u> <u>Taylor</u> <u>Coleridge</u>. Edited by E.L.
      Griggs. Oxford: Clarendon Press, 1956 ff., 5: 34.
          Coleridge reports Wordsworth's contempt for Scott, and
      goes on, "My criticism was <u>confined</u> to the <u>one</u> point of the
      higher degree of intellectual Activity implied in the
      reading and admiration of Fielding, Richardson & Sterne--in
      moral, or if that be too high and inwardly a word, in
      <u>mannerly</u> manliness of Taste the present age and it's [<u>sic</u>]
      writers have the decided advantage." However, nothing Scott
      has done in character painting approaches Lovelace or "Miss
      Byron, Emily, Clementina in Sir C. Grandison," or Uncle
      Toby or Parson Adams.
          Cf. 2: 507, where Coleridge cites Richardson, with
      Sterne, Fielding, and Swift, as examples of "the poetry of
      witty logic."

3   GARAT, DOMINIQUE-JOSEPH. <u>Mémoires</u> <u>historiques</u> <u>sur</u> <u>la</u> <u>vie</u> <u>de</u>
      <u>M.</u> <u>Suard,</u> <u>sur</u> <u>ses</u> <u>écrits,</u> <u>et</u> <u>sur</u> <u>le</u> <u>dix-huitième</u> <u>siècle</u>.
      Paris: Armand Belin, 2: 146.
          Sterne's Maria is as powerful as Richardson's Clarissa
      or Clementina in "ouvrant . . . les sources de toutes
      les larmes."

4   HUNT, LEIGH. "The Destruction of the Cenci Family and Tragedy
      on that Subject." <u>The</u> <u>Indicator</u> No. 41 (July 19).
      Reprinted in <u>The</u> <u>Indicator</u>. 2v. London: Joseph
      Appleyard, 1820, 1822.
          With "all its undoubted genius" he would as soon read
      <u>Clarissa</u> again "as see a man run the gauntlet from here to
      Land's End. The pain is too long drawn out, and the
      author's portrait looks too fat and comfortable." See
      1821.2.

5   [TALFOURD, THOMAS NOON.] "British Novels and Romances." <u>New</u>
      <u>Monthly</u> <u>Magazine</u> 13: 206-7.
          <u>Clarissa</u> is "one of the few books which leave us
      different beings." Richardson's works have extraordinary

range: both the sternest professions of virtue and the
freest libertinism, "the most stately idea of paternal
authority, the the most elaborate display of its abuses."
Richardson's wealth of detail allows him to influence us in
any way he wants. Through the vast accumulation of detail
we are convinced that the tendency of his books is moral;
through it Richardson creates another world. Yet, in spite
of our conviction that the books are moral, reading Tom
Jones after them is a relief; one steps from "a palace of
enchantment . . . illumined by a light not quite human
and not quite divine" into the healthful light of day.

5   SCHLEGEL, FRIEDRICH VON. Geschichte der alten und neuen
    Litteratur: Vorlesungen gehalten zu Wien im Jahre 1812.
    2nd rev. ed. 2v. Vienna: Mayer, 2:198-99.
        As the portrayer of contemporary social life Richardson
    perhaps takes the first place; French writers take him for
    a model. But now he is out of date; his striving toward
    ideal characters and the high style was not successful, and
    his verbosity is wearisome. Perhaps his case proves that
    idealization cannot be joined to realism and prose.

                              1821

1   BYRON, GEORGE GORDON, lord. Diary entry for January 4.
    Letters and Journals of Lord Byron. . ., ed. Thomas
    Moore, 3d ed. London: John Murray, 1833, 3: 87-88.
        Prefers Fielding to Richardson, the "vainest and
    luckiest" of authors; notes with delight the newspaper
    account of a murderess whose bacon was wrapped in a leaf of
    Pamela.

2   HUNT, LEIGH. The Indicator No. 69 (Jan. 31). Reprinted in
    The Indicator. 2v. London: Joseph Appleyard, 1820, 1822,
    2: 134.
        Comparison of Clarissa, unfavorably, with Lamb's
    "Rosamund Gray"; accuses Richardson of sadism toward his
    characters. " . . . He writes the most affecting books,
    in a spirit, which to us appears one of the most unfeeling
    imaginable. . . . He wants humanity. He neither knows
    what vice nor what virtue is, properly speaking," and often

makes them change sides; his vicious characters are
sympathetic to others, his virtuous ones to nobody but
themselves. His endless detail of preparation before the
slaughter of innocence robs virtue of all its dignity;
there is a "pedantry and ostentation of virtue" in his
outlook.

1824

1   ANON. Review of Scott's Essays on the Lives and Writings of
     the British Novelists. Blackwood's Edinburgh Magazine 15:
     406-18.
          "Who reads Richardson?" The perfection of a few scenes
     and conceptions is undeniable; but so large "a heap of
     lumber" as Clarissa outweighs "the sublime catastrophe,"
     and the "Shakespearean madness" of Clementina is not worth
     all the cedar-parlors of Grandison. Pamela is both
     unnatural and insufficiently moral.

2   SCOTT, SIR WALTER. "Prefatory Memoir of Richardson." The
     Novels of Samuel Richardson . . . Edinburgh: J.
     Ballantyne & Co. (Border Press); Published by Hurst,
     Robinson and Co., London, 6:i-xlviii.
          Perhaps the single most influential nineteenth-century
     criticism of Richardson. Scott praises Richardson the man,
     the "simplicity" and "truth to nature" of the first part of
     Pamela, and the sublimity of Clarissa. He is almost the
     first critic to prefer Pamela I to Sir Charles Grandison;
     "Clementina is the real heroine of the work." He treats
     Richardson's works as lessons in practical morality--the
     reader is to imitate the actions of Pamela, Clarissa, and
     Sir Charles Grandison--and as such finds them wanting.
     Stylistically, Richardson is "heavier" than Fielding and
     perhaps too labored; but in "deeper scenes of tragedy"
     Richardson is unequalled.

3   SHERIDAN, FRANCES. Memoirs of the Life and Writings of Mrs.
     Frances Sheridan. London: G. and W.B. Whittaker, pp.
     86-88, 197-98.
          Material on Frances Sheridan's professional debt to
     Richardson and on his melancholy.

1   ALLART de MÉRITENS, HORTENSE [PRUDENCE de   SAMAN.]   Les
     Enchantements de Prudence. First published 1872. Paris:
     Calmann Lévy, 1877, p. 85.
         In 1825 Clarissa serves as a touchstone for a   liberated
     Romantic Frenchwoman to judge a lover by. (1924.2, p.   97,
     misconstrues this passage.)

1826

1   HAZLITT, WILLIAM. "On Reading Old Books." Opinions on Books,
     Men, and Things. London: Henry Colburn, 2: 61-84.
         Miscellaneous appreciation of Richardson; the books are
     not too long, could never be too long for him. A footnote
     on p. 78 tells of his admiration for Napoleon, who had
     identified Lovelace as "the hero [sic] of Richardson's
     romance."

1827

1   HAZLITT, WILLIAM. "Why the Heroes of Romance Are Insipid."
     New Monthly Magazine 20:417÷23.
         Sir Charles is "the prince of coxcombs," and B is
     insipid; Lovelace, however, is attractive. "There is a
     regality about him. Pamela delights us, but "is far from a
     regular heroine."

1828

1   BEYLE, HENRI [STENDHAL]. In Courrier anglais.   Edited by
     Henri Martineau.   Paris: Editions du Divan, 1935,
     3:378-79.
         Reviewing Villemain's Lecture 27 (see 1858.2), Stendhal
     says that Richardson's influence on the eighteenth century
     was comparable to the contemporary influence of Scott, but
     no one reads him now; to contemporary Frenchmen nothing
     seems more boring than "les lettres infinies de
     Richardson." He would hardly be remembered if it were not
     for a proverbial expression: "lorsqu'on parle d'un homme
     qui, à force de vouloir paraître parfait, devient aussi

dépourvu de caractère qu'une nature morte, on dit couramment: C'est un Grandisson."

1829

1   BALZAC, HONORÉ de. Letter to the duchesse d'Abrantès [1829]. Correspondance. Paris: Calmann Lévy, 1876, 1:87.
      "Clarisse, dans Richardson, est une fille chez qui la sensibilité est à tout moment étouffée par une force que Richardson a nommé vertu." On p. 409, to Madame Hanska, May 20, 1838, he says that he knows of no book that has painted "l'amour heureux, l'amour satisfait . . . Rousseau y met trop de rhétorique et Richardson trop de prédication." Cf. 1838.1.

1830

1   HAZLITT, WILLIAM, and JAMES NORTHCOTE. Conversations of James Northcote, R.A., by William Hazlitt. London: Henry Colburn and Richard Bentley.
      Conversations 19 and 20 deal extensively with Richardson and Fielding. Clarissa might tempt another author to be lascivious, but Richardson's imagination is never contaminated; "if there had been the least hint of an immoral tendency, the slightest indication of a wish to inflame the passions, it would have been all over with him." Richardson is more admirable than Fielding because of the nature of his characters; the virtues of Fielding's are those of dogs or horses, but Clarissa presents the beauty of an ideal.
      First published in The New Monthly Magazine and The Atlas.

2   MUSSET, PAUL de. Biographie de Alfred de Musset, sa vie et ses oeuvres. 5th ed. Paris: G. Charpentier, 1877, p. 97.
      At the first night of La Nuit vénitienne, December 1, 1830, Musset inserted a quotation from one of Lovelace's letters to Belford into the scene between Laurette and the Prince, expecting the audience to catch the allusion; they didn't, and on the second night he added the words "comme

dit Lovelace" after the quotation. But "le nom de Lovelace provoqua le ricanement de la bêtise et de l´ignorance." (98) Musset´s opinion that Clarissa was "le premier roman du monde" is well-known.

1831

*1   ANON.   Journal des Débats (Sept. 2, 1831).
     Who reads Richardson now? "Qui veut acheter au prix de trente volumes mortellement ennuyeux, la belle folie de Clémentine, les admirables lettres de Lovelace et la catastrophe sublime de Clarisse?" Very few. Richardson pandered too much to the taste of his age, but his charac ter-drawing will always endure.
     Source: 1924.2, p. 97.

2   WILSON, JOHN DOVER [CHRISTOPHER NORTH]. Blackwood´s Edinburgh Magazine 30:533.
     Richardson is too long; even Clarissa "has sunk under the weight of her eight volumes." Cf. his Critical and Miscellaneous Essays (Philadelphia: 1829) 1: 74: "That good old proser Richardson" was "a sort of idiot, who had a strange insight into some parts of human nature, and a tolerable acquaintance with most parts of speech . . ." (Source for this quotation: 1926.2, p. 363).

1832

1   GENT, THOMAS. The Life of Mr. Thomas Gent, Printer, of York. London: Thomas Thorpe, p. 146.
     Refers briefly to jobbing for Richardson during the printing of the Polyglot Dictionary. (Written about 1746.)

1833

1   BEUDIN, J.F., GOUBAUX, P.P., and LEMOINE, G. [M. DINAUX]. Clarisse Harlowe; drame, en cinq actes et en prose, par M.

Dinaux, représentée pour la première fois, à Paris, sur le
Théâtre-Français, le 27 mars
1833. Paris: Barba, 76 pp.
    Very sympathetic to Lovelace; assumes a basic previous
knowledge of the major events of the novel, such as the
fire-scene and the function of Col. Morden. "Rien n´est
plus froid, plus languissant que . . . ce drame,"
commented the Annuaire historique universelle of March 1833
(source for this quote: 1924.2, p. 220).

2   LAMB, CHARLES. Last Essays of Elia. London: Edward   Moxon,
    pp. 52-54.
        Anecdotes about reading Richardson.

3   PUSHKIN, ALEKSANDR SERGEEVICH. Evgenii Onegin´ roman´ v´
    stikhakh´. Sanktpeterburg´: V´ tip. Departamenta nar.
    prosveshchenija. [Eugene Onegin, novel in verse. St.
    Petersburg: Printing Office of the Department of Popular
    Enlightenment.] 8 pts, 1825-32, Part 2, stanzas 30-31.
        Tatiana "would glory/ In Richardson and in Rousseau,"
finding them equally (and, one imagines, similarly)
romantic. Her mother has never actually read Richardson,
but has heard of Lovelace and Grandison from her cultured
Moscow cousin, Princess Aline--and not too accurately; her
lover is that impossible thing, "a Grandison attached to
cards,/A beau, a sergeant in the Guards" (Babette Deutsch´s
translation). One could argue that Eugene Onegin himself
is a remote descendant of Lovelace, through Bednaya Liza,
but the passage argues more strongly that some Russian
intellectuals of the period knew more of some version of
Richardson than does Princess Aline. See for further
discussion Eugene Onegin...translated..., with a
Commentary, by Vladimir Nabokov. 2v. Princeton:
Princeton (Bollingen), 1981, 1:140; 2: 288-291.

4   VIGNY, ALFRED de. Journal d´un poète. First published 1833.
    Edited by Fernand Baldensperger. London: Scholartis
    Press, 1928, pp. 78, 80.
        Clarissa is a work of strategy "worthy of Vauban."
Grandison, a perfect man, cannot be interesting; "only
clockwork moves by principles; men make principles and act
against the very ones they make."

1834

1   COLERIDGE, SAMUEL TAYLOR.   "Table-Talk," July 5.   Complete
    Works.   Ed. W.G. Shedd.   New York: Harper and Brothers,
    1853, 6: 521.
        "To take [Fielding] up after Richardson is like emerging
    from a sick-room heated by stoves into an open lawn on a
    breezy day in May."

2   CRABBE, GEORGE.   "Belinda Waters."   Posthumous Tales.   Poetical
    Works of the Rev. George Crabbe.   Edited by the Rev.
    George Crabbe [jr.].   8v.   London: John Murray, 1834, Vol.
    8, Tale 15.
        Belinda took up Clarissa with enthusiasm, but could not
    grasp its truth, "nor a tale would read/ That could so
    slowly on its way proceed;/ And ere Clarissa reached the
    wicked town,/The weary damsel threw the volume down" in
    favor of more modern fiction.

*3 SHAL´, ---.   "Tom Dzhons" Fil´dinga i "Klarissa Garlov"
    Richardsona.   Sin otechestva, M., 1834, t. XIV, s.
    283-97.   [Shawl, ---.   "Tom Jones" by Fielding and
    "Clarissa Harlowe" by Richardson.   Son of the Fatherland
    14: 283-97.] All-Union State Library, Moscow
        Source: Card index of the All-Union Public Library of
    V.I. Lenin.

1835

1   DUDEVANT, AURORE [GEORGE SAND].   André.   Paris: Félix
    Bonnaire, Victor Magen, Publications de la Revue des Deux
    Mondes, p. 19.
        Mentions "la grande et pâle Clarisse" among Andre´s
    favorite reading, which is Romantic and full of "chastes
    créations."

2   MACKINTOSH, Sir JAMES.   Memoirs of the Life of the Right
    Honorable Sir James Mackintosh, ed. Robert James
    Mackintosh.   London: Edward Moxon. 1: 247; 2: 126-35,
    233-34.
        1:247: dated July 18, 1805, on the Correspondence.
    Though it is often rather dull, even Richardson's dullness
    interests Mackintosh; the picture of him it paints is on
    the whole "admirable." Mackintosh disagrees with Barbauld´s
    censure of Pamela; in that book Richardson aimed at no

higher   than   a   practical   morality.   2:   126-35,   Mackintosh
shows himself influenced by sympathy for Richardson in a
discussion   of   Tom   Jones,   with   occasional   references   to
Clarissa.   233-34:   dated   March   27,   1812.   Reading
Grandison,   he   compliments   Richardson   for   "extraordinary
genius for   truth   in painting";   he   finds   Sir   Charles
blameworthy   not   for   improbable   excellence,   but   for
commonplace   moral   sentiments.   Sir   Charles   is   less
improbable a character than Lovelace, whom "no reader would
wish . . . anything but the gallows." Richardson is a
stranger   to   fashionable   life   and   has   no   talent   for   shades
of character; "his genius triumphs in scenes of powerful
passion."

1836

1   CHATEAUBRIAND,   FRANCOIS-RENÉ,   vicomte   de.   Essai   sur   la
     littérature   anglaise   et   considérations   sur   le   génie   des
     hommes,   des   temps,   et   des   révolutions .. . .   2v.   Paris:
     Furne et Charles Gosselin, 1836. Repr. Oeuvres complètes.
     Paris: Pourrat frères, 1837, 34:   282.
         In the 1790's Richardson "dormoit oublié" because of the
     apparent   lowness   of   his   style.   If   he   really   cannot   write
     stylishly, he is dead; but Richardson's style may not be
     low, only specifically bourgeois, and thus may revive.

2   COLERIDGE, SAMUEL TAYLOR. Literary Remains of Samuel Taylor
     Coleridge,   collected   and   ed.   by Henry Nelson Coleridge.
     London: W.   Pickering.   Volume   1   (1836).   Repr.   in
     Complete   Works.   Ed.   W.G.   Shedd.   New York: Harper and
     Brothers, 1853, 4:330.
         "I do loathe the cant which can recommend Pamela and
     Clarissa Harlowe as strictly moral, though they poison the
     imagination of the young with continued doses of tinct.
     lyttae [tincture of madness], while Tom Jones is prohibited
     as loose. . . . There is a cheerful, sunshiny, breezy
     spirit   that   prevails   everywhere   [in Fielding],   strongly
     contrasted with the close, hot, day-dreamy continuity of
     Richardson." A rephrasing of 1834.1.

*3   HEINE,   HEINRICH.   Chapter   10.   Die   Romantische   Schule.
     Hamburg: Hoffmann and Campe.
         Heine groups Sterne, Fielding, and Richardson together

among favorite authors; "Richardson gibt uns die Anatomie der Empfindungen." (I have seen only modern editions.)

4   BEYLE, HENRI [STENDHAL]. <u>Vie</u> <u>de</u> <u>Henry</u> <u>Brulard</u>. Written in 1836. Edited by Henri Martineau. Paris: Garnier frères, 1953, p. 279, 352.

Describes reading <u>Grandison</u> "en fondant en larmes de tendresse" surreptitiously in his childhood (about 1796-99), but by 1836 Richardson is a dead letter for Stendhal and <u>Clarissa</u> has sunk to becoming "le bréviaire des provinciaux." In <u>De</u> <u>l'Amour</u> he comments acerbically that Clarissa died from feminine pride (Paris: Editions de Cluny, 1938, p. 103).

1837

1   STE.-BEUVE, CHARLES AUGUSTIN. "Pensees d'août." Written 1837. In <u>Poésies</u> <u>complètes</u>. Paris: Charpentier et Cie., 1869, p. 352.

Brief impressions of Clarissa and Clementina.

1838

1   BALZAC, HONORÉ de. <u>Lettres</u> <u>a</u> <u>l'Etrangère</u> <u>1833-1842</u>. Paris: Calmann-Lévy frères, 1930.

April 1, 1838, p. 471: Balzac has read <u>Pamela</u> and <u>Grandison</u> for the first time each, and has just reread <u>Clarissa</u>. The first two he finds "horriblement ennuyeux et bêtes. Quelle destinée pour Cervantes et Richardson de ne faire qu'une seule oeuvre . . .!" He seems to have studied the author (May 20, 1838); he has read <u>Clarissa</u> at least three times (April 29, 1844). (As he didn't know English, it would have been one of the French <u>Clarissas</u>.) 1924.2, p. 269, cites Edmond Werdel, <u>Portrait</u> <u>intime</u> <u>de</u> <u>Balzac</u> (1859) to the effect that Richardson's example caused Balzac to print his own early works. See also 1843.1.

*2   DOUDAN, XAVIER. <u>Lettres</u> . . . Paris: C. Lévy, 1879. Vol. 1.

Under date June 24, 1838, he asks Richardson's pardon;

having read <u>Clarissa</u> in English, he finds the ending
pathetic, splendid. The translators (i.e. presumably
Prévost) have taken the strangest liberties with the story
and have cut out the saddest parts. Source: 1924.2, p.
97.

1839 NONE

1840

1   ROSCOE, THOMAS. <u>The</u> <u>Works</u> <u>of</u> <u>Henry</u> <u>Fielding</u> . . .   London:
    Henry Washbourne [etc.], 1: xxiii.
       Glories that Fielding´s reputation is rising while
    Richardson´s   "long,   wearisome,   thrice-elaborated
    productions" sleep "undisturbed upon their shelves."

1841

1   DE QUINCEY, THOMAS. <u>Posthumous</u> <u>Works</u> . . . Ed. Alexander
    H. Japp. London: William Heinemann, 1891, 1: 114.
       Criticizes Richardson, who, "though a man of great
    genius," was unbearably obsequious to the "fine gentleman"
    Lovelace. Neither de Quincey nor Japp seems to have read
    Richardson.

2   KÄSTNER, ABRAHAM GOTTHELF. <u>Abraham</u> <u>Gotthelf</u> <u>Kästners</u>
    <u>Gesammelte</u> <u>Poetische</u> <u>und</u> <u>Prosaische</u> <u>Schönwissenschaftliche</u>
    <u>Werke</u>. Berlin: Theod. Christ. Friedr. Enslin. 4:3-5.
       Undated letter in which Kästner, who is supposed to have
    participated in the translations of <u>Pamela</u> and <u>Sir</u> <u>Charles</u>
    <u>Grandison</u> (1932.7, p. 190n1), compares Fielding´s Amelia
    unfavorably, at length, with Pamela. Kästner has read
    <u>Pamela</u> in English, German, and French.

3   MACAULAY, THOMAS BABINGTON. Speech on the Copyright, Feb. 5,
    1841. <u>The</u> <u>Miscellaneous</u> <u>Writings</u> <u>and</u> <u>Speeches</u> <u>of</u> <u>Lord</u>
    <u>Macaulay</u>. London: Longmans, Green, Reader, and Dyer, 1:
    615-16.
       Richardson´s novels are used as a test case against   the

extension of the copyright; had the copyright descended to
his grandson, who thought novel-reading sinful, these great
classics would not have been reprinted. [But see 1753.2.]

4   RUSKIN, JOHN. Journal entry of November 17. The Works of
     John Ruskin. Ed. E.T. Cook and Alexander Wedderburn.
     London: George Allen; New York: Longmans, Green and Co,
     35 (1907): 308.
          He has read the Clementina episodess of Sir Charles
     Grandison. "I never met with anything which affected me so
     powerfully; at present I feel disposed to place this work
     above all other works of fiction I know. It is very, very
     grand; and has, I think, a greater practical effect on me
     for good than anything I ever read in my life." See 1903.7.

1842 NONE

1843

1   BALZAC, HONORÉ de. Paméla Giraud. First performed at the
     Théâtre de la Gaîté, Sept. 26, 1843. In Oeuvres complètes
     de Honoré de Balzac. Edited by Marcel Bouteron and Henri
     Longnon. Paris: Louis Conard, 1929, 34:315-427.
          Louise Pamela Giraud is the virtuous daughter of
     porters, "l'espoir de [leurs] cheveux blancs" and "digne du
     prix de vertu," who is asked to say, falsely, that she has
     "given up her honor" to Jules Rousseau on the night when he
     is suspected of having engaged in a conspiracy. By doing
     so she will save him from trial. After crises of
     conscience she agrees. Jules is so impressed by her virtue
     in sacrificing her honorable name that, although far above
     her in social station, he marries her. Kidnaping and the
     opposition of upper-class relatives add to the
     Richardsonian atmosphere.
          Until the discovery of the original manuscript of Paméla
     Giraud, in Balzac's hand, the rumor persisted that the play
     was not his; it was arranged for the stage by "MM. Bayard
     et Jaime" from a play that had apparently been written
     about five or six years before 1843, and failed so
     completely that it was often thought Balzac had simply lent
     his name to it. Balzac's letter to Mme. Hanska (see

1838.1) suggests that the play is a reaction to his reading
<u>Pamela</u> and tentatively sets its date of composition at
1838.

2   GIRARDIN, SAINT-MARC. "Du Suicide dans le Roman et au
     Théâtre." <u>Revue de Paris</u> 4th ser. 21: 297-330.
         Praises Pamela for her "moral vitality" and expresses
     his admiration for the pond scene, "qui m´a toujours
     beaucoup ému." (314)

*3   GRAY, THOMAS. <u>Correspondence of Thomas Gray and the Rev.</u>
     <u>Norton Nicholls.</u>
         Gray "knew no instance of a story so well told" as
     <u>Clarissa.</u>" He "spoke with the highest commendation of the
     strictly dramatic propriety, and consistency of the
     characters, perfectly preserved, and supported from the
     beginning to the end, in all situations and circumstances,
     in every word, action, and look." He preferred it to <u>Tom</u>
     <u>Jones</u>. Source: 1926.3.

                              1844

*1   ANON. "Standard Novels." <u>Monthly Review</u> 3:533-58.
         Richardson (pp. 538-39) is moral but tedious and was
     supplanted by Fielding and Sterne.

                         1845   NONE

                              1846

1   ANON. <u>La Nouvelle Clarisse Harlowe</u>.
         See under 1846.5.

2   ANON. <u>La Pamela. Cancion nueva</u>. . . . Folded broadside.
     Barcelona: F. Valles, pp. [1]-[2]. BM.
         Virtuous young girl describes common modern vices; no
     connection with original Pamela except that the virtuous
     girl is apparently called generically a "Pamela."

3   BARBA, J.N. <u>Souvenirs</u>. Paris: Ledoyen et Giret, pp. 53-54.
      Discusses with Pigault-Lebrun a proposed abridgment of
      <u>Clarissa</u>, which the latter refuses to do; "j´aimerais
      mieux me couper le bras. . . que de mutiler ce chef
      d´oeuvre."

*4   CHASLES, [VICTOR EUPHÉMIEN] PHILARÈTE. "Fielding et
      Richardson." <u>Le</u> <u>dix-huitième</u> <u>siècle</u> <u>en</u> <u>Angleterre</u>. 2v.
      Paris, 1: [361]-382.
      So listed in table of contents of Volume 2; first
      volume not available.

5   DUMANOIR, P.F.P., L.F.N. CLAIRVILLE, and LEON GUILLARD.
      <u>Clarisse Harlowe. Drame en 3 actes, mêlé de chant, par MM.</u>
      <u>Dumanoir, Clairville et Guillard; représentée pour la</u>
      <u>première fois, à Paris, sur le théâtre du</u>
      <u>Gymnase-Dramatique, le 5 août 1846</u> . . . Paris:
      Michel-Lévy frères, 58 pp. NN.
      Adaptation of Janin´s <u>Clarisse</u>. According to 1924.2,
      pp. 220-21, it ran for over 100 performances, lasting as
      late as July 1847; two imitations (one, <u>La Nouvelle</u>
      <u>Clarisse Harlowe</u>, a parody) ran simultaneously,
      capitalizing on its success. Reviewed in <u>L´Epoque</u>,
      August-September 1846; by Eugène Maron, in the "Revue
      théâtrale" of the <u>Revue indépendante</u>, August 1846; and in
      the <u>Revue et gazette des théâtres</u>, July 15, 1847.

*6   ---. <u>Clara Harlowe</u>. Trans. Wenceslao Ayguals de Izco.
      Madrid: Imprenta de Wenceslao Ayguals de Izco, 35 pp.
      Source: 1935.2, pp. 62-63.

*7   ---. <u>Clara Harlowe. Traducido del frances</u>. Madrid:
      Sociedad Literaria, 35 pp. MWelC
      Source: <u>NUC</u>. Translation apparently by Ayguals de
      Izco.

*8   ---. <u>Clara Harlowe</u>. Trans. Ramon Navarrete y Fernández
      Landa. In <u>Biblioteca Dramatica</u>. Vol. V. Madrid:
      Librería Perez.
      Source: 1935.2, pp. 62-63.

*9   ---. <u>Clara Harlowe. Drama en tres actos, arreglada a la</u>
      <u>escena española por D. Ramon de Navarrete</u>. Madrid: V. de
      Lalama. Bib. Nac. de Argentina.
      Source: Catalog of the Bib. Nac. de Argentina.

10   JANIN, JULES. <u>Clarisse Harlowe, de Samuel Richardson, par M. Jules Janin; précédée d'un essai sur la vie et les ouvrages de l'auteur.</u> 2v. Paris: Amyot.
The title is exact; this is not Richardson's <u>Clarissa</u>, but "de" Richardson and clearly "par" Janin. Janin, influenced by Villemain, finds the only barrier to his appreciation of <u>Clarissa</u> is the excessive presence of the book itself; his task is to rediscover <u>Clarissa</u>, "retrouver <u>Clarisse Harlowe</u> tout entière de ces décombres, tout démolir, mais pour choisir dans ces matériaux épais, les belles parties du monument qui était à refaire . . ." (xxiii-xxiv). To do this, he cuts out all the sermons (though adding some new ones), eliminates the repetitions, partially discards the epistolary format, and rewrites the plot, adding much of his very own. The drugged rape (2:296 ff.) now includes an orgy, at which Clarissa appears raving. Clarissa's last moments are soothed by Anna Howe, who is married to Solmes ("une vengeance que Richardson n'a pas osé indiquer," Janin comments, p. xxxv). Lovelace, not Belford, is present at "Saint-Clair's" deathbed. Patrick Macdonald, whose role is greatly changed, attends Clarissa's funeral and makes an oration. All of Lovelace's friends are at the duel in which he is killed, and his last words are addressed to Belford. Janin prefers the action of the book to its psychology and sees Lovelace as a Byronic hero-villain, borrowing bits from Byron himself, as well as Shakespeare and Milton, to flesh out the conception. (See, e.g., 1:136 ff.) Janin's life of Richardson owes much to his conception of the novelist as a Romantic child of nature, like Shakespeare, and little to biographical facts.
Although Amédée Achard, in <u>L'Epoque</u> (April 13, 1846), approved of the book, <u>L'Univers</u> (July 8, 1846) found it mechanical; Auguste Vacquerie in <u>L'Evénement</u> (October 9, 1848) agreed, since Janin had removed the conclusion, and the <u>Revue et gazette des théâtres</u> (August 9, 1846) called it "treachery." (All from 1924.2, p. 97.) However, it was extremely popular; see below.

11   ---. <u>Clarisse Harlowe, de Samuel Richardson, par M. Jules Janin.</u> Semaine littéraire du Courrier des Etats-Unis, series 13, vol. 3. New York: Courrier des Etats-Unis, 224 pp.
Omits most of the preface.

12   ---. <u>Clarisse</u> <u>Harlowe.</u> <u>Précédée</u> d'un <u>essai</u> <u>sur</u> <u>la</u> <u>vie</u> <u>et</u> <u>les</u>
      <u>ouvrages</u> <u>de</u> <u>l'auteur</u> <u>de</u> <u>Clarisse</u> <u>Harlowe,</u> <u>Samuel</u>
      <u>Richardson.</u> 2v. La Haye: Chez Les Héritiers Doorman.
      Koninklikje Bib.

13   ---. <u>Clarisse</u> <u>Harlowe.</u> 2v. Bruxelles: Meline. BZK, Statni
      knihovna ČSR.

*14   ---. <u>Clarisse</u> <u>Harlowe.</u> <u>Nach</u> <u>dem</u> <u>Plane</u> <u>Jules</u> <u>Janins</u> <u>im</u> <u>Ausg.</u>
      <u>bearb.</u> <u>von</u> <u>H.</u> <u>Bode.</u> 3 Tle. Leipzig: Gerhart.
            Source: Heinsius. A second edition or issue the next
      year.

15   LACY, THOMAS HAILES, and JOHN COURTNEY. <u>Clarissa</u> <u>Harlowe.</u> <u>A</u>
      <u>tragic</u> <u>drama</u> <u>in</u> <u>three</u> <u>acts.</u> <u>Founded</u> <u>on</u> <u>Richardson's</u>
      <u>celebrated</u> <u>novel</u> . . . <u>First</u> <u>performed</u> <u>at</u> <u>the</u> <u>Princess's</u>
      <u>Theatre,</u> <u>London,</u> <u>August</u> <u>28th,</u> <u>1846.</u> London: Lacy's Acting
      Edition of Plays, Vol. 77 [1846?], 46 pp. BM.
            Adapted from Janin, probably unconsciously maximizing
      the pattern of delusion and trickery in his adaptation; in
      the Lacy-Courtney adaptation each act revolves around a
      delusion or trick. The ending is more melodramatic than
      Janin's; psychology is further replaced by action.

*16   RICHARDSON, SAMUEL. <u>Clarisse</u> <u>Harlowe</u> <u>par</u> <u>Richardson.</u> <u>Traduit</u>
      <u>sur</u> <u>l'édition</u> <u>originale</u> <u>par</u> <u>l'abbé</u> <u>Prévost,</u> <u>précédé</u> <u>de</u>
      <u>l'Eloge</u> <u>de</u> <u>Richardson</u> <u>par</u> <u>Diderot.</u> 2v. Paris: Boulé.
      Bib. municipale de Besançon.
            Abridged? Source: Catalog of the Bibliothèque
      municipale de Besançon.

                            <u>1847</u>

1   HUNT, LEIGH. "A Novel Party." <u>Men,</u> <u>Women</u> <u>and</u> <u>Books</u> . . .
      London: Smith, Elder and Co, 1: 96-113.
            Sketches of characters from the three novels; soft and
      friendly criticism of Richardson's morality.

2   SHAW, THOMAS B. <u>Outlines</u> <u>of</u> <u>English</u> <u>Literature.</u> London:
      John Murray, pp. 311-17.
            To Defoe's realism Richardson added characterization.
      His works show "feminine" minuteness, melancholy,
      penetration into character, and purity of morality. His

method is to tell "a natural story of ordinary life"
illuminated by character and dramatized through accretion
of detail. In general, he suffers from lack of contact
with the upper classes, as <u>Grandison</u> in particular shows;
it is slow, unreal, inordinately long, clumsily written.
Richardson is "a great, profound, creative, and . . .
truly original genius . . ." but "no longer very
generally read." (315)

1848

1   AQUILIUS [PSEUD.] "A Few Words about Novels--A Dialogue, in a
Letter to Eusebius." <u>Blackwood's</u> <u>Magazine</u> 64:459-74.
      <u>Pamela</u> is successful as a how-to book for aspiring
chambermaids; <u>Clarissa</u> is disguised as morally suitable
for young people; but both are indecent.

*2   ---. <u>Samuel</u> <u>Richardson</u> <u>i</u> <u>ego</u> <u>epocha</u>. <u>B-ka</u> <u>dlja</u> <u>chtenija</u>,
SPB., 1848, t. XCI, Otd. III, s. 1-24, T. XCII, otd.
III, s. 1-22. [Samuel Richardson and his Epoch. <u>The</u>
<u>Library</u> <u>for</u> <u>Reading</u> (St. Petersburg), Vol. 91, pt. 3:
1-24; 92, 3: 1-22.] All-Union State Library, Moscow.
      Source: Catalog of the All-Union State Library, Moscow.

3   HUNT, LEIGH. <u>The</u> <u>Town</u>. 2v. London: Smith, Elder & Co.,
1:76-77, 117-27.
      A biographical sketch, drawing on Sir John Hawkins and
the <u>Correspondence</u>. The Stationers' Hall portrait is
described on 76-77: a face "as uneasy as can well be
conceived,--flushed and shattered with emotion."

*4   RICHARDSON, SAMUEL. <u>Klarissa</u> <u>ili</u> <u>istorija</u> <u>o</u> <u>junoi</u> <u>barishne,</u>
<u>soderzhashchaja</u> <u>v</u> <u>cebe</u> <u>vazh-</u> <u>neishie</u> <u>dela</u> <u>chastnoi</u> <u>zhizni</u> <u>s</u>
<u>osobennim</u> <u>ukazaniem</u> <u>na</u> <u>bedstvija,</u> <u>mogushchie</u> <u>proizoiti</u> <u>ot</u>
<u>durnogo</u> <u>obraza</u> <u>deistvovanija</u> <u>roditelei</u> <u>i</u> <u>detei</u> <u>v</u> <u>otnoshenii</u>
<u>k</u> <u>braku</u>. B-ka dlja chtenija, SPB., 1848, t. LXXXVII, Otd.
II, s. 137-240. t. LXXXVIII, s. 29-244, t. LXXXIX, s.
1-96. [Clarissa, or The History of a Young Lady,
Containing The Most Important Affairs of Private Life, with
Special Attention to the Distresses which Can Arise from
Evil Modes of Behavior in Parents and Children in Relation
to Marriage. <u>Library</u> <u>for</u> <u>Reading</u>, St. Petersburg, 1848,
Vol. 87, Part 2: 137-240; 88: 29-244; 89: 1-96.]

All-Union State Library, Moscow
　　Source: Catalog of the All-Union State Library, Moscow.

1849 NONE

1850

1　ANON. "Piozziana." <u>GM</u> 96, NS 34:267.
　　Richardson's genius in the Italian scenes in <u>Grandison</u>.

2　BARBEY D'AUREVILLY, JULES. <u>Lettres de J. Barbey d'Aurevilly</u>
　　<u>à Trébutien</u>. Paris: Lecampion, Blaizot, 1908, 1: 181,
　　231.
　　　　P. 181 (letter of May 20, 1850): Quotes "Robert
　　Lovelace, que j'aime mieux que Robert Lindet" as preface to
　　an account of an epistolary intrigue he is carrying on with
　　the Finance Minister in the character of an
　　eighteen-year-old girl. P. 231 (letter of June 6, 1851):
　　discussing his Vellini, defends the right of painting evil
　　characters; "n'y a-t-il plus à peindre, sous peine de
　　mettre tout en péril, que des Grandissons?"

*3　DRUZHININ, A.V. "Gallereja zamechatel'neishikh romanov.
　　Klarissa Garlov Samuela Richardsona." <u>Sovtremennik</u>, Spb.,
　　1850, t. XIX, otd. IV, s. 1-40. [Druzhinin, A.V. "A
　　Gallery of Outstanding Novels: Clarissa Harlowe, by Samuel
　　Richardson." <u>Contemporary</u> (St. Petersburg) Vol. 19, pt.
　　4: 1-40.] All-Union State Library, Moscow
　　　　Source: Catalog of the All-Union State Library, Moscow.

1851

*1　RICHARDSON, SAMUEL. <u>Clarisse Harlowe</u> .　.　. <u>Traduction</u>
　　<u>nouvelle par André de Goy</u>. Les <u>Veillées littéraires</u>
　　<u>illustrées</u> 9. Paris: n.p.. BN .
　　　　Abridged? Source: B.N. Catalog.

1852

1   EVANS, MARY ANN [GEORGE ELIOT]. Letter to Bessie Rayner
     Parkes, Oct. 30. Letters of George Eliot. Ed. Gordon S.
     Haight. 7v. New Haven: Yale University Press, 1954-55,
     1:240; cf. 2:65; 6:320.
         Expresses her favorable opinion of Grandison--"I should
     be sorry to be the heathen that did not like that book";
     prefers Lady G. to Harriet Byron, who is "too proper and
     insipid."

2   MITFORD, MARY RUSSELL.   "Letters of Authors. Samuel
     Richardson." In her Recollections of a Literary Life. 3v.
     London: R. Bentley, 3:41-63.
         Considering its subject, does not wonder that Clarissa
     is no longer read, "but as my friend, Sir Charles
     Grandison, has no other sin to answer for than that of
     being very long, very tedious, very old-fashioned, and a
     prig, I cannot help confessing that . . . I think there
     are worse books printed now-a-days . . . " Richardson's
     great virtue is in making his persons a part of everyday
     life.   Largely extracts from and commentary on the
     Correspondence.

3   POOLEY, CHARLES. "Richardson's 'Choice of Hercules.'" N&Q 1st
     ser. 6:485.
         Pooley, the executor of Richardson's granddaughter's
     will, thinks he owns a poem by Richardson. Hannaford, item
     473, suggests it is by Bishop Lowth.

1853

1   ANON. "The Progress of Fiction as an Art." Westminster Review
     60:355-56.
         Although the manners of Richardson's characters are
     antiquated, they have the feelings and passions of human
     nature in all ages. The coarseness and viciousness of the
     eighteenth century make his picture of life "revolting" to
     the fastidious, and he may have been unwise to unveil
     "scenes of vice which the pure need never witness," but the
     scenes are never made to "pander to the evil passions of
     human nature." The innocent person is as disgusted by them
     as by the reality they represent. Fielding, on the other

hand, is merely gross.

2   DUMANOIR, P.F.P., L.F.N. CLAIRVILLE, and LÉON GUILLARD.
    Clara Harlowe. Drama en tres actos, contremeiado de canto.
    Por M.M. Dumanoir, Clairville e Guillard. Traduisido por
    A. Rego . . . Bibliotheca dramatica. [Maranhão.] 35
    pp. NN.
        Translation of 1846.5.

3   THACKERAY, WILLIAM MAKEPEACE. The English Humourists.
    London: Smith, Elder and Co., pp. 257÷58.
        Richardson was a Cockney "mollycoddle and a milksop" who
    wrote "endless volumes of sentimental twaddle" and whose
    "squeamish stomach" sickened at Fielding's hearty rough
    fare.

4   [YONGE, CHARLOTTE M.] The Heir of Redclyffe. . . . 2v.
    London: John W. Parker.
        To the literary influences that Prof. Robert Lee Wolff
    notes in The Heir of Redclyffe can be added Sir Charles
    Grandison. Sir Charles, who must fight against anger,
    seems an insufferable "piece of self-satisfaction" to the
    hero, Sir Guy Morville, whose own struggle against
    hereditary bad temper and toward Christian perfection is a
    major theme of the book. Two major secondary characters
    are named, but perhaps by coincidence, Charles and
    Charlotte. See Robert Lee Wolff, Gains and Losses (New
    York: Garland, 1977), pp. 127 ff.

1854 NONE

1855

*1   BOULLÉE, Monsieur. Etude sur Clarissa Harlowe. Metz.
     Source: BZK.

*2   ELWIN, REV. WHITWELL. Quarterly Review (December).
     Richardson, with his lengthiness, "tedious trivialities
     and mawkish prose" is seldom read. Source: 1926.2, pp.
     426-27.

<u>1856</u> NONE

<u>1857</u>

1   BAUDELAIRE, CHARLES. "Danse macabre." <u>Les</u> <u>Fleurs</u> <u>du</u> <u>Mal</u>, no.
     97.   Reprinted in <u>Oeuvres</u> <u>complètes</u>. Paris: Bibliothèque
     de la Pléiade, 1961.
          "Antinoüs flétris, dandys à face glabre,/ Cadavres
     vernissés,   lovelaces chénus .   .   . ": Baudelaire
     comments on this passage in a letter to Calonne, quoted in
     a note to the lines on p. 1546 of the Pléiade edition.   Is
     "Lovelace" a substantive or a proper noun?   Baudelaire
     decides for the former; "en somme, Lovelace est presque un
     substantif de conversation" in the French of 1857.
          In <u>La</u> <u>Fanfarlo</u> Baudelaire speaks of "la force
     absolutrice de Valmont ou de Lovelace . . . " <u>Oeuvres</u>,
     p. 501.

2   CARLYLE, THOMAS.   "Burns." <u>The</u> <u>Collected</u> <u>Works</u> <u>of</u> <u>Thomas</u>
     <u>Carlyle</u>. London: Chapman and Hall, 2:209.
          In descriptive writing, Defoe and Richardson are hardly
     below the supreme artist, Homer. All three are garrulous,
     detailed, lovingly exact; "Homer's fire bursts through .
     . . but Defoe and Richardson have no fire."

                         <u>1858</u>

1   THACKERAY, WILLIAM MAKEPEACE. <u>The</u> <u>Virginians:</u> <u>A</u> <u>Tale</u> <u>of</u> <u>the</u>
     <u>Last</u> <u>Century</u>. 2v. London: Bradbury and Evans.
          In Chapter 26 Richardson makes a brief appearance--"a
     printer, his name is Richardson, he wrote <u>Clarissa</u> you know
     . . . a good, fat old man." Thackeray treats him more
     kindly than in 1853 and regrets giving his shade the news
     that <u>Clarissa</u> may no longer be read by modest young women.

2   VILLEMAIN, ABEL FRANÇOIS. "Lecture 27." <u>Cours</u> <u>de</u> <u>littérature</u>
     <u>française</u>. Paris: Didier, 2:336-60.
          Richardson was one of the English artists most
     frequently imitated by the French, and with good reason;
     the <u>roman</u> <u>moral</u>, Richardson's forte, is in some sense the
     epic of our time. His influence may be discovered in all

of the dramatic innovations of the novel at that time,
innovations that have so completely proven themselves
since. The art of Richardson is distinguished by ardor,
vivacity, and moral seriousness; though the length of his
works is a difficulty, it takes time to see all of
Richardson´s world. The narrator varies appropriately with
time and situation. His realism and his morality go
together; in his books one sees morality in action.
Villemain discusses principally <u>Clarissa</u>, a great work
because of its variety, its vivacity, its fecundity of
thought; the original English version is much preferable
to the too-French one of Prévost. Richardson´s eloquence
itself comes from realism, as in De la Tour´s final letter:
"Il n´y a pas d´éloquence au delà de ce récit; c´est la
nature retrouvée par la génie du peintre." (360) Janin was
influenced by an early version of this lecture to begin his
study of <u>Clarissa</u>; see 1846.10, pp. vii-viii.

1859

1   MASSON, DAVID. <u>British Novelists and their Styles</u>. Cambridge
     and London: Macmillan and Co., pp. 99-121, 132-36.
         Praise for Richardson´s profundity, originality, and
     intelligence. Though the books are long and not much read
     now, their style is perhaps the most original in English
     fiction. Richardson paints, not the manners of his time,
     but the essential principles of human nature. "His
     peculiar power consists . . . in the subtle imagination
     of progressive states of feeling rather than of changing
     external scenes . . . " (113) and from this comes a
     certain disconnection of his characters from their
     surroundings, an air of unreality. But allow him this, and
     he is remarkable. His style is "plain, full, somewhat
     wordy . . . , not always grammatically perfect; but
     each page is a series of minute touches . . . from a
     thorough conception of the case which he is presenting."
     (115) So completely does he concentrate on the "minute
     representation of feeling in its progress" that the
     characters stand before us, not as types, but rather as
     "names for certain protracted courses of action or
     suffering." (115) Though no longer to be read in family
     gatherings, his works are genuinely moral; even the
     prudential morality of <u>Pamela</u> is good enough for the

character. Their effect lies "in the whole power of the work to stir and instruct the mind . . . The addition which it makes to the total mind, the turn or wrench which it gives to the mind, . . . are the measures of its value even morally." (118) Clarissa is morally magnificent, although Richardson may be accused of a too-exclusive concern with the love-interest, which has harmed the later English novel. Masson compares Richardson to Fielding and Smollett, and prefers him to both. Reviewed by British Quarterly Review 30:443-65.

1860

1   MEREDITH, GEORGE. Evan Harrington: or, He Would Be a Gentleman. Once a Week, Oct. 13, p. 425.

In Chapter 47, an in-joke for readers of Grandison. The Countess de Saldar de Sancorvo (who has recently, and rather summarily, been converted to Catholicism) finds that the Jesuits remind her of Sir Charles Grandison. "The same winning softness! the same irresistible ascendancy over the female mind!" Only a Catholic, she feels, can be a gentleman. Of course, she has missed the point of Grandison's heroism in the Clementina episode. Meredith delighted in Grandison; there are several other references to the book in his works, and Sir Willoughby Patterne, with his many perfections and many women, may descend comically from Grandison. Meredith compares Richardson and Fielding, briefly, in the Essay on Comedy (1877).

2   ROSCOE, WILLIAM CALDWELL. Poems and Essays. London: Chapman and Hall, 2:301.

Pamela is, morally, a worse character than Iago to read: on "the prurient minute details of a seduction" we would not now "tolerate such minuteness for an instant."

3   THACKERAY, W.M.. "Nil Nisi Bonum." Cornhill Magazine 1:129-34. Reprinted in Roundabout Papers. Reprinted from the "Cornhill Magazine." With Illustrations. London: Smith, Elder & Co., 1863 [1862].

Here first appears the often-told story of Macaulay's rhapsodies over Clarissa at Ootacamund; see 1876.2.

1861

1   DELANY, MARY GRANVILLE. The Autobiography and Correspondence
     of Mary Granville, Mrs. Delany. Ed. Lady Llanover.
     Vols. 2 and 3. London: Richard Bentley.
          Richardson is mentioned frequently. Mrs. Delany´s
     reactions to Clarissa are at 2:523,561,603,614; 2:622 has
     a possible mention of Grandison; Mrs. Delany discusses
     Sir Charles Grandison at 3:242-49,251-52,257.

1862

*1   TEN, I. Literatura i iravy Anglii v XVIII stoletii. Vremja,
     SPB., 1862, t. VII, fevr., s. 463-72. [Ten, I. "The
     Literature and Morals of England in the Eighteenth
     Century." Time (St. Petersburg), 7(February):463-72.]
     All-Union State Library, Moscow.
          Source: Catalog of the All-Union State Library, Moscow.

1863

1   TAINE, HIPPOLYTE. Histoire de la littérature anglaise.
     Paris: Librairie de L. Hachette et Cie., 3:280-303.
          Both Fielding´s and Richardson´s works are born of the
     "grand débat de la règle et de la nature" (280). In
     Richardson, psychology and morality go together, "la
     casuistique chrétienne est une sorte d´histoire naturelle
     de l´âme." (281) Thus he has under his hand all the cordes
     humaines and can make them vibrate. His Pamela is fresh
     and sublime; his Clarissa shows the dangers of a
     too-strong will. Her sense of duty is pathetic but
     insufficiently moral; "j´ajoute bien bas, tout bas, que la
     sublime Clarisse est un petit esprit; sa vertu ressemble à
     la piété des dévotes . . . " (298), and her duty is
     simply une consigne. As for Sir Charles, he should be
     canonized and stuffed. Richardson´s small soul cannot
     create great ones in his characters; he cannot recognize
     the element of rebellion in the human soul. Taine attacks
     Richardson´s poetic justice; there is no art in his
     writing, he is a mere "greffier archiviste," fearing his
     genius and trusting only his conscience. "Vous ne savez

pas aimer [la Nature], et votre punition est que   vous   ne
pouvez pas la voir." (303)

<u>1864</u> NONE

<u>1865</u>

1   ANON. "Clarissa" (review). <u>Littell's</u> <u>Living</u> <u>Age</u> 87:92-95.
       Review of the 1864 Tauchnitz edition.

*2   ---. "Richardson." <u>Fraser's</u> <u>Magazine</u> 71:83-96. Also in
       <u>Littell's</u> <u>Living</u> <u>Age</u> 84:215-16.
          Summarizes   novels   and   notes   Richardson's
       characterization of Sir Charles and Clarissa, his morality,
       and his portrayal of manners; he deserves to be read more
       than he is. Source: Hannaford, item 427.

*3   KNIGHT, CHARLES. "Samuel Richardson." In his <u>Shadows</u> <u>of</u> <u>the</u>
       <u>Old</u> <u>Booksellers</u>. London: Bell and Daldy, pp. 125-53.
          Life, especially life as a   printer, with brief
       commentary on the novels; source: Hannaford, item 446.

<u>1866</u> NONE

<u>1867</u> NONE

<u>1868</u>

1   C., F.W.. <u>N&Q</u> 4th ser. 1:285-86.
          Criticizes Leslie Stephen's article in the <u>Cornhill</u> (see
       1868.5. below); Richardson was an earnest moralist as far
       as his "twopenny-tract-morality" allowed him   to be.
       Reprints Richardson's letter of November 9, 1749, accusing
       a correspondent (Frances Grainger?) of laziness for not
       replying to a letter.

2   FITZGERALD, EDWARD.   Letter to W.F.   Pollock, January 9.
     Letters and Literary Remains of Edward Fitzgerald. London:
     Macmillan and Co., Ltd., 1903, 2:246-47.
          Discusses 1868.5.. Richardson's novels are too long;
     Fitzgerald has himself made an abridgment, which he will
     not publish because it would be unprofitable.   "When the
     Writer [Stephen] talks of Grandison and Clarissa being the
     two Characters [worth note in Richardson's works]--oh,
     Lovelace himself should have made the third: if unnatural
     (as the Reviewer says) yet not the less wonderful: quite
     beyond and above anything in Fielding." He repeats his
     opinion of Lovelace in a letter to Pollock of Dec.   24
     [1871] (3:8) and adds that "Richardson (with all his
     twaddle) is better than Fielding, I am quite certain."

3   RICHARDSON, SAMUEL. Clarissa: A Novel .   ...   Edited [and
     greatly abridged] by E.S. Dallas. 3v. London: Tinsley
     Bros.
          Abridged least at both ends, heavily in center.   Dallas
     often shortens individual letters and consistently removes
     Richardson's moralizing, which "is an intolerably tedious
     and solemn joke when it starts from fiction" (1:xvi).
     Nevertheless, the book "ranks above all others in prose,"
     (1:xx) needing only to be shorn of its eighteenth-century
     clumsiness to become a masterpiece of nineteenth-century
     realism. Richardson has written a genuine tragedy, a genre
     usually beyond the novel, and has handled his "unseemly"
     subject well; Lovelace is subtle and agreeable, though
     impossible (1:xxvii), but "we who can read him aright know
     that his wit . . . [is] but the luminous unwholesome
     vapours that play upon graves . . . " (1:xxxi).
     Doubtless Richardson had trouble in creating Lovelace; he
     could make heroines but never heroes, as witness Sir
     Charles. Richardson's influence has been felt on the
     Continent, and perhaps will reach England again once it has
     tired of the "insular" Fielding. Dallas prefers Clarissa
     and, after it, Grandison to Pamela. Though Richardson was
     no intellectual, he could tell a story well and had "a good
     heart"; without being versatile, within his range he was
     "wonderfully true." Reviewed in The Christian Remembrancer
     56:330-55; St. James's Magazine NS 2(1868-69):251-55;
     Westminster Review 91 (1869):48-75; and by Stephen
     (1868.6) and Forman (1869.2).

4   RICHARDSON, SAMUEL. <u>Clarissa Harlowe.</u> <u>A</u> <u>new</u> <u>and</u> <u>abridged</u>
      <u>edition</u> <u>by</u> <u>Mrs.</u> [Harriet] <u>Ward</u>. London: G. Routledge
      and Sons, Routledge's Railway Library [n.d.].
           Mrs. Ward's edition emphasizes the moral Richardson at
      the expense of all else;   it is a mix of letters and
      linking notes, attempting to show Clarissa's edifying death
      as completely as possible while blackening Lovelace's
      character.
           Frequently reprinted without date of republication.

5   [STEPHEN, LESLIE.]. "Richardson's Novels." <u>Cornhill</u> <u>Magazine</u>
      17:48-69.
           Richardson's feminine qualities of analysis made him
      successful as a novelist; his moralizing was ineffective.
      His women characters are far finer than the ordinary male
      novelist's.   The epistolary form is unnatural, hardly
      realistic, and demanding (Stephen counsels skipping two
      letters out of every three), but creates extraordinarily
      minute genre-painting.   The   epistolary   narrator   is
      inevitably immodest;   Grandison is offensive and even
      Clarissa not wholly above suspicion. But these two are his
      two original and lasting creations; "Grandison has passed
      into a proverb . . . the model fine gentleman of the
      eighteenth century . . ." Clementina is rather too
      conventional. Grandison, though a "prig of the first
      water," is not impossibly beyond arousing a certain
      affection in the reader; he has a delicate mind and some
      spirit, seems as attractive as good men in real life, and
      fails only because virtuous men in novels are required to
      have no passions.   The minor characters are animated and
      amusing and <u>Grandison,</u> on the whole, is much to be
      preferred to <u>Pamela</u>.
           <u>Clarissa</u> is Richardson's masterpiece, though a faulty
      one, prolix and incredible. Clarissa would "make a good
      governess" and Lovelace, though a "fancy character," has
      "every merit but that of existence." Richardson lacks humor
      and appreciation of nature; his views of morality are
      constricted;   he has a somewhat defective perception of
      character and can bore the reader. But his genius puts him
      with the French masters of fiction in the affecting
      qualities of his situations, the exquisite proportions of
      the story, the unity of interest, the marvelous closeness
      of observation, and "the astonishing and often
      ungrammatical fluency by which he is possessed, and which
      makes his best passages remind us of the   marvelous

malleability of some precious metal."

1869

1   ANON. <u>N&Q</u> 4th ser. 3:375-78.
     Richardson was not merely a "manufacturer of
     twopenny-tract morality"; he felt he had a mission, as
     shown in his letter to Miss G. [Frances Grainger] on
     parental authority, dated January 22, 1749-50. The letter
     discusses Lovelace's and Anna Howe's characters, but is
     largely on parental authority. Reply to 1868.1.

2   FORMAN, H. BUXTON. "Samuel Richardson, as Artist and
     Moralist." [A review of Dallas's edition of <u>Clarissa</u>.]
     <u>Fortnightly Review</u> 71 (N.S. 34): 428-43.
     Apologizes for Richardson's "ultra-moralising" [but this
     is a review of the far more moralistic Dallas abridgment];
     there is a conflict in Richardson, nevertheless, between
     "an importunate moral idea and an uncontrollable artistic
     force." Finds in this force the excuse for Lovelace's
     character and for the epistolary mode, the point of which
     is "the overwhelming of the minds of his audience with a
     moral engrossed and made irresistible by a wealth of
     circumstantial detail." Approves of the Dallas edition, a
     good abridgment for the modern reader.

3   OLIPHANT, MARGARET. "Historical Sketches, X. The Novelist."
     <u>Blackwood's Edinburgh Magazine</u> 105, no. 641:253-76.
     Reprinted as part of her <u>Historical Sketches of the Reign
     of George II</u>. Edinburgh: Blackwood's, 1870.
     A review of Richardson's life and works with frequent
     comparison to Fielding. Richardson's Salisbury Court may
     be said to have taught worldly knowledge as effectively as
     Fielding's Covent Garden, and Richardson's feminist slant
     encouraged him to give conversation an important place in
     his work. <u>Pamela</u> is not to the taste of modern readers;
     the book "abounds in nauseous details as explicit as the
     frankest of French novels" and perhaps it is immortal only
     through having produced <u>Joseph Andrews</u>. But <u>Clarissa</u> is a
     wonder. From the "little printer" one would expect
     sentimental love-stories--Clarissa is instead "one of the
     finest tragic efforts of genius" though "the story in its
     chief point is revolting." Richardson's moral seriousness

is shown in his refusal to compromise the ending. Lovelace
is essentially a woman´s hero; his vices are full of
passionate excitement, vices as seen by a woman. Compared
with him, Tom Jones´s "fundamental easy-minded uncleanness
[is] infinitely nastier, infinitely more innocent."
(244-45) Richardson´s conception of his novel surpasses
Fielding´s, though Fielding´s execution outdoes
Richardson´s. Sir Charles Grandison and its hero are too
sweet for the common taste; the double ending secures both
the happy conclusion his friends preferred and "the unhappy
ending which he himself approved." The book is "a
housemaid´s ideal, the perfection of everything that is
fine," but Sir Charles is somehow saved from being a fool.
   (Repr. in book form, 1870; page numbers taken from
that ed.)
   Compare Oliphant to John Blackwood, February 3, 1869:
she finds less difficulty reading Richardson than Fielding
and confesses actually to prefer Lovelace to Tom Jones, but
believes it a feminine prejudice. Autobiography and
Letters of Mrs. M.O.W. Oliphant . . . Edinburgh and
London: William Blackwood, 1899, p. 221.

1870

1   RICHARDSON, SAMUEL. Clarissa Harlowe. A novel. London:
    Milner and Sowerby [1870], 384 pp. BM, VaU.
       Highly abridged and moralistic edition retold in a
    combination of narrative and extracted letters, clumsily
    tied together. The editor freely preaches ("Lovelace,
    under all the horrors of a self-accusing conscience") and,
    like Mrs. Ward, cuts deeply into the earlier part of the
    novel to present Clarissa´s edifying death intact.

1871

1   FORSYTH, WILLIAM. The Novels and Novelists of the Eighteenth
    Century, in Illustration of the Manners and Morals of the
    Age. London: John Murray, pp. 213-57.

"Few, very few" read Richardson's novels now, and
generally with just cause; to Forsyth "Clarissa Harlowe is
an unpleasant, not to say odious, book." (215) All the
books lack morality, story, and taste. The best of them is
Sir Charles Grandison; Forsyth's favorite character, and
the best-drawn in the three novels, is Lady Clementina, and
Harriet's kidnapping is a fine scene, Richardson's best.
But the story does go to astounding lengths. Richardson's
faults are humorlessness and ignorance of upper-class
manners.

1872

1   TOCQUEVILLE, ALEXIS DE. Correspondence and Conversations of
     A. de Tocqueville with N.W. Senior from 1834 to 1859.
     Edited by M.C.M. Simpson. 2v. London: Henry S. King &
     Co., 2:176.
         Records "weeping over Lady Clementina" and hearing
     Grandison read aloud in his childhood in the First Empire.

1873

1   RICHARDSON, SAMUEL. Pamela, or Virtue Rewarded. Edited by
     Thomas Archer. London: George Routledge & Sons,
     Routledge's Railway Library [1873], 544 pp. BM, Cambridge
     University Library.
         Archer's introduction claims that Pamela, though not
     wholly blameless, is less shocking than many modern novels;
     the present edition has been slightly abridged of passages
     "tedious, unnecessary, or . . . likely to be offensive
     to modern taste." Based on the 1801 edition of Pamela; see
     1978.4.

2   ---. The History of Sir Charles Grandison. Edited by Mary
     Howitt. London: George Routledge & Sons, Routledge's
     Railway Library [1873], 554 pp.
         Sympathetically and carefully cut, with nothing added
     and no linking narrative.

1874

1   RICHARDSON, SAMUEL. Clarissa, or, The history of a young lady
    . . . Condensed by C.H. Jones. New York: Henry Holt &
    Co., 515 pp.
        Somewhat redresses the moralistic bias of the Dallas,
    Ward, and 1870 London editions, but omits major episodes of
    the middle portions of the novel, distorting the psychology
    of both main characters and particularly of Lovelace.
    Extremely popular and reprinted, usually without date, well
    into the twentieth century. (The latest edition I have
    seen dates from 1939.)

2   STEPHEN, LESLIE. "Richardson's novels." Hours in a Library
    [first series]. London: Smith, Elder & Co., pp. 59-112.
        Reprint with slight changes of 1868.5.

1875

*1 GUILLEMOT, ERNEST.   Clarisse   Harlowe.   Bibliotheque
    anglo-francaise 1. Poitiers: Chez tous les libraires, 151
    pp. BN.

2   SCHMIDT, ERICH. Richardson, Rousseau, und Goethe: Ein
    Beitrag zur Geschichte des Romans im 18. Jhdt. Jena:
    Eduard Frommann, 331 pp; pp. 6-81 are particularly
    devoted to Richardson.
        Certainly not the first, even in his century, to note
    Richardson's influence abroad, Schmidt was the most
    assiduous scholar of that influence before Texte and Price.
    Schmidt does not particularly care for Richardson, though
    freely admitting his influence over the German novel;
    however, he finds that Richardson's larmoyante style is
    often gripping and sometimes effectively pathetic.
    Perfection is the infirmity of all Richardson's characters;
    it prevents them from changing and developing, they remain
    fertige. The book also suffers from a want of invention in
    characters and incidents, Sir Charles Grandison a bit less
    than the other two. Richardson's influence is particularly
    marked over Gellert; Schmidt sees his influence on Goethe
    as coming principally through Rousseau, and thinks of his
    importance in 1875 as largely historical.   Reprinted in
    1924.

1876

1   STEPHEN, LESLIE. <u>History of English Thought in the Eighteenth</u>
     <u>Century</u>. London: Smith, Elder & Co., 2:380, 440.
          Fielding is the essential eighteenth-century novelist,
     Richardson far inferior in "sheer intellectual vigor . .
     . though a greater artist" (380).   His popularity among
     women shows the "weight of emotion without adequate vent .
     . . accumulating behind the old . . . barriers of
     moral convention"; he discovered "how a sincere profession
     of the narrowest code of morality might excuse a systematic
     dallying with seductive images." Cf. 1904.3.

2   TREVELYAN, GEORGE OTTO. <u>Life and Letters of Macaulay</u>.   2v.
     London: Longmans, Green, & Co., 1:377÷78.
          Again, the Ootacamund story (the <u>Clarissa</u> delirium at
     Macaulay's hill station in 1834-35), which had also
     appeared in Thackeray's <u>Roundabout Papers</u> (see 1860.3).
     Trevelyan comments in a footnote that "degenerate readers
     of our own day have actually been provided with an
     abridgment of Clarissa [actually four] . . . A wiser
     course . . . would be to commence the original at the
     Third Volume. In the same way, if anyone, after obtaining
     the outline of Lady Clementina's story from a more
     adventurous friend, will read Sir Charles Grandison,
     skipping all letters to Italians, from Italians, and about
     Italians, he will find that he has got hold of a
     delightful, and not unmanageable, book."

1877

1   CROMPTON, SAMUEL. "Richardson's Clarissa annotated." <u>N&Q</u> 5th
     ser. 8: 101-3.
          Lady Bradshaigh's notes on the first edition of <u>Clarissa</u>
     and Richardson's notes on the notes; shows Richardson at
     his most characteristic and frank. See 1933.4. (This
     unique copy of <u>Clarissa</u> is now [1982] in the possession of
     Prof. T.C. Duncan Eaves.)

2   GRIMM, FRIEDRICH MELCHIOR, baron, et al. <u>Correspondance</u>
     <u>littéraire</u>. Ed. Maurice Tourneux. 16v. Paris: Garnier,
     1877-82.
          Contains many references to Richardson and

Richardsoniana, the most important of which have been discussed under their original dates in this bibliography.

3 STEVENSON, ROBERT LOUIS. Letter to A. Patchett Martin, December. Reprinted in Letters of Robert Louis Stevenson to his Family and Friends. Edited by Sidney Colvin. New edition. 4v. New York: Charles Scribner's Sons, 1911, 1:255-56.

Recommends to Martin "one of the rarest and certainly one of the best of books--Clarissa Harlowe. For any man who takes an interest in the problems of the two sexes, that book is a perfect mine of documents. And it is written, sir, with the pen of an angel." He writes that he is planning a dialogue on the book. This "Dialogue on Men, Women, and Clarissa Harlowe" was actually written late in that year or early in 1878, but was not published. In the Stevenson sale in New York, 1914, it was sold as Lot 366 in Part II; its current location is not known. In the same sale (Lot 469) appeared Stevenson's set of the Mangin edition of Richardson, which, according to the sale catalogue, "contain[ed] many interesting pencil notes by Stevenson on the margins of four of the volumes." (Again, the current location is unknown.) Stevenson's affection for Clarissa Harlowe remained unchanged; in "A Gossip on Romance," 1882, he compared it with Robinson Crusoe and found Clarissa "a book of far more startling import, worked out, on a great canvas, with inimitable courage and unflagging art. It contains wit, character, passion, plot, conversations full of spirit and insight, letters sparkling with unstrained humanity . . . And yet a little story of a shipwrecked sailor . . . goes on from edition to edition, ever young, while Clarissa lies upon the shelves unread." (Information kindly supplied me by Mr. Roger Swearingen.) See also 1888.4.

1878

1 ANON. A Sequel to the History of Sir Charles Grandison. London: William Clowes. Bodleian.

A delightful book, the product of well-informed dislike. Sir Charles is revealed to be a highwayman and is hung; the della Porrettas meet an even more colorful end, and the burning of Grandison Hall destroys an enormous mass of correspondence.

1879

1   G.,F. and others. "Richardson´s House at the Grange, North
     End,   Hammersmith."   <u>N&Q</u>   5th   ser.
     12:264-65,295,318,337÷38,358,417,437.
          A long attempt to tell the right from the left end. See
     1935.10.

1880

1   WELSCHINGER, HENRI. <u>Le</u> <u>Théâtre</u> <u>de</u> <u>la</u> <u>Révolution,</u> <u>1789-1799</u>.
     Paris: Charavey Frères, pp. 55-60.
          Material on François de Neufchâteau´s <u>Pamela</u>, judged
     counterrevolutionary because Pamela was rewarded for
     aristocratic blood, not virtue. See 1793.3, 1795.2.

<u>1881</u> NONE

<u>1882</u> NONE

1883

1   LANIER, SIDNEY. <u>The</u> <u>English</u> <u>Novel</u>. New York: Charles
     Scribner´s Sons, pp. 1169-74, 176.
          "<u>Pamela,</u> <u>or</u> <u>the</u> <u>Reward</u> <u>of</u> <u>Virtue</u>" is "silly and
     hideous"; Mr. B.´s reformation, such as it was, was far
     better rewarded. <u>Clarissa</u> is "a patient analysis of the
     most intolerable crime in all history or fiction," and thus
     <u>Sir</u> <u>Charles</u> <u>Grandison</u> is "certainly less hideous."

2   RICHARDSON, SAMUEL. <u>The</u> <u>Works</u> <u>of</u> <u>Samuel</u> <u>Richardson.</u> <u>With</u> <u>a</u>
     <u>prefatory</u> <u>chapter</u> <u>of</u> <u>bibliographical</u> <u>criticism</u> <u>by</u> <u>Leslie</u>
     <u>Stephen</u> . . . 12v. London and Manchester: Henry

Sotheran & Co. Vols. 1-3, Pamela; 4-8, Clarissa; 9-12,
Sir Charles Grandison.

Stephen's introduction, 1:ix-lv, is reprinted with some
changes and additions from his Cornhill article of 1868 and
the essay of 1874. Among the additions are a powerful
concluding paragraph on the necessary connection in
Richardson's works between moral and artistic success; new
material on Richardson's connection with the Sentimental
movement (xxiv-xxv), in which Stephen takes a different
position on Richardson's sympathy to passion; and a few
biographical addenda, not all accurate. The edition is
reviewed in the Athenaeum, No. 2994 (1884):399-400;
Saturday Review 55:114-15; Spectator 56:1284-85; and
below.

3   TRAILL, H.D. "Samuel Richardson." Contemporary Review 44, 4
     (October): 529-45. Reprinted in his New Fiction. London:
     Hurst and Blackett, 1897, pp. 104-36.

     A review of the Stephen edition. Richardson is now
     quite unread; the epistolary form seems prolix and
     handicapping, and the didacticism ruins, in particular,
     Pamela, the title character of which is too much a
     chambermaid-soubrette to be a good heroine. She is
     calculating; the other characters are crudely drawn, and
     Richardson is too deferential to Mr. B.--Joseph Andrews is
     the more moral book. Clarissa reverses Pamela--"virtue
     defeated, outwitted, betrayed"; and to understand how
     happiness may come from such a situation the moralist must
     cease preaching and begin to analyze. Clarissa gains from
     Lovelace's masterly vigor; though the man and his plots
     could not exist in human nature, he is like Iago a
     masterpiece of "imaginative truth." Sir Charles Grandison
     is inferior, but not wholly bad, and the epistolary method,
     though tedious to all and soporific to some, works like the
     dropping of water on a stone; with thousands of tiny
     details Richardson channels deep impressions in our minds.

1884

1   TRAILL, H.D.. "Richardson and Fielding." The New Lucian being
     a Series of Dialogues of the Dead. London: Chapman &
     Hall, Ltd., pp. 200-15.

     A warm dispute about their intended audiences and goals,

pitting Fielding the Laughing Cavalier against Richardson the "harem-preacher," realism vs. idealism, "corruption" vs. "preachifying". Fielding concludes that, though they have raised a statue to him and may raise one to Richardson, "they do not read either of us." (215)

1885

1　TRAILL, H.D. "The Novel of Manners." Nineteenth Century 18:561-76. Republished in his New Fiction. London: Hurst and Blackett, 1897, pp. 137-69.
　　Disagrees with Johnson's distinction between Fielding and Richardson; both portray human nature.

1886

1　JUSSERAND, JULES. Le Roman anglais. Paris: Ernest Leroux, pp. 47-54.
　　Richardson reveals the charm of analysis and opens the way for the modern novel; perhaps surpassed, he is still a génie créateur.

2　LESSING, GOTTHOLD EPHRAIM. Sämtliche Schriften. Ed. K. Lachmann. 32v. Stuttgart: G.J. Goschen, 1886-1924.
　　Frequent references in Lessing's Collected Works testify to the influence of Richardson over him: e.g., 4:407; 5:17, 165, 398-99, 433, 453; 7:18-19, 31, 73, 74, 399, 442n.; 8:110; 9:271; 15:62; 19:54, 57-58, 62. 1937:3 comments on Lessing's early admiration of Richardson, and quotes Schmidt (1:277): "Es sind die Jahre, wo [Lessing] Richardsons Romane mit dem unbeschränkste Lob überschüttet: der unsterbliche Schöpfer einer Pamela, einer Clarissa, eines Grandison könne nichts Mittelmässiges spenden, niemand verstehe sich besser auf Bildung des Herzens, Einflössung der Menschenliebe, Beförderung der Tugend, auf die im Zauberkleid gefälliger Poesie das Gemüt bezwingende Wahrheit." Lessing later found fault with Richardson but "continued to be Richardson's follower in fact," as Liljegren asserts in discussions of Miss Sara Sampson, Emilia Galotti and Minna von Barnhelm (58).

3   RICHARDSON, SAMUEL, edited by "John Oldcastle." <u>Sir Charles
     Grandison by Samuel Richardson: with Six Illustrations
     from the Original Copper-Plates engraved in 1778 by Isaac
     Taylor: and a preface by John Oldcastle</u>. The Leadenhall
     Press Sixpenny Series: Illustrated Gleanings from the
     Classics 1. London: Field & Tuer, The Leadenhall Press .
     . . New York: Scribner & Welford [1886], 34 pp.
         "That leisurely and voluble author who delighted our
     grandmothers" is now a subject for delicate patronization,
     especiallly his third novel, the most "conspicuously
     unknown." The author prefers the minor characters,
     especially Charlotte, but castigates them, the Italians in
     particular, for their eagerness to wallow in emotions.

                                1887

1   WOLFF, EUGEN. "Preface." In Lessing, K.G. <u>Die Mätresse</u>.
     <u>Deutsche Litteraturdenkmale des 18. und 19. Jhdts</u>. 28.
     Heilbronn: Gebr. Henniger, pp. iii-xx.
         See 1780.5.

2   ---. "Die Sturm- und Drangkomödie und ihren fremden
     Vorbilder." <u>ZVL</u> N.S. 1: 192-220, 329-47.
         Discussion of <u>Sturm und Drang</u> drama influenced by
     Richardson, among others.

                                1888

1   GERSTENBERG, HEINRICH WILHELM VON. <u>Briefe über
     Merkwürdigkeiten der Litteratur</u>. Ed. Alexander von
     Weilen. <u>Deutsche Litteraturdenkmale des 18. und 19.
     Jhdts</u>. Heilbronn: Gebr. Henniger.
         Weilen's introduction summarizes Gerstenberg's
     preference of Richardson to Fielding and mentions a long,
     uncompleted project, "[eine grössere] Dichtung, 'Clarissa
     im Sarge.'" (lxxii) See 1916.1. The <u>Briefe</u> themselves
     contain references to Richardson, indexed in this edition.

2   HARDY, THOMAS. "The Profitable Reading of Fiction." <u>Forum</u> 5,
     3: 57÷71.
         Richardson's only real claim to being placed on a level

with Fielding is in his grasp of form; though the heroine
is cold and the circumstances unnatural, <u>Clarissa</u> forms a
"circumstantial whole," a fine example of constructive art.
    See 1925.2 for an expanded version of this article,
which has been reprinted in its original form in <u>Thomas
Hardy's Personal Writings</u>. Edited by Harold Orel.
Lawrence, Kans.: University of Kansas Press, 1969, pp.
121-22.

3   STEVENSON, ROBERT LOUIS. "Some Gentlemen in Fiction."
    <u>Scribner's Magazine</u> 3: 764-68.
        Richardson, "undeniably not a gentleman," can create
them, while Fielding cannot. With Sir Charles, Stevenson is
personally unacquainted---"the day [<u>Grandison</u>] overtakes
me, Baron Gibbon's fortress shall be beat about his ears,
and my flag shall be planted on the formidable ramparts of
the second part of <u>Faust</u>"--but Richardson's hero seems by
repute a gentleman, and Lovelace, M--, and Col. Morden are
all indisputably far beyond Booth or Dr. Harrison. Cf.
1877.3.

1889

*1   BRINK, JAN TEN. <u>De Roman in Brieven</u> <u>1740-1840</u>. Amsterdam:
    Elsevier.
        Richardsonian adaptations and imitations in Holland,
France, and Germany. (Information courtesy of Dr. Maryka
Rudnik.)

2   GOSSE, EDMUND "The Novelists." <u>A History of Eighteenth-Century
    Literature</u>. London: Macmillan & Co., pp. 245-51.
        Richardson has genius though he is slow, tedious, and
clumsy; he can "preserve the general proportions of a
scheme" better than Fielding or Smollett. <u>Clarissa</u>, though
not often read, is a masterpiece.

3   LANG, L.B.. "Morals and Manners in Richardson." <u>National
    Review</u> 14, 3: 321-40.
        Mrs. Andrew Lang considers that Richardson may not be
read by unmarried women without expurgation, and attacks
his characters for gross vulgarity and outrages of
morality. <u>Clarissa</u> is Richardson's finest novel, all the
more so because of the flaws in the heroine's character, if

it were not for Richardson´s urging that "a reformed rake
makes the best husband" [!]. The death scene is entirely
natural. So is not Lovelace, like B "not in the least a
real man," brutal and wholly uncharming, but he is better
than "the galvanized puppet that struts to and fro under
the title of Sir Charles Grandison", or any of Grandison´s
friends except the "delightful" Charlotte Grandison. Her
Letters on Literature (1889), which I have not seen,
contains some material on Grandison, pp. 135-46; see
Hannaford, item 448.

*4   LUCAS, ELIZA. "An Essay in Criticism." In A Library of
      American Literature. Edited by E.C. Stedman and E.M.
      Hutchinson. 11v. New York: William Evarts Benjamin,
      2:446-47.
           "A clever mock letter on Pamela II, noting the defect .
      . . of writing at length how others praise
      her"--Hannaford, item 455.

*5   WILLS, WILLIAM G. Clarissa. Unpublished play. L.
      Chamberlain´s Office, MS. No. 240.
           Source: 1964.27, p. 25.

                              1890

*1   BUCHANAN, ROBERT. Clarissa. Unpublished play. L.
      Chamberlain´s Office, MS. No. 245.
           Source 1964.27, p. 25.

2   GASSMEYER, MAX. Richardsons Pamela: ihre Quellen und ihr
      Einfluss auf die englische Literatur. Leipzig and
      Reidnitz: Oswald Schmidt, 83 pp. MH.
           Material on the sources and influence of Pamela. The
      name is from the Arcadia; details on pronunciation.
      Sources: Marivaux, perhaps; Richard Glover´s Leonidas;
      Locke; Télémaque; the moral weeklies; and The London
      Merchant. Richardson´s characters, even Pamela, are all
      fertige und nicht werdende. (44) Notes on the
      continuations and some imitations: Moore´s The Foundling,
      The Maid of the Mill, Joseph Andrews, and David Simple;

also suggests, not very convincingly, an influence on Aaron
Hill´s The Fatal Interview. Appendices argue that
Richardson knew neither Latin nor French (but this
information comes from Richardson himself).

3   HENLEY, WILLIAM ERNEST. "Richardson." In his Views and
     Reviews. London: David Nutt, pp. 215-22.
          Pamela is unsurpassably vulgar, Grandison deadly dull,
     but Clarissa with all its faults is the best book in the
     world--is there anything better than Lovelace, "the
     completest hero in fiction"? Admires Anna Howe and the
     minor characters. Though Clarissa is a moral pedant, she
     speaks for women´s right to independence. "Not the Great
     Pyramid itself is more solidly built nor more incapable of
     ruin" than Clarissa.

4   JUSSERAND, JULES. The English Novel in the Time of
     Shakespeare. Translated by Elizabeth Lee. Revised
     edition. London: T. Fisher Unwin, pp. 123-24,
     169,249-50. Revised and enlarged from his Roman au temps
     de Shakespeare. Paris: C. Delagrave, 1887.
          Richardson´s moralizing and his debt to the Arcadia.

*5   PEET, WILLIAM H. "Booksellers´ Sales in the Eighteenth
     Century." N&Q 7th ser. 9:301-2.
          Copyright prices for the three novels in 1766: Pamela,
     288; Clarissa, 600; Sir Charles Grandison, 480. Source:
     Hannaford, item 471.

*6   RICHARDSON, SAMUEL. Clarissa. Roman. Aus dem Englischen
     übersetzt und bearbeitet von R[udolfine] und E[mma]
     Ettlinger. Mit einem Vorrede von Franz Müncker. 2v.
     Karlsruhe: Braun. BZK.
          Abridged. See 1927:6.

7   WARD, WILLIAM C. "Samuel Richardson." GM 268:74-86.
          A general introduction. Richardson creates living and
     beautiful characters; he is tender and his books are not
     too long. Ward sets him higher than Fielding or Smollett,
     puts Clarissa first for tragedy, but "for a book to live
     with" prefers Sir Charles Grandison.

1891

*1   ETTLINGER, JOSEF. "Wielands <u>Clementina</u> <u>von</u> <u>Porretta</u> und ihr
      Vorbild." <u>ZVL</u> N.S.4: 434-39.
          Source: 1953.5, item 523.

2   MAGNUSSEN, JOHANNES. <u>Samuel</u> <u>Richardson:</u> <u>et</u> <u>Afsnit</u> <u>af</u>
      <u>Romanens</u> <u>Historie</u>. Copenhagen: Jakob H. Mansas, 179 pp.
          General introduction to Richardson in Danish.

1892

1   BIRRELL, AUGUSTINE. "Samuel Richardson: A Lecture." <u>Res</u>
      <u>Judicatae</u>. New York: Charles Scribner's Sons, pp. 1-38.
          An appreciation of Richardson's work and life. Though
      his <u>Pamela</u> is vulgar, it is meant for the vulgar, and "you
      feel as you read a fine affinity between the communicating
      medium, the language, and the thing communicated, the
      story." (15) <u>Clarissa</u> is realistic, pathetic, and
      courageous; though Fielding is the better writer of the
      two, so far as mere writing goes, Richardson's characters
      are better and his books more interesting. Fielding "has
      no more of the boldness than he has of the sublimity" of
      Richardson. (3) His works show the new importance of women
      at the expense of the Restoration ideal of the triumphant
      male, Lovelace. Richardson's books are unread by most, but
      Birrell protests against being proud that one does not read
      them. Reprinted in 1908.

2   HEINE, CARL. <u>Der</u> <u>Roman</u> <u>in</u> <u>Deutschland</u> <u>von</u> <u>1774</u> <u>bis</u> <u>1778</u>.
      Halle an S.:   Max Niemayer.   140 pp., especially pp.
      29-37. MH.
          Heine believes that the whole group of German
      <u>Gelassenheitsromane</u> in this period may be said to come from
      Richardson's work, and estimates that a third of all the
      novels he studies are <u>Richardsonaden</u>. (This figure is
      likely to be exaggerated since Heine includes all
      <u>Geschichte</u> <u>der/des</u> titles, not all of which are influenced
      by Richardson.) In the generality of novels of the period
      is much that is similar to the <u>Richardsonaden</u>, if not to
      Richardson himself.

3   HILL, G.B. <u>Writers</u> <u>and</u> <u>Readers</u>. London: T.   Fisher Unwin,
      pp. 85-91.
          Praise of Richardson, who, however, has now entirely

"passed away"; even in Hill's boyhood it was a wonder for someone to have read Grandison from beginning to end. "For one reader of his novels there are perhaps ten readers of his rival's, neglected though Fielding now is."

1893

1   BURNEY, FRANCES, later d'Arblay. Diary and letters of Mme. d'Arblay. Ed. Charlotte Barrett. Rev. ed. 4v. London: Bickers and Son, 1:17, 45, 48, 51, 99, 158, 290, 520.
        Miscellaneous references and reactions to Richardson and his works. Pp. 290, 520 record "tediousness" and "melancholy" of Grandison, 1780 and 1783.

1894

1   DOBSON, AUSTIN. "Richardson at Home." Eighteenth-Century Vignettes, 2d ser. New York: Dodd, Mead & Co., pp. 56-83.
        General, chatty introduction to the "tea-partying" and "womanizing" Richardson. His works are long, no longer than Les Misérables, but with a minimum of action, and, as Janin, Prévost, Dallas, and Ward have proved, impossible to cut down; his prolixity is his style. Fielding and he are essentially opposed.

2   LARROUMET, GUSTAVE. Marivaux: Sa Vie et ses Oeuvres. Paris: Hachette et Cie., pp. 313-18.
        Asserts incontestable influence of Marivaux over Richardson.

3   RALEIGH, WALTER. "Richardson and Fielding." The English Novel. London: John Murray, pp. 143-62. Reprinted St. Clair Shores, Mich.: Scholarly Press, 1970.
        A general introduction, not favorable to Richardson, who is criticized for having failed to understand male characters, since he wrote his books entirely for women. His morality is either uninspiring or disgusting on the whole, but in Clarissa his "tropical luxuriance of sentiment" bears all before it. Though Grandison himself is unpleasant, the book is well-constructed. Richardson is

a formal moralist, stressing a code of conduct and
conformity to a social standard; Fielding, on the
contrary, is a romantic moralist, laying most stress on
goodness of heart and the individual´s conformity to his
better self.

4   ROBERTSON, J.G.   "The Beginnings of the German   Novel."
     Westminster Review 142: 183-95.
        "Richardson was the father of the novel in Germany .   .
     . The German realistic novel of ordinary life, . . . an
     alien growth, . . . owed its origin to the author of
     Clarissa." (183) Discusses Fanny Wilkes and Sophiens Reise,
     Das Fräulein von Sternheim, Agathon, and others. The
     subjectivity of the German novel and its tendency to deal
     with ethical principles and problems rather than with
     incident is traceable back to Richardson.

                              1895

1   RICHARDSON, SAMUEL.   Letters from Sir Charles Grandison,
     selected with a biographical introduction and connecting
     notes by George Saintsbury. With illustrations by Chris.
     Hammond . . . 2v. London: George Allen.
        A Dresden-china edition of Sir Charles Grandison, highly
     abridged and stressing its domesticity, but pleasant to
     read and a delightful piece of bookmaking.

*2   RIDDERSHOFF, CUNO.   "Sophie von La Roche, die Schülerin
     Richardsons und Rousseaus." Diss. Einbeck. Univbib.
     Wien.
        Source: Catalog of the Universitätsbibliothek Wien.

3   TEXTE, JOSEPH.   Jean-Jacques Rousseau et les origines du
     cosmopolitisme littéraire, étude sur les relations
     littéraires de la France et de l´Angleterre au 18e.
     siècle. Paris: Hachette, ca. 450 pp.
        Richardson is dealt with particularly in Book 2,
     chapters 3 and following. Texte fits Richardson into the
     context of his European influence; his novels are among
     the influences preparing the French for Rousseau´s
     cosmopolitanism, and he readies the French and the rest of
     Europe for the novel of bourgeois morality (171).
     Richardson is compared to Prévost and Marivaux, as well as

to Rousseau. His defects are preciosity, grossness, a
heavy emphasis rather than solemnity, and a love for the
roman documentaire-- Richardson's novels, says Texte, are
"le triomphe de la paperasserie" (203). The epistolary
mode is clumsy, far from neatly organized, and thus not
French, but in its way very successful--"if realism is the
art of giving the impression of real life, Richardson is
the greatest of realists." (210) One of the strengths of
both Richardson and Rousseau is that they put their
portraits of bourgeois life in the context of the
romanesque, but Richardson's triumphs and failures are all
in the context of realism. It is this that gives the
violence and horror in his novels their value; as with the
Dutch realists, it allows him to pick an unimportant
subject, since the subject gains importance in its
treatment. His heroes fail completely on the side of
realism; "everyone in his works is a parvenu" including
Lovelace (221), and Grandison fails because Richardson has
no idea of the high society he draws. He is better at
women. His true value is in bringing to his "lecteurs
inquiets" a taste for the interior life, a sense of
stillness and thoughtfulness in the midst of everyday
distractions; in this he is profoundly moral, and under
his hands the novel becomes an instrument for analyzing the
soul. Rousseau takes from Richardson the "English
coloration" of his novel, the storyline, and individual
characters, but most particularly the capacity to look at
large, grave problems. (302) Copious material on
Richardson's influence in France in the generations of
Rousseau and of the Revolution.

Page numbers of these citations taken from the second,
revised edition of 1909 (q.v.). It was translated into
English in 1899 by J.W. Matthews as Jean-Jacques Rousseau
and the Cosmopolitan Spirit in Literature. London:
Duckworth; New York: Macmillan. Leslie Stephen commented
on the book in "The Cosmopolitan Spirit in Literature."
Studies of a Biographer, 4th ser. (1902), pp. 230-59.

1896

1   BARBIER, P.J., and P. CHOUDENS. Clarisse Harlowe [opera].
     Paris: C. Lévy, 99 pp. Bib. de l'Institut.
        Melodramatic attempt to treat Clarissa as Gounodesque

opera; the final scene features the simultaneous deaths of
Clarissa by poison and Lovelace by Morden´s hand, while a
chorus of nymphs sing from a small boat in the distance,
"Dors, dors . . ." Much is made of Rosebud. Probably
unproduced.

2   DONNER, JOAKIM O.E.. Richardson in der deutschen Romantik.
     Sonderabdruck aus der ZVL [N.S. 10 (1896)]. Weimer: Emil
     Felber, n.d. [1896], 16 pp.
         Richardson´s influence on Tieck´s William Lovell and
     Achim von Arnim´s Gräfin Dolores.

3   STEPHEN, LESLIE. "Samuel Richardson." DNB.   London: Smith,
     Elder & Co.   First   appeared   in 1896.   Repr.   16(1909):
     1129-33.
         Remarkable chiefly for its picture of Richardson as a
     vain, sentimental, and tedious author, a change in tone
     from his attitude of e.g. 1883; summarizes biographical
     material. Now outdated.

4   WELLS, BENJAMIN W.   "Richardson   and   Rousseau."   MLN   11:
     225-32.
         Owes a considerable debt to 1895.3.   From Richardson
     Rousseau takes the epistolary form, the "tone of the lay
     confessional," the substitution of bourgeois characters for
     the aristocratic, romantic, or burlesque types of earlier
     fiction, a taste for prolix digressions, and some of his
     characters.   Richardson prepares the way for Rousseau and
     has himself been prepared for by Free-Masonry, the "sweet
     simplicity of Sensational philosophy," and English science.
     Prevost further contributes to his success by Frenchifying
     him.   Richardson has no style, but his psychology is more
     brilliant than Fielding´s; like Rousseau, he has an
     essentially feminine soul.

                            1897

1   HILL, GEORGE BIRKBECK, ed.   Johnsonian   Miscellanies.   2v.
     Oxford: Clarendon Press.
         Frequent references to Richardson, showing Johnson´s
     addmiration for the works and, to a somewhat lesser degree,
     for the man.

*2   KETTNER, GUSTAV. "Lessings Emilia Galotti und Richardsons
         Clarissa." ZDU 11: 442-61.
               Source: 1953.5, item 522.

3   RICHARDSON, SAMUEL. In A Library of the World's Best
         Literature, Ancient and Modern. Ed. Charles Dudley
         Warner. New York: The International Society, 31:
         12225-46.
               Extracts with an introduction. Richardson is the father
         of "the modern analytic novel of society" by having written
         Pamela, a great new thing in fiction since a girl of the
         lower classes is for the first time found worthy of being
         presented at full length.   Pamela herself is naive.
         Clarissa, Richardson's masterpiece, is somewhat slow-moving
         for modern taste; in Lovelace Richardson has given a name
         to the "genus fine-gentleman profligate." (12227) Grandison
         is a failure, a Sir Willoughby Patterne taken seriously.
         Richardson may be regarded as having inspired Fielding's
         career.
               The selections are the "sunflower" episode from Pamela
         and Harriet's kidnaping and the description of Sir Charles
         from Grandison; there is nothing from Clarissa.

4   TENNYSON, HALLAM, baron. Alfred Lord Tennyson: A Memoir.
         London and New York: Macmillan & Co., 2:372.
               "I like those great still books," the poet says of
         Clarissa--"I wish there were a great novel in hundreds of
         volumes that I might go on and on."

                              1898

1   ELOESSER, ARTHUR. Das bürgerliche Drama: seine Geschichte im
         18. und 19. Jhdt. Berlin: Wilhelm Hertz, 218 pp.
               Richardson comes in as a general influence on the
         Aufklärung.

                              1899

1   WHITE, WILLIAM HALE [Mark Rutherford]. Letter to Sarah Fabian
         Colenutt, August 16, 1899. Letters to Three Friends.
         Oxford: Humphrey Milford, 1924, p. 95.

                              165

He does not find <u>Clarissa</u> wearisome; the "slow walking
pace" allows him to see everything delightfully, and "the
genius of Richardson is sufficient to carry me on without
any sense of fatigue." But "this incessant circling and
hovering round" the central fact of the story "makes [it]
more immoral by far than anything Fielding ever wrote."

1900

*1   STRAUSS, LOUIS A. "The Ethical Character of the English Novel
       from Lilly to Richardson." Ph.D. dissertation, University
       of Michigan.
           Source: 1975.2, item D93.

2   THOMSON, CLARA LINKLATER. "An Historic House." <u>Athenaeum</u>, No.
       3770, p. 115.
           Describes The Grange.

3   ---. <u>Samuel Richardson: a Biographical and Critical Study</u>.
       London: Horace Marshall & Son, 308 pp. Reprinted Port
       Washington, N.Y.: Kennikat Press [1978?].
           Half-biographical and half-critical. Richardson
       develops the novel past Marivaux and the romances. The
       heroine of <u>Pamela</u>, the worst of the books, is "anything but
       pure-minded" and very conventional but a perfect
       characterization; the book is too long after the marriage.
       <u>Clarissa</u> is felt to be so unfamiliar to the ordinary reader
       that it must be summarized. The epistolary style exactly
       represents the inching-forward of Clarissa's agony, but it
       is highly improbable. Clarissa, though of lifelike
       perfection, shares with her creator the definition of
       virtue as "insusceptibility to temptation" and suffers from
       the vices of pride, obstinacy, and respectability.
       Lovelace is a "dazzling monster," inconsistent in order to
       advance the plot; vanity rules him. Grandison's "divided
       passion" is ignoble and the two heroines unattractive: the
       delicacy of love conflicts with the "objectionable candour"
       of an epistolary world. The book is skillfully constructed
       but lacks suspense.
           Richardson's art is all in the subject; he has no
       thought for form, although the epistolary novel gives him
       some advantages: laying bare the heart, writing to the
       moment, moving a large cast and giving the reader a

thorough acquaintance with each. But it is impossibly slow
and   difficult,   and   makes   his   plots   unbelievable   and
hackneyed.   Though he is a minute realist in execution,   in
intention and conception his books are the work of an
idealist.   He influenced many authors of   the   later
eighteenth century and gave expression to sentimentalism.
          Reprinted in 1969.

1901

1   ANON. Samuel Richardson: His Writings and his Friends.   New
          York: Cruscup & Sterling Co, [1901], 32 pp.
               First   modern   analytical   novelist;   "gentle feminine
          kindness" of the man; the twentieth century will see a new
          awakening of interest in him. An advertising pamphlet for
          the Phelps edition of the novels.

1A   ---. "Samuel Richardson and George Meredith." Macmillan's
          Magazine 85:356-61.
               They are joined by an interest in women as people.

2   BERTANA, EMILIO. "Pro e Contro i romanzi del Settecento."
          GSLI 37:339-52.
               Discusses   eighteenth-century   novel   in   terms   of
          contemporary theories of utility of the novel; Richardson
          mentioned on pp. 350-52.

3   FORMAN, H. BUXTON. "Richardson, Fielding, and the Andrews
          Family." Fortnightly Review 76, n.s. 70, no. 420:949-59.
               Finds Richardson outdated, sanctimonious, and funny, "a
          virtous man with [possibly] a dissolute mind" (p. 957),
          but has nothing but praise for Clarissa;   uses Richardson
          and Fielding as sticks with which to beat each other, but
          feels we have each to thank for creating the other's
          genius.   The Familiar Letters are so unknown that Forman
          must assure his readers the book exists; he believes that
          Pamela is read by fewer persons even than Clarissa, and
          does not bother to mention Sir Charles Grandison.

4   HOWELLS, W.D. Heroines in Fiction.   New York: Harper &
          Bros., 1: 3-5.
               Finds the epistolary form of Clarissa, with its constant
          necessity of writing, "unlifelike," but the character

herself is modern, "a masterpiece in the portraiture of
that Ever-Womanly which is of all times and places" (p.
3).

*5   MARSTON, E.. Sketches of Booksellers of Other Days. No. 4.
      Samuel Richardson.
          Source: Catalog of the St. Bride's Foundation Library,
      London.

6   RICHARDSON, SAMUEL. The Novels of Samuel Richardson.
     Complete and unabridged . . . With a life of the author
     and introductions by William Lyon Phelps. 19v. New York:
     Croscup & Sterling, 1901-02.
         Vols. 1-4, Pamela; 5-12, Clarissa; 13-19, Sir Charles
     Grandison. The introduction to Pamela apologizes for its
     morality but appreciates the character; that to Grandison
     deprecates its social portraiture and the "deserts of
     talk," ruefully makes the best of Sir Charles, but finds
     Harriet praiseworthy. Clarissa is the best of the novels,
     "a masterpiece of Morality and Art." Richardson, though not
     sufficiently read, deserves modern readers.
         Material from the introductions appeared also in "The
     Richardson Revival." The Independent 53:2743-47 and in
     "Richardson." In his Essays on Books. New York:
     Macmillan, 1922, pp. 16-128. The edition was reviewed by
     A.M. Logan, The Nation 73:489-90 (with the Chapman and
     Hall edition, below) and in Academy 61:485-86.

7   [ST. BRIDE FOUNDATION INSTITUTE, LONDON.] Conversazione to
     commemorate the VIIth anniversary of the opening of the
     Institute, and the presentation of a bust of Samuel
     Richardson, by J. Passmore Edwards, Esq., Wednesday,
     November 20, 1901. [London: 1901.] 12 pp., 5 pl., 3
     facsim. NN, BM.
         On the occasion of the unveiling of George Frampton's
     bust of Richardson; genteel adulation of native son
     mingled with wry sense that his works are not very
     important now.

8   THORNE, W.B.. "A Famous Printer: Samuel Richardson." Library
     n.s. 2:396-404.
         A short history of Richardson as a printer, now
     superseded.

9   VREELAND, WILLIAMSON UP DIKE. <u>Etude</u> <u>sur</u> <u>les</u> <u>Rapports</u>
    <u>Littéraires</u> <u>entre</u> <u>Genève</u> <u>et</u> <u>l´Angleterre</u> <u>jusqu´à</u> <u>la</u>
    <u>Publication</u> <u>de</u> <u>la</u> Nouvelle Héloïse. Dissertation, Geneva.
    Geneva: Librairie Henry Kundig, pp. 139-95.
        <u>Genève</u> is Rousseau, and <u>l´Angleterre</u>, for all of Part 2,
    is Richardson. Praises Richardson for his realistic
    depiction of the bourgeois life and his painting of
    "tranquil emotions." Rousseau takes from Richardson the
    epistolary style, the characterization of Clarissa and
    Anna, the heavy, inflexible fathers, and the feeble
    mothers. But differences outweigh similarities: Julie
    feels a greater warmth toward love and marriage; her book
    has a fundamental moral unity, while <u>Clarissa</u> does not;
    Rousseau paints pictures of love, delights in nature, and
    tries to reconcile <u>les</u> <u>dévots</u> and <u>les</u> <u>incrédules</u>, while
    Richardson does not; St.-Preux is not Lovelace;
    Richardson is a painter of the real world, Rousseau of the
    ideal one. Rousseau´s debt to Richardson is on balance
    "very small." (194) There are a number of factual errors in
    the book.

10 WHITE, R.N., and COLEMAN, EVERARD HOME. <u>N&Q</u> 9th ser.   8:163,
    271.
        White asks for information on the date and place of
    Richardson´s birth; Coleman corresponds to report failure.

                               <u>1902</u>

*1 CHESTERTON, G.K. "England´s Novelists in the National
    Portrait Gallery." <u>Bookman</u> 14:465.
        Describe´s Highmore´s portrait of Richardson. Source:
    Hannaford, item 690.

2   DOBSON, AUSTIN. <u>Samuel</u> <u>Richardson</u>. English Men of Letters.
    London: Macmillan & Co., 213 pp.
        A useful though biographically outdated introduction to
    Richardson´s life with some comments on the works.
    Intimates that had Richardson himself died at fifty he
    would have been a nicer man (189-91); in the conditions of
    modern life he is probably not due for a revival, since his
    books are far too long to be read and "in spite of their
    admitted <u>longueurs</u> and <u>langueurs</u>, appear to defy
    compression." (197) Pamela is much too clever for an

ingenue and nobody reads her continuation, and "in
Grandison, though the manner is perfected, and the method
matured, the movement of the story for the most part
advances no more than a rocking-horse" (94). Nevertheless,
if one forgives much long-windedness, self-consciousness,
and ignorance of society in the last book, it is
marvellously successful and the hero remains, on the whole,
extraordinarily interesting. (157) Clarissa is
indisputably the masterpiece; though the story is "in some
respects repulsive" (86) and Lovelace is "concocted" (88),
though in any real England things would never have been
suffered to go so far, there is no explanation but genius
for the vivacity of the Howe abduction letter, the travesty
of "Lady Betty" and "Cousin Charlotte," and the scenes at
Mrs. Smith's. Like Pamela, Clarissa is a little too warm
in spots. (102) "Had his genius been less individual, and
his artistic method more worthy of emulation" he would have
been as great in England as he was in Germany and France.
(198) Reviewed by Athenaeum (January 17, 1903), pp. 71-73;
Bookman 17 (1903): 98-99; Lamp 26 (1903):216-17; Nation
76 (1903):177.

*3   KRETSCHMER, ELIZABETH. Gellert als Romanschriftsteller.
      Dissertation, Heidelberg. Breslau: n.p., 53 pp.
          His relationship to English, French, and German
      novelists. Source: 1953.5, item 512.

*4   MOSS, MARY. "Why We Read Richardson." Lippincott's Magazine
      69:489-91.
          Notes the current Richardson "boom" and feels his
      reputation is deserved in spite of his "tedium,
      artificiality, and revolting impropriety." Source:
      Hannaford, item 811.

5   RICHARDSON, SAMUEL. The Complete Novels of Mr. Samuel
      Richardson. With a prefatory note by Austin Dobson, and a
      life and introduction by William Lyon Phelps. 20v.
      London: William Heinemann.
          Limited edition. Pamela, vols.1-5; Clarissa, 6-13,
      Grandison, 14-20.

6   ---. The Complete Novels. . . . 19v. London: William
      Heinemann.
          Same format as above, but with Pamela reduced to four
      volumes; ordinary trade edition.

7   ---. The <u>Novels</u> <u>of</u> <u>Samuel</u> <u>Richardson</u> <u>.</u> <u>.</u> <u>.</u> <u>With</u> <u>an</u>
      <u>introduction</u> <u>by</u> <u>Ethel</u> <u>M.</u> <u>M.</u> <u>McKenna</u>. 20v. Philadelphia:
      J.B. Lippincott Co.
          Vol. 1-4, <u>Pamela</u>; 5-13, <u>Clarissa</u>; 14-20, <u>Sir</u> <u>Charles</u>
      <u>Grandison</u>. Illustrations reproduced, misleadingly, from
      the engravings by Thomas Stothard, E.F. Burney, et al.
      Also published in London: Chapman and Hall.

9   ---. <u>Pamela,</u> <u>or</u> <u>Virtue</u> <u>Rewarded</u>. The English Comédie
      humaine, 1st ser., vol. 2. New York: Century Co., 533
      pp.
          Reprinted 1903, 1904, 1905, 1906, 1920 (at least).

<u>1903</u>

1   B.; W.; H.,L.; COLEMAN, E. H.; SKEAT, W.W.; and
      PICKFORD, B. J. "Owl-light." <u>N&Q</u> 9th ser. 11: 349, 411,
      412, 452.
          A correspondence on the word "owl-light," used by
      Richardson.

3   CANBY, HENRY SEIDEL. "Pamela abroad." <u>MLN</u> 18:206-13.
          Notes on several comedies made from <u>Pamela</u>, including
      those of Goldoni and François de Neufchateau.

4   MARCHESI, GIAMBATTISTA. <u>Studi</u> <u>e</u> <u>Ricerche</u> <u>intorno</u> <u>ai</u> <u>nostri</u>
      <u>Romanzieri</u> <u>e</u> <u>Romanzi</u> <u>del</u> <u>Settecento</u>. . . . Bergamo:
      Istituto Italiano d´Arti Grafiche, pp. 18-21, 431;
      (imitations and <u>Richardsonaden</u>) chapters 2-4. BM.
          Notes individual imitations and prevalence of epistolary
      form in eighteenth-century Italian fiction.

5   MORITZ, CARL PHILLIP. <u>Reisen</u> <u>eines</u> <u>Deutschen</u> <u>in</u> <u>England</u> <u>im</u>
      <u>Jahre</u> <u>1782</u> <u>v.</u> <u>Carl</u> <u>Philipp</u> <u>Moritz</u>. Edited by Otto zur
      Linde. Deutsche Litteraturdenkmale des 18. und 19.
      Jhdts. 126. Heilbronn: Gebr. Henniger, pp. v-xxix.
          Zur Linde´s introduction discusses Moritz´s Anglomania
      and the effect on him of English authors, including
      Richardson.

6   RUSKIN, JOHN. <u>The</u> <u>Works</u> <u>of</u> <u>John</u> <u>Ruskin</u>. Edited by E.T. Cook
      and Alexander Wedderburn. 37v. London: George Allen;
      New York: Longmans, Green & Co., 1903-8.

References to Richardson scattered throughout Ruskin's writings document his love of, in particular, <u>Grandison</u>; see, for example, 5: 373n; 15: 227; 25: 355; 35: 542; and 36: 193 ("I am again divided between Sir Charles Grandison and Don Quixote"). For Ruskin, Richardson was the most moral English novelist.

*7   ŠALDA, F.X. <u>Ottův slovník naučný</u> 21: 732. Statni knihovna ČSR.
       Source: Catalog of the Statni knihovna ČSR.

8   SMITH, RICHARD HORTON; PRIDEAUX, W.F.; and TAYLOR, C.S.. <u>N&Q</u> 9th ser. 12: 141, 330.
       Richardson's pronunciation is the one now current in England, but not that in general use in the eighteenth century, as witness Pope's "Epistle to Mrs. Martha Blount." W.F. Prideaux notes "Pamēla" in Drayton's "Goe you my lynes . . . " and C.S. Taylor cites the case of a parishioner, "Pamělla."

1904

1   LOW, CONSTANCE BRUCE. "Wieland and Richardson." <u>MLQ</u> 7:142-48.
       Richardson's influence over Wieland, with particular notice of <u>Clementina von Porretta</u>.

*1A   MCCRAE, THOMAS. "George Cheyne, an Old London and Bath Physician." <u>Johns Hopkins Hospital Bulletin</u> 15:1-29.
       Discusses Cheyne's correspondence with Richardson (see also 1943.1). Source: Hannaford, item 787.

2   RICHARDSON, SAMUEL. <u>Letters from Sir Charles Grandison; selected with a biographical introduction and connecting notes, by George Saintsbury, with illustrations by Chris. Hammond</u>. London: George Allen.
       One-volume reprint of 1895 edition.

3   STEPHEN, LESLIE. <u>English Literature and Society in the Eighteenth Century</u>. London: Gerald Duckworth, 1904. Reprinted London: Methuen & Co., University Paperbacks, 1962, pp. 93-96.
       Richardson is treated as a middle-class Sentimentalist with the narrow intellectual limitations of his class, and

yet this mild, narrow-minded man wrote a book that made a whole generation throughout Europe weep, <u>Clarissa Harlowe</u>. This popularity is due probably to his having been the first "sentimentalist," that is, the first writer indulging in "emotion for its own sake.." <u>Clarissa</u> affects Stephen with a kind of "disgust" because of Richardson´s eagerness to rub our noses in every detail of Clarissa´s agony; it owes some of its success, however, "to the very fact that [it is] in bad taste." Fielding´s revolt against this "mawkish and unmanly" insistence on moral questions produced the novel in its definitive form.

1905 NONE

1906

1   LUCAS, E.V.. <u>Life of Charles Lamb</u>.   3d ed.   2v.   London: Methuen & Co., 1: 385; 2: 323.
Joking reference to Richardson.

1907

*1A   BÖÖK, F.. <u>Romanens och prosaberattelsens historie i Sverige intill 1809</u>.   Stockholm.
Source: 1966.13, p. 423n12.

2   DOYLE, A. CONAN. <u>Through the Magic Door</u>.   London: Smith, Elder & Co., pp. 139-51.
The author of the Brigadier Gerard series improbably prefers Richardson to Fielding, comparing the two at length. Richardson drew the better women but also the finer gentlemen; Lovelace, in spite of aberrations, "had possibilities of greatness and tenderness" not hinted at in Tom Jones, and "in Grandison he has done what has seldom or never been bettered." (141) Richardson is also the finer writer, excelling in character-drawing and analysis of the soul, avoiding the "scuffles" of Fielding´s writing. Though he is prolix, one cannot bear to cut him; surely it is better to read one masterpiece, three times as long as

an ordinary book, than to read three ordinary books.
Praises Richardson's "beautiful style, . . . so correct
and yet so simple that there is no page which a scholar may
not applaud nor a servant-maid understand." The epistolary
style, however, is inherently unrealistic. Fielding's
handling of the lewd is not a guarantee of artistry;
Richardson drew vice with some freedom to condemn it, and
showed himself a moralist.

3   HUCHON, RENÉ LOUIS, ed. <u>Mrs. Montagu and her Friends,</u>
        <u>1720-1800</u>. London: John Murray, pp. 23, 83⸴
        Correspondence about <u>Clarissa</u>.

*4   TYNAN, KATHERINE. "The Romance of a Bookseller." <u>Cornhill</u>
        <u>Magazine</u> NS 22:678-89⸴
           "Thinly fictionalized account of Richardson"--source:
        Hannaford, item 873.

5   UHRSTRÖM, WILHELM. <u>Studies in the Language of Samuel</u>
        <u>Richardson</u>. Uppsala: Almqvist & Wiksell, 186 pp.
        Reprinted: [Folcroft, Pa.:] Folcroft Press, 1969.
           An enumeration of all the ways in which Richardson's
        language differs from "modern" speech (i.e., that of 1907);
        it is outdated from time to time ("harpsichord" is not now
        "obsolete in all its senses") and somewhat misleading.
        Uhrstrom does not mention Richardson's idiosyncratic use of
        "naughty" in <u>Pamela</u> and omits the respectable "slut";—nor
        does he note the uses of (significantly) obsolete
        swear-words in <u>Clarissa</u>. See also 1951.4.

6   WATERHOUSE, OSBORN. "The Development of English Sentimental
        Comedy in the Eighteenth Century." <u>Anglia</u> 30:137÷72,
        269-305.
           Richardson appears briefly in this study of
        Sentimentalism and its audience.

<u>1908</u>

1   ANON. "The Grandisonian Manner." <u>The Dial</u> 45:75-77⸴
           Not-too-serious recommendation that the manners of the
        present age be raised by the persistent reading of
        <u>Grandison</u>.

*2   FRISCHMEYER, ILSE S. "Einfluss Richardsons und Rousseaus auf
      Goethes <u>Werther</u>." Ph.D. dissertation, University of Texas
      at Austin.
      Source: McNamee.

 3   GRAHAM, HENRY GREY. <u>Literary</u> <u>and</u> <u>Historical</u> <u>Essays</u>.   London:
      Adam & Charles Black, pp.   170-218.
            <u>Pamela</u> is highly offensive and <u>Grandison</u> feeble, but
      <u>Clarissa</u> shows Richardson possessed by some superhuman
      power, going (for once) beyond his didactic purposes,
      painting   "a pure, noble-hearted girl exposed to the
      machinations of an unscrupulous rake," who is nevertheless
      a very lively fellow--so much so that one wonders how
      Richardson could have made him.   Richardson's style is
      nothing, "dreary wastes of epistolary irrelevancies" (190);
      in the long run of his novels, however, his power and
      genius show themselves. Again, Graham feels it necessary
      to introduce readers to Richardson, as he is felt to be
      entirely unfamiliar to all.

 4   H., A.C., and HODSON, LEONARD J. <u>N&Q</u>, 10th ser. 9:   510;
      10: 96.
            Speculations, since proven wrong, about Richardson's
      family.

 5   HORNE, C.F.. <u>The</u> <u>Technique</u> <u>of</u> <u>the</u> <u>Novel</u>.   New York and
      London: Harper & Bros., pp. 105-263.
            Richardson's works are frequently cited as examples of
      novelistic technique. Particularly to be noted: <u>Clarissa</u>
      is one of the few examples of the highest possible type of
      the novel, "the inevitable" (116-23): Richardson's realism
      is compromised by his moral purpose, but it is a realism of
      emotions (152).

 6   JACKSON, HOLBROOK. <u>Great</u> <u>English</u> <u>Novelists</u>. London: Grant
      Richards, pp. 39-63.
            A general introduction to Richardson, characterized as a
      fairly uneducated person, somewhat feminine in outlook, and
      highly moralistic, who wrote domestic romances.   <u>Pamela</u>,
      the first analytical novel, is "a simple tale"; <u>Clarissa</u>
      is fine though long, but <u>Sir</u> <u>Charles</u> <u>Grandison</u> is "trivial
      in the extreme . . . Passion is out of his sphere. His
      medium is sentiment," but in this he is master.   Fielding
      is the true father of the novel, Richardson only its
      grandfather.

7   POETZSCHE, ERICH.   Samuel   Richardsons   Belesenheit.   Kieler
       Studien   zur   Englischen   Philologie n.s.   4.   Kiel: Robert
       Cordes, 121 pp.
          Largely a reference guide to the citations of other
       authors in the three novels and the Correspondence. (This
       list of books should be supplemented by those in the third
       part of 1733.1.) To it is added a reprint of the dedication
       to Pamela, a list of alterations in Clarissa (not
       complete), and a discussion of the extent and nature of
       Richardson's knowledge of other authors, "verhältnismässig
       grosse" according to Poetzsche. But cf. 1936.5, p. 141,
       and 1948.2A.

8   READE, ALEYN LYELL, and DOBSON, AUSTIN. "Richardson's Pamela:
       Her Original." N&Q, 10th ser. 9:361-63, 503-5.
          Reade conjectures that neither Elizabeth, Countess
       Gainsborough, nor Hannah, Lady Hazlerigg, has a claim to be
       the original Pamela, and that Mr. B's name really began
       with B.   Dobson suggests Thomas Boothby of Tooley Park,
       Peckleton, Leics., and his third wife, Sarah.   Notes the
       possibility that Spectator no. 375, attributed to John
       Hughes, served as the original of the story, though doubts
       it in view of Richardson's known honesty.

9   READE, ALEYN LYELL. "Samuel Richardson's Supposed Kinsfolk at
       Derby." N&Q, 10th ser. 9:261-63.
          The Derby Richardsons are not related to Richardson.

10   RICHARDSON, SAMUEL. Clarissa. Aus dem Englischen übertragen
       und ausgewählt von Wilhelm und Fritz Miessner. Englische
       Romane des 18.   Jhdts., 522 pp.   Deutsche Staatsbib.,
       Öster. Nationalbibliothek.

1909

1   BURTON, R.. "Eighteenth Century Beginnings: Samuel
       Richardson." In his Masters of the English Novel. New
       York: Henry Holt & Co., pp. 23-47.
          A general introduction, factually far from accurate.
       Pamela is distinguished only by "chambermaid" style and
       morality and Grandison is "by common consent the poorest of
       the three fictions" (40), though Harriet Byron and
       Clementina are good characters and Clementina's mad scenes

are fine. <u>Clarissa</u> shows the conflict between a good woman
under the stress of sorrow and a man whose nature is far
from bad. Richardson will always have a place in English
fiction because he is the first novelist interested in
characters rather than incident. This, rather than
realism, is the starting-point of the novel.

*2   PFEIFER, NINA. <u>Richardson</u> <u>Samuel</u> <u>a</u> <u>német</u> <u>irodalomban</u>.
      [Samuel Richardson in German literature.] Budapest, 53 pp.
      Országos Széchényi Konytvar.
         Source: Catalog of the Országos Széchényi Konytvar.

3   TEXTE, J.. <u>Jean-Jacques</u> <u>Rousseau</u> <u>et</u> <u>les</u> <u>origines</u> <u>du</u>
      <u>cosmopolitisme</u> <u>littéraire</u>: <u>étude</u> <u>sur</u> <u>les</u> <u>relations</u>
      <u>littéraires</u> <u>de</u> <u>la</u> <u>France</u> <u>et</u> <u>de</u> <u>l'Angleterre</u> <u>au</u> <u>10e</u> <u>siècle</u>.
      2d ed. Paris: Hachette, pp. 171-309.
         See 1895.3.

1910

1   ANON. <u>Book</u> <u>Prices</u> <u>Current</u> 24:66.
         Richardson's printer's notebook described. [This
      notebook or another has recently been rediscovered.]

2   DIBELIUS, WILHELM. <u>Englische</u> <u>Romankunst.</u> <u>Die</u> <u>Technik</u> <u>des</u>
      <u>englischen</u> <u>Romans</u> <u>im</u> <u>18.</u> <u>und</u> <u>zu</u> <u>Anfang</u> <u>des</u> <u>19.</u> <u>Jhdts.</u>
      2v. Berlin: Mayer & Müller, 1:57÷84, 217-20, 226, 232-35,
      354-59, 385, 403-6; 2:3-109 passim, chap. 12 passim.
         Richardson's novels are one of the two <u>Ur</u>-forms of the
      novel in his day. He is influenced neither by Defoe nor by
      Marivaux, although there are similarities; he is a
      novelist of experiences, not adventures, whose
      <u>Konstruktionsmotiv</u> is the theme of love. His principal
      character is the suffering woman, in his hands a universal
      type. He treats the split between good and evil in human
      nature with complexity and subtlety. As he becomes more
      skilled as a novelist, Richardson develops
      characterizational technique, form, and "objectivity." The
      letter form leads to some unrealities, as when Grandison
      must tell all of what Olivia has done, but Richardson is
      the first novelist for whom technique and art seem
      important. The Puritan interest in the soul is central to
      Richardson, far from Fielding, and they are opposed through

their interest in technique vs. characterization, large
social canvases vs. small realistic detail, "subjective
omniscience" vs. the epistolary style and didacticism.
However, they are not so far apart, and traits of both may
be found in almost any later novelist; The Vicar of
Wakefield, for example, is a synthesis of Fielding and
Richardson. Ambrosio, Mackenzie´s "Man of the World,"
Falkland, and the characters in Inchbald´s Nature and Art
are compared with Richardson´s; the character of the
attractive doomed man becomes the pre-Romantic and Romantic
hero, while Richardson´s pathos develops into
sensationalism and terror. Dibelius discusses Richardson´s
influence on women writers from Burney to Austen, on George
Eliot in particular, and on Scott.

3 GESCHKE, EMIL H.F. Untersuchungen über die beiden Fassungen
   von Musaeus´ Grandisonroman. Dissertation,
   Albertus-Universität zu Königsberg i. Pr.: Karg &
   Manneck, 88pp.
      Comparison of the 1760 and 1781 versions of Grandison
   der Zweyte; discussion of the point of Musaeus´s parody of
   Richardson.

3 KALFF, GERRIT. Geschiedenis der Nederlandsche Letterkunde.
   Groningen: J.B. Wolters. Vol. 6.
      Notes Richardson´s influence on Rhijnvis Feith, Wolff
   and Deken, Gellert, Bellamy and Bruno Daalberg.

5 MORNET, DANIEL. "Enseignements des bibliothèques privées."
   RHL 17:449-96.
      A study of private libraries in France between 1750 and
   1780 shows Pamela to be the second most popular novel,
   Clarissa the fourth, in the period.

*6 STRAUS, RALPH. Robert Dodsley. London and New York. P.
   355.
      Prints two of Richardson´s printing-bills; source:
   Hannaford, item 858.

7 YOUNG, EDWARD. Edward Youngs Gedanken über die Originalwerke
   in einem Schreiben an Samuel Richardson, übersetzt von H.E.
   von Teubern, hrsg. von Kurt Jahn. . . Bonn: A. Marcus
   und E. Weber. NN; Vatican.
      Reprint of 1760.16.

1911

*1   BOOKWORM, A. [pseud.] "Dublin pirate publishers: on the case
      of Samuel Richardson and George Faulkner." Irish Book Lover
      3:46-47.
          See also reply by A.G., ibid., 60-61. Source: Mr. Alf
      Mac Lochlainn, Director, National Library of Ireland.

2   BOAS, F.S.. "Richardson's Novels and their Influence." E&S
      2:37-70.
          Richardson's influence upon the Continent is even
      greater than in England; discusses epistolary technique,
      which is "a gigantic make-believe," and characters. Pamela
      is "depraved," Grandison a "miscellaneous" assortment of
      virtues, and Clementina boring, but Emily Jervois is
      delightful, as is Anna Howe--an ideal type, like Beatrice
      or Rosalind--and Clarissa, of course, is fine. Boas traces
      the influence of Richardson's epistolary form into
      nineteenth-century fiction and wonders, "Is it fanciful to
      suggest that in the twentieth century we are returning in
      some respects to the Richardsonian tradition" of epistolary
      form and sentimental analysis?

*3   BUCHOLZ, JOHANNES. Johann Timotheus Hermes Beziehungen zur
      englischen Literatur. Dissertation, Marburg. Göttingen,
      67 pp.
          Source 1953.5, item 434.

3A   DOBSON, AUSTIN [A.D.]. "Samuel Richardson." Encyclopedia
      Britannica. 11th ed. 29v. New York: Encyclopedia
      Britannica Company, 1910-11, 23:300-2.
          Balanced and generally sympathetic review of
      Richardson's works, with quotations from contemporaries;
      biographical sketch.

4   GRAF, ARTURO. L'Anglomania e l'Influsso Inglese in Italia nel
      Secolo XVIII. Torino: Ermanno Loescher, pp. 280-82. BM.
          General influence of Richardson on Goldoni, Chiari,
      Cerlone, and some French imitators.

*5   HUBL, ALFRED. "Richardsons Pamela." Dissertation, Wien.
      Univbib. Wien.
          Source: Catalog of the Universitätsbibliothek Wien.

*5A   HULME, WILLIAM H.   "Shenstone   on   Richardson's   Pamela."   MLN
        26:158-59.
           Uses a Shenstone letter to suggest (wrongly) that Pamela
        was published as early as July 1739. John Edwin Wells
        refutes this in The Nation 93:120 and Anglia 35
        (1912):177-80. Source: Hannaford, items 936,1002-3.

6   KAYE-SMITH, SHEILA, ed.   Introduction.   Samuel   Richardson.
        London: Herbert and Daniel, 368 pp.
           General introduction to life and works;   not wholly
        accurate, and inclined to praise the works at the expense
        of their author. Richardson is praised for his realism and
        disliked for its limits, especially for the preference of
        moral purpose to realism. The greater part of the book
        consists of selections from the three novels.

7   MORGAN, CHARLOTTE A.   The Rise of the Novel of Manners: A
        Study of English Prose Fiction between 1600 and 1740.   New
        York: Columbia University Press.
           Material on Richardson's debt to earlier   writers;
        influence on him of Euphues, the Arcadia, and Defoe
        (Religious Courtship and The Family Instructor).   The
        epistolary form, the stock characters, his sentimentality,
        his morality, "his excessive detail," and "his favorite
        situation of virtue contending with vice . . . not only
        existed, but were common" in fiction before him.

8   READE, ALEYN LYELL.   "Samuel Richardson's Supposed Derbyshire
        Connections." N&Q 11th ser.   3:123-24.
           More candidates for the Derbyshire connection; they are
        not related to Richardson.

9   WARD, H.G..   "Samuel Richardson and the English Philosophers."
        N&Q 11th ser.   3:5-6.
           Richardson's novels contain references to Shaftesbury,
        Mandeville, Berkeley, and Locke.

10   ---.   "Samuel Richardson and the Methodists." N&Q 11th ser.
        3:124.
           Richardson's   references   to   the   Methodists   are
        differentiated by character; however, their general tone
        is positive and reflects a change of attitude parallel to
        that expressed by Lady Mary Wortley Montagu's letters of
        1741-1759.

11   ---. "Samuel Richardson's Birth." Ibid., p. 127.
      Is there any more information since 1902?

12   ---. "Anna Howe and Charlotte Grandison." Ibid., pp. 164-65.
      Richardson himself first pointed out the similarity, as,
      later, did Mary Wortley Montagu and Lessing.

13   WILLIAMS, H. "Samuel Richardson." In Two Centuries of the
      English Novel. London: Smith, Elder & Co., pp. 33-52.
      Richardson has no story and much morality, but of a
      vulgar kind. Pamela is vulgar and Grandison insufferable;
      in Clarissa, however, "there is not a word too much" of the
      elaborate analysis of "ideal womanhood," although Lovelace
      is only a partial success. In Richardson there is no sense
      of the mystery of human character; it is a subject to be
      dissected. He may be said to have originated the sexual
      problem novel.

1912

1   BALDWIN, EDWARD CHAUNCEY. "Marivaux's Place in the
      Development of Character Portrayal." PMLA 27:168-87.
      On Marivaux's Spectateur francais. Some comparison
      between Marianne and Pamela: they are both coldly
      calculating; however, Baldwin does not believe Richardson
      read Marianne, though he may have known the Spectateur.

*1A   BATYUSHKOV, F.D. ["On the Eve of the Nineteenth Century." In
      History of Western Literature. Vol. 1. Edited by F.
      Batyushkov. Moscow: n.p., pp. 26-29.] All-Union State
      Library, Moscow.
      Source: Catalog of the All-Union State Library.

2   ELTON, OLIVER. A Survey of English Literature 1780-1830.
      London: Edward Arnold, 1:170-75.
      Cites Richardson as a great inventor of types. He is
      often, but not significantly, referred to in Elton's
      chapter on the novel of manners.

3   HOLLIDAY, C. English Fiction from the Fifth to the Twentieth
      Centuries. New York: n.p., pp. 219-28.
      Pamela is "dangerously suggestive" to our time though
      not to its own, and Clarissa, though a masterpiece,

disappoints us by its ending; innocence is crushed, not
vindicated. Grandison is "a monster of gentility," but
Clementina´s madness, Harriet´s mock marriage, and the
subtle analysis interest us. Richardson´s "appreciation of
the . . . human soul is so keen and so unabating that
the reading of this author´s three books is rather wearing
on the nerves." They demand the closest attention to detail
and discover states of mind rather than deeds.

*4   MUSKALLA, KONSTANTIN. Die Romane von Johann Timotheus Hermes.
      BBL 25, 87 pp.
          Influence of Richardson. Source: 1953.5, item 519.

*5   RODE-BRUCKNER, SOPHIE. "Frauen im Leben und in den Romanen
      Richardsons und Fieldings." Dissertation, Wien. Univbib.
      Wien.
          Source: Catalog of the Universitätsbibliothek Wien.

6   WARD, H.G. "Richardson´s Character of Lovelace." MLR
      7:494-98.
          Lovelace derives from Rowe´s Young Lothario.

7   WOLFF, SAMUEL LEE. The Greek Romances in Elizabethan Prose
      Fiction. Columbia University Studies in Comparative
      Literature. New York: Columbia University Press, p.
      463n1.
          Notes Richardson´s debt to the Arcadia in Clarissa´s
      threat of suicide to save her honor and in Harriet Byron´s
      abduction; they may derive from Philoclea´s threat of
      suicide and the abduction of the Arcadian princesses.

*8   WUSTLING, FRITZ. Tiecks William Lovell. Ein Beitrag zur
      Geistesgeschichte des 18. Jhdts. Bausteine zur Geschichte
      der neueren deutschen Literatur, vol. 7. Halle: n.p.,
      pp. 115-20.
          The influence of Richardson´s Clarissa over William
      Lovell. Source: 1953.5, item 301a.

                                1913

1   BREWSTER, DOROTHY. Aaron Hill: Poet, Dramatist, Projector.
      New York: Columbia University Press, pp. 254-73.
          Richardson´s dislike of Pope as a man was probably

largely due to Hill's and Cibber's unpleasant experiences
with the <u>Dunciad</u>; Richardson himself did not know Pope
well. Chapter 7, "Hill and Richardson," is a general
overview of the relations between the two men, taken
largely from material in the <u>Correspondence</u> and Hill's
<u>Works</u> (which, Brewster speculates, may have been published
by Richardson to aid Hill's family).

1   CAZAMIAN, LOUIS. "Richardson." In <u>The Cambridge History of
    English Literature</u>. Vol. 10. Edited by A.W. Ward and
    A.R. Waller. Cambridge: Cambridge University Press; New
    York: Putnam. pp. 1-19, 411-13.
        Short background sketch and biography of Richardson;
    outlines three novels, sketches reputation, influence, and
    decline. Considers Richardson a "Puritan" author.
    Bibliography, pp. 411-13; superseded by <u>NCBEL</u>.

*2   DONÁTH, LÉO. "Richardson Samuel és az érzelmes regény
    helyzete az aol régeny történetében." [Samuel Richardson
    and the Position of the Sentimental Novel in the History of
    the English Novel.] Dissertation, Budapest. Országos
    Széchényi Konytvar.
        Source: Catalog of the Országos Széchényi Konytvar.

3   JONES, T. LLECHID. <u>N&Q</u> 11th ser. 7:250.
        Wishes to know whether he owns a volume of the first
    edition of <u>Clarissa</u>.

4   KAYE-SMITH, SHEILA. Introduction. <u>Samuel Richardson</u>.
    Chicago: F.G. Browne, 368 pp.
        American edition of 1911.6.

5   MACAULAY, G.C. "Richardson and his French Predecessors." <u>MLR</u>
    8:464-67.
        Quotes from Warburton's preface to the fourth volume of
    <u>Clarissa</u>, which provides "a definitive statement . . .
    that . . . [Richardson] had been following the lead" of
    Marivaux and other contemporary French writers. See
    1875.3, 1912.1, 1915.5, 1917.5, 1919.1, 1919.3, 1925.1,
    1936.3, 1938.6, and 1940.6.

6   SAINTSBURY, GEORGE. <u>The English Novel</u>. London: J.M. Dent;
    New York: E.P. Dutton, pp. 82-103. Reprinted St. Clair
    Shores, Mich.: Scholarly Press, 1971; New York, AMS
    Press, 1976.

It is a mistake to separate novel of incident from novel of character, a fault that made Johnson think Fielding shallower than Richardson. Saintsbury prefers the former to the latter, finding Pamela and Clarissa both less than perfect heroines, the books too long, and Richardson´s male figures, Lovelace and Grandison, unbelievable. But Richardson gathered up the scattered elements of the novel into the novel itself, infused it with psychological interest, and caught the attention of his readers to a greater degree than any novelist before him. His "unhealthiness" and bad breeding are the defects of the epistolary method and his ignorance as much as they are of the author himself. His greatest work is to have created his successor, Fielding, who is more dramatic, more detailed, and far less improper.

1914

1   HUGHES, H.S. "Characterization in Clarissa Harlowe." JEGP 13:110-23.
       Compares the opinions of several eighteenth- and nineteenth-century writers on the verisimilitude of Clarissa, Lovelace, and Anna Howe; the last is most truthful because least imbued with the author´s morality. Notes the closeness of Clarissa to the heroine of seventeenth-century heroic tragedy and eighteenth-century sentimental comedy (Clélie, Tyrannic Love).

2   PHELPS, WILLIAM LYON. Essays on Books. New York: Macmillan, pp. 16-128.
       A biographical-critical study. Though the morality of Pamela is "defective," it is a great book, and Clarissa "produces upon the readers of today, all things considered, about the same effect that it produced in the eighteenth century," deserving its many readers in spite of the moral problem of Clarissa´s terrible pride; "we are purified by this spectacle of pain." Lovelace, an "essentially Romantic character," duly impresses us in spite of his unreality. On the whole Phelps does not like Sir Charles Grandison, though he considers many parts of it admirable and forgives Richardson gladly; but there is too much talk and the Italians bore intolerably. Though Defoe was the first realistic novelist, Richardson was the first analytic

realist, and "one of the most stern and uncompromising . . . bolder and more honest than Fielding." In his very earliest writing, Richardson completely changed the idea of fiction. Phelps traces his influence on Brooke, Sterne, and even the Wesleys, his German following, and his effect on the French Revolution.

3   RICHARDSON, SAMUEL. <u>Pamela</u>. Introduced by George Saintsbury. 2v. London: J.M. Dent, Everyman's Library; New York: E.P. Dutton, Everyman's Library.
     <u>Pamela</u> I is in Vol.1, II in Vol.2. Frequently reprinted, but I more frequently than II. Unfortunately, a corrupt text; see 1977:17, 1978.4.

4   SHELLEY, HENRY. <u>Life</u> <u>and</u> <u>Letters</u> <u>of</u> <u>Edward</u> <u>Young</u>. London: Sir Isaac Pitman & Sons, 289 pp.
     Information on Young's long friendship with Richardson and on the Duchess of Portland's acquaintance with Richardson, taken largely from the <u>Correspondence</u>; see especially pp. 216-70.

                               <u>1915</u>

1   BERNBAUM, ERNEST. <u>The</u> <u>Drama</u> <u>of</u> <u>Sensibility</u>. Boston and London: Ginn & Co., pp. 164-65. Reprinted Gloucester, Mass.: Peter Smith, 1958.
     Parallels between <u>Sylvia</u> and <u>Pamela</u>, <u>Clarissa</u> and Charles Johnson's <u>Caelia</u>.

2   GOODWIN, GWENDOLINE. "Samuel Richardson." <u>N&Q</u> 11th ser. 12:320.
     Has Richardson's birthplace yet been discovered?

3   HUDSON, W.H. <u>A</u> <u>Quiet</u> <u>Corner</u> <u>in</u> <u>a</u> <u>Library</u>. First published 1915. Reprinted Freeport, N.Y.: Books for Libraries Press, 1968, pp. 163-218.
     Overview of Richardson, who lacks "virility." <u>Pamela</u> is vulgar; thinking of <u>Clarissa</u> as a great book is "wild talk . . . reckless and absurd . . . [the book is] repulsive and at times absolutely nauseating" but intermittently, and in total effect, is "extremely powerful." The epistolary style lacks the merit of simplicity, drawing attention too grossly to itself. Lovelace seems more interesting than Clarissa, a study of

supreme villainy, though inhuman and unconvincing.
Grandison is "desperately dull." The advantage of the
epistolary mode is psychological detail; its disadvantage,
the scattering of the story interest. Its pretense at
realism fools no one. Richardson is beneath our notice
today but has a secure place in literary history.

4   PLOMER, HENRY R.   A Short History of English Printing
     1476-1900.   London: Kegan Paul Trench Trubner & Co.
          Scattered references to Richardson as a creditable
     printer.

5   SCHNEIDER, FERDINAND JOSEF. "Studien zu Th. G. von Hippels
     Lebenslaufen: (1) Die Lebenslaufe und Sophiens Reise von
     Memel nach Sachsen." Euphorion 22:471-82.
          Material on Richardson's influence on Hippel.

6   SCHROERS, CAROLA. "Ist Richardsons Pamela von Marivauxs Vie
     de Marianne beeinflusst?" Es 49:220-54.
          Schroers suggests that Richardson might well have been
     able to read Marianne in French in spite of his
     disclaimers, but if there is any influence it is only that
     of the first three parts. Pamela, unlike Marianne, belongs
     to a coherent new literary genre.

7   THORNTON, RICHARD H. N&Q 11th ser. 12:333.
          The French translation of Pamela was placed on the Index
     in 1745. Cf. 1935.12.

                              1916

1   GERSTENBERG, HEINRICH WILHELM VON. "Clarissa Harlowe, eine
     tragische Cantate." Edited and introduced by Albert Malte
     Wagner. Archiv 134 (n.s. 34):3-5.
          The undated MS, in the Hof. und Staatsbib. zu München,
     had not previously been published, says Wagner [but see
     1815.1]. The "tragic cantata" is bits of Clarissa woven
     luridly together in reminiscence of the last part of Faust
     I.

2   SAINTSBURY, GEORGE. The Peace of the Augustans . . .
     London: G. Bell and Sons, 1916. Reprinted London:
     Oxford University Press, World's Classics, 1946, pp.

116-20.

    Pamela is not as moral as one might wish, but it is "very much the liveliest" story to its date; Saintsbury prefers it to Clarissa and Grandison, which he rates about equal to each other for entertainment value. He cannot s´amuser franchement at either of them.

3   TIEJE, ARTHUR. The Theory of Characterization in Prose Fiction prior to 1740. University of Minnesota Studies in Language and Literature, no. 5. Minneapolis, Minn.: Bulletin of the University of Minnesota, pp. 47-48.

    Traces Grandisonian concepts of heroism and sentiment back to sources in seventeenth century and earlier.

1917

*1   BATYUSHKOV, F. Richardson, Pushkin i Lev Tolstoi. Zhurnal ministerstva narodnogo prosveshchenija, Spb., 1917, ch. 71. Novaja serija, No. 9, sent., s. 1-17. ["Richardson, Pushkin, and Lev Tolstoy." Journal of the Ministry of Popular Enlightenment (St. Petersburg), NS 71, 9: 1-17.] All-Union State Library, Moscow.

    Source: Catalog of the All-Union State Library.

2   DANIELOWSKI, EMMA. Richardsons erster Roman. Entstehungsgeschichte . . . Ph.D. dissertation, Tübingen. Berlin: Mayer & Müller, 161 pp.

    General study of intellectual origins of Pamela in earlier fiction and in the periodical essays. Part I of a two-part study, the second half of which was published as Die Journale der frühen Quäker (see 1921.1).

3   DICKSON, FREDERICK S. N&Q 12th ser. 3:7-8.

    Compares Richardson´s and Fielding´s publishing records on the Continent, Great Britain and Ireland; Fielding comes off favorably.

4   DOBSON, AUSTIN. Bookman´s Budget. London: Humphrey Milford, pp. 79, 108-109.

    The pronunciation of Pamela and a silhouette by Hugh Thomson taken from Susanna Highmore´s drawing.

5   HUGHES, H.S. "Translations of the <u>Vie</u> <u>de</u> <u>Marianne</u> and their
     Relations to Contemporary English Fiction." <u>MP</u> 15:491-512.
          In writing <u>Pamela</u> Richardson had access to only the
     first six parts of <u>Marianne</u>, which was not Englished
     completely until 1742. (Cf. 1915.5.) However, the more
     important influence was probably that of earlier French and
     English writers upon both.

                              1918

*1   LACZER, ISTVÁN. "Richardson S.: Clarissa or the history of a
     young lady c.   regényének hatása Rousseau Julie ou la
     nouvelle Héloïse c.   regényére." [The Influence of S.
     Richardson's <u>Clarissa</u> <u>or</u> <u>the</u> <u>History</u> <u>of</u> <u>a</u> <u>Young</u> <u>Lady</u> on
     Rousseau's <u>Julie</u> <u>ou</u> <u>la</u> <u>Nouvelle</u> <u>Heloise</u>.] Dissertation,
     Budapest, 31 pp. Országos Széchényi Konytvar.
          Source: Catalog of the Országos Széchényi Konytvar.

2   WHITEFORD, R.N. "Samuel Richardson, Fielding, Sarah Fielding
     and Tobias Smollett." <u>Motives</u> <u>in</u> <u>English</u> <u>Fiction</u>. New
     York, pp. 90-93.
          Clarissa is colorless and lacks passion; Lovelace is
     "almost if not quite a piece of consistent characterization
     of unmorality."

                              1919

*1   BIRON, Sir HENRY CHARTRES.   "The First English Novelist."
     <u>Littell's</u> <u>Living</u> <u>Age</u> 303:98-106.
          Compares Richardson with Henry James;   analyzes
     characters of Clarissa and Lovelace. Source: Hannaford,
     item 873.

2   CRANE, R.S. "A Note on Richardson's Relations to French
     Fiction." <u>MP</u> 16: 495-99.
          Reply to 1913.5. It is unlikely that Warburton's
     preface to the fourth volume of the first edition of
     <u>Clarissa</u> reliably reflects Richardson's point of view,
     given Warburton's critical temperament and the substitution
     of another preface in later editions. The question of
     Richardson's relationship to French fiction remains open.

3   HAVENS, GEORGE R. "The Sources of Rousseau's Edouard
     Bomston." MP 17:13-27.
          Among them is Richardson's Grandison, known to Rousseau
     through Prévost's Nouvelles Lettres anglaises.

4   HUGHES, H.S. "Richardson and Warburton." MP 17:45-50.
          On the Richardson-Warburton falling-out over Warburton's
     quarrel with Thomas Edwards. Reply to Crane, above.

5   PRICE, L.M. English>German Literary Influences: Bibliography
     and Survey. University of California Publications in
     Modern Philology 9, part 1. Berkeley: University of
     California Press, 616 pp.
          Includes information on Richardson's influence over
     German authors as well as citations of articles and
     dissertations on this influence written before 1914.
     Revised in 1932 and 1953 (qq.v).

*6   RICHARDSON, SAMUEL. Pamela vainottuna. Suomentanut ja
     johdannolla varustanut V. Hameen-Anttila. [Pamela or
     Virtue Rewarded. Translated (into Finnish) and introduced
     by V. Hameen-Anttila.] Kariston klassillinen kirjasto 12.
     Hameenlinna, 466 pp. Helsinki Univ. Library
          Source: Catalog of the Helsinki University Library.

7   RIVINGTON, SEPTIMUS. The Publishing Family of Rivington.
     London: Rivington, pp. 33-37, 40, 41, 49, 52-54, 64.
          Some references to the printing history of Pamela, but
     most important for a facsimile opposite p. 52 of a letter
     from Richardson, dated April 24, 1750, unpublished
     elsewhere and not in the E&K list of letters, in which it
     appears that Richardson drew up Charles Rivington's will.
     The letter is to John Rivington in reply to his of the same
     date and refers to Rivington's marriage to Elizabeth Miller
     Gosling.

                              1920

1   ANON. "Richardson's Illustrators." TLS, Dec. 16, 1920, p.
     864.
          A note on the sale of the originals of the Highmore
     illustrations to Pamela (now in the Fitzwilliam, Cambridge,
     the National Gallery, and the National Gallery of Victoria,

Melbourne) and on illustrated editions of Richardson's works.

2   DIGEON, AURÉLIEN. "Autour de Fielding." Revue germanique 11:209-19. ("Sarah Fielding, Henry Fielding, et Richardson".)

       Influence of Fielding and Richardson on each other. It is mutual and reciprocal; there are more tears in the later Fielding, more laughter in the later Richardson, though Richardson does not take his "enfant terrible," Charlotte Grandison, from Fielding. Fielding's early reaction to Richardson is shown in his preface to his sister's Familiar Letters between the Principal Characters in David Simple (1747) and in Tom Jones, which is "plein d'allusions malignes à Richardson . . . " (219). Amelia is not like Clarissa, but "faite tout entière de renoncement" (219). The same people, including Sarah Fielding, liked and read both writers.

3   HUFFMAN, CHARLES HERBERT. The Eighteenth-Century Novel in Theory and Practice. Dayton, Virginia: Ruebush-Kieffer Co., 131 pp.

       Richardson, caught like most writers in his period by the necessity of being moral, tried to make virtue fashionable; he was the first begetter of the "matter-of-fact novel of realism" with a democratic tendency.

4   KANY, CHARLES E. "The Beginnings of the Epistolary Novel in the Romance Languages." Ph.D. dissertation, Harvard. Published as 1937.2.

*5   NORESS, H. La Vie de Marianne von Marivaux und Richardsons Pamela. Ph.D. dissertation, Marburg, 1920? Marburg: n.p.

       Source: 1948.2, item 57. Not reported by any European or American library.

6   REYNOLDS, MYRA. The Learned Lady in England, 1650-1760. Boston and New York: Houghton Mifflin Co., pp. 337÷42.

       "Richardson was the first to make feminism an issue in fiction" and his correspondence with Lady Bradshaigh shows him holding advanced views about female education.

1921

1   DANIELOWSKI, EMMA. Die Journale der frühen Quäker. Berlin:
     Mayer und Muller, 138 pp.
          Second part of 1917.2. Studies development of Pamela
     and the sentimental bourgeois novel from the confessional
     journals of early Quakerism, considered as a type of
     bourgeois spiritual autobiography. Notes the connection
     between realism, as an aesthetic manner, and the spiritual
     concerns of this Ur-Latitudinarianism. Though Pamela, as a
     novel of manners and a Charakterroman, is out of the
     tradition, "durch Gliederung, Form und Stil [das Buch
     bleibt] mit den Journalen der frühen Quäker verwandt."
     (114) Contains the table of contents for 1917.2, pp.
     115-118.

*2   EVERETT, EDWARD. "The Greater Family in the Novels of Samuel
     Richardson   and   his   Immediate   Successors."   Ph.D.
     dissertation, U. of Michigan.
          Source: McNamee.

3   KANT, IMMANUEL. Vermischte Schriften.   Grossherzog Wilhelm
     Ernst Ausgabe.   I.   Anthropologie, Didaktik.   Leipzig:
     Insel Verlag, 1:339.
          Refers briefly to Clarissa. (Courtesy of Dr.   Gertrude
     F. Weisskopf.)

4   LEVY, LILLI. "Der Einfluss der moralischen Wochenschriften
     auf Richardsons Romane." Ph.D. dissertation, Konigsberg.
     Abstract in Inaug.-Diss. d. phil. Fak. Konigsberg i.
     Pr. 1921, pp. 65-66.
          By far the most important literary influence on
     Richardson was the moral weeklies such as the Tatler and
     Spectator. In these are detailed psychology, lovingly
     detailed death scenes, urging against duelling, interest in
     the problems of education, paraphrases of psalms, and other
     features to be found in Richardson, as well as
     plot-parallels with Clarissa (forced marriage) and
     Grandison (a good man between two women). Levy suggests
     that Lovelace originates in Hamilton's Comte de Grammont
     and Mandeville's Fable of the Bees. (Abstract courtesy
     MiU. The original thesis may have disappeared in the war;
     a copy was once in the Deutsche Bücherei.)

5   LUBBOCK, PERCY. The Craft of Fiction. London: Jonathan
     Cape, pp. 152-55.
         Compares the epistolary novel with James's method in The
     Ambassadors.   The former is wonderfully accurate in
     psychological detailing but impracticable because of its
     lack of verisimilitude and its terrible length.

                                1922

1   ANON. Miscellanea Genealogica et Heraldica and the British
     Archivist. 5th ser. 4, part 10 (June 1922):   215-17.
         Richardson's will reprinted.

2   CRANE, R.S. "Richardson, Warbuton, and French Fiction." MLR
     17:17-23.
         The connection between French fiction and Richardson is
     completely accidental in Warburton's preface to the first
     edition of Clarissa, since Warburton later uses   the
     parallel for Marivaux and Fielding. Crane notes with
     Aurélien Digeon (1920) that Richardson and Fielding were
     "rivaux sur le même terrain" since Warburton transferred
     not only his allegiance but his actual words so easily from
     one to the other. See 1919.1, 3.

3   ETIENNE, SERVAIS. Le Genre romanesque en France depuis
     l'apparition de la "Nouvelle Héloïse" jusqu'aux approches
     de la Révolution. Academie royale de Belgique, classe des
     Lettres et des Sciences morales et politiques, mémoires 2.
     ser. 17. Bruxelles: Lamertin; Paris: Colin, 440 pp.
         Refers frequently to Richardson, whose influence he
     nevertheless finds "vraiment féconde" only in the
     nineteenth century, with Balzac (58).   Through his
     obsession with moralizing, Richardson leads out of its
     rightful path the "roman antiromanesque" he had so boldly
     conceived; nevertheless he seems the "Titan" of the Age of
     Louis XIV. Richardson's works are analyzed, 109 ff.;   his
     influence on Prévost is minimal; rather, he and Prévost
     were conflated in France into a single tradition (120 ff.).
     Etienne includes considerable material on French
     Revolutionary Richardsonaden (68 ff. and Chapters 6 and
     7), not all of which has been included in Appendix A.
         Rev.: G. Cohen in RBP 3 (1924): 884-88; A. Francois
     in AJJR 15 (1923):   368;   D. Mornet in RHL 30 (1923):

90-92; A. Schinz in <u>Etat</u> <u>present</u> <u>des</u> <u>travaux</u> <u>sur</u> <u>J.-J.</u>
<u>Rousseau</u>. New York: MLAA, 1941, pp. 98, 214, 406.

4   HUGHES, H.S. "A Letter to Richardson from Edward Young." <u>MLN</u>
     37:314-16.
         Correcting a letter from Young in the <u>Correspondence</u>;
     Barbauld has telescoped two letters of 1758 and 1751.
     Hughes asks for a general reevaluation of the reliability
     of the <u>Correspondence</u>.

*5   MEINECKE, HERBERT. "Das bürgerliche Drama in Deutschland und
     Samuel Richardsons Familienromane. Ein Beitrag z.
     vergleich. Literaturgeschichte." Ph.D. dissertation,
     Heidelberg, 194 pp.
         Once in the Deutsche Staatsbibliothek, but now probably
     destroyed. Source: Deutsche Staatsbibliothek.

6   READE, A.L. "Samuel Richardson and his Family Circle." <u>N&Q</u>
     12th ser. 11:181-83, 224-26, 263-64, 303-05, 342-44,
     383-86, 425-27, 465-67, 506-08.
         Material on the Richardsons and their relatives and
     friends.

                              <u>1923</u>

*1   FOLLETT, WILSON. <u>The</u> <u>Modern</u> <u>Novel</u>. Rev. ed. New York:
     Alfred A. Knopf, pp. 71-99.
         Hypocrisy, vanity, and blind optimism define
     sentimentality. Though Richardson incomparably
     psychologizes characters, he is disastrous for the novel
     because he espouses sentiment.

*1A GHIJSEN, H.C.M. "Wolff en Dekens Romans uit haar bloeitijd."
     <u>De</u> <u>Gids</u> 87:114-39, 241-64.
         "Two Dutch women novelists of the eighteenth century
     [Elizabeth Beker Wolff and Agathe Deken] in their relation
     to Richardson." Source: 1948.2, item 124.

2   HUGHES, HELEN SARD. "English Epistolary Fiction before
     <u>Pamela</u>." <u>Manly</u> <u>Anniversary</u> <u>Studies</u> <u>in</u> <u>Language</u> <u>and</u>

Literature. Chicago: University of Chicago Press, pp. 156-69.
_____ Sources of the epistolary novel in literary forms before 1740; Hughes finds the principal source to be real-life letters. See 1966.3, 1969.26.

3   READE, A.L. "Samuel Richardson and his Family Circle." N&Q 12th ser. 12:6-8, 44-47, 56, 83-85, 126-30, 167÷70, 209-11, 247÷50, 287-89, 329-30, 366-68, 410-11, 446-47, 469-72, 504-06.
     See 1922.6.

*4   RICHARDSON, SAMUEL. Pamela naimisissa. [Pamela in her Exalted Condition.] Englanninkielesta suomentanut [translated from English (into Finnish) by] Valfrid Hedman. Kariston klassillinen kirjasto 22. Hameenlinna, 422 pp. Helsinki U. Library.
     Source: Catalog of the Helsinki University Library.

5   UTTER, R.P. "On the alleged tediousness of Defoe and Richardson." University of California Chronicle 25:175-93.
     The very qualities that make Richardson unreadable--"femininity, minuteness, length--are the main elements of his strength." The minuteness of his realism makes one exhausted, not bored, by Richardson; one sits above the action, helplessly omniscient, "watching mortals attempt to evade their fate." Detail produces monumentality, a sense of the passage of time. Clarissa´s ending is compared favorably with Job´s; the only possible compensation for such suffering is the knowledge of the favor of God, with which no other reward can equate.

6   WILCOX, FRANK H. "Prévost´s Translations of Richardson." Ph.D. dissertation, University of California, Berkeley.
     Published in part in 1927.(q.v.).

7   WILLIAMS, IOLO A. "Two Kinds of Richardsons." LM 7:382-86.
     Transcripts of letters, including the autobiographical letter to Stinstra (in part) and a letter on Richardson´s knowledge of foreign languages. The other "kind" is Jonathan Richardson.

1924

1   GRIMM,   CHARLES.   "Encore   un   fois   la   question
      Marivaux-Richardson." RLC 4:590-600.
            Richardson read the Vie de Marianne, parts 1-6, in
      English and used it to create Pamela. Unconvincing
      reasoning.

*1A   GUTERMUTH, ELSE. "Das Kind im englischen Roman von Richardson
      bis Dickens." Ph.D. dissertation, Giessen.
            Source: 1975.2, item D51.

2   PARTRIDGE, ERIC. The French Romantics' Knowledge of English
      Literature, Bibliothèque de la RLC 14. Paris: Librairie
      ancienne Edouard Champion, 370 pp.
            Bibliographically useful for Richardson's influence in
      France in the early nineteenth century. Partridge
      correctly sees Richardson's influence declining in France
      in the early nineteenth century, but has missed many basic
      references.

*3   ---. The History of Sir Charles Grandison. Ed.   Thomas
      Archer. London: G. Routledge & Sons. [1924?]
            "Thomas Archer" a mistake for "Mary Howitt"?   See
      1873.2.

4   SCHÜCKING, LEVIN L. "Die Grundlagen des Richardson'schen
      Romans." GRM 12:21-42, 88-110.
            Attacks contrast of Richardson to Fielding; Richardson
      is above all a Tendenzschriftsteller who brings together
      the social outlooks of different spheres, though intending
      to give preference to the Puritan- bourgeois ideal. In
      many places he is a modern social critic, especially in his
      attitude toward women. His picture of the process by which
      two distinct social groups are fused into a single class
      ideal will maintain his reputation even if his literary
      reputation has largely disappeared.

1925

1   BIRKHEAD, EDITH. "Sentiment and sensibility in the
      eighteenth-century novel." E&S 11:92-116.
            Short definition of "sentiment" and "sensibility" as
      used by Sterne and Richardson. See also 1951.4, 1974.4,
      and Michel Foucault's Folie et déraison . . . for

further   discussions   of   "sentiment"   applicable   to
Richardson.

2   HARDY, THOMAS. <u>Life</u> <u>and</u> <u>Art</u>:   <u>Essays,</u> <u>Notes,</u> <u>and</u> <u>Letters</u>.
     Introduction by Ernest Brennecke Jr. New York: Greenberg,
     p. 70.
          Expanded version of 1888.2 (q.v.).

3   HUNTER, ALFRED C. <u>J.-B.-A.</u> <u>Suard,</u> <u>Un</u> <u>Introducteur</u> <u>de</u> <u>la</u>
     <u>littérature</u> <u>anglaise</u> <u>en</u> <u>France</u>. Paris: Champion, p. 102.
          Disagrees with Texte's contention that Richardson was an
     important literary figure in the Romantic period; he did
     only what others did.

4   MCKILLOP,   ALAN   DUGALD.   "Richardson,   Young,   and   the
     <u>Conjectures</u>." <u>MP</u> 22:391-404.
          Points out that Richardson took an active role in the
     composition of the <u>Conjectures</u>; under his influence, Young
     conflated the themes of original and moral genius.

5   MORNET, DANIEL. Introduction. <u>La</u> <u>Nouvelle</u> <u>Héloïse</u>.   Paris:
     Hachette. Vol. 1.
          Contains material on Richardson's influence on Rousseau
     and (pp.   335-85) a list of French novels of the period,
     including some <u>Richardsonaden</u>.

6   NAIRN, J.A. "Samuel Richardson and the Merchant Taylor's
     School." <u>N&Q</u> 149:421.
          A Samuel Richardson appears in the lists of the Merchant
     Taylor's   School   in   1701   and   1702;   as far as is
     ascertainable, the name does not appear on the rolls of any
     other London school at that period.

7   PRICE, LAWRENCE MARSDEN. "Richardson in the Moral Weeklies of
     Germany." <u>Studies</u> <u>in</u> <u>German</u> <u>Literature</u> <u>in</u> <u>Honor</u> <u>of</u>
     <u>Alexander</u> <u>Rudolph</u> <u>Hohlfeld</u> . . . University of Wisconsin
     Studies in Language and Literature 22. Madison, Wisc.:
     University of Wisconsin Press, pp. 169-83.
          The moral weeklies of Germany show Richardson steadily
     falling in favor, as idealistic characters become less
     prized than realistic ones.

8   PRINSEN, J. <u>De</u> <u>Roman</u> <u>in</u> <u>de</u> <u>18e</u> <u>Eeuw</u> <u>in</u> <u>West-Europa</u>.
     Groningen and the Hague: J.B. Walters, pp. 291-313.
          General introduction to Richardson's works and survey of

his influence in the eighteenth century. (In Dutch.) Rev. PG 2 (1926): 351.

1926

1   BINZ-WINIGER, E. _Erziehungsfren_ _in_ _den_ _Romanen_ _von_ _Richardson,_ _Fielding,_ _Smollett,_ _Goldsmith_ _und_ _Sterne_. Ph.D. dissertation, Zurich. Weida i. Thur.: Druck von Thomas und Hubert, pp. 6-15.
     Finds that projects of education in Richardson are too abstract; there are few children in his works, and those are unreal by our standards, since the boundaries between childhood and adulthood are set very early and depend on behavior. Discusses Richardson´s debt to Locke in _Pamela II_.

*1A CHEVALLEY, ABEL. "Monsieur Psalmanazar." RAA 5:308n.
     Doubts Richardson´s story of how _Pamela_ originated. Source: Hannaford, item 910.

2   BLANCHARD, FREDERIC T. _Fielding_ _the_ _Novelist:_ _A_ _Study_ _in_ _Historical_ _Criticism_. New Haven: Yale University Press, 655 pp.
     Richardson is referred to _passim_ in this study of Fielding´s reputation, for which Blanchard gathers together an extraordinary list of references and _obiter_ _dicta_; it has been used as a source for this survey. _Caveat_: the index is not complete; Blanchard´s use of later editions sometimes leads him astray; and Blanchard contends injudiciously that "during his lifetime Fielding´s most continuously active enemy" was Richardson, whose "insidious and malignant attempts to undermine his fellow craftsman" were fortunately unmasked by the _Correspondence_.

3   COLLINS, A.S. "The Growth of the Reading Public during the Eighteenth Century." RES 2:284-94,428-38.
     Richardson is referred to as part of the growth of prose fiction.

4   ERNLE, ROWLAND E.P., lord. "Samuel Richardson." _Edinburgh Review_ 243:139-57. Reprinted in his _Light_ _Reading_ _of_ _our_ _Ancestors_. 1927; reprinted 1970.
     General biographical and critical introduction.

*5   [FIELDING, HENRY.] An Apology for the Life of Mrs. Shamela Andrews . . . Introduced by R. Brimley Johnson. Waltham St. Lawrence: Golden Cockerel Press, 90 pp.

6   HILLHOUSE, JAMES T. The Grub-Street Journal. Durham: Duke University Press, pp. 156-57.
      Notes a MS annotation by Richardson to a letter of Eustace Budgell (BM Add. MSS 37,232, f. 137).

7   HUGHES, H.S. "The Middle-Class Reader and the English Novel." JEGP 25:362-78.
      Discusses Richardson's and Fielding's novels as materials for the development of the middle-class audience.

8   PRICE, LAWRENCE MARSDEN. "On the Reception of Richardson in Germany." JEGP 25:7-33.
      History of the German editions of Richardson's work and Richardson's German reputation until 1800.

1927

*1   BINNION, RUBY IRENE. "A History of Richardsonian Criticism in the Eighteenth Century." M.A. dissertation, Illinois/Urbana.
      Source: University of Illinois/Urbana Library.

2   FACTEAU, BERNARD A. Les Romans de Richardson sur la scène française. Paris: Presses Universitaires de France, 142 pp.
      Eighteenth- and particularly nineteenth-century influence of Richardson on French literature; Facteau counts seventeen "nouvelle Pamélas," fifteen "Clarissas," and five "Lovelaces," counting only direct and extensive French-English parallels (q.v.); however, he rather neglects Grandison. There is a three-page appendix of parallels.

3   FORSTER, E.M. Aspects of the Novel. London: Edward Arnold, pp. 26-27.
      Similarities between Richardson and Henry James.

4   FOSTER, JAMES R.   "The Abbé Prévost and   the   English   Novel."
     PMLA 42: 443-64.
          Traces development of the Radcliffean   novel   from
     Richardson and Prévost, through the influence of their
     works and their imitators´ (Mmes de Tencin, Riccoboni, and
     de Genlis, and Baculard d´Arnaud).

5   PRIESTLEY, J.B.   The English Novel.   London: Thomas Nelson &
     Sons, Ltd., pp. 16-19.
          Richardson is betrayed by his method, intolerably slow
     and prolix, but chiefly by the quality of his mind, not
     that of a great novelist; his priggish Grandison and the
     "chit," Pamela, are transformed to heroism only by "the
     curiously unhealthy hothouse atmosphere that   envelops   all
     [his] novels."

6   SCHLICHTING,   HERTHA-MARIA   von.   Frauengestalten   bei
     Richardson. Freiburg im Breisgau: J. Weibel, 62 pp.
          Richardson´s psychological attitude to women   comes   out
     of   his   personal   experience   and   changes with his
     development; Clarissa and Harriet Byron are his ideal
     women,   while Pamela is only an apprentice-work.   In
     creating them he owes debts to Defoe, Steele, and the
     "Ladies´ Library." Richardson creates the domestic novel;
     his goal is to give a knowledge of ethical duty;   he is
     limited by the tendency of his era to Puritanism.
     (Probably a Freiburg dissertation.)

7   SONDHEIM, MORIZ. Gesammelte Schriften .   .   .   Frankfurt
     a.M.: [J. Baer & Co.], pp. 104-5.
          Review of the Ettlingers´ Clarissa (1890.3); Richardson
     cannot be read today in complete versions, beautiful though
     the original Clarissa is.

8   VAN TIEGHEM, PAUL. "Les droits de l´amour et de l´union libre
     dans le roman français et allemand (1760-1790)." Neophil
     12:96-103.
          Richardson serves as the direct ancestor of   the
     passionate Sentimental novel of 1760-90.

9   ---. "Quelques aspects de la sensibilité pré-romantique dans
     le roman européen au 18e s." Edda 26:146-75.
          The   establishment   of   the   Sentimental   words
     "Empfindlichkeit," "belle âme," and "sentimental" itself is
     due in part, but only in part, to the influence of

Richardson; "[il] ne marque," in the history of ideas and
in linguistic history, "que le triomphe et la diffusion
européene de tendances déjà visibles . . ." (159).
Richardson is typical of writing of the Age of Sentiment in
having an essentially passive, feminine nature and in
expounding the malheur d'être sensible; Grandison is one
of the classic cases of sensibility becoming the foundation
of honor and virtue.

10   WILCOX, FRANK HOWARD. "Prévost's Translations of Richardson's
      Novels." University of California Publications in Modern
      Philology 12: 341-411.
           Illustrates certain characteristics of
      eighteenth-century French sensibility by examining the
      changes Prévost introduced into Richardson's novels.
      Prévost's goals: to adapt Richardson's text to French
      dislike of vulgarity, extravagance, and unrestrained
      expressions of feeling; to accentuate the realism,
      especially in descriptions of mental states; to lessen the
      moralizing.

                              1928

1   DOTTIN, PAUL. "Du nouveau sur Richardson (documents
      inédits)." RAA 5:557-61.
           How Richardson came to write the continuation of Pamela:
      material reprinted from the Forster Collection, purporting
      to be a letter from Richardson to James Leake in early
      August 1741, but see McKillop's review of Down's
      Richardson, PQ 8 (1929): 199 in which the letter is
      identified as a conflation of two letters, the second to
      George Cheyne.

2   DOWNS, BRIAN W. Richardson. Republic of Letters, No. 5.
      London: George Routledge & Sons; New York: E.P. Dutton,
      248 pp. Reprinted New York: Barnes and Noble, London:
      Frank Cass, 1969.
           Biographical-critical study (the biographical material
      is outdated). Much material on continuations, influence.
      There are ethical objections to be urged against both
      Clarissa and Pamela; Grandison, though inferior to both,
      is technically perfect, with an "almost Shakespearian"
      opening sentence. Richardson's epistolary art makes up for

much--essential improbability of plots, insufficient
differentiation of characters from book to book; it draws
attention to the major theme of Richardson's psychological
study, the divided mind, and serves as a disguised
stream-of-consciousness. Richardson is typical of earlier
Sentiment, advocating conduct based on feeling; he is "the
laureate of the Christian family." (190)

    Rev.: YWES 9:273-74; TLS, Jan. 31, 1929, p. 77;
A.D. McKillop, PQ 8 (1929): 199; A. Birrell,
National-Atheneum 44: 14, 490-91; W. King, Criterion,
April 1929, 536-38; K. Hornbeak, SRL 5:832; P. Dottin,
RELV 46 (1929):164-67; Commonweal 10 (1929):83; W.
Cross, Yale R 19 (1929):181-83. (These all review Downs'
edition of the Familiar Letters as well; see below.)

3   ELTON, OLIVER. A Survey of English Literature 1730-1780.
    London: Edward Arnold, 1: 164-81.

    Richardson invented types well, had great analytic
power, maintained suspense with skill, and "though not a
great poet ...took the risks of one." (175) His poverty of
ideas and of language are against him; he barely lives
today, but he played an important role in the European
revolt against reason.

4   HEIDLER, J.B. History from 1700-1800 of English Criticism of
    Prose Fiction. University of Illinois Studies in Language
    and Literature 13, part 2. Urbana, Ill.: University of
    Illinois Press, 188 pp.

    Attempts to differentiate individual conceptions of
prose fiction in writers of the period, including
Richardson. Richardson's "apparent indifference" to
technical matters extended only to criticism of them
(51-52); he obviously thought about issues of technique
and considered them important, as he did moral value,
consistency of characters, truth to nature, but not strict
realism, at least in Grandison. (61) He was indebted to
dramatic theory. After Diderot's Eloge, he was considered
the champion of emotional writing. Includes material on
Richardson's influence and criticism of him by the
eighteenth century.

*5   KRASENSKY, OTTOKAR. "Goethes Verhältnis zu den Hauptvertreten
    des sentimentalen englischen Romans des 18. Jhdts.,
    Richardson, Fielding, Smollett, Sterne und Goldsmith."
    Diss. Wien 1928.

Source: Universitätsbibliothek Wien.

6   LANZISERA, FRANCESCO. "I Romanzi di Samuel Richardson in
    Italia." Reale Istituto Orientale di Napoli--<u>Annali</u> 1 (but
    Anno 7):148-79.
        Richardson is a convinced Puritan, so much so that his
    "angelico Grandison" is allowed to be an exception to his
    rule of social realism in characterization. He influences
    English and European writing toward pathos and
    sentimentalism. Lanzisera cites numerous novels and dramas
    owing something to Richardson.

7   MCKILLOP, ALAN DUGALD. "Notes on Smollett . . . II.
    Smollett and Richardson." <u>PQ</u> 7:369-71.
        Notes on Smollett's apologies to Richardson for a bad
    notice in the <u>Critical Review</u> (1756.1).

8   RICHARDSON, SAMUEL. <u>Familiar Letters on Important Occasions</u>.
    With an introduction by Brian W. Downs. London: G.
    Routledge; New York: Dodd, Mead, 292 pp.
        Downs stresses the literary qualities of the <u>Familiar
    Letters</u>, gives their history, and draws parallels with the
    novels.
        Rev.: See 1928.2.

9   ---. <u>Selections from Richardson and Fielding</u>. Selected by
    the Department of English, College of Liberal Arts,
    Northwestern University. N.p.: n.p., 32 pp.
        All Richardson selections are from <u>Clarissa</u>.

10 THOMSEN, EJNER. <u>Studier i Richardsons romaner</u>. Studier fra
    Sprog- og Oldtidsforskning utgivna af det
    Filologisk-Historiske Samfund Nr. 150. Copenhagen & Oslo:
    Jespersen og Pios Forlag, 88 pp.
        Largely on <u>Pamela</u> and <u>Clarissa</u>; introduction to and
    summary of foreign criticism, with material on Richardson's
    European influence.

*11 WHITLEY, W.T. <u>Artists and their Friends in England,
    1700-1799</u>. London. Pp. 47÷50.
        Richardson's relationships with Highmore and Young.
    Source: Hannaford, item 886.

1   BECKSTEIN, J. <u>Richardsons</u> <u>Pamela</u> <u>nach</u> <u>ihrem</u> <u>Gedankengehalt</u>
     <u>betrachtet.</u> <u>Mit</u> <u>einem</u> <u>Anhang:</u> <u>die</u> <u>Quellenfrage</u> <u>bei</u> <u>der</u>
     <u>Pamela</u>. Ph.D. dissertation, Erlangen, 1930 [?]. Bremen:
     H Engelke, 154 pp.
         Study of moral purpose of <u>Pamela</u>, noting sources in
     moral theology; general remarks on characters, structure,
     method, concluding that Richardson works through
     influencing the feelings.

2   DOTTIN, PAUL. "Du Nouveau sur Richardson (documents
     inédits)." <u>RAA</u> 7:55-59, 258-61.
         Richardson and the Society for the Encouragement of
     Learning; why and how Richardson left North End.

3   FORD, FORD MADOX. <u>The</u> <u>English</u> <u>Novel</u>. London and
     Philadelphia: J.B. Lippincott, pp. 71-77, 80-84, 89-90,
     112, 115.
         Richardson is the progenitor of "the modern novel which
     does not avoid the problems of the day," of everything
     opposed to the commercial "nuvveling" of Thackeray and
     Dickens, and thus the father of everything Ford considers
     valuable in the novel. Ford compares him to Flaubert,
     James, and Anthony Trollope, whom he thinks the first real
     disciple of Richardson in English fiction, and considers
     him to be one of the few utterly original geniuses (with
     Trollope, Jane Austen, and Shakespeare) in English writing.

4   LAWRENCE, D.H. <u>Pornography</u> <u>and</u> <u>Obscenity</u>. Criterion
     Miscellany No. 5. London: Faber & Faber, p. 11.
         Defends his writing by comparing it with the "slightly
     indecent . . . titillations" of <u>Pamela</u>, <u>Anna</u> <u>Karenina</u>
     and <u>The</u> <u>Mill</u> <u>on</u> <u>the</u> <u>Floss</u>; <u>Clarissa</u> is also cited as a
     model of an insulting approach to sexuality in literature.

5   PROPER, COENRAAD BART ANNE. <u>Social</u> <u>Elements</u> <u>in</u> <u>English</u> <u>Prose</u>
     <u>Fiction,</u> <u>1700-1832</u>. Amsterdam: H.J. Paris, pp. 47÷49.
         Richardson is a novelist of moral, but not social,
     equality; he influences <u>Anna</u> <u>St.</u> <u>Ives</u>, <u>Hermsprong</u>,
     <u>Desmond</u>, <u>The</u> <u>Fool</u> <u>of</u> <u>Quality</u>, and <u>The</u> <u>Man</u> <u>of</u> <u>the</u> <u>World</u>, but
     there is no special place in his novels for discussion of
     social issues.

6   RICHARDSON, SAMUEL. <u>Pamela;</u> <u>or,</u> <u>Virtue</u> <u>Rewarded.</u> <u>A</u>
     <u>Facsimile</u> <u>Reproduction</u> <u>of</u> <u>the</u> <u>Edition</u> <u>of</u> <u>1769,</u> <u>with</u> <u>an</u>
     <u>Introduction</u> <u>by</u> <u>A.</u> <u>Edward</u> <u>Newton</u>. Berwyn, Pa.:

Privately printed, 181 pp.
See 1930.1.

7   ---. The <u>Shakespeare</u> <u>Head</u> <u>Edition</u> <u>of</u> <u>the</u> <u>Novels</u> <u>of</u> <u>Samuel</u>
     <u>Richardson</u>. 18v. [Stratford-upon-Avon: Printed at the
     Shakespeare Head Press and published for the press by Basil
     Blackwell, Oxford, 1929-31.]
          Vols. 1-4, <u>Pamela</u>; 5-12, <u>Clarissa</u>; 13-18, <u>Sir</u> <u>Charles</u>
     <u>Grandison</u>. Currently the standard edition, but the texts
     are not markedly superior; the cautious writer should stay
     with Richardson's own editions. Reprinted New York:
     Houghton Mifflin, 1930-31. Reviewed: <u>TLS</u> (1932), p. 266.

SCHÜCKING, LEVIN L. <u>Die</u> <u>Familie</u> <u>in</u> <u>Puritanismus</u>.
     See 1964.21, 1969.15.

8   SWANN, GEORGE ROGERS. <u>Philosophical</u> <u>Parallelisms</u> <u>in</u> <u>Six</u>
     <u>English</u> <u>Novelists</u>: <u>The</u> <u>Conception</u> <u>of</u> <u>Good</u> <u>and</u> <u>Evil</u> <u>in</u>
     <u>Human</u> <u>Nature</u>. Ph.D. dissertation, University of
     Pennsylvania. Philadelphia: [University of Pennsylvania].
          Chapter 3, "Richardson and the Idealism of the Moral
     Will," compares Richardson with Kant; social ties are
     all-important, religion is identified with unworldliness
     (but is the most useful means of dealing with the world),
     and "the basic factor in human personality . . . is the
     will." Richardson, like Kant, bases his conception of the
     good on moral perfection, not happiness.

                              1930

1   ANON. "Newbery's edition of Pamela, 1769." <u>TLS</u>, p. 196.
          Notes on A. Edward Newton's privately printed facsimile
     of this edition (see 1929.6).

2   ADDLESHAW, S. "A Pioneer--Samuel Richardson." <u>Church</u>
     <u>Quarterly</u> <u>Review</u> 110, part 220 (July 1930):297÷315.
          General introduction to Richardson, who is now a "great
     but unvisited deity" since it is difficult to find an
     unabridged edition of his works; he must be taken whole in
     order that his elaborate and slow analysis may be
     appreciated. The reader who abandons impatience will find
     undoubted genius, original thought, unusual feminism for

his day, "a complete world."

3   BAKER, ERNEST A. The History of the English Novel. Vol. 4.
     Intellectual Realism from Richardson to Sterne. London,
     pp. 16-76 (and elsewhere).
         Richardson's   novels   perpetuate   much   that   is
     characteristic of the old romances, but fundamentally he is
     a realist whose central theme is action; analysis of
     feeling leads directly to a study of motive and to scrutiny
     of will and action. His observation is directed inward,
     observing himself, and all of his characters engage to some
     extent in the same self-analysis, a way of life that
     explains   Grandison's   ludicrous   side.   (However, in
     technique, characterization, and amusement value, Grandison
     is superior to Pamela.) Testing and development of
     character form the necessary groundwork of each story and
     find   their   fullest   expression in Clarissa. Baker
     appreciates Richardson's epistolary technique, which allows
     the "mental story" of his books "a coherence, and the
     impending tragedy . . . an inevitableness, beyond [the]
     questions of the adequacy or inadequacy of the machinery"
     and apart from Richardson's inexperience in the social
     sphere he wrote about. Useful on Marivaux, Richardson's
     moral development, and Richardson's place in the history of
     individualism in the novel.

4   DOTTIN, PAUL. "Du nouveau sur Richardson (documents
     inédits)." RAA 7:432-34.
         "Richardson as matrimonial agent"; an unpublished
     letter of October 9, 1750, from the Forster Collection.

5   ---. "L'Accueil fait à Paméla." RAA 7:505-19.
         Personal and literary tributes paid to the book just
     after its publication. Rev. A.D. McKillop, PQ 10 (1931):
     207.

6   ---. "Les Continuations de Paméla." RELV 47:444-61.
         Principally on Kelly's Pamela's Conduct in High Life.
     This, the two articles above, and 1929.2 were re-used in
     Dottin's Samuel Richardson the next year.

*6   [FIELDING, HENRY.] An Apology for the Life of Mrs. Shamela
     Andrews.   Attributed   to   Henry   Fielding.   With an
     Introduction by Brian W. Downs. Cambridge (England):
     Gordon Fraser, 71 pp.

7   FORD, FORD MADOX. <u>The English Novel</u>.   London: Constable &
     Co.
         See 1929.3.

*8   GIBSON, STRICKLAND, and Sir WILLIAM HOLDSWORTH. "The Case of
     Samuel Richardson, of London, Printer." <u>OBS</u> 2:320-25.
         Reprints <u>The Case of Samuel Richardson</u> .   .   .   (see
     1753.23).
         Source: <u>YWMLS</u>.

9   KRUTCH, J.W. "Samuel Richardson." <u>Atlantic Monthly</u> 146:50-59,
     205-15.   Reprinted in <u>Five Masters</u>. New York; London:
     Jonathan Cape, 1931, pp.   117-74;   Bloomington, Indiana:
     Indiana University Press, 1959; Gloucester, Mass.:   Smith,
     1968.
         A highly unsympathetic account of Richardson as an
     "essentially vulgar soul" with "tradesman's virtue [and]
     tradesman's conscience," whose creations, <u>Pamela</u> and
     <u>Clarissa</u>, share his vulgarity. In particular, <u>Clarissa</u>
     "<u>became, above all else, the model for sentimental fiction,
     . . . that vulgar sortof demi-tragedy produced when
     goodness is substituted for greatness</u>" and the hero or
     heroine tamely acquiesces in the forces that destroy him or
     her. Richardson's discovery of this unworthy pattern
     explains his great popularity in his time. But, though
     <u>Clarissa</u> is no longer much read, it is still an
     astonishingly gripping book; Pamela, though not Clarissa,
     is a triumph of characterization; and Richardson, while
     eliminating "every human experience above his own range, .
     . . examined what remained with a minuteness never known
     before."

10   LOVERING, STELLA. "L'Activité intellectuelle de l'Angleterre
     d'après l'ancien 'Mercure de France' 1672-1778." Paris:
     Boccard, pp.   275-78.
         Richardson was appreciated in the <u>Mercure de France</u>;
     however, Fielding was even more popular.

11   MARTIN, BURNS. "Richardson's Removal to Salisbury Court." <u>MLN</u>
     45:469.
         An advertisement dated from Salisbury Court, January 11,
     1724, seems to prove that Richardson moved there no later
     than late 1723.

12　　MILLER, GEORGE MOREY and C.J.　LONGMAN.　"The　Publisher　of
　　　　　Pamela."　TLS, pp.　628, 684.
　　　　　　　　Miller identifies Richardson´s　bookseller　friends　and
　　　　　partners　in the publication of Pamela as Charles Rivington
　　　　　and John Osborn Sr.　C.J.　Longman replies that the　second
　　　　　partner　was not Thomas Longman´s partner, John Osborn, but
　　　　　another John Osborn at the Golden Ball in Paternoster-Row.

13　　PRICE, LAWRENCE MARSDEN.　"Richardson, Wetzlar and Goethe." In
　　　　　Mélanges　offerts　à　Fernand　Baldensperger.　Paris:
　　　　　Librairie ancienne Honoré Champion, 2:174-87.
　　　　　　　　Goethe was influenced in the　composition　of　Werther,
　　　　　literarily　and　personally,　by the "zartere Sittlichkeit"
　　　　　and　"Empfindlichkeit"　transmitted　to　Germany　by
　　　　　Richardson´s works, especially　as　they were seen in the
　　　　　work of Sophie von La Roche, with　whose　family　Goethe
　　　　　stayed　just before composing Werther.　" .　.　. When the
　　　　　reading of an author becomes a part of the education　of　a
　　　　　succeeding　generation,　when his ideal principles become a
　　　　　part of its code, when that code again leads to a　poignant
　　　　　situation of real life, and when that situation is rendered
　　　　　into a work of art that　surpasses　that　of　the　original
　　　　　master,　then　it　would　seem that we have one of the rare
　　　　　authentic　instances　of　literary　influence." (187) See
　　　　　1875.3, 1937.3.

14　　　---.　Pamela, ou La Vertu récompensée.　Traduction　de　l´abbé
　　　　　Prévost.　Introduction　et　notes　par Pierre Melèse.　Les
　　　　　Cent Chefs-d´oeuvre étrangers.　Paris:　La　Renaissance　du
　　　　　Livre [1930], 187 pp.

*15　　SALE, WILLIAM MERRITT, JR.　"Samuel Richardson:　Master
　　　　　Printer." Ph.D.　dissertation, Yale.
　　　　　　　　Early version of 1950.10 and 1936.9.

1931

1　　　BECKWITH, F.　"The Anti-Pamelas." TLS, p.　135.
　　　　　　　　On The　True　Anti-Pamela,　Haywood´s　Anti-Pamela　and
　　　　　Mauvillon´s French translation, and Villaret´s Anti-Pamela,
　　　　　ou mémoires de M.　D.　.　.　., with　reviews　from　the
　　　　　Bibliothèque britannique.

*2   DISTENFELD, FELICIA.   "Richardsons   Menschen."   Diss.   Wien.
      Univbib.   Wien.
          Source: Catalog of the Universitätsbibliothek Wien.

 3   DOTTIN, PAUL.   <u>Samuel   Richardson,   1689-1761,   imprimeur   de
      Londres,   auteur   de   Pamela,   Clarissa,   et   Grandison</u>.   Paris:
      Perrin, 534 pp.   (Two editions in this year.)
          "One must read Richardson for neither the story, nor the
      moral, but the psychology." Dottin summarizes the books and
      the   correspondence   associated   with   them,   as   well   as
      twentieth-century   critical   reaction   to   Richardson   in
      France;   for this the most relevant chapters are those   on
      the   response to the three novels (Chs.   7, 11, 15) and the
      material   on Richardson´s   reading   and   his   influence   in
      Europe.
          Rev: L. Cazamian, <u>RH</u> 158:395-97;   J.W.   Draper, <u>PQ</u>
      10:320;   J.A.   Falconer, <u>ES</u> 14 (1932):37-40;   E.   Legouis,
      <u>RAA</u> 9:151-52;   A. McKillop, <u>MLN</u> 47 (1932): 120-22;   <u>TLS</u>,
      July 16, 1931, p.   561 (with the SHE <u>Clarissa</u>);   S.   Gwynn,
      <u>QuarterlyR</u> 259:315-30 (with the Everyman <u>Clarissa</u>).

 4   DOWNS, BRIAN W. <u>TLS</u>, p.   154.
          Reply to Beckwith, distinguishing the three books.

 5   DUDLEY, O.H.T. <u>TLS</u>, p.   116.
          Reply to A.L.   Reade, below;   Richardson might have been
      a   private   pupil   at Christ´s Hospital, as Warren Hastings
      was, and may have been there during his apprenticeship, not
      before. (But see 1783.5A.)

 6   MCKILLOP, A.D.   "The Personal Relations between Fielding   and
      Richardson." <u>MP</u> 28:423-33.
          Richardson´s   and Fielding´s   relationship   underwent
      several changes.   Richardson would have been able to follow
      Fielding´s career as a dramatist in <u>The Prompter</u> and would
      have   been aware of Fielding´s anti-Walpole campaign in <u>The
      Champion</u>, since he printed the   chief   Walpole   organ,   <u>The
      Gazetteer</u> (which Fielding attacked in Book II, chapter xvii
      of <u>Joseph Andrews</u>).   It was trade   knowledge   at   the   time
      that   <u>Shamela</u> was Fielding´s,   and Richardson knew from
      George Cheyne that <u>Joseph Andrews</u> also was his even   before
      the   book was published.   But with   Fielding´s generous
      praise of <u>Clarissa</u> the   relationship   warmed   for   a
      time--McKillop speculates   that Fielding had a copy of the
      fifth volume of <u>Clarissa</u> from   Richardson--only   to   cool

again with the success of <u>Tom</u> <u>Jones</u> and Richardson's contempt for it, a contempt that may have motivated <u>Sir</u> <u>Charles</u> <u>Grandison</u>. In the minds of the two authors' friends there was no diametrical opposition between them.

7   READE, ALEYN LYELL.   "Samuel   Richardson   and   Christ's
     Hospital." <u>TLS</u>, p.   99.
         Richardson's name is not on the books of Christ's
     Hospital. Cf. 1931.5 and 1783.5A.

8   TRAHARD, PIERRE.   <u>Les</u> <u>Maîtres</u> <u>de</u> <u>la</u> <u>Sensibilité</u> <u>française</u> <u>au</u>
     <u>18e.</u> <u>s.</u> <u>(1715-1789)</u>. 4v. Paris: Boivin, 1931-33.
         Richardson appears frequently as an influence in French
     sensibility, particularly over Prévost (1:171 ff.), Diderot
     (2:168 ff.), Rousseau and Julie de Lespinasse (3:259 ff.),
     and Laclos (4:52).

9   ZEYDEL, EDWIN H. <u>Ludwig</u> <u>Tieck</u> <u>and</u> <u>England:</u> <u>A</u> <u>Study</u> <u>in</u> <u>the</u>
     <u>Literary</u> <u>Relations</u> <u>of</u> <u>Germany</u> <u>and</u> <u>England</u> <u>During</u> <u>the</u> <u>Early</u>
     <u>Nineteenth</u> <u>Century</u>. Princeton: Princeton   University
     Press, pp. 14-15.
         Influence of <u>Sir</u> <u>Charles</u> <u>Grandison</u> and <u>Clarissa</u> on
     <u>William</u> <u>Lovell</u>.

<u>1932</u>

1   BOND, RICHMOND P.   <u>English</u> <u>Burlesque</u>   <u>Poetry</u>   <u>1700-1750</u>.
     Cambridge, Mass.: Harvard University Press, pp. 425-26.
         <u>Pamela,</u> <u>or</u> <u>the</u> <u>Fair</u> <u>Impostor</u> described.

2   BOYD, JAMES. <u>Goethe's</u> <u>Knowledge</u> <u>of</u> <u>English</u>   <u>Literature</u>.
     Oxford: Clarendon Press, pp. 118-24.
         Goethe's knowledge of Richardson discussed; covers
     material in <u>Die</u> <u>Laune</u> <u>des</u> <u>Verliebten,</u> <u>Werther,</u> <u>Wilhelm</u>
     <u>Meisters</u> <u>Lehrjahre,</u> <u>Versuch</u> <u>über</u> <u>die</u> <u>Dichtungen</u>, and
     Goethe's letters.

3   BROWN, HERBERT R.   "Richardson and Sterne in the <u>Massachusetts</u>
     <u>Magazine</u>." <u>NEQ</u> 5:65-82.
         The vogue of <u>Richardsonaden</u> is shown in the
     <u>Massachusetts</u> <u>Magazine</u> in themes of seduction and resulting
     misery, the combination of sentiment and seduction, the
     appeal to the female reader, the frequent use of the

epistolary form, and moral didacticism. Brown´s summaries of the <u>Mass</u>. <u>Mag</u>. material are not reliable.

4   JOHNSON, THOMAS H.
Edwards read <u>Grandison</u> with pleasure and had favorable opinions of the other books.

5   LYNCH, KATHLEEN M.   "<u>Pamela</u> <u>Nubile</u>, <u>L´Ecossaise</u>, and <u>The English Merchant</u>." <u>MLN</u> 47:94-96.
<u>Pamela</u> <u>nubile</u> supplied some plot details to <u>L´Ecossaise</u> and Colman added another detail, probably from the same source, in his translation of the play, <u>The English Merchant</u>.
See 1970.11.

6   MACCARTHY, DESMOND. "Richardson and Proust." In <u>Criticism</u>. London and New York: Putnam, pp. 210-15.
Richardson and Proust both concentrate on the texture of everyday life, in the social context of the day. Richardson´s work is sentimental and moral; Proust´s, esthetic, amoral, and cynical.

7   PRICE, LAWRENCE MARSDEN. <u>The Reception of English Literature in Germany</u>. Berkeley: University of California Press, 606 pp.; see especially Chapters 7, 12, 13, and pages 111-29, 190-231.
Price maintains, <u>inter alia</u>, that Richardson exerted an important influence in Germany in the years 1746-70 and was "a way of life" in Wetzlar and perhaps in other unrecorded communities in the ´70s; thereafter his influence fell off, a decline signaled by Blankenburg´s <u>Versuch über den Roman</u> (1774). A revision of 1919.4 with materials from 1925.7, 1926.5, and 1930.13; to be further revised as 1953.5, with material from 1950.6.

8   REICHENBURG, MARGUERITE. "Essai sur les Lectures de Rousseau." <u>AJJR</u> 21:178, 197÷98.
Documents Rousseau´s reading of Richardson. Reprinted as a pamphlet in Philadelphia: n.p., 1934.

9   RICHARDSON, SAMUEL. <u>Clarissa or the History of a Young Lady</u>. 4v. London: J.M. Dent; New York; E.P. Dutton; Everyman´s Library.
Text of third edition. Frequently reprinted. Rev.: S. Gwynn, <u>QuarterlyR</u> 259:315-30.

10   TOMPKINS, J.M.S. The Popular Novel in England, 1770-1800.
      London: Constable & Co, 402 pp.
         Extremely valuable study of trends and individual
      writers in last part of eighteenth century; much material
      on Richardsonaden, not always identified as such. A second
      edition was published in 1961 and reprinted in 1969. Rev.:
      Graham Greene, Spectator, August 20, 1932, pp. 238-39.

                          1933

1   BLACK, FRANK GEES.   "The Technique of Letter Fiction in
      English from 1740 to 1800." Harvard Studies and Notes in
      Philology and Literature 25: 291-312.
         Using material taken from the C.N. Greenough Catalogue
      of prose fiction at Harvard and from other sources, Black
      describes twelve types of epistolary novel popular between
      1740-1800.   Though the epistolary vein was "worked out
      within fifty years" (compare 1933.13), epistolary writing
      called attention to the narrative problem of point of view,
      brought reader and story into closer association, gave the
      story circumstantial realism, a modern domestic air, and a
      "generous inclusiveness and leisureliness of style," and
      allowed the author to mix discussion and commentary with
      the narrative.   Black estimated that of 3000 novels
      published in the period, 506 were epistolary and at least
      fifty-five of these contained borrowings from Richardson.
      [This is a conservative estimate.]

2   BROADUS, E.K. "Mr. Richardson Arrives." London Mercury 28:
      425-35.
         Chatty   general   introduction,   intimating   that
      Richardson's novels were the fruit of his early anonymous
      letters--in the novels Richardson is giving unasked advice
      to grown-ups--but finding that "even to the jaded and
      cynical modern reader the fourth volume [of Clarissa] is
      curiously compelling."

3   EDGAR, PELHAM. "Richardson and the Epistolary Novel." In The
      Art of the Novel from 1700 to the Present Time. New York:
      Macmillan, pp. 46-51.
         Richardson's techniques for motivating the use of the
      letter form seem clumsy, and in varying the tone of his
      letters he is less successful than Smollett. But "as a

generating influence no other English novelist can compare
with him." His influence on the analytical novelist of
today is indirect, and he is less read than Fielding.

4   H., A.J. "Lady Bradshaigh, Richardson´s Correspondent." N&Q
     164: 192-93.
          Corrects 1877.1 and says that brief extracts from
     Richardson´s correspondence were published in Elegant
     Epistles, a book of letters for the moral education of the
     young, which had editions in 1791, 1807, 1821, and 1822.

*5   LASLEY, ROBERT L. "The Reputation of Samuel Richardson,
     1740-1832: A Study in the Origins of the English Novel."
     Ph.D. dissertation, University of Wisconsin.
          Source: 1975.2, item D63.

6   LEFEVER, CHARLOTTE. "Richardson´s Paradoxical Success." PMLA
     48: 856-60.
          Richardson´s books are real rather than ideal, books of
     "human nature".

7   MCCLELLAND, JOHN. "The Course of Realism in the English Novel
     from Addison and Steele through Sir Walter Scott." Ph.D.
     dissertation, Stanford.
          Richardson aimed for unity of action, emphasized
     character and emotions, and centered his novels in domestic
     life.

8   MCKILLOP, A.D. "Richardson´s Early Years as a Printer." RES
     9: 67-70.
          Material on Richardson´s printing and associates from
     1715-25.

*9   MATHESIUS, VILEM. Dějiny anglické literatury od poloviny 15.
     stol. do poloviny 18. stol. [History of English
     Literature from the 15th to the 18th centuries.] Spolek
     posluchačů filosofie a studentské sekce britské
     společnosti. Práha: n.p., pp. 218-23. Statni knihovna
     ČSR.
          General introduction to Richardson in Czech. Source:
     Catalog of the Statni knihovna ČSR.

*10 RAILO, EINO, ed. In Englantilaisen kirjallisuuden kultainen
     kirja. [The Golden Book of English Literature.] Porvoo &
     Helsinki: n.p., pp. 263-69. Helsinki U. Library.

Source: Catalog of the Helsinki University Library. Short biography of Richardson and extracts from <u>Pamela naimisissa</u> (1919) and <u>Clarissa</u>. Aila Lassila of the Helsinki University Library concludes, since this is the only work of criticism in Finnish on Richardson, "In collecting information about Samuel Richardson's influence on Finnish literary life, one had to draw the conclusion that there was almost no influence at all."

11 SALE, WILLIAM, MERRITT, JR. "<u>Sir Charles Grandison</u> and the Dublin Pirates." <u>YULG</u> 7: 80-86.
Partial description of the Yale University Library copy of the first pirated edition of <u>Grandison</u> and summary of the circumstances under which it appeared.

12 SINGER, GODFREY FRANK. <u>The Epistolary Novel</u>. Philadelphia: University of Pennsylvania Press, 276 pp.
Singer discusses the epistolary tradition before 1740, in which the <u>Familiar Letters</u> are "most important," and criticizes the three novels from moral and epistolary points of view; <u>Grandison</u> receives high marks on both scores. Surveys continental epistolary fiction to 1800, American and English fiction past 1800, and suggests that many of them were influenced by editions of Richardson's novels and by the various abridgments. Richardson is the best writer in the epistolary form; his "many successors and imitators serve but to emphasize this fact for us." (216) Pp. 217÷55 contain a bibliography of epistolary fiction. Rev.: <u>YWES</u> 14:34,304; <u>RES</u> 11:356-57.

13 WEBB, GEOFFREY. "Architecture and the Garden." In <u>Johnson's England</u>. Edited by A.S. Turberville. 2v. Oxford: Clarendon Press, 2:102-3.
Richardson's description of Grandison Hall is cited as the ideal country house and treated as a realistic description.

<u>1934</u>

1 BIRNBAUM, JOHANNA. <u>Die 'Memoirs' um 1700; eine Studie zur Entwicklung der realistischen Romankunst vor Richardson</u>. Ph.D. dissertation, Gottingen. Halle: Max Niemeyer, 117 pp.

A decreased interest in dogma as such and a greater interest in this world open the way for, first, memoirs and books of edification, then the novels of Richardson. The art of the memoir provides Richardson with the art of his fiction, particularly plot, thematic parallels, and realism.

*2   BORCHERDT, RUDOLF. <u>Pamela.</u> <u>Komödie</u> <u>in</u> <u>drei</u> <u>Akten.</u> <u>Neu</u> <u>erfunden</u>. Berlin: Dreimasken-Verlag, 211 pp. BZK. Source: Bayerische Zentralkatalog.

3   BOSWELL, JAMES. <u>The</u> <u>Life</u> <u>of</u> <u>Samuel</u> <u>Johnson,</u> <u>LL.D.</u> Edited by G.B. Hill, revised by L. Powell. 6v. Oxford: Clarendon Press, 1934-50.
      Frequent references to Richardson (see index); valuable biographically and for contemporary opinions of Richardson.

4   CRANE, R.S. "Suggestions toward a Genealogy of the ´Man of Feeling.´" <u>ELH</u> 1: 205-30.
      Sir Charles Grandison is one of the examples taken up in this discussion of the origin and development of the cult of "moral weeping".

*5   DE HAAN, M.H. <u>Adrian</u> <u>Loosjes</u>. Ph.D. dissertation, Leiden. Utrecht: n.p.
      Contains material on the influence of Richardson on Loosjes´ novel, <u>Susanna</u> <u>Bronkhorst</u>.
      Source: <u>YWMLS</u>.

6   HORNBEAK, KATHERINE GEE. <u>The</u> <u>Complete</u> <u>Letter</u> <u>Writer</u> <u>in</u> <u>English.</u> Smith College Studies in Modern Languages 15, pts. 3-4 (April-July): introduction and Chapter 4.
      Richardson was indebted to previous letter-writing compendia for his subjects in the <u>Familiar</u> <u>Letters</u>, but his book contained more and longer letters; was interested in ethics, not rhetoric or "correct forms"; had a preponderance (57%) of letters by and about women, and a preponderance of letters about love, but a great distrust of the cavalier style; contained groups of letters; contained characterization, even in single letters; and made use of a dramatic and novelistic concretization. Hornbeak gives some history of the <u>Familiar</u> <u>Letters</u>, parts of which she found appearing in letter-writing manuals published as late as 1924.

*7   LANGBROEK, M. <u>Liebe</u> <u>und</u> <u>Freundschaft:</u> <u>Bei</u> <u>Klopstock</u> <u>und</u> <u>im</u>
      <u>niederländischen</u> <u>empfindsamen</u> <u>Roman</u>. Ph.D. dissertation,
      Amsterdam. Purmerend: J. Muusses.
            Source: <u>YWMLS</u> 5: 174: the work "discusses the
      influence of Richardson in the Netherlands by way of
      Germany."

 8   MARSHALL, RODERICK. <u>Italy</u> <u>in</u> <u>English</u> <u>Literature,</u> <u>1755–1815</u>.
      Columbia University Studies in English and Comparative
      Literature, No. 116. New York: Columbia University
      Press, p. 13.
            During the period in which the Italian character was
      considered almost uniformly vicious, <u>Sir</u> <u>Charles</u> <u>Grandison</u>
      was "the only important English novel .   .   .   to give
      [Italians] prominence."

*9   RIVA, SERAFINO. "Pamela a Venezia." <u>Annuario</u> <u>1933–34</u> <u>del</u>
      <u>Reale</u> <u>Istituto</u> <u>Tecnico</u> <u>Provinciale</u> <u>Pareggiato</u> <u>Jacopo</u>
      <u>Riccati</u> <u>di</u> <u>Treviso</u>. Treviso.
            Source: <u>BELL</u> 1934.

*10   SEILLÈRE, ERNEST. "Le Père du Roman Victorien." <u>Figaro</u>, 11
      March 1934.
            Source: <u>BELL</u> 1934.

 11   SMITH, WARREN H. <u>Architecture</u> <u>in</u> <u>English</u> <u>Fiction</u>. New Haven:
      Yale University Press, pp. 65–70.
            The "Romantic" or "Gothic" architecture in <u>Clarissa</u> and
      <u>Pamela</u> and the Renaissance style of Grandison Hall.

                                1935

 1   BLACK, FRANK GEES. "Edward Kimber, Anonymous Novelist of the
      Mid–Eighteenth Century." <u>Harvard</u> <u>Studies</u> <u>and</u> <u>Notes</u> <u>in</u>
      <u>Philology</u> <u>and</u> <u>Literature</u> 17: 27÷42.
            Though Kimber is more indebted to Smollett than to
      Richardson, he consistently attempts to reproduce the
      character of Sir Charles Grandison in the virtuous young
      heroes of <u>The</u> <u>Generous</u> <u>Briton</u> and <u>James</u> <u>Ramble,</u> <u>Esq</u>., as
      well as in Breyfield in <u>The</u> <u>Happy</u> <u>Orphans</u> and Col.
      Beaumont in <u>Maria</u>; other of his elderly men have
      Grandisonian characteristics, and he produces many
      libertines on the model of Lovelace.

2   COE, ADA M. "Richardson in Spain." <u>HR</u> 3: 56–63.
     General review of Richardson´s literary presence in
     Spain, through plays and translations, up to 1847. " . .
     . It seems quite certain that whenever a careful study of
     the novels can be made it will show conclusively that the
     works of this English novelist . . . led Spanish writers
     to imitate him." (63)

3   COX, J. CHARLES, H. ASKEW, and F. WILLIAMSON. "Samuel
     Richardson´s birthplace." <u>N&Q</u> 169: 263, 300–301.
     Askew asks if any information has been discovered since
     1921.   J.   Charles   Cox   identifies   himself   as   a
     great–great–gran–nephew of the novelist. Williamson
     replies that Cox is not a member of the family and proves,
     by subtracting 1689 from 1706 and getting 7, that
     Richardson could not have been born later than 1682.

4   DE HAAN, M.H. "De Invloed van Richardson op Jane Austen en op
     Nederlandsche auteurs." <u>De Nieuwe Taalgids</u> 29: 274–80.
     Influence of Richardson over Austen, Wolff and Deken,
     and Adrian Loosjes (<u>Susanna Bronkhorst</u>); compares the
     various pictures in these authors of the "gentle and
     sensitive mind".

5   EWALD, EUGEN. <u>Abbild und Wunschbild der Gesellschaft bei</u>
     <u>Richardson und Fielding</u>.   Ph.D.   dissertation,   Köln.
     Wuppertal–Elberfeld: Wuppertaler Druckerei A–G, 108 pp.
     Both teach the ideal, and for both the artistic form is
     only the most important of the means by which they show
     society. Their common starting–point is the individual,
     bound to other individuals through friendship and love, to
     a circle, a family, finally to a whole society; therefore
     reform of the society must begin with reform of the
     individual personality. The two agreed on this, and
     disagreed only on the role of social class and profession.

6   GREEN, FREDERICK C. <u>Minuet: A Critical Survey of French and</u>
     <u>English Literary Ideas in the Eighteenth Century</u>. London:
     J.M. Dent, see esp. pp. 365 ff., 399–409.
     Attacks Texte´s contention (1895.3) that Richardson
     influenced the eighteenth–century French novel widely;
     finds his influence weak, if present at all, in Rousseau,
     Restif de la Bretonne, and Marivaux, to all of whom he is
     inferior.

7   RONTE, HEINZ.   <u>Richardson</u> <u>und</u> <u>Fielding</u>:   Geschichte   ihres
     <u>Ruhms</u>:   literärsoziologischer   Versuch.   Ph.D.
     dissertation, Köln. Kölner Anglistische Arbeiten No.   25.
     Leipzig: Tauchnitz, 217 pp. Reprinted New York: Johnson
     Reprint   Corp.,   1966.   (Another   edition:
     Bochum-Langendreer: Poppinghaus, 217 pp.)
          Comparison   of Richardson's and Fielding's views   on
     several   moral and formal questions. The greater part of
     the book is devoted to a study of their reputation, leaning
     heavily on 1926.2, but it should be titled "ihres Ruhms in
     England," since   there   is   nothing   on   Fielding's   not
     inconsiderable or Richardson's enormous influence outside
     England.   Anti-Fieldingites   tend   to   be   listed   as
     pro-Richardsonian, misleadingly.
          Rev. H. Heuer, <u>LGRP</u> 59 (1938): 95-96; L.   Stettner,
     <u>NJWJ</u> 12 (1936): 376; E. Deckner, <u>Ang.</u> <u>Bbl.</u> 47 (1936):
     367-68; G. Kitchin, <u>MLR</u> 32 (1937): 662; A. Potthoff,
     <u>NS</u> 45: 133-34.

8   SALE, WILLIAM MERRITT, JR. "The First Dramatic Version of
     <u>Pamela</u>." <u>YULG</u> 9:83-88.
          Distinguishes various editions of Henry Giffard's play,
     <u>Pamela</u>,   from   <u>Pamela,</u> <u>or</u> <u>Virtue</u> <u>Triumphant</u>, which is
     possibly to be ascribed to James Dance, a.k.a. James Love.

9   ---. "Samuel Richardson and <u>Sir</u> <u>William</u> <u>Harrington</u>." <u>TLS</u>, p.
     537.
          On the basis of BM Add. MS.   28,097, identifies Anna
     Meades as the author of <u>The</u> <u>History</u> <u>of</u> <u>Sir</u> <u>William</u>
     <u>Harringon</u>, which Richardson read and corrected. Thomas
     Hull, to whom the authorship was previously ascribed, may
     have edited the book.

10   ---. "Samuel Richardson's House at Fulham." <u>N&Q</u> 169: 133-34.
          Material on the ownership and tenancy of the house
     rented by Richardson at North End, Fulham.

11   ---. "The Singer Copy of <u>Sir</u> <u>Charles</u> <u>Grandison</u>." <u>University</u>
     <u>of</u> <u>Pennsylvania</u> <u>Library</u> <u>Chronicle</u> 3: 42-45.
          A <u>cancellandum</u> at 2:349-50, accidentally preserved in
     the Singer copy of the first edition of <u>Grandison</u>, explains
     a bibliographical problem: a copy with this feature may
     have been used to set the text of the third edition.

12   SCHLECK, FLORIAN J. "Richardson on the Index." TLS, p. 272.
         Pamela, with Eliza Haywood's Anti-Pamela, was placed on
         the Index in 1744; from 1758-1900 the French translations
         only were prohibited, but in 1900 the French versions were
         again replaced by the English. In 1930 both were still
         indexed (together with Sterne's Sentimental Journey).
         Clarissa and Grandison never appeared on the Index. Cf.
         1915.6.

*13   TODD-NAYLOR, URSULA. "Richardson's Influence on the Women
         Novelists of the Eighteenth Century." Dissertation, U. of
         London (University College).

*14   ZINKEL, ELSBETH. Der Abbé Prévost als Übersetzer aus dem
         Englischen mit besonderem Besichtigung der Werke von S.
         Richardson. Dissertation, Vienna. Univbib. Wien.

1936

1   BLACK, FRANK GEES. "The Continuations of Pamela." RAA 13:
         499-507.
         Black provides a short summary of three continuations of
         Pamela (Pamela's Conduct in High Life, Pamela in High
         Life--another title for Pamela's Conduct--and The Life of
         Pamela). While themselves "without any merit," they show
         the "great vogue of the Pamela legend."

2   BOAS, F.S. "Richardson's Novels and their Influence." In his
         From Richardson to Pinero. London: John Murray.
         Reprint of 1911.2.

3   DOTTIN, PAUL. "Samuel Richardson et le roman épistolaire."
         RAA 13: 481-99.
         Richardson, the "first and last of the great epistolary
         novelists," varies the patterns and content of his
         epistolary fiction in a masterful manner in Clarissa,
         though the form of Grandison is too heavy and too much
         concerned with mere epistolary stylization. Contains a
         discussion of the pros and cons of epistolary writing,
         largely from the point of view of psychological realism.
         Richardson's epistolary technique influenced Rousseau and
         Goethe.

*3A   GARNETT, DAVID. "Richardson, Fielding, and Smollett." In The
       English Novelists. Edited by Derek Verschoyle. 1936;
       reprinted Folcroft, Pa.: Folcroft Press, 1969, pp. 71-82.
       General   critical   introduction;   emphasizes
       middle-classness; feels Richardson had little influence
       but praises dramatic intensity of Clarissa.   Source:
       Hannaford, item 737.

4   H.,C. "Another Pamela." TLS, p. 1035.
       A real-life parallel to Pamela dating from 1789.

5   MCCKILLOP, ALAN DUGALD. Samuel Richardson, Printer and
       Novelist. Chapel Hill, N.C.: University of North Carolina
       Press, 369 pp. Reprinted Hamden, Conn.: Shoe String
       Press, 1960; London: Mark Paterson, 1961 (rev. Bernhard
       Fabian, Archiv 201 [1964]: 378).
       Detailed discussion of publication and reception of the
       three novels, Richardson's reputation, and his influence.
       Additional material on Richardson's biography, particularly
       relating to his business. A major study.
       Rev.: TLS, p. 270 (with Sale, below); J.W.   Beach,
       JEGP 36 (1937): 438-40 (with Sale and Shepperson, below);
       H. Williams, RES 14 (1938): 106-7; L.   Kronenberger,
       NYTBR, Dec. 27, 1936, p. 5; C.G. Stillman, New York
       Herald Tribune Book Supplement, Jan. 10, 1937, p. 17; G.
       Kitchin, MLR 33 (1938): 77-79; SRL 15: 16; F.T. Wood,
       ES 72: 115-17.

6   MITRANI, CHARLES. "Richardson and Mme de Souza." Philological
       Papers (West Virginia University), W. Virginia University
       Bulletin Series 37, No. 14, part 1: 28-35.
       Adelaîde de Souza is a follower of Richardson, writing
       good little books about private people who did simple and
       humble deeds, performed their duties, preached moderation
       and morality, and loved, especially matrimonially and
       filially. Richardson's influence is felt in plot details,
       concreteness of detail, diversity of plot, and religious
       scruples.

7   SALE, WILLIAM MERRITT.   "A   Bibliographical   Note   on
       Richardson's Clarissa." The Library 4th ser. 16: 448-51.
       Determines the first state of Clarissa's second preface
       and draws attention to a letter in the Correspondence
       assigning the preface to Warburton.

8   ---. <u>Samuel</u> <u>Richardson</u>:   <u>A</u> <u>Bibliographical</u> <u>Record</u> <u>of</u> <u>his</u>
       <u>Literary</u> <u>Career</u> <u>with</u> <u>Historical</u> <u>Notes</u>.   New Haven: Yale
       University Press, 165 pp.   Reprinted: Hamden, Conn.:
       Archon Books, 1969.
           Bibliographical description, with illustrations, summary
       of contents and background of publication, of the English
       editions of Richardson´s works published   during   his
       lifetime, with supplementary material on Richardson´s
       periodical publications and on works inspired by
       Richardson´s.   Complete, as far as the English works go,
       except for the York <u>Aesop´s</u> <u>Fables</u> of 1753;   on those,
       definitive.   Does not include Continental editions of the
       same period.
           Rev.: G. Tillotson, <u>RES</u> 16 (1940):   100-1;   E.A.
       Baker, <u>MLR</u> 32 (1937): 614-15;   D.A. Randall, <u>Publishers´</u>
       <u>Weekly</u> 131 (1937):   1347÷48;   <u>Reading</u> <u>and</u> <u>Collecting</u> 1
       (1937):   13;   see also 1936.5 above. Reprinted (Hamden,
       Conn.: Archon Press) 1969.

9   SHEPPERSON, ARCHIBALD BOLLING.   "Richardson and Fielding:
       Shamela and Shamelia." In his <u>Novel</u> <u>in</u> <u>Motley</u>: <u>A</u> <u>History</u>
       <u>of</u> <u>the</u> <u>Burlesque</u> <u>Novel</u> <u>in</u> <u>English</u>.   Cambridge, Mass.:
       Harvard University Press, pp. 9-38.
           History of the <u>Antipamelas</u>, concentrating on <u>Shamela</u>,
       which is to be preferred to <u>Pamela</u> for its normal, natural
       interpretation of its heroine´s motives. Other references
       to parodies of Richardson are scattered through the book
       (not all are indexed). Not wholly reliable.   Rev. J.W.
       Beach, <u>JEGP</u> 36 (1937): 440-42;   see <u>PQ</u> 17 (1938): 181.

10   STREETER, HAROLD W. <u>The</u> <u>Eighteenth-Century</u> <u>English</u> <u>Novel</u> <u>in</u>
       <u>French</u> <u>Translation</u>. New York: n.p., 224 pp.
           Bibliographical study with short section on Richardson
       individually;   much material on <u>Richardsonaden</u>.

                                1937

*1   BOGOSIAN, EZEKIEL. "The Perfect Gentleman: A Study of an
       Esthetic Type in the Novels of Richardson, Jane Austen, and
       Henry   James."   Ph.D.   dissertation.   University   of
       California/Berkeley.
           Source: McNamee.

2   KANY, CHARLES E. <u>The</u> <u>Beginnings</u> <u>of</u> <u>the</u> <u>Epistolary</u> <u>Novel</u> <u>in</u> <u>France,</u> <u>Italy,</u> <u>and</u> <u>Spain</u>. University of California Publications in Modern Philology 21, part 1. Berkeley, Calif.: University of California Press, 168 pp.

      An account of the formative period of the epistolary novel in Continental literature, centuries before Richardson, Rousseau, and Goethe; scattered references to possible specific originals for aspects of Richardson´s novelistic form.

3   LILJEGREN, STEN B. <u>The</u> <u>English</u> <u>Sources</u> <u>of</u> <u>Goethe´s</u> <u>Gretchen-Tragedy</u>. Skrifter Utgivna av Kungl. Humanistiska Vetenskapssam fundet i Lund, No. 24. Lund: C.W. Gleerup, 278 pp.

      The influence of Richardson on the novels and dramas of the late eighteenth and early nineteenth century literature of Germany was far-reaching and subtle, extending to an estimated 200 novels and plays; Liljegren discusses this influence in detail, particularly but not exclusively with regard to Goethe. It was felt in similarities of situation, moral definition, and character portrayal.

4   ORIANS, G.H. "Censure of Fiction in American Romances and Magazines 1789-1810." <u>PMLA</u> 52: 207-8.

      Richardson is sometimes an exception to the general dislike of novels in this period.

5   UTTER, R.P. and G.B. NEEDHAM. <u>Pamela´s</u> <u>Daughters</u>. London: Lovat Dickson; New York: Macmillan, 528 pp.

      Finds that "<u>every</u> heroine of eighteenth-century fiction" is in some sense an imitation of Pamela; concerned largely, however, with stereotypes of femininity in popular fiction from 1740 to the twentieth century, using Pamela and Clarissa, among others, as examples.

6   WARNER, J.H. "Eighteenth-Century English Reactions to the <u>Nouvelle Héloïse</u>." <u>PMLA</u> 52: 812-14.

      Cites frequent comparisons paralleling Richardson and Rousseau.

7   WRIGHT, WALTER FRANCIS. <u>Sensibility</u> <u>in</u> <u>English</u> <u>Prose</u> <u>Fiction,</u> <u>1760-1814:</u> <u>A</u> <u>Reinterpretation</u>. Illinois Studies in Language and Literature 22, parts 3-4: 16-19.

      Importance of Richardson as a seminal figure for the English writers after 1760.

1938

1   FISHER, HENRY C. "Realism and Morality in English Fiction
     before   1750."   Ph.D.   dissertation, University   of
     Pittsburgh.
         Relationship between moral fiction and realism in novels
     including Richardson´s.

2   HORNBEAK, KATHERINE GEE. "Richardson´s <u>Aesop</u>." Smith College
     Studies in Modern Languages 19, pt. 2: 30-50.
         Richardson´s edition has considerable emendations,
     additions and omissions from the edition by Sir Roger
     l´Estrange on which it is based.   Richardson keeps
     l´Estrange´s three-part format (fable, moral, reflection)
     but rewrites the reflections to omit the pervasive
     politicizing of the earlier edition, arguing instead for
     filial duty, benevolence, altruism, service to the
     community, and education of the young to trade, and against
     superstition,   bawdiness,   doubtful   expressions,   and
     "lawyering." Richardson takes some congenial ideas from
     l´Estrange but dilutes his epigrammatic phrasing. As a
     whole, Richardson´s edition is clearer and simpler than
     l´Estrange´s and designed in a cheaper format for a less
     educated audience, with fewer fables and a smaller size,
     but more pictures.

3   ---. "Richardson´s <u>Familiar</u> <u>Letters</u> and the Domestic Conduct
     Books." Ibid., 1-29.
         Like many other letter-writers, Richardson´s <u>Familiar</u>
     <u>Letters</u> is concerned not solely with forms of salutation
     and address, but counsels proper domestic conduct, "How to
     Think and Act <u>Justly</u> and <u>Prudently</u>." Background of other
     conduct books.
         Rev. (with 1938.2): A.D. McKillop, <u>MLN</u> 53: 551; E.
     Decker, <u>Ang. Bbl</u>. 49: 368-70.

4   PURDIE, EDNA. "Some Adventures of <u>Pamela</u> on the Continental
     Stage." In <u>German</u> <u>Studies</u> <u>Presented</u> <u>to</u> <u>Professor</u> <u>H.G.</u>
     <u>Fiedler</u> . . . Oxford: Clarendon Press, pp. 352-84.
     Reprinted in her <u>Studies</u> <u>in</u> <u>German</u> <u>Literature</u> <u>of</u> <u>the</u>
     <u>Eighteeth</u> <u>Century</u> . . . London: Athlone, 1965, pp.
     62-89.
         <u>Pamela</u> serves as an index to changes in taste in
     eighteenth-century Europe; dealing with the numerous
     versions and productions of plays of <u>Pamela</u> in the 1700´s,

Purdie concludes that by the publication of <u>Anton</u> <u>Reiser</u> (1785-90) "virtue rewarded had ceased to be so enthralling as virtue betrayed."

5   SLAGLE, KENNETH C. <u>The</u> <u>English</u> <u>Country</u> <u>Squire</u> <u>as</u> <u>Depicted</u> <u>in</u> <u>English</u> <u>Prose</u> <u>Fiction</u> <u>1740-1800</u>. Ph.D. dissertation, University of Pennsylvania. Philadelphia: n.p., 158 pp.
     Scattered remarks on depiction of Richardsonian characters, primarily B.

*6   SWAEN, A.E.H. "Marianne-Pamela." <u>Neophil</u> 23: 409-11.
     "Denies influence of Marianne on Pamela; in Dutch." <u>YWMLS</u> 10 (1940): 61-62.

1939

1   BARKER, RICHARD HUNDRY. <u>Mr.</u> <u>Cibber</u> <u>of</u> <u>Drury</u> <u>Lane</u>. Morningside Heights, N.Y.: Columbia University Press, pp. 250-55.
     Some material on Cibber's response to <u>Grandison</u> and on the friendship among Richardson, Hill, and Cibber, which influenced Richardson's response to Fielding, particularly in the case of <u>Shamela</u>.

2   FISCHER, WALTHER. "Ein unbekannter Brief David Garricks an Samuel Richardson." <u>Anglia</u> 63: 436-44.
     Prints a letter from Garrick to Richardson, dated Sept. 4, 1753, thanking him for a prepublication copy of <u>Grandison</u> and referring to the Dublin piracy. (Letter subsequently published as item 133 in the <u>Letters of David Garrick</u>.)

3   SHENSTONE, WILLIAM. <u>Letters</u>. Ed. Marjorie Williams. Oxford: Basil Blackwell. Letters 15, 42, 111, 113, 114, 160, 162, 164, 216, 269, 294.
     Critical judgments on the three novels and on Richardson's qualities as a novelist. Dislikes his low style and believes "he wants ye Art of abridgment in everything he has yet wrote" (393), but in later years "I never Look into his works, but with greater Admiration of his Genius--and then, if we regard ye extensive good they [his works] were <u>so</u> <u>well</u> calculated to promote, there are Few Characters to whom the Nation may be said to <u>owe</u>

greater Honours." (625)

4   TAUPIN, RENÉ. "Richardson, Diderot, et l'art de conter." FR
     12: 181-94.
          The influence of Richardson on Diderot summarized:
     parallels of situation, characterization, language, and
     detail. Pamela and Clarissa provide motifs for La
     Religieuse, but in complexity of character and in the
     relationships between individual situations and the book as
     a whole, Diderot's book is inferior to Richardson's.
     Richardsonian themes are behind Les Deux Amis de Bourbonne
     (the goal of faire le drame des situations, the use of
     pathos as a necessary element of the story, the utilization
     of pantomime and the notation of details of voice and
     gesture), as well as behind "Ceci n'est pas une conte" (the
     fiction of "authentic narrative") and Jacques le fataliste
     (the author and the novel part company, so that the text is
     not a "fiction" but a truth). Diderot learns from
     Richardson to admire the effect of "le beau désordre de la
     vie" but develops it in his own fashion.

5   TOBIN, JAMES E. Eighteenth-Century Literature and its
     Cultural Background: A Bibliography. New York: Fordham
     University Press, pp. 149-50.
          Short bibliography of Richardson (49 items).

6   WHITE, WILLIAM. "Richardson: Idealist or Realist?" MLR 34:
     240-41.
          The contrast between Pamela and letters 138-139 of the
     Familiar Letters shows Richardson's realism; the daughter
     of the Familiar Letters leaves a dangerous situation, while
     Pamela puts her pride in her pocket and Clarissa, having
     nothing to lose, can "satisfy her outraged vanity . . .
     Richardson, knowing women's motives as he did, either
     consciously or unconsciously made his female characters do
     the most selfish thing in each case." (241)

                                1940

1   BLACK, FRANK GEES. The Epistolary Novel in the Late
     Eighteenth Century. University of Oregon Monographs,
     Studies in Literature and Philosophy, no. 2, April 1940.
     Eugene, Ore.: University of Oregon, 190 pp.

Richardson is a leading influence on epistolary fiction
in the later eighteenth century, both through his own works
and in the works of those who imitate him. Extensive
bibliography of epistolary fiction.

*2   CAVENDER, MARY HUMPHRIES. "Samuel Richardson--Realist and
     Satirist." Ph.D. dissertation, Southern Methodist
     University.
          Source: Abstracts of Theses, Southern Methodist
     University, No. 7, pp. 41-42.

*3   ROBERTO, MADIA. Samuel Richardson, con una racolta delle sue
     migliore pagine. Napoli.
          Source: Catalog of the Bib. Naz. Centrale de Firenze.

4   RODDIER, HENRI. Review of Claire-Eliane Engel's L'Abbé
     Prévost en Angleterre. RLC 20: 122-25.
          Suggests that the works of Penelope Aubin "a
     probablement contribué" to the genesis of both Manon and
     Pamela.

5   TRAUGER, WILMER K. "Pedagogues and Pupils: A Study in
     Eighteenth-Century Fiction." Ph.D. dissertation, Harvard
     University.
          Education in novels including Richardson's.

6   VAN TIEGHEM, PAUL. "Le Roman sentimental en Europe de
     Richardson à Rousseau." RLC 20: 129-51.
          In a study of the sentimental novel 1740-61, claims that
     Richardson exerted little influence on the form before
     Rousseau joined his influence to that of Prévost's
     translations, although he had followers in Germany and
     among female novelists. Prévost was the more popular
     writer for imitation.

                              1941

1   DOWNS, BRIAN W. "Samuel Richardson." Cambridge Bibliography
     of English Literature. Ed. F.W. Bateson. Vol. 2.
     Cambridge: Cambridge University Press; New York:
     Macmillan, pp. 514-17.
          Superseded by NCBEL.

2   GIRAUDOUX, JEAN. Littérature. Paris: Grasset, pp. 75-79.
        Compares Clarissa and Les Liaisons dangereuses, with
     remarks on the letter novel, which "must be ended by
     death."

3   HILBISH, FLORENCE M.A. Charlotte Smith, Poet and Novelist
     (1749-1806). Philadelphia: University of Pennsylvania
     Press, pp. 356, 373, 496-99.
        Her heroines and heroes are of the Richardsonian ideal
     type and are shown in Richardsonian patterns (e.g., an Anna
     Howe setting off a Clarissa). Specific instances of
     imitation in Desmond, The Young Philosopher, and Emmeline;
     criticism of Richardson in The Old Manor House.

4   QUINLAN, MAURICE J. Victorian Prelude. New York: Columbia
     University Press, pp. 191, 228.
        Cites the Eclectic Review's estimate of Richardson as
     "too general and obscure" in his Christianity, and H.
     Murray's censorship of him in The Morality of Fiction for
     indelicacy, failure to stress religious principles, and
     encouragement of servants to rise above their station.
     Both opinions date from 1805.

*5   WATTERS, REGINALD J. "The Vogue and Influence of Samuel
     Richardson in America, A Study of Cultural Conventions,
     1742-1825." Ph.D. dissertation Wisconsin.
        Source: University of Wisconsin Summaries of Doctoral
     Dissertations. . . 6: 295-97.

                              1942

1   BOWEN, ELIZABETH. English Novelists. London: William
     Collins, pp. 14-19.
        Comparison of Fielding and Richardson; out of their
     practice of the novel comes that of every other English
     novelist. Both have as their subject "the predicament of
     the conscience," although Fielding's sense of the moral
     question is lived, Richardson's theoretical. Both have
     "the idea--or--ideal--of the rational passion," which has
     limited the English novel, while the French and Russians
     have been free to explore the inherent disorder and pain of
     love. Of Richardson's three novels, Pamela shocks "more
     than a little" because of its "success philosophy" and

founders on B´s character and the marital question, treating both with "unconscious cynicism." Grandison lacks emotional power. Richardson´s masterpiece, Clarissa, succeeds because of Richardson´s "unfailing sense of detail in art" as well as the moral atmosphere he creates: "Clarissa has a compactness (in spite of its length) and a saturation in its own moral atmosphere to which few novels have so completely attained. It has a convincingness nothing can break through . . .."

2   PETTIT, HENRY. "The Text of Edward Young´s Letters to Samuel Richardson." MLN 57: 668-70.
     Notes that the text of the Young letters printed in the Monthly Magazine in 1813-19 is far superior to that in the Barbauld edition of the Correspondence; provides a guide to the letters, which have since been printed in Pettit´s Correspondence of Edward Young (1971).

3   "SENEX." [PSEUD.] "Richardson and Philology." N&Q 182: 120.
     The false pretensions to philology of one of Pamela´s children.

1943

1   CHEYNE, GEORGE. The Letters of Dr. George Cheyne to Samuel Richardson (1733-1743). Edited with an introduction and notes by Charles F. Mullett. University of Missouri Studies 23, no. 1. Columbia, Mo.: University of Missouri, 137 pp.
     Reviews the career of Dr. Cheyne, Richardson´s doctor and one of the authors whose books Richardson printed; includes 82 letters from Cheyne to Richardson.
     Rev.: Louis A. Landa, PQ 43 (1944): 174-76; Richard H. Shryock, AHR 49: 279.

*2   CORDASCO, FRANCESCO. "La Fortuna di Samuel Richardson in Italia." Rivista universitaria 1: 37-58.
     Source: 1948.2.

3   EAVES, T.C. DUNCAN. "´The Harlowe Family´ by Joseph Highmore: A note on the illustration of Richardson´s Clarissa." HLQ 7: 89-96.
     Reidentifies a picture long thought to be "The Green

Room, Drury Lane" by Hogarth, and notes the precision of detail in Richardson that allowed Highmore to paint the Harlowe family recognizably.

*4   EKEBERG, GLADYS W. "The English Novel as a Vehicle of Tragedy, Richardson through Hardy." Ph.D. dissertation, University of Wisconsin.
Source: McNamee.

5   MCKILLOP, A.D. "Samuel Richardson's Advice to an Apprentice." JEGP 42: 40-54.
Identifies The Apprentice's Vade Mecum (1733, though with date 1734) as Richardson's; provides a bibliographical description and a summary of its background, the circumstances of its publication and advertising, and its content. Also suggests that some additions to the fourth edition (1738) of Defoe's Complete English Tradesman may have been written by Richardson.

6   WAGENKNECHT, EDWARD. Cavalcade of the English Novel. New York: Henry Holt, pp. 46-57.
"Richardson was a moralist; like Bernard Shaw, he would not have faced the labor of writing a single sentence for art's sake alone." (54) His best-crafted book is Grandison. Few today would read it; yet not until Meredith did another male writer understand women so well.

1944

1   BAKER, C.H. COLLINS. "Joseph Highmore, Samuel Richardson, and Lady Bradshaigh." HLQ 7: 316-20.
Identifies the picture over the fireplace in the full-length Highmore portrait of Richardson, now in the National Portrait Gallery, with a group portrait of the Bradshaighs; therefore identifies the NPG portrait with the one Dorothy Bradshaigh commissioned from Highmore in the summer of 1750. Highmore may have painted a "Pamela" and a "Clementina" as well.

2   EAVES, T.C. DUNCAN. "Graphic Illustrations of the Principal English Novelists of the Eighteenth Century." Ph.D. dissertation, Harvard University.
"Descriptive catalogue of all discoverable

illustrations" of major English novelists to 1810.

3   ENGEL, CLAIRE-ELIANE. "English Novelists in Switzerland in the Eighteenth Century." <u>CLS</u> 14-15:2-8.
       Notices of Richardson in eighteenth-century Switzerland and in the Dutch <u>Bibliothèque</u> <u>raisonnée</u>.

4   HOPKINSON, H.T. "Robert Lovelace, the Romantic Cad." <u>Horizon</u> [London] 10: 80-104.
       Lovelace is the supreme example of the cad, the man whose relationships with women are the center of his life, but who is driven by pride and lust of the chase to destroy tranquillity, provoke worry, annihilate normal life. He is compared with Valmont, Tom Jones, and du Roy (<u>Bel</u> <u>Ami</u>). The book, <u>Clarissa</u>, though dull, long-winded, and boring, resembles "the frightful slowing-down of a river as it nears a waterfall . . . " (98) as Lovelace destroys what he wants.

1945

*1 ELISTRATOVA, A. Richardson. V kn.: Istorija angliiskoi literatury, t. I, v. 2, M.: L., 1945, s. 390-408. ["Richardson." <u>History</u> <u>of</u> <u>English</u> <u>Literature</u>. Moscow/Leningrad. Vol. 1, pt. 2: 390-408.]
       Source: Catalog of the All-Union State Library, Moscow.

2   SHERWOOD, IRMA ZWERGEL. "The Influence of Digressive Didacticism on the Structure of the Novels of Richardson and Fielding." Ph.D. dissertation, Yale.
       Didactic technique in both Richardson and Fielding expresses itself through digressions; Richardson differs in details of stylization rather than in fundamentals.

1946

1   EAVES, T.C. DUNCAN. "Joseph Highmore's Portrait of the Reverend Edward Young." <u>SP</u> 43:668-74.
       Richardson was involved in getting Young to sit for it.

2   MCCULLOUGH, BRUCE. "Samuel Richardson." In his Representative
     English Novelists, Defoe to Conrad. New York: Harper, pp.
     23-41.
         General introduction to Richardson, considered as a
     Puritan writer and one who seldom rose above his
     middle-class culture; "there is surely some vulgarity in
     the display of so much virtue." However, in Clarissa, "for
     all its admonitory stuffiness and haggling morality, there
     sounds.   . .a genuine human cry." A connection between
     action and feeling distinguishes Richardson's work from
     earlier novelists'; he is particularly good in depiction
     of personality.

3   PRITCHETT, V.S. "Clarissa." In his Living Novel. London:
     Chatto and Windus, pp. 9-17.
         "Richardson was mad about sex" and the power struggle;
     in Clarissa's and Lovelace's struggle, Clarissa's greatness
     is conferred by the starkness of her defeat. Pritchett
     finds difficulty in believing that Richardson could have
     created either character, notes the "slavery" of the
     epistolary method, but praises Richardson's ability to
     shake it off and achieve style.

                              1947

1   HOWE, ELLIC. The London Compositor: Documents Relating to
     Wages, Working Conditions and Customs of the London
     Printing Trade 1785-1900. London: Bibliographical
     Society, pp. 30-32, 36, 39.
         30-32, Richardson's chapel-rules reprinted (BM MS. Add.
     27,799, f. 88; see 1734.1). 36, 39: References to
     Richardson's career as an important printer and employer,
     under whom at least five other future master printers
     served, and as a "high-flyer" in contemporary lists of
     printers. (Howe's earlier From Craft to Industry [1946]
     contains little on Richardson.)

*2   KOWALKOWSKI, A. Od sławy do zapomnienia. Wielkości czasów
     wobec s ądu potomnych. Gazeta zachodnia no. 22, p. 4.
         Source: Bib. Jagiellońska.

3   MACK, EDWARD C. "Pamela´s Stepdaughters: The Heroines of
      Smollett and Fielding." CollE 8: 293-300.
          "The pretty marzipan female leads" of Smollett,
      Fielding, Scott, and Dickens owe their being to Pamela.

4   MCKILLOP, A.D. "The Mock Marriage in Pamela." PQ 26: 285-88.
          Speaks of real contemporary parallels to the fictional
      mock-marriage, for instance, those between William, Earl
      Cowper, and Elizabeth Cummings and between Mary de la
      Rivière and her cousin, John Manley.

5   RODDIER, HENRI. "Robert Challes, Inspirateur de l´abbé
      Prévost et de Richardson." RLC 81: 5-38.
          Suggests that Robert Challes´ Angelique de Contamine of
      the Illustres francaises foreshadows Pamela and that M. de
      Contamine´s mother´s opposition suggests that of Lady
      Barbara Davers, "mais il reste de substantielles
      différences" and the evidence is largely that of dates.
      Richardson may have been influenced by Challes,
      particularly by the preface to the Illustres françaises,
      toward a combination of realism and sens morale pratique.
          Also published separately: Paris: Boivin, n.d.
      [1948?], 23 pp.

*6   SCOWCROFT, RICHARD P. "Anti-Pamela, the Problem of
      Retribution as it Affected Women in the Eighteenth-Century
      Novel." Ph.D. dissertation, Harvard.
          Source: Catalog of Widener Library, Harvard University.

7   SMITH, PHYLLIS PATRICIA. "The Eighteenth-Century Gentleman:
      Contributing Theories and their Realization in Sir Charles
      Grandison." Ph.D. dissertation, Radcliffe.
          Sir Charles Grandison is a summa of seventeenth- and
      eighteenth-century theories of practical morality.
      Valuable unpublished study.

                              1948

1   CARTER, A.E. "The Greatest English Novelist." UTQ 17:
      390-97.
          General introduction to Richardson, who deserves the
      title "greatest" for his powers of psychological insight,
      though he is the least read of great English novelists;

Lovelace is his finest creation, but the perfect virtue of
Clarissa damages the book.

2   CORDASCO, FRANCESCO. Samuel Richardson: A List of Critical
     Studies Published from 1896 to 1946. Eighteenth-Century
     Bibliographical Pamphlets, No. 3. Brooklyn: Long Island
     University Press, 12 pp.
          Unannotated list of critical studies; 131 items.
          Rev.: PQ 29: 294-96.

2A   CULLER, A. DWIGHT. "Edward Bysshe and the Poet's Handbook."
     PMLA 63: 870-71n.
          As part of a longer article, notes that Richardson used
     Bysshe's Art of English Poetry (1702) as a quarry for
     quotations in, primarily, Clarissa.

*3   GUELICH, ERNESTINE D.   "The Relationship between Goethe's
     Werther and Samuel Richardson's Novels." Ph.D.
     dissertation, Fordham. Fordham U. Dissertations 15:
     49-54.
          Source: McNamee; 1953.5, item 516.

*4   HELSZTYŃSKI, STANISŁAW. "Dwóchsetlecie "Clarissy" Samuela
     Richardsona." Od Fieldinga do Steinbecka. Warszawa:
     Stanisław Cukrowski, pp. 24-33.
          Source: Bib. Jagiellońska.

*5   ---. "Dwóchsetlecie Clarissy." Norwiny literackie, No. 49,
     pp. 1-2.
          Source: YWMLS.

6   LEAVIS, F.R. The Great Tradition. London: Chatto and
     Windus, pp. 3-4.
          Comparison of Richardson and Fielding; feels
     Richardson's works excite "a more inward interest" and
     finds his "strength in the analysis of emotional and moral
     states .   .   .   a matter of common acceptance," but the
     works are too long and vulgar and can enter into the main
     line of English literary development only via Fanny Burney
     and Austen.

7   MAYO, R.D. The English Novel in the Magazines, 1740-1815.
     Evanston, Ill.: University of Illinois Press, 705 pp.

Richardson's influence, like Fielding's, is comparatively slight in magazine fiction, since sensibility had entered the magazines well before his time; Mayo suggests an influence of, in particular, the <u>Tatler</u> and <u>Spectator</u> over popular novelists, Richardson included. However, his name is invoked frequently.

8   MCADAM, E.L. "A New Letter from Fielding." <u>YR</u> 38: 300-310.
    Reprints a letter from Fielding to Richardson dated Oct. 15, 1748, praising <u>Clarissa</u>, and gives its background.

9   MCKILLOP, A.D. "A Letter from Richardson to Alexis Claude Clairaut." <u>MLN</u> 63: 109-13.
    A letter of July 5, 1753, giving information on <u>Grandison</u> and on translations of <u>Clarissa</u>.

10 MOORE, ROBERT E. <u>Hogarth's Literary Relationships</u>. Minneapolis: University of Minnesota Press, pp. 68, 187-88.
    Hogarth's projected illustrations for <u>Pamela</u>; Richardson's debt in the <u>Familiar Letters</u> to Hogarth's <u>Harlot's</u> and <u>Rake's Progress</u>.

11 SHERBURN, GEORGE. <u>The Restoration and Eighteenth Century (1660-1789)</u>. Vol. III of <u>A Literary History of England</u>. Edited by Albert C. Baugh. New York: Appleton-Century-Crofts, p. 952.
    Richardson's "prolix fondling of episodes" is "more indecent than vulgarity." General introduction.

*12 SIGAUX, GILBERT. "Clarisse Harlowe. 1748." <u>La Nef</u>, Oct. 1948, pp. 101-4.
    Bicentennial introduction.

13 WHEATLEY, KATHERINE E. "Andromache as the 'Distrest Mother.'" <u>RR</u> 39: 3-21.
    Discusses Pamela's remarks on <u>The Distrest Mother</u> and comments, "By far the most detailed and in a sense most judicious criticism of [the play] comes from the pen of the novelist, Samuel Richardson." (Courtesy Prof. Susan Staves.)

1949

1   FOSTER, JAMES R. <u>History</u> <u>of</u> <u>the</u> <u>Pre-Romantic</u> <u>Novel</u> <u>in</u>
<u>England</u>. MLA Monographs, No. 17. New York: Modern
Language Assn. of America, pp. 1-127.
       Description of "pre-Romantic" novel and discussion of
English and Continental fiction, including much material on
Richardson and <u>Richardsonaden</u>. Is inclined to make
Prevost, rather than Richardson, responsible for much of
the "pre-Romantic" tendencies in Rousseau and Gellert.
Rev.: <u>TLS</u> (1949), p. 645; <u>PQ</u> 29 (1950): 253-54; <u>RES</u> NS
2 (1951): 187-89; <u>MLN</u> 68 (1953): 42-46.

*2   GLÄTTLI, WALTER. "Richardson." In his <u>Behandlung des</u> <u>Affekts</u>
<u>der</u> <u>Furcht</u> <u>im</u> <u>Englischen</u> <u>Roman des 18.</u> <u>Jhdts.</u> Zurich:
Juris, pp. 57-70.
       Source: Hannaford, item 738. Richardson's use of fear,
especially in conjunction with persecuted innocence.

3   HIGHET, GILBERT. "Fiction." In his <u>Classical</u> <u>Tradition</u>. New
York and London: Oxford University Press, pp. 340-41.
       The influence of <u>Télémaque</u> and the <u>Arcadia</u> on <u>Pamela</u>.

4   MCKILLOP, A.D. "Wedding Bells for Pamela." <u>PQ</u> 28: 323-25.
       Variants of the Herschel anecdote about the blacksmith
reading <u>Pamela</u> to his neighbors, who rang the church bells
at her wedding.

5   SALE, W.M., JR. "From <u>Pamela</u> to <u>Clarissa</u>." In <u>The</u> <u>Age</u> <u>of</u>
<u>Johnson:</u> <u>Essays</u> <u>Presented</u> <u>to</u> <u>Chauncey</u> <u>Brewster</u> <u>Tinker</u>.
Ed. F.W. Hilles. New Haven: Yale University Press, pp.
127-38.
       "Disturbing social forces" are at work in the merging of
Pamela's and Clarissa's lives with those of the higher
classes. The double position of Richardson's males, as
aristocrat and potential lover, creates tensions: B would
be less ambiguous and Pamela less scheming if B were only
man, not master. Clarissa and Lovelace cannot be tucked
into the social structure; Clarissa is seeking freedom, a
naturally tragic situation. Like Meredith, Richardson is
fascinated by the rape of the lower classes by the higher;
he is the first English novelist to convey this
fascination.

*6   VIDYARTHY, D.P. "Sentiment and Sensibility in English Prose
Fiction from Samuel Richardson to Ann Radcliffe, with
Special Reference to Character-Delineation." Ph.D.

dissertation, University of London (King´s College).
Source: McNamee.

7   WATT, IAN. "The Naming of Characters in Defoe, Richardson,
     and Fielding." <u>RES</u> 25: 322-34.
          Historical and literary echoes and puns in the names
     "Pamela,"   "Clarissa,"   "Harriet,"   "Lovelace,"   and
     "Grandison."

<u>1950</u>

1   BREDVOLD, LOUIS I. "The Sentimental Novel: Richardson." In
     <u>The</u> <u>Literature</u> <u>of</u> <u>the</u> <u>Restoration</u> <u>and</u> <u>the</u> <u>Eighteenth</u>
     <u>Century</u>. <u>A</u> <u>History</u> <u>of</u> <u>English</u> <u>Literature</u>. Edited by
     Hardin Craig. New York: Oxford University Press, pp.
     414-16.
          Richardson is a master of pathos and psychology.

2   GALBRAITH, LOIS H. <u>The</u> <u>Estabished</u> <u>Clergy</u> <u>as</u> <u>Depicted</u> <u>in</u>
     <u>English</u> <u>Prose</u> <u>Fiction</u> <u>1740-1800</u>. Philadelphia: n.p., pp.
     1-13.
          Richardson´s treatment of Arthur Williams, the Rev. Mr.
     Peters, Elias Brand, Dr. Lewen, Dr. Bartlett, the Rev.
     Mr. Dobson and others as representative of the state of
     the clergy in his time; Richardson´s treatment shows
     unusual respect.

*2   HOPKINSON, TOM. "The English Novel--II. The Printer Who
     Wrote a Masterpiece." <u>The</u> <u>Listener</u>, Jan. 26, pp. 162-63.

3   KERMODE, FRANK. "Richardson and Fielding." <u>Cambridge</u> <u>Journal</u>
     4: 106-14.
          Fielding, not Richardson, is the moralist of the Good
     Heart, but the crucial test of the Good Heart, Tom´s
     incest, is evaded by good luck and "not without a parade of
     theatrical dexterity." Richardson is rather the mythmaker,
     "essentially tragic" as opposed to the "essentially comic
     (Meredithian)" mode of Fielding; his fiction is not
     dependent on the surprises and delights of plot, which are
     contrivance. The surprises of Richardson "are organic, and
     therefore more acutely satisfying." Analysis of passages
     from <u>Clarissa</u> shows Richardson´s ability to surprise and
     please.

*4   LOHSE, MINNA. "Die ´Liaisons dangereuses´ von Laclos in ihrem
      Verhältnis zu den Romanen Richardsons und Crébillons."
      Ph.D. dissertation, Hamburg. Deutsche Staatsbib.,
      Deutsche Bücherei
         Source: Catalogs of the Deutsche Staatsbibliothek and
      Deutsche Bücherei.

5   MCKILLOP, A.D., ed. Critical Remarks on Sir Charles
      Grandison, Clarissa, and Pamela, by a Lover of Virtue
      (1754). Augustan Reprint Society, No. 21. Los Angeles:
      W.A. Clark Memorial Library, 69 pp.
         See 1754.10. McKillop, who gives a five-page
      introduction to this facsimile edition, sketches the early
      history of Richardsonian criticism and discusses the
      Critical Remarks.

6   PRICE, L.M. C.H. Schmid and his Translations of English
      Dramas, 1767-1789. UCPMP 26 (1942-1950, pub. 1950):
      1-122.
         Schmid translated Diderot´s Eloge into German and wrote
      an important article, "Über die verschiedenen
      Verdeutschungen von Richardsons Klarisse" in the JVFD in
      1792; as well, he translated and completed the version of
      Clarissa in Reichard´s Bibliothek der Romane. See 1792.15
      and 1926.5.

7   RICHARDSON, SAMUEL. or, The History of a Young Lady.
      Clarissa; or, The History of a Young Lady. Ed. with an
      introduction by and abridged by John Angus Burrell. New
      York: Modern Library, 800 pp.
         See 1972.17 for summary of editing principles of this
      abridged edition.

8   RODDIER, HENRI. J.-J. Rousseau en Angleterre au XVIIIe
      siècle: l´oeuvre et l´homme. Paris: Boivin, 435 pp.
         Frequently compares Richardson and Rousseau and
      discusses influence of former on latter.

9   SALE, WILLIAM MERRITT. Samuel Richardson: Master Printer.
      CSE 37. Ithaca, N.Y.: Cornell University Press, 399 pp.
         Definitive study of books printed by Richardson,
      valuable for history of English printing as well as for
      background of novels. Lists books printed by Richardson,
      booksellers for whom he printed, his apprentices;
      reproduces his printer´s ornaments. See 1969.12.

Rev.: Herbert Davis, <u>RES</u> n.s. 4 (1953): 79-81;
Hellmut Lehmann-Haupt, <u>CRC</u> 14; A.W. Secord, <u>JEGP</u> 52
(1953): 423-26; Austin Wright, <u>MP</u> 48 (1951): 274-75;
A.T. Hazen, <u>MLN</u> 67 (1952): 484-85; <u>TLS</u>, June 19, 1951,
p. 412; <u>NCF</u> 5: 337-38; Harold Williams, <u>Library</u> 6:
228-29.

*10   SHOUP, LOUISE. "The Use of the Social Gathering as Structural
      Device in the Novels of Richardson, Fielding, Smollett, and
      Sterne." Ph.D. dissertation, Stanford. <u>Stanford
      University Abstracts of Dissertations</u> (1950): 139-41.
      Source: <u>BELL</u> 30 (1950-52), item 6477.

11   SINCLAIR, UPTON. An<u>other</u> <u>Pamela</u>: <u>or</u>, <u>Virtue Still Rewarded</u>.
      New York; London: Werner Laurie, 1952, 314 pp.
          From the preface it is clear that Sinclair does not
      expect his audience to have read the original <u>Pamela</u>, whose
      story is quoted <u>in extenso</u> in the book and is wept over by
      her "great-great-great-granddaughter," a William Millerite
      parlormaid in 1920's California, serving in the household
      of the rich and dissolute Harries family. Pamela Andrews
      II, a sweet religious girl, becomes a Socialist and
      criticizes <u>Pamela</u> from the Socialist point of view; Pamela
      I married a "wicked and treacherous" man because of the
      class system, but Pamela II, a private secretary making a
      hundred dollars a week, need not marry for any reason but
      love and virtue. Under the influence of Eugene V. Debs,
      she reforms Charles Harries and marries him, but insists on
      keeping her job. No kidnapping, no Mrs. Jewkes.
      Curiously similar to R.M. le Suire's <u>Pamela francaise</u>
      (1804).

12   VAN GHENT, DOROTHY. "Clarissa and Emma as Phèdre." <u>PR</u> 17:
      820-33.
          "Vénus toute entière à sa proie attachée"--the center of
      significance of the love-myth in <u>Clarissa</u>, as in <u>Phèdre</u> and
      <u>Mme Bovary</u>, is "no longer renewal of life through death,
      but the relationship between individual and group--with the
      taboos, rebellion of instinct, outrage of law, and defeat
      that this relationship implies." In <u>Clarissa</u> the death of
      the heroine, a deity of love, demands our admiration and
      gives "supernatural sanction to the social abstraction and
      impotence," the "Harlowe-economy of death" of which
      Lovelace is the principal instrument. Symbols of this
      economy of rape and subsequent death include the word "man"

(used as a loaded word), clothes, stabbing, rent tissue, flowing liquid (female tears), and limp bodies. Her death scene, technically a tour de force, exalts the "cult of sterility" of "that acquisitive idealism that has been morally rationalized by Puritanism and afforded religious depth by fear, perverted sexuality, and death-wish. It is a paean to death, with the rape-motif central."

1951

1   BONNARD, G.A. "Samuel Richardson and G.A. de Luc." MLR 46: 440-41.
Records a friendship with the son of a friend of Rousseau; Richardson sent de Luc a complete set of his works in 1759, and de Luc replied in 1760 with a medal of Geneva.

2   EAVES, T.C. DUNCAN. "Graphic Illustrations of the Novels of Samuel Richardson, 1740-1810." HLQ 14: 349-83.
English illustrations of Richardson's novels, concentrating on the work of Gravelot, Highmore, Hayman, and Stothard.

3   ---. "An Unrecorded Children's Book Illustration by Thomas Bewick." Library 5th ser. 5: 272-73.
An edition of Pamela in the library of the American Antiquarian Society in Worcester, Mass., possibly contains woodcuts by Thomas Bewick, described here. See 1779.3.

4   ERÄMETSÄ, ERIK. A Study of the Word "Sentimental" and of Other Linguistic Characteristics of Eighteenth-Century Sentimentalism in England. Ph.D. dissertation, Helsinki. Helsinki: Helsingen Liikekirjapaino Oy, 169 pp. PaU
Description of the "dialect of sentiment", in which Richardson is frequently quoted. See 1952.2.

5   HAUSER, ARNOLD. The Social History of Art. New York: Alfred A. Knopf, 2: 562-66.
"It is hardly possible to speak of a romantic movement in the real sense before . . . Richardson," since he contains it in germ: the psychologizing, which allows the new middle class to express its own qualities in the "emotional intensity and inwardness" of the novel; the

wish-fulfillment   of   the   success-morality;   the
autobiographical form, which emotionally chains reader to
characters and "invites the reader to romanticize his
existence." "Richardson's moralizing novels contain the
germ of the most immoral art that has ever existed, namely
the incitement to indulge in those wish-fantasies in which
decency is only a means to an end, and the inducement to
occupy oneself with mere illusions," Hauser concludes from
Q.D.   Leavis, ascribing Richardson's influence to the
position he holds in the development of bourgeois art; his
"mediocre" but "felicitous formula" suited the temper of
his age.

6   KEAST, W.R. "The Two Clarissas in Johnson's Dictionary." SP
     54: 429-39.
          Notes frequent references in the Dictionary both to
     Clarissa (96 references) and to the Collection of . . .
     Sentiments (78 references).

7   KETTLE, ARNOLD. An Introduction to the English Novel.
     London: Hutchinson's, 1: 65-71.
          Attacks Pamela for technical crudity and "unadmirable"
     morality   but   finds   Clarissa   remarkable,   subtle,
     fascinating, psychologically complex, a tragedy that is
     simply insoluble in its social context. Though Richardson
     is sentimental, calling up feeling for its own sake,
     Clarissa is not, asserting a woman's dignity; its moral is
     the "irrevocability of human action" (Downs). Lovelace
     terrifies, "so much an eighteenth-century gentleman," with
     "a great deal of . . . elegance of manner . . . and
     at the same time unspeakable." Though Richardson must be
     read historically, his art has relevance to our own.

8   MCKILLOP, A.D. "Epistolary Technique in Richardson's Novels."
     Rice Institute Pamphlets 38: 36-54. Rep. in Studies of
     the Literature of the Augustan Age in Honor of A.E.   Case.
     Ann Arbor: University of Michigan Press, 1952.
          The epistolary novel's peculiar advantage is that the
     characters are "writing, editing, even reading a novel
     within a novel" so that "the relation of the earlier
     letters in an epistolary novel to the later may thus be
     quite different from the relation of the earlier chapters
     of a novel to the later." Letters are used as falsification
     or corroboration of events, as commentary, as denial or
     affirmation of other letters, as journals; they are shown

to an audience (or not shown); they are opened
prematurely, received at the wrong time, or intercepted;
they both reflect and become the action. McKillop notes
the division of narrators in <u>Clarissa</u> and comments
extensively on the refinement of epistolary narration in
<u>Grandison</u>.

9.   MOORE, R.E. "Dr. Johnson on Fielding and Richardson." <u>PMLA</u>
     66: 162-81.
          Disagrees with Johnson's comments on Richardson; notes
     similarities between Richardson and Fielding.

                              1952

1   ANON. ". . . A Novelist's Coffin." <u>Illustrated</u> <u>London</u>
     <u>News</u> 221:65.
          Photograph of Richardson's coffin, recovered from the
     war-damaged St. Bride's.

1A   BISHOP, ALISON. "Richardson Discusses his <u>Clarissa</u> and <u>Sir</u>
     <u>Charles</u> <u>Grandison</u>." <u>Boston</u> <u>Public</u> <u>Library</u> <u>Quarterly</u> 4:
     217-21.
          In a letter of May 17, 1754, to Lady Echlin, Lady
     Dorothy Bradshaigh's sister, Richardson discusses
     Lovelace's reformation, the ending of <u>Grandison</u>, the
     Catholic compromise with the Porrettas, and Sir Charles's
     preference of Harriet to Clementina.

2   ERÄMETSÄ, ERIK. "Notes on Richardson's Language." <u>NM</u> 53:
     18-20.
          A summary of some of the points made about Richardson in
     1951.4. Richardson shares with other sentimental authors a
     frequent use of the "nominal style," in which absence of
     strong transitive verbs is compensated for by an abundance
     of the <u>nomina</u> <u>agentis</u> ending <u>-er</u>; "there is usually a
     marked emotional colouring combined with a kind of upstart
     familiarity attached to these words . . . ." Nouns and
     adjectives become verbs ("to handkerchief," "to ugly");
     "over-" becomes "out-" ("out-argued"); coinages are
     frequent ("doggesses," "kill-times," "to unlook") and many
     abusive terms are derived from family relationships ("to
     mamma-up"). Clarifies and supplements but does not replace
     1951.4.

3   HOLMES, WILLIAM C.   "Pamela Transformed." <u>Music</u> <u>Quarterly</u> 38:
      581-94.
           On Goldoni's <u>Pamela</u> <u>nubile</u> and Piccinni's <u>La</u> <u>buona</u>
      <u>figliuola</u>.

4   JOHNSON, SAMUEL. <u>Letters</u> <u>of</u> <u>Samuel</u> <u>Johnson</u>. Ed. R.W.
      Chapman. 3v. Oxford: Clarendon.
           Letters to Richardson and references to him and his
      works; no significant criticism.

5   LESSER, SIMON O. "A Note on <u>Pamela</u>." <u>CollE</u> 14: 13-17.
           In spite of its "occasionally nauseating moral coating,"
      <u>Pamela</u> appeals because of the strength of its story, which
      is the Cinderella story, and its well-rounded characters.
      Parallels with Cinderella discussed at length. [It should
      be noted, however, that <u>Cinderella</u> was not actually
      available in English when <u>Pamela</u> was written.]

*6   RICHARDSON, SAMUEL. <u>Pamela o la virtu premiata</u>. Versione di
      A.M. Speckel. Narratori italiani e stranieri 3. Milano:
      Ed. A.P.E. (Busto Arsizio, Tip. A. Pianezza), 269 pp.
           Sources: Bib. Naz. Centrale di Firenze; CUBI.

7   WATT, IAN. "Defoe and Richardson on Homer: A Study of the
      Relationship of Novel and Epic in the Early Eighteenth
      Century." <u>RES</u> n.s. 3: 325-40.
           Defoe was anti-Homer; Richardson expressed a private
      liking for Homer but publicly deplored the Homeric
      influence. Fielding's filiation with the epic is also
      covered.

                              <u>1953</u>

1   [FIELDING, HENRY.] <u>An Apology for the Life of Mrs. Shamela</u>
      <u>Andrews</u>. Ed. i.n. Sheridan W. Baker, Jr. Berkeley and
      Los Angeles: University of California Press, 122 pp.
           Introduction discusses relationship between <u>Shamela</u> and
      <u>Pamela</u>.

2   HANSFORD, F.E., F.R.S.A., and G.A.C. EVANS. <u>The Story of the</u>
      <u>Grange, North End Crescent, Fulham</u>. London: Fulham

Historical Society Publications, No. 1, 12 pp.
Printed as a protest against the destruction of the
house in North End, Fulham, lived in by Richardson and
later by Burne-Jones. Inaccurate on biographical details.

3   HAUSER, ARNOLD. <u>Sozialgeschichte der Kunst und Literatur</u>.
    2v. München: C.H. Beck.
    See 1951.5.

*4 PHILLIPSON, JOHN S. "Richardson in the Twentieth Century."
    Ph.D. dissertation, Wisconsin. <u>University of Wisconsin
    Abstracts of Theses</u> 14 (1954): 443-45.
    Source: McNamee; BELL, 31 (1953-54), item 4861.

5   PRICE, LAWRENCE MARSDEN. <u>English Literature in Germany</u>.
    UCPMP 37. Berkeley, Calif.: University of California
    Press, 556 pp.
    Revisions of 1919.4 and 1932.7. See in this edition pp.
    49-50 for Price's revisions of the "wave theory" of German
    literary history and their implications for Price's
    estimate of Richardson's influence.

*6 RICHARDSON, SAMUEL. <u>Pamela. Traduzione e prefazione di
    Vittoria Ottolenghi</u>. 2v. Collezione di classici inglesi a
    cura di S. Rosati. Milano: A. Garzanti.
    Sources: Bib. Naz. Centrale Vittorio Emanuele II,
    Roma; Bib. Naz. Centrale di Firenze; Uff. Inf. Bib.;
    CUBI.

7   VAN GHENT, DOROTHY. "On <u>Clarissa Harlowe</u>." In her <u>English
    Novel: Form and Function</u>. New York: Rinehart, pp. 45-64
    (see also 307-21).
    Clarissa tends "to convert the external forms of
    life--social customs, physical action, material
    quantities--into subjective quality and spiritual value,"
    and thus the book is a dramatization of emotional states,
    particularly eroticism (bodily violence, violence done to
    clothes, equation of purity and debility), and of myths and
    inappropriate myths of parental authority, conformity, and
    social dependance, in which nonconformity leads to death.
    The epistolary form is dictated by the subjective nature
    and the "vital immediacy" of both Clarissa's and Lovelace's
    experiences and emotions.

1954

1   BARBIER, C.P. "Letters of an Italian Nun and an English
     Gentleman (1781), A Bibliographical Problem." RLC 28:
     75-89.
          Cites several French imitations of Pamela.

2   MCKILLOP, A.D. "Richardson's Early Writings: Another
     Pamphlet." JEGP 53: 72-75.
          The case for Richardson's authorship of the pamphlet, A
     Seasonable Examination of the Pleas and Pretensions of the
     Proprietors of, and Subscribers to, Play-Houses . . .
     See 1735.1.

3   RICHARDSON, SAMUEL. Samuel Richardson's Introduction to
     Pamela. Edited with an introduction by Sheridan W. Baker,
     Jr. ARS No. 48. Los Angeles: William Andrews Clark
     Memorial Library, 52 pp.
          Reprints in facsimile the text of the second-edition
     introduction; discusses changes the preface and the
     complimentary letters went through from edition to edition.
     Conjectures the probable authors of the complimentary
     letters; notes Aaron Hill's particular involvement.

3A   SCRUTTON, MARY. "Bourgeois Cinderellas." Twentieth Century
     155:351-55.
          Notes that the Cinderella story of
     success-through-marriage does not fit the moral structure
     of Pamela.

4   SHAW, E. "Malesherbes, l'Abbé Prévost, and the First French
     Translation of Sir Charles Grandison." MLN 69: 105-9.
          Corrects 1927.10: Malesherbes did give permission for
     Grandison to be printed, and, moreover, he helped sales of
     the books by dissuading another publisher, J.N. Bruyset of
     Lyons, from bringing out another translation. [But Bruyset
     did eventually bring out an edition.]

5   SHIPLEY, JOHN B. "Richardson and Pamela." N&Q 199: 28-29.
          The petition for the royal license to publish Pamela
     (Jan. 7, 1741/2) reprinted.

<u>1955</u>

1   BESTERMAN, THEODORE, ed. <u>Voltaire's</u> <u>Complete</u> <u>Works</u>. Geneva,
     later Banbury, Oxf.: Voltaire Foundation, 1955 ff.
          References to Richardson by Voltaire and members of the
     Voltaire circle. Mme du Deffand praises the novels, Oct.
     28, 1759 (20: 424); Voltaire writes to her about them,
     Apr. 12, 1760 (21: 233), Apr. 24, 1769 (34: 421); to
     Marie-Louise Denis, Oct. 1, 1753, he writes of "un ouvrage
     dans le goust de Pamela," which he is contemplating making
     of her imprisonment (14: 270; see 1963.10 for an
     identification of this work). Charles des Brosses writes
     to Charles Catherine Loppin, about May 27, 1761, comparing
     <u>Clarissa</u> to <u>Julie</u>; he prefers the former (23: 229).
     (Citations courtesy of Prof. Alexander Jovicevich)

2   DAVYS, MARY. <u>Familiar</u> <u>Letters</u> <u>between</u> <u>a</u> <u>Gentleman</u> <u>and</u> <u>a</u> <u>Lady</u>.
     Edited with an introduction and notes by R.A. Day. ARS
     no. 54. Los Angeles: William Andrews Clark Memorial
     Library.
          Refers to Richardson in the introduction; useful for
     Richardson's relationship to earlier epistolary fiction.
     Contains a bibliography of epistolary fiction.

3   HILL, CHRISTOPHER. "Clarissa Harlowe and her Times." <u>EC</u> 5:
     315-40.
          <u>Clarissa</u>, "one of the greatest unread novels," displays
     moral problems in a social context. Both Lovelace and
     Clarissa, as characters, criticize the "market morality";
     Richardson's "Puritan morality" and his humanity look
     forward to the <u>idéologues</u> of the French Revolution.
     Reprinted in his <u>Puritanism</u> <u>and</u> <u>Revolution</u> (1958).

4   MCKILLOP, A.D. "Two Eighteenth-Century 'First Works'."
     <u>Newberry</u> <u>Library</u> <u>Bulletin</u> 4: 10-13.
          Notes on the Newberry Library copy of the <u>Apprentice's</u>
     <u>Vade</u> <u>Mecum</u>.

5   RODDIER, HENRI. <u>L'Abbé</u> <u>Prévost,</u> <u>l'homme</u> <u>et</u> <u>l'oeuvre</u>. Paris:
     Hatier-Boivin, pp. 166-76.
          Prévost's translations of Richardson and his role in
     popularizing and extending the "Richardson influence" in
     France.

*6   ROSSELOT, E. LAVELLE. "Samuel Richardson et son influence en
     France avant la Révolution." Ph.D. dissertation,
     Université de Laval.

Source: Bib. de l´U. de Laval.

1956

1   DAICHES, DAVID. "Samuel Richardson." In his <u>Literary Essays</u>.
      London: Oliver and Boyd, pp. 26-50.
          Richardson suffers from his historical   period   in
      defining virtue as self-approval and the approval of
      others; this definition is dramatized in the epistolary
      form by the ever-present fictional audience.

2   ERÄMETSÄ, ERIK. "Der sprachliche Einfluss Richardsons auf
      Goethes <u>Werther</u>." NM 57: 118-25.
          Notes many English-sounding constructions, words, and
      idioms in <u>Werther</u> paralleling Richardson´s coinings and
      formulae: among others, the use of "head" and "heart"
      formulae for the emotions, the demi-personification of the
      feelings through the present participle ("the pitying
      tear," "my doubting eye," "meinem strebendem, sehnenden
      Busen," "eure staunende Seele"), the use of the word
      <u>sensibility</u> ("Empfindlichkeit" or "Fühlbarkeit"), and the
      idealization of the simple life and domestic joys, "die
      Glückseligkeit des häuslichen Lebens."

3   [FIELDING, HENRY.] <u>An Apology for the Life of Mrs. Shamela
      Andrews</u> . . . Introduction by Ian Watt. ARS No. 57.
      Los Angeles: William Andrews Clark Memorial Library, 81
      pp.
          Summarizes Fielding´s use of Richardson; notes,
      however, substantial parodies of Cibber, Conyers Middleton,
      Administration politics, and Methodism.

4   FRYE, NORTHROP. "Towards Defining an Age of Sensibility." <u>ELH</u>
      23: 144-52.
          Richardson is mentioned as a writer giving an impression
      of literature as a process.

5   MCKILLOP, A.D. <u>The Early Masters of English Fiction</u>.
      Lawrence, Kans.: University of Kansas Press, pp. 47-97.
          General overview of Richardson´s three novels. Notes
      the social clash in <u>Pamela</u>, the lack of it in <u>Clarissa</u>.

Hermetic distortion in Clarissa exists for didactic
purposes, not social: to show Lovelace's inability to be
improved, Clarissa's self-deception. Appreciation of
Richardson's brevity. Fielding's admiration for Clarissa
noted. Sir Charles Grandison discussed in relation to
Richardson's influence over the late eighteenth century.

6   RABKIN, NORMAN. "Clarissa: A Study in the Nature of
    Convention." ELH 23: 204-17.
        Conflict in Clarissa is that of "Nature" vs.
    convention, Lovelace vs. Clarissa. Clarissa is
    exaggeratedly conventional; Lovelace too, too natural.
    Only the minor characters can actively balance the two
    forces and live in peace.

7   RODDIER, HENRI. "L'abbé Prévost et le probleme de la
    traduction au XVIIIe siècle." Les Courants internationaux
    de l'art français . . . Paris: CAIEF, pp. 173-81.
        Presents evidence that Prévost did not translate Pamela.

8   WENDT, ALLAN EDWARD. "Richardson and Fielding: A Study in
    the Eighteenth-Century Compromise." Ph.D. dissertation,
    Indiana University.
        Discusses ethical beliefs of the eighteenth century and
    their reflections in Richardson's and Fielding's major
    novels. Sees Richardson as developing from the right-wing
    orthodoxy associated with Mandeville toward a more liberal
    position of Shaftesburyan benevolence.

9   SHUMAN, R. BAIRD. "Censorship as a Controlling Theme in
    Pamela and Clarissa." N&Q 201: 30-32.
        Censorship is a metaphor for restraint, while free use
    of pen and ink implies freedom. Shuman connects Pamela and
    Clarissa with authors silenced by the Licensing Act of
    1737, while B, Lovelace, and James Harlowe Jr. represent
    the Government.

*10 ŠTĚPANÍK, K., and A. TICHÝ. Istorija anglijskoi literatury.
    Moskva: Učpedgiz.
        Short article on Richardson; source: Statni knihovna
    ČSR.

<u>1957</u>

1   BRADBROOK, FRANK W. "Samuel Richardson." In <u>A</u> <u>Guide</u> <u>to</u>
     <u>English</u> <u>Literature</u>. Ed. Boris Ford. 5v. London:
     Cassell, 4: 285-304.
          "This vulgar, complacent little bookseller" nevertheless
     had   great   influence   over   later   fiction;   a   general
     introduction   to   Richardson,   with   minor   factual
     inaccuracies. See also A.R. Humphreys´ article, "Fielding
     and Smollett," in the same volume.

1A   COCKSHUT, A.O.J. "Sentimentality   in   Fiction."   <u>Twentieth</u>
     <u>Century</u> 161:354-64. Thorough and honest analysis of
     emotions precludes sentimentality; <u>Pamela</u> is sentimental,
     but <u>Clarissa</u> is not.

*2   D´AGOSTINO, NEMI. "The History of Clarissa Harlowe." In his
     <u>L´Ordine</u> <u>e</u> <u>il</u> <u>caos.</u> <u>Studi</u> <u>sugli</u> <u>Augustei</u>. Trieste: Ed.
     Universita,   Istituto   de   filologia   germanica   (Tip.
     Smolars), pp. 199 ff.
          Source: Bib. Naz. Centrale di Firenze.

3   DUNCAN-JONES, E.E. "Proposals of Marriage in <u>Pride</u> <u>and</u>
     <u>Prejudice</u> and <u>Pamela</u>." <u>N&Q</u> 202: 76.
          Mr. B´s proposal, which begins, "In vain, my Pamela, do
     I struggle against my affection for you," may have provided
     Austen with the germ of Mr. Darcy´s first proposal.

4   REID, BENJAMIN LAWRENCE. "Justice to Pamela." <u>Hud</u> <u>R</u> 9:
     527-28. Reprinted in <u>The</u> <u>Long</u> <u>Boy</u> <u>and</u> <u>Others</u>. Athens,
     Ga.: University of Georgia Press, 1957; repr. 1969.
          <u>Pamela</u> is good because of its solid specificity and its
     practical morality, more useful than a heady idealism, but
     it succeeds in spite of rather than for its Puritanism.

5   SHERBO, ARTHUR. "Time and Place in Richardson´s <u>Clarissa</u>."
     <u>Boston</u> <u>University</u> <u>Studies</u> <u>in</u> <u>English</u> 3: 139-46.
          <u>Clarissa</u> is set, Sherbo speculates, somewhere between
     1728-33, and possibly in the leap year 1732. Though
     Richardson   carefully   avoids   identifiable   places   in
     Hertfordshire,   where   Harlowe   Place   is   located,   or
     Bedfordshire, where M. lives, there are a number of easily
     identifiable locations in London: the Belle-Savage on
     Ludgate Hill, the Four Swans in Bishopsgate, and Flask Walk
     in Hampstead, among others.

6   TAYLOR, DICK, JR. "Joseph as Hero of <u>Joseph Andrews</u>." <u>TSE</u> 7: 91-109،
       Refers to <u>Pamela</u> in establishing the scheme of burlesque in Fielding's novel.

7   WATT, IAN. <u>The Rise of the Novel: Studies in Defoe, Richardson and Fielding</u>. Berkeley: University of California Press; London: Chatto and Windus, 319 pp.
       Roots in Puritanism, the emerging freedom of women, the psychological and social components of romantic love, and other moral and social preoccupations of the age, of Richardson's conception of the novel. These forces also help to shape the actions of Pamela, Clarissa, and Lovelace; "Clarissa's tragedy reflects the combined effects of Puritanism's spiritual inwardness and its fear of the flesh," for instance. The effect of Richardson's psychological insight is to give the novel the terrifying ambiguity of life. Compares <u>Clarissa</u> and <u>Tom Jones</u>; Fielding allots characterization much less space in his novel.
       Rev.: <u>TLS</u>, Feb. 15, p. 98; <u>Listener</u> 57: 483, 485; Charles B. Woods, <u>MLN</u> 57: 622-25; A.D. McKillop, <u>MP</u> 55: 208-10; F.K. Stanzel, <u>Anglia</u> 76: 334-36; V.S. Pritchett, <u>New Statesman</u> 53: 355-56; M. Roberts, <u>EC</u> 8: 428-38; J.Bennett, <u>Cambridge Review</u> 78: 597-99; J.R. Moore, <u>MLQ</u> 21 (1960): 373-75; R. Weimann, <u>ZAA</u> 8 (1960): 315-17; F. Wolcken, <u>Archiv</u> 196 (1960): 214-15.

1958

1   BRADBROOK, FRANK W. "Richardson and Joseph Conrad." <u>N&Q</u> 203: 119.
       Notes several similarities between Richardson's novels and Conrad's <u>Victory</u>: moral structure, realistic presentation, a "hot-house atmosphere," rhetorical speech used at emotional high points, and several specific similarities in character presentation and phrasing.

2   BRISSENDEN, R.F. <u>Samuel Richardson</u>. Writers and their Work, No. 108. London and New York: The British Council, 42 pp.
       General introduction to Richardson's life and work, with a history of his reputation. Includes a bibliography.

3   BRONSON, BERTRAND H.   <u>Printing</u> <u>as</u> <u>an</u> <u>Index</u> <u>to</u> <u>Taste</u> <u>in</u>
     <u>Eighteenth-Century</u> <u>England</u>.   New York: New York Public
     Library, pp. 15, 21.
            Strictures on Richardson as a printer. Also appeared in
     <u>BNYPL</u> (Aug.-Sept. 1958).

4   NEWCOMB, ROBERT.   "Franklin and Richardson." <u>JEGP</u> 57:   27-35.
            The influence of Richardson on <u>Poor</u> <u>Richard's</u> <u>Almanac</u>.

5   NOYES, ROBERT G.   <u>The</u> <u>Neglected</u> <u>Muse</u>.   Brown University
     Studies 24.   Providence: Brown University Press, pp.
     70-71, 93-94, 117-18, 159, 171.
            Richardson's ideas on poetic justice and opinions on
     plays (quotations from the letters and from <u>Pamela</u> and
     <u>Clarissa</u>).

6   RICHARDSON, SAMUEL.   <u>Pamela</u> or <u>Virtue</u> <u>Rewarded</u>.   Introduced by
     William M. Sale, Jr. New York: Norton, 533 pp.
            Introduction stresses inherent contradiction between
     "new sensibility" and temporal rewards of virtue in <u>Pamela</u>,
     gives general history of book and critical introduction to
     its reputation and problems.

7   STERN, G.   "A German Imitation of Fielding: Musäus, <u>Grandison</u>
     <u>der</u> <u>Zweite</u>." <u>CL</u> 10:   335-43.
            Musäus's <u>Grandison</u> <u>der</u> <u>Zweite</u> (1760-62) helped topple
     "that   dictator   Richardson" and establish an era of
     Fielding-admiration in German fiction, in which dramatic
     irony   played a greater role in fiction.   Summarizes
     <u>Grandison</u> <u>der</u> <u>Zweite</u>, but does not give separate treatment
     to <u>Der</u> <u>deutsche</u> <u>Grandison</u>.

                              <u>1959</u>.

1   COLEY, W.B.   "Gide and Fielding." <u>CL</u> 11: 1-15.
            Relates some of Gide's novelistic preoccupations to his
     reading in Defoe, Fielding, and Richardson.

*2   HORNÁT, J. "Pamela, Shamela a Joseph Andrews." <u>Časopis</u> <u>pro</u>
     <u>moderni</u> <u>filologii</u> 49.
            Source: Statni knihovna ČSR. A comparative analysis.

3   KINKEAD-WEEKES, MARK.   "Clarissa Restored?" RES n.s.   10:
      156-71.
           Perhaps the standard third edition of Clarissa is not
      really preferable to the first; by the third edition
      Richardson's desire to explain his book perfectly has
      driven him to some uncomfortable didactic positions, while
      the Letters and Passages Restored to Clarissa provides
      valuable clues to his original intentions. See 1973.33.

4   KRUTCH, J.W. Five Masters. Gloucester, Mass.:   Smith, 328
      pp.
           See 1930.9, 1931.6.

5   MCKILLOP, A.D.   "Supplementary Notes on Richardson as a
      Printer." SB 12: 214-18.
           Notes that Richardson printed The Matchless Rogue
      (1725); gives additional information on the first and
      second editions of Hervey's Meditations and Reflections;
      gives details from Dr. Thomas Birch on Richardson's
      printing business; notices fictional characters working
      for "Mr. Richardson, the parliament printer," in the novel
      The Life and Imaginations of Sally Paul (1760).

6   MCWATTERS, K.G.   "Stendhal, Richardson, et l'Edinburgh
      Review." Stendhal Club 1: 229-30.
           Stendhal disliked Richardson's work except at the
      beginning and end of his own literary career, where there
      are favorable allusions to Richardson.

7   WEINSTEIN, LEO. Metamorphoses of Don Juan. Stanford Studies
      in Language and Literature 18. Stanford: Stanford
      University Press, pp. 39-41, 83.
           Lovelace is not a Don Juan since he falls passionately
      in love, and with only one woman; but notes, p. 83, a
      dissenting reference in Musset's Namouna (1832), in which
      Lovelace is characterized as a cold-hearted roué, a man who
      only loves himself.

8   WHITE, WILLIAM.   "Samuel Richardson." Today's Japan:
      Orient/West 5: 65-74.
           Biographical introduction to Richardson with summaries
      of the three novels.

1960

1   BLAGDEN, CYPRIAN. The Stationers' Company: A History.
     1403-1959. London: George Allen & Unwin, pp. 230-31,
     234, 276.
          Information on Richardson's mastership of the
     Stationers' Company in 1754, on his business sense, and on
     the unusual loyalty he was able to instill in his
     employees.

2   CARROLL, JOHN. "The Reasoning Imagination." Ph.D.
     Dissertation, Harvard.
          General study of the novels and of Richardsonian
     dichotomies: critic vs. artist, artist vs. moralist,
     self-will vs. benevolism.

2A   DAICHES, DAVID. "The Novel from Richardson to Jane Austen."
     In A Critical History of English Literature. New York:
     Ronald Press, 2:700-13.
          General critical introduction, concentrating on
     Clarissa.

3   EAVES, T.C. DUNCAN. "Dr. Johnson's Letters to Richardson."
     PMLA 75: 377-81.
          Corrects and clarifies points in Chapman's edition of
     the Letters; provides some further biographical material
     on Johnson's relationship to Richardson (e.g., that he
     apparently read Grandison in MS).

4   --- and BEN D. KIMPEL. "The Publisher of Pamela and its
     First Audience." BNYPL 54: 143-46.
          Identifies the John Osborn who published Pamela and
     establishes the nature of the business relationship between
     that John and his son John Osborn; provides biographical
     material on Elizabeth Midwinter, who lived with the
     Richardsons from 1736-42.

5   FIEDLER, LESLIE. Love and Death in the American Novel. New
     York: Criterion, passim to p. 125.
          Richardson, with Rousseau and Goethe, is the "founding
     father" of the American novel and Lovelace and Clarissa are
     its Ur-characters. Fiedler constructs a tradition
     stretching from Richardson and the other Sentimentalists to
     Melville's Lucy, Hawthorne's Hilda, and James's Daisy
     Miller, and connects the class war of Sentimental fiction

with its analogues in the war between male and female,
conceived of as the negative intellectual principle and its
corresponding female emotional principle. Cites many minor
American novels influenced by Richardson. "There is
scarcely a nineteenth-century book written by an American,
whether avowedly in the analytical school that derives from
Pamela, or in the Gothic tradition . . . which does not
accept the standards of the . . . sentimental Love
Religion, inextricably bound up with the example of
Richardson . . . " (45) But this sensibility is also a
"universal calamity," replacing ideas by either facts or
feelings. During the course of Richardson's influence the
Clarissa-novel with a female heroine is transformed into a
novel with a male hero, Lovelace. Grandison exerts almost
no influence because "mythically, Grandison does not exist
at all . . ." (51).

6   FOLKIERSKI, W. "L'Anglais de Diderot." RLC 34:   226-34.
       Richardson's stylistic influence over   Diderot   and
     Diderot's knowledge of English.

*7   GUERRINI, SANDRA. "La donna nei romanzi di Richardson." Ph.D.
     dissertation, Universita del Sacro Cuore, Milan.
       Courtesy Prof. Carl Berkhout.

8   KREISSMAN, BERNARD. Pamela-Shamela: A Study of Burlesques,
     Parodies, and Adaptations of Richardson's Pamela. N.p.
     [Lincoln]: University of Nebraska Press, 98 pp.
       Criticism of Pamela I and II as well as of the
     adaptations;   finds Richardson's original hypocritical and
     dull;   covers Shamela and the pro-Pamela criticism.
       Rev.: R.   Paulson, JEGP 61 (1962):   410-13;   A.D.
     McKillop, CollE 22:   205.

9   MANDELKOW, KARL ROBERT. "Der deutsche Briefroman.   Zum
     Problem der Polyperspektive im Epischen." Neophil 44:
     200-208.
       Richardson is cited as the founder of the
     "polyperspectival" novel, which in Clarissa achieved new
     expressive and formal possibilities. From the point of
     view of narrative, Richardson's and Fielding's novels are
     antitypes of each other, Fielding's narrative theory being
     that of standortfestes Erzahlen, Richardson's standortloses
     (203). While Blankenburg praises the standortfest type as
     being more true to life, the "nihilistic, unbalanced

generation of <u>William Lovell</u>" finds entirely adequate
expression in the <u>Briefroman</u>, which is the classic type of
<u>standortlos</u> narrative. <u>Werther</u> adds further distancing to
the epistolary form, since it is a letter novel with a
narrator. Mandelkow compares the aesthetic and
epistemological sense of the epistolary novel to Broch's
work and to the Heisenberg Uncertainty Principle in its
acknowledgment of the distortions set up when the observer
is introduced into the field of observation.

10

    Item deleted.

11   MEAD, WILLIAM. "<u>Les Liaisons dangereuses</u> and Moral
        Usefulness." <u>PMLA</u> 75: 563-70.
        Laclos should be considered as writing against the
    extreme <u>sensibilité</u> that is represented by both Rousseau
    and Richardson.

12   NACHTIGALL, ELSBETH. <u>Die Mémoires der Marguerite de Valois
        als Quelle zu Richardsons Clarissa</u>. Romanisches Seminar an
        der Universitat Bonn. Ph.D. dissertation, Bonn. Bonn:
        n.p., 140 pp.
        Marguerite de Valois's <u>Memoirs</u>, and particularly the
    Mlle de Tournon episode, may have served as a source for
    Richardson, given his proven interest in memoirs of the
    French court; parallels are cited between the two.

13   VOSS, ERNST THEODOR. <u>Erzählprobleme des Briefromans</u> . . .
        Ph.D. dissertation, Bonn, 1960? Bonn: n.p., 360 pp.
        In the German novel as in the English, Richardson was
    not the "discoverer" of the epistolary novel; to
    Richardson's and Rousseau's influence must be added that of
    many other authors. The Richardsonian influence makes
    itself felt in Germany in a sudden rush of epistolary
    fiction; however, the first real German epistolary novel
    is <u>Grandison der Zweyte</u>.

14   WENDT, ALLAN. "Clarissa's Coffin." <u>PQ</u> 39: 481-95.
        "Clarissa's coffin . . . dominates the book" as a
    symbol of Christian death; Clarissa, the spiritual person,
    is unable to live in the world. Relates <u>Clarissa</u> to its
    roots in eighteenth-century Benevolism.

*15   WHITE, WILLIAM. "Samuel Richardson: Novelist of the Sewing
        Circles." <u>Today's Japan: Orient/West</u> 5: 65-74.
        Source: <u>BELL</u> 35, item 3463.

1961

1   BLOCK, ANDREW. The English Novel 1740-1850: A Catalogue. 2d
     ed. London: Dawsons of Pall Mall.
          Numerous references to Richardsonaden; editions cited
     are not always the first.

2   BOYCE, BENJAMIN. "The Effect of the Restoration on Prose
     Fiction." Tennessee Studies in Literature 6:77-83.
          As part of study of Restoration fiction, concludes that
     Clarissa owes more to middle-class than to courtly
     concerns.

*3   CHALKER, JOHN. "´Virtue Rewarded´: The Sexual Theme in
     Richardson´s Pamela." LHY 2: 58-64.
          Source: YWMLS.

4   EAVES, T.C. DUNCAN, and BEN D. KIMPEL. "Richardsoniana." SB
     14: 232-34.
          Description of the bound volume of Richardsoniana in the
     Forster Collection, which contains Remarks on Clarissa
     (listed by Richardson as by Sarah Fielding), Answer to a
     Letter . . . Objecting to the Warmth of a Particular
     Scene in . . . Clarissa, material from the GM, Copy of a
     Letter to a Lady, and Answer to a Letter from a Friend.

5   FARRELL, WILLIAM J. "Rhetorical Elements in the
     Eighteenth-Century English Novel." Ph.D. dissertation,
     University of Wisconsin.
          Notes similarities between compositional techniques in
     Richardson (and Fielding, Smollett, Sterne) and techniques
     of traditional rhetoric. Though Richardson condemns
     eloquence, it plays a prominent role in characterizing
     Clarissa and Lovelace.

6   [FIELDING, HENRY.] Shamela/Joseph Andrews. Edited with an
     introduction and notes by Martin C. Battestin. Boston:
     Houghton Mifflin (Riverside Press), pp. 1-40.
          Battestin´s introduction summarizes the history of the
     Pamela-Shamela publications and controversy (though less
     sympathetically than 1968.38), suggesting that Fielding
     substituted for the "technical and intellectual
     inadequaciess of Pamela . . . a mature and antithetic
     alternative," Joseph Andrews.

7   GRIFFITH, PHILIP MAHONE.   "Fire-Scenes   in   Richardson's
     Clarissa and Smollett's _Humphrey Clinker:_ A Study of a
     Literary Relationship in the Structure of the   Novel."   _TSE_
     11: 39-51.
          Suggests Smollett looked back on _Clarissa_ in   the
     epistolary format of _Humphrey Clinker_ but used fire-scenes
     for comic rather than tragic effect, ridiculing Richardson
     in the process. Notes some parallels between Melford and
     Lovelace   and   the   presence   of   posteriors   in   both
     fire-scenes.

*8   KONIGSBERG, IRA. "Samuel Richardson and the Rise of the
     Dramatic Novel." Ph.D. dissertation, Stanford University.
     Revised as 1968.28. Source: McNamee.

*9   MALLIK, B.R. _Richardson's_ _Clarissa_ _Harlowe._ Delhi: S.
     Chand, 34 pp.
          Source: Catalog of the National Library of India.

10   PEAKE, CHARLES. "Samuel Richardson and Wit." _Books,_ No. 335,
     pp. 83-87.
          Discusses Richardson as conscious artist; compares his
     use of wit favorably with Fielding's. Though Fielding was
     witty about his characters, Richardson showed the uses of
     wit in real life, creating witty sympathetic characters and
     using wit to make a moral judgment on irresponsible use of
     words. His use of wit, Peake suggests, was one of the
     elements attracting Jane Austen to him.

11   PONS, CHRISTIAN. "Richardson et la _Nouvelle_ _Héloïse._" _EA_ 14:
     350-51.
          Discusses similarities and differences   between   _La_
     Nouvelle _Héloïse_ and, in particular, _Pamela_ _II_ and
     Grandison, concentrating on the two men's conception of
     Christian duties and of "reasonable marriage."

*12 RICHARDSON, SAMUEL. _Pamela_ _o_ _la_ _Virtud_ _Recompensada._   In
     Maestros _ingleses._ Barcelona: Planeta, pp. 1272-1649.
          Source: Catalog of the National Library of Chile.

*13 SEN, S.E. "Richardson and Fielding: Moral Sense and Moral
     Vision." _Bulletin_ _of_ _the_ _Department_ _of_ _English,_ _University_

of Calcutta 2:   38-40.
Source: BELL 36, item 3630.

14   SUTHERLAND, JAMES. "The Paradox of Richardson." The Times
      (London), July 4, 1961, p. 11.
         A note on the two-hundredth anniversary of Richardson's
      death.   How,   asks   Sutherland, could such a rigid,
      narrow-minded,   bourgeois, unpleasant little man have
      written such great novels?   Praises the first part of
      Pamela, Clarissa, and, surprisingly, Grandison, which,
      though it "lacks the compelling situation" of the other
      two, "abounds in observation, and has a good deal of comedy
      and wit."

15   TEN HARMSEL, HENRIETTA. "The Villain-Hero in Pamela and Pride
      and Prejudice." CollE 23: 104-8.
         The "villain-hero," B. or Darcy, by his assertion of
      aristocratic privilege makes the heroine abhor him, while
      his "good looks, wealth and aristocracy make him all that
      she wants." Cites numerous similarities between the two
      novels, including the ambiguous social position of the
      heroine and a series of almost insuperable obstacles
      between her and the hero, arising from her birth or family;
      an about-face in a condescending proposal; similar scenes
      between Pamela-Lady Barbara and Elizabeth-Lady Catherine;
      and a certain difficulty in characterizing the hero after
      his defeat.

16   TUCKER, SUSIE I.   "Predatings from Samuel Richardson's
      Familiar Letters." N&Q 206: 56-57.
         Notes several word-usages in Richardson that predate the
      OED's earliest examples: "blessed" in the sense of
      "cursed," "domesticate," "matronise," "school-age," and
      "free-masonry" in the pejorative transferred sense.

*17   VIVIANI, ELENA GIOVANNA. "Pamela: studio." Diss. Universita
      del Sacro Cuore, Milan.
         Courtesy Prof. Carl Berkhout.

*18   WHITE, WILLIAM. "Samuel Richardson." ABC 11: 11-20.
         Source: BELL.

1962

*1   BARKER, GERARD A. "Form and Purpose in the Novels of Samuel
     Richardson." Ph.D. dissertation, Stanford University.
          Source: McNamee.

2   EAVES, T.C. DUNCAN, and BEN D. KIMPEL. "Richardson's London
     houses." <u>SB</u> 15: 135-48.
          Locations, dates, and uses of Richardson's London
     houses; incorporated into E&K.

3   FIEDLER, LESLIE. "Le viol des Temple: de Richardson à
     Faulkner." <u>Preuves</u>, No. 138, pp. 75-81.
          French summary of 1960.5, discussing the man-woman
     conflict as the essential theme of the Romantic tradition.

*4   MOJAŠEVIC, MILKA. "Richardsonovi romani i Goetheov Werther."
     <u>Filologija</u> 3: 97-108.
          The influence of Richardson's works on <u>Werther</u>. Source:
     <u>BELL</u>.

5   RICHARDSON, SAMUEL. <u>Clarissa; or, The History of a Young
     Lady</u>.   Abridged and ed. with an intro. by George
     Sherburn. Boston: Houghton Mifflin (Riverside Press), 537
     pp.
          According to 1972.17, the most usable of the three
     modern abridgments of <u>Clarissa</u>. See 1971.8A.

6   ---. <u>Clarissa, or the History of a Young Lady</u>. Intro.   by
     John Butt. 4v. London: J.M. Dent (Everyman).
          Text of third edition. General introduction (1: v-xi)
     by John Butt makes comparisons with <u>Pamela</u> and Milton,
     discusses the character of Lovelace and relates   the
     epistolary form to Richardson's concept of virtue.

7   ---. <u>Pamela, or Virtue Rewarded</u>. Introduced by   Mark
     Kinkead-Weekes. 2v. London: J.M. Dent (Everyman).
          Reset edition of 1914, with new introduction but same
     corrupt Cooke text;   includes both parts of <u>Pamela</u>. See
     1977.17, 1978.4.

8   ROMBERG, BERTIL. "Clarissa." In <u>Studies in the Narrative
     Technique of the First-Person Novel</u>. Stockholm, etc.:
     Almqvist and Wiksell, pp. 177-235.
          Actually on <u>Clarissa</u> and <u>Pamela</u>, as well as on the
     theory of the first-person novel (pp.   46-55) and the
     <u>Briefwechselroman</u> (a very valuable section, pp. 72 ff.).

257

Detailed   discussion   of   epistolary   form   in   <u>Clarissa</u>
concentrates   on   epistolary   form   as   function   of
psychological   realism,   function   of   editor,   place   of
audience,   and   role   of   multiple   narrators   (especially
Lovelace)   in   raising   story   to   tragedy.   Compares
Richardson's narrative format with that of Marivaux (which
he finds quite different), Keller's in <u>Der grune Heinrich</u>
and Durrell's in <u>The Alexandria Quartet</u>.

9   ROUSSET, JEAN. "Une Forme littéraire: le roman par lettres."
       In his <u>Forme et Signification: Essai sur les structures</u>
       <u>littéraires de Corneille à Claudel</u>.   Paris: Corti, pp.
       65-108.
             The   letter-novel   as   drama   and   formal   analogue   of
       realism, with special attention to the "symphonic novel" or
       <u>Briefwechselroman</u>.   <u>Clarissa</u> is discussed as an example.
       Jacques Derrida discusses Rousset's work in <u>Critique</u>, Nos.
       193-94.

10   SHERBURN, GEORGE.   "Samuel Richardson's Novels   and   the
       Theater: A Theory Sketched." <u>PQ</u> 41: 325-29.
             Richardson read plays (rather than seeing them); he is
       indebted to them for a focused plot, character-types, and
       vivid, extensive dialogue, as well as for his writing-style
       itself; he wrote for the ear.

11   SLATTERY, WILLIAM CARLIN. "The Correspondence between Samuel
       Richardson and Johannes Stinstra, the Dutch Translator of
       <u>Clarissa</u>." Ph.D. dissertation, University of Arkansas.
             Published with modifications and additions as 1969.17.

*12   ZIGERELL, JAMES J. "Choosing a Mate in the Novels of Samuel
       Richardson." Ph.D. dissertation, University of Chicago.
             (Appears in McNamee as "Patterns of Courtship and
       Marriage . . ."; this title from ICU.)

                                 1963

*1   ---. <u>Dějiny anglické literatury</u>. [History of English
       Literature.] Edited by Hardin Craig; translated from
       English by Eliška Hornátová and Jaroslav Hornăt.   Práha:
       SNKL, pp. 83-85. Bib. Jagiellońska
             Source: Catalog of the Bib. Jagiellońska.

2   CARROLL, JOHN.   "Richardson on Pope and Swift." UTQ 33:
     19-29.
          Extracts from his edition of the Selected Letters;
     notes importance of Swift in characterization of Lovelace.

3   CLELAND, JOHN. Memoirs of a Woman of Pleasure.   Edited with
     an introduction by Peter Quennell. New York: Putnam, 256
     pp.
          See 1749.2A; Quennell's introduction suggests, p.   xi,
     that Fanny Hill is to be counted among anti-Richardsonian
     fiction. The book is epistolary but not greatly indebted
     to Richardson (though cf. 1972.6).

4   DONOVAN, R.A. "The Problem of Pamela, or Virtue Unrewarded."
     SEL 3:   377-95.   Reprinted in his Shaping Vision:
     Imagination in the English Novel from Defoe to Dickens.
     Ithaca: Cornell University Press, 1966, pp.   47-67.
          Pamela is "about morality" only as a means of limiting
     the sphere of action to the impact of the new middle class
     upon the old aristocracy.   Pamela's values and conduct
     express her social aspirations, while Mr. B.'s libertinism
     is limited by his sense of class.

5   DREW, ELIZABETH. "Clarissa." The Novel. New York: Norton,
     pp. 39-59.
          Richardson was "the pioneer in the analytical study of
     individual behavior in conflict with an oppressive social
     code, and also in the analytical study of conflict within
     the individual consciousness"; as such, though cruder than
     any of them, he was the progenitor of George Eliot,
     Flaubert, James and Tolstoy.

6   FARRELL, WILLIAM J. "The Style and the Action in Clarissa."
     SEL 3: 365-75.
          Traditional and conventional formulae in Clarissa's
     speeches and Lovelace's letters show Richardson adapting
     the conventions of literary prose to the artistic needs of
     his realism. Special discussion of tragic "high style" and
     courtly rhetoric.

7   GOLDEN, MORRIS.   Richardson's Characters.   Ann Arbor:
     University of Michigan Press, 214 pp.
          Richardson is "unique in his time" in the perception of
     the hidden bases of character, particularly the roots of
     action in sadistic dominance and lust for power.   Such

urges inform even Richardson's attitude towards his readers
and turn his major male characters into "modifications . .
. of certain urges, rather than rational actors chosen for
moral or artistic reasons." (27-28) Grandison is no
exception to this rule, while the woman achieve power by
suffering or yielding. Among the prudent bourgeois, lust
for power is "restrained and channeled through the
admirable, disinterested dispensing of money." (106) The
conflict of wills is the central action in Pamela and
Clarissa; where it is not, in Grandison, the result seems
"mythically . . . inferior."
 See also Golden's *Fielding's Moral Psychology* (Amherst,
Mass.: University of Massachusetts Press, 1966), in which
Richardson is frequently mentioned and Richardsonian
preoccupations, such as the enclosed self, are discussed.
 Rev.: David Daiches, MassR 6 (1965): 208-17; Owen
Jenkins, MLQ 25 (1964): 372-74; Ian Watt, ELN 20
(1964-65): 136-38; Martin Battestin, JEGP 63 (1964):
797-800; TLS, June 18, 1964, p. 529.

8 GREANY, HELEN TERESA. "A Study of Process in the Novels of
 Samuel Richardson." Ph.D. dissertation, Columbia
 University.
  Discusses Richardson's style as a function of interest
 in the psychology of the moment and in Sentimentalim;
 general study of the three novels.

9 HUGHES, LEO. "Theatrical Conventions in Richardson: Some
 Observations on a Novelist's Technique." In Restoration and
 Eighteenth-Century Literature: Essays in Honor of Alan
 Dugald McKillop. Edited by Carroll Camden. Chicago:
 University of Chicago Press (for W.M. Rice University),
 pp. 211-35.
  Draws attention to theatrical costuming and conventional
 theatrical gestures in Richardson's work--handkerchiefs,
 the hand to the brow, the white satin of innocence,
 etc.--and notes the source of some of them in Cibber's
 writings and Hill's Art of Acting.

10 JOHNSON, SAMUEL. The Yale Edition of the Works of Samuel
 Johnson. Volume II: The Adventurer. Edited by W.J.
 Bate, J.M. Bullitt, and W.F. Powell. New Haven and
 London: Yale University Press, pp. 331-32n, 486n.
  Richardson was asked to contribute to The Adventurer,
 but declined. Johnson always supposed that Robert Nelson,

author of <u>Feasts</u> <u>and</u> <u>Fasts</u>, was the original of Sir Charles
Grandison.

11 JOVICEVICH, ALEXANDER. "A Propos d´une ´Paméla´ de Voltaire."
<u>FR</u> 36: 276-83.
    The book that Voltaire speaks of as "dans le goust de
<u>Pamela</u>" is his <u>Lettres</u> <u>d´Amabed</u> (1769), an olio of
real-life and fictional adventures. Apart from the
epistolary form and the theme of persecuted virtue,
however, the <u>Lettres</u> <u>d´Amabed</u> are not at all like <u>Pamela</u>.
(Courtesy Prof. Alexander Jovicevich)

12 MCBURNEY, WILLIAM HARLAN, edited and introduced. <u>Four</u> <u>Before</u>
<u>Richardson</u>:   <u>Selected</u> <u>English</u> <u>Novels,</u> <u>1720-1727</u>. Lincoln,
Neb.: University of Nebraska Press, 428 pp.
    35-page introduction notes Richardsonian elements in
pre-Richardsonian fiction. Body of text reprints four
novels: Arthur Blackmore´s <u>Luck</u> <u>at</u> <u>Last</u>, W.P.´s <u>The</u>
<u>Jamaica</u> <u>Lady,</u> <u>or</u> <u>the</u> <u>Life</u> <u>of</u> <u>Bavia</u>, Eliza Haywood´s
<u>Philidore</u> <u>and</u> <u>Placentia,</u> <u>or</u> <u>L´Amour</u> <u>trop</u> <u>Delicat</u>, and Mary
Davy´s <u>The</u> <u>Accomplished</u> <u>Rake,</u> <u>or</u> <u>Modern</u> <u>Fine</u> <u>Gentleman</u>.
Reprinted in 1964.

13 MACCHIA, G. <u>La</u> <u>Scuola</u> <u>dei</u> <u>Sentimenti</u>. Arethusa: Collezione
di Litteratura 19. Roma: Salvatore Sciascia, pp. 160-64.
    Discusses Lovelace as part of libertine tradition and
compares him with Valmont; considers him one of precursors
of Mozart´s Don Giovanni.

14 MAY, GEORGES. <u>Le</u> <u>Dilemme</u> <u>du</u> <u>roman</u> <u>au</u> <u>XVIIIe</u> <u>siècle:</u> <u>Etude</u>
<u>sur</u> <u>les</u> <u>rapports</u> <u>du</u> <u>roman</u> <u>et</u> <u>de</u> <u>la</u> <u>critique</u> <u>(1715-1761)</u>.
New Haven: Yale University Press; Paris: PUF, 294 pp.
    Important background for Richardson in France and moral
questions in the novel; Richardson is referred to but not
at length.

15 MOORE, JOHN ROBERT. "Daniel Defoe: Precursor of Samuel
Richardson." In <u>Restoration</u> <u>and</u> <u>Eighteenth-Century</u>
<u>Literature</u> . . . (see 1963.9 above), pp. 351-69.
    Defoe is a "dramatic novelist" in his use of dialogue
(e.g. in <u>The</u> <u>Family</u> <u>Instructor</u> and <u>Religious</u> <u>Courtship</u>);
he also writes epistolary fiction of a sort, and letters
are used in his work to relate offstage action and to
signal climaxes. Notes Defoe´s connections with printing.

15A   PARNELL, PAUL E. "The Sentimental Mask." PMLA 78:529-35.
       As part of a study on Steele, Cibber and sentimental
comedy, notes that the sentimental heroine and hero are
raised above their sex and hated for their virtue; quotes
Richardson´s description of Clarissa as an example of "the
Christlike mask."

16   SHERBURN, GEORGE. "Writing to the Moment: One Aspect." In
       Restoration and Eighteenth-Century Literature . . . (see
       1963.9 above), pp. 201-10.
       Richardson and dramatic writing: specifies examples of
physical detail and visual imagination.

17   SIEGEL, JUNE SIGLER. "Diderot and Richardson: A Confluence
       of Opposites." Ph.D. dissertation, Columbia.
       Study of complex influence of Richardson upon Diderot;
both develop a new kind of prose reflecting conflict,
internal character tensions, antithesis, paradox, and an
"unprecedented exploration of psychological motifs." "From
their involvement in conflict and contradiction . . .
arises a new kind of expression which is at once lyrical
and empirical . . . [providing]
expression-by-representation of an increasingly complex and
incomprehensible world."

*18   SIEGEL, JUNE SIGLER. "Grandeur--Intimacy: the Dramatist´s
       Dilemma." DS 4.
       "Attributes Diderot´s failure as a dramatist to his
attempts to translate to the stage the techniques of
Richardsonian novel"--YWMLS 25: 79.

19   SKLEPOWICH, LOIS ANNE. "Providential Labyrinth: The
       Development of Richardson´s Christian Comedy." Ph.D.
       dissertation, University of Virginia.
       Examines Richardson´s fiction as representation of a
Latitudinarian world-order; concentrates on plot and style
as mirroring Christian providence.

20   SOUTHAM, B.C. "Jane Austen and Clarissa." N&Q 208: 191-92;
       and E.E. Duncan-Jones, ibid: 350.
       Southam queries whether the Rev. Elias Brand is a
possible source for Mr. Collins; Duncan-Jones affirms
that Austen read Clarissa, noting a reference to the rape
scene in a letter to Cassandra Austen, September 18, 1796.

21   VAN HEYNINGEN, CHRISTINA. <u>Clarissa:</u> <u>Poetry</u> <u>and</u> <u>Morals</u>.
      Pietermaritzburg: University of Natal Press, pp. 1-44.
           Analysis of the presence of moral purpose in major
      episodes of the book and in Richardson's technique. Rev.:
      R. Lee, <u>English</u> <u>Stud</u> <u>in</u> <u>Africa</u> 7 (1964): 235-37 (courtesy
      Saltykov-Shchedrin Library).

*22   WILSON, J.S. "Novel into Play: The Influence of Richardson,
      Fielding, Smollett, and Sterne upon the Later English
      Drama." Ph.D. dissertation, Rice University.
           Source: 1975.2, item D110.

*23   WÜRZBACH, NATASCHA. "Die Struktur des Briefromans und seine
      Entstehung in England." Ph.D. dissertation, Munich.
           Source: 1971.15.

                              <u>1964</u>

*1   ANIKST, A., Edited by and trans. "Richardson." <u>Dĕjiny</u>
      <u>anglické</u> <u>literatury</u> [History of English Literature].
      Práha: SPN, pp. 153-55.
           Translated from 1956.10. Courtesy Statni knihovna ČSR.

2   AUCHINCLOSS, LOUIS. <u>The</u> <u>Rector</u> <u>of</u> <u>Justin</u>. Cambridge, Mass.:
      Houghton Mifflin, 341 pp.
           The narrator, Brian Aspinwall, admires Richardson--the
      small portrait of Richardson writing at his desk is
      Aspinwall's most prized possession--but he does not realize
      that he is serving as a Richardsonian narrator. The novel
      is in modified epistolary form.
           When asked why Aspinwall admires Richardson, Mr.
      Auchincloss replied, "He <u>would</u>. <u>Clarissa</u> enables him to
      escape longer and deeper into fiction than any other
      novel," and added that he shares the sentiment. (Letter
      from Mr. Auchincloss to SWRS, November 27, 1978.)

3   BAKER, SHERIDAN. "The Idea of Romance in the
      Eighteenth-Century Novel." <u>PMA</u> 49: 507-22.
           Discusses patterns of romance in eighteenth-century
      fiction, noting Richardson's use of them (515-16).

                              263

4   BROICH, ULRICH. "Fielding's Shamela und Pamela or the Fair
      Imposter, zwei Parodien von Richardsons Pamela." Anglia 82,
      pt. 2: 172-90.
          In Richardson's attempt to separate his heroine from the
      tradition of the picara, Puritan "realism" and "moral
      idealization" war with what Fielding sees as hypocritical
      efforts to hide the crossing of class lines. Pamela, or
      the Fair Imposter relies on mock-epic to diminish
      Richardson's heroine. Both parodies are in the rearguard
      of conservative writing and war with the new bourgeois
      literature.

5   BULLEN, JOHN SAMUEL. "A Search for a Method: The Novels of
      Samuel Richardson." Ph.D. dissertation, Stanford
      University.
          General study of the three novels, concentrating on:
      the differences among groups of Richardson's readers; the
      use of time and space as analogues of novelistic
      intentions; the problems of plausible narration; and the
      effect of narrative modes on the presentation of character.

6   CARROLL, JOHN, selected, introduced, and edited. Selected
      Letters of Samuel Richardson. Oxford: Clarendon, 350 pp.
          128 letters or parts of letters from Richardson to
      various correspondents; the letters have been selected
      largely for their relevance to "the themes and characters
      of Richardson's novels . . . his craftsmanship and
      literary judgements . . . and his own personality." The
      most convenient, the most textually reliable, and the only
      annotated edition of Richardson's letters, but does not
      claim to be complete. Carroll's 35-page introduction
      discusses Richardson's correspondence and epistolary
      theory. Rev.: S. Read, Canadian Lit, Winter 1966, pp.
      76-77; V.S. Pritchett, New Statesman, January 26, 1965,
      p. 324; Robert Halsband, NYTBR, April 4, 1965, pp.
      18-19; JNL 25 (1965): 4-5; TLS, February 18, 1965, p.
      128; J.C. Reid, AUMLA, No. 24 (1965): 302-3; Morris
      Golden, JEGP 64 (1965): 740-42; D.M. Low, New Rambler,
      June 1965, pp. 43-44; Rachel Trickett, RES 17 (1966):
      323-26; John Preston, MLR 61 (1966): 499-501; Donald F.
      Bond, MP 64 (1966): 164-65; Ian Watt, UTQ 35 (1966):
      211-12.

7   DEMAREST, DAVID PORTER. "Legal Language in the
     Eighteenth-Century Novel: Readings in Defoe, Richardson,
     Fielding, and Austen." Ph.D. dissertation, University of
     Wisconsin.
          Metaphors of legal language; Clarissa appies legal
     language to Lovelace and triumphs through her "will." ". .
     . Defoe and Richardson share the same rigoristic vision."

8   DUNCAN-JONES, E.E. "The Misses Selby and Steele." TLS,
     September 10, 1964, p. 845.
          Suggests that the Steele girls, Nancy and Lucy, in Sense
     and Sensibility are called, with slight parody, after Nancy
     and Lucy Selby in Grandison; the Steele girls have friends
     named Richardson.

9   DUSSINGER, JOHN A. "Richardson's Clarissa: ´A Work of Tragic
     Species." Ph.D. dissertation, Princeton.
          The influence on Richardson of the Deist controversy,
     the Evangelical revival, and contemporary theories of
     tragedy.

10   EAVES, T.C. DUNCAN, and BEN D. KIMPEL. "Richardson and his
     Family Circle." N&Q 209: 212-18, 264-70, 300-304, 343-47,
     362-71, 402-6, 467-69; 212 (1968): 448-50.
          Biographical material on Richardson and his family and
     friends. 212 ff.: Material on the Wildes, John Wilde's
     ancestry, and his life as a printer. 264 ff.: The Leakes,
     family of Richardson's second wife. 300 ff.: Richardson's
     will. 343 ff.: Richardson's ancestry. 362 ff.:
     Richardson's immediate family, birthplace, and possible
     date of birth. 402 ff.: William Richardson, brother of
     the novelist. 467 ff.: Benjamin Richardson, another
     brother. In December 1968 (see 1968.20) some errors in
     these data are corrected and Eaves and Kimpel discuss
     material from the tax records of the City of London,
     relating principally to Richardson's London addresses.
     Incorporated into E&K.

11   ENOMOTO, FUTOSHI. "Clarissa Harlowe's Pursuit of Happiness."
     SEL (Tokyo) 40: 167-84.
          The novel's apparent theme is the pursuit of happiness
     through marriage, but Clarissa finds her happiness only
     through death. Richardson identifies with Lovelace.
     Clarissa is sinful, in a sense particularly Puritan, not
     only in her nature as a human being but in her denial of

her sin.

*12   GREINER,   M.   <u>Die</u>   <u>Entstehung</u>   <u>der</u>   <u>modernen</u>
       <u>Unterhaltungsliteratur</u>.   <u>Studien</u> <u>zum</u> <u>Trivialroman</u> <u>des</u> <u>18.</u>
       <u>Jhdts</u>. Reinbek bei Hamburg: Rowohlt, 153 pp.
            Source: <u>YWMLS</u> 26: 449-50.

*13   JAUSS,   HANS   ROBERT.   "Nachahmungsprinzip   und
       Wirklichkeitsbegriff in der Theorie des Romans von Diderot
       bis Stendhal." In his (ed.) <u>Nachahmung</u> <u>und</u> <u>Illusion:</u>
       <u>Kolloquium</u> <u>Giessen</u> <u>Juni</u> <u>1963,</u> <u>Vorhanden</u> <u>und</u> <u>Verhandlungen</u>.
       Munich: Eidos, pp. 157÷78.
            Source: <u>CBFL</u>, item 5176.

14   KNIGHT, CHARLES A.   "<u>Clarissa</u>:   an   Analysis."   Ph.D.
       dissertation, University of Pennsylvania.
            Unchanging thematic unity of <u>Clarissa</u> is contrasted with
       major characters´ changing ideas of themselves; general
       study focusing on relationships between theme and
       technique.   McNamee lists under title: "Pattern and
       Identity in Richardson´s <u>Clarissa</u>: A Critical Analysis."

15   MARKS, WILLIAM SOWELL. "The Novel as Puritan Romance: A
       Comparative Study of Samuel Richardson, the Brontës, Thomas
       Hardy, and D.H.   Lawrence." Ph.D dissertation, Stanford
       University.
            Studies Richardson´s novels as exemplars of Miltonic
       idea of "romantic marriage," emphasizing psychological
       aspects of heroines´ moral dilemmas; Clarissa and Lovelace
       shown as archetypes of Victorian heroine and "demon lover."
       Cf. 1960.5.

16   MCKENZIE, D.F. "Richardson, Mr. W., and Lady T." <u>N&Q</u> 210:
       pp. 299-300.
            Previously unrecorded letter of Richardson to Charles
       Acres, a printer, dated 30 January 1745/6, and probably
       concerning the relationship between Ethelreda, Lady
       Townshend, and Thomas Winnington.

17   PRICE, MARTIN. "Clarissa and Lovelace." <u>To</u> <u>the</u> <u>Palace</u> <u>of</u>
       <u>Wisdom</u>. New York: Doubleday, pp. 278-284.
            Clarissa´s limited self-awareness leads to her tragedy.

18   RAWSON, C. "´Nice´ and ´sentimental´: A parallel between
        <u>Northanger Abbey</u> and Richardson´s correspondence." <u>N&Q</u> 210:
        180.
            Catherine´s "nice" (in the Chapman edition, pp. 107-8)
        compares in scope and vagueness with "sentimental" as Lady
        Bradshaigh says it was used in 1749 (<u>Corr</u>, 4: 282-83).

19   RICHARDSON, SAMUEL. <u>Clarissa: Prefaces, Hints of Prefaces,</u>
        <u>and Postscript</u>. Edited with an introduction and notes by
        R.F. Brissenden. ARS No. 103. Los Angeles: W.A. Clark
        Memorial Library, 57 pp.
            The introduction by Brissenden distinguishes between
        Richardson´s ability to express a critical sense of his
        work and his critical intuitions themselves, which were
        "sound" in Brissenden´s opinion. Richardson himself notes
        the division of <u>Clarissa</u> by narrators (first Clarissa and
        Anna, then Lovelace, then Belford), the necessary
        "minuteness," the characterization for <u>both</u> individuality
        and moral value, the necessity of Clarissa´s rejecting
        Lovelace, the superiority of the symphonic mode of multiple
        narration to the single voice of the novelist, "whence
        different Styles, Manners, etc., that make Episodes
        useless." Defends his ending under sanction of Aristotle´s
        theory of tragedy and Biblical reliance on the Divine;
        also defends Hickman and the necessity of the
        "objectionable" scenes. Defines idea of love in Clarissa;
        shows why Lovelace is not an infidel. Haller is quoted and
        recapitulated.

20   SACKS, SHELDON. <u>Fiction and the Shape of Belief: A Study of</u>
        <u>Henry Fielding with glances at Swift, Johnson and</u>
        <u>Richardson</u>. Berkeley and Los Angeles: University of
        California Press, pp. 234 ff.
            Sack´s important study discusses Fielding and Richardson
        (concentrating on <u>Pamela</u>), arguing that aesthetic and moral
        purposes cannot be separated in their fiction; though the
        major references to Richardson are in the pages cited
        above, the whole book is useful. Rev.: Ronald Paulson,
        <u>JEGP</u> 65 (1966): 602-4; Martin C. Battestin, <u>CollE</u> 27
        (1966): 654; C.T.P. in <u>ABC</u> 14 (1966): 5; Frank Brady,
        <u>JGE</u> 17 (1966): 332-35.

*21   SCHÜCKING, LEVIN L. <u>Die Puritanische Familie in</u>
        <u>Literarsoziologischer Sicht</u>. 2. verb. Aufl. Bern und
        München: Francke.

Material on Milton, Defoe, Bunyan, and Richardson;   see 1969.15. Source: <u>NUC</u>.

22   SCHULTZE, EDVIGE.   "Pamela e le sui origine." <u>Istituto Orientale di Napoli</u>--<u>Annali</u>, Sezione Germanica, 7: 143-74.
        Those who look for discussion of social problems in Richardson should not ignore the preeminence of the moral problem. Argues for great influence of Defoe on Richardson, going so far as to say that Defoe may have been Richardson's mysterious gentleman correspondent; Defoe prefigured Richardson in being the first to create the modern novel's blend of moral comment, picturing of bourgeois life, and aesthetic realism. Specific parallels between <u>Moll Flanders</u> and <u>Pamela</u>; other parallels with Haywood.

23   SHARROCK, ROGER. "Richardson's <u>Pamela</u>: the Gospel and the Novel." <u>DUJ</u> 57: 67-74.
        Richardson embodies in Pamela "the truths of the doctrine of Grace," while marvelously keeping her an ordinary person as well; through this combination she becomes a heroine of romance. Richardson combines the stream-of-consciousness style with a Christian style influenced by the Bible; the result is comparable to Augustine's <u>sermo humilis</u>.

24   TEN HARMSEL, HENRIETTA. <u>Jane Austen: A Study in Fictional Conventions</u>. SEL 4. La Hague: Mouton, p. 51.
        Willoughby's "rescue" of Marianne from the gypsies in <u>Sense and Sensibility</u> is a parodic reference to the kidnap of Harriet in <u>Grandison</u>.

25   WESTBROOK, JAMES SEYMOUR, JR. "Sensibility and Society. A Study in Themes." Ph.D. dissertation, Columbia.
        Chapter One discusses the relations between sensibility and society in <u>Grandison</u>.

26   WILSON, STUART. "The First Dramatic Version of <u>Clarissa</u>." <u>ELN</u> 2: 21-25.
        Summary of 1788.4.

27   WOLFF, ERWIN.   "Die gesellschaftliche Welt als Erlebnis: Samuel Richardson." In his <u>Englische Roman im 18. Jhdt. Wesen und Formen</u>. Gottingen: Vandenhoeck und Ruprecht, pp. 39-48.

Richardson, like most English authors, considers the novel more as an instrument for understanding life than as an aesthetic form. His characters seek an emotional experience rather than the practical and factual knowledge of the world gained through, for instance, travel; in this the novels are books for women.

1965

1   BAXTER, CHARLES L., JR. "A Study of Clarissa." Ph.D. dissertation, Columbia
        Discusses Clarissa in terms of theories of "history" and of familiar epistolary correspondence, neoclassic image of "the world"; technical discussion of distancing devices such as ritual.

*2   BRISSENDEN, R.F. Samuel Richardson. London: Longmans, Green & Co. for the British Council and National Book League, 40 pp.
        Slightly revised from 1956 edition (additions to bibliography).

3   BULLEN, JOHN SAMUEL. Time and Space in the Novels of Samuel Richardson. Utah State University Monograph Series 12, pt. 2. Logan, Utah: Utah State University Press, 53 pp.
        Richardson's use of time for fictional ends: it hardly exists in Pamela, is rigidly present in Clarissa, and is very odd in Grandison, where there is no organic connection of dates and events. Space depends in Richardson's fiction on the consciousness of the writer; it often reflects causality and emotional lines of force and frequently has a tragic dimension. Confined spaces and distances, the process of confinement or release, and the confinement of the writer are weighted with emotional implications.

4   COLLYER, MARY, trans., adapt., and part author. The Virtuous Orphan, or the Life of Marianne, Countess of * * *. Edited by with a critical introduction and notes by William Harlin McBurney and Michael Francis Shugrue. Carbondale and Edwardsville, Ill.: Southern Illinois University Press, 532 pp.
        On xxvii ff., xxxiii, the editors note the influence of the Richardsonian novel on The Virtuous Orphan but do not

mention that Mary Collyer was well-known to Richardson, and he and his work to her, when her translation of the Vie de Marianne first appeared in 1748. They note as "Richardsonian" the "reformation" of the heroine from the "sin of coquetry," the increased prominence of the vicar, M. de Rosaud, the replacement of Marivaux´s irony by "open platitude or subconscious guilt," and an increase in the morality and sentimentality of the book. On p. xxxiii there is more on the Pamela-Marivaux controversy; the editors note that it is Fielding, not Richardson, who seems deeply indebted to Marivaux, and note unmistakable influences on Sterne and Fanny Burney.

5 GOPNIK, IRWIN. "Verbal Structures and Richardson´s Clarissa." Ph.D. dissertation, University of Pennsylvania.
   Critique of the methodology of stylistic analysis and proposal of a new model, revealing "the esthetic integrity of an extremely complex but masterfully ordered ironic manipulation of language" in Clarissa. Richardson´s stylistic usage in Clarissa "anticipates the ultimate stylistic development of the form in the twentieth century." See 1970.14.

6 GREENE, MILDRED S.E. "Love and Duty: The Character of the Princesse de Clèves as Reflected in Certain Later English and American Novels . . ." Ph.D. dissertation, University of New Mexico.
   The Princesse de Clèves serves as a prototype of English and American heroines protesting against the "mariage de raison" from a firm sense of duty to themselves. Both she and Clarissa Harlowe are "ultimately unable to combine love and duty."

7 JENKINS, OWEN. "Richardson´s Pamela and Fielding´s ´Vile Forgeries.´" PQ 44: 200-210.
   Pamela II is a reply to Shamela, as Joseph Andrews is Pamela rewritten in Fielding´s Augustan mode. The question of Richardson´s art, and his aesthetic accomplishment in Pamela, is largely ignored by both writers. Cf. 1978.11, 1967.1.

8 JENNINGS, EDWARD MORTON, III. "Reader-Narrative Relationships in Tom Jones, Tristram Shandy, and Humphrey Clinker." Ph.D. dissertation, University of Wisconsin.
   Some discussion of reader-narrative relationships in

Pamela.

9   LYLES, A. "Pamela´s Trials." <u>CLAJ</u> 8: 290-92.
    Metaphors and situations of trial in <u>Pamela</u>.

*10 MAHIEU TERRAGUSO, ANTOINETTE. "Balzac, émule de Richardson,
    ou les traquenards du roman épistolaire." Universidade
    Católica de São Paulo, Faculdade de Filosofia, Ciências e
    Letras "Sedes Sapientiae," <u>Anuário</u>, 1965-66, pp. 31-40.
    Source: Prof. Carl Berkhout.

11 MAY, GEORGES. "The Influence of the English Novel on the
    French Mid-Eighteenth Century Novel." <u>Aspects of the
    Eighteenth Century</u>. Edited by Earl Wasserman. Baltimore:
    John Hopkins University Press; London: Oxford University
    Press, pp. 265-80.
       Discusses   the   complexity   of   French-English
    interinfluence in the eighteenth century. Uses material
    from 1910.4, 1936.10, and the <u>Eloge</u> to gauge depth of
    influence;   uses Diderot to note the twin perceived themes
    in Richardsonian writing, moral effect and the illusion of
    reality. Suggests that for the French, Richardsonian
    "realism" had limits; "the kind of ism the French were
    prepared to appreciate . . . was the kind to which they
    had already grown accustomed through reading the novels of
    Richardson´s   French   predecessors,   especially Lesage,
    Prévost, and Marivaux." The combination of middle-class
    moralism and "a virile realism devoid of prudishness"
    appealed more to the French audience. The most
    far-reaching effect of English fiction was to make the
    writing of novels respectable.

*12 MEAD, W. <u>Jean-Jacques</u> <u>Rousseau</u> <u>ou</u> <u>le</u> <u>Romancier</u> <u>enchainé</u>.
    Paris: PUF, 120 pp.
       The <u>Nouvelle</u> <u>Héloïse</u> follows Richardsonian techniques.
    "Amply documented but overstates similarities"--<u>YWMLS</u> 28
    (1966): 102.

13 PIERCE, ROBERT B. "The Novel of the 1750s." <u>PQ</u> 44: 73-87.
       Notes in the novels of the 1750s the frequency of
    instantaneous true love after kidnappings and rescues,
    generous young men, scenes against duelling, female
    faintings, prudence and practicality, and an interest in
    moral growth. Upper-class life portrayed in these books is
    usually not realistic. Largely about Fielding and his

imitators, but some direct references to Richardson.

14   PIERSON, ROBERT C. "A Study of the Text of Richardson's <u>Sir</u>
      <u>Charles</u> <u>Grandison</u>." Ph.D. dissertation, University of
      Arkansas.
          Collation and comparison of the first through fourth
      editions and the edition of 1801. Summarized in 1968.34.

15   SHERBO, ARTHUR. "Anecdotes by Mrs. LeNoir." <u>DUJ</u> NS
      26:166-69.
          Anecdotes about Richardson and the reception of
      <u>Clarissa</u>.

16   SLATTERY, WILLIAM C. "Richardson and the Netherlands: Early
      Reception of his Work." <u>PELL</u> 1: 20-30.
          Richardson's relations with the Dutch translator
      Johannes Stinstra and representative comments on his work
      in Dutch periodicals.

*17   SUZUKI, ZENZO. "A Study of Samuel Richardson with Special
      Reference to the Development of his Trilogy." <u>ARFALTU</u> 16:
      67-123.
          In Japanese; English summary on p. 256. Courtesy
      Prof. Carl Berkhout.

18   WATT, IAN. "Samuel Richardson." <u>The</u> <u>Listener</u> 73: 177-80.
          Argues for the complexity and ambiguity of <u>Pamela</u>,
      suggesting a discrepancy between conscious moral purpose
      and aesthetic achievement and locating the source of the
      discrepancy in the function of the first person; the use
      of the "I" makes possible a heretofore unknown
      identification between heroine and reader through the first
      person's lack of definition, and thus allows "the supreme
      object of mass art, that total (and sickening) collusion of
      two 'I's', the hero's and the audience's . . . ."

19   WINTEROWD, WALTER ROSE. "The Poles of Discourse: A Study of
      Eighteenth-Century Rhetoric in <u>Amelia</u> and <u>Clarissa</u>." Ph.D.
      dissertation, University of Utah.
          Studies effect of eighteenth-century rhetorical theory n
      two novels; <u>Amelia</u> is Aristotelian, <u>Clarissa</u> Ciceronian.

20   WORTLEY MONTAGU, LADY MARY. <u>Complete</u> <u>Letters</u> <u>of</u> <u>Lady</u> <u>Mary</u>
      <u>Wortley</u> <u>Montagu</u>. Edited by Robert Halsband. 3v. Oxford:
      Clarendon, 1965-67.

Frequent comments, especially in Volume 3, on Richardson's fiction.

1966

1   BALL, DONALD L.   "Samuel Richardson's Theory of Fiction."
    Ph.D. dissertation, University of North Carolina at Chapel
    Hill.
        Construction of Richardson's theory of fiction, based on
    his statements about fiction and his practice. See 1971.2.

2   CLANCEY, RICHARD WALLACE. "The Augustan Fair-Sex Debate and
    the Novels of Samuel Richardson." Ph.D. dissertation,
    University of Maryland.
        The debate over the nature, education and status of
    women as reflected in Richardson's works. Richardson's
    novels depict the lot of women with amazing accuracy and
    defend their rights, although he takes the conservative
    position that women are by nature inferior.

3   DAY, ROBERT ADAMS. Told in Letters: Epistolary Fiction
    before Richardson. Ann Arbor: University of Michigan
    Press, 281 pp.
        Through examinations of over 200 epistolary novels that
    appeared in England between 1660 and 1740, shows that
    "Richardson's work may be viewed historically as the
    culmination of a process of development [of epistolary
    fiction] rather than as a literary eruption." But
    Richardson crystallized the inchoate tendencies of the
    epistolary style in Pamela. In the epistolary form before
    1740, letters introduce a subjective element through
    revealing emotions. Rev.: TLS, p. 738; Novel 1 (1967):
    83-85; SAQ 66 (1967): 121-22; MP 65 (1968): 389-91.

4   ---. "Richardson, Aaron Hill and Johnson's Life of Savage."
    N&Q 212: 217-19.
        Speculates on the relationships between Richardson and
    Johnson and notes that Richardson advised Hill not to read
    the Life of Savage because of Hill's former unpleasant
    relations with Savage over The Tragedy of Sir Thomas
    Overbury.

5   Item deleted.

6   DUSSINGER, JOHN A. "Conscience and the Pattern of Christian Perfection in Clarissa." PMLA 81: 236-45.
         Richardson attempts to represent in his heroine the ultimate refinement of sensibility as the condition of salvation.

7   EAVES, T.C. DUNCAN, and BEN D. KIMPEL. "Cowper's 'An Ode on Reading Mr. Richardson's History of Sir Charles Grandison.'" PLL 2: 74-75.
         Description of Forster MSS copy of Cowper's "Ode," which differs substantially from the version in Cowper's collected poems.

*8   ELISTRATOVA, A. Angliiskii roman epokhi Prosveshchenija. Moskva: 1966, s. 155-214. [Elistratova, A. The English Novel of the Age of Enlightenment. Moscow: n.p. given, pp. 155-214.] All-Union State Lib., Moscow.

*9   FAUST, BEATRICE. "Richardson's Novel." Ph.D. dissertation, University of Melbourne.
         In Baillieu Library, University of Melbourne; courtesy Mr. Christopher Harrison, Acting Director, Rare Book Division, National Library of Australia.

10   GUTHKE, K.S. "Friedrich von Hagedorn und das literarische Leben seiner Zeit im Lichte unveröffentlicher Briefe an J.J. Bodmer." JFDH, pp. 1-108.
         Material on Hagedorn's knowledge of Richardson.

11   HALSBAND, ROBERT. "Lady Mary Wortley Montagu and Eighteenth-Century Fiction." PQ 45: 145-56.
         Lady Mary Wortley Montagu's relationships to fiction (both what she read and what she wrote) explain her attitude to Richardson.

12   HILLES, F.W. "The Plan of Clarissa." PQ 45: 236-48.
         The unity of Clarissa is shown in its time-scheme (one year, from January to December), its use of symbolic language (e.g., language of height and depth), its differentiation of the narrative through several narrators, and its imagery of devices such as the serpent with its tail in its mouth, emblem of Fate, eternity and Clarissa's

circularity. "From the beginning Richardson had clearly in mind the ´triumphant´ ending, the deaths of Clarissa and Lovelace."

13   JOST, FRANÇOIS. "Le Roman épistolaire et la technique narrative au 18e siècle." <u>CLS</u> 3: 397-427.
      The superiority of the epistolary genre for certain kinds of action, including the tragic, and its drawbacks. Compares narrative methods of Fielding, Goethe, Richardson, and Laclos.

14   KEARNEY, A.M. "Richardson´s <u>Pamela</u>: The Aesthetic Case." <u>REL</u> 7: 78-90.
      In <u>Pamela</u>, Richardson´s authorial tone tends to take over from his narrative one. "Yet, despite its technical crudities, Richardson´s first novel represents a brave attempt to harmonize the two worlds of fiction: the internal and the external narrative viewpoint."

15   ---. "<u>Clarissa</u> and the Epistolary Form." <u>EC</u> 16: 44-56.
      In <u>Clarissa</u>, style is "a sure means of judging character"; the contrasting styles of the characters and the variations in style within characters during the course of the novel chart differing moral values.

*15A KLUGE, WALTER. "Die Szene als Bauelement des Erzählers im englischen Roman des achtzehnten Jahrhunderts." Ph.D. disseratation, Munich.
      Source: 1975.2, item D59.

16   KONIGSBERG, IRA. "The Tragedy of <u>Clarissa</u>." <u>MLQ</u> 27: 285-98.
      What does Richardson mean by calling <u>Clarissa</u> a tragedy? Discusses literary context of tragic drama, concentrating on power of tragedy to "teach and delight" by purging emotions and to inspire "terror and fear" but especially "pity." Discusses Clarissa´s near-perfection as a character; there is a potential conflict between her quality as a heroine of a tragedy and her role as model for her sex, and she must have a tragic flaw. Discusses unities in <u>Clarissa</u>. No other writer but Hardy has been able to make the novel truly tragic. See also 1967.6.

*17   MARCO, J. [Notes on translator´s prefaces to the Spanish edition of <u>Pamela Andrews</u>, 1794-95.] <u>Boletín de la Real Academica Española</u> 46: 113-24.

275

Source: <u>YWMLS</u> 28: 220-21.

*18   OSSOWSKA, MARIA. "Wątki moralne w powieści" [Fielding vs.
       Richardson] and "Wątki moralne u Richardsona." <u>Myśl moralna
       oświecenia angielskiego</u>. Warszawa: Państwowe Wydawnictwo
       Naukowe, pp. 240-41, 256-61.
       Source: Bib. Jagiellońska.

19   PARK, WILLLIAM. "Fielding <u>and</u> Richardson." <u>PMLA</u> 80: 381-88.
       Fielding and Richardson have in common: nostalgia for a
       Tudor-Stuart past;   leanings toward the Tory country
       gentry, even to Pantisocracy;   benevolism;   a Rococo
       structuring of their novels, an almost invisible basic
       structure covered by profusion;   discussions of "moral
       nature" and "nature as it should be"; the ideal of the
       happy family; moral exempla; stock figures; stock plots
       (country to city to country);   ideals of benevolence,
       chastity, and prudence, and dislike of selfishness, folly,
       and promiscuity; the use of "contrast plots"; discussions
       of corrupt society and the place of pride. Notes
       difference in use of their similarities;   discusses
       rationale of popularity of rape scenes in
       eighteenth-century fiction.

20   RICHARDSON, SAMUEL, abr. and trans. by RUTH SCHIRMER.
       <u>Clarissa</u> <u>Harlowe.</u> <u>Roman.</u> <u>Aus</u> <u>dem</u> <u>Englischen</u> <u>übersetzt</u> <u>und</u>
       <u>bearbeitet</u> <u>von</u> <u>Ruth</u> <u>Schirmer</u>. Manesse-Bibliothek der
       Weltliteratur. [Zurich:] Manesse Verlag, 573 pp.
       Source: Württ. Landesbib.

21   SPEARMAN, DIANA. "Richardson." In her <u>Novel</u> <u>and</u> <u>Society</u>.
       London: Routledge Kegan Paul, pp. 173-98.
       Richardson's characters are compared with real
       eighteenth-century persons;   the differences far outweigh
       the similarities. In terms of contemporary social
       realities, the Harlowes' behavior throughout the first part
       of the book is "incredible";   they should have been
       motivated to give their daughter to Lovelace, not Solmes.
       Richardson's "social realism" is not real and subordinates
       itself to the psychological necessity of getting Clarissa
       isolated with Lovelace and raped. Lovelace, "though not a
       real man . . . is a real psychological case," a fine
       study in sadism "with a touch of paranoia." It is largely
       Richardson's own personality, not social reality, that is
       expressed in the books.

*22   STRANDBERG, VICTOR H.   "A Palm for Pamela: Three   Studies   in
        the Game of Love." WHR 20:   37-47.
               Covers Shakuntala, Romeo and Juliet, and A   Farewell   to
        Arms.   Source: YWMLS 28:   220.

23   TUCKER, SUSIE I. "Richardsonian Phrases." N&Q, 464-65.
               "Tell it not in Gath" and "the nature of the beast".

24   WOLFF, CYNTHIA GRIFFIN.   "The Puritan Sources of Richardson's
        Psychological Realism." Ph.D. dissertation, Harvard.
               Revised as 1972.26.

25   ZIRKER, MALVIN R., JR.   "Richardson's Correspondence: The
        Personal Letter as Private Experience." In The Familiar
        Letter in the Eighteenth Century. Edited by H.   Anderson,
        P.   Daghlian, and I. Ehrenpreis.   Lawrence, Kansas:
        University of Kansas Press, pp. 71-91.
               Characteristics   of   Richardson's   epistolary   style
        discussed;   believes that Richardson was "unhealthily"
        concerned with the act of writing letters, which were for
        him an "emotional life in other than the conventional terms
        of human intercourse."

                              1967

1   BROOKS, DOUGLAS. "Richardson's Pamela and Fielding's Joseph
        Andrews." EC 17: 158-67.
               " . . . In writing Joseph Andrews Fielding was, in
        fact, rewriting Pamela in his own mode." Parallels between
        the two include clothes-imagery; the wedding scenes; Lady
        Booby's conflicts, which parallel B's; parallels between
        characters (Joseph--Mr.   B and Pamela;   Fanny--Pamela;
        Pamela of Joseph Andrews--Lady Barbara Davers;   Mrs.
        Jewkes--Mrs.   Slipslop;   Adams--Williams);   parallel
        between bedroom scenes in Joseph Andrews and second
        attempted rape in Pamela.   Discusses possible parallels
        with Pamela II.   Fielding was rewriting Pamela in the
        Augustan mode, damping the psychological element;
        "Fielding's novel stands as a symbol of Augustanism,
        opposed to Pamela, the real voice of the future." (167) See
        1965.8, 1968.7, 1968.25, 1978.11.

                              277

*2   CHAKRABARTI, S.C. <u>Samuel</u> <u>Richardson</u>: <u>Clarissa</u> <u>Harlowe</u>: <u>A</u>
        <u>Critical</u> <u>Study</u>. Calcutta: Nababharat, 206 pp.
              Source: Catalog of the National Library of India.

3   CLEMENTS, FRANCES MARION. "Social Criticism in the English
        Novel: 1740-1754."   Ph.D.   dissertation, Ohio State
        University.
              Compares social conditions in novels of Richardson,
        Fielding and Smollett with actual social conditions; finds
        the novels realistic and particularly concerned with
        mistreatment of women, children, and prisoners. See also
        her "Rights of Women in the Eighteenth-Century Novel."
        <u>Enlightenment</u> <u>Essays</u> 4 (1973): 63-70 (brief references to
        Richardson).

4   COULET, HENRI. <u>Le</u> <u>Roman</u> <u>jusqu´à</u> <u>la</u> <u>Révolution</u>.   2v.   Paris:
        Armand Colin.
              A volume of text and a volume of extracts document
        literary history of French novel in the period; much
        reference to Richardson.

5   DUSSINGER, JOHN A. "Richardson´s ´Christian Vocation.´" <u>PLL</u>
        3: 3-19.
              Richardson´s religious orientation and its effect on his
        novels;   importance of the theme of Christian perfection,
        particularly necessary for understanding <u>Sir</u> <u>Charles</u>
        <u>Grandison</u>;   material   on   religious   background   and
        controversies of the period.

6   ---. "Richardson´s Tragic Muse." <u>PQ</u> 46: 18-33.
              Definition of <u>Clarissa</u> as "a work of <u>tragic</u> species"
        examined   through Richardson´s interest in the drama.
        Clarissa evolves from the seventeenth-century distressed
        heroine, but is influenced by the "affective tragedy" of
        Rapin; thus she has a real kinship with post-Restoration
        theater   heroines,   a   kinship   partly   explaining   the
        "pornographic" qualities of the novel. See also 1962.10,
        1963.9, 1966.16.

7   EAVES, T.C. DUNCAN, and BEN D. KIMPEL. "Richardson´s Helper
        in Creating the Character of Elias Brand." <u>N&Q</u> n.s. 16:
        414-15.
              Conjectures that R. Smith (d.   1754), a letter from
        whom, signed "Elisha Brand" and in the Brand manner, is in
        the FMSS, contributed the Latin tags to the Elias Brand

letters.   Smith was Richardson's corrector and could
translate Latin correspondence.

8   ---. "Richardson's Revisons of *Pamela*." <u>SB</u> 20: 61-88.
There is no reason to regard any edition of *Pamela* as
standard. They report on the last edition of the book
revised by Richardson, published in 1801 and 1810. It has
more   paragraphs   and   more   italics;   contractions   are
expanded;   there are extensive word-changes aimed at making
the book more "genteel" (these are listed <u>in extenso</u>). See
also 1978.4.

9   ENOMOTO, FUTOSHI. "Richardson's Theory of Fiction." <u>SEL</u>
(Tokyo) 43; 181-95.
Richardson reacted against the tradition of the romance
and epic, but developed a fiction closely allied with
traditional fiction.

10   GOLDEN, MORRIS. "Richardson's Repetitions." <u>PMLA</u> 82: 64-67.
Issues and situations are repeated in the works for
several reasons: as an exercise in technique, as a moral
lesson, as a spur to discussion of the   characters'
alternatives, as an index to Richardson's fascination with
the repeated situation, and perhaps through lack of
imagination.

11   KIMPEL, DIETER. <u>Der</u> <u>Roman</u> <u>der</u> <u>Aufklarung</u>.   Stuttgart:
Metzler, pp. 67-71.
Sets Richardson in German literary perspective;
contains extensive bibliography.

12   LEED, JACOB. "Pa-mé-la--Pám-e-la." <u>JNL</u> 27: 11.
Richardson changed the pronunciation to make the name
resemble his.

13   MUECKE, D.C. "Beauty and Mr. B." <u>SEL</u> <u>1500-1900</u> 7: 467-74.
Parallels between *Pamela* and <u>Cinderella</u>, <u>Guy of Warwick</u>,
Spenser, and <u>Beauty</u> <u>and the</u> <u>Beast</u>.

14   NEPPI MODONI, MARIE LOUISE. "Les Premières réactions de la
critique française devant les oeuvres de Richardson
(1742-1762)." <u>LS</u> 16, pt. 1: 16-33.
Early reactions to the three novels; *Pamela* was the
most popular.

15   ---. "Le Rôle de l'abbé Prévost dans le succès de Richardson
        en France." <u>LS</u> 16, pt. 2: 7-9.
            The prestige of Prevost had nothing to do with the
        success of Richardson's first and most popular novel.

*16   OKA, TERUO. "Samuel Richardson's View of Moderate Rakery."
        <u>SEL</u> (Tokyo) 44: 15-24.
            Source: <u>YWMLS</u>.

17   PAULSON, RONALD. "Fielding the Anti-Romanticist." In his
        <u>Satire</u> <u>and</u> <u>the</u> <u>Novel</u> <u>in</u> <u>Eighteenth-Century</u> <u>England</u>. New
        Haven and London: Yale University Press, pp. 106-31; cf.
        211-16, 279-83.
            Fielding satirizes the subjectivism of <u>Pamela</u> in <u>Shamela</u>
        and <u>Joseph</u> <u>Andrews</u>; the subjectivizing force of the first
        person works against satire in <u>Pamela</u> itself. Notes satire
        in the treatment of courtship in <u>Clarissa</u> and <u>Grandison</u>.

18   TALBUT, NANCY E.B. "The Use of Family Relationships for
        Dramatic Effect in the Novels of Samuel Richardson." Ph.D.
        dissertation, University of Arkansas.
            Discusses various uses of family relationships for
        dramatic effects: to create dramatic tensions; to
        dramatize situations and reveal characters; to complicate
        plots.

*19   WEBER, ANTAL. "A szentimentális stilusirány elméleti es
        történeti kérdéseirol." <u>Irodalomtörténeti</u> <u>Közlemények</u> 71:
        125-39.
            Includes Richardson <u>passim</u>. Courtesy Prof. Carl
        Berkhout.

20   WILPERT, GERO VON, and ADOLF GÜHRING. <u>Erstausgaben</u> <u>deutscher</u>
        <u>Dichtung</u> <u>.</u> <u>.</u> <u>.</u> 1600-1900. Stuttgart: Alfred Kröner
        Verlag, 1481 pp.
            Useful as a bibliographical reference for German
        <u>Richardsonaden</u>.

21   WILSON, ANGUS. "Evil in the English Novel." <u>Kenyon</u> <u>R</u> 39:
        167-94.
            Richardson is at the beginning of that period in the
        novel in which evil is taken less and less seriously.
        However, in <u>Clarissa</u> there is still a supernatural element
        in Lovelace's evil that gives the book a "titanic quality."
        Compares his attitude to James's; in both evil possesses a

"curious, half-concealed, sexual, sensual quality."

1968

1   ABRAHAM, DAVID. "Clarissa and the Two Meanings of Death." MSE
     1: 96-99.
          Clarissa is compared with Tess of the d'Urbervilles;
     for Clarissa rape is spiritual death, to be followed
     naturally by physical dissolution. She is an example of
     the Puritan ethic of living according to the way things
     should be.

2   BALL, DONALD L. "Pamela II: A Primary Link in Richardson's
     Development as a Novelist." MP 65: 334-42.
          Pamela II develops Richardson's skills in narrative,
     characterization, and epistolary technique, as he designs
     new conflicts, improves his skills in timing narrative
     events and drawing detailed scenes, broadens his range of
     characterization, and develops new techniques for
     presentation of character. It is Richardson's first
     genuine epistolary narrative.

2A   BARNETT, GEORGE L. Eighteenth-Century British Novelists on
     the Novel. New York: Appleton-Century-Crofts, pp. 72-89.
          A brief introduction by Barnett precedes the Postscript
     to the fourth edition of Clarissa (1751).

3   BATTESTIN, MARTIN C. "On the Contemporary Reputations of
     Pamela, Joseph Andrews and Roderick Random: Remarks by an
     'Oxford Scholar'." N&Q n.s. 17: 450-52.
          The author of 1748.9 is an antipamelist, echoing Parson
     Oliver's objections in Shamela.

4   BEER, GILLIAN. "Richardson, Milton and the Status of Evil."
     RES n.s. 19: 261-70.
          In Clarissa, Miltonic allusions provide "a stable
     structure of judgment" (269). Discusses parallels between
     Richardson and Milton in narrative, imagery, verbal
     texture, and epic treatment. Richardson, working with
     human figures (unlike Milton), like Milton invests them
     with transcendence and tragic grandeur.

5   BENOIST, HOWARD, III.   "The Morality is the Message: A Study
     of Samuel Richardson's A Collection of the Moral and
     Instructive Sentiments, Maxims, Cautions, and Reflexions,
     Contained in the Histories of Pamela, Clarissa, and Sir
     Charles Grandison." Ph.D.   dissertation, University of
     Pennsylvania.
         Discusses   the   Collection as   literary   theory   and
     autobiographical   statement.   Notes   changes   between
     Collection texts and novels from which texts were taken.
     Texts emphasize social duties, vices and virtues (sexual
     morality tends to stand for all forms of moral   rectitude),
     and ethical and theological ideas; Benoist notes the
     importance of the Collection as helping to define
     Richardson's "sentimentalism."

6   BERGGREN, NOEL DAVID.   "Grandisonian Depths: A Study of
     Richardson's Last Novel." Ph.D. dissertation, Yale.
         Discusses Grandison as precursor of social fiction of
     later eighteenth century, notes sophistication of its
     technique, and suggests possible critical approaches: the
     theme of power, the interrelation of relationships, the
     drawing-room as metaphor of the body politic.

6A   BORINSKI, LUDWIG.   "Richardson." In his Englische Roman des
     18.   Jhdts.   Frankfurt-am-Main and Bonn: Athenäum, pp.
     98-148.
         Richardson   is   influenced   by   conduct-books   and
     theological writers.   Borinski compares him with Rowe,
     Young, Marivaux; gives details of his art (writing to the
     moment,   circumstantial detail, character study, epistolary
     form); and considers that he is at his best in individual
     scenes.   In Clarissa, the tragedy is augmented because the
     age has begun to secularize tragedy. Grandison is compared
     with sermons of Barrow and Tillotson on the duties of
     gentlemen;   Sir   Charles   is   important   as   the
     eighteenth-century gentleman-ideal.

7   BROOKS, DOUGLAS. "Pamela and Joseph Andrews." EC 18: 348-49;
     19: 348-50.
         Correspondence with A.M.   Kearney about 1967.1,
     defending the parallels he has cited and expanding on his
     discussion of "Augustan" qualities in Joseph Andrews.   See
     1968.25.

8   BROOKS, PETER. The Novel of Worldliness. Princeton, N.J.:
     Princeton University Press, pp. 105-13 and elsewhere.
          This book on eighteenth-century French fiction suggests
     a connection between marivaudage and Richardson's "dramatic
     writing"; discusses also the connection between dramatic
     writing and libertine language. Some discussion of
     Richardson's effect on the Nouvelle Heloise.

9   CAIN, ROY E., and WILLIAM C. SLATTERY. "Richardson's Role in
     an Attack on Hume and Bolingbroke." PLL 4: 330-34.
          Richardson suggested that a very harsh attack on these
     two Deists in Peter Packard's A Dissertation on Revelations
     XI.13 should be softened, but for the sake of Packard's
     argument and not for the men's intrinsic merits--Richardson
     said, very strongly for him, that he "despised"
     Bolingbroke.

*10 CHAKRABARTI, S.C. Samuel Richardson: Sensibility in Sir
     Charles Grandison. Calcutta: Nababharat, 86 pp.
          Source: Catalog of the National Library of India.

*11 ---. Samuel Richardson: Sentimental Culture in Pamela.
     Calcutta: Nababharat, 95 pp.
          Source: Catalog of the National Library of India.

12   COHEN, MURRAY A. "Forms of True Judgment in the
     Eighteenth-Century Novel." Ph.D. dissertation, Johns
     Hopkins.
          Richardson is one of a number of eighteenth-century
     novelists addressing the problem of judging meaning in
     society.

13   COHEN, RICHARD. "The Literary Aims of Samuel Richardson."
     Ph.D. dissertation, University of Massachusetts, Amherst.
          Examines Richardson's literary aims through: his
     interpretation and use of eighteenth-century literary
     terminology; his references to past and contemporary
     writers; his rejection of the contemporary dictum of
     distinct genre; his use of psychological effects for
     "implicit" rather than obvious didactic purposes.
     Published as 1970.5.

14   COPELAND, EDWARD WALTON. "Clarissa. Didacticism and
     Narrative Technique." Ph.D. dissertation, Harvard.
          Discusses both Pamela and Clarissa. Richardson makes

uninteresting didactic material come alive through
vignette, character, anecdote, and imagery. Discusses
morality of styles, dubiousness of "allegory," dramatic
value of irony, ambivalence of imagery; shows how
Richardson also uses allegory and imagery (of animals,
hunt, imperialism, monarchy and invasion) to structure
Clarissa. Notes contrast in action of book between ideal
choices and possible actions.

15   DOODY, MARGARET A.   "A   Comparative   Study   of   Samuel
      Richardson's Clarissa and Sir Charles Grandison." Ph.D.
      dissertation, Oxford University.
          Published with additions as 1974.10.

16   DETIG, JOSEPH, S.V.D.   "Pamela and her Critics." LSS 2:242-49.
          Summarizes major critical opinion about Pamela.

*17   ---. "Samuel Richardson and his Modern Critics." FJS 1:
      55-70.
          Source: MLA Bibliography, 1969, item 5001.

18   DUSSINGER, JOHN A.   "Richardson and Johnson: Critical
      Agreement on Rowe's The Fair Penitent." E Stud 49:45-47.
          "While comparing Rowe's The Fair Penitent to Clarissa,
      Johnson essentially follows Richardson's own suggestions as
      expressed in Belford's letter to Lovelace [of Thursday,
      August 17]." Discussion of the title, the characters of
      Lothario and Calista, and the power of domestic tragedy.

19   EAVES, T.C. DUNCAN, and BEN D. KIMPEL. "The Composition of
      Clarissa and its Revision before Publication." PMLA 83:
      416-28.
          Uses detailed chronology of composition to demonstrate
      that Richardson revised Clarissa thoroughly before
      publication but did not change his basic plan.   The authors
      believe that the novel may have been completed as early as
      July 1744, certainly early in 1746;   between that time and
      publication Richardson revised the book once, possibly
      twice, working to reduce its length, blacken Lovelace's
      character, clarify his characters' motives, and elevate
      their language.

20   ---. "Richardson and his Family Circle." N&Q 212: 448-50.
          See 1964.10.

21   ---. "Richardson's Connection with <u>Sir William Harrington</u>."
        <u>PLL</u> 4: 277-78.
                In letters to Anna Meades (BM Add. MSS. 28,097),
        Richardson suggested copious revisions to the text of <u>Sir
        William Harrington</u>, covering moral issues, characterization
        and consistency, probability, and details of wording and
        propriety. These were apparently not used, and Anna
        Meades' final editor was Thomas Hull.

22   ---. "Two notes on Richardson: Richardson's Chapel Rules;
        The Printer of the <u>Daily Journal</u>." <u>Library</u> 5th ser. 23:
        242-47.
                Identifies "Rules and Orders to be Observed by the
        Members of this Chapel" (BM Add. MSS. 27,799, fol. 88)
        as Richardson's chapel-rules (cf. 1947.1, 1734.1);
        suggests that James Purser and T. Cooper "were both
        protecting the more prominent and well-established
        Richardson [from prosecution] by allowing their names to be
        used as the printers of the <u>Daily Journal</u>."

*22A   ENOMOTO, FUTOSHI. "Richardson to Atarashisa." <u>EigoS</u> 114:
        586-87.
                Newness of Richardson. Source: <u>MLA Bibliography</u>, 1970,
        item 3685.

23   GARMON, GERALD MEREDITH. "The Development of Tragic Realism
        in English Literature: 1720-1820." Ph.D. dissertation,
        Auburn University.
                Richardson's works are discussed as examples of the
        development of realism as a proper tragic mode.

*24   HARRIS, JOCELYN M. "Sir Charles Grandison and the Little
        Senate, The Relation Between Samuel Richardson's
        Correspondence and his Last Novel." Ph.D. dissertation,
        University College, University of London.
                Source: McNamee; Catalog of the University College
        Library.

25   JOST, FRANÇOIS. "L'évolution d'un genre: le roman
        épistolaire dans les lettres occidentales." In <u>Essais de
        litterature comparée</u>. Freiburg: Editions universitaires;
        Urbana, Ill.: University of Illinois Press, pp. 89-179.
                Richardson is part of the development of the genre in
        Western literature, but not the inventor of the form, which
        is to be found in all European cultures. Bibliography of

epistolary fiction.

26   KEARNEY, ANTHONY M.   "Pamela and Joseph Andrews." EC 18:
      105-7, 479-80.
          Correspondence with Douglas Brooks (see above, 1967 and
      1968), disagreeing with the conclusions of 1967.1; the two
      novelists are neither as closely "in parallel" nor as
      ideologically opposed as Brooks believes.

27   ---. Samuel Richardson. Profiles in Literature. London:
      Routledge and Kegan Paul; New York: Humanities Press, 123
      pp.
          A short introduction to Richardson's life, reputation,
      and writings, for the student and the general reader,
      combined with extracts and criticism exploring five areas
      of Richardson's art: the basic situation of a moral
      conflict; character portrayal, with special emphasis on
      the doubled, external/internal portrayal of character that
      the epistolary style allows; setting and atmosphere (close
      confinement, restriction);   epistolary technique;   the
      range and achievement of his fiction.   Discusses his
      drawbacks, which are moral tags and great length; compares
      him to Fielding; notes that in him descriptive realism is
      modified by a strong tinge of fantasy. Bibliography.
      Rev.: TLS, p. 579; YWES 49:254.

28   KISSANE, JOSEPH M.   "Richardson and Jane Austen." Ph.D.
      dissertation, Columbia University.
          Discussion of parallels in character-portrayal through
      three similar characters, the rake, the young lady, and the
      gentleman-hero.

29   KONIGSBERG, IRA. "The Dramatic Background of Richardson's
      Plots and Characters." PMLA 83: 42-53.
          The influence on Richardson's fiction of English drama:
      attempted seduction of chaste heroine by libertine "hero,"
      attempted forced marriage, suffering heroine.   Striking
      resemblance between Clarissa and Charles Johnson's Caelia
      (1732).   Grandison is also influenced by the   drama,
      especially Sir Charles himself, the playwrights' "man of
      sense."

30   ---. Samuel Richardson and the Dramatic Novel. Lexington,
      Ky.: University of Kentucky Press, 142 pp.
          Notes the dramatic dimension of Richardson's novels,

"physically and temporally conceived," and traced his
knowledge of plays and dramatists, his use of dramatic
characters and rixes, his characters' use of plays and the
play form, and his melding of drama and narrative into a
"narrative-dramatic" form. Dislikes Grandison but sees in
it a new kind of conflict, one "possible in a world of
non-villainous characters--a conflict between values that
are correct, but incompatible."
     Rev.: Andrew Wright, YES 1 (1971): 271-74; Edward
Bloom, Novel 3 (1970): 173-76; JNL 28: 7; PQ 48 (1969):
385-86; ECS 3 (1970): 562-63.

31   KURTH, LIESELOTTE E. "Formen der Romankritik im achtzehnten
     Jahrhundert." MLN 83: 655-93 (Richardson: 663-65, 677-78,
     688-89 and mentioned passim).
        Richardson's place in the development of a theory of the
     novel in the eighteenth century. Attacks idea that with
     the exception of Blankenberg there was no theory of fiction
     in Germany until the "Höhe der Klassik" and notes that
     Richardson's novels helped form an implicit literary theory
     through being both imitated and parodied.

32   MACINTOSH, CAREY. "Pamela's Clothes." ELH 35: 75-83.
        Social and sexual symbolism of clothing in Pamela and
     its role in the action.

33   MILLER, NORBERT. Der empfindsame Erzähler. München: Carl
     Hauser Verlag, Serie Literatur als Kunst, 478 pp.
        Richardson is noted passim, but see especially pp.
     171-86, "Johann Timotheus Hermes und Richardson," in which
     Richardson serves as the source of the mehrstimmige Roman
     of Hermes. Discusses use of tenses in the letter novel;
     realism in letter fiction; the special role of first
     letters in letter fiction.

34   PIERSON, ROBERT CRAIG. "The Revisions of Richardson's Sir
     Charles Grandison." SB 21: 163-89.
        Collation of the four revised editions of Grandison to
     establish a proper copy-text; concludes that the first
     edition, together with the substantive changes in the
     second, third, and 1810 editions and those occurring in the
     seventh volume of the fourth edition (1762), should form
     the basis of a modern text of Grandison.

35   RABKIN, NORMAN. "Clarissa: A Study in the Nature of Convention." <u>ELH</u> 23: 204-17.
Clarissa struggles between instinct and decorum; since her primary urge is to do what is proper, she distrusts the violence of her passions and denies herself life. Lovelace is not only "the villain" but "represents man untrammeled by the rules of society." Richardson shows that neither stance is right; neither can stand alone and both die. "If there is a ´moral´ in <u>Clarissa</u>, it is that life does not break down into absolutes . . . ."

36   REED, JOSEPH, W., JR. "A New Samuel Richardson Manuscript." <u>YULG</u> 42: 215-31.
A transcription and discussion of "Private Thoughts on a Certain Proposal . . . ," discussing the marriage-settlement of Mary Richardson on her marriage to Philip Ditcher. Shows Richardson´s taste for law (cf. 1919.6).

37   RICHETTI, JOHN J. "The Uses of Fiction, 1700-1739: Popular Narrative Before Richardson." Ph.D. dissertation, Columbia.
Published as 1969.18 (<u>q.v.</u>).

38   ROTHSTEIN, ERIC. "The Framework of <u>Shamela</u>." ELH 35: 381-402.
Draws attention to satire in <u>Shamela</u> on Cibber, Conyers Middleton, Hervey, Walpole, and the Methodists, and suggests that though Fielding "obviously disliked" <u>Pamela</u>, "<u>Shamela</u> is rather an exploitation than an expose of its older, soberer sister."

*39   SCHULZ, DIETER. "Studien zur Verführungsszene im englischen Roman (1660-1760)." Ph.D. dissertation, University of Marburg.
Source: 1974.12, bibliography.

40   SCOTT, SIR WALTER. "Prefatory Memoir of Richardson." In <u>Sir Walter Scott on Novelists and Fiction</u>. Edited by Ioan Williams. London: Routledge Kegan Paul, pp. 19-45.
Reprint of 1824.4.

*41   SINKO, ZOFIA. "Recepja powieści Richardsona, Rousseau i Goethego." <u>Powieść zachodnioeuropejska w kulturze polskiego Oświecenia</u>. Instytut Badań literackich Polskiej Akademii

Nauk. Studia z Okresu Oświecenia 8. Wrocław: Ossolineum, pp. 142–203.
   On the reception in Poland of Richardson's works, Rousseau's, and Goethe's. Source: Catalog of the Bib. Jagiellońska.

42   SOLOMON, STANLEY. "Irony and the Eighteenth-Century Novel: Value and Vision from Richardson to Jane Austen." Ph.D. dissertation, Temple University.
   Discusses the use of moral irony in novelists basing their work on Richardson, Fielding and Smollett; some discussion of Richardson's use of irony.

43   STEWART, KEITH. "History, Poetry, and the Terms of Fiction in the Eighteenth Century." MP 66: 110–20.
   In a discussion of the terms "history," "poetry," and "romance," compares Richardson's and Fielding's definitions of novel-writing and in particular their uses of the word and concept "history".

44   VERSINI, LAURENT. "Laclos et Richardson ou la fausse affinité." *Laclos et la Tradition*. Paris: Klincksieck, pp. 481–519 (and passim).
   Though seeing many similarities, concludes that the "influence reste au niveau du détail et de la matière." (519) Richardson is too moralizing, too unstylish, and too conservative to exert a real influence on Laclos; the truer "Richardsonian" influence is that of Crébillon *fils*.

1969

1   BARKER, GERARD A. "The Complacent Paragon: Exemplary Characterization in Richardson." *SEL* 9: 503–19.
   Suggests that in Richardson's work, the "adjectival value" of goodness (in Lovejoy's terms) is mistaken for its "terminal value"; the self-approval of Richardson's good characters is contradictory and inconsistent, but "constitutes a necessary concomitant of virtue" in the Calvinistic scheme, "confirming the validity of personal judgment." See 1956.1.

2   CARROLL, JOHN, editor. Richardson: A Collection of Critical
     Essays. Englewood Cliffs, N.J.: Prentice-Hall, 185 pp.
           Contains an introduction on Richardson´s critical
     reputation by John Carroll and the following essays: M.
     Kinkead-Weekes´   1962   introduction   to   Pamela;   A.M.
     Kearney, "Richardson´s Pamela: The Aesthetic Case"; W.M.
     Sale, Jr., "From Pamela to Clarissa"; Dorothy Van Ghent,
     "On Clarissa Harlowe";   Ian Watt, from The Rise of the
     Novel; F.W. Hilles, "The Plan of Clarissa";   William J.
     Farrell, "The   Style   and   the Action in Clarissa";
     Christopher Hill, "Clarissa Harlowe and Her Times";   A.D.
     McKillop, from The Early Masters of English Fiction (on Sir
     Charles   Grandison)   and   "Epistolary   Technique   in
     Richardson´s Novels";   George Sherburn, "Writing to the
     Moment: One Aspect"; and Morris Golden, from Richardson´s
     Characters.
           Rev. Andrew Wright, YES 2 (1972): 281.

3   COLEMAN, VIRALENE JOHNSON. "The English Dramatic Adaptations
     of Richardson´s Pamela in the 1740s." Ph.D. dissertation,
     University of Arkansas.
           Discusses four adaptations of the 1740s: Dance´s,
     Giffard´s, and Edge´s adaptations, and "Pamela the Second,"
     a play-poem based not on the novel but on a closely
     parallel case (see 1742.4).   Concludes that "none fully
     realize the thematic conflict of Pamela."

4   COWLER, ROSEMARY, editor.   Twentieth-Century Interpretations
     of Pamela. Englewood Cliffs, N.J.: Prentice-Hall, 122 pp.
           Contains an introduction by Rosemary Cowler and material
     from David Daiches, Literary Essays (1956); McKillop,
     Early Masters (1956);   Reid   (1957);   Watt   (1957);
     Brissenden (1958); Kinkead-Weekes´ introduction to Pamela
     (1962); Golden (1963); Sacks (1964); Kearney (1966);
     McIntosh (1968); Hornbeak, "Richardson´s Familiar Letters
     . . . " (1938);   Fiedler (1960);   Sherburn (1961);
     Lyles (1965); Jenkins (1965); Bullen (1965); Day (1966);
     Park (1966);   and Kreissman (1960).   Chronology and
     bibliography.

5   GENETTE, GÉRARD. "La Littérature et l´espace," "Les
     Frontières du récit," and "Vraisemblance et motivation."
     Figures II. Paris: Seuil, Tel Quel, pp. 43-99.
           Discussions of spatial relationships and language, of
     the   letter-novel,   and   of   the   connection   between

characterization   and   the   <u>romanesque</u>;   important
Richardsonian   background,   although   Richardson   is   not
mentioned.

6   GOLDKNOPF, DAVID. "Studies in the Novel's Search for Form."
Ph.D. dissertation, Syracuse University.
Tension in the novel between the consciousness of the
self and the consciousness of the world; Chapter 3, "The
I-Narrator in the Pseudo-Memoir and the Epistolary Novel,"
compares Defoe's novels with <u>Clarissa</u>, concluding that the
epistolary   novel   expresses   the   impulse   toward
self-dramatization.

7   KNIGHT, CHARLES A. "The Function of Wills in Richardson's
<u>Clarissa</u>." <u>TSLL</u> 11: 1183-90.
Wills express personal power, order worldly goods, honor
merit or family connections, call for prudence in the
executor, and create new patterns of relationship and
conflict.

8   KURTH, LIESLOTTE E. <u>Die zweite Wirklichkeit: Studien zum
Roman des achtzehnten Jahrhunderts</u>.   Chapel Hill, N.C.:
University of North Carolina Press, <u>passim</u>.
Discusses Richardson's role in: use of virtuous love as
subject;   perspectives and points of view; epistolary
fiction;   popularization of Locke;   theory of German
fiction. Compares Richardson and Fielding, pp. 50-64;
notes Richardsonian material and criticism in <u>Grandison der
Zweyte</u> and <u>Don Sylvio</u>; discusses influence on Lessing's
early favoring of idealization (114).

9   MASLEN, KEITH.   "Samuel Richardson and Smith's 'Printer's
Grammar.'" (Note 322.) <u>BC</u> 18: 518-19.
Maslen has found about 100 books evidently printed by
Richardson and not listed in Sale (1950.10), and about 150
Richardsonian printers' ornaments to add to Sale's 103.
Among the books now known to be printed by Richardson is
Smith's <u>Printer's Grammar</u> (1755).

10   MILES, KATHLEEN. "A Note on Richardson's Response to
Fielding's Felon." <u>SNNTS</u> 1: 373-74.
Notes a reference to <u>Jonathan Wild</u> in <u>Clarissa</u>:
"<u>Goodness</u>, I thought, was <u>greatness</u>."

11   MOYNIHAN, ROBERT DUNCAN. "Richardson and Esthetic Compromise in <u>Clarissa</u>." Ph.D. dissertation, University of Arizona.
      Discusses cultural milieu of <u>Clarissa</u> and Richardson's cultural and esthetic compromises.

*12   PARKER, DOROTHY. "The Time Scheme of <u>Pamela</u> and the Character of B." <u>TSLL</u> 11: 695-704.

13   PONS, CHRISTIAN. <u>Richardson et la littérature bourgeoise en Angleterre</u>. Aix-en-Provence: Ophrys, 661 pp.
      Richardson's grandeur is connected to his roots in Christian humanism, leading to Sentimentalism, a blind and bourgeois optimism that faith is rewarded in this life. Much information on relation of Richardson to major and minor fiction of the eighteenth century.
      Originally presented as his thesis, Aix-Marseille.

14   RICHETTI, JOHN J. <u>Popular Fiction before Richardson: Narrative Patterns 1700-1739</u>. Oxford: Clarendon, 283 pp.
      Richardson's (and Defoe's) success is the result of their community of feelings with other writers, their capacity for heightened artistic exploration of the same raw materials. These are largely concerned with social fantasies: "In eighteenth-century popular narrative, action itself tends to be depicted as impious aggression against a natural or social order or against innocent and therefore virtuously passive characters. Popular fiction tends . . . to develop this basic conflict by means of a rhetoric and a frame of reference that make secular and religious the most accurate critical terms to describe the novelistic ideology. . . ." Richetti discusses several early eighteenth-century genres: the rogue or criminal novel, the whore-biography, the pirate-novel, the scandal-novel, and the rape-novel; there is much material on female novelists.
      Rev: Leon M. Guilhamet, <u>ECS</u> 5 (1971): 192-95; Maximillian E. Novak, <u>MP</u> 68 (1971): 312-15; Andrew Wright, <u>YES</u> (1971): 271-74.

15   SCHÜCKING, LEVIN L. "The Family as a Literary Problem: Samuel Richardson." In his <u>Puritan Family: A Social Study from the Literary Sources</u>. Translated from the German (1964.21) by Brian Battershaw. London: Routledge and Kegan Paul, New York: Schocken Books [1970], pp. 145-58.
      Richardson is a didactic figure, having become

superflous as a literary figure. Study of the Puritan
family in <u>Clarissa</u> shows a Janus-headed attitude: on the
one hand, his characters behave like Puritans; on the
other, they make no reference to religion or religious
arguments, solving their problems with the aid of
principles of humanity rather than rigid religious
dogmatism.

16   SHARP, RUTH MARIAN MCKENZIE. "Rational Vision and the Comic
      Resolution: A Study in the Novels of Richardson, Fielding,
      and Jane Austen." Ph.D. dissertation, University of
      Wisconsin.
           Discussion of problem of "rectification"--alteration of
      imitation of reality in the direction of an ideal order--in
      the novels; the ideal order in this case is that of
      rational vision, and in the comic novels of all three (with
      <u>Clarissa</u> out of consideration), character is defined
      according to this ideal, and growth and change of character
      come to be defined in terms of rational insight. "The
      central problem examined in each novel is the author's
      success or failure in producing an illusion based on the
      ideal integration of rational vision with chance."

17   SLATTERY, WILLIAM C., editor, introducer, translator. <u>The
      Richardson-Stinstra Correspondence and Stinstra's Prefaces
      to Clarissa</u>. Carbondale and Edwardsville, Ill.: Southern
      Illinois University Press; London and Amsterdam: Feffer
      and Simons, 270 pp.
           Correspondence between Richardson and his Dutch
      translator, Johannes Stinstra; translations of Stinstra's
      introductory essays, 1752-55. Major points: necessity to
      conjoin realism with moral aims; Richardson's grasp of
      detail and style; proper function of imagination and
      reason in novel-reading; powerful moral force of the
      ending. Slattery supplies information on Dutch imitations,
      parodies, adaptations, and translations of Richardson's
      novels.
           Rev.: <u>TLS</u>, September 25, 1969, pp. 1105-6; <u>JNL</u> 29:
      9-10; Andrew Wright, <u>YES</u>, 1 (1971): 271-74; R.A. Day,
      <u>Novel</u> 5 (1972): 189-92.

*18   SUZUKI, YOSHIKO. "Juhachi Seiki Eikoku Shosei Kenkyu." <u>EigoS</u>
      115: 298-99.
           "Study of the eighteenth-century English novel; focus
      on Richardson." <u>MLA</u> <u>Bibliography</u>, 1970, item 3696.

*19   SZEGEDY-MASZÁK, MIHÁLY. "A XVIII. századi angol irodalom a
       kutatás   tükrében."   Irodalomtörténeti   Közlemények 73:
       315-30.
              Includes Richardson. (Courtesy Prof. Carl Berkhout.)

20   TOPF, MELVYN A. "An Inquiry into Some Relations between the
       Epistemology   of   the   Novel and its Origins." Ph.D.
       dissertation, Pennsylvania State University.
              Defoe, Fielding, and Richardson as inheritors of the
       tradition of Copernicus and Galileo; Pamela is considered
       as deriving from Cartesian rationalism.

21   VAN MARTER, SHIRLEY ANN. "Richardson's Aesthetic Theory and
       Practice   in   Variant   Editions   of Clarissa." Ph.D.
       dissertation, University of Chicago.
              Comparison of editions of Clarissa discussing changes in
       intended effect among early editions.

22   WÜRZBACH, NATASCHA, edited and introduced by. The Novel in
       Letters. Epistolary Fiction in the Early English Novel,
       1678-1740. London: Routledge Kegan Paul, 322 pp.
              Elements of epistolary fiction that would be combined by
       Richardson are traced from the Lettres portugaises to 1740.
       Selected texts include material from Five Love-Letters from
       a Nun to a Cavalier (i.e., the Lettres portugaises), 1678;
       Captain Ayloffe's Letters, 1701; From a Lady to a Lady,
       1711;   A Letter from Mrs. Jane Jones, 1737, The Lover's
       Week, 1718;   The Double Captive, 1718;   The Constant
       Lovers, 1731;   The Polite Correspondence (1740?); and
       Love-Letters between a Nobleman and his Sister, 1684.
       Selected bibliography.

                                    1970

1   BARKER, GERARD A.   "Clarissa's Command of her Passions:
       Self-Censorship in the Third Edition." SEL 10: 525-39.
              Richardson attempts to re-characterize Clarissa's
       feeling for Lovelace from at-first-unconscious love in the
       first edition to a mere "conditional liking" in the third.
       Two key passages (4:60; 4:297-98) interpolated in the
       third edition suggests that Clarissa is in command of her
       passions once she recognizes their nature. But this change
       shifts the emphasis from Clarissa's conflict within herself

to "a banal melodrama of seduction"; her guilt and self-contempt after the rape seem inordinate and prudish; and Richardson, by attempting to make his heroine quite exemplary, has subverted her.

2   BELL, MICHAEL DAVITT. "Pamela´s Wedding and the Marriage of the Lamb." <u>PQ</u> 49: 100-112.
     Suggests that Richardson´s stereotypes of romantic love, language and courtship are based on theological language and the metaphor of judging souls; but <u>Pamela</u> is not in any sense a Christian allegory. Earthly meanings of "grace," "tender," and "goodness" are confused or simply conflated with their spiritual meanings. Richardson´s treatment of love in <u>Pamela</u> may be compared with the Christolatry of the Great Awakening, leading to union with Christ in death, in "the Marriage of the Lamb"; by importing its vocabulary into the realm of romantic love, Richardson is able to tap its vein of anxiety about external rewards.

3   BENOIST, HOWARD, III. "An Unpublished Letter of Samuel Richardson." <u>LC</u> 36: 63-66.
     A letter from Richardson to Benjamin Kennicott, author of the preface to the <u>Collection of Moral and Instructive Sentiments</u> (1755.11); Richardson disparages the book as "the Instruction without the Delight," no doubt, says Benoist, to draw a demurral from Kennicott.

4   BROPHY, ELIZABETH BERGEN. "The Conscious Art of Samuel Richardson." Ph.D. dissertation, Columbia University.
     Notes that Richardson was both a conscious artist and a deliberate moralist and discusses techniques used to combine these goals; argues, however, that in his last two novels Richardson fails to show his virtuous characters suffering real moral trials. Published with revisions as 1974.5.

*4A   CHATTERJEE, AMBARNATH. "Around the Mid-Century: The Progress of the Novel (Richardson)." In <u>A Study of the English Novel in the Eighteenth Century</u>. Masters of English Literature 24. Allahabad: Kitab Mahal, pp. 35-43.
     General introduction summarizing novels and pointing out Richardson´s strengths: subjectivity, circumstantial detail, and portraying of emotion. Source: Hannaford, item 595.

5   COHEN, RICHARD. <u>Literary</u> <u>References</u> <u>and</u> <u>their</u> <u>Effects</u> <u>upon</u>
       <u>Characterization</u> <u>in</u> <u>the</u> <u>Novels</u> <u>of</u> <u>Samuel</u> <u>Richardson</u>.
       Bangor, Maine: Husson College Press, 46 pp.
           Analyzes Richardson's attitude to his characters through
       his and their use of literary references in the Bible,
       ancient and contemporary authors, and Renaissance conduct
       books. Discusses Richardson's view of contemporary genres
       and his rejection of the eighteenth-century idea of
       distinct genres. In his works, literary references express
       didacticism, literary theory, and character. Based on
       1968.13.

6   COSTA, RICHARD H. "The Epistolary Monitor in <u>Pamela</u>." <u>MLQ</u> 31:
       38-47.
           Pamela addresses her letters not only to her parents
       but, once she knows he is reading them, to B; they become
       part of her courtship of him.

7   DALES, JOANNE. "The Novel as Domestic Conduct Book:
       Richardson to Jane Austen." Ph.D. dissertation, Cambridge
       University.
           Didactic function of eighteenth-century fiction
       including Richardson's.

8   DALZIEL, MARGARET. "Richardson and Romance." <u>AUMLA</u> 33: 5-24.
           Richardson's differences from the romance lie largely in
       the area of espousal of romantic love; he takes from the
       romance many details of plot, characterization, and
       subject.

9   DETIG, JOSEPH E. "Clarissa and her Modern Critics." <u>LSS</u> 4:
       131-38.
           General overview of some major modern criticisms of
       <u>Clarissa</u>.

10   DIRCKS, RICHARD J. "Cumberland, Richardson, and Fielding:
       Changing Patterns in the Eighteenth-Century Novel." <u>RSWSU</u>
       38: 291-99.
           Discusses Cumberland's sentimentalism in <u>Arundel</u> and
       <u>Henry</u> with respect to <u>Grandison</u> and Fielding; suggests
       aspects of a definition of Sentimentalism.

10A   DONALDSON, IAN. "The Clockwork Novel: Three Notes on an
       Eighteenth-Century Analogy." <u>RES</u> NS 21: 14-22.
           Imagery of clocks and time in Richardson and Fielding.

11   DUCKWORTH, COLIN. "Madame Denis's Unpublished <u>Pamela</u>: A Link
      Between Richardson, Goldoni, and Voltaire." <u>SVEC</u> 76:
      37-53.
          Madame Denis's manuscript <u>Pamela</u> is largely a
      translation and adaptation of <u>Pamela</u> <u>nubile</u> and, from
      internal evidence, was written in 1759. She replaces
      Goldoni's heroine's dilemma with the choice between
      separation and seduction, voluntarily assented to;
      seduction for her is mutual dishonor, and she makes
      explicit the social egalitarianism of <u>Pamela</u>. Duckworth
      speculates that the theme of <u>Pamela</u> may have had some
      relevance to the personal relationship between Mme. Denis
      and Voltaire, and that her play perhaps suggested to him
      the writing of <u>L'Ecossaise</u>.

12   DUSSINGER, JOHN A. "What Pamela Knew: An Interpretation."
      <u>JEGP</u> 69: 377-93.
          Pamela's style reflects her creator's Cartesian world,
      "where thinking amounts to doubting, fearing, longing, and,
      in short, to anxiety." The matriarchal pattern of the B
      family is broken by old Lady B's death; the Lincolnshire
      episode dramatizes Pamela's hysteria, arising from her
      sexual awakening, and is resolved in an "ideal friendship
      that embraces formerly individual relationships in a new
      harmonious family," ending with the restoration of a
      benevolent matriarchy under the new Lady B, Pamela.
      Reprinted with some changes as Chapter 2 in 1974.11.

13   FRIEDMAN, ARTHUR. "Aspects of Sentimentalism in
      Eighteenth-Century Literature." In <u>The</u> <u>Augustan</u> <u>Milieu</u>:
      <u>Essays</u> <u>Presented</u> <u>to</u> <u>Louis</u> <u>A.</u> <u>Landa</u>. Edited by Henry
      Knight Miller, Eric Rothstein, and G.S. Rousseau. Oxford:
      Clarendon, pp. 247-61.
          <u>Pamela</u> and <u>Clarissa</u> are cited as examples of Sentimental
      works, which are defined as works possessing a moral
      disposition in their characters; producing an effect on
      the reader or spectator through the characters' distresses,
      not their faults; and using the Christian tendency of the
      works as a means to make suffering pleasurable to the
      audience.

14   GOPNIK, IRWIN. <u>A</u> <u>Theory</u> <u>of</u> <u>Style</u> <u>and</u> <u>Richardson's</u> <u>Clarissa</u>.
      La Hague and Paris: Mouton, 135 pp.
          A linguistic study of formal realism, using a linguistic
      theory of style and a theory of literary value to

investigate verbal structure in the novel, using <u>Clarissa</u>
as a test case. Characterizes style of <u>Clarissa</u> as ironic
transformation of both traditional rhetoric and "normal"
language; notes numerous special cases of linguistic use;
and disagrees with other characterizations of Richardson's
style, such as Watt's.
> Rev.: Shirley Van Marter, <u>MP</u> 69 (1972): 352-55;
Morris Golden, <u>Style</u> 6 (1972): 74-76.

15   GRAVES, WILLIAM THOMAS. "National Characters in the Novels of
      Henry Fielding, Samuel Richardson, and Tobias Smollett."
      Ph.D. dissertation, New York University.
> Stereotypes of nationality in novels including
Richardson's.

16   HUGHES, FREDERICK A. "An Examination of the Changes among the
      First Three Editions of Richardson's <u>Clarissa</u>." Ph.D.
      dissertation, SUNY/Buffalo.
> Discusses textual changes among first three editions,
suggesting that artistic and moral goals pulled Richardson
in opposite directions and that, by the third edition, he
had chosen the moral rather than the artistic. Uses
correspondence to substantiate discussion of Richardson's
reaction.

17   HUMPHREYS, A.R. "Richardson's Novels: Words and the
      'Movements Within'." <u>E&S</u> 23: 34-50.
> Richardson's "awkward" style is gifted and innovative;
devices of style and syntactic subtleties in his language
accurately transmit psychological idiosyncracies. "Curious
passive and indirect verb-forms" indicate social rigor;
the conditional "erodes" certainty; and double and even
triple negatives add to the curiously claustrophobic air of
the whole. Richardson is a master of the <u>style indirect
libre</u>, often for ironic effect, and his epistolary
narrative allows the assimilation of inner and outer event
into a single category.

18   LEVIN, GERALD H. "Lovelace's Dream." <u>L&P</u> 20: 121-27.
> Discusses Lovelace's relationship with Clarissa and his
fantasies about her in terms of sadism/masochism and
Oedipal fantasies. See 1978.9.

19   MACANDREW, MARY ELIZABETH. "The Debate Between Richardson and
      Fielding." Ph.D. dissertation, Columbia University.
           Discusses <u>Pamela</u> <u>I</u>, <u>Shamela</u>, <u>Pamela</u> <u>II</u>, and <u>Joseph</u>
      <u>Andrews</u> as "a veritable debate in literary form between
      Richardson and Fielding."

*20   MCWATTERS, K.G. <u>Australian</u> <u>Journal</u> <u>of</u> <u>French</u> <u>Studies</u> 7: 1-2.
           "Proposes an influence of Richardson's <u>Clarissa</u> on
      [Gide's] 'Geneviève' trilogy, in the question of feminism
      and in the situations." <u>YWMLS</u> 33 (1971): 191.

20A   MANHEIM, LEONARD H. "The Absurd Miss Pamela and the Tragic
      Miss Clarissa: A Brief Study of Samuel Richardson as a
      Developing Artist." <u>Nassau</u> <u>Rev</u> (Nassau [NY] Community
      College) 2, pt.1: 1-10.
           <u>Pamela</u> is "preposterous" and the heroine only
      technically virtuous, but the book is a new kind of
      writing, an original examination of middle-class morals;
      <u>Clarissa</u> is a pioneering work in analyzing behavior under
      the stress of social codes.

22   METCALFE, ALVIN C. "<u>Sense</u> <u>and</u> <u>Sensibility</u>: A Study of its
      Similarity to <u>The</u> <u>History</u> <u>of</u> <u>Sir</u> <u>Charles</u> <u>Grandison</u>." Ph.D.
      dissertation, Kent State University.
           Austen examines notions, concepts, and sentiments that
      have previously appeared in <u>Grandison</u>, but treats them
      originally.

23   NEEDHAM, GWENDOLYN B. "Richardson's Characterization of Mr.
      B. and Double Purpose in <u>Pamela</u>." <u>ECS</u> 3: 433-74.
           Though there is a potential conflict between the moral
      and the realist interpretation of Pamela's marriage to Mr.
      B., Richardson effectively fuses the two interpretations by
      taking care to create a B. who is not simply a "booby."
      B., given sufficiently strong motivation, is capable of
      correcting and disciplining himself; his state of
      indecision between love and pride allows Richardson to
      characterize him subtly and not to condemn him; when he
      finally makes the decision to wed Pamela, we feel that both
      characters have learned to rise above potential character
      defects, and that while Virtue may be Rewarded, Vice need
      not be Punished. Individualizing both Pamela and B.
      allows Richardson to secure moral and social approval of
      their marriage.

23   PARK, WILLIAM. "What Was New about the ′New Species of
      Writing′?" SNNTS 2: 112-30.
           Discussion of an important Richardsonian critical term.

24   PRAZ, MARIO. The Romantic Agony. Second edition. Foreword
      by Frank Kermode. Oxford: Oxford University Press, pp.
      97-102.
           " . . . the unctuous pietism of Richardson′s novels
      succeeds in covering only in appearance their sensual,
      turbid background." His moralizing is "little more than a
      veneer," though perhaps not conscious hypocrisy. His works
      are compared with Darles de Montigny′s Thérèse philosophe
      (1748) and with the Liaisons dangereuses. Originally
      appeared in Italian; first edition in English appeared
      1933.

24A   PRESTON, JOHN. "Clarissa (i): A Process of Estrangement" and
      "Clarissa (ii): A Form of Freedom." The Created Self: The
      Reader′s Role in Eighteenth-Century Fiction.   London:
      Heinemann, pp. 38-93.
           The epistolary form exists in an existential or
      Pascalian present, alienated from past and future and from
      the formalized definition of personality, looking
      apprehensively toward the future. Reading and writing are
      the essential actions of the book. Distinguishes varieties
      of the present tense and discusses writer and reader
      representations within the book; notes importance of the
      privileged position given by cross-referencing; suggests
      that the editor is a referent for the reader, but not
      always clearly so. Concludes that the novel includes
      within its form the material of its tragedy; it cannot
      avoid the Lovelace-world of fantasy although it advocates
      Clarissa′s world of real relationships.

25   RICHARDSON, SAMUEL. Paméla ou la Vertu Récompensée, traduit
      par l′abbé Prévost. Bordeaux: Ducros, 381 pp.

*26   ---. Pamela.S engelskog preveo [translated from English by]
      Berislav Grgić. 2v. Zagreb: Zora.
           First Serbo-Croation translation; sources: Nacionalna
      i Sveučilišna Biblioteka, Zagreb; Narodna in univerzitetna
      knjižnica, Ljubljana.

27   SCHMITZ, ROBERT M. "Death and Colonel Morden in <u>Clarissa</u>."
      <u>SAQ</u> 69, [346]-53.
           Morden serves both as character and embodiment of
      Clarissa's salvation through death.

28   TEMPLE, EUAN R.A. "The Somber World of <u>Clarissa</u>." Ph.D.
      dissertation, University of Arkansas.
           Pessimism of world-view of <u>Clarissa</u>. Clarissa and
      Lovelace are defeated sexually; the book as a whole is
      "the futile grasping of people at events in useless effort
      to control destiny."

29   WARDE, WILLIAM BOOTH, JR. "Revisions in the Published Texts
      of <u>Clarissa</u>." Ph.D. dissertation, University of Arkansas.
           Collates the first through fifth editions and the
      edition of 1792 with <u>Letters</u> <u>and</u> <u>Passages</u> <u>Restored</u> . . .
      (1751); notes sharpening of language, developing of
      character psychology, and greater emphasis on morality and
      instruction. Cf. 1969.27, 1970.1, 1970.16.

30   ---. "Revisions of the Published Texts of Samuel Richardson's
      Preface to <u>Clarissa</u>." <u>SCB</u> 30: 232-34.
           Revisions are intended to stress the moral value, the
      pleasure and instruction of the work, the value of
      friendship, the stylistic advantages of "writing to the
      moment," and the character of Clarissa, exemplary but not
      perfect.

31   WILLIAMS, IOAN, editor. <u>Novel</u> <u>and</u> <u>Romance,</u> <u>1700-1800:</u> <u>A</u>
      <u>Documentary</u> <u>Record</u>. London: Routledge Kegan Paul, 496 pp.
           Richardson is an important figure both in Williams'
      introductory essay and in the documentation; for Williams,
      Richardson is the most important figure in the conservative
      school of moral fiction. His conservatism is unfortunate
      both for him (leading him from <u>Clarissa</u> to the far inferior
      <u>Grandison</u>) and for writers who followed him, but it
      provides a firm base for the development of conservative
      criticism, the Gothic novel, and sentimental fiction.
      Compares the effects of Richardson's and Fielding's
      theories of fiction. Documentary material includes: the
      introductory material of the first and second edition of
      <u>Pamela</u>; the preface to the first edition of <u>Clarissa</u>;
      Elizabeth Carter's comparison of <u>Clarissa</u> and Tom Jones in
      a letter to Catherine Talbot, June 20, 1749; Haller's
      discussion of <u>Clarissa</u> (1749.6); a letter from Mrs.

Donellan to Richardson, September 25, 1750, suggesting the outline of <u>Grandison</u>; Richardson to Mrs. Donellan on <u>Amelia</u>, February 22, 1752; Philip Skelton to Richardson on <u>Grandison</u> and the necessity for adventures and drama, December 28, 1752; William Whitehead on Richardson and Fielding in <u>The</u> <u>World</u>, May 10, 1753; Mary Wortley Montagu (1760); <u>Critical</u> <u>Review</u> (1761); Blair (1759); Barthe (1796); Pratt's <u>Liberal</u> <u>Opinions</u>, 1777 (see 1785.9); Knox (1777); Anna Seward (1777); Beattie (1783); Cumberland (1786); Henry Pye, from <u>A</u> <u>Commentary</u> <u>Illustrating</u> <u>the</u> <u>Poetics</u> <u>of</u> <u>Aristotle</u>, 1786; The <u>Analytical</u> <u>Review</u> 18 (1794): 357-66; and Moore (1797).

<u>1971</u>

1   BAKER, MARTHA CAREY. "The Philosophical Seducer." Ph.D. dissertation, Yale University.
      Discusses analysis of social values in Crébillon <u>fils</u>, Restif de la Bretonne, and Richardson through the figure of the "philosophical seducer" who practices seduction from rationally thought-out motives.

2   BALL, DONALD L. <u>Samuel</u> <u>Richardson's</u> <u>Theory</u> <u>of</u> <u>Fiction</u>. De Proprietatibus Litterarum, Series Practica 15. La Hague and Paris: Mouton, 323 pp.
      Published version of 1966.1. Gathers together Richardson's statements about fiction (in the novels and the correspondence) under four headings: techniques of narrative structure, epistolary technique, characterization, and presentation of moral doctrine. Examines his practice in each category in detail. Concludes that in all areas his practice is more comprehensive than his theory, and that in the area of presentation of moral doctrine his theory and practice are seriously at odds, subverting his first two novels morally. However, in general "his achievements were in accord with his intentions." Several appendices tabulate Richardson's method in detail.

3   BEASLEY, JERRY C. "The Minor Fiction of the 1740s: A Background Study of the Novels of Richardson, Fielding, and Smollett." Ph.D. dissertation, Northwestern University.
      Study of minor fiction of the period with frequent

references to Richardson. Material from this study has appeared most recently in Beasley's <u>Fiction of the 1740s</u> (1982), and also in 1972.2A, 1973.2, and 1976.5.

4   BREWSTER, JACK. "The Virtuous Heroes of the English Novel." Ph.D. dissertation, Indiana University.
Grandison, as central character and moral exemplar, is under considerable pressure: through him the moral system of the novel must be shown performing dramatically. Concludes that the most successful heroes, such as Grandison, must have a value system perfectly in accord with their authors´.

5   CARROLL, JOHN. "Samuel Richardson" [bibliography]. <u>NCBEL</u>. Edited by George Watson. Cambridge: Cambridge University Press. 3: Cols. 917-925.
Unannotated. Most complete bibliography before Hannaford.

6   COPELAND, EDWARD W. "Samuel Richardson and Naive Allegory: Some Beauties of the Mixed Metaphor." <u>Novel</u> 4: 231-39.
Relationship between emblematic rhetoric and psychological insight, between psychological representation, in the near-mythic form in which Richardson gives it (<u>a</u> Clarissa, <u>a</u> Lovelace), and rhetoric of the novels; argues that Richardson´s failure to distinguish between mimetic and didactic concerns is useful. Richardson uses naive allegory as an index to "proper meaning" in <u>Pamela</u>. In <u>Clarissa</u> "two completely developed rhetorical styles," Clarissa´s and Lovelace´s, refer ironically to each other; allusion within the novel becomes almost completely internal, one set of allegories commenting on the other.

7   DAICHES, DAVID. "Samuel Richardson." In <u>The Penguin Companion to English Literature</u>. New York: McGraw-Hill, pp. 443-44.
Short general introduction.

8   EAVES, T.C. DUNCAN, and BEN D. KIMPEL. <u>Samuel Richardson: A Biography</u>. Oxford: Clarendon Press, 746 pp.
Referred to <u>passim</u> here as "E&K", this is the definitive biography, supplanting all previous work in depth and accuracy. Contains emormous amounts of new data, including material on Richardson´s birthplace, life as a printer, and

contemporary reputation. Universally respected for its depth of scholarship on Richardson's life, but has been criticized for its attitude toward the works, in particular <u>Grandison</u>.

Failing a complete edition of the correspondence, their appendix (pp. 620-704) is the only reliable guide to Richardson's letters; to it may be added a letter of 24 April 1750 from Richardson to John Rivington, in reply to Rivington's of the same date to him, concerning his marriage settlement with Elisabeth Miller Gosling and mentioning that Richardson drew Charles Rivington's will. The letter is reproduced and transcribed in 1919.7. On p. 630 the letter of 27 January 1742 should be from Richardson to an anonymous correspondent (courtesy Prof. T.C. Duncan Eaves). See also John August Wood. "The Chronology of the Richardson-Bradshaigh Correspondence of 1751." <u>SB</u> 33 (1980):182-91, which provides slight revisions. The portrait referred to on p. 525, n22, has been located (it is in a private collection in America).

Rev.: <u>TLS</u>, July 9, 1971, p. 807 (see also 1971.10, below); D.J. Enright, <u>The Listener</u>, August 19, 1971, pp. 245-46; <u>JNL</u> 31: 1-2; F.W. Hilles, <u>YR</u> 61: 109-17; <u>DQR</u> 1: 175-79; (in 1972) <u>PQ</u> 51: 752-54; John Carroll, <u>RES</u> NS 23:504-8; Ellen Moers, <u>NYRB</u>, Feb. 10, 1972, 27-31; William B. Warde, Jr., <u>SoHR</u> 6: 417-18; (in 1973) Christian Pons, <u>EA</u> 26: 296-308 (v. 1973.29); R.F. Brissenden, <u>ECS</u> 6: 518-20; R.A. Day, <u>Archiv</u> 210: 397-402; Pat Rogers, <u>N&Q</u> n.s. 20: 234-35; Ronald Paulson, <u>SNNTS</u> 5: 110-16 (v. 1971.15, 1973.27); (in 1974) Wolfgang Zach, <u>GRM</u> 55: 248-51.

8   FREEMAN, CAROL MARIA CREANZA. "Richardson and the Uses of Romance: A Study of Art, Morality, and Ambiguity in <u>Clarissa</u>." Ph.D. dissertation, Yale University.

Richardson suggests, then explodes, the conventions of romance to show "the tenuous nature of truth and the difficulty of acting in an ambivalent world." However, he takes from the romance the idealism of striving for the ideal, even though it cannot be achieved.

9   KAPLAN, FRED. "'Our Short Story': The Narrative Devices of <u>Clarissa</u>." <u>SEL</u> 11: 549-62.

Discusses Richardson's expertise in narrative technique.

10   HALSBAND, ROBERT. <u>TLS</u>, August 6, p. 945.
        In a letter replying to the review of <u>Samuel</u> <u>Richardson:</u>
      <u>A</u> <u>Biography</u>, Halsband writes that George Sherburn "couldn´t
      stay awake while reading the complete [<u>Clarissa</u>]";   E&K
      mentioned that Sherburn "didn´t like" his own abridgment.

11   KEARNEY, A.M. "A Recurrent Motif in Richardson´s Novels."
      <u>Neophil</u> 55: 447-50.
        The male-female relationships in Richardson are seen as
      an unwary female bird trapped in a male fowler´s snare, an
      image used in connection with B, Lovelace, and comically in
      <u>Grandison</u> with "the creeping Mr. Fowler." Another example
      of Richardson´s artistry in small things.

12   LEVIN, GERALD H. "Richardson´s <u>Pamela</u>: Conflicting Trends,"
      <u>AI</u> 28: 319-29.
        Masochistic traits in B and Pamela: a Freudian reading
      of their relationship and of the masochistic component of
      Sentimentalism.

13   MCKENZIE, ALAN T.   "Two Letters from Giuseppe Baretti to
      Samuel Johnson." <u>PMLA</u> 86:218-24.
        In a letter of July 21, 1762, Baretti mentions his great
      regard for Richardson and gives his opinion of what is
      probably Diderot´s <u>Eloge</u>.

14   MORTON, DONALD E. "Theme and Structure in <u>Pamela</u>." <u>SNNTS</u>
      3:242-57.
        Discusses <u>Pamela</u> as a "kind of <u>Paradise</u> <u>Lost</u> and
      <u>Paradise</u> <u>Regained</u>" in which Puritan values--the salvation
      of souls, principally B´s--are the end at issue, rather
      than Pamela´s merely secular good.   Provides Puritan
      definition of virtue and suggests that rhetoric of novel
      provides a serious religious framework, a Providential
      design in which we are to see Pamela´s successes as
      spiritual.

15   OTTEN, KURT. "Samuel Richardson." In his <u>Englischen</u> <u>Roman</u> <u>vom</u>
      <u>16.</u> <u>zum</u> <u>19.</u> <u>Jhdts</u>. Berlin: E. Schmidt, pp. 61-71.
        In Richardson´s fiction, love-interest becomes central,
      the integration of the bourgeoisie is portrayed, and the
      epistolary form is connected with psychological drama.
      Discusses sociological relevance and style.

*16   PAVITT, MAGDA. "The Concept of Libertinage in Richardson's
       <u>Clarissa</u> and Laclos's <u>Les Liaisons dangereuses</u>." M.A.
       thesis, McGill University. Université de Laval.
           Source: Catalog of the Bib. de l'U. de Laval.

*17   PUTNAM, MARGARET ALICE SCOBEY. "Style and Sentimentality in
       Three   Novels: <u>Clarissa</u>,   <u>Charlotte   Temple</u> and <u>The</u>
       <u>Coquette</u>." M.A. thesis, University of Texas at Austin.
           Source: Catalog of the U. of Texas at Austin Library.

18   RICHARDSON, SAMUEL. <u>Pamela.</u> Edited with an introduction by
       T.C.   Duncan Eaves and Ben D. Kimpel. Boston: Houghton
       Mifflin (Riverside), 438 pp.
           Based on the first edition. Reviewed briefly by Ronald
       Paulson, <u>SNNTS</u> 5 (1973): 115-16.

19   ---. <u>Clarissa; or, The History of a Young Lady.</u> Edited and
       abridged with an introduction by Philip Stevick. San
       Francisco: Rinehart, 569 pp.
           1972.17 (q.v.) praises the introduction but feels this
       is the weakest of the three modern abridgments.

20   STEELE, Sir RICHARD. <u>Plays.</u> Edited by Shirley Strum Kenny.
       Oxford: Clarendon, pp. 7, 202.
           Notes use of Steele's plays in Richardson's fiction;
       see also 1963.9.

*21   SUZUKI, ZENZO. "Locke and Richardson." <u>ARFALTU</u> 21:   37-56.
       [In Japanese; English summary on pp. 176-77.]
           Courtesy Prof. Carl Berkhout.

22   VAN BETTEN, HERMAN. "Richardson in Holland and his Influence
       on Wolff and Deken's <u>Sara Burgerhart</u>." Ph.D. disseration,
       University of Southern California.
           Background study on Richardson's influence in Holland
       and Richardsonian techniques in <u>Sara Burgerhart</u>; concludes
       that the book succeeds both as Richardsonian novel and as
       native Dutch fiction.

23   YOUNG, EDWARD. <u>Correspondence of Edward Young, 1689-1765.</u>
       Edited by Henry Pettit. Oxford: Clarendon, 624 pp.
           Letters to and from Richardson reprinted from the
       <u>Monthly Magazine</u> (see 1813.4) and elsewhere. The most
       textually reliable appearance of these letters.

1972

1　ALLENTUCK, MARCIA. "Narration and Illustration: The Problem
of Richardson's *Pamela*." PQ 51: 874-86.
　　Notes a "curious alienation between text and
illustration" in the Hayman-Gravelot illustrations to
Pamela; they lack the "feeling of the moment" and indicate
instead Pamela's relation to the moral world,
oversimplifying and distorting Richardson's creation.

2　ANDERSON, HOWARD. "Answers to the Author of *Clarissa*: Themes
and Narrative Techniques in *Tom Jones* and *Tristram Shandy*."
PQ 51: 859-73.
　　Mutual trust, in the worlds of *Tom Jones* and *Tristram
Shandy*, is mirrored in the narrative by the reader's
dependence on the narrator; in contrast, the reader of
Clarissa is alone.

2　BEASLEY, JERRY C. *A Check List of Prose Fiction Published in
England 1740-1749.* Charlottesville, N.C.: University of
North Carolina Press.
　　Continues McBurney; contains editions of Richardson's
works and Richardsoniana.

3　CARROLL, JOHN. "Lovelace as Tragic Hero." UTQ 42: 14-25.
　　Lovelace's role as tragic conqueror is indicated by
references to historical conquerors and rapists (Alexander,
Peter the Great, Jupiter) and to Lucifer. His ambitions
are cosmic; he wishes both to destroy virtue and to
possess its essence. Nothing outside himself has value;
"his imagination, his will, his intellect have absolute
value." His punishment is to be shackled to a convention,
that of the libertine. We pity him; he loses his soul.

4　COHEN, RICHARD. "The Social-Christian and Christian-Social
Doctrines of Samuel Richardson." HSL 4: 136-46.
　　Moral-social classifications create a double doctrinal
approach in Richardson's novels; each half must be
considered as part of the compound whole.

5　COPELAND, EDWARD W. "Allegory and Analogy in *Clarissa*: The
'Plan' and 'No-Plan'." ELH 39: 254-65.
　　The source of what might be called the mythic power of
Clarissa is the "misuse" of the formal figurative modes of
allegory ana analogy, which function as both a tool of

rhetoric and a form of logic. The image and its spiritual anagogue are identified but not identical in Clarissa's flight from her father's house, her rape, and her death. The "Plan" of the novel, allegory elevating the book to cosmic significance, and the "No-Plan," returning metaphors, allusions, and symbolism to the social world of the novel, move in opposite directions.

6   ---. "Clarissa and Fanny Hill: Sisters in Distress." <u>SNNTS</u> 4: 343-52.
      Compares similarities of technique and convention in the virtuous sensibility of <u>Clarissa</u> and the eroticism of <u>Fanny Hill</u>; suggests a possible fundamental similarity between their nature and effects. A sensual connection between individual gratification and general benevolence leaves open questions of method and effect in "chaste" sentimental fiction.

7   FINK, GUIDO. "Da Pamela a Shamela (e viceversa)." <u>Paragone</u> 266: 3-35.
      Comparison of <u>Pamela</u>, <u>Shamela</u>, and <u>Joseph Andrews</u>; discussion of "personal calculation," the double standard of male and female sexual behavior, and the letter form as self-expression and parody. Notes "twinship" structure; two characters go from a relationship of antagonism to one of reciprocation.

8   FOLKENFLIK, ROBERT. "A Room of Pamela's Own." <u>ELH</u> 39: 585-96.
      Imagery of invasion of spatial order on three levels: of social order, of the house, and of Pamela herself. Spatial locutions are prevalent; action is referred to by space-names ("closet-work," "summer-house trick"). Pamela's only truly free space is within her letters; after her marriage they lose their "existential urgency" and the novel becomes dull. The marriage itself is symbolized by Pamela's new space and privacy, but within Mr. B's house.

9   FOUGÈRES, MICHEL. "Le Thème de la <u>Liebestod</u> dans le roman français, anglais et allemand au dix-huitième siècle." Ph.D. dissertation, New York University.
      Discusses the resurgence of the theme of tragic love in novels including <u>Clarissa</u>. Published as 1974.13.

10   GEETTER, JOAN T. "Richardson's <u>Clarissa</u>: Five Views of an
      Epistolary Novel." Ph.D. dissertation, University of
      Connecticut.
          Discussion of epistolary form, man-woman psychology,
      sexual categorization and assumptions, effect of the
      theater, and myth of romance in <u>Clarissa</u>.

11   GUILHAMET, LÉON M. "From <u>Pamela</u> to <u>Grandison</u>: Richardson's
      Moral Revolution in the Novel." In <u>Studies in Change and
      Revolution: Aspects of English Intellectual History
      1640-1800.</u> Edited by Paul J. Korshin. Menston, Yorks.:
      Scolar Press, pp. 191-210.
          The central issue in Richardson's novels is not social
      realism, but "an imaginative ideal of sincerity" that
      seemingly insincere external dramatization (e.g. the
      bended knee) attempts to visualize. Richardson's moral
      revolution is the development in his novels of a coherent
      moral ideal.

12   HOHENDAHL, PETER UWE. "Empfindsamkeit und gesellschaftliches
      Bewusstsein: Zur Soziologie des empfindsamen Romans am
      Beispiel von <u>La Vie de Marianne</u>, <u>Clarissa</u>, <u>Fräulein von
      Sternheim</u>, und <u>Werther</u>." <u>JDSG</u> 16: 176-207.
          Attempt to define the "bourgeois reader" through
      discussion of the relationships between social reality and
      Sentimental writing; finds <u>Clarissa</u> difficult to
      characterize as either bourgeois or antibourgeois.
      Clarissa herself articulates the contradiction between the
      simple material reward of virtue and its larger moral
      values; she protests dehumanizing class-interests that
      victimize the individual, particularly women. "Clarissa
      wird zum Gegenspieler der eigenen Klasse, weil sie deren
      humane Ideale verwirklichen will."

13   KIEHL, JAMES MILLINGER. "Epic, mock-heroic and novel:
      1650-1750." Ph.D. dissertation, Syracuse University.
          Discusses decline of traditional epic, rise of
      mock-heroic and novel; notes analogies to epic in several
      novels, including <u>Clarissa</u> and <u>Tom Jones</u>.

14   MCALLISTER, HAROLD STANWOOD. "Apology for Bad Dreams: A
      Study of Characterization and the Use of Fantasy in
      <u>Clarissa</u>, <u>Justine</u> and <u>The Monk</u>." Ph.D. dissertation,
      University of New Mexico.
          Fantasy as an element of characterization and audience

response. Character-clusters of male persecutor, male observer, female victim, and female predator allow each author to work out anti-social fantasies, Richardson most satisfyingly.

15   MORTON, ANN RUTH. "The Structure of Samuel Richardson's Novels." Ph.D. dissertation, University of Oregon.
     Discussion of structural patterns in the three novels. Pamela has a bipartite structure; the three-part structure of Clarissa heightens the tragic inevitability of the novel; Sir Charles Grandison is organized around character groups rather than events.

16   NIKLAUS, R. "Crébillon fils et Richardson." SVEC 89: 1169-85.
     Crébillon fils and Richardson have similarities, but Richardson presents us with insoluble moral conflicts between two codes; he possesses the moral vision Crébillon lacks.

17   PALMER, WILLIAM J. "The Abridgments of Clarissa." JNL 32 pt. 2: 8-9.
     Compares the three modern abridgments for their value as teaching aids. Sherburn (1962) and Burrell (1950) include parts of as many letters as possible, while Stevick (1971) omits whole groups of letters apparently in order to make the novel faster-moving. Both Sherburn and Burrell omit Lovelace's fantasy-rape of Anna Howe and her mother; Stevick, with a predisposition to psychological approaches, includes the letter in its entirety (although it is not from his base-text, the first edition; see 1973.33). Sherburn makes great cuts in the impersonation scene with Widow Bevis, which Burrell summarizes and Stevick omits. All three omit Belton's death and the letters relating to the whores' fates. Stevick includes Sinclair's death but destroys the continuity of the plot and the integrity of Richardson's characterizations and social themes, particularly in the part of the book following Clarissa's rape. He omits the ball scene, which Burrell and Sherburn do not, and the letters that describe Clarissa's last escape from Mrs. Sinclair's. Minor omissions throughout Stevick destroy any possibility of discussing narrative viewpoint or imagery and damage the characterizations of Clarissa, Lovelace and Belford. In short, Stevick's fine introduction is coupled with a bad abridgment; Burrell's

introduction is "insensitive" to Richardson's complexity; and Sherburn's introduction, plodding though sometimes witty, is joined with the best teaching abridgment available. However, Palmer feels, no one should teach Clarissa in abridgment without telling students how much they are missing.

18   RICHARDSON, SAMUEL. The History of Sir Charles Grandison. Edited with an introduction and notes by Jocelyn Harris. 3v. London: Oxford University Press.
        Text of first edition. Reviewed by Shirley Van Marter, ECS 9 (1975): 125-28; TLS.

19   SACKS, SHELDON. "Clarissa and the Tragic Traditions." In SECC 2. Edited by Harold D. Pagliaro. Cleveland: Press of Case Western Reserve University, pp. 195-221.
        Tragedy is given a new form of action, narrative rather than dramatic, in the sentimental novel of which Clarissa is the perfect example. By stressing both that the outcome results from the character's own psychologically blameless actions and that the character assents to that outcome through the ethical choices s/he has learned to make, tragedy involves us most fully; Richardson initiates a tradition of such novels in English.

19A   STASKIEL, Sister M. PACELLI, C.S.B. "The Divine Clarissa: Secular Sanctity in the Eighteenth Century." Ph.D. dissertation, Duquesne University.
        Compares Clarissa with seventeenth- and eighteenth-century conduct books of the religious life, particularly Jeremy Taylor's Holy Living and Holy Dying; indicates that "Richardson's moral philosophy basically agreed with eighteenth-century Christian teachings."

20   STEIN, WILLIAM B. "Pamela: The Narrator as Unself-Conscious Hack." BuR 20: 39-66.
        Characterizes Pamela as a novice author writing a "potboiler," her own letters, based on the stereotypes of current literary themes, which exalt her into a heroine; she is "simply the stereotyped mouthpiece of the reigning ethos, the arbiter of the puritanic decorums of the frighteningly artificial codes of respectability." Metaphors of novel-writing, card-games, gaming, hypocrisy and cheating pervade the book; notes particularly the political and linguistic implications of Pamela's game of

whist.   Thinks   of   the   book   as   a   politically   and
aesthetically Augustan jeu d´esprit.

21   ULMER, GREGORY L.   "Clarissa and La Nouvelle Héloïse." CL   24:
      289-308.
            Rousseau   inverts   Clarissa,   overturning   Richardson
      aesthetically   and   psychologically   while   attempting   to
      maintain the earlier author´s didactic   conclusions.   This
      inversion   is   explored   through   two   major   interrelated
      themes, the moral ordeal and a "sexual   ordeal,"   comparing
      St.-Preux (rather than Julie) to Clarissa. The influence
      of Richardson on Rousseau shows the   latter´s   originality;
      he   extends   the   subject   of   the earlier book to confront
      problems raised by it but left unresolved.

*22   VINCENT, THOMAS BREWER.   "The   Influence   of   Ontological   and
      Epistemological   Assumptions   on   Form and Structure in the
      Eighteenth-Century Novel: A   Study   of   the   Major   Works   of
      Richardson,   Fielding,   Smollett,   and   Sterne." Ph.D.
      dissertation, Queens [Canada].
            Courtesy of the Bib. de l´U. de Laval.

23   VOPAT, JAMES BERNARD.   "The Denial of Innocence: The Theme of
      Social   Responsibility   in   the Early British Novel." Ph.D.
      dissertation, University of Washington.
            Discusses   several   novels,   including   Pamela   and   Tom
      Jones,   in   which   the   central   character begins in a state of
      innocence or inexperience, comes to learn the necessity for
      self-control, and assumes social responsibility.

24   WASSERMAN, JERRY S.   "Concrete Mimetic Form and the   Languages
      of   Silence   in   English   Fiction." Ph.D.   dissertation,
      Cornell University.
            Clarissa   is   among   novels   using   silence   and   visual
      structure   to   get   at the nature of experiences beyond the
      reach of words.

25   WINNER, ANTHONY.   "Richardson´s Lovelace: Character   and
      Prediction." TSLL 14:   53-75.
            Richardson´s achievement consists   in   circumstancing   a
      general   myth   in   a   particular   society,   working   out   a
      Christian Providential   lesson   in   the   circumstantial
      darkness and ambiguity of the novel.   Lovelace is a type of
      the heroic criminal, his emotionalism a dark commentary   on
      Sentimentalism: "Clarissa is . . . [both] the fictional

source of a sentimental revolution and a largely pejorative examination of the implications of such a revolution." In later fiction, the novelist would be concerned with the corruption itself, not with its presence in the secure anagogic structure of Richardson's novel.

26   WOLFF, CYNTHIA GRIFFIN. <u>Samuel Richardson and the Eighteenth-Century Puritan Character</u>. Hamden, Conn: Shoe String Press, 259 pp.
        Richardson initially used Puritan modes of characterization, but was increasingly forced into examination of the social significance of Puritan characters, and hence into a secularized mode of thought and characterization. Defines "Puritanism" as it relates to Richardson and shows how use of it in his work led to the beginnings of the novel of manners.
        Reviewed by Richard W. Noland, <u>HSL</u> 6 (1974): 193-96.

1973

1   ALLEN, WALTER. "Letters as Literature: The Virtues of the Epistolary Novel." <u>TLS</u>, January 26, pp. 97-98.
        Its great virtue is dramatization; Allen praises <u>Clarissa</u> highly, though conceding that "nowadays it . . . belongs almost entirely to university departments of English," discusses history of the epistolary form, and suggests it may still be of interest.

2   BEASLEY, JERRY C. "English Fiction in the 1740s: Some Glances at the Major and Minor Novels." <u>SNNTS</u> 5: 155-75.
        Notes in novels of the 1740s: lip-service at least to formal realism; moral realism; familiar and topical narratives; new, Christian definition of heroism. Discusses various genres of novels and their roots in other literature including conversion narratives and political memoirs, the influence of foreign literature, the careers of individual writers.

2A   BRAUDY, LEO. "The Form of the Sentimental Novel." <u>Novel</u> 7: 5-13.
        The Sentimental novel commits itself to "nonliterary, even inarticulate expression," a conscious anti-artistry that implies a found form and subject. Braudy connects

this with the problem of being a literary person, a source
of literature; the writers and narrators of Sentimental
fiction indirectly express the problem, assert the value
and energy of partial meaning, bring themselves out of
isolation   through   telling   their   stories,   and   feel
threatened by the end of their story. "The essence of the
form that gives them life its its tentativeness and its
groping response to the nuances of feeling."

3   BRÜCKMANN, PATRICIA C. "The Settings in Pamela." TSJSNW 6:
     1-10.
        The movement of the action from Bedfordshire to
     Lincolnshire   has   emblematic   significance,   since
     Lincolnshire is traditionally associated with gloom and
     melancholy;   the   move   reflects   Pamela´s   growth in
     experience.

4   CARROLL, JOHN. "Richardson at Work: Revisions, Allusions,
     and Quotations in Clarissa." In Studies in the Eighteenth
     Century: Papers Presented at the Second David Nicol Smith
     Memorial   Seminar,   Canberra   1970.   Edited   by   R.F.
     Brissenden.   Toronto: University   of   Toronto   Press,
     2:53-71.
        Documents Richardson´s meticulous care in revising his
     work, extending even to the typography and possibly to the
     printers´ ornaments.   Richardson revises for emphasis,
     for elegance, and to dramatize Lovelace´s hardheartedness and
     Clarissa´s difficult position. Concludes that since the
     first edition is less "blighted" by overcorrectness and
     less "warped . . . by failures among his readers," the
     best copytext is probably the first edition, with the
     addition in textual notes of the critically significant
     changes.   Notes Richardson´s use of the word "great." See
     also 1973.33.

5   COWARD, D.A. "Laclos and the denouement of the Liaisons
     dangereuses." ECS 5: 431-39.
        Analyzes the implications of Laclos´s praise of
     Richardson in his review of Cecilia (1784).

6   DAVIS, ELIZABETH ALDRICH.   "The Spirit of the Letter:
     Richardson and the Early American Novel. A Study in the
     Evolution of Form." Ph.D. dissertation, Yale University.
        The lack of an authoritative style in Clarissa, a
     stylistic norm reflecting norms of behavior and genre, is

brought into the early American novel as an intrinsic
generic instability. Discussion of this phenomenon in the
works of W.H. Brown, Hannah Foster, Brackenridge, C.B.
Brown, Cooper, and Hawthorne.

7   ENGEL, GISELA. "Familie und Familienbeziehungen in den
     Romanen Richardsons." Ph.D. dissertation, University of
     Frankfurt.
         Published as 1974.12.

8   FORTUNA, JAMES L., JR. "'The Unsearchable Wisdom of God': A
     Study of Providence in Richardson's Pamela." Ph.D.
     dissertation, University of Florida.
         The nature and working of Providence provides a
     traditional Christian theme in Richardson's first novel.
     Published in 1981.

9   GOLDKNOPF, DAVID. "The Meaning of the Epistolary Format in
     Clarissa." In his Life of the Novel. Chicago: Chicago
     University Press, pp. 59-78.
         The letter-novel dramatizes literacy, the writing of
     letters; through it Clarissa Romantically dramatizes her
     own drama and the part she plays in it. The epistolary
     format allows us to see the self-creation of the
     characters; their lives progress from chaos, to dream, to
     wish-fulfillment sent out into the world through their
     letters.
         Reviewed: TLS, March 9.

*10   GUYNN, ROBERT H. "The Pleasures of Righteousness: A Study of
     the Fantasy Materials and Affective Structures of
     Richardson's Clarissa." Ph.D. dissertation, University of
     California, Berkeley.
         Source: 1975.2, item D52.

11   HARRIS, JOCELYN. "Twenty-Eight Volumes of Sir Charles
     Grandison." N&Q n.s. 20: 18-19.
         Not a massive Ur-Grandison, but twenty-eight manuscript
     volumes.

12   HIGBIE, ROBERT GRIGGS. "Characterization in the English
     Novel: Richardson, Jane Austen, and Dickens." Ph.D.
     dissertation, Indiana University.
         Suggests that Richardson's major contribution to
     characterization in the novel is the creation of characters

with "internal tension," that is, with forces acting on them outside the demands of the plot or of the didactic purposes of the novel.

13   JOST, FRANÇOIS. "Prévost traducteur de Richardson." Expression, Communication and Experience in Literature and Language. Proceedings of the XII Congress of the International Federation for Modern Languages and Literatures Held at Cambridge University, 20-26 August 1972. Edited by Ronald G. Popperwell. [London:] Modern Humanities Research Association, pp. 297-300. [Abstract only.]

Prévost's translation makes Clarissa more elegant and centers the action more completely around the heroine. Cutting the number of correspondents in half results in a different form of book: while the English novel creates correspondents to give the protagonists a tiers to whom to write, the French novel has its principal figures "s'affront[ant], par un commerce épistolaire direct, ressort de l'action." Rousseau, Restif and Laclos follow Prévost's Richardson in this, not Richardson's. Prévost also largely suppresses multiple narration of the same event, and Rousseau follows him in this; Laclos follows Richardson. Richardson's method totally eliminates omniscient narration, but Prévost, cutting the book greatly, reintroduces omniscient narration by narrating some of the plot. Richardson's contribution to world literature through the Prévost translation is not a method of telling a story but the psychological vivisection of a soul; and Prévost, while not offering "l'autoanalyse, la véritable substance de Clarissa," powerfully disposes French spirits toward the English book and England. Cf. 1927.10.

*14   JOYCE, VICTORIA. "Imagery and Symbolism in Richardson's Clarissa." Ph.D. dissertation, University of London.
Source: 1975.2, item D57.

15   KAY, DONALD. "Pamela and the Poultry." SNL 10 pt. 1: 25-27.
Use of fowl imagery in Pamela.

16   KELSALL, MALCOLM. "Introduction." In Sarah Fielding. The Adventures of David Simple. Edited with an introduction by Malcolm Kelsall. Oxford, London, New York: Oxford University Press.

Kelsall's introduction draws attention to dissimilarities between this work and Richardson's, but notes that <u>Volume the Last</u> contains much of the Sentimental pessimism of its contemporary, <u>Sir Charles Grandison</u>. (See 1744.2, 1753.13.)

17   KINKEAD-WEEKES, MARK. <u>Samuel Richardson: Dramatic Novelist</u>. Ithaca, N.Y.: Cornell University Press; London: Methuen, 516 pp.
       Detailed exploration of the interrelatedness of the moral problems of Richardson's characters, their psychological nature, and Richardson's own success as a technician. "Richardson's greatest achievements came when his <u>form</u> enabled him to free himself from his moralistic straitjacket." Discusses nature of "dramatic writing" in Richardson; distinguishes varieties of dramatic usage; analyzes interplay in Richardson between moral "second voice," that part of the characters that speaks for the author, and their psychology as realistic characters; suggests ways in which dramatic techniques reflect characters' or readers' mental processes. Compares with Defoe and Fielding. Discusses "unconsciousness" of Richardson's art, arguing that its unconscious quality proceeds not from naïveté but from the inability of any single persona, including that of "Mr. Richardson, author," to express the full range of meaning that the dramatic form allows. Detailed analyses of all three books and valuable discussions of style, particularly challenging in the case of Sir Charles's style (pp. 448 ff.). Concludes with a discussion of the approaches of other modern critics.
       Reviewed by: Dieter Mehl, <u>Erasmus</u> 26 (1974): 355-60; C.J. Rawson, <u>DUJ</u> 36 (1974):120-22; Benjamin Boyce, <u>ELN</u> 12 (1974): 146-49; <u>TLS</u>, 25 January 1975; Bertil Romberg, <u>Samlaren</u> 95 (1974): 224-25; <u>JNL</u> 35 (1975): 4-5; <u>PQ</u> 53 (1974): 785-87; <u>RES</u> NS 27 (1976): 81-84; <u>SEL</u> 4 (1974): 465-67.

18   LABAN, LAWRENCE FREDERICK. "The Sense of Place in the Fiction of Samuel Richardson." Ph.D. dissertation, Indiana University.
       Place as means of realism, structure, and metaphor.

19   LAUTERMILCH, STEVEN JAMES. "The Marriage of Realism and
      Romance in the Eighteenth-Century English Novel." Ph.D.
      dissertation, University of Michigan.
          Studies the adaptation to each other of romance and
      realism through the concept of "history"; detailed
      discussion of Clarissa.

20   LEED, JACOB. "Richardson's Pamela and Sidney's." AUMLA 40:
      240-45.
          Comparisons with Sidney's Pamela; concludes that
      similarities between the two argue a favorable attitude
      toward romance in Richardson's novel, and that Richardson
      has a definite, though limited, debt to romance.

21   LENNOX, CHARLOTTE. The Female Quixote. Edited with an
      introduction and notes by Margaret Dalziel. London,
      Oxford, New York: Oxford University Press, 446 pp.
          Besides other references to Richardson by Lennox herself
      (see pp. 253, 314, and 377, and 1752.6), this edition
      contains a useful appendix by Dalziel on "Johnson,
      Richardson, and The Female Quixote," pp. 418-27.

22   LEVIN, GERALD. "Character and Fantasy in Richardson's Sir
      Charles Grandison." ConnR 7 pt. 1: 93-99.
          Discusses Grandison as a fantasy-variation of the
      Freudian "neurotic's family romance"; the women embody
      moral masochism, the energies of which "pass into stoicism
      and serve as a means of confining the dangerous passions."

23   LINDLEY, ARTHUR DEAN LEE. "Samuel Richardson and the Novel of
      Soliloquy." Ph.D. dissertation, Rutgers University.
          Dramatic influence in Richardson's fiction;
      Richardson's works are "shaped by his effort to reconcile
      fluid and subjective reality with timeless moral and social
      categories." Concludes that Richardson's thematic content
      is "dictated by" his form; discusses all three novels.
      Compare 1973.17.

*24   MORGAN, SUSAN JENNIFER. "The Changing Novel: Richardson,
      Austen, and Scott." Ph.D. dissertation, University of
      Chicago.
          Courtesy University of Chicago Library.

*25   O'CONNELLY, JIM. <u>Mistress</u> <u>Pamela</u> (motion picture). Based on
        the novel <u>Pamela, or Virtue Rewarded</u> by Samuel Richardson.
        Merlot Films, produced and directed with a script by Jim
        O'Connelly, distributed by MGM/EMI.
            A British sex farce based very loosely on <u>Pamela</u>. Not
        released in America. Source: American Film Institute
        Library, Washington DC; Motion Picture Institute of
        America Research Department, New York; British Film
        Institute Library, London. Reviewed by <u>The</u> <u>Times</u> (London),
        November 2, 1973, p. 13; R. Combs, <u>MFB</u> (1973), p. 253:
        "What the makers clearly had in mind was <u>Carry</u> <u>On</u> <u>Tom</u>
        <u>Jones</u>."

26   PALMER, WILLIAM J. "Two Dramatists: Lovelace and Richardson
        in <u>Clarissa</u>," SNNTS 5: 7-21.
            Argues that Lovelace, the "objective correlative" for
        Richardson's subconscious and the reflection of his
        unacknowledged desire for control over others, is in
        control of <u>Clarissa</u>; connects Richardson's
        self-identification as Lovelace with his obsessions as an
        artist.

27   PAULSON, RONALD. "All About Richardson." <u>SNNTS</u> 5:110-16.
            Review of E&K, noting a few additional biographical
        details. Paulson approves of E&K the researchers "but
        whenever the novels are in question [they are] replaced by
        a critic persona . . . a crusty, grumpy, somewhat
        old-fashioned type" who seems unaware that one can now be
        enthusiastic about the books. Discusses the moral-social
        confusion in Richardson, the moralistic versus the
        imaginative self, the liberating potential of the letter
        for the imaginative self.

28   PAWLYK, JOHN E. "<u>The</u> <u>Expedition</u> <u>of</u> <u>Humphrey</u> <u>Clinker</u>: Methods
        and Consequences of a Multiple First-Person Focus." Ph.D.
        dissertation, Syracuse University.
            Discusses Richardson, in particular <u>Pamela</u>, in
        comparison with Smollett's novel; concludes that Fielding
        may have influenced Smollett more greatly.

29   PONS, CHRISTIAN. "Richardson en 1973: à propos de <u>S.</u>
        <u>Richardson, A Biography</u>." <u>EA</u> 26: 296-308.
            Review of E&K, focused largely on Richardson's
        historical place in the development of bourgeois ideology
        and on his relevance for us today. Discards notion of

Richardson as a mediocre Puritan businessman taken "out of himself" by unconscious genius--in fact, Richardson was not strictly speaking a Puritan. Notes that some of his ideas, such as love from esteem and stress on earthly rewards, were in keeping with his time. Suggests that his bourgeois nature and his romanticism blended into naturalism.

30   RADER, RALPH W. "Defoe, Richardson, Joyce and the Concept of Form in the Novel." In <u>Autobiography, Biography and the Novel: Papers Read at the Clark Library Seminar, May 13, 1972</u>. Edited by William Matthews and Ralph W. Rader. Los Angeles: William Andrews Clark Memorial Library, 72 pp.
      <u>Pamela</u> is discussed specifically on pp. 34-40. A work of serious fiction, which <u>Pamela</u> is and <u>Moll Flanders</u> is not, is an objective fantasy that "suggests the possibility . . . of cathartically working out the shape of desire against the resistance of our ideals . . . and the objective conditions of experience." The "covert sense of potential prosperity" in <u>Pamela</u> is due not to the heroine's vulgarity but to the pressure of those desires, as is every detail in the book; detailed discussion of Mrs. Jewkes as an example of this.

31   SCHULZ, DIETER. "'Novel,' 'Romance,' and Popular Fiction in the First Half of the Eighteenth Century." <u>SP</u> 70: 77-91.
      Distinguishes between the romanticized novel or novella, the old high romance, and the new fiction; suggests that the third is a reaction against the first rather than the second. The terms "novel" and "romance" are not distinguished by Richardson or any other major writer but Smollett.

32   STAMPER, DONALD R. "Success and Openness in English Fiction from Richardson through Jane Austen." Ph.D. dissertation, University of Arkansas.
      Richardson's characters define success in terms of truth to conscience or recognition of their individuality by other characters.

33   STEEVES, EDNA L. "Pre-Feminism in Some Eighteenth-Century Novels." <u>Texas Quarterly</u> 16,3: 48-57.
      Women in Richardson are by nature limited, domestic, and subordinate to men.

34   TAYLOR, GORDON R. <u>The</u> <u>Angel-Makers</u> . . . Revised edition.
      London: Secker and Warburg.
         Richardson   is   cited   as   evidence   of   the
      eighteenth-century   search   for   perfection,   especially in
      women.

35   TOPF, MEL A. "<u>Pamela</u>." <u>PMLA</u> 88: 1190-91.
         Reply to Wilson, below. Suggests that it is not
      Pamela′s   scheming   but   her   subjectivism   that   Fielding
      attacks in <u>Shamela</u>, which is an attempt to discredit
      solipsism and "the implication that reality [is] an affair
      of the feelings."

36   VAN MARTER, SHIRLEY. "Richardson′s Revisions of <u>Clarissa</u> in
      the Second Edition." <u>SB</u> 26: 107-32.
         The revisions in the second edition of <u>Clarissa</u> reflect
      not   only   Richardson′s reactions to contemporary criticism
      but his development as an artist; they may be traced back
      to patterns of change begun eight to ten years before. The
      revisions show "his considerable strengths and special
      weaknesses."

*37   WATT, IAN. <u>Narodziny powiesci. Studia o Defoe′em,</u>
      <u>Richardsonie i Fieldingu</u>. Warszawa: Państwowy Instytut
      Wydawniczy, 402 pp.
         Polish   translation   of   1957.7.   Courtesy   of   Bib.
      Jagiellońska.

38   WERNIGG, FERDINAND. <u>Bibliographie österreichischer Drucke</u>
      <u>während der ′erweiterten Preisfreiheit′ 1781-1795</u>. Wiener
      Schriften, hft.   35.   Wien-München: Verlag Jugend und
      Volk.
         Material on <u>Richardsonaden</u> in novels   and   dramas;
      Richardson′s works were not printed in Austria during this
      period.

39   WILCOX, DELMAR C. "The Importance of Traditional Moral and
      Religious Analogies in the English Novel 1666-1760: Four
      Essays." Ph.D. dissertation, Brandeis University.
         Chapter 3, on <u>Pamela</u>, discusses Richardson′s use of
      traditional religious emblems to create a moral frame.

40   WILSON, STUART. "Richardson′s <u>Pamela</u>: An Interpretation."
      <u>PMLA</u> 88: 79-91.
         Discusses Pamela as an evolving character, tracing her

development from childish near-hysteria to an adulthood
free from trauma; much of the "action" and
"characterization" reflects her fears and erotic desires
and should be taken as her projection rather than as
objective narration. Replied to by 1973.32.

41   WOLFF, RENATE C. "Pamela as Myth and Dream." Costerus 7:
      223-35.
            Pamela is a dream-fantasy, revealing aspects of
      Richardson's imagination and social class as well as human
      nature; its heroine appropriates qualities of two
      conflicting codes and shows a divided mind about sex,
      social mobility, and the question of privacy vs.
      publicity.

42   WOOTEN, ELIZABETH HARPER. "Biblical Allusion in the Novels of
      Richardson." Ph.D. dissertation, University of Tennessee.
            Notes Biblical allusions in Richardson's three novels
      and discusses their uses, e.g. to show his moral and
      doctrinal position.

1974

1   ARORA, SUDESH VAID. "The Divided Mind: A Study of Selected
      Novels of Defoe and Richardson." Ph.D. dissertation, Kent
      State University.
            Analyzes Pamela and Clarissa, with Roxana and Moll
      Flanders, as expressions of the authors' feminism and in
      the light of Kate Millett's Sexual Politics; concludes
      that both are ambivalent toward feminism and that this
      ambivalence affects their novels.

2   BEHRENS, LAURENCE. "Plotting the Eighteenth-Century Novel:
      Narrative Constructs from Defoe to Goldsmith." Ph.D.
      dissertation, U.C.L.A.
            Chapters 4 and 5 examine Pamela and Clarissa, suggesting
      that the first works best as a melodrama and that the
      second succeeds at least partially through the skillfulness
      with which its plot is constructed.

3   BRAUDY, LEO. "Penetration and Impenetrability in Clarissa."
      In New Approaches to Eighteenth-Century Literature:
      Selected Papers from the English Institute. Edited by

Phillip Harth. New York and London: Columbia University Press, pp. 177-206.

The "praise of the necessary repression of sexuality" in Clarissa reflects a new concern with the nature of identity and the fear of its loss. Clarissa's sexual fear is connected with her fear of losing her identity; in the end she asserts her psychic independence by turning against her physical, vulnerable body. Notes use of language as an agent of attack and defense. (Cf. 1974.7.)

4   BRISSENDEN, R.F. Virtue in Distress: Studies in the Novel of Sentiment from Richardson to Sade. London: Macmillan, pp. 159-86 and passim.

Though Richardson is dealt with specifically in part 2, chapter 1 ("Clarissa: The Sentimental Tragedy"), all of Part 1, on the definition and history of Sentiment, is important background material. Notes the frequency with which the concept of benevolence is exploded in Clarissa, in which almost all relationships are dominated by the lust for power and the metaphor of warfare. "And yet one of the morals to be drawn from [this "sad and sorry story"] is that life without love is impossible: in a negative and perverse but yet profoundly moving way it demonstrates both the truth and the falsity of the assertion that man is by nature a benevolent creature."

Reviewed by Jocelyn Harris, SoRA 9 (1976): 151-54; Marilyn Butler, N&Q (1976), pp. 373-74.

5   BROPHY, ELIZABETH BERGEN. Samuel Richardson: The Triumph of Craft. Knoxville: University of Tennessee Press, 149 pp.

Discusses relationship between Richardson's expressed moral purpose and his artistic practice. His precepts were artistic purpose, moral purpose, reader engagement, and realism through the epistolary form. Real moral tension and art go together in his books; the lack of them seriously damages Pamela II and Sir Charles Grandison, while a lack of art in presenting B's character damages Pamela. An appendix argues that Richardson's "nervous complaint" was Parkinson's disease.

Reviewed by Marilyn Butler (see 1974.4).

6   BUTLER, SYDNEY JAMES. "Masks of Reality: The Rhetoric of Narration in the Eighteenth-Century English Novel." Ph.D. dissertation, University of British Columbia.

Modes of narration as conveyor of realism in

eighteenth-century fiction including Richardson's.

7   BYRD, MAX. <u>Visits</u> <u>to</u> <u>Bedlam</u>: <u>Madness</u> <u>and</u> <u>Literature</u> <u>in</u> <u>the</u>
     <u>Eighteenth</u> <u>Century</u>. Columbia, S.C.: University of South
     Carolina Press, pp. 89-90.
         Letter 153 of the <u>Familiar</u> <u>Letters</u> shows an unusual
     charity toward the mad. Notes the connection in Richardson
     between sensuality and loss of personality. (Cf. 1974.3.)

8   CARROLL, JOHN. "Richardson." In <u>The</u> <u>English</u> <u>Novel</u>: <u>Select</u>
     <u>Bibliographical</u> <u>Guides</u>. Edited by A.E. Dyson. London:
     Oxford University Press, pp. 56-70.
         Analytic introduction to the basic critical approaches
     to Richardson, with a bibliography.

9   COHAN, STEVEN M. "Fiction and the Creation of Character."
     Ph.D. dissertation, U.C.L.A.
         Chapter 3 studies the characters of <u>Clarissa</u>.

10   DOODY, MARGARET A. <u>A</u> <u>Natural</u> <u>Passion</u>: <u>A</u> <u>Study</u> <u>of</u> <u>the</u> <u>Novels</u>
     <u>of</u> <u>Samuel</u> <u>Richardson</u>. Oxford: Clarendon Press, 410 pp.
         Critical synthesis and survey of the novels with due
     attention to <u>Pamela</u> <u>II</u>. Special emphases on Richardson's
     sources and their effect on his imagery; the originality
     of that imagery; the theme of the inner world of emotion;
     the interrelationship of the novels; the implications of
     "heroinism"; and the process of consciousness as an
     aesthetic shaping force. Detailed and sympathetic
     discussion of the "much underrated" <u>Grandison</u>.
         Reviewed by Jocelyn Harris, <u>ECS</u> 10 (1976);   F.W.
     Bradbrook, <u>N&Q</u> (1976), pp. 371-73; <u>EA</u> 29 (1976): 611-12;
     <u>RES</u> NS 27 (1976): 81-84; <u>PQ</u> 55: 515-18.

11   DUSSINGER, JOHN A. "<u>Pamela</u>: Toward the Governance of Time"
     and "<u>Clarissa</u>: The Curse of Intellect." In his <u>Discourse</u>
     <u>of</u> <u>the</u> <u>Mind</u> <u>in</u> Eighteenth-Century <u>Fiction</u>. SEL 80. The
     Hague: Mouton, pp. 53-126.
         In <u>Pamela</u>, fiction is a representation of how the mind
     orders experience; "Richardson's fictional art is of a
     piece with the century's <u>episteme</u> and represents the self
     as the role-playing of multiple identities in unstable
     relationships with others." The discourse of <u>Pamela</u> is both
     a wish-fulfillment and a picture of "thinking . . . ever
     an instant short of completion," in which the "individual
     mind [is] passive in consciousness, continually deluded in

judgments of the moment, and finally dependent on
involuntary processes for stability." The conflict is
finally that among the various levels of a mind.
Clarissa's behavior is explicable in terms of Freud's
theory of the death instinct; her rebellion against
parental and male authority is expressed by rejecting the
body.

12 ENGEL, GISELA. Individuum, Familie, und Gesellschaft in den
    Romanen Richardsons: eine literatursōziologische Studie.
    [Frankfurt am Main:] Akademische Verlagsgesellschaft, 212
    pp.
        The Richardsonian family is both a structure in itself
    and a reflection of the real nature of bourgeois family
    life in the eighteenth century. Richardson dramatizes
    bourgeois individualism as an economically necessary
    principle propagated by Protestantism. Pamela's various
    relationships show the dilemmas of bourgeois individualism,
    developing bourgeois society, and the economic role of
    women. Engel draws attention to imagery of wealth and to
    discussions of social climbing. Clarissa, whose book is
    more realistic than Pamela and set in a higher social
    sphere, is an object of speculation for her family and a
    rebel from it; the book contains imagery of control and
    duties and many familial patterns. In the atmosphere of
    the time, familial social problems are perceived as moral
    problems. The family structure appears to break down
    before the principle of individualism. Sir Charles
    Grandison presents a family structure of organized
    individuals; but many of the conflicts have been removed,
    as we may see particularly through the absence of
    conventional family structures and in the special treatment
    given Sir Charles. Bibliography, pp. 198-212.

13 FOUGÈRES, MICHEL. "Clarissa." In his Liebestod dans le Roman
    français, anglais et allemand au dix-huitième siècle.
    Ottawa: Naaman, pp. 87-122.
        The criteria of the Liebestod theme are: fatal love;
    exceptional protagonists; the consecration of love through
    the death of the heroic protagonists; the sublimation of
    love through a union beyond death. Puts Clarissa in the
    tradition, attacking the idea that the heroine is
    masochistic (rather, "[elle] est de la race des grandes
    amoureuses . . . [mais] dans la contradiction de
    l'attirance du coeur et de l'effroi des sens") and

suggesting common elements linking Lovelace to Don Juan, Faust, and Tristan.

*14   GHIGI POGGI, VALENTINA.   Messaggio e mito in Clarissa di Samuel Richardson. Modena: Goliardica, 185 pp.
         Source: MLA Bibliography.

15   GREENSTEIN, SUSAN MITCHELL. "The Negative Principle and the Virtuous Character Undercutting in the Work of Richardson, Austen and James." Ph.D. dissertation, Indiana University.
         Examines the process of undercutting the good character to disarm envy and obtain belief in the character's virtue. Clarissa establishes in English fiction the device of "situational undercutting," to bring the patterns of social intercourse into question.

16   HARDWICK, ELIZABETH. "Seduction and Betrayal." In her Seduction and Betrayal: Women and Literature. New York: Random House, pp. 177-208.
         Psychological study of Clarissa and Lovelace as victim and seducer; Hardwick is impressed by the "sordid" power of the novel and by its style. "The novelist . . . understands cruelty in his own angular, disguised way." Discusses connection between subject and epistolary form.

17   HURLEY, ANDREW. "In a Manner of Speaking: Narrative Aesthetics for Non-Third-Person Fiction." Ph.D. dissertation, Rice University.
         Aesthetics of the limited point of view; Chapter 5 discusses Pamela as an example of epistolary fiction.

18   KURTH-VOIGHT, LIESELOTTE E. Perspectives and Points of View: The Early Works of Wieland and their Background. Baltimore: Johns Hopkins University Press, pp. 23, 44, 51-52, 114, 126.
         Briefly discusses effect of Richardson's works on Wieland. Courtesy Prof. Lieselotte Kurth.

19   LIEBOWITZ, JUDITH. "The Poetics of Salvation in Clarissa, La nouvelle Héloïse, and Die Leiden des jungen Werthers." In Proceedings: Pacific Northwest Conference on Foreign Languages. 25th Annual Meeting . . . 25 pt. 1 (Literature and Linguistics). Corvallis, Ore.: Oregon State University, pp. 242-45.
         The quality of the feelings, not the abnegation of the

self, becomes increasingly the eighteenth-century criterion
of salvation. Traces the process from <u>Clarissa</u> toward the
Romantics.

*20   LYONS, PETER A. "Confidante to the Principal: A Study of
       Richardson's Use of Anna Howe." <u>Graduate</u> <u>English</u> <u>Papers</u>
       (Arizona) 6 pt. 1: 7-8.
          Source: <u>MLA</u> <u>Bibliography</u>.

*21   METCALF, BRIAN R. "The New Fiction of Samuel Richardson."
       Ph.D. dissertation, University of Toronto.
          Source: Bib. de l'Université de Laval.

22   MILLER, NANCY KIPNIS. "Gender and Genre: An Analysis of
       Literary Femininity in the Eighteenth-Century Novel." Ph.D.
       dissertation, Columbia University.
          Nine novels, including <u>Clarissa</u> and <u>Pamela</u>, discussed as
       generic representations of femininity. Each has in common
       a "founding opposition of virtue to non-virtue--chaste vs.
       non-chaste," and each includes three "significant moments
       of the feminine trajectory." Semantic and structural
       discussion.

23   OLDERMAN, STAR SCHECHTER. "Public and Private Values in the
       World of Richardson's Novels." Ph.D. dissertation, Indiana
       University.
          Discussion of clash between private, questioning
       morality and the moral certainty of a powerful and hostile
       world.

24   OLIVIER, THEO. "'Pamela' and 'Shamela': A Reassessment." <u>ESA</u>
       17 pt. 2: 59-70.
          Denies that Fielding satirizes the "true" <u>Pamela</u> in
       <u>Shamela</u>, since Richardson's moral oppositions in his first
       novel are by no means simple; however, Fielding does begin
       to discover the true Fielding, using satire to inculcate
       positive values.

25   PARTRIDGE, ERIC. <u>The</u> <u>French</u> <u>Romantics'</u> <u>Knowledge</u> <u>of</u> <u>English</u>
       <u>Literature</u>. Geneva: Slatkine.
          Reprint of 1924 edition.

26   RAWSON, C.J. "Language, Dialogue, and Point of View in
       Fielding: Some Considerations." In <u>Quick</u> <u>Springs</u> <u>of</u> <u>Sense</u>:
       <u>Studies</u> <u>in</u> <u>the</u> <u>Eighteenth</u> <u>Century</u>. Edited by Larry S.

Champion.   Athens,   Ga.:   University of Georgia Press, pp.
137-56.
   Linguistic indicators in Fielding and Richardson   as   an
index of class, personal character, and degree of authorial
intervention.

27   RICHARDSON, SAMUEL and   others.   Richardsoniana.   25v.   New
York: Garland Publishing Co., 1974-75.
   Part of the   series,   Life   and   Times   of   Seven   Major
British Writers. All are facsimile editions.
   Volume 1: Richardson, Samuel.   The Apprentice's Vade
Mecum   (1734)   and   A   Seasonable   Examination   (1735).   2:
Richardson, Samuel.   Aesop's   Fables   (1739).   3:   Pamela
Parodied   I: [Fielding, Henry?]   An Apology for the Life of
Mrs.   Shamela Andrews .   .   .   (1741).   Pamela Censured
(1741).   4,5:   Pamela Imitated I: Kelly, John.   Pamela's
Conduct in High   Life   (1741).   6:   Pamela   Parodied   II:
[Haywood, Eliza?] Anti-Pamela . . 7: Pamela Imitated II:
[Villaret, Claude?] Antipamela .   .   .   (1742).   Lettre sur
Pamela (1742).
   9:   Pamela Imitated IV: Pamela   in   High   Life   (1741).
10:   Anti-Pamela: Povey, Charles.   The Virgin in Eden .   .
. (1741);   Memoirs   of   the   Life   of   Lady   H   .   .   .
(1741--not,   incidentally,   in   any   strict   sense   an
"anti-Pamela").   11:   Pamela   Summarized: The   Life   of
Pamela   (1741).   12:   Pamela   on   Stage: Dance,   James.
Pamela .   .   .   (1741).   Giffard,   Henry.   Pamela   (1741).
Edge, Mr. Pamela .   .   .   (1742). Goldoni, Carlo. Pamela
(1756).   13:   Critical   Remarks   on   Clarissa: Remarks   on
Clarissa (1749).   CriticalRemarks on Sir Charles Grandison,
Clarissa and Pamela (1754). Plum[m]er, Francis.   A   Candid
Examination   .   .   .   (1754).   14:   Richardson Adapted for
Children: The Paths   of   Virtue Delineated (1756).   15:
Richardson   on   Clarissa: Richardson, Samuel.   Meditations
Collected from   the   Sacred Books .   .   .   (1750).   16-19:
Richardson's   England: Defoe,   Daniel.   A Tour thro' the
Whole Island of Great Britain (1742).   20-21:   Reviewed   by
Richardson: Lussan,   Marguerite   de.   The Life and Heroic
Actions   of   Balbe   Berton   .   .   .   (1760).   22-25:   A
Richardsonian   Novel: Meades,   Anna.   The History of Sir
William Harrington (1771).

28   RICHARDSON, SAMUEL.   Pamela.   Ed. M.F.   Shugrue.   4v.   New
York: Garland Publishing.
   Facsimile reprint of 1801 text of Pamela I and   II;   in

the series, The Flowering of the Novel. See 1978.4. The
same base-text, with variants from the 1810 edition, was
published by Penguin in 1981, edited by Peter Sabor with an
introduction by Margaret Doody.

29   ---, abridged by ?. The History of Pamela; or, Virtue
       Rewarded. Abridged from the Works of Samuel Richardson,
       Esq. Norristown [Pa.]: David Sower, 1799. Repr.
       Millwood, N.Y.: KTO Microform, 2 sheets.
            Rosenbach Collection of Early American Children's
       Literature, item 248. See 1799.7.

30   ---. The History of Pamela . . . Worcester [Mass.]:
       Isaiah Thomas, 1794. Repr. Millwood, N.Y.: KTO
       Microform, 2 sheets.
            Rosenbach 182; see 1794.2.

31   ---. The Paths of Virtue Delineated . . . Philadelphia:
       W. Woodhouse, 1791. Repr. Millwood, N.Y.: KTO
       Microform, 2 sheets.
            Rosenbach 152; see 1791.8. This is Clarissa only.

32   ---. The Paths of Virtue Delineated . . . Cooperstown: E.
       Phinney, 1795. Repr. Millwood, N.Y.: KTO Microform, 2
       sheets.
            Rosenbach 199; see 1795.7. Clarissa only.

32A   ROGERS, PAT. "Richardson." In his Augustan Vision. London:
       Weidenfeld and Nicolson, New York: Harper and Row, pp.
       267-74.
            Richardson in his Augustan context; biographical and
       critical introduction.

33   ROUSSEL, ROY. "Reflections on the Letter: The Reconciliation
       of Distance and Presence in Pamela." ELH 41: 375-99.
            In the familiar letter the writer both withdraws from
       the world and asserts a presence in it. Distance is used
       to symbolize the protective separation between the lower
       class and the structured social conventions of the higher;
       love attempts to transcend this separation, a transcendence
       allowed partly through "exposure" (Roussel notes importance
       of dress and disrobing as metaphors). Love forms a Divine
       society, which is created by writing, and the status of
       writing is explicitly associated with the status of the
       self that flows from the writing.

34   RUSSELL,   ANN   ZIMMERMAN.   "The   Image   of   Women   in
        Eighteenth-Century   English   Novels."   Ph.D.   dissertation,
        Brandeis University.
            Compares real eighteenth-century women with the
        "idealized heroine" of eighteenth-century novels including
        Pamela and Clarissa.

35   TAYLOR,   ETHEL   FRANKLIN.   "Imagery   in   Samuel   Richardson´s
        Clarissa."   Ph.D.   dissertation,   Indiana   University.
            Discussion of patterns of imagery, concentrating on
        sensory,   archetypal,   and   figurative   images;   finds   that
        sensory   imagery   predominates   at   beginning   of   book,
        figurative more and more toward end.

36   VAN MARTER, SHIRLEY. "Hidden Virtue: An Unsolved Problem in
        Clarissa." YES 4:   140-48.
            Revisions in the character of Hickman, as well as in
        Clarissa and Lovelace´s characters, in the editions of 1748
        through 1759 show Richardson trying to balance the
        competing claims of artistry and morality.   Hickman´s
        character ought both to embody a particular type of good
        and to fulfill a necessary supporting role in the novel;
        Richardson does not succeed, even through revision, in
        wholly harmonizing the two functions.

*37   VIGLIENO, LAURENCE. "Richardson et Rousseau devant la loi du
        père: Tentative de psychocritique comparée." In Etudes et
        recherches de littérature générale et comparée. Annales de
        la Faculté des Lettres et Sciences Humaines de Nice 22.
        [Paris:] Belles Lettres, pp. 167-79.
            Source: MLA Bibliography 1978, item 5523.

38   WATT, IAN. Der bürgerliche Roman . . .   [Frankfurt a.M.:]
        Suhrkamp, 402 pp.
            German translation of 1957.7.

39   WILLS, ANTONY. "The World of Clarissa." Rendezvous 9, 1:
        1-14.
            "The world of Clarissa" is one of moral absolutes,
        embodied in sexual-Biblical linguistic equations, the
        psychological relations between Lovelace and Clarissa, and
        the many references to vice; points out deep pessimism of
        book, in which "the world" becomes defined as the Johannine
        kosmos, that world that is the Christian´s enemy.

1975

1   BLONDEL, MADELEINE. "Images de la femme dans le roman anglais
     de 1740 à 1771." Ph.D. dissertation, University of Paris
     III. Published: 2v. Lille: Atelier réproduction des
     thèses, Paris: Librairie Honoré Champion, 1976.
          Richardson's characters are cited as examples of various
     categorizations of women.

2   BOUDREAUX, DAVID ELLIOTT. "An Annotated Bibliography of the
     Criticisms and Editions of Samuel Richardson (1895-1974)."
     Ph.D. dissertation, University of Arkansas.
          Annotated, indexed, organized by subject.

3   CARROLL, JOHN. "On Annotating <u>Clarissa</u>." In <u>Editing
     Eighteenth-Century Novels: Papers on Fielding, Lesage,
     Richardson . . . Given at the Conference on Editorial
     Problems, University of Toronto, November 1973.</u> Edited by
     Gerald E. Bentley, Jr. Toronto: Hakkert, pp. 49-66.
          On the problems of annotating <u>Clarissa</u>: Richardson,
     though frequently drawing on familiar sources, is also
     often obscure. Notes on apppriateness of quotations, their
     sources.

3   CLARK, JOHN R. "Unnoticed Satire: <u>Pamela</u>'s Shape and Form."
     <u>ScholS</u> 1 pt. 1: 32-37.
          Points out scabrous puns and double-entendres as well as
     the "hourglass" shape of the book.

4   CONNAUGHTON, MICHAEL EDWARD. "Samuel Richardson's Novels:
     Style and the Uses of Literature." Ph.D. dissertation,
     Indiana University.
          Points out uses of allusion in the novels; notes
     Richardson's large debt to Bysshe's <u>Art of English Poetry</u>.
     (Cf. 1948.2A.)

*5   DANEK, DAUNTA. "Nos a żydka: O powieściowych spisach
     rzeczy." <u>Teksty</u> 22: 50-71.
          On the use of indexes in novels; material on
     Richardson. Source: <u>YWMLS</u>.

6   FRANK, FREDERICK S. "From Boudoir to Castle Crypt:
     Richardson and the Gothic Novel." <u>RLV</u> 41: 49-59.
          Richardson prefigures several important elements of the
     Gothic novel: episodes of terror, the "Gothic esthetic of

pleasure in pain," the polarization of the sexual contest in melodrama, an interest in the psychology of evil, and an ambivalence in its presentation.

7   GRIEDER, JOSEPHINE. <u>Translations</u> <u>of</u> <u>French</u> <u>Sentimental</u> <u>Prose</u> <u>Fiction</u> <u>in</u> <u>Late</u> <u>Eighteenth-Century</u> <u>England:</u> <u>The</u> <u>History</u> <u>of</u> <u>a</u> <u>Literary</u> <u>Vogue</u>. Durham, N.C.:   Duke University Press, 136 pp.
     Bibliographic background material.

8   HILSON, J.C. and ROSALIND NICOL. "Two Notes on <u>Sir</u> <u>Charles</u> <u>Grandison</u>:   1.   The Name ´Grandison´;   2.   Grandison´s Italian Journey: A Source." <u>N&Q</u> 22:492-93.
     The Earl of Grandison, dedicatee of Ogilvie´s translation of Pietro Giannone´s <u>Civil</u> <u>History</u> <u>of</u> <u>the</u> <u>Kingdom</u> <u>of</u> <u>Naples</u>, which Richardson printed in 1729, may have served as a source for Sir Charles, sharing the name and the domestic virtue. The crossing of Mont Cenis may have been taken from <u>An</u> <u>Account</u> <u>of</u> <u>the</u> <u>Glacieres</u> <u>or</u> <u>Ice</u> <u>Alps</u> <u>in</u> <u>Savoy</u> (1744); since parts of the text in <u>Grandison</u> resemble the French original more than its English translation, the person who helped Richardson compose the letter may have known French.

9   HOFFELD, LAURA DIAMOND. "The Servant Heroine in Eighteenth- and Nineteenth-Century British Fiction: The Social Reality and its Image in the Novel." Ph.D. dissertation, New York University.
     Studies <u>Pamela</u> as one of the two patterns of servant behavior in fiction, "the woman as moral template for man."

10   JACOBSON, MARGARET CHARLOTTE KINGSLAND. "Women in the Novels of Defoe, Richardson and Fielding." Ph.D. dissertation, University of Connecticut.
     Feminist critique of eighteenth-century novels including Richardson´s (Chs. 2,3), concentrating on implications of "instruction" of women and "delight" of readers. Discusses popularity of persecuted maiden theme.

11   KEARNEY, ANTHONY. <u>Samuel</u> <u>Richardson:</u> <u>Clarissa</u>. SEL 55. London: Edward Arnold, 65 pp.
     Ably introduces <u>Clarissa</u> to the general reader; suggests patterns of design, compares Clarissa and Lovelace, warns against too purely social reading, notes disparity between stated and actual themes. Feels that

"The first parts of <u>Clarissa</u> stand up very well to a comparison with Austen and James, and in some things one feels he really bettered them," though more crudely.
Reviewed by F.W. Bradbrook, <u>N&Q</u> 1976, pp. 520-21.

12   MACANDREW, ELIZABETH. "Courtly-Genteel or Moral-Didactic?   A Response to Carey McIntosh." <u>SECC</u> 4:155-59.
Suggests that the nominal style of <u>Clarissa</u> (see 1975.23 below) supports, not her gentility, but her moral discrimination.

13   MCINTOSH, CAREY. "Quantities of Qualities: Nominal Style and the Novel." <u>SECC</u> 4: 139-53.
On the use of the nominal style (depending heavily on nouns rather than verbs) in <u>Clarissa</u> and other novels; in the early volumes of <u>Clarissa</u> it "adds a certain presumptive dignity" to the Harlowes´ schemes, while in later volumes Clarissa herself uses it to express complicated states of mind. It is used to stress not action but the quality of possessing a certain attribute; it allows extensive and subtle personification of qualities; it implies mutual obligation; and it fits in well with the epistolary style, a relatively actionless format in which "the abstractions being balanced and arranged are . . . psychological and moral."

14   MOYNIHAN, ROBERT D. "Clarissa and the Enlightened Woman as Literary Heroine." <u>JHI</u> 36: 159-66.
The moral and religious freedom of women (as exemplified in, for instance, Defoe´s <u>Religious Courtship</u> and <u>Family Instructor</u>, both printed by Richardson) is set in <u>Clarissa</u> against the moral opacity of the Harlowes´ "family interest." Clarissa´s isolated and tragic grandeur come from her sense of feminine dignity and worth.

15   MUNRO, JAMES S. "Richardson, Marivaux, and the French Romance Tradition." <u>MLR</u> 70: 752-59.
The presence in Richardson´s work of the French romance convention, the "surprise de l´amour," throws light on his relationship with Marivaux and on the origins of the theme of psychological analysis in the French and English novel.

16   NAPIER, ELIZABETH R. "´Tremble and Reform´: The Inversion of Power in Richardson´s <u>Clarissa</u>." <u>ELH</u> 42: 214-23.
Clarissa, originally a passive victim, becomes the

victor; metaphors and themes of power and its exchange, of drama, hunting, predators, disguises, temporal control, the "moment," houses, and Fate are transmuted to serve her.

17   RICHARDSON, SAMUEL. The Apprentice's Vade Mecum. Edited with an introduction by Alan Dugald McKillop. ARS 169-70. Los Angeles: Clark Memorial Library, UCLA, 84 pp.

*18   ---. Pamela, Translated into Oriya [an Indian language] by Subodh Kumar Chattopadhyay. Cuttack: Agraduta, 67 pp.
          Presumably an abridgment. Courtesy National Library of India.

19   ROGERS, PAT. "Samuel Richardson and Defoe's Tour (1738): The Evidence of Bibliography." SB 28: 305-7.
          Deduces that Richardson acted as editor as well as printer of the second edition of the Tour.

20   SIEGEL, JUNE SIGLER. "Diderot and Richardson: Manuscripts, Missives, and Mysteries." DidS 18: 145-67.
          Argues that Richardson's influence over Diderot was most marked from autumn 1761 to summer 1762; summarizes Richardson's uses for the Grimm-Diderot circle (largely as a stick to beat Rousseau with); discusses whether the French or English Clarissa was used in the Eloge; analyzes two episodes from the Eloge.

21   SKONNORD, JOHN ANDREW. "Richardson, Rousseau, Goethe and Laclos: A Study of Four Epistolary Novelists." Ph.D. dissertation, University of Minnesota.
          Analyzes effect, structure, reader relationship to book in four novels including Clarissa; shorter discussion of Pamela.

22   SMIDT, KRISTIAN. "Character and Plot in the Novels of Samuel Richardson." CritQ 17: 155-66.
          Argues that in Richardson character and plot work together well, though his success is partially obscured by his moralizing and lack of economy.

23   SMITH, SARAH W.R. "Mastering the Heart: From the Moral Novel to a Theoretics of Value in the Work of Samuel Richardson." Ph.D. dissertation, Harvard University.
          General study of Richardson's works with emphasis on convergence of moral purpose and style to create an

emergent Sentimentalism. The problem of the split in characterization between exemplarity and individuality is solved by making the paradigmatic exemplar an exemplary action, knowledge of the self; both Clarissa and Lovelace fail at this in similar ways, and <u>Clarissa</u> shows the almost complete inability of the new psychological novel to carry didactic moral force. Suggests that <u>Sir Charles Grandison</u> is a fully Sentimental novel but that its "comic" triumph is partial and fragmentary; the Sentimental novel at its best is an essentially pessimistic and anti-didactic form.

24   VAN MARTER, SHIRLEY. "Richardson's Revisions of <u>Clarissa</u> in the Third and Fourth Editions." <u>SB</u> 28: 119-52.
        Argues that the first and third editions of <u>Clarissa</u> are the only ones from which an editor might select a copy-text; suggests that the revisions in later editions of the book are not primarily motivated by criticism from contemporary readers.

1976

1   ANON. <u>Pamela Censured</u> <u>(1741)</u>. Edited with an introduction by Charles Batten, Jr. ARS 175. Los Angeles: Clark Memorial Library, UCLA, 83 pp.

2   ALBERT, THEODORE GIBBS. "1. The Law vs. Clarissa Harlowe. . . . " Ph.D. dissertation, Rutgers University.
        Part 1 of this dissertation discusses relationship of <u>Clarissa</u> to eighteenth-century law.

3   BABB, HOWARD S. "Richardson's Narrative Mode in <u>Clarissa</u>." <u>SEL</u> 16: 451-60.
        Notes the power of the epistolary mode to create constant motion through a constant choice of alternatives that, when chosen, solidify themselves and beget further alternatives. Example of Lovelace's letter from St. Albans.

4   BALL, DONALD L. "Richardson's Resourceful Wordmaking." <u>SAB</u> 41 pt. 4: 56-65.
        Richardson's invented words subtilize the processes of inward perception; they describe conduct compactly and denominate manners, attitudes, and acts. Richardson uses

the noun as a major part of his wordmaking, creates an
equivalent for <u>marivaudage</u>, and to a limited extent
develops a specifically feminine dialect.
      Cf. 1951.4 and 1975.13.

5   BEASLEY, JERRY C. "Romance and the ´New´ Novels of
      Richardson, Fielding and Smollett." <u>SEL</u> 16: 437-50.
            Parallels between popular novels of the 1740s and the
      "new fiction" include the use of romance and satire,
      especially political satire, a prejudice against the
      marvellous, and the advocacy of the theory of <u>la belle</u>
      <u>nature</u>. Though this fiction has debts to romance it is
      generally anti-romantic, socially relevant, and realistic.

6   COHAN, STEVEN M. "<u>Clarissa</u> and the Individuation of
      Character." <u>ELH</u> 43: 163-83.
            <u>Clarissa</u> is the first novel to exploit the tension
      between the personal and the typical, creating character by
      it; the epistolary form allows us to see characters both
      internally and externally, from both their own viewpoint
      and others´, in both the ´single, portentous moment´ and
      the flux of changing identity. In both main characters,
      egocentric drive tends to compensate for lack of true
      knowledge of self.

7   COX, RICHARD ALLEN. "Judgment of Character in Richardson´s
      Novels." Ph.D. dissertation, University of Texas at
      Austin.
            Christian faith, prayerfulness, humility, and
      subservience to Providence form the basis of Richardson´s
      judgment of his characters; he expects his readers to
      judge them similarly. Discusses Richardson´s similarity to
      Locke in advocating self-control as the basis for education
      toward virtue.

8   DRUCE, ROBERT. "Jane, Heiress to Pamela?" <u>DQR</u> 6: 164-90.
            Compares <u>Pamela</u> and <u>Jane Eyre</u>.

9   DUPREE, NANCY BARKER. "The Comic in the Novels of Samuel
      Richardson." Ph.D. dissertation, Auburn University.
            Theory of comedy and process of production of comedy in
      Richardson´s novels; comedy is used in highly complex ways
      as indication of character and moral value.

10   ERICKSON, ROBERT A. "Mother Jewkes, Pamela, and the
      Midwives." <u>ELH</u> 43: 500-516.
            Much of the success of the passages detailing Pamela´s

struggles with Mrs. Jewkes comes from the connection of both characters with the "folklore of midwifery and witchcraft." Parallels descriptions of Jewkes with those of witches and (bad) midwives; notes power of birth-death metaphors and sexual linguistic overtones.

11   GILLIS, CHRISTINA MARSDEN. "Images of Privacy in Richardson's Clarissa." Ph.D. dissertation, Bryn Mawr.
        "The epistolary novel . . . is particulaly concerned with the publicizing of private space." The structure of the novel involves continual transformation of private experience into public form through metaphors of space, "exposure" of the heart, and language of confinement and release.

12   HARRIS, JOCELYN M. "The Reviser Observed: The Last Volume of Sir Charles Grandison." SB 29: 1-31.
        Explains the oddness of the last volume of Grandison--"aesthetically wayward, digressive, and often distorting to characterisation and probability"--by suggesting that Richardson revised in proof in order to make his work "morally invulnerable." Correlates criticism and revisions.

13   HUNT, RUSSELL A. "Johnson on Fielding and Richardson: A Problem in Literary Moralism." HAR 27:412-20.
        Johnson dispraises Fielding because Fielding's morality depends on "good nature," which becomes a substitute for virtue. But Richardson's ethic is based on reason, and Richardson's idea of mixed characters is more profound than Fielding's.

14   KELLY, GARY. The English Jacobin Novel. Oxford: Clarendon, 303 pp.
        Finds Richardson's influence strong in all the four major authors studied (Bage, Inchbald, Holcroft, and Godwin); discusses individual cases of influence.

15   LEGATES, MARLENE. "The Cult of Womanhood in Eighteenth-Century Thought." ECS 10:21-39.
        Among models for the chaste maiden and obedient wife, the new ideals of the eighteenth century, are Pamela and Clarissa, "divine" because embodying traditional ideals of religion, family, and the state. They marry or die but cannot rebel. Virtue is an upper-class characteristic

(Pamela's reward is rise to her "true" class). Richardson's novels are about the rise of the bourgeois family.

16   NOBLE, YVONNE. "Clarissa: Paradise Irremediably Lost." SVEC 154: 1529-45.
      Clarissa is a re-imagining of Paradise Lost, relocating moral conflict in the modern private family; but here Paradise is irremediably lost. "Clarissa is a myth of life as unliveable" in which conscious Christian impulse is transmuted into a "lowering fatalistic imagination," the cosmic panorama is fragmented into local empirical time and multiple points of view, and the ending proves the impotence of Clarissa's transcendence. Cf. 1968.4.

17   PARK, WILLIAM. "Clarissa as Tragedy." SEL 16: 461-71.
      Compares Clarissa and Tom Jones, seeing many similarities in themes and language, but noting Richardson's strategies for turning potential comedy, even Lovelace's, into tragic form.

18   POOVEY, MARY. "Journeys from This World to the Next: The Providential Promise in Clarissa and Tom Jones." ELH 43: 300-315.
      Disagrees with Park, above; Fielding and Richardson are not similar since their characters and their conceptions of the nature of truth differ widely. Both books are "fictionalized expressions of the Christian epic" but Richardson perceives that absolute realism is incompatible with temporal rewards, while Fielding believes the two can be reconciled metaphorically. The significant understanding in Clarissa is the heroine's understanding of herself while in Tom Jones "social situations and behavior . . . provide vehicles for the controlling providential metaphor"; progress is defined by clarification rather than development; and characterization is often static and single-principled. The narrator serves as a perceptual norm.

*19   RAY, J. KAREN. "The Feminine Role in Robinson Crusoe, Roxana and Clarissa." ESRS 24 pt. 3: 28-33.
      Comparison of femininity in Defoe and Richardson; source: MLA Bibliography.

20   ROGERS, KATHARINE M. "Sensitive Feminism vs. Conventional
      Sympathy: Richardson and Fielding on Women." Novel 9:
      256-70. Reprinted in The Authority of Experience: Essays
      in Feminist Criticism. Edited by Arlyn Diamond and Lee R.
      Edwards. Amherst: University of Massachusetts Press,
      1977, pp. 118-36.
         While Fielding's women are submissive by socially
      trained instinct, Richardson's women show the author
      examining traditional assumptions about male-female
      relationships, though in the context of his time; he
      dramatizes the negative elements of the myth of romantic
      love through Anna Howe's suppressed hostility and
      Lovelace's character. The greater positive femininity of
      Richardson's characters is shown by their submission to the
      moral law, the women's greater capacity for friendship with
      other women, their radical attitudes toward marriage, and
      the possibility of intellectual equality between men and
      women.

21   ROUSSEAU, G.S. "Sensibility." Studies in the Eighteenth
      Century 3. Edited by R.F. Brissenden and J.C. Eade.
      Toronto and Buffalo: University of Toronto Press, pp.
      137-57.
         Richardson is among authors cited in an article on
      Locke, Willis, and the rise of sensibility from
      physiological theory.

22   SACKS, SHELDON. "Novelists as Storytellers." MP 73, 4, pt.
      2: 97-109.
         Defends the story as not merely aesthetic dead weight;
      discusses and defends Clarissa.

23   SANDLER, SUSAN JANET. "'A Continual Fervour': Samuel
      Richardson and the Making of Clarissa." Ph.D.
      dissertation, New York University.
         Discussion of Clarissa as "conscious and deliberate art
      of a high order."

*24   SCIULLO, L. "Pamela da Richardson a Goldoni." Quaderni di
      Lingue e Letterature, Universita degli Studi (Padova
      [published in Pisa]) 1: 117-21.
         Courtesy Prof. Carl Berkhout and Dott. Gian Albino
      Ravalli Modoni (Director, Bib. Naz. Marciana).

25   SLATTERY, WILLIAM C. "From Richardson to Wolff and Deken:
      Comic Devices in Willem Leevend." In Reisgidsen vol
      Belluno´s en Blauwbaarden: Opstellen over S. Vestdijk en
      anderen aangeboden aan Dr. H.A. Wage. Leiden: Vakgroep
      Nederlandse Taal- en Letterkunde, pp. 141-47.
         The variety of epistolary styles, taken over from
      Richardson, gives strength to Wolff and Deken´s humor in
      Willm Leevend. (Thanks to Prof. Slattery.)

26   SPACKS, PATRICIA MEYER. "The Sense of Audience: Samuel
      Richardson, Colley Cibber." In her Imagining a Self . . .
      Cambridge, Mass.: Harvard University Press, pp. 193-226.
         Writing is performance, process, revelatory affectation,
      and intrinsically meaningful act in Pamela and Cibber´s
      Apology. Writing provokes questions of language,
      narratorial identity, and genre ("in a sense her pride as
      author protects her virtue": Pamela´s becoming B´s
      mistress would not have made a sufficiently unusual story).
      Each dramatizes directly to an audience; Spacks notes the
      pervasive theatricality and "the power of external
      judgment" in Pamela, in which reality is gained through the
      successful manipulation of appearance. "The pursuit of
      honor and the awareness of audience" shapes each book.

27   WATT, IAN. Le Origini del romanzo borghese. Translated by
      Luigi Del Grosso Destrieri. Milan: Bompieri.
         Italian translation of 1957.7.

28   ZACH, WOLFGANG. "Richardson and the Dedication to the Earl of
      Grandison in Ogilvie´s Civil History of the Kingdom of
      Naples." Archiv 213: 343-45.
         Richardson may have taken the name "Grandison" from the
      dedication to John, Earl Grandison, in Ogilvie´s book and
      may even have written the dedication. (Compare 1975.8.)

*29   ---. "Richardson und der Leser." ArAA 1: 65-105.
      Source:MLA Bibliography, 1976, item 4823.

                              1977

1   BROWNSTEIN, RACHEL MAYER. "´An Examplar [sic] to her Sex´:
      Richardson´s Clarissa." YR 67: 30-47.
         The "Examplar," the perfect didactic heroine of a

realistic fiction, serves as a convention to oppress women. Clarissa transmutes her "Examplarity," as she does houses, clothes, and finally letters, from externally imposed symbol to personal artifact, active emanation of her personality. She is an emblem to herself, as is Lovelace; but Lovelace's rake-symbol does not similarly express him, and for each, finally, the symbolism they choose is not adequate. Is each to blame for remaining in such a character?

2   COCKSHUT, A.O.J. "Richardson and Fielding." In his <u>Man</u> <u>and</u> <u>Woman</u>: <u>A</u> <u>Study</u> <u>of</u> <u>Love</u> <u>and</u> <u>the</u> <u>Novel</u> <u>1740-1940</u>. London: Collins, pp. 32-45.
    Moral choice and sexual ethics in Fielding and Richardson.

3   EAVES, T.C. DUNCAN. "Amelia and Clarissa." In <u>A</u> <u>Provision</u> <u>of</u> <u>Human</u> <u>Nature</u> . . . Edited by Donald Kay. University, Ala.: University of Alabama Press, pp. 95-110.
    Tentatively dates beginning of composition of <u>Amelia</u>, which is influenced by <u>Clarissa</u> in that Amelia is the perfect heroine that Clarissa does not become until the end of her life. But Fielding's book is flawed by his failure to dramatize the internal struggles of the characters.

*4   HARTVEIT, LARS. "Samuel Richardson, <u>Pamela</u> <u>I</u>. The Impact of Moral Exemplum: The Dilemma of the Didactic Writer." <u>The</u> <u>Art</u> <u>of</u> <u>Persuasion</u>: <u>A</u> <u>Study</u> <u>of</u> <u>Six</u> <u>Novels</u>. Bergen: Universitetsforlaget (distributed through Columbia University Press), pp. 14-32.
    Courtesy Prof. Robert R. Allen.

5   JEFFREY, DAVID K. "The Epistolary Format of <u>Pamela</u> and <u>Humphrey</u> <u>Clinker</u>." In <u>A</u> <u>Provision</u> <u>of</u> <u>Human</u> <u>Nature</u> . . . (see 1977.1 above), pp. 145-54.
    Parallels Pamela with Humphrey and Lydia Melford; both authors focus to some degree on the choices their heroines must make, isolate them through the epistolary format, and enable them to "construct their own portraits of themselves."

6   JONNES, DENIS. "The Family as Fiction: The Authoritarian-Sentimental Family in the Works of Richardson, Diderot and Lessing." Ph.D. dissertation, Brown University.

Defines the "authoritarian-sentimental" family pattern and discusses Richardson's works as exemplifying the first of three stages of its development and use in fiction.

7   JOSEPHS, HERBERT. "Diderot's Eloge de Richardson: A Paradox on Praising." In Essays on the Age of Enlightenment in Honor of Ira O. Wade. Edited by Jean Macary. Geneva: Droz, pp. 169-82.
      Diderot perceived a drama in Richardson's fiction clearly separable from moral intention, though not perhaps from "the moralizing strategies of the human psyche." Notes the blurring in the Eloge of distinction between "truth" and "moral efficacy," "fiction" and "real world"; "beautiful ethical act" vs. passive enjoyment of representations of ethical actions; admiration of self-effacement and self-control vs. the rhapsodizing of the Eloge. The style and qualities of the book become a justification of the reader, Diderot, a sensitive soul made perfect by the very passion of his reading of Richardson. Compares the Diderot persona in the Eloge with the neveu de Rameau.

8   KLOTMAN, PHYLLIS R. "Sin and Sublimation in the Novels of Samuel Richardson." CLAJ 20: 365-73.
      Though consciously focusing on the moral order, Richardson unconsciously is fascinated by the sublimation of sexual desires; the epistolary form is one aspect of this. Notes sadism, masochism, and in particular voyeurism in Richardson; suggests that his books provide a historical perspective for understanding distorted psychosexual patterns in women.

9   LEVEY, STEPHEN BARRY. "The Lady's Legacy: A Study of Richardson's Clarissa." Ph.D. dissertation, SUNY at Buffalo.
      Concentrates on characterization, psychological themes as expressed in metaphor, and male-female relationships in eighteenth-century England as expressed or distorted by Clarissa and Lovelace.

10   LITWACK, DAVID MICHAEL. "Clarissa and La Nouvelle Héloïse: A Comparative Study." Ph.D. dissertation, Boston University.
      Both portray a clash between morality and social utility; concludes that Rousseau's novel and Richardson's come to similar conclusions by differing means, Rousseau

using linguistic tools rather than the trappings of classical tragedy.

11　LYNCH, LAWRENCE W. "Richardson´s Influence on the Concept of the Novel in Eighteenth-Century France." <u>CLS</u> 14: 233-43.
　　Richardson is the prime source of the change in the French concept of the novel from a collection of adventures to an exalted, Horatian concept, a form espousing both entertainment and instruction. Prévost, Diderot, Rousseau and Laclos put Richardson´s fiction either among the best of the century or in a metacategory beyond the <u>roman</u>; Rousseau´s later change of heart seems due to personal rivalry with Diderot.

12　MARTIN, ANGUS, MYLNE, VIVIENNE, and FRAUTSCHI, RICHARD. <u>Bibliographie du genre romanesque français 1751-1800</u>. London: Mansell; Paris: France Expansion, 529 pp.
　　Invaluable bibliographical information on French and other <u>Richardsonaden</u> in the latter part of the century; referred to in this bibliography as MMF, but not all of its Richardsonian imitations appear here. Annotations allow for easy identification of subject-matter and form.

*13　MICHELE, LAURA DI. "Il Realismo come expressione dei sentimenti e delle emozioni in S. Richardson." In <u>L´Educazione del Sentimento: La Crisi del Romanzo inglese fra Gotico a Sentimentale (1750-1800)</u>. Napoli: Istituto Universitario Orientale, pp. 66-92.
　　Source: Hannaford, item 803.

14　NOEL-BENTLEY, ELAINE. "An Allusion to ´Sir Charles Grandison´ in Jane Austen´s Letters." <u>N&Q</u>, p. 321.
　　A previously unnoticed reference to <u>Grandison</u>.

15　RICHARDSON, SAMUEL. <u>Samuel Richardsons Sittenlehre für die Jugend</u> . . . Translated by G.E. Lessing. Afterword by Thomas Hohle. Leipzig: Insel-Verlag, 399 pp.
　　Facsimile of 1757.3, with an afterword (28 pp.) by Thomas Hohle. Courtesy Deutsche Bücherei.

*16　ROBERTSON, ELIZABETH. "Dreams Sleeping and Dreams Waking: A Psychological Study of Richardson´s <u>Clarissa</u>." Ph.D. dissertation, McMaster University.
　　Source: McMaster University Library.

17   SABOR, PETER. "The Cooke-Everyman Edition of <u>Pamela</u>." <u>Library</u>
        32: 360-66.
            Information on the Cooke edition of 1811 and its
        reprints; though textually extremely corrupt, this edition
        has been used for the Everyman edition of <u>Pamela</u>, the
        long-standard twentieth-century text.

*18   ---. "Samuel Richardson, His Critics, and the Revisions of
        <u>Pamela</u> 1740-1801." Ph.D. dissertation, University of
        London.
            Source: Prof. Peter Sabor.

19   SCHMITZ, ROBERT M. and WILT, JUDITH. "Lovelace and
        Impotence." <u>PMLA</u> 92: 1005-6.
            An exchange on 1977.23. Schmitz argues that the phrase
        "I can go no further" is a <u>Leitmotiv</u> and does not support
        Wilt´s thesis, nor does Lovelace´s conclusion that Clarissa
        is pregnant. Wilt disagrees.

20   SPECTOR, JUDITH ANN. "Sexual Dialectic in Four Novels: The
        Mythos of the Masculine Aesthetic." Ph.D. dissertation,
        Indiana University.
            Sexual dialectic--male thesis vs. female antithesis--in
        four novels including <u>Clarissa</u>, which is given a close
        reading in Chapter 1.

21   TRAUGOTT, JOHN. "<u>Clarissa</u>´s Richardson: An Essay to Find the
        Reader." In <u>English</u> <u>Literature</u> <u>in</u> <u>the</u> <u>Age</u> <u>of</u> <u>Disguise</u>.
        Edited by Maximillian E. Novak. Berkeley: University of
        California Press, pp. 157-208.
            Separates the "silly . . . pedestrian" moralist
        Richardson from Richardson the artist and from <u>Clarissa</u>.
        Richardson sets the worlds of Restoration comedy and
        sentimental realism, Lovelace´s world and Clarissa´s,
        against each other, then invites the reader to judge which
        is right; the relocation of the rake figure from comedy to
        the real world means that Richardson must take libertinism
        to its ultimate and allow Lovelace to collapse under his
        burden of freedom. He does so by providing a perfect
        audience in Clarissa, then emptying Lovelace´s theater by
        her death. Richardson shows his mastery by transmuting
        moralistic material to art.

22   WEIBEL, KATHRYN. <u>Mirror</u> <u>Mirror</u>: <u>Images</u> <u>of</u> <u>Women</u> <u>Reflected</u> <u>in</u>
      <u>Popular</u> <u>Culture</u>. New York: Doubleday, Anchor Books.
          Richardson's fiction and fictional formulae connected
      with popular imagery of women.

23   WILT, JUDITH. "He Could Go No Farther: A Modest Proposal
      about Lovelace and Clarissa." <u>PMLA</u> 92: 19-32.
          Argues that not Lovelace, but Sinclair, is the prime
      mover in the rape scene; Richardson equates Sin and Death
      with femaleness, thus compromising Clarissa.

                                  1978

1   BROPHY, ELIZABETH BERGEN. "A Richardsonian Letter: 'Carpers'
      or 'Carvers'?" <u>N&Q</u> 25: 44-45.
          On the basis of another use of the word by Richardson,
      suggests "carvers."

2   CRABTREE, PAUL RICHARD. "Richardson and Rousseau: Looking
      Backward in the Eighteenth Century." Ph.D. dissertation,
      SUNY at Buffalo.
          Compares <u>Sir</u> <u>Charles</u> <u>Grandison</u> and Rousseau's <u>Discours</u>
      <u>sur</u> <u>l'Inégalité</u>; finds in Richardson's work a "code of
      reactionary sentimentality." Both share a reaction to
      rationalism.

*3   DUCROCQ, JEAN. "<u>Clarissa</u> <u>Harlowe</u> (1747-48)" and "Samuel
      Richardson (1689-1761): L'Exploration de la Caverne." In
      <u>Roman</u> <u>et</u> <u>société</u> <u>en</u> <u>Angleterre</u> <u>au</u> <u>dix-huitième</u> <u>siècle</u>.
      Edited by Jean Ducrocq, Suzi Halimi, and Maurice Lévy.
      Paris: Presses Universitaires, pp. 87-94, 78-86.

4   GASKELL, PHILIP. "Richardson's <u>Pamela</u>." <u>In</u> <u>his</u> <u>From</u> <u>Writer</u> <u>to</u>
      <u>Reader</u>. Oxford: Clarendon, pp. 63-79.
          On editing texts, including <u>Pamela</u>. General information
      on changes in the various revisions. The last version is
      quite different from the earlier ones, which were revised
      largely for linguistic refinement; however, for the 1801
      edition "Richardson virtually rewrote the book in his
      artistic maturity, producing a version of <u>Pamela</u> with the
      skill and assurance of <u>Clarissa</u> and <u>Grandison</u>." For <u>Pamela</u>,
      therefore, "copy-text cannot be chosen in the ordinary way,
      for the editor has got to choose between main versions of

the work . . . ." Information on the Cooke–Everyman
edition (see 1977.17).

5   HARVEY, A.D.   "Clarissa and the Puritan Tradition." EIC 28:
     38-51.
          Puritanism, with its special definition of virginity,
     clashes to some degree with Richardson's book; discusses
     Lovelace's (long-past) virginity, the lack of distinction
     in Puritan eyes between deflowering and fornication, and
     the reification of female "virtue." Concludes that since
     Clarissa's rape was a physical "union" with Lovelace, thus
     in the opinion of some divines a marriage, she cannot be
     married unless to him and cannot be an old maid, therefore
     must die.

*6   KOVACS, ANNA–MARIA. "Pamela's Poverty." RLV 44: 3-14.
          Source: MLA Bibliography (1978), item 5516.

*7   LANSBURY, CORAL.   "The Triumph of Clarissa: Richardson's
     Divine Comedy." Thalia: Studies in Literary Humor (Ottawa)
     1 pt. 1: 9-17.
          Source: MLA Bibliography (1978), item 5517.

*8   LAUREN, BARBARA. "Clarissa and The Newgate Calender (1768):
     A Perspective on the Novel Twenty Years Later." MLS 8 pt.
     3: 5-11.
          Source: MLA Bibliography (1978), item 5518.

9   LEVIN, GERALD. Richardson the Novelist: The Psychological
     Patterns. Costerus n.s. 9. Amsterdam: Rodopi, 177 pp.
          Studies Richardson as novelist of psychological fantasy
     with special reference to Freudian theories of masochism
     and comparisons with Lawrence; attempts to explain appeal
     of Sentimentalism in Freudian terms.   Chapter 2 is a
     reprint of 1971.10; other material in the book is adapted
     from other Levin articles.
          Reviewed by E.B. Brophy, WHR, Spring 1979, pp. 155-58.

*10 OKA, TERUO. "'Tegami' to 'Shokan': Richardson to Pope."
     ["Letters" and "Epistles":   Richardson and Pope.] EigoS
     124: 412-14.
          Source: MLA Bibliography, 1978, item 5520.

11   SABOR, PETER. "Joseph Andrews and Pamela." BJECS 1: 169-81.
             Not merely a second Shamela, Joseph Andrews provides a
        profound critique of Richardson's type of fiction, of which
        the use of Pamela and Booby as minor characters, the
        parallelisms between Joseph and Pamela, and the frequent
        allusions to Richardson's novel (especially to Pamela II)
        are the outward signs.

12   SIEGEL, JUNE SIGLER. "Lovelace and Rameau's Nephew: Roots of
        Poetic Amoralism." DidS 19: 163-74.
             Lovelace and Rameau's Nephew are alike in their "refusal
        of   containment,   [their]   anarchic   nature,"   their
        impenitence; they have in common "abnormal energy or
        intensity of life, . . . dichotomy, and . . . poetic
        expansion." Suggests that the Richardsonian influence over
        Diderot is double;   while the suffering saint Clarissa
        appears in La Religieuse, the "agonized cynic" Lovelace
        influences the Neveu.

13   SPACKS, PATRICIA MEYER. "The Dangerous Age." ECS 11: 417-38.
             A study of fictional adolescence referring among other
        books to Clarissa and Pamela. Finds that with Clarissa the
        basic adolescent decision of whether to be woman or child
        is resolved by death and reads the book as a fantasy of
        adolescent rebellion;   notes   the   connection   between
        Pamela's   adolescence   and   "the   ambiguous   adult   status
        possible for women," feeling that both women and
        adolescents are severely punished by society. Discerns
        ambiguity about goal of social maturity in all novels
        studied;   the adolescent serves artificially to separate
        good and evil--good in the self, evil in the world--and
        allows the author both to criticize that world and to
        insist on the adolescent's dependence on it.

14   SPACKS, PATRICIA MEYER. "Early Fiction and the Frightened
        Male." In Towards a Poetics of Fiction. Edited by Mark
        Spilka. Bloomington, Indiana: Indiana University Press,
        pp. 255-65.
             Sexual and social power in fiction including Clarissa.

15   VAN MARTER, SHIRLEY. "Richardson's Debt to Hester Mulso
        Concerning the Curse in Clarissa." PLL 14: 22-31.
             Strengthens the case made by E&K that Hester Mulso
        influenced Richardson's treatment of the parental curse in
        the third edition of Clarissa, citing material from her

347

three letters to him.

16   VAN SANT, CAROL ANN JESSIE. "Masters of the Heart: A Study
      of the Uses of Sentimentalism in the Novels of Richardson,
      Fielding and Sterne." Ph.D.   dissertation, University of
      California, Berkeley.
          Origins of Sentimentalism and use of fictional
      strategies in Sentimental novelists; Chapter 3, dealing
      directly with Richardson, concludes that by "dramatizing
      the opposition between the ideal of wit, play, and artifice
      and   the   sentimental   ideal   he   accommodates   the
      attractiveness   of   each   and explores the nature of
      idealism." He both "elicits and controls sadistic impulses"
      and   contrasts Lovelace´s artificiality with Clarissa´s
      sentimental idealism to make her more attractive.

17   WARNER, WILLIAM BEATTY. "Clarissa´s Undoing: The Struggles
      of Interpretation in and about Richardson´s <u>Clarissa</u>."
      Ph.D. dissertation, Johns Hopkins.
          Reading   of   the   novel   as   a   struggle   among
      interpretations: Clarissa´s vs. Lovelace´s, Richardson´s
      vs. his contemporary readers´, and subsequent readers´ of
      the novel vs. each other´s. Published with alterations as
      <u>Reading</u> <u>Clarissa</u> (1979).

Appendix A: "Richardsonian" Novels

This list of fiction excludes novels purporting to be adaptations of Richardson's works, which will be found in the main body of the bibliography; juvenilia and adaptations of Richardson for children, which will be found in Appendix C; and novels written in the 1740s. These last, generally criticism as well as <u>Richardsonaden</u>, appear in the main body of the bibliography. Some later works are also discussed further there.

Eliza Haywood. <u>History of Miss Betsy Thoughtless</u>. 4v. 1751.

Sarah Fielding. <u>The Adventures of David Simple</u>. <u>Volume the Last</u>. 1752.

Anon. <u>The Memoirs of Sir Charles Goodville and his Family, in a Series of Letters to a Friend</u>. 1753. (Not seen; Sale, who has found only advertisements for this book, conjectures it was published on the coattails of <u>Grandison</u>.)

Eliza Haywood. <u>The History of Jemmy and Jenny Jessamy</u>. 3v. 1753.

Anon. <u>De hollandsche Pamela of de zegenpralende Deugd</u>. 2v. 1754. Reprinted abridged as <u>De Godvrugtige Hollandsche Schoonheid</u>. 1759.

Pietro Chiari. <u>La Ballerina onorata</u>. 2v. 1754.

P.P. Jolyot de Crébillon <u>fils</u>. <u>Les Heureux orphelins, histoire imitée de l'anglois</u>. 4v. 1754.

William Dodd. <u>The Sisters; or The History of Lucy and Caroline Sanson</u>. 2v. 1754.

John Shebbeare. <u>The Marriage Act</u>. 2v. 1754.

John Kidgell. <u>The Card</u>. 2v. 1755.

Edward Kimber. <u>The Life and Adventures of James Ramble, Esq</u>. . . . <u>from his own Manuscript</u>. 2v. 1755, 1770. (Not as Richardsonian as 1935.1 would have us believe. Kimber's debts are largely to <u>Pamela</u> and to Grandison's eccentric benevolism.)

Charles de Fieux, chevalier de Mouhy. <u>Le Financier</u>. 4 pts. 1755.

Johann Gebhard Pfeil. <u>Geschichte des Grafen von P</u>. 1755.

C.M. Wieland. <u>Sympathien: As Soul Approuches Soul</u> [sic]. 1756.

[Richard and Elizabeth Griffith.] <u>A Series of Genuine Letters between Henry and Frances</u>. 2v. 1757. Republished as <u>The Delicate Distress</u>. The Griffiths' actual letters, but rewritten along Richardsonian lines.

John Piper. <u>The Life of Miss Fanny Browne, (A Clergyman's Daughter)</u>. 1760. Possibly also published as <u>The Life of Miss Fanny Browne, or Pamela the Second</u>.

Pietro Chiari. <u>La Viaggiatrice</u>. 1760 or 1761.

Frances Sheridan. <u>Memoirs of Miss Sidney Bid[d]ulph</u>. Originally 2v.; eventually, in numerous revised republications, 5v. 1761 ff.

François Thomas Baculard d'Arnaud. "Nancy, ou la nouvelle Paméla." In <u>Le Discoureur</u>, 1762; repr. (unauthorized) as <u>Fanni ou l'heureux</u>

répentir, 1764; repr. (authorized) as <u>Fanni ou la nouvelle Paméla</u>, 1767 et seq.

Frances Moore Brooke. <u>The History of Lady Julia Mandeville</u>. 2v. 1761?

Pietro Chiari. <u>La Donna che non se trova</u>. 1762.

The Miss Minifries, of Fairwater, in Somersetshire. <u>The History of Lady Frances S</u>. <u>and Lady Caroline S</u>. 3v. 1763.

Mme G.D. de St. Germain, author or translator. <u>Lettres d´Henriette et d´Emilie</u>. Possibly a translation of the anonymous <u>Letters between Emilia and Harriet</u>. 1763.

A.L.M.D. Elie de Beaumont. <u>Lettres du marquis de Roselle</u>. 2v. 1764.

[Edward Kimber.] <u>Maria; the Genuine Memoirs of a Young Lady of Rank and Fortune</u>. 2v. 1764. Translated as <u>Mariane ou la nouvelle Paméla</u>. <u>Histoire véritable</u> . . . 2v. ; also as <u>Maria, ou les Veritables Mémoires d´une Dame illustre par son Mérite</u> . . . 2v. 1765.

Marie-Jeanne Riccoboni. <u>Histoire de Miss Jenny, écrite et envoyée par elle à milady Comtesse de Roscomond</u> . . . 4v. 1764.

[Edward Kimber.] <u>The Generous Briton</u> . . . 2v. 1765.

Henry Brooke. <u>The Fool of Quality; or, The History of Henry Earl of Moreland</u>. 5v. 1766.

F.T. Baculard d´Arnaud. <u>Sidney et Silli</u>. 1766. Republished as <u>Sidney et Volsan, histoire anglaise</u>. 1770.

Johann Timotheus Hermes. <u>Geschichte der Miss Fanny Wilkes</u>. 2v. 1766. Completed as: <u>Geschichte der Miss Fanny Wilkes, so gut als aus dem Englischen übersetzt, zweite verbesserte Auflage</u>. 3v. 1770.

C.M. Wieland. <u>Geschichte des Agathon</u>. 2v. 1766-67.

Hugh Kelly. <u>Memoirs of a Magdalen or, The History of Louisa Mildmay</u>. 2v. 1767.

J.M. Leprince de Beaumont. <u>La Nouvelle Clarice, Histoire véritable</u>. 2v. 1767. (In German:) <u>Clarissa, eine wahrhafte Geshichte</u>. ? and 1778.

Anon. <u>The History of Miss Emilia Beville</u>. 2v. 1768.

Frances Moore Brooke. <u>The History of Emily Montague</u>. 4v. 1769.

Antoine Sabatier de Castres. <u>Betsi ou les Bizarreries du destin</u>. 2v. 1769. Republished as <u>La Nouvelle Orpheline Angloise, ou les Bisarreries du Destin</u>. 2v. 1770. (Curiously, the frontispiece strikingly anticipates Stothard´s well-known illustration of the chariot rescue from <u>Grandison</u>.)

"A Lady" [pseud.] <u>Jessy; or, The Bridal Day</u>. 1771.

Claude Dorat. <u>Les Sacrifices de l´Amour, ou Lettres de la Vicomtesse de Senanges et du Chevalier de Versenai; suivies de Sylvie et Moléshoff</u>. 2 pts. 1771.

Sophie von La Roche. <u>Geschichte des Fräulein von Sternheim</u>. <u>Von einer Freundin derselben aus Original-Papieren und andern zuverlässigen Quellen gezogen</u>}. 2 pts. 1771. Translated (into Dutch): <u>De Hoogduitsche Clarissa, of Geschiedenis van de Freule van Sternheim</u> . . .

[The German Clarissa . . .]. 2v. 1772; (into English:) The History of Lady Sophia Sternheim. 2v. 1776.

Anon. Genuine Memoirs of Miss Harriet Melvin and Miss Leonora Stanley. In a Series of Letters. 1772.

[Anne Dawe.] The Younger Sister; Or, The History of Miss Somerset. 2v. 1772. (First published 1770?)

Claude Dorat. Les Malheurs de l´Inconstance, ou Lettres de la Marquise de Syrcé et du comte de Mirbelle. 2 pts. 1772.

Anon. The History of Miss Pamela Howard. 2v. 1773.

Henry Mackenzie. The Man of the World. 2v. 1773.

Friedrich Nicolai. Das Leben und die Meinungen des Herrn Magister Sebaldus Nothanker. 3v. 1773.

Anon. Les Amans vertueux, ou Lettres d´une jeune dame . . . 2 pts. 1774.

Frances Moore Brooke. All´s Right at Last; or the History of Miss West. 2v. 1774.

J.W. von Goethe. Die Leiden des jungen Werthers. 2 pts. 1774.

N.G. Léonard. La Nouvelle Clémentine, ou Lettres de Henriette de Berville. 1774.

Anon. L´Amour Vainqueur du vice, ou Lettres du Marquis de Cousanges. 2 pts. 1775.

J.J. Dusch. Geschichte Carl Ferdiners. 3v. 1776? (See 1776.3.) Republished much altered in 1785.

Elizabeth Griffith. The Story of Lady Juliana Harley. 2v. 1776.

Johann Martin Miller. Siegwart; eine Klöstergeschichte . . . 2v. 1776; second edition, 1777.

Henry Mackenzie. Julia de Roubigné. A Tale. In a Series of Letters. 2v. 1777.

Frances Burney. Evelina; or A Young Lady´s Entrance into the World. 3v. 1778.

Johann Martin Miller. Die Geschichte Karls von Burgheim und Emiliens von Rosenau. In Briefen. 4v. 1778-79.

MarieJeanne Riccoboni. Paméla françoise. Ou, La Vertu en célibat et en mariage;; dépeinte dans les Lettres de Messrs. de Talbert et Mozinge, rédigées dans le Goût des Lettres de Clarisse et Grandison . . . 4 pts. 1778. Originally published, and better known, as the Lettres du colonel Talbert.

Anon. The History of Lady Bettesworth and Captain Hastings. In a Series of Letters. 2v. 1780.

Anon. Letters between Clara and Antonia. 2v. 1780.

Anon. Histoire de Miss Elise Warwick, trad. angl. 2 pts. 1781. A translation or an original work.

Robert Bage. Mount Henneth. 2v. 1782.

P.P.A. Choderlos de Laclos. Les Liaisons dangereuses. 1782.

Sophie de Genlis. Adèle et Théodore . . . 3v. 1782.

Marie-Jeanne Riccoboni or Mlle de la Guesnerie. Les Ressources de la Vertu. 4 pts. in 2v. 1782.

F.T. Baculard d´Arnaud. Délassements de l´homme sensible. 12v. 1783-87.

Elisabeth Wolff and Agatha Deken. Historie van Mejuffrouw Sara Burgerhart. 2v. 1783.

Anon. The History of Julia Benson . . . 2v. 1784?

N.G. Restif de la Bretonnne. Le Paysan et la paysanne pervertis, ou Les Dangers de la ville . . . 4v. 1784. Restif de la Bretonne got the idea for the book, but little else, from Pamela.

Elisabeth Wolff and Agatha Deken. Historie van den Heer Willem Leevend. 9v. 1784.

Pietro Chiari. Storia della virtuosa Portoghese. 1784.

Rhijnvis Feith. Ferdinand en Constantia. 2v. 1785.

Anon. The Errors of Innocence. 5v. 1786.

Charlotte de Bournon Malarme. Tout est possible a l´amitié, ou Histoire de milord Loverose et de Sophie Mostain. 2v. 1786. (Charlotte de Bournon Malarme was a prolific producer of what seem from their titles to be Richardsonian fiction. I have not seen most of them.)

Anon. Alphonse d´Inange, ou Le nouveau Grandisson. 4 pts. in 2v. 1787.

"M.A.L.D.G.A." La Femme vertueuse ou le Débauché converti par l´amour. 2 pts. in 1v. 1787.

J.T. Hermes. Fur Töchter edler Herkunft. 3 pts. 1787.

Elisabeth Wolff and Agatha Deken. Brieven van Abraham Blankaart. 3v. 1787.

Anon. The Twin Sisters; or, The Effects of Education: A Novel; In a Series of Letters. 4v? 1788.

[Elizabeth Helme.] Clara and Emmeline; or, The Maternal Benediction. 2v. 1788.

J.C.F. Schulz. Albertine. 5v. 1788-89; retitled and possibly revised as Clarisse in Berlin. 5v. 1797.

[William Hill Brown.] The Power of Sympathy: or, The Triumph of Nature. 2v. in 1. 1789.

Georg Karl Claudius [Franz Ehrenburg]. Leonore Schmidt. 2v. 1789-91.

Richard Cumberland. Arundel. 2v. 1789.

Anon. The History of Charles Mandeville . . . 2v. 1790. A sequel to Frances Moore Brooke´s History of Lady Julia Mandeville, and possibly by her.

J.J. de Cambon. Clementina Bedford, in Brieven. 1791; (in English) 1796.

Elizabeth Inchbald. A Simple Story. 4v. 1791.

Susanna Rowson. Charlotte. 1791. (1960.5 overstates his case; the book contains echoes of Clarissa, but comparatively faint ones.)

D.A.F. de Sade. Justine, ou les Malheurs de la vertu. 2v. 1791.

Revised as part of <u>La Nouvelle Justine</u>, <u>ou les Malheurs de La Vertu</u>, . .
. <u>suivie de l'Histoire de Juliette</u>, <u>sa soeur</u>[, <u>ou les Prospérités du vice</u>]. 10v. 1797.
    Thomas Holcroft. <u>Anna St. Ives</u>. 7v. 1792.
    Nikolai M. Karamzin. "Bednaya Liza." [Poor Liza.] <u>Moskovskii Zhurnal</u>. 1792.
    "An American Lady" [pseud]. <u>The Hapless Orphan</u>, <u>or Innocent Victim of Revenge</u> . . . 1793.
    William Godwin. <u>Things as They Are</u>: <u>Or</u>, <u>the Adventures of Caleb Williams</u>. 3v. 1793.
    Elisabeth Wolff and Agatha Deken. <u>Historie van Mejuffrouw Cornelia Wildschut</u>. 6v. 1793.
    J.L. Tieck. [<u>Geschichte des Herrn</u>] <u>William Lovell</u>. 3v. 1795.
    William Beckford ["Lady Harriet Marlow"]. <u>Modern Novel Writing</u>; <u>or</u>, <u>The Elegant Enthusiast</u> . . . 2v. 1796.
    J.J. Dusch, completed by J.G. Muller. <u>Die Pupille</u>. <u>Eine Geschichte in Briefen</u> . . . 2v. 1798.
    [Hannah Lee.] [<u>Clara Lennox or the Unfortunate Widow</u>.] Translated into French as <u>Clara Lennox ou la Veuve</u> infortunée. 2v. 1798.
    Charles Brockden Brown. <u>Ormond</u>; <u>or</u>, <u>The Secret Witness</u>. 1799.
    Sophie Ristaud, dame Cottin. <u>Claire d'Albe</u>. 1799?
    [Elizabeth Hamilton.] <u>Memoirs of Modern Philosophers</u>. 3v. 1800.
    Charles Brockden Brown. <u>Clara Howard</u>: <u>In a Series of Letters</u>. 1801.
    Charles Brockden Brown. <u>Jane Talbot</u>, <u>a novel</u> . . . 1801.
    Maria Edgeworth. <u>Moral Tales for Young People</u>. 5v. 1801.
    Sophie von La Roche. <u>Schönes Bild der Resignation</u>. 2v. 1801.
    F.J. Villemain d'Abancourt. <u>Maria ou l'Enfant de l'Infortune</u>. 1801.
    [Ugo Foscolo.] <u>Ultime lettere di Iacopo Ortis</u>. 1802.
    F.T. Baculard d'Arnaud. <u>Les Epreuves du Sentiment</u>. 1803.
    F.T. Baculard d'Arnaud. <u>Eustasia</u>, <u>histoire italienne</u> . . . 2v. 1803.
    R.M. le Suire. <u>La Paméla française</u>, <u>ou Lettres d'une jeune Paysanne et d'un jeune çi-devant</u> . . . 4v. 1803.
    Anon. <u>Miss Charlotte</u>, <u>ou La Nouvelle Paméla</u>. 4v. 1806.
    Pierre Cuisin. <u>Le Bâtard de Lovelace et la Fille naturelle de la Marquise de Merteuil</u>, <u>ou les Moeurs vengées</u>. 4v. 1806.
    Janos Kis. <u>A Magyar Pamela</u>. [The Hungarian Pamela.] In <u>Flora</u>. 4v. 1806-08.
    Adriaan Loosjes. <u>Historie van mejuffrouw Susanna Bronkhorst</u>. 6v. 1806-07.
    Heinrich von Kleist. <u>Die Marquise von O--</u>. <u>Vollständiger Abdruck im Phöbus</u> 2. 1808.
    J.W. von Goethe. <u>Die Wahlverwandtschaften</u>. <u>Ein Roman</u>. 2v. 1809.
    Achim von Arnim. <u>Armuth</u>, <u>Reichthum</u>, <u>Schuld und Büsse der Gräfin Dolores</u>. . . . 2v. 1810.
    Jane Porter. <u>The Scottish Chiefs</u>: <u>A Romance</u>. 5v. 1810.

Mary Brunton. Self-Control. 3v. 1811.
Susanna Rowson. Sarah, or The Exemplary Wife. [1813?]
Anon. Confessions de Clémentine. 2v. 1817.
Jane Austen. [Sanditon.] Written 1817.
Maria Edgeworth. Ormond. 1817.
Anon. Laideur et Beauté, ou le Nouveau Lovelace. 1825.
Mme --- Moraux d´Omâtre. Ninon et Paméla, ou l´Influence d´une Première Lecture. 1825. (Reported, not seen; possibly a juvenile and possibly not having to do with Pamela.)
Jules Janin. Clarisse Harlowe. 2v. 1846. So thorough an adaptation that it may be listed as an original work.
J.A. Froude. "The Spirit´s Trials." Shadows of the Clouds. 1847.
J.A. Froude. The Nemesis of Faith. 1848.
Charlotte Yonge. The Heir of Redclyffe. 2v. 1853.
George Meredith. Evan Harrington. 1860.
[Rev. Francis Edward Paget.] Lucretia; or, The Heroine of the Nineteenth Century . . . 1868. Parodies Richardsonian cliches among others.
Anon. A Sequel to the History of Sir Charles Grandison. 1878.
Upton Sinclair. Another Pamela. 1950.

Appendix B: "Richardsonian" Dramas

Louis de Boissy. <u>Pamela</u> <u>en</u> <u>France</u>. First performed 1743, published 1745.

Claude Godard d'Aucourt. <u>La Déroute des Pamela</u>. First performed 1743, published 1744.

Pierre Claude Nivelle de la Chaussée. <u>Pamela</u>. First performed 1743, published 1762; (in German) 1768.

Carlo Goldoni. <u>La Putta onorata</u>. 1748.

Carlo Goldoni. <u>Pamela</u> (later <u>Pamela nubile</u>) 1750; (in English) 1756; (in German) 1756, 1758, 1761, etc.; (in French) 1759; (in Portuguese) 1766; (in Spanish) 1787. Many Italian adaptations.

Carlo Goldoni. <u>Gastalda</u>. 1751.

Carlo Goldoni. <u>L'Incognita perseguitata</u>. 1751.

Carlo Goldoni. <u>La Moglie saggia</u>. 1752.

Pietro Chiari. <u>L'Amica Rivale</u>. Before 1753.

Pietro Chiari. <u>La Pamela maritata</u>. 1753, 1759.

G.E. Lessing. <u>Miss Sara Sampson</u>. 1755.

Johann Gebhard Pfeil. <u>Lucy Woodvil</u>. About 1755.

Denis Diderot. <u>Le Père de famille</u>. 1758.

Carlo Goldoni. <u>Pamela maritata</u>. Written 1759; first performed 1760; published (in German) 1763, (in Italian) 1765.

Voltaire (F.M. Arouet). <u>L'Ecossaise</u>. 1760.

George Colman. <u>Polly Honeycombe</u>. 1760.

C.M. Wieland. <u>Clementina von Porretta</u>. 1760.

C. Lanfranchi Rossi. <u>Pamela Schiava et Combattuta</u>. 1764. (Based vaguely on Richardson's character, but far, far from Richardson.)

Isaac Bickerstaffe. <u>The Maid of the Mill</u>. 1765. Isaac Bickerstaffe. <u>The Maid of the Mill</u>. 1765.

Francesco Cerlone. <u>Pamela nubile</u> and <u>Pamela maritata</u>. 1765.

J.H. Steffens. <u>Clarissa, ein bürgerliches Trauerspiel</u>. 1765.

Antonio Bianchi. <u>La Buona Figliuola Supposta Vedova</u>. 1766.

G.E. Lessing. <u>Minna von Barnhelm oder Das Soldatenglück</u>. 1767.

Anon. <u>Clary ein Schauspiel</u> (?). 1770.

J.-A. Perreau. <u>Clarisse</u>. 1771.

G.E. Lessing. <u>Emilia Galotti</u>. 1772.

Samuel Foote. <u>The Handsome Housemaid; or, Purity in Pattens</u>. 1773.

J.W. von Goethe. <u>Clavigo</u>. 1774.

Jacob M.R. Lenz. <u>Die Soldaten</u>. 1775.

Anon. <u>Clarissa oder das unbekannte Dienstmädchen</u>. 1776. (Based on <u>Pamela</u>.)

Thomas Holcroft. <u>The Maid of the Vale</u>. 1776.

Heinrich Leopold Wagner. <u>Die Kindermörderin</u>. 1776.

Jacob M.R. Lenz. <u>Der Engländer eine dramatische Phantasey</u>. 1777.

Anon. <u>Lovelace og Clarissa</u> . . . 1780.

K.G. Lessing. Die Mätresse. 1780.

W.C.S. Mylius. Puf van Vlieten. 1780. (An adaptation of L´Ecossaise.)

Antonio Piazza. Giulietta. 1780.

Antonio Piazza. Narcisa o La Virtu coronata dal premio. 1780.

Antonio Piazza. La Pazza per amore. 1780.

--- Bievre. Le Séducteur. 1783.

Friedrich Schiller. Kabale und Liebe. 1784. (See 1784.3.)

J.F. Née de la Rochelle. Clarisse Harlove. 1786.

Giovanni Greppi. Teresa e Claudio, Teresa Vedova, and Teresa e Wilk (a trilogy). 1786.

Robert Porrett. Clarissa. 1788.

Giovanni di Gamerra. Angelica Perseguitata, Angelica Fuggitiva, Angelica Tradita, and Angelica Vendicata (a quadrilogy based on Clarissa). 1789.

J.W. von Goethe. Faust. 1790.

Anon. I Arete tis Pamelas (in Greek) 1791, 1806.

Anon. Clarisse ou la Vertu malheureuse. 1792.

Louis-Jean Nepomucène Lemercier. Lovelace. 1792. Revived in 1795 as Clarissa Harlowe.

Nicolas-Louis François de Neufchâteau. Paméla, ou la Vertu récompensée . . . 1793; printed 1795.

[Jane Austen?] Sir Charles Grandison [a fragment]. 1799?

Anon. Clarice. 1800.

Anon. Pamela, dramma comico. 1800.

G. Foppa. Pamela, commedia buffa. 1804.

Antonio Marques Espejo. Miss Clara Harlove. 1804.

Benoît Pelletier-Volméranges and Michel de Cubières-Palmézeaux. Pamela mariée, ou La Tiomphe des épouses . . . 1804.

Gaetano Rossi. La Pamela maritata (musical comedy). 1804.

Anon. Pamele (sic). Opéra-Bouffon en un Acte. (Performed in Amsterdam.) 1806.

Felix Enciso Castrillon. Pamela casada [opereta]. 1806.

Anon. Pamela oder die belohnte Tugend. 1807.

[Gaetano Rossi and Giuseppe Foppa; music by Pietro Generali?] Pamela nubile. Farsa in musica. First performed sometime before 1810; printed in 1810.

Heinrich von Kleist. Das Käthchen von Heilbronn, oder Die Feuerprobe. 1810.

Henri Louis Blanchard. Clarisse et Lovelace; ou, Le Séducteur . . . First performed 1815; printed 1817.

Anon. Pamela Gpandros. (In Greek.) 1817.

Anon. Pamela nubil, farca . . . 1819.

J.F. Beudin, P.P. Goubaux, and G. Lemoine ["M. Dinaux"]. Clarisse Harlowe, drame . . . 1833.

[Honoré de Balzac.] <u>Paméla Giraud</u>. 1843.

Anon. <u>La Nouvelle Clarisse Harlowe</u>. 1846.

Philippe F.P. Dumanoir, L.F.N. Clairville, and Léon Guillard. <u>Clarisse Harlowe</u> . . . <u>Drame</u> . . . <u>mêlé de chant</u>. 1846. (Trans. Wenceslas Ayguals de Izco) <u>Clarissa Harlowe</u>. 1846. (Trans. Ramon Navarrete and Fernandez Landa) <u>Clara Harlowe</u>. 1846. (Trans. A. Rigo) <u>Clara Harlowe</u>. 1853. (All based on Janin.)

Thomas Hailes Lacy and John Courtney. <u>Clarissa Harlowe</u>. 1846. (Based on Janin.)

William C. Wills. Clarissa. 1899. (Unpublished.)

Robert Buchanan. Clarissa. 1890. (Unpublished.)

P.J. Barbier and P. Choudens. <u>Clarisse Harlowe</u> (opera). 1896. Published but probably not produced.

Appendix C: Juvenilia

Most of these are anonymous abridgments of the three novels. Their textual relationships deserve further study.

Den belonnede Dyd, eller Pamela sodskende barn. 1751.

The Paths of Virtue Delineated; or, The History in Miniature of the Celebrated Pamela, Clarissa Harlowe, and Sir Charles Grandison. 1756, 1764, 1777. (In German:) Die Wege der Tugend . . . 1765, 1769-76. (In Dutch:) Het Pad der deugd . . . 1766. (Another version:) Pamela, Clarissa, en Grandison. Verkort. Met platen. 1808.

The Paths of Virtue Delineated, or the History of the Celebrated Sir Charles Grandison, in miniature. 1757, 1770.

Sittenlehre für die Jugend. 1757. Translation of Richardson's Aesop.

The History of Pamela: or, Virtue Rewarded. 1769, 1779(?), 1793, 1796.

[The History of Clarissa(?).] [1779?]

The History of Sir Charles Grandison, abridged . . . Before 1783 [1779?], 1795.

M.G. de Cambon. De Kleine Grandisson . . . 1782. (See 1782.3.) Later appeared as De Jonge Grandisson. (In French:) Le Petit Grandisson. 1787. (In English:) Young Grandison. 1790. The History of Little Grandison. 1791.

J.C.F. Schulz. Albertine. 5v. 1788-89. Retitled and possibly revised as Clarisse in Berlin. 5v. 1797. See 1788.3.

M.G. de Cambon. De kleine Klarissa . . . (See 1790.2). (In English:) Letters and Conversations between Several Young Ladies . . . 1790.

The Paths of Virtue Delineated; Or the History in Miniature of the Celebrated Clarissa Harlowe . . . 1791, 1795.

The Pleasing History of Pamela. 1793.

De Geschiedenis van Sir Charles Grandison Verkort. Ten nutte der Nederlandsche jeugd . . . 1793.

Clarissa; or, The History of a Young Lady . . . 1795, 1798.

The History of Miss Clarissa Harlowe . . . 1798.

Appendix D: Minor Poetry Addressed to Richardson or About his Works

More substantial poetry will be found in the main body of the bibliography.

Anon. "Advice to Booksellers (After Reading Pamela)." *Daily Advertiser*, April 8, 1741.

Poetry on fans painted with scenes from *Pamela*. *Daily Advertiser*, April 28, May 2, 1741.

William Whitehead. *On Nobility*. 1744.

"Belinda" [pseud.]. "To the Author of *Pamela*." *GM* 15. 1745.

Rev. Josiah Relph. "Wrote after Reading Pamela or Virtue Rewarded." *A Miscellany of Poems*. 1747.

"Pamela B. Junior" [pseud.]. Elegiac couplet, "Scire hominum mores varios . . ." *GM* 19. 1749.

William Dodd. *A Day in Vacation at College*. 1751.

John Duncombe. *An Evening Contemplation in a College*. 1753.

John Duncombe. *The Feminead*. 1754.

Anon. "A Poem on the Invention of Letters and the Art of Printing Addrest to Mr. *Richardson* . . . " 1758.

Anon. "Sent to Miss C--, with *Clarissa*." *Imperial Magazine* 1. 1760.

Mrs. --- Bennett. "Upon an Alcove, Now at Parson's Green." In *A Collection of Poems*. Edited by R. Dodsley. 1763. 5: 296-97.

Index

This index contains interfiled subject, title, and author headings. Some authors appear both in capitals and in standard upper and lower case; the latter entries are subject headings, while the former refer to writings by the author.

Entries in the appendices are not indexed.

A Mais Heroica Virtude, ou a Virtuosa Pamella   1766.2.
"A Propos d'une 'Paméla' de Voltaire."   1963.11.
"A XVIII. szazadi angol irodalom." 1969.19.
Aaron Hill: Poet, Dramatist, Projector.   1913.1.
Abbé Prévost als Übersetzer 1935.14.
"Abbé Prévost and the English Novel."   1927.4.
Abbild und Wunschbild der Gesellschaft bei Richardson und
    Fielding.   1935.5.
ABBT, THOMAS [B.].   1765.1.
Abraham Gotthelf Kästners Gesammelte Werke. 1841.2.
ABRAHAM, DAVID.   1968.1.
Abrantès, duchesse d', letter to.   1829.1.
Abridgment of Clarissa: or, The History of a Young
    Lady 1756.7.
Abridgments 1743.3, 1743.8, 1751.11, 1756.7, 1756.12, 1764.4,
    1765.4, 1766.3, 1779.2, 1789.4, 1798.4, 1805.4, 1808.7,
    1846.3, 1846.10, 1868.2, 1868.3, 1869.2, 1870.1, 1873.1,
    1874.1, 1875.1, 1876.2, 1892.1, 1894.1, 1902.2, 1908.10,
    1927.7, 1927.10, 1930.2, 1950.7; 1962.5, 1966.20, 1971.10,
    1972.17, 1973.13, 1975.18.
"Abridgments of Clarissa"   1972.17.
"Absurd Miss Pamela and the Tragic Miss Clarissa."   1970.20.
Account of the Life and Writings of James Beattie   1759.1.
"Accueil fait à Pamela."   1930.5.
Acres, Charles, letter to   1964.16.
"Activité intellectuelle de l'Angleterre."   1930.10.
ADAMS, ABIGAIL.   1785.1.
ADDLESHAW, S.   1930.2.
Address to the Public   1753.17, 1754.7.
Adèle et Théodore, ou Lettres sur l'education.   1782.6.
Adrian Loosjes.   1934.5.
Adventures of David Simple   1744.2.
Advice to an Apprentice   1943.5, 1955.4.
Adviser   1797.1.
Aesop's Fables   1739.1, 1747.3, 1753.15, 1753.16, 1938.2,
    1974.27; 1977.15.
AIKIN, JOHN.   1793.2, 1813.2.
ALBERT, THEODORE GIBBS.   1976.2.
Albertine   1788.3.

1900.3, 1902.2, 1907.3, 1908.5, 1912.6, 1914.1, 1914.2,
1918.2, 1921.3, 1929.4, 1930.3, 1936.3, 1936.7, 1944.4,
1946.2, 1948.1, 1948.2, 1948.4, 1948.5, 1948.9, 1948.12,
1950.3, 1950.6, 1950.7, 1951.6, 1951.7, 1951.8, 1952.1,
1953.7, 1956.6, 1957.2, 1957.5, 1957.7, 1960.5, 1960.14,
1962.8, 1962.9, 1963.2, 1963.6, 1963.13, 1964.2, 1964.9,
1964.11, 1964.14, 1964.17, 1964.19, 1964.26, 1965.1, 1965.5,
1965.6, 1965.19, 1966.6, 1966.12, 1966.15, 1966.16, 1967.2,
1967.6, 1967.7, 1967.21, 1968.1, 1968.4, 1968.14, 1968.19,
1968.29, 1968.35, 1969.6, 1969.7, 1969.11, 1969.15, 1969.21,
1970.1, 1970.9, 1970.14, 1970.16, 1970.18, 1970.20, 1970.24,
1970.27, 1970.28, 1970.29, 1970.30, 1970.31, 1971.1, 1971.6,
1971.8, 1971.9, 1971.10, 1971.16, 1971.17, 1972.3, 1972.5,
1972.6, 1972.9, 1972.10, 1972.12, 1972.14, 1972.17, 1972.19,
1972.24, 1972.25, 1973.1, 1973.4, 1973.9, 1973.10, 1973.13,
1973.14, 1973.17, 1973.26, 1973.36, 1974.1, 1974.2, 1974.3,
1974.4, 1974.9, 1974.10, 1974.11, 1974.12, 1974.13, 1974.14,
1974.15, 1974.16, 1974.19, 1974.20, 1974.22, 1974.31,
1974.32, 1974.34, 1974.35, 1974.36, 1974.39, 1975.3,
1975.11, 1975.12, 1975.13, 1975.14, 1975.16, 1975.20,
1975.21, 1975.23, 1975.24, 1976.2, 1976.3, 1976.6, 1976.11,
1976.16, 1976.17, 1976.18, 1976.20, 1976.22, 1976.23,
1977.1, 1977.3, 1977.8, 1977.9, 1977.10, 1977.16, 1977.19,
1977.20, 1977.21, 1977.23, 1978.3, 1978.5, 1978.7, 1978.8,
1978.12, 1978.13, 1978.15, 1978.17.
"Clarissa (i): A Process of Estrangement." 1970.24.
"Clarissa (ii): A Form of Freedom" 1970.24.
"Clarissa and Emma as Phedre."   1950.12.
"Clarissa and Fanny Hill: Sisters in Distress"   1972.6.
"Clarissa and her Modern Critics." 1970.9.
"Clarissa and La Nouvelle Heloise" 1972.21, 1977.10.
"Clarissa and Lovelace."   1964.17.
"Clarissa and the Enlightened Woman"   1975.14.
"Clarissa and the Epistolary Form." 1966.15.
"Clarissa and the Individuation of Character"   1976.6.
"Clarissa and The Newgate Calender (1768)" 1978.8.
"Clarissa and the Puritan Tradition"   1978.5.
"Clarissa and the Two Meanings of Death."   1968.1.
"Clarissa as Tragedy"   1976.17.
Clarissa Harlowe   1966.20.
"Clarissa Harlowe (1747-48)"   1978.3.
"Clarissa Harlowe and her Times."   1955.3.
"Clarissa Harlowe, eine tragische Cantate." 1916.1.
Clarissa Harlowe. A new and abridged edition by Mrs. Ward.
     1868.4.
Clarissa Harlowe. A novel. 1870.1.
Clarissa Harlowe. A tragic drama, in three acts.   1846.15.
"Clarissa Harlowe's Pursuit of Happiness." 1964.11.

CLELAND, JOHN.   1749.3, 1963.3.
Clementina von Porretta. Ein Trauerspiel   1760.11.
CLEMENTS, FRANCES MARION.   1967.3.
COE, ADA M. 1935.2.
Coelebs in Search of a Wife 1808.6.
COHAN, STEVEN M.   1974.9, 1976.6.
COHEN, MURRAY A.   1968.12.
COHEN, RICHARD.   1968.13, 1970.5, 1972.4.
COLEMAN, E.H.   1901.10, 1903.1.
COLEMAN, VIRALENE JOHNSON. 1969.3.
Colenutt, Sarah Fabian, letter to. 1899.1.
COLERIDGE, SAMUEL TAYLOR.   1805.2, 1808.3, 1813.3, 1820.2,
        1834.1, 1836.2.
COLEY, W.B. 1959.1.
Collected Letters of Samuel Taylor Coleridge   1820.2.
Collection of . . . Sentiments 1968.5, 1970.3.
Collection of the Moral and Instructive Sentiments 1755.7,
        1777.4.
Collection of...Sentiments 1951.6.
COLLYER, MARY, trans., adapt., and part author.   1965.4.
COLLYER, MARY.   1744.1.
Colman, George   1932.5.
COLMAN, GEORGE.   1760.3.
"Comic in Novels of Samuel Richardson"   1976.9.
"Commencement and Progress of Romance"   1797.5.
"Comparative Study of Samuel Richardson's
        Clarissa." 1968.15.
"Complacent Paragon."   1969.1.
Complete English Tradesman 1737.1.
Complete Letter Writer in English. 1934.6.
Complete Letters of Lady Mary Wortley Montagu.   1965.20.
Complete Novels   1902.5, 1902.6.
"Composition of Clarissa." 1968.19.
"Concept of Libertinage"   1971.16.
"Concrete Mimetic Form and the Languages of
        Silence" 1972.24.
Conduct books   1972.19.
"Confidante to the Principal"   1974.20.
Conjectures on Original Composition 1759.7, 1813.4, 1925.4.
Conjectures on Original Composition.   1910.7.
CONNAUGHTON, MICHAEL EDWARD.   1975.4.
Conrad, Joseph   1958.1.
"Conscience and the Pattern of Christian
        Perfection." 1966.6.
"Conscious Art of Samuel Richardson."   1970.4.
"Contented Porter" 1799.5.
"Continual Fervour" 1976.23.
"Continuations de Pamela." 1930.6.

"Continuations of Pamela"   1936.1.
Conversations of James Northcote.   1830.1.
Conversazione   1901.7.
"Cooke-Everyman Edition of Pamela" 1977.17.
COPELAND, EDWARD W. 1971.6, 1972.5, 1972.6.
COPELAND, EDWARD WALTON.   1968.14.
"Copy of a Letter to a Lady"   1754.11.
CORDASCO, FRANCESCO.   1943.2, 1948.2.
Correspondance littéraire   1751.5, 1753.10, 1754.4, 1756.6,
    1758.2, 1761.8, 1762.6, 1762.7, 1763.4, 1782.1, 1877.2.
Correspondence   1753.12, 1804.2.
Correspondence (see also under Biographical
    material) 1919.7, 1922.4, 1942.2, 1971.8.
Correspondence and Conversations of Tocqueville.   1872.1.
"Correspondence between Samuel Richardson and Johannes Stinstra."
    1962.11.
Correspondence of Edward Young   1971.23.
Correspondence of Thomas Gray.   1843.3.
Correspondence with Henrietta G.   1799.3.
COSTA, RICHARD H.   1970.6.
COULET, HENRI.   1967.4.
Courrier anglais.   1828.1.
Cours de littérature française.   1858.2.
Course of Lectures on Oratory and Criticism.   1777.3.
"Course of Realism in the English Novel."   1933.7.
"Courtly-Genteel or Moral-Didactic?"   1975.12.
COWARD, D.A.   1973.5.
COWLER, ROSEMARY, editor.   1969.4.
Cowper, William   1966.7.
COWPER, WILLIAM.   1754.3.
"Cowper's 'An Ode on Reading Mr. Richardson's
    History.'" 1966.7.
COX, J. CHARLES, H. ASKEW, and F. WILLIAMSON.   1935.3.
COX, RICHARD ALLEN. 1976.7.
CRABBE, GEORGE.   1834.2.
CRABTREE, PAUL RICHARD.   1978.2.
Craft of Fiction. 1921.5.
Cranch, Lucy, letter to.   1785.1.
CRANE, R.S. 1919.1, 1922.2, 1934.4.
Created Self   1970.24.
"Crébillon fils et Richardson"   1972.16.
Critical Remarks on Sir Charles Grandison, Clarissa and Pamela
    1754.5.
Critical Remarks on Sir Charles Grandison, Clarissa, and Pamela
    1950.5, 1974.27.
Criticism 1789.4.
Criticism, general (see also under individual
    titles) 1747.1, 1748.4, 1748.6, 1749.2, 1749.6, 1749.7,
    1749.9, 1749.10, 1750.2, 1750.4, 1750.5, 1750.8, 1750.9,

"Greater Family in the Novels of Samuel
      Richardson." 1921.2.
"Greatest English Novelist."   1948.1.
GREEN, FREDERICK C. 1935.6.
GREENE, MILDRED S.E.   1965.6.
GREENSTEIN, SUSAN MITCHELL. 1974.15.
GREINER, M. 1964.12.
GRGIC, BERISLAV   1970.26.
GRIEDER, JOSEPHINE. 1975.7.
GRIFFITH, PHILIP MAHONE.   1961.7.
GRIMM, CHARLES.   1924.1.
[GRIMM, FRIEDRICH MELCHIOR, and DENIS DIDEROT?]   1756.6.
GRIMM, FRIEDRICH MELCHIOR, baron, et al.   1877.2.
[GRIMM, FRIEDRICH MELCHIOR, baron.] 1751.5, 1754.4, 1758.2,
      1761.8, 1762.6, 1762.7, 1763.4, 1764.1.
"Grundlagen des Richardson'schen Romans."   1924.4.
GUELICH, ERNESTINE D.   1948.3.
GUERRINI, SANDRA.   1960.7.
GUHRING, ADOLF   1967.20.
GUILHAMET, LEON M.   1972.11.
GUILLARD, LEON.   1846.5, 1853.2.
GUILLEMOT, ERNEST.   1875.1.
GUTERMUTH, ELSE.   1924.1.
GUTHKE, K.S.   1966.10.
GUTIERREZ, JOSE MARCOS   1794.1.
GUYNN, ROBERT H.   1973.10.
H., A.C., and HODSON, LEONARD J.   1908.4.
H., A.J.   1933.4.
H., L.   1903.1.
H.,C.   1936.4.
Hagedorn, Friedrich von.   1966.10.
HAGEDORN, FRIEDRICH VON.   1749.6.
HALLER, ALBRECHT von.   1749.7, 1753.11.
HALSBAND, ROBERT.   1966.11, 1971.10.
HAMANN, J.G.   1762.8.
[HAMILTON, ELIZABETH.]   1800.3.
HANSFORD, F.E., F.R.S.A., and G.A.C. EVANS.   1953.2.
HARDWICK, ELIZABETH.   1974.16.
HARDY, THOMAS.   1888.2, 1925.2.
"'Harlowe Family' by Joseph Highmore."   1943.3.
HARRIS, JOCELYN M. 1968.24, 1976.12.
HARRIS, JOCELYN.   1973.11.
HARTVEIT, LARS.   1977.4.
HARVEY, A.D.   1978.5.
HAUSER, ARNOLD.   1951.5, 1953.3.
HAVENS, GEORGE R.   1919.3.
HAWKESWORTH, DR. JOHN.   1790.5.
HAYLEY, WILLIAM.   1785.4.

KIDGELL, JOHN.   1755.5.
KIEHL, JAMES MILLINGER.   1972.13.
Kimber, Edward   1935.1.
KIMPEL, BEN D.   1971.8.
KIMPEL, DIETER.   1967.11.
KIMPEL,BEN T.   1966.7; 1967.7; 1968.19, 1968.20, 1968.21,
        1968.22, 1971.8.
"Kind im englischen Roman von Richardson bis
        Dickens." 1924.1.
Kinkead-Weekes, Mark   1962.7.
KINKEAD-WEEKES, MARK.   1959.3, 1973.17.
KISSANE, JOSEPH M.   1968.28.
Klarissa   1785.11.
Klarissa, oder, die Geschichte eines jungen
        Frauenzimmers 1790.10.
Klarissa.   1848.4.
Klarissa: Roman   1805.3.
Kleine Grandisson verkort   1792.4.
Kleine Grandisson, of de Gehoorzaame Zoon.   1782.3.
Kleine Klarissa   1790.2.
KLOPSTOCK, FRIEDRICH GOTTLOB.   1750.8.
KLOPSTOCK, META.   1757.1.
KLOTMAN, PHYLLIS R. 1977.8.
KLUGE, WALTER.   1966.15.
KNIGHT, CHARLES A.   1964.14, 1969.7.
[KNOX, VICESIMUS, ed.]   1790.7.
[KNOX, VICESIMUS.]   1777.2.
KONIGSBERG, IRA.   1961.8, 1966.16, 1968.29, 1968.30.
Konigsbergschen Gelehrten und Politischen
        Zeitungen.   1767.3.
Kosegarten, L.T., trans.   1790.9.
KOVACS, ANNA-MARIA.   1978.6.
KOWALKOWSKI, A.   1947.2.
KRASENSKY, OTTOKAR.   1928.5.
KREISSMAN, BERNARD.   1960.8.
KRETSCHMER, ELIZABETH.   1902.3.
KRUTCH, J.W.   1930.9, 1959.4.
KURTH, LIESELOTTE E.   1968.31, 1969.8.
KURTH-VOIGHT, LIESELOTTE E.   1974.18.
LA CHAUSSÉE, PIERRE-CLAUDE NIVELLE DE.   1743.7, 1762.10.
LA PORTE, JOSEPH DE, abbé.   1751.6.
LA ROCHE, SOPHIE VON.   1791.5.
LABAN, LAWRENCE FREDERICK.   1973.18.
"L'abbé Prévost et le problème de la traduction."   1956.7.
L'Abbé Prévost, l'homme et l'oeuvre.   1955.5.
"Laclos and the denouement of the Liaisons
        dangereuses" 1973.5.
"Laclos et Richardson ou la fausse affinité."   1968.44.

MOORE, R.E. 1951.9.
MOORE, ROBERT E.   1948.10.
"Morality is the Message." 1968.5.
Morality of Richardson´s works   1741.11, 1741.12, 1741.13,
        1741.14, 1741.15, 1741.19, 1741.20, 1741.32, 1742.7,
        1742.13, 1745.5, 1748.2, 1748.7, 1749.2, 1749.6, 1750.2,
        1750.7, 1751.14, 1753.22, 1754.5, 1755.7, 1755.10, 1759.1,
        1759.2, 1759.3, 1759.4, 1760.8, 1760.10, 1762.5, 1766.2,
        1767.4, 1769.4, 1773.1, 1774.1, 1774.2, 1775.3, 1780.3,
        1782.6, 1785.1, 1785.2, 1785.5, 1785.6, 1785.7, 1785.8,
        1786.3, 1787.4, 1787.6, 1787.8, 1790.6, 1790.11, 1792.8,
        1797.6, 1798.1, 1798.3, 1799.3, 1801.2, 1808.3, 1808.4,
        1808.5, 1809.2, 1810.4, 1811.2, 1819.2, 1820.5, 1824.2,
        1830.1, 1835.2, 1836.2, 1841.1, 1847.1, 1847.2, 1858.1,
        1858.2, 1859.1, 1860.2, 1862.1, 1863.1, 1868.1, 1868.3,
        1868.4, 1869.2, 1870.1, 1871.1, 1873.1, 1876.1, 1883.2,
        1883.3, 1889.3, 1892.1, 1894.3, 1899.1, 1900.1, 1900.3,
        1901.3, 1901.9, 1902.2, 1903.6, 1904.3, 1907.2, 1911.6,
        1914.2, 1920.3, 1923.5, 1927.10, 1929.1, 1929.5, 1929.8,
        1930.3, 1932.3, 1933.12, 1935.7, 1938.1, 1939.3, 1942.1,
        1947.7, 1950.3, 1951.7, 1952.5, 1955.3, 1956.1, 1956.8,
        1957.7, 1960.11, 1960.14, 1961.11, 1961.13, 1963.4, 1963.14,
        1963.19, 1963.21, 1964.4, 1964.9, 1964.20, 1964.21, 1964.22,
        1964.23, 1965.11, 1966.6, 1966.24, 1967.5, 1968.4, 1968.5,
        1968.9, 1968.14, 1968.27, 1968.42, 1969.1, 1969.8, 1969.14,
        1969.17, 1970.2, 1970.4, 1970.16, 1970.23, 1970.29, 1970.30,
        1970.31, 1971.2, 1971.8, 1971.14, 1972.4, 1972.7, 1972.11,
        1972.16, 1972.19, 1972.20, 1972.22, 1972.25, 1972.26,
        1973.8, 1973.17, 1973.27, 1973.39, 1974.4, 1974.5, 1974.10,
        1974.23, 1974.36, 1974.39, 1975.9, 1975.13, 1975.23, 1976.7,
        1976.12, 1976.16, 1976.18, 1977.7, 1977.21, 1978.5.
"Morals and Manners in Richardson.".   1889.3.
Moralske tanker   1744.3.
MORE, HANNAH.   1780.3, 1808.6.
MORGAN, CHARLOTTE A.   1911.7.
MORGAN, SUSAN JENNIFER.   1973.24.
MORITZ, KARL PHILIPP.   1783.6, 1785.6, 1903.5.
MORNET, DANIEL.   1910.5, 1925.5.
MORTON, ANN RUTH.   1972.15.
MORTON, DONALD E.   1971.14.
"Mother Jewkes, Pamela, and the Midwives"   1976.10.
motion pictures   1973.25.
MOYNIHAN, ROBERT D. 1975.14.
MOYNIHAN, ROBERT DUNCAN.   1969.11.
Mr. Cibber of Drury Lane.   1939.1.
"Mr. Richardson Arrives." 1933.2.
Mrs. Montagu and her Friends, 1720-1800.   1907.3.
MUECKE, D.C.   1967.13.

MULLER, JOHANN GOTTWERTH.   1784.1.
MÜNCKER, FRANZ.   1890.6.
MUNRO, JAMES S.   1975.15.
MURPHY, ARTHUR.   1753.14.
Musaeus, J.K.A. von   1765.1, 1958.7, 1960.13, 1969.8.
MUSAEUS, JOHANN KARL AUGUST von.   1760.9, 1770.4, 1781.3.
Musaeus, K.G..   1910.3.
MUSENHOLD, DER PLAUDERER, and SINCERINUS. [pseuds.].
        1761.9, 1761.10.
MUSKALLA, KONSTANTIN.   1912.4.
MUSSET, ALFRED de. 1830.2.
MUSSET, PAUL de.   1830.2.
MYLNE, VIVIENNE   1977.12.
"Nachahmungsprinzip und Wirklichkeitsbegriff."   1964.13.
NACHTIGALL, ELSBETH.   1960.12.
NAIRN, J.A. 1925.6.
"Naming of Characters in Defoe, Richardson, and
        Fielding." 1949.7.
Nanine   1749.12.
Nansouty, Mme de, letter to.   1815.3.
NAPIER, ELIZABETH R.   1975.16.
Narodziny powiesci 1973.37.
"Narration and Illustration"   1972.1.
"National Characters in the Novels of Henry
        Fielding." 1970.15.
Natural Passion   1974.10.
NÉE DE LA ROCHELLE, JEAN-FRANÇOIS. 1786.5.
NEEDHAM, G.B.   1937.5.
NEEDHAM, GWENDOLYN B.   1970.23.
"Negative Principle and Virtuous Character Undercutting . . . "
        1974.15.
Negotiations   1740.1.
NEPPI MODONI, MARIE LOUISE. 1967.14, 1967.15.
Neue Zeitungen von Gelehrten Sachen 1754.2.
"New Clementina, from the French of d'Arnaud.".   1783.1.
"New Fiction of Samuel Richardson" 1974.21.
"New Letter from Fielding." 1948.8.
"New Samuel Richardson Manuscript." 1968.36.
NEWCOMB, ROBERT.   1958.4.
"'Nice' and 'sentimental'." 1964.18.
NICHOLS, JOHN.   1782.8, 1812.1.
NICOL, ROSALIND   1975.8.
Nieuwe Grandison.   1770.4.
NIKLAUS, R. 1972.16.
NOBLE, YVONNE.   1976.16.
NOEL-BENTLEY, ELAINE.   1977.14.
NORESS, H. 1920.5.
"Nos a łydka"   1975.5.

1967.1, 1967.8, 1967.14, 1967.15, 1968.2, 1968.3, 1968.7,
1968.11, 1968.14, 1968.26, 1968.38, 1969.3, 1969.12, 1970.2,
1970.6, 1970.12, 1970.20, 1970.23, 1970.26, 1970.31, 1971.6,
1971.12, 1971.14, 1971.18, 1972.1, 1972.7, 1972.8, 1972.20,
1972.23, 1973.3, 1973.8, 1973.17, 1973.20, 1973.25, 1973.28,
1973.30, 1973.35, 1973.39, 1973.40, 1973.41, 1974.1, 1974.2,
1974.10, 1974.11, 1974.12, 1974.17, 1974.22, 1974.24,
1974.28, 1974.29, 1974.30, 1974.33, 1974.34, 1975.3, 1975.9,
1975.21, 1976.8, 1976.10, 1977.4, 1977.5, 1977.17, 1977.18,
1978.4, 1978.6, 1978.11, 1978.13.
"Pamela a Venezia." 1934.9.
"Pamela abroad." 1903.3.
Pamela als Mutter. Ein ruhrendes Lustspiel in drey Aufzugen
    1764.3.
"Pamela and Joseph Andrews."   1968.7.
"Pamela and Joseph Andrews."   1968.26.
"´Pamela´ and ´Shamela´: A Reassessment"   1974.24.
"Pamela and the Poultry"   1973.15.
Pamela Andrews, o La Virtud Recompensada   1794.2.
Pamela Andrews, ou a virtude recompensada   1807.3.
"Pamela as Myth and Dream" 1973.41.
Pamela Censured   1974.27.
"Pamela da Richardson a Goldoni"   1976.24.
"Pamela e le sui origine." 1964.22.
Pamela eller Den belonnede Dyd   1743.9.
Pamela eller den Belonta Dygden.   1783.8.
Paméla en France   1743.2, 1745.3.
Paméla Giraud.   1843.1.
"Pamela II."   1968.2.
Pamela in High Life 1936.1, 1974.27.
Pamela maritata   1760.4.
Pamela naimisissa. 1923.4.
"Pamela Nubile, L´Ecossaise, and The English
    Merchant." 1932.5.
Pamela o la virtu premiata. 1952.6.
Pamela o la Virtud Recompensada.   1961.12.
Pamela oder die belohnte Tugend   1742.24.
Pamela oder die Belohnte Tugend   1742.25.
Pamela of de Beloonde Deugd 1741.30.
Pamela or Virtue Rewarded. 1958.6.
Paméla ou la Vertu Récompensée.   1970.25.
"Pamela Transformed."   1952.3.
Pamela vainottuna. 1919.6.
Pamela, a Comedy   1741.8, 1741.9.
Pamela, Clarissa en Grandison   1808.7.
Pamela, Clarissa en Grandison Verkort   1805.4.
Pamela, Comedy   1742.9.
Pamela, ili nagrazhdennaja dobrodetel´   1796.3.

PLOMER, HENRY R.   1915.4.
"Plotting the Eighteenth-Century Novel"   1974.2.
[PLUMMER, FRANCIS?] 1754.6, 1755.6, 1974.27.
Poems and Essays.   1860.2.
"Poetics of Salvation"   1974.19.
Poetry based on Richardson's works (see also Appendix
        D) 1743.10, 1744.4, 1753.12, 1754.3, 1754.12, 1791.3,
        1815.1, 1916.1, 1969.3.
POETZSCHE, ERICH.   1908.7.
"Poles of Discourse."   1965.19.
Polish literature and Richardson   1968.41.
Pollock, W.F., letter to.   1868.2.
Polly Honeycombe. A Dramatic Novel in One Act   1760.3.
POLYCLETUS UND CRITO [pseuds.]   1750.2.
PONS, CHRISTIAN.   1961.11, 1969.13, 1973.29.
POOVEY, MARY.   1976.18.
Pope, Alexander   1978.10.
Popular Fiction before Richardson. 1969.14.
Popular Novel in England.   1932.10.
Pornography and Obscenity.   1929.4.
Porrett, Robert   1964.26.
PORRETT, ROBERT.   1788.2.
Porten, Catherine, letter to.   1756.3.
PORTER, JANE.   1803.3.
Portland, Duchess of, letter to.   1748.6.
Portrait of Richardson   1792.2.
Portuguese literature and Richardson (includes translations)
        1766.2, 1807.3, 1853.2.
Posthumous Works.   1841.1.
POVEY, CHARLES.   1741.19, 1741.20, 1974.27.
Practical View of Prevailing Religious System   1797.6.
PRATT, SAMUEL JACKSON ["Courtney Melmoth"]. 1785.7.
PRAZ, MARIO.   1970.24.
"Predatings from Samuel Richardson's Familiar
        Letters." 1961.16.
"Prefatory Memoir of Richardson"   1824.2.
"Prefatory Memoir of Richardson."   1968.40.
"Premières réactions de la critique française."   1967.14.
PRESTON, JOHN.   1970.24.
Prévost d'Exiles, A.F.   1741.31, 1751.5, 1751.8, 1751.9,
        1751.10, 1755.1, 1755.3, 1755.8, 1756.6, 1758.1, 1758.2,
        1758.3, 1762.4, 1762.11, 1838.2, 1846.16, 1895.3, 1896.4,
        1923.6, 1927.4, 1927.10, 1930.14, 1935.14, 1940.4, 1940.6,
        1947.5, 1949.1, 1954.4, 1955.5, 1956.7, 1965.11, 1967.15,
        1977.11.
"Prévost traducteur de Richardson" 1973.13.
"Prévost's Translations of Richardson."   1923.6.
"Prévost's Translations of Richardson's Novels."   1927.10.

PRICE, LAWRENCE MARSDEN.   1919.5, 1925.7; 1926.8, 1930.13,
    1930.14, 1932.7, 1950.6, 1953.5.
PRICE, MARTIN.   1964.17.
PRIDEAUX, W.F.   1903.8.
PRIESTLEY, J.B.   1927.5.
PRIESTLEY, JOSEPH.   1777.3.
PRINSEN, J. 1925.8.
Printing   1734.1, 1936.5, 1943.1, 1947.1, 1950.9, 1958.3,
    1959.5, 1960.1, 1963.15, 1968.22, 1969.9.
Printing as an Index to Taste in Eighteenth-Century England.
    1958.3.
PRITCHETT, V.S.   1946.3.
"Pro e Contro i romanzi del Settecento."   1901.2.
"Problem of Pamela, or, Virtue Unrewarded"   1963.4.
"Profitable Reading of Fiction.".   1888.2.
Progress of Romance 1785.8.
PROPER, COENRAAD BART ANNE. 1929.5.
"Proposals of Marriage in Pride and Prejudice and
    Pamela." 1957.3.
Proust, Marcel   1932.6.
"Providential Labyrinth."   1963.19.
Psychological criticism   1950.12, 1953.7, 1957.7, 1960.5,
    1963.7, 1964.15, 1966.21, 1966.24, 1970.18, 1971.6, 1971.12,
    1972.10, 1973.9, 1973.17, 1973.22, 1973.40, 1973.41,
    1974.11, 1974.16, 1974.37, 1974.39, 1975.6, 1975.13, 1977.8,
    1977.9, 1977.16, 1978.9, 1978.16.
"Public and Private Values" 1974.23.
"Publisher of Pamela and its First Audience."   1960.4.
"Publisher of Pamela."   1930.12.
Publishing Family of Rivington.   1919.7.
PURDIE, EDNA.   1938.4.
"Puritan Sources of Richardson's Psychological
    Realism." 1966.24.
Puritanische Familie in Literärsoziologischer
    Sicht.   1964.21.
Puritanism 1972.26.
PUSHKIN, ALEKSANDR SERGEEVICH.   1833.3.
PUTNAM, MARGARET ALICE SCOBEY.   1971.17.
Quakerism   1921.1.
"Quantities of Qualities"   1975.13.
Quarterly Review.   1855.2.
"Quelques aspects de la sensibilité
    pré-romantique." 1927.9.
Quennell, Peter   1963.3.
Quiet Corner in a Library.   1915.3.
RABKIN, NORMAN.   1956.6, 1968.35.
Radcliffe, Anne   1927.4.
RADER, RALPH W.   1973.30.

1972.17.
"Reputation of Samuel Richardson." 1933.5.
Restoration and Eighteenth Century (1660–1789).   1948.11.
"Retardierende Person"   1795.3.
Review of Coelebs   1809.2.
Review of Fatal Revenge   1810.5.
Review of L'Abbé Prévost en Angleterre.   1940.4.
Review of New System   1809.1.
Review of Richardson's Life and Correspondence   1804.1.
Review of The Wanderer   1815.2.
"Reviser Observed" 1976.12.
"Revisions in the Published Texts of Clarissa."   1970.29.
"Revisions of Richardson's Sir Charles Grandison." 1968.34.
"Revisions of the Published Texts of Samuel Richardson's Preface."
        1970.30.
REYNOLDS, MYRA.   1920.6.
rhetoric   1961.5, 1963.6, 1965.19, 1971.6, 1972.5.
"Rhetorical Elements in the Eighteenth-Century English Novel."
        1961.5.
RICCOBONI, MARIE-JEANNE   1787.4.
"Richardson"   1974.8.
"Richardson and Esthetic Compromise."   1969.11.
"Richardson and Fielding." 1884.1, 1894.3, 1950.3, 1961.13.
"Richardson and Fielding: A Study in the Eighteenth-Century
        Compromise." 1956.8.
"Richardson and Fielding: Shamela and Shamelia." 1936.9.
"Richardson and his Family Circle." 1964.10, 1968.20.
"Richardson and his French Predecessors." 1913.5.
"Richardson and Jane Austen."   1968.28.
"Richardson and Johnson: Critical Agreement."   1968.18.
"Richardson and Joseph Conrad."   1958.1.
"Richardson and Mme de Souza."   1936.6.
"Richardson and Pamela."   1954.5.
"Richardson and Philology." 1942.3.
"Richardson and Proust."   1932.6.
"Richardson and Romance."   1970.8.
"Richardson and Rousseau"   1978.2.
"Richardson and Rousseau."   1896.4.
"Richardson and Sterne."   1932.3.
"Richardson and the Dedication to the Earl of
        Grandison" 1976.28.
"Richardson and the Epistolary Novel."   1933.3.
"Richardson and the Netherlands." 1965.16.
"Richardson and the Uses of Romance."   1971.8.
"Richardson and Warburton." 1919.4.
"Richardson at Home."   1894.1.
"Richardson at Work"   1973.4.
"Richardson Discusses his Clarissa and Sir Charles Grandison."
        1952.1.

RICHARDSON, SAMUEL, trans. FRIEDRICH WILHELM STREIT. 1765.4.
RICHARDSON, SAMUEL, translated and abridged by ?   1771.5.
RICHARDSON, SAMUEL. 1753.7.
[RICHARDSON, SAMUEL.].   1741.22, 1741.23, 1741.24, 1741.25,
    1741.26, 1741.27, 1741.28, 1741.29, 1741.30, 1741.31,
    1742.15, 1742.17, 1742.18, 1742.19, 1742.20, 1742.21,
    1742.22, 1742.23, 1742.24, 1742.25, 1746.4, 1746.5, 1747.4,
    1750.12.
RICHARDSON, SAMUEL. 1739.1, 1740.1, 1743.8, 1743.9, 1748.9,
    1748.10, 1749.9, 1749.10, 1749.11, 1751.7, 1751.8, 1751.9,
    1751.10, 1751.11, 1751.12, 1751.13, 1751.14, 1752.5, 1752.6,
    1752.7, 1753.16, 1753.17, 1753.18, 1753.19, 1753.20,
    1753.21, 1754.7, 1754.8, 1754.9, 1754.10, 1754.11, 1755.7,
    1755.8, 1755.9, 1756.7, 1756.8, 1756.9, 1756.10, 1756.11,
    1756.12, 1757.2, 1759.5, 1759.6, 1762.11, 1765.5, 1766.3,
    1771.4, 1779.2, 1780.4, 1783.7, 1783.8, 1787.7, 1790.9,
    1790.10, 1791.6, 1791.7, 1792.1, 1792.2, 1793.5, 1793.6,
    1793.7, 1793.8, 1794.1, 1794.2, 1796.3, 1797.1, 1797.2,
    1797.3, 1798.4, 1801.3, 1804.2, 1804.3, 1804.4, 1805.4,
    1807.3, 1808.7, 1808.8, 1811.3, 1846.10, 1846.16, 1848.4,
    1851.1, 1868.3, 1868.4, 1870.1, 1873.1, 1873.2, 1874.1,
    1883.2, 1890.6, 1895.1, 1897.3, 1901.6, 1902.5, 1902.6,
    1902.7, 1902.9, 1904.2, 1908.10, 1914.3, 1919.6, 1923.4,
    1928.8, 1928.9, 1929.6, 1929.7, 1932.9, 1950.7, 1952.6,
    1953.6, 1954.3, 1958.6, 1961.12, 1962.5, 1962.6, 1962.7,
    1964.19, 1970.25, 1970.26, 1971.18, 1972.18, 1974.28,
    1975.17, 1975.18, 1977.15.
[RICHARDSON, SAMUEL.]   1723.1, 1733.1, 1734.1, 1735.1,
    1736.1, 1740.2, 1741.21, 1742.15, 1746.3, 1747.3, 1748.8,
    1750.11, 1753.15.
[RICHARDSON, SAMUEL?]   1799.5.
Richardson, Thomas Verren, letter to.   1804.3.
"Richardson, Warburton, and French Fiction."   1922.2.
"Richardson, Wetzlar and Goethe."   1930.13.
"Richardson, Young, and the Conjectures."   1925.4.
Richardson-Stinstra Correspondence. 1969.17.
"Richardson."   1913.1.
Richardson. 1928.2.
Richardson. 1945.1.
"Richardson."   1964.1, 1966.21.
Richardson: A Collection of Critical Essays.   1969.2.
"Richardson: Idealist or Realist?" 1939.6.
Richardsonaden (see also under Pamela, Clarissa, Grandison, and in
    Appendix A)   1744.1, 1744.2, 1746.2, 1749.5, 1752.3,
    1752.4, 1755.5, 1769.5, 1784.2, 1790.2, 1790.3, 1792.5,
    1795.3, 1796.2, 1802.2, 1803.2, 1892.2.
"Richardsonian Letter"   1978.1.
"Richardsonian Phrases."   1966.23.

"Samuel Richardson's <u>Advice to an Apprentice</u>." 1943.5.
Samuel <u>Richardsons Belesenheit</u>. 1908.7.
"Samuel Richardson's Birth." 1911.11.
"Samuel Richardson's birthplace." 1935.3.
"Samuel Richardson's House at Fulham" 1935.10.
Samuel <u>Richardson's Introduction to</u> Pamela. 1954.3.
"Samuel Richardson's Novels and the Theater." 1962.10.
"Samuel Richardson's Novels: Style and Uses of
    Literature" 1975.4.
"Samuel Richardson's Supposed Derbyshire
    Connections." 1911.8.
"Samuel Richardson's Supposed Kinsfolk at Derby.". 1908.9.
"Samuel Richardson's Theory of Fiction." 1966.1.
Samuel <u>Richardson's Theory of Fiction</u>. 1971.2.
"Samuel Richardson's View of Moderate Rakery." 1967.16.
SANDERSON, THOMAS. 1805.5.
SANDLER, SUSAN JANET. 1976.23.
SCHEDONI, PIETRO. 1810.4.
SCHILLER, FRIEDRICH. 1784.2.
Schirmer, Ruth 1966.20.
SCHLECK, FLORIAN J. 1935.12.
SCHLEGEL, FRIEDRICH VON. 1820.5.
SCHLICHTING, HERTHA-MARIA von. 1927.6.
Schmid, C.H. 1950.6.
SCHMID, C.H. 1771.6.
[SCHMID, C.H.] 1792.7.
SCHMIDT, ERICH. 1875.2.
SCHMITZ, ROBERT M. and WILT, JUDITH. 1977.19.
SCHMITZ, ROBERT M. 1970.27.
SCHNEIDER, FERDINAND JOSEF. 1915.5.
SCHROERS, CAROLA. 1915.6.
SCHÜCKING, LEVIN L. 1924.4, 1964.21, 1969.15.
SCHULTZE, EDVIGE. 1964.22.
SCHULZ, DIETER. 1968.39.
SCHULZ, J.C.F., trans. and adapt. 1788.3.
SCIULLO, L. 1976.24.
<u>Scots Magazine</u> 1761.10.
SCOTT, SIR WALTER. 1824.2, 1968.40.
[SCOTT, SIR WALTER.] 1810.5.
SCOWCROFT, RICHARD P. 1947.6.
<u>Scuola dei Sentimenti</u>. 1963.13.
"Search for a Method." 1964.5.
<u>Seasonable Examination</u> 1735.1, 1954.2.
<u>Seasonable Examination . . .</u> 1974.27.
<u>Séducteur</u>. 1783.3.
"Seduction and Betrayal" 1974.16.
SEILLÈRE, ERNEST. 1934.10.
<u>Selected Letters of Samuel Richardson</u>. 1964.6.

"Stendhal, Richardson, et l´Edinburgh Review."   1959.6.
STEPANIK, K., and A. TICHY.   1956.10.
Stephen, Leslie   1868.1, 1868.2, 1883.2, 1883.3.
[STEPHEN, LESLIE.]   1868.5.
STEPHEN, LESLIE.   1874.2, 1876.1, 1896.3, 1904.3.
STERN, G.   1958.7.
Sterne, Laurence   1925.1.
STEVENSON, ROBERT LOUIS.   1877.3, 1888.3.
STEVICK, PHILIP   1971.569.
STEWART, KEITH.   1968.43.
Stinstra, Johannes 1752.5, 1756.11, 1962.11, 1965.16, 1969.17.
STOCKDALE, PERCIVAL.   1809.3.
Story of the Grange.   1953.2.
STRANDBERG, VICTOR H.   1966.22.
STRAUSS, LOUIS A.   1900.1, 1900.3.
STREETER, HAROLD W. 1936.10.
Structuralism   1974.22.
"Structure of Samuel Richardson´s Novels"   1972.15.
Studi e Ricerche intorno ai nostri Romanzieri.   1903.4.
"Studien zu Th. G. von Hippels." 1915.5.
"Studien zur Verführungsszene."   1968.39.
Studier i Richardsons romaner.   1928.10.
Studies in the Language of Samuel Richardson.   1907.5.
"Studies in the Novel´s Search for Form." 1969.6.
"Study of Clarissa."   1965.1.
"Study of Process in the Novels of Samuel
     Richardson." 1963.8.
"Study of Samuel Richardson."   1965.17.
"Study of the Text of Richardson´s Sir Charles
     Grandison." 1965.14.
Study of the Word "Sentimental".   1951.4.
"Sturm- und Drangkomödie und ihren fremden
     Vorbilder.". 1887.2.
"Style and Sentimentality in Three Novels" 1971.17.
Style and stylistic questions   1970.14, 1970.17.
"Style and the Action in Clarissa." 1963.6.
Suard, J.-B.-A.   1762.11.
"Success and Openness in English Fiction" 1973.32.
"Suggestions toward a Genealogy of the ´Man of
     Feeling´" 1934.4.
"Supplementary Notes on Richardson as a Printer." 1959.5.
Survey of English Literature.   1928.3.
Survey of nglish Literature.   1912.2.
SUTHERLAND, JAMES. 1961.14.
SUZUKI, YOSHIKO.   1969.18.
SUZUKI, ZENZO.   1965.17, 1971.21.
SWAEN, A.E.H.   1938.6.
SWANN, GEORGE ROGERS.   1929.8.